C0-ATE-331

CAMBRIDGE STUDIES IN
ANGLO-SAXON ENGLAND

17

THE HYMNS OF THE
ANGLO-SAXON CHURCH

CAMBRIDGE STUDIES IN
ANGLO-SAXON ENGLAND

GENERAL EDITORS
SIMON KEYNES
MICHAEL LAPIDGE

ASSISTANT EDITOR: ANDY ORCHARD

THE HYMNS OF THE ANGLO-SAXON CHURCH

A STUDY AND EDITION OF THE 'DURHAM HYMNAL'

INGE B. MILFULL

Department of Literature and Linguistics
The Catholic University of Eichstätt

CAMBRIDGE
UNIVERSITY PRESS

BX
1999.85
.A3
D876
1996

Published by the Press Syndicate of the University of Cambridge
The Pitt Building, Trumpington Street, Cambridge CB2 1RP
40 West 20th Street, New York, NY 10011–4211. USA
10 Stamford Road, Oakleigh, Melbourne 3166, Australia

© Cambridge University Press 1996

First published 1996

Printed in Great Britain at the University Press, Cambridge

A catalogue record for this book is available from the British Library

Library of Congress cataloguing in publication data

Milful, Inge B.
The hymns of the Anglo-Saxon church: a study and edition of the
Durham Hymnal / Inge B. Milful.
p.   cm. – (Cambridge studies in Anglo-Saxon England; 17)
Originally presented as the author's thesis (Ph.D.)
– Ludwig-Maximilians-Universität, 1991.
Includes bibliographical references.
ISBN 0 521 46252 5
1. Catholic Church. Durham hymnal. 2. Durham hymnal.
3. Antiphonaries – Texts. 4. Catholic Church – Hymns.
5. Hymns, Latin (Medieval and modern) – England – Durham.
6. Hymns, Latin (Medieval and modern) – England – Durham – History and criticism.
7. Manuscripts, Latin (Medieval and modern) – England – Durham.
8. Manuscripts, English (Old) – England – Durham.
9. Durham (Eng.) – Church history. 10. Durham Cathedral. Library.
I. Title. II. Series.
BX1999.85.A3D876   1996
264'.2–dc20   95-51247   CIP

ISBN 0 521 46252 5 hardback

Contents

Illustrations

Preface

When Christianity was introduced into Anglo-Saxon England at the end of the sixth century, the practice of singing hymns in the liturgy of the Office was already well established. The hymnal that the missionaries brought with them was replaced during the Benedictine Reform in the tenth century by another body of hymns, itself introduced from the Continent. Later on, the Normans in their turn brought their hymns with them.

This edition assembles the textual evidence, some of it hitherto unpublished, for hymns in England up to the Norman Conquest. The hymnal in an eleventh-century manuscript from Canterbury, Durham, Cathedral Library, B. III. 32 was chosen as the core of the edition and base manuscript. This hymnal is accompanied by an Old English interlinear gloss, known as the 'Durham Hymnal Gloss'. The 'Durham Hymnal Gloss', also edited here, is of considerable linguistic interest as an adaptation made in Canterbury of a Late West Saxon original.

This book replaces and extends J. Stevenson's unreliable edition, *The Latin Hymns of the Anglo-Saxon Church* (1851). It was originally a project of Helmut Gneuss's and in a sense represents a continuation of his seminal work, *Hymnar und Hymnen im englischen Mittelalter* (1968); it was accepted as a PhD dissertation by the Ludwig-Maximilians-Universität, Munich, in 1991.

I am indebted for advice and information to M. Y. Ashcroft, Günter Bernt, Susan Boynton, Franz Brunhölzl, Patrick Conner, Birgit Gansweidt, Andreas Haug, Michael Herren, Walter Hofstetter, Michel Huglo, Lucia Kornexl, Michael Lapidge, David McDougall, H. Mussett, Alan Piper, Susan Rankin, Karlheinz Schlager, and especially Fred Büttner, without whose help ch. 4 of the Introduction could not have been written.

I also have to thank Alfred Bammesberger, Susan Johnson, Gabriele Knappe, Dorothee Krien, Ursula Lenker, Jenny Potts, Renate Rößle, Frederick Schwink, Gabriele Waxenberger, Renate Weiß and Sophie Weiß for their generous assistance.

For access to their collections, I thank the staffs of the Bodleian Library, the British Library, the Cambridge University Library and the Lambeth Palace Library, the Dean and Fellows of Corpus Christi College, Cambridge, and St John's College, Cambridge, and the Dean and Chapter of Durham Cathedral. To the staff of the Brotherton Library, Leeds, I owe thanks for the photographs of the Ripon fragments.

I thank the British Library, the Dean and Fellows of Corpus Christi College and the Dean and Chapter of Durham Cathedral for their permission to use reproductions of their manuscripts.

I am also indebted to the Ludwig-Maximilians-Universität, Munich, for a two-year research grant and to Michael Lapidge for including this book in the Cambridge Studies in Anglo-Saxon England.

Above all, however, my gratitude is due to Helmut Gneuss, who is the giant on whose shoulders a dwarf stood to gain a wider view of the field of hymnology. If the dwarf should have squinted at any time, let nobody find fault with the giant.

Abbreviations

AH	*Analecta Hymnica Medii Aevi*, ed. Dreves, Blume and Bannister
ASE	*Anglo-Saxon England*
ASNSL	*Archiv für das Studium der neueren Sprachen und Literaturen*
BL	British Library
Bulst	*Hymni Latini Antiquissimi LXX. Psalmi III*, ed. Bulst
Campbell	Campbell, *Old English Grammar*
CCM	Corpus Consuetudinum Monasticarum (Siegburg)
CCSL	Corpus Christianorum Series Latina (Turnhout)
Cluny BCG	*Consuetudines Cluniacensium Antiquiores*, ed. Hallinger, versions B, C and G
CSEL	Corpus Scriptorum Ecclesiasticorum Latinorum (Vienna)
Dewick	*The Leofric Collectar*, ed. Dewick and Frere
Dewick, *Horae*	*Facsimiles of Horae de Beata Maria Virgine*, ed. Dewick
EEMF	Early English Manuscripts in Facsimile (Copenhagen)
EETS	Early English Text Society Publications, Original Series (London)
F	*Consuetudines Floriacenses*, ed. Davril
Gneuss	Gneuss, *Hymnar und Hymnen im englischen Mittelalter*, pp. 263–413 (edition of the *Expositio hymnorum*)
Gneuss, *HHEM*	Gneuss, *Hymnar und Hymnen im englischen Mittelalter*
HBS	Henry Bradshaw Society Publications (London)
Hogg	Hogg, *A Grammar of Old English*, vol. I
Hy	Hymn of the New Hymnal (cited by number and line of this edition, e.g. *Hy 1/1*)

ICL	Schaller and Könsgen, *Initia carminum Latinorum saeculo undecimo antiquiorum*
Isidore of Seville	*Isidori Hispalensis episcopi etymologiarum sive originum libri XX*, ed. Lindsay
Ker	Ker, *Catalogue of Manuscripts containing Anglo-Saxon* (cited by number)
Korhammer, *MC*	Korhammer, *Die monastischen Cantica im Mittelalter und ihre altenglischen Interlinearversionen*
Lindelöf	*Rituale Ecclesiae Dunelmensis. The Durham Collectar*, ed. Lindelöf
MGG	*Die Musik in Geschichte und Gegenwart. Allgemeine Enzyklopädie der Musik*, ed. F. Blume, 17 vols. (Kassel, 1949–86)
MGH	Monumenta Germaniae Historica
Auct. Ant.	Auctores Antiquissimi
NHy	Hymn of the New Hymnal (cited by number and line in this edition)
O	Odilo of Cluny, *Liber tramitis aevi*, ed. Dinter
OHy	Hymn of the Old Hymnal (cited according to Gneuss's numbering; see below, pp. 473–4)
Prudentius	*Aurelii Prudentii Carmina*, ed. Cunningham
RES	*Review of English Studies*
RS	Rolls Series (London)
SB	Brunner, *Altenglische Grammatik. Nach der Angelsächsischen Grammatik von Eduard Sievers*
SChr	Sources Chrétiennes (Paris)
Stäblein	*Hymnen (I). Die mittelalterlichen Hymnenmelodien des Abendlandes*, ed. Stäblein (melodies cited by number)
Temple	Temple, *Anglo-Saxon Manuscripts 900–1066* (cited by number)
Virgil	*P. Vergili Maronis Opera*, ed. Mynors
Walpole	*Early Latin Hymns*, ed. Walpole
Wieland	*The Canterbury Hymnal*, ed. Wieland

For manuscript sigla, see below, p. 108. References to Old English forms and words in the 'Durham Hymnal Gloss' are given in ch. 3 by hymn number and line of this edition: *1/1*, *1/2*, *1/3* etc.

1

Sources of the Anglo-Saxon hymnals

Like Christianity itself, hymns were introduced to Anglo-Saxon England from the Continent.

ST AMBROSE AND THE OLD HYMNAL

So, if it is praise and it is not praise of God, it is not a hymn. If it is praise and is praise of God and is not sung, it is not a hymn. Therefore, if it is uttered in praise of God and is sung, then it is a hymn.

Thus concludes a definition of *hymnus* compiled from the works of Isidore of Seville and known to the Anglo-Saxons.[1] Songs in praise of God were not invented by the Christians, of course. Isidore's definition itself mentions David as the first singer of hymns and thereby acknowledges the debt of Christian poetry to the Psalms and Jewish tradition.[2] Pagan antiquity had a tradition which the Christians were less eager to acknowledge. Nevertheless, hymns in the narrower sense in which the term is to be used in this book originated in Milan towards the end of the fourth century AD.

In this narrower sense hymns are stanzaic songs in metrical or rhythmical Latin verse and in regular liturgical use in the Office (but not the mass). The first of these hymns were composed by St Ambrose, archbishop of Milan (374–97), for the encouragement of the Catholic party, which was being persecuted by Arian heretics and at one point was even besieged by them in the cathedral. They combined a new metre, the iambic dimeter, which Ambrose had virtually invented, with striking imagery and popular appeal. In spite of their immediate purpose these

---

[1]   Gneuss, *HHEM*, pp. 265 (edition of the definition) and 199 (comments).
[2]   *Ibid.*, p. 265.

hymns lent themselves to regular use in that they proclaimed central religious truths, rather than details of doctrine. Each of them also had reference to a specific time of day or a specific feast of the church,[3] so they could readily be introduced into the Office, as it developed, and provided the basic framework for a liturgical cycle of hymns. We can reconstruct such a cycle from later evidence for Milan from early times onwards; it is preserved in the so-called Ambrosian liturgy.[4] This original cycle of hymns, known as the Old Hymnal, spread during the following centuries. We find our earliest evidence for it in the sixth century, in a monastic environment in Italy and southern Gaul.

A primitive form of the cycle is presupposed in the first half of the sixth century by St Benedict of Nursia in the *Regula S. Benedicti*, as Gneuss has proved.[5] Benedict prescribes the use of a hymn for each of the eight canonical hours of the Office, namely Vespers, Matins, Lauds, Prime, Tierce, Sext, None and Compline. At approximately the same time Caesarius, bishop of Arles from 503 to 542, gives us, apparently, the incipits of the hymns in use in the monastery of Lérins in southern Gaul, where he had been a monk. He and a successor of his as bishop of Arles, Aurelian, introduced these hymns in three newly founded Gaulish monasteries. They

---

[3] Because of their originality, Ambrose's hymns have received the most attention in literary history. They are treated by J. Szövérffy, *Die Annalen der lateinischen Hymnendichtung: ein Handbuch*, 2 vols. (Berlin, 1964–5) I, 46–68, and F. J. E. Raby, *A History of Christian-Latin Poetry from the Beginning to the Close of the Middle Ages*, 2nd ed. (Oxford, 1953), pp. 28–41. See also *Ambroise de Milan: Hymnes*, texte établi, traduit et annoté sous la direction de J. Fontaine (Paris, 1992). This work and H.-M. Jullien, 'Les sources de la tradition ancienne des quatorze *Hymnes* attribuées à Saint Ambroise de Milan', *Revue d'histoire des textes* 19 (1989), 57–189, came to my attention too late to be taken into account.

[4] The possibility cannot be excluded, however, that there was a break in the hymn tradition at Milan at some point. At any rate it cannot be proved whether the hymn cycle really developed in Milan or elsewhere. See Gneuss, *HHEM*, pp. 15 and 29. Gneuss's account of the history of the hymns from St Ambrose up to the tenth century has completely superseded all preceding ones and, supplemented by his article 'Latin Hymns in Medieval England: Future Research', remains the most comprehensive treatment to date.

[5] *Benedicti Regula*, ed. R. Hanslik, 2nd ed., CSEL 75 (Vienna, 1977), pp. 60–79 (chs. 9, 12, 13, 17 and 18). See Gneuss, *HHEM*, pp. 13, 29–31 and 38–40. See also A. G. Martimort, 'La place des hymnes à l'office dans les liturgies d'occident', in *Studi Ambrosiani in onore di Mons. Pietro Borella*, ed. C. Alzati and E. Majo, Archivio Ambrosiano 43 (Milan, 1982), 138–53.

are fundamentally the same as Benedict's, with minor adaptations and additions.[6]

Since Gregory the Great was a champion of St Benedict, as is clear from his *Dialogi*,[7] we might expect that the monks of the English mission, led by Augustine, would have brought the Benedictine cycle to England in 597. In fact there was a manuscript preserved until the beginning of the fifteenth century in St Augustine's Abbey, Canterbury, but subsequently lost, which was claimed to have been sent to St Augustine by Gregory and which contained a hymnal resembling the Benedictine cycle, as Thomas of Elmham reports. He lists the incipits of the hymns, as follows:[8]

Mediae noctis tempus est	*pro medio noctis*
Aeterne rerum conditor	*ad gallicantum*
Splendor paternae gloriae	*ad matutinas*
Venite fratres ocius	*ad primam*
Iam surgit hora tertia	*ad tertiam*
Bis ternas horas explicans	*ad sextam*
Ter hora trina volvitur	*ad nonam*
Deus creator omnium	*ad vesperas*
Te deprecamur domine	*ad completorium*
Christe qui lux es et dies	*in quadragesima*
Rex aeterne domine	*pro die dominico*
Intende qui regis Israel	*de natali domini*

6   Caesarius of Arles, *Regula virginum*, ed. and trans. A. de Vogüé, in *Oeuvres Monastiques I. Oeuvres pour les Moniales*, ed. A. de Vogüé and J. Courreau, SChr 345 (Paris, 1988), 35–273, with hymns mentioned pp. 254, 260 and 264 (chs. 66 and 69). Aurelian's text is virtually the same. See Gneuss, *HHEM*, pp. 15–16.

7   See Gregory the Great, *Dialogi*, ed. A. de Vogüé II, 120–249 (bk II, Life of St Benedict), esp. 242 (praise of his Rule).

8   Thomas of Elmham, *Historia Monasterii S. Augustini Cantuariensis*, ed. C. Hardwick, RS (London, 1858), p. 97; see Gneuss, *HHEM*, pp. 16–17, 24 and 33–4, and 'Latin Hymns', pp. 417–18. It should be noted that *matutinas* here as in the Anglo-Saxon manuscripts means 'Lauds', not 'Matins'. These hymns are nos. 1, 2, 8, 15, 17, 19, 21, 26, 33, 30, 3, 34, 39, 42 and 43 in Gneuss's table of all hymns evidenced for the Old and the Frankish Hymnal (*HHEM*, pp. 24–5). Reference to the numbers of the hymns in this table will henceforth be made as 'OHy', while hymns of the New Hymnal will be referred to as 'NHy' or, outside comparisons with the Old and Frankish Hymnals, as 'Hy'. The numbering given for the New Hymnal is that of the hymns in this edition and based on that of Gneuss, *HHEM*, pp. 60–8, which is in its turn based on Durham, Cathedral Library, B. III. 32. Note, however, that my numbering of hymns not included in the manuscript is different (Hy 134–62). See below, p. 105.

3

Hic est dies verus dei	*in Pascha*
Apostolorum passio	*in festo apostolorum Petri et Pauli*
Amore Christi nobilis	*de S. Iohanne Evangelista*

While the manuscript may not have belonged to St Augustine himself, it (or its exemplar) must have been of considerable antiquity, pre-tenth century at the very least, as we shall see. There is even a chance that the link with St Augustine was authentic. We have corroborative evidence for the early liturgical use of three of these hymns by the Anglo-Saxons in London, BL, Cotton Vespasian A. i (England, s. viii[1]; provenance: Canterbury). Bede (d. 735) quotes from seven of them as familiar examples in his treatise *De arte metrica*.[9]

Meagre as this evidence is, nothing suggests that there was any other type of hymnal in use in Anglo-Saxon England until the Benedictine Reform in the tenth century – except possibly among the Irish missionaries of the seventh century and for a time in the sphere of their immediate influence. So it may be the hymns included in this hymnal that Aldhelm and Felix of Crowland mention in passing, if indeed they are talking about hymns proper.[10]

As has been hinted above, the series is not quite identical with the cycle that can be reconstructed for Benedict and the early Milanese church. The first two hymns were apparently intended for two different parts of the Night Office, *pro medio noctis* and *ad gallicantum*. This feature agrees with the use of Lérins rather than the *Regula S. Benedicti*, which has only one hymn for Nocturns. The hymn for Prime is also distinctive and was perhaps specifically English. The usual hymn for Compline was restricted to Lent in favour of *Te deprecamur domine*. This series could arguably derive

---

[9] For Cotton Vespasian A. i, see below, pp. 56–7. For the hymn incipits in Bede, see 'De arte metrica et schematibus et tropis', ed. C. B. Kendall and M. H. King, *Bedae Venerabilis Opera, Opera didascalica I*, CCSL 123A (Turnhout, 1975), 135–6 and 139. They are discussed by Gneuss, *HHEM*, pp. 35–6. On the treatise as a whole, see M. Irvine, 'Bede the Grammarian and the Scope of Grammatical Studies in Eighth-Century Northumbria', *ASE* 15 (1986), 15–44.

[10] For Aldhelm, see his third *carmen ecclesiasticum*, 'In ecclesia Mariae a Bugge exstructa', *Aldhelmi Opera*, ed. R. Ehwald, MGH, Auct. Ant. 15 (Berlin, 1919), 14–18, esp. p. 17, line 52, and the footnote to this line in *Aldhelm: the Poetic Works*, trans. M. Lapidge and J. L. Rosier (Cambridge, 1985), p. 236, n. 25. For Felix, see *Felix's Life of Saint Guthlac*, ed. B. Colgrave (Cambridge, 1956), p. 86. OHy 3 (NHy 31) has been suggested as source of the beginning of the OE poem 'Guthlac B'; see *The Guthlac Poems of the Exeter Book*, ed. J. Roberts (Oxford, 1979), pp. 38–9.

from an unknown continental source; but Gneuss has suggested that it might have been adapted for English use by St Augustine himself. He has also suggested that Benedict Biscop, who was a monk in Lérins for two years and in charge of St Augustine's from 669 to 671, might be the influence behind the Gaulish elements in the Night Office.[11]

It should also be noted that such evidence as we have for its use is exclusively monastic. Moreover, we have an authentic early text of only three of these hymns in Vespasian A. i, but this is in fact the earliest direct witness to the text of the hymns of the Old Hymnal altogether.

On the Continent, we find only the Old Hymnal up to the second half of the eighth century. The evidence is too sparse to determine whether it was adopted by all the monasteries (regardless of the rule they followed) and how far it was taken over by the secular clergy. We find hymns in non-monastic contexts in some regions of Gaul, but not in Rome, for hymns were not adopted there until much later.[12]

THE DEVELOPMENT OF THE NEW HYMNAL

During the period extending from the second half of the eighth century to the early ninth, a new type of hymnal is found in a group of six manuscripts originating in either northern or eastern Francia or Alemannia; five of these are certainly monastic. This type is called the 'Frankish Hymnal' by Gneuss.[13] Its most striking characteristic is the provision of a different hymn for Lauds on each day of the week. The type may have reached England, but there is a dearth of Anglo-Saxon evidence in the ninth century.

The Frankish Hymnal, however, was replaced as early as the ninth

---

[11] The hymns are discussed by Gneuss, *HHEM*, pp. 16–17, 34 and 36–8. The importance of Benedict Biscop was suggested to me personally by Gneuss. On his career, see Stenton, *Anglo-Saxon England*, p. 132.

[12] On this question, see Wagner, *Einführung in die gregorianischen Melodien* I, 162–74. According to Wagner Rome appears to have introduced the hymns at some point in the twelfth century (pp. 166–7). Cf. also P. Batiffol, *Histoire du bréviaire romain*, 3rd ed. (Paris, 1911), pp. 205–18.

[13] Gneuss, 'Latin Hymns', pp. 409–10. The name 'Frankish Hymnal' replaces 'Old Hymnal II', as he had designated this type in *HHEM*. In *HHEM* its sources and its innovations are fully described (pp. 19–28). It differs not only with regard to Lauds, but also substitutes another series for the Day Hours from Prime to None. There are also changes in the small set of hymns Proper for Seasons and for Saints.

century by a third type, the so-called New Hymnal, which spread rapidly and from the tenth century on is found everywhere except in Milan. It clearly originated somewhere in the Frankish empire. Gneuss suggests that it developed in northern France and assumes a monastic origin for it; he associates its spread with Benedict of Aniane. Bullough and Corrêa argue that an authoritative copy was kept in the chapel of Louis the Pious; they suggest it was compiled by members of the secular clergy, without excluding monastic influence completely.[14]

There must have been a powerful motivation behind two successive attempts at reforming the time-honoured Old Hymnal within less than a century, and the introduction of the New Hymnal must have been backed by the authorities for it to succeed so speedily. The net result of the change was certainly a larger and more complex hymnal with a stable cycle of ferial hymns providing different hymns for Vespers, Lauds and Matins each day of the week[15] and an extended, but rather more variable, set of hymns for feasts and saints' days. This is in line with the inclusion of additional Lauds hymns in the Frankish Hymnal, but in fact that set of Lauds hymns was discarded and quite a few other hymns of the Frankish Hymnal were discarded, too – which could indicate that the two did not originate in the same centre.[16]

---

[14] On the development of the New Hymnal and the earliest manuscripts, see Gneuss, *HHEM*, pp. 41–54, 'Latin Hymns', pp. 411–12, and Bullough and Corrêa, 'Texts, Chant'. For Benedict of Aniane and the Chapel of Louis the Pious respectively, see Gneuss, *HHEM*, pp. 50–2, 'Latin Hymns', p. 412, and Bullough and Corrêa, 'Texts, Chant', pp. 496–7 and 503–5. See also M.-H. Jullien, 'Les hymnes dans le milieu alcuinien', in *De Tertullien aux Mozarabes: mélanges offerts à Jacques Fontaine*, ed. L. Holtz and J.-C. Fredouille, 2 vols. (Paris, 1992) II, 171–82, and A. L. Harting-Corrêa, 'Make a Merry Noise! A Ninth-Century Teacher Looks at Hymns', in *The Church and the Arts: Papers Read at the 1990 Summer Meeting and the 1991 Winter Meeting of the Ecclesiastical History Society*, ed. D. Wood (Oxford, 1992), pp. 79–86.

[15] The high stability of the ferial cycle can be followed in the index of Mearns, *Early Latin Hymnaries, passim*. This was a pioneering work and is still extremely valuable. However, it does not give precise information on the diverging use of hymns and does not attempt to cover the period after 1100 completely.

[16] Gneuss, *HHEM*, pp. 51–2. There are six hymns common to the Old and the Frankish Hymnals in the New Hymnal (OHy 2, 3, 8, 30, 34 and 44 = NHy 4, 31, 15, 12, 39 and 117), one is largely confined to the Old Hymnal (OHy 26 = NHy 2) and one may or may not have been part of the Old Hymnal (OHy 31 = NHy 11). The New Hymnal took over the hymns for Lent and Easter from the Frankish Hymnal (OHy 36–8, 40 and 41 = NHy 51–2, 54, 70 and 72), but only one of its specific ferial hymns (OHy 25

What is more, there was a period of flux. Both Gneuss and, subsequently, Bullough and Corrêa have attempted to reconstruct a primitive set of ferial hymns for the New Hymnal which is actually less complex than that of the Frankish Hymnal and some types of Old Hymnal.[17] If the reconstruction is correct, the reason for replacing the old hymns was perhaps that they seemed too long for everyday use or that they were less satisfactory metrically.[18]

The question is relevant to the Anglo-Saxon situation in that the theory is supported by Anglo-Saxon evidence. This evidence consists in hymns written by three scribes of Chester-le-Street *c.* 970 in Durham, Cathedral Library, A. IV. 19 (the 'Durham Ritual') and an eleventh-century Anglo-Saxon liturgical textbook, the so-called 'Benedictine Office'.[19] Another relevant text, the *Indicium regule quomodo*, is found in an eleventh-century English manuscript.[20] Each of these could also represent a selection from a fuller hymnal, however. The scribes of the 'Durham Ritual' at any rate were certainly not aiming at comprehensiveness. If the 'Durham Ritual' (or the Benedictine Office) should represent an earlier stage of the New

= NHy 53). Not all of these were equally firmly established in the New Hymnal; see, for example, below, p. 24, n. 94. Others turn up sporadically during the early stages of the New Hymnal (Gneuss, *HHEM*, p. 50).

[17] Gneuss, *HHEM*, p. 49; Bullough and Corrêa, 'Texts, Chant', p. 503.

[18] The normal length of hymns of the Old and Frankish Hymnals is eight stanzas, while those of the New Hymnal tend to run to only four. Metrical irregularity, of course, does not apply to the hymns of St Ambrose, but as regards the others compare, for example, the metre of NHy 31 (OHy 3), which is quite 'Merovingian', with the standard maintained in the ferial hymns of the New Hymnal. Note in this context that Bullough and Corrêa are willing to consider the possibility that the New Hymnal was not, in the main, compiled from older texts and that most of the hymns were recent, i.e. Carolingian, compositions ('Texts, Chant', pp. 506–7).

[19] Gneuss, *HHEM*, p. 49 ('Durham Ritual'), Bullough and Corrêa, 'Texts, Chant', p. 503 ('Durham Ritual' and Benedictine Office). For the 'Durham Ritual', see below, pp. 57–8. The hymn incipits in the Benedictine Office in Oxford, Bodleian Library, Junius 121 (Worcester, s. xi$^{3/4}$) are discussed by Gneuss, *HHEM*, pp. 120–1, where he explains their peculiarities differently and more convincingly. The text has been edited by J. M. Ure as *The Benedictine Office: an Old English Text*, Edinburgh University Publications, Language and Literature 11 (Edinburgh, 1957).

[20] The 'Indicium regule', ed. Bateson, is transmitted in Cambridge, University Library, Ll. 1. 14 (England, s. xi^{ex}). See Gneuss, *HHEM*, p. 45, n. 14, and 'Latin Hymns', pp. 412 and 423, n. 19. If it was indeed, as Gneuss suggests, composed by Benedict of Aniane or one of his followers, it is surprising that NHy 5 and 6 are already included here, as they do not appear in any ninth-century hymnal (Gneuss, *HHEM*, pp. 49–50).

Hymnal, it might further be suggested that this form came to England comparatively early, in spite of the late date of the manuscripts.

In any case the full New Hymnal seems only to have been introduced in connection with the English Benedictine Reform in the tenth century. Not only is there no evidence for its use before that time, but our two earliest witnesses, the *Regularis concordia* and the Bosworth Psalter, both come from centres of reform, namely Winchester and Canterbury respectively. The *Regularis concordia* is itself the work of Bishop Æthelwold of Winchester, a leading figure of the Benedictine Reform, and the Bosworth Psalter has been connected with another leading figure, Archbishop Dunstan.[21]

The evidence for the New Hymnal from the period between the late tenth century and the Norman Conquest will be discussed in detail in the next section. The New Hymnal proved extremely stable, but the *proprium* and the *commune sanctorum* retained and developed certain regional characteristics. After the Norman Conquest, as was to be expected, Norman practices were imposed on the English hymnals. The result was the 'revised' New Hymnal, as Gneuss tentatively calls it, which underlies most English Benedictine hymnals and also the Sarum Hymnal, which was the most influential among secular clergy.[22] Later monastic orders brought their hymnals with them from the Continent. The Cistercians based theirs on the Milanese hymnal, which had developed from the Old Hymnal. In the seventeenth century the New Hymnal was thoroughly overhauled to conform to new demands made on literary form and doctrinal content. In that form it is still in use in the Roman Catholic church and has remained basically the same, except that in this century it has receded more and more before the vernacular tradition it inspired.[23]

THE NEW HYMNAL IN ANGLO-SAXON ENGLAND

There is some, though not plentiful, manuscript evidence for the New Hymnal in England between the presumed date of its introduction in the

---

[21] On the *Regularis concordia* and Bosworth Psalter, see below, pp. 9–10, and on the Bosworth Psalter, pp. 41–3.

[22] Gneuss, *HHEM*, pp. 75–83. For the Sarum Use, see *Breviarium ad usum insignis ecclesiae Sarum*, ed. Proctor and Wordsworth. It is compared with the hymnal in the Bosworth Psalter by Gneuss, 'Latin Hymns', pp. 418–21.

[23] For the monastic hymnal of today, see *Liber hymnarius cum invitatoriis & aliquibus responsoriis*, Antiphonale Romanum secundum liturgiam horarum 2 (Solesmes, 1983).

tenth century and the changes that resulted in the 'revised type' of the later Middle Ages. Five hymnals which are complete – or nearly so – survive from the period:

B   London, BL, Add. 37517 (Canterbury, s. x^{ex})
C   Cambridge, Corpus Christi College 391 (Worcester, *c.* 1065)
D   Durham, Cathedral Library, B. III. 32 (Canterbury, s. xi^1)
H   London, BL, Harley 2961 (Exeter, s. xi^{med})
V   London, BL, Cotton Vespasian D. xii (?Canterbury, s. xi^{med})

There are also two copies of the *Expositio hymnorum*. This is a schoolbook, a prose version of the complete hymn cycle with a few added explanations.[24] One of these is combined with the hymnal in V. (*Vm* will henceforward be used to signify the hymnal and *Vp* the *Expositio*.) The other is London, BL, Cotton Julius A. vi (?Canterbury, s. xi^{med}(J)).[25]

Of these hymnals BCDJV were intended for the use of Benedictine monks,[26] while H was intended for secular canons; it differs from BCDJV both in the hymns it contains and in the liturgical use prescribed for them. However, a collectar included in the same manuscript (H) largely agrees with the directions for the use of hymns.[27]

The Anglo-Saxon monastic hymnals

BCDJV in their turn represent two different sub-types of the New Hymnal and may be grouped accordingly as BDVm and CJVp. Since CJVp agree with the directions given in Ælfric's letter to the monks of Eynsham (founded 1005)[28] and with the comments on Sundays in Lent in

---

[24] For a typology of liturgical manuscripts, see M. Huglo, *Les Livres de chant liturgique*, Typologie des sources du moyen âge occidental 52 (Turnhout, 1988) and, for Anglo-Saxon England in particular, Gneuss, 'Liturgical Books in Anglo-Saxon England and their Old English Terminology', in *Learning and Literature*, ed. Lapidge and Gneuss, pp. 91–141. Gneuss also lists the relevant surviving manuscripts. For the grammatical principles according to which the *Expositio hymnorum* re-arranges the text, see Korhammer, *MC*, pp. 128–37.

[25] For details of these manuscripts, see below, pp. 26–55.

[26] The mere fact that BCDJV all contain monastic *cantica* proves that they are Benedictine.

[27] See below, pp. 48–9.

[28] 'Aelfrici abbatis epistula', ed. Nocent, chs. 13 and 50. See Gneuss, *HHEM*, pp. 60–8

his mentor Æthelwold's *Regularis concordia*,[29] Gneuss[30] regards this type as the one in use in Winchester. It was also in use in Worcester, the provenance of C. As other liturgical texts in C appear to be influenced by Winchester usage,[31] the hymnal, too, may derive from a Winchester source. On the other hand the provenance of BDVm is clear proof that this type was current in Canterbury. The fact that JVp, too, appear in (presumably) Canterbury manuscripts is irrelevant, since the *Expositio* is a schoolbook and as such would have been useful at any centre, even if it did not agree precisely with the actual liturgical usage of that centre. As we shall see, it was inconvenient only in that it did not treat all the hymns in use in Canterbury.

These two types of monastic hymnal were accordingly called 'Winchester Hymnal' and 'Canterbury Hymnal' by Gneuss.[32] There is not enough evidence to ascertain whether these were the only types of monastic hymnal extant at the time or how influential they were. Even the Canterbury evidence may be valid only for Christ Church.[33] However, the use of the Canterbury Hymnal must have been a little more widespread than that, since its influence can clearly be traced in the post-Conquest hymnal of the convent of Barking, Essex.[34]

The Winchester Hymnal may have been more widely used. Æthelwold would probably have introduced it in the monasteries that he founded or reformed just as Ælfric later introduced it at Eynsham. If the Winchester Hymnal was introduced in Worcester as early as the time of Bishop Oswald, he would also have passed it on to the monasteries that he founded or reformed. It may be a measure of influence that this is the type for which the *Expositio* was written. It also had whatever authority the *Regularis concordia* may have been able to give it.

If the New Hymnal was only introduced in England during the Benedictine Reform, why were there two significantly different types already current in the 970s or 980s, as attested by the Bosworth Psalter and the *Regularis concordia*? At first sight it seems quite likely that the Winchester and the Canterbury Hymnals were introduced to England

---

and 119–20 and M. McC. Gatch, 'The Office in Late Anglo-Saxon Monasticism', in *Learning and Literature*, ed. Lapidge and Gneuss, pp. 341–62.

[29] *Regularis concordia*, ed. Symons, pp. 25 (= ch. 28); 'Regularis concordia', ed. Symons and Spath, ch. 39.

[30] Gneuss, *HHEM*, pp. 70–1.   [31] See below, p. 44.   [32] Gneuss, *HHEM*, p. 71.

[33] *Ibid*. See below, pp. 40–2 and 54–5.   [34] Gneuss, *HHEM*, pp. 71 and 81.

from different continental sources. Gneuss's attractive hypothesis is that >this is the result of the well-known connections between Ghent and Dunstan of Canterbury on the one hand and between Fleury and Æthelwold of Winchester and Oswald of Worcester on the other.[35]

The differences between the Canterbury Hymnal and the Winchester Hymnal are of various kinds.[36] The Canterbury Hymnal has provision for more feasts and has more hymns in it, although some only appear in the two later manuscripts DV. (The reason why some hymns are lacking in B is that it is the oldest manuscript; not only does it represent an earlier stage of the Canterbury type than D and Vm, but it also represents an earlier stage of the New Hymnal than CJH.) It does not agree with the Winchester Hymnal in all its instructions for the liturgical use of hymns. It has full texts in some cases where the Winchester Hymnal has abbreviated ones.

Hymns in the Canterbury Hymnal for feasts for which the Winchester type has no provision are Hy 35 for St Andrew, Hy 88 for St Laurence and Hy 54, 56_1 and 56_2 for Sundays in Lent. There are hymns in DV for feasts not accounted for in the Winchester Hymnal, which are not yet found in B. These are Hy 69, processional hymn for Maundy Thursday, and Hy 60, once again for Sundays in Lent. Hy 101 for St Martin is only in B and D. That a hymn for the Canterbury saint Dunstan (Hy 82) is found in the Canterbury Hymnal and not in the Winchester Hymnal, is hardly surprising. Annunciation is also provided for only in the Canterbury Hymnal. Hy 65_1, 65_2 and 66, the prescribed hymns, are in the

---

[35] *Ibid.*, pp. 72–4. The influence of Ghent and Fleury on the leaders of the Benedictine Reform has been extensively discussed with regard to the *Regularis concordia*; cf. Symons in the introduction to his edition of the text, pp. xix and xxi–xxii. An abbreviated version of this introduction is included in 'Englands Brauchtexte im 10./11. Jahrhundert', ed. K. Hallinger in *Consuetudinum saeculi X/XI/XII monumenta. Introductiones*, ed. Hallinger, pp. 371–93, at 373–89, where the corresponding pages are 379 and 381–2. Hallinger's comments follow on p. 393. Note, however, that there was also contact between Winchester and Ghent and, on the other hand, between Canterbury and Fleury; see P. Wormald, 'Æthelwold and his Continental Counterparts' and M. Lapidge, 'Æthelwold as Scholar and Teacher' in *Bishop Æthelwold*, ed. Yorke, pp. 13–42 and 89–117 respectively, esp. pp. 23 and 98–9. See also Korhammer, *MC*, pp. 71–2.

[36] For the following, see Gneuss, *HHEM*, pp. 60–8, 69 and n. 5 and 130–2. See also below, pp. 67–9, and the apparatus of my edition of the hymns in question.

Winchester Hymnal as well, where the first two are prescribed for Candlemas and the third for the Assumption of Mary.[37]

There are other hymns found in the Canterbury Hymnal, but not in the Winchester Hymnal. The Canterbury Hymnal has one more hymn for Christmas, Hy 37, and one more for Pentecost, Hy 78. The later manuscripts of the Canterbury Hymnal, DV, also have a version of *Aeterna Christi munera* especially for Apostles (Hy 103), the original version (Hy 117) being reserved for Martyrs. They have another hymn for St Stephen, too, Hy 41. The Marian hymns Hy 90–4 are added in DV after the Assumption of Mary. It goes without saying that the liturgy of each of these feasts must have been affected by these differences. In the case of the feast of St Stephen and the Assumption of Mary, however, the details are unclear because of the vagueness of the rubrics in DV.

There are hymns that are used in different ways in the Canterbury and the Winchester Hymnals. At Christmas the additional hymn of the Canterbury Hymnal, Hy 37, was assigned to Matins. It is not clear at which hour the Matins hymn of the Winchester type, Hy 39, was sung at Canterbury.

At Pentecost only the Canterbury type provides special hymns for Tierce, Sext and None, Hy 79–81. These are originally part of a single hymn, which is specified for use at Vespers in the Winchester type. Hy 76 and 77 are not assigned to the same canonical hours either (Hy 76: Vespers (Canterbury), Matins (Winchester); Hy 77: Matins (Canterbury), Lauds (Winchester)). This leaves the Canterbury type's additional hymn, Hy 78, for Lauds.

The Canterbury type has three hymns for the feast of a Confessor, the Winchester type only two, with Hy 123 doubling for Vespers and Matins. The Canterbury type's third hymn, Hy 122, is assigned to the feast of the Apostles in the Winchester Hymnal. For these feasts B has only two hymns, while DV supply the additional version of Hy 117 for Apostles,

---

[37] BCDJV do not give cross-references if a hymn is used on two separate occasions. As the hymnal follows the church calendar, one would expect each hymn to be given on the first occasion of its use in the liturgical year. So Hy 65 was presumably not used at Candlemas in the Canterbury Hymnal and Hy 66 was not used at Annunciation in the Winchester Hymnal. On the other hand Hy 65 and 66 could have also been used at the Assumption of Mary in the Canterbury Hymnal and Hy 65 at the Annunciation in the Winchester Hymnal, for Candlemas precedes Annunciation and Annunciation precedes the Assumption of Mary. See, however, below, p. 17.

Hy 103. Hy 44 is assigned to Epiphany in the Canterbury Hymnal, to Candlemas in the Winchester type. The arrangements for either feast are not completely clear in either hymnal. However, the Epiphany hymns Hy 43 and 45 are assigned to Vespers and Lauds by the Canterbury type; in the Winchester type it is the other way around. While the same hymns are provided in both types for the feast of St Michael (Hy 95–7) and for All Saints (Hy 98–100), they are directed for use at different canonical hours.

The Winchester type has abbreviated hymns in some cases. The stanzas omitted are Hy 44, stanzas 6 and 7, Hy 45, stanzas 3 and 5, Hy 66, stanzas 2 and 6, Hy 73, stanzas 2, 4, 6 and 8, Hy 74, stanzas 2, 4 and 7 and Hy 81, stanza 3.

A hymnal for the canons of Exeter

In comparing H, the hymnal for canons, with the two monastic types at these points, we find it agreeing sometimes with Winchester, sometimes with Canterbury, sometimes with neither.[38]

H does not include a hymn for the feast of St Andrew. If H's hymnal agreed with H's collectar at this point, it did not include hymns for St Laurence or Maundy Thursday, although the relevant section is missing in the manuscript. It does, however, contain a hymn to St Martin, but not the same as that in the Canterbury Hymnal.[39] In the case of the hymns for Lent, hymnal and collectar do not agree. While the collectar agrees with the Canterbury type, in the hymnal Hy 57, which is included in both monastic types, is missing. On the other hand H contains not only the additional hymns typical for Canterbury (Hy 54 and 56), but two more. The liturgical use of this set of hymns is not completely clear, but is obviously quite distinct from that of the monastic hymnals.[40]

Annunciation is apparently not provided for in H's hymnal (although the first half of the hymnal has no rubrics). Hy 65 and 66 are assigned to Candlemas and the Assumption of Mary as in the Winchester type, although the latter is directed for use at Compline.[41] This hour is not

[38] For the following, see the list of hymns in H (below, pp. 475–8) and pp. 47–9.

[39] Hy 145.

[40] The two additional hymns are Hy 139 and 140. Oddly, there are three hymns assigned to None (Hy 53, 54 and 55) and three to Compline (Hy 60, 139 and 140).

[41] The hymnal in H resumes after a gap in the middle of what seems to be the section on the Assumption of Mary. Note that H gives cross-references and Hy 65 appears both for Candlemas and Assumption. H provides two hymns (Hy 138 and 144) for the

normally assigned a special hymn in the monastic hymnals. H's collectar, however, confuses the issue. Even though it agrees with the hymnal, it prescribes Hy 65 and 66 for Annunciation as well, as in the Canterbury type, with the difference that here Hy 66 is a Vespers hymn, as in the Winchester type.

As regards the other additional hymns typical of the Canterbury type, Hy 41, 90–4 and 103 are also found in H's hymnal, but not Hy 37 and, perhaps, Hy 78, which may, however, be missing due to a gap in the manuscript, together with the other hymns for Pentecost. On the other hand Hy 37, 41, 78 and 90–3 are not included in H's collectar. Note that H's hymnal apparently assigns Hy 90–4 to a different liturgical use (and so, in the case of Hy 94, does the collectar).[42]

The arrangements for Christmas differ with regard to both monastic types and agree with the Winchester type only in not including Hy 37. At Pentecost they basically agree with the Winchester type, but details are reminiscent of the Canterbury type. However, for this section only the collectar is extant.

In H, Hy 122 is a hymn for the Apostles as in the Winchester type, but H also includes DV's Hy 103 for Lauds and Hy 122 is only an alternative hymn for Vespers, possibly for the feast of St John the Evangelist. He is the only Apostle who is assigned this hymn in H's collectar, which otherwise designates Hy 122 for Confessors, thereby agreeing with the Canterbury type.

Hy 44 is assigned to Candlemas by H (hymnal and collectar) as in the Winchester type, but also to Christmas, where it appears in neither of the monastic hymnals. The arrangements for Epiphany differ from both monastic types.

At Michaelmas H agrees with the Winchester Hymnal, at All Saints H's collectar agrees with the Canterbury type (the omission of Hy 99 is probably accidental), but H itself (the hymnal) disagrees. It is, however, closer to Canterbury than to Winchester.[43]

Nativity of Mary, which otherwise does not appear to have had specific hymns, that is, hymns not used earlier in the year. In fact, in the hymnal, but not the collectar, Hy 138 is already given among the Candlemas hymns and this agrees with V.

[42] Hy 94 is assigned to Advent (and in the collectar to Annunciation). Hy 90–3 are added after Candlemas instead of after Assumption and their precise function remains unclear. See above, p. 12.

[43] Canterbury type: Vespers, Hy 98, Matins, Hy 99, Lauds, Hy 100; Winchester type:

Hy 44 and 66 are unabbreviated in H. In Hy 45 one stanza, the third, is omitted, but it is used by itself for Matins of the Holy Innocents. Hy 73, 74 and 81 are lost.

With the exception of Hy 57, H contains all the hymns that are common to both types of monastic hymnal, if the gap in the manuscript is taken into account. In addition there are some hymns which H only shares with one of B, V or D: Hy 115 (also a later addition in V), 116, 134, 138 and 140. What is more, H includes *Pange lingua*, which is not commonly found in English hymnals until later,[44] as well as *Agnoscat omne saeculum*, *Corde natus*, *Infantum meritis* and *Gaude visceribus*, hymns that were not in universal use in later times either, some of them even rare.[45] Moreover, *Rex angelorum praepotens*, *Fratres unanimes*, *Rex Christe factor* and *O Nazarene lux* are not otherwise found in English hymnals at all.[46] Apart from the expected differences between a secular and a monastic hymnal, there may be another influence at work. As we shall see, there is some reason to suspect a (more direct) continental element here.

CONTINENTAL SOURCES

Returning to the question of continental sources for the differences between the Winchester and the Canterbury Hymnals, we are faced with the difficulty that we do not have a hymnal from either Ghent or Fleury which is earlier than (or even from approximately the same period as) the Anglo-Saxon hymnals. We therefore have to rely on indirect sources of information.

The customaries

In respect of customaries, in particular, our situation has improved a little since 1968, although the new evidence may be thought to have obscured

---

Vespers, Hy 98, Matins, Hy 100, Lauds, Hy 99; H: Vespers, Hy 99, Matins, Hy 98, Lauds, Hy 100.

[44] Hy 143. See Gneuss, *HHEM*, p. 78, and Mearns, *Early Latin Hymnaries*, p. 65.

[45] Hy 135, 136, 137 and 144. Hy 135 and 136 were, however, used in the York Hymnal; see Gneuss, *HHEM*, p. 426–7. Hy 137 and 144 are not listed as occurring in other English manuscripts either by Gneuss, *HHEM*, pp. 77–9 and 425–30, or Mearns, *Early Latin Hymnaries*, pp. 43 and 36. However, Gneuss does not mention them as *not* occurring in English manuscripts in *HHEM*, p. 109.

[46] Hy 139, 141, 142 and 145. See Gneuss, *HHEM*, p. 109.

matters, rather than clarified them. At the time, Gneuss concluded that there appeared to be one tangible parallel between the Winchester type and presumed Fleury usage on Sundays in Lent.[47] However, in the light of our new information on Fleury, this parallel seems much more doubtful than before. It depended on the assumption that Fleury took over much of the liturgical usage of Cluny, when it was reformed on Cluniac lines, but the description of the *consuetudines* of Fleury in the tenth century by Theoderic of Fleury and Amorbach, recently discovered by Anselme Davril,[48] proves that this was not the case. The usage of Fleury appears to have been closer to that of the monasteries in Lotharingia and Flanders, which it may have influenced. At the same time, it is clear from Theoderic that Fleury was on the whole more conservative than had been thought hitherto. This means that the later and more extensive customary of Fleury, which dates from the thirteenth century,[49] may represent considerably older traditions even where it cannot be checked against Theoderic. While Theoderic has nothing to say about hymns, the later customary does, even if it does not give the complete hymn cycle. The hymns have, of course, been added to, but the core is likely to be old.

Concerning Sundays in Lent it disagrees with the Winchester type and the *Regularis concordia* as well as Cluny in providing special hymns.[50] The hymns prescribed are Hy 55 for Matins, Hy 60 for Lauds and *Iesu sacrator* for Vespers. Of these, Hy 55 is common to all Anglo-Saxon hymnals, Hy 60 is included in DV and in H, and the third appears to be unusual, being

---

[47] Gneuss, *HHEM*, pp. 73–4.

[48] A. Davril, 'Un coutumier de Fleury du début du XIe siècle', *Revue Bénédictine* 76 (1966), 351–4. See also his 'Un moine de Fleury aux environs de l'an mil: Thierry, dit d'Amorbach', in *Etudes ligériennes d'histoire et d'archéologie médiévale*, ed. R. Louis (Auxerre, 1975), pp. 97–104, and, in the same volume, L. Donnat, 'Recherches sur l'influence de Fleury au Xe siècle', pp. 165–74. The text has been edited by A. Davril and L. Donnat as 'Consuetudines Floriacenses Antiquiores', *Consuetudinum saeculi X/XI/ XII monumenta non-Cluniacensia*, CCM 7.3 (Siegburg, 1984), 3–60; the introduction to the text is by K. Hallinger and A. Davril, 'Fleury's Bräuche um die Wende des 10./11. Jahrhunderts', *Consuetudinum saeculi X/XI/XII monumenta. Introductiones*, ed. Hallinger, pp. 331–70, esp. 347–50 (comparison of Theoderic with the Cluniacensians) and 354–9 (comparison of Theoderic with the Synod of Winchester and the *Regularis concordia*).

[49] *Consuetudines Floriacenses*, ed. Davril; see esp. pp. xliv–xlv of the Introduction.

[50] See Hallinger, *Gorze-Kluny*, pp. 914–16, *Regularis concordia*, ed. Symons and Spath, ch. 39, and *Consuetudines Floriacenses*, ed. Davril, ch. 80A.

known to Mearns only from Moissac, Jumièges and Verona.[51] Thus, while Winchester and Cluny agree on Sundays in Lent, Cluniac influence cannot have reached Winchester via Fleury in this case. Apart from Hy 60 no other hymns are mentioned in the Fleury customary which occur in the Canterbury, but not in the Winchester, type.

In a few other instances the thirteenth-century customary may throw light on how much or how little the Winchester type was influenced by Fleury. In some cases it is possible to compare the older customs of Cluny, which exist in various redactions, the archetype of which actually goes back to the tenth century, and the *Liber tramitis* of Odilo of Cluny.[52] Unfortunately, the other early customaries do not yield any relevant information.

As regards the Marian hymns and the question of their use at Annunciation, Hy 65 was used at Matins at Candlemas both in Fleury and Cluny as in the Winchester type. It was sung at other feasts of Mary as well, but apparently not at Annunciation as in the Canterbury type.[53] Hy 66 was used for all feasts of Mary at Lauds or at Tierce in Fleury, but not for Matins as in Canterbury. In Cluny Hy 66 was a Vespers hymn and sung at the Assumption of Mary as in Winchester, but also at Candlemas.[54]

At Christmas both Cluny and Fleury assign Hy 39 to (first) Vespers, which does not agree with any Anglo-Saxon hymnal,[55] but least of all with the Canterbury type. But they also appear to have disagreed among themselves. At any rate Odilo and Fleury differ on the hymn for Matins.[56] It should also be noted that in Cluny Hy 39 was also used on the Vigil of Epiphany, but not, it appears, in Fleury.[57]

At Pentecost Hy 79–81 appear to be one single hymn in both Fleury

[51] Mearns, *Early Latin Hymnaries*, p. 47.

[52] In the following notes 'Cluny BCG' will refer to the three oldest versions of the Cluniac customary, *Consuetudines Cluniacensium antiquiores*, ed. Hallinger, 'O' to Odilo of Cluny's *Liber tramitis aevi*, ed. Dinter, and 'F' to the *Consuetudines Floriacenses*, ed. Davril. All are quoted by chapter.

[53] Cluny BC 27, G 82, O 100, 109, F 241, 354 and 373. See above, pp. 11–12.

[54] Cluny BCG 57, B 58, G 63.6, O 31, 51, 100 etc., F 243, 261, 354, 355, 362, 373 and 509.

[55] Cluny BCG 18, O 12.3 and F 25. See above, p. 12.

[56] O 13.1 (Hy 36) and F 26 (Hy 46). Odilo (O 13.3) agrees with H in using Hy 44 at Christmas, but not for the same hour; see above, p. 14.

[57] Cluny BCG 25, O 22.1 and F 42.

and Cluny, but Cluny agrees even further with Winchester in assigning this hymn to Vespers, while it is a Matins hymn in Fleury.[58]

At the feast of St Michael both Cluny and Fleury agree with Winchester in assigning Hy 96 to Vespers. However, Fleury has only two hymns for this feast, not three as the Anglo-Saxon hymnals, and uses Hy 97 for both Matins and Lauds. The same appears to be true of Cluny.[59]

At All Saints, Fleury and Cluny agree with Winchester in having Hy 99 sung at Lauds, but with Exeter (H) in having Hy 98 sung at Matins. There is no third hymn mentioned at Cluny. Hy 100 may have been unknown there, but at Fleury it is sung at Vespers.[60]

This is to say that whereas usage at Fleury at these points is closer to the Winchester than to the Canterbury type except in the question of Sundays in Lent, Cluny is even closer to the Winchester type at the Assumption of Mary and at Pentecost as well as on Sundays in Lent. On the other hand, in two cases Fleury and Cluny agree against the Anglo-Saxon monastic hymnals (St Michael, All Saints).

There is one further instance of agreement between the Winchester type and the customs of Fleury. Hy 44 is assigned to Candlemas (Lauds) by both. However, at Fleury it was sung at Epiphany as well, not at Matins as in Canterbury, but at the Lauds of the Vigil of Epiphany.[61] Here there appears to be no early information from Cluny.

With regard to the Cluniac customs it may be noteworthy that even the older redactions all include hymns which are not found in the Anglo-Saxon monastic hymnals except as later additions: *Iam Christe sol iustitiae* and *Pange lingua* with its *divisio*,[62] *Lustra sex*.[63]

Thus the results of the comparison are somewhat indecisive. They could indicate that Cluniac customs influenced the Winchester type directly or by other routes than via Fleury. Unfortunately, our data are neither complete nor reliable enough to venture such a hypothesis. The statements

---

[58] Cluny BG 47, O 74, F 178 and 179. See above, p. 12.

[59] Cluny BCG 63, O 115, F 393 and 395. See above, p. 13.

[60] Here we have no evidence for Cluny earlier than Odilo (O 125). F 418–24.

[61] F 41, 241 and 512.

[62] Longer hymns could be divided up into sections each of which was used at a different hour of the feast in question; cf. Hy 79–81 above, p. 12. Such sections are called *divisiones*.

[63] Cluny BCG 34 and 37. The latter is Hy 143 and included in H; see above, p. 15. Both are added by a hand of s. xi^ex or xii^in in V; see below, pp. 52–3.

in the Cluniac customs may not, after all, go back to the tenth-century archetype and the customs at Fleury may have been subject to change at just those feasts. What is more, it is by no means clear that the relevant liturgical features were typical of Cluny and could not have been derived independently from another source, for example Ghent. Still, the material does suggest that the Winchester type may have been influenced by Fleury or Cluny, but was not taken over from either monastery directly. It seems quite possible, however, that Hy 100, which is in all Anglo-Saxon hymnals, was borrowed directly from Fleury.[64]

Four Frankish hymnals

While the Flemish customs are silent on the matter of the hymns and there is no hymnal of St Peter's in Ghent available for comparison, we do have one fairly early Flemish hymnal, that of Saint-Bertin (Boulogne-sur-Mer, Bibliothèque Municipale, 20, written *c.* 1000).[65] It is interesting not only in being Flemish, but also in that both Saint-Bertin and St Peter's were reformed by the followers of Gerard of Brogne.[66]

Moreover, there is abundant evidence for ecclesiastical and political contacts between Saint-Bertin and England. For example, Grimbald of Saint-Bertin, who came to England *c.* 886 and was made abbot of the New Minster in Winchester, may or may not already have known the New Hymnal. The monks who fled from the reform of Saint-Bertin in 944 to find refuge with King Edmund certainly would have.[67] The abbot of Saint-Bertin maintained friendly relations with Dunstan and his successors at Canterbury, Æthelgar (988–90) and Sigeric (990–4).[68]

---

[64] For Hy 100, see below, p. 23.

[65] See Leroquais, *Les Psautiers manuscrits* I, 94–101 and Mearns, *Early Latin Hymnaries*, *passim*.

[66] Hallinger, *Gorze-Kluny*, pp. 79, 290–1 and 300, and Wormald, 'Æthelwold and his Continental Counterparts', pp. 25–6.

[67] Stenton, *Anglo-Saxon England*, pp. 271 and 447.

[68] 'Epistola Odberti ad Æthelgarum archiepiscopum', 'Epistola Odberti abbatis ad Sigericum archiepiscopum', both ed. W. Stubbs in his *Memorials of Saint Dunstan*, pp. 384–5 and 388–9 respectively. Note also the activities of Goscelin of Saint-Bertin in England and his relations with Sherborne and Wilton; see F. Barlow, *Edward the Confessor*, 2nd ed. (London, 1979), p. 233. On relations between Anglo-Saxon royalty and the monastery of Saint-Bertin, see, for example, Stenton, *Anglo-Saxon England*, p. 355. Note also that the *Encomium Emmae Reginae* (ed. A. Campbell, Camden 3rd

Another hymnal which might be relevant here is that of Corbie. It might be thought to have had an influence on the Winchester type especially, if the chronicle of Æthelwold's monastery, Abingdon, correctly reports that Æthelwold had a chanter come from Corbie to teach the monks of Abingdon.[69] The fact that Anglo-Saxon neumes of this period are most closely related to the style of Corbie is surely of importance here.[70] From Corbie we have a rather late manuscript hymnal from the eleventh century.[71]

These two hymnals, from Saint-Bertin and Corbie, and two Norman hymnals from Jumièges and Lyre[72] are the earliest extant from northwest Francia,[73] that is, from Francia north and west of the Ile de France. It was

Series 72 (London, 1949)) was written by a monk of Saint-Bertin (or, perhaps, Saint-Omer): see pp. xix–xxiii and 37. Cf. Ortenberg, *The English Church and the Continent*, pp. 21–40.

[69] 'ex Corbiensi coenobio, quod in Francia situm est, ecclesiastica ea tempestate disciplina opinatissimo viros accersiit solertissimos, quos in legendo psallendoque sui imitarentur', *Chronicon monasterii de Abingdon*, ed. J. Stevenson, 2 vols., RS (London, 1858) I, 129. This is not a contemporary document, but a twelfth-century chronicle; cf. Stenton, *Anglo-Saxon England*, p. 699.

[70] This is discussed by Rankin, 'Neumatic Notations in Anglo-Saxon England', pp. 131–2. See also Hartzell, 'An Eleventh-Century English Missal Fragment', pp. 45–97, on the possible influence of Corbie, Saint-Denis and Saint-Vaast on the missals of Winchester and Worcester.

[71] Amiens, Bibliothèque Municipale, 131; see E. Coyecque, *Amiens, Catalogue général des manuscrits des bibliothèques publiques de France, Départements* 19 (Paris, 1893), 61–2 and Mearns, *Early Latin Hymnaries*.

[72] Rouen, Bibliothèque municipale, 56 (A. 347) (Jumièges, s. xii^{ex}) and Rouen, Bibliothèque Municipale, 57 (A. 431) (Jumièges, s. xii^{ex}), both containing the identical hymnal, and Evreux, Bibliothèque Municipale, 70 L. (Lyre, s. xi², hymnal slightly later than the rest of the manuscript); see M.-C. Garand, G. Grand and D. Muzerelle, *Ouest de la France et Pays de Loire*, 2 vols., Catalogue des manuscrits en écriture latine portant des indications de date, de lieu ou de copiste 7 (Paris, 1984) I, 465 and 501. Note that the Evreux manuscript had previously been assigned to the church of Saint-Ouen in Rouen, by V. Leroquais, *Les Psautiers manuscrits* I, 196–7, and to Saint-Amand in Rouen by S. Corbin, 'Valeur et sens de la notation alphabétique, à Jumièges et en Normandie', *Jumièges* II, 913–24, at 918.

[73] The hymnal of Jumièges, however, is preserved in two other manuscripts of approximately the same date, which have not been indexed by Mearns, *Early Latin Hymnaries*: Rouen, Bibliothèque Municipale, 226 (A. 276) and 227 (A. 367), s. xii^{ex} and xiiiⁱⁿ respectively. See R.-J. Hesbert, 'Les manuscrits liturgiques de Jumièges', *Jumièges* II, 855–72, at 867.

this region of the Continent, directly across the Channel, that the Anglo-Saxons were in most immediate contact with and whose influence can be traced in Anglo-Saxon pontificals and missals.[74] The four hymnals are therefore worth looking at as a group as well as singly. They may give us an idea of what the hymnals of other influential centres of the region might have looked like, even though no early version survives.

Normandy itself is a possible source of influence. There was traffic across the Channel before the time of Queen Emma and her son Edward and some of the contacts were of an ecclesiastical nature.[75] However, the Norman church was in a bad state for most of the tenth century, even if the monasteries of Normandy were being reformed by William of Dijon in the early eleventh century. Gneuss has already set out the differences between Anglo-Saxon and Norman hymnals by demonstrating the considerable impact which the Norman Conquest had on the use of hymns in England.[76]

The most noticeable feature of the four Frankish hymnals (when compared with the common stock of the Anglo-Saxon hymnals) is that a considerable number of hymns is lacking in all of them.[77] This has already been pointed out by Gneuss for the Norman hymnals, but with the exception of Hy 2 and 124 all the hymns missing in the two early Norman hymnals are missing at Corbie and Saint-Bertin as well. This is also true of Hy 57, included in all Anglo-Saxon hymnals except that of Exeter. Looking at the hymns that were only introduced into the Anglo-Saxon hymnals after the late tenth century and are thus not yet included in B, we find that only Hy 39 and 75 are present in all four continental hymnals or even in all three later ones (excluding Saint-Bertin).[78] So Hy 39 and 75 could be assumed to have been borrowed because they were

[74] *Two Anglo-Saxon Pontificals: the Egbert and Sidney Sussex Pontificals*, ed. H. M. J. Banting, HBS 104 (London, 1989), xvii–xxxiv. See above, p. 20, n. 70.

[75] L. Musset, 'Les contacts entre l'église Normande et l'église d'Angleterre de 911 à 1066' and N. Bulst, 'La réforme monastique en Normandie: étude prosopographique sur la diffusion de la réforme de Guillaume de Dijon', in *Les Mutations socio-culturelles au tournant des XIe – XIIe siècles*, ed. Foreville, pp. 67–84 and 317–30 respectively.

[76] Gneuss, *HHEM*, pp. 81–3.

[77] Hy 38, 42, 52, 53, 58, 68, 95, 100 and 122, plus, of course, the hymns for English saints, which are not considered here. Hy 114 is a special case, since it is part of the series Hy 104–16, and its inclusion presupposes that of the series.

[78] The others are Hy 40, 43, 46, 63 and 64.

newly and universally popular across the Channel,[79] but not the others. Fewer of the hymns that are common to the Anglo-Saxon hymnals are lacking in the hymnal of Corbie than in the other three Frankish hymnals, but the number of shared hymns is probably too small to be significant.[80]

The comparison of the Canterbury type with these hymnals yields ambiguous results. Of the six early Canterbury hymns, three[81] are missing in all four of the Frankish hymnals; one (Hy 54) is included in all of them, one (Hy 56) is found only in the Norman hymnals and one (Hy 78) only at Saint-Bertin. Of the later hymns, those common to D and V, Hy 41, 69 and 90–3 are missing in all four hymnals. Hy 60 and 103 do not appear in Saint-Bertin, but in the other, later, hymnals. This leaves Hy 94, which is included in the hymnals of Saint-Bertin and Corbie, but not in the Norman hymnals.

Each of the four hymnals also contains hymns not (or only sporadically) represented in the Anglo-Saxon hymnals. It is perhaps noteworthy that *Pange lingua* (Hy 143) is in all of them, even in Saint-Bertin, which makes the Anglo-Saxon monastic hymnals look a little old-fashioned. Corbie shares Hy 141 with H.

If any of the three types of hymnal in Anglo-Saxon England derived from a single source, it is not likely to have been a hymnal of this region. The Canterbury type was not borrowed from Ghent, unless the hymnal of Ghent was quite different from the hymnal of Saint-Bertin.

Hymns from further abroad

The Anglo-Saxon hymns seem to be of mixed provenance, as far as they can be traced in Mearns's sources. From his data it appears that of the thirteen hymns common to the later Anglo-Saxon monastic hymnals,[82]

---

[79] In its older version as OHy 34, Hy 39 had, of course, already been known in England, see above, p. 4.

[80] Corbie does not lack any hymns of the common Anglo-Saxon stock which are included in all the other three manuscripts and it does have Hy 63, 74 and 127–9 (all lacking in Saint-Bertin, Jumièges and Lyre), Hy 2 and 124 (lacking in Jumièges and Lyre) and Hy 46 and 104$_2$ (lacking in St Bertin and Jumièges). Hy 39, 127–9, 143 and 160 are already included in the ninth-century hymnal in 'Corbie *a-b* script', Düsseldorf Universitätsbibliothek cod. B. 3; see Bullough and Corrêa, 'Text, Chant', pp. 498–9 and H. Dausend, *Das älteste Sakramentar der Münsterkirche zu Essen* (Essen, 1920), p. 33.

[81] Hy 35, 37 and 88.

[82] Hy 38, 40, 42, 43, 52, 53, 57, 58, 64, 68, 95, 100 and 122.

but missing in the four northern Frankish hymnals, there is one (Hy 42) that is not attested outside England. Five[83] were clearly going out of use. Two of these five (Hy 52 and 53) had been fairly common in France. Eleven of the thirteen hymns under discussion, however, were either very rare in France or not attested at all. This leaves Germany and Italy.[84] Some of the eleven were never common anywhere, others were more or less current in both countries, but Hy 68 was virtually restricted to Germany and Hy 95 to Italy.[85]

The borrowing of hymns from German sources would most likely take place via Lotharingia. Italian hymns could have been introduced by Anglo-Saxon pilgrims to Rome. Gneuss is also prepared to consider the Cluniac connections with southern Italy as a possible link, but one would surely have expected hymns backed by Cluniac influence to spread further.[86] It should be noted that in the case of Hy 100 the Anglo-Saxons seem to have borrowed the southern French and Spanish, not the Italian and German, version, perhaps via Fleury.[87]

There are a few hymns of the Canterbury Hymnal not yet accounted for.[88] For them Mearns's results are similar. Hy 35 is found only in one Italian hymnal, Hy 37 seems to have been borrowed from Lotharingia[89] and Hy 88 was in use in both Germany and Italy. Of the hymns only introduced in DV, Hy 91–3 are not attested outside England, while Hy 90 is attested sparsely in Germany and Italy and Hy 41 is rare.[90] Nowhere among the other hymnals that Mearns lists is there one that bears a striking resemblance to the Anglo-Saxon ones. So unless further research radically alters the picture, it would seem that the Anglo-Saxons borrowed

---

[83] Hy 38, 40, 52, 53 and 122. See Mearns, *Early Latin Hymnaries*, pp. 12, 40, 56, 66 and 21 respectively. For Hy 43, 57, 58, 64, 68, 95 and 100, see Mearns, *ibid.*, pp. 48, 47, 23, 52, 11, 56 and 64 respectively.

[84] Spain does not appear to have played a significant role, even if Mearns's material is scanty; we would hardly expect it to be influential in the tenth century.

[85] Its increase in popularity later on was due to its use by the Cistercian order, as the distribution in Mearns's *Early Latin Hymnaries* shows.

[86] See above, pp. 15–19.   [87] Gneuss, *HHEM*, p. 73.

[88] Hy 35, 37, 41, 88, 90–3; see Mearns, *Early Latin Hymnaries*, pp. 57, 83, 77, 55, 53, 36 and 53 respectively.

[89] Gneuss, *HHEM*, p. 73, n. 16.

[90] Hy 69, being a processional hymn, cannot be expected to be listed regularly in hymnaries, so Mearns's index is not reliable evidence for its use. See Gneuss, *HHEM*, p. 73, n. 14.

widely in assembling their hymn cycles. As for Hy 42 and 91–3, they may well be by an English author, as are the more obviously English hymns for SS Augustine, Cuthbert and Dunstan.[91]

THE STRUCTURE OF THE ANGLO-SAXON HYMNALS

The Anglo-Saxon hymnals are laid out according to a common liturgical scheme. They are divided up into *ordinarium de tempore*, hymns for normal Sundays and weekdays, *proprium de tempore*, hymns for feasts of the Lord (Christmas, Easter etc.), *proprium sanctorum*, hymns for the feasts of particular saints, and *commune sanctorum*, hymns for feasts of unspecified saints. Except for the hymnal in C the two *propria* are run together in the Anglo-Saxon hymnals.[92]

The first section gives the hymns for the Hours of a normal Sunday, the first day of the week, then those for Vespers, Matins and Lauds of the rest of the week. (The other Hours do not change.) For the first Vespers, Matins and Lauds of Sunday and for Compline two hymns are given, a shorter and a longer one. According to the *Regularis concordia* and Ælfric, Hy 2, 5, 6 and 11 are to be sung from the octave of Pentecost until 1 November and Hy 1, 3, 4 and 12 are to replace them in winter and during Lent.[93] This rule agrees with the instructions of the *Indicium regule* and the customs of Fleury.[94] The collectar in H does not agree with

---

[91] Hy 83–5, 61 and 82 in D, cf. also Hy 116.

[92] The terms used for these sections are *termini technici*; they do not actually occur in the hymnal rubrics. In D the sections correspond to Hy 1–31, 32–101 and 102–26.

[93] 'Regularis concordia', ed. Symons and Spath, chs. 39 and 91 and 'Aelfrici abbatis epistula', ed. Nocent, chs. 13 and 54. On these texts, see above, pp. 9–10. Actually the *Regularis concordia* contradicts itself on the matter of Sundays in Lent, which may reflect its use of conflicting sources. (On Sundays in Lent, see also above, pp. 16–17.) Neither the *Regularis concordia* nor Ælfric is clear about the hymn for Compline to be sung in the period between Passion and Pentecost.

[94] 'Indicium regule', ed. Bateson, and *Consuetudines Floriacenses*, ed. Davril, ch. 225. The agreement is not precise, since the 'Indicium' and the *Consuetudines* are based on hymnals that did not include Hy 2. On Hy 2 in the New Hymnal, cf. Gneuss, *HHEM*, p. 50. The hymnal on which the 'Durham Ritual' entries are based may not have included Hy 2, as Hy 1 appears beside Hy 11; see above, p. 71, and below, pp. 57–8. The Cluniac custom was to begin with Hy 12 in November, but to commence singing Hy 3 and 4 on the first of October; see *Consuetudines Cluniacensium antiquiores*, ed. Hallinger, chs. 15 and 48, and cf. *Consuetudinum saeculi X/XI/XII monumenta. Introductiones*, ed. Hallinger, pp. 354 and 366.

this.[95] The instructions there for the interchange between Hy 1 and 2 look a little confused, as if they reflected conflicting usage, but, roughly speaking, Hy 2 is only sung from August to the end of October. The interchange between Hy 3 and 5 and between 4 and 6 apparently takes place on the octave of Epiphany and in the third week of November. The arrangements for Compline are complicated by the inclusion of special hymns for Compline in Lent and another for Sundays between Epiphany and Septuagesima. The collectar in H often offers alternatives so that it appears to be a composite document or to reflect ongoing change or perhaps both.

In the *Proprium* the arrangement follows the liturgical year, beginning with Advent. A full set of hymns for a feast or festal season consists of three hymns, for Vespers, Matins and Lauds. If there is only one hymn available or if there are only two, a hymn may be divided into two or three *divisiones* like Hy 86. It may also be sung repeatedly or, if the feast in question is a saint's day, an appropriate hymn from the *commune sanctorum* may be used. Important feasts such as Pentecost may also have special hymns for the Day Hours Tierce, Sext and None. It is typical of H, the non-monastic hymnal, that it has special hymns for Compline on these feasts, too, for example Hy 66 for the Assumption of Mary.

While the *ordinarium de tempore* developed quite early in the history of the New Hymnal and then remained extremely stable, the two *propria* were subject to much change and it is in this section in particular that the Anglo-Saxon hymnals disagree among each other and with other types of New Hymnal.[96]

Only the most important of the saints were included in the *proprium sanctorum*. At the feasts of other saints the appropriate hymns from the *commune sanctorum* were selected. This section provides hymns for feasts of apostles, a single martyr, several martyrs, confessors and holy virgins.

The *commune sanctorum* is followed by hymns for the Dedication of the Church. This feast is unlike others in that its date would depend on the church concerned. Finally, a number of new hymns not originally included are appended to the hymnals proper in D, V and J.

[95] On the collectar, see below, pp. 48–9.
[96] Most of the hymns discussed above, pp. 11–24, are *proprium* hymns.

2

The transmission of hymns in
Anglo-Saxon manuscripts

This chapter contains descriptions of those Anglo-Saxon manuscripts in which texts of hymns are found and on which this edition is based. Most of them contain other liturgical texts. They are grouped by type of manuscript, beginning with the hymnals and the *Expositio hymnorum*.[1] Special attention is given to Durham Cathedral Library, B. III. 32, both here and in the edition.

The edition does not necessarily include all the hymns ever used liturgically in Anglo-Saxon England. Some have probably been lost. In other cases it is difficult to determine whether or not a hymn-like poem functioned as a liturgical hymn because the manuscript context does not definitely indicate it and there are no other sources that could throw light on its use. This is particularly true of religious poetry in honour of saints, especially Anglo-Saxon ones. Their liturgical use would have been strictly localized and possibly short-lived and so less likely to be attested in our sources. Such texts, not included here, are the hymns to St Æthelwold, St Swithun and St Birinus ascribed to Wulfstan of Winchester[2] and all but one of the hymns written by Bede.[3] There are others.[4] Likewise excluded

---

[1] On types of liturgical manuscripts available in Anglo-Saxon England, see H. Gneuss, 'Liturgical Books in Anglo-Saxon England and their Old English Terminology'.

[2] For these hymns, see Wulfstan of Winchester, *Life of Æthelwold*, ed. Lapidge and Winterbottom, pp. xxiii–xxx, cxiii–cxv and cxviii, Gneuss, *HHEM*, pp. 117–18 and 246–8 and *AH* 48, 9–18. There are indications that at least two of them were used liturgically. Hy 83–5 have also been ascribed to Wulfstan of Winchester.

[3] For Bede's hymns, see Gneuss, *HHEM*, pp. 53–4, *AH* 50, 96–116, Bede, 'Opera Rhythmica', ed. Fraipont, pp. 405–39 and, for the hymn to St Æthelthryth, Bede, *Historia ecclesiastica* IV.20 (*Bede's Ecclesiastical History of the English People*, ed. Colgrave and Mynors, pp. 396–400). The only hymn by him in this edition is Hy 73.

[4] For example, the hymns to St Judoc ed. M. Henshaw, 'Two Hymns on St Judocus',

here are the manuscripts of works by Sedulius and Prudentius, for even if a couple of hymns were originally excerpted from them, they clearly represent a completely different textual tradition.[5]

While two of the hymnals, V and D, include what is clearly a processional hymn for Maundy Thursday (Hy 69), processional hymns are not in general included here, and in fact it is not easy to decide if a text might have been used for processions.

Some of the evidence for the use of hymns in Anglo-Saxon England consists in hymn incipits given in a number of liturgical texts. A few of these have already been mentioned. Others will be discussed below.[6] There are also allusions to hymns in non-liturgical texts. These tend to be unspecific about liturgical use, but are evidence for the familiarity of the texts.[7]

HYMNALS AND *EXPOSITIO HYMNORUM*

Besides the five manuscripts already mentioned in ch. 1 there is also a hymnal fragment (Ri) to be discussed here.

D = *Durham, Cathedral Library, B. III. 32 (the 'Durham Hymnal')*

List of contents:[8]

Speculum 21 (1946), 325–6, and the hymn to St Machutus (*AH* 43, 222–4 (no. 373)). Hymns transmitted in post-Conquest manuscripts may nevertheless be by Anglo-Saxon authors; cf. K. D. Hartzell, 'A St. Albans Miscellany in New York', *Mittellateinisches Jahrbuch* 10 (1975), 20–61.

[5] Gneuss, *HHEM*, pp. 116–17. The same would certainly apply to manuscripts of the poetry of Venantius Fortunatus, but only fragments are preserved; see R. W. Hunt, 'Manuscript Evidence for Knowledge of the Poems of Venantius Fortunatus in Late Anglo-Saxon England' (with an Appendix by M. Lapidge, 'Knowledge of the Poems in the Earlier Period'), *ASE* 8 (1979), 279–95.

[6] See above, pp. 7 and 9–10, and below, pp. 45, 48–9 and 58–9. Cf. Gneuss, *HHEM*, pp. 107, 109, 111–12 and 118–21.

[7] See above, p. 4, for allusions to hymns of the Old Hymnal. The most specific allusion to a hymn of the New Hymnal is in *Byrhtferth's Enchiridion*, ed. P. S. Baker and M. Lapidge, EETS s.s. 15 (1995), 114, where stanzas I and IV of Hy 7 are translated.

[8] The manuscript is Ker no. 107, Temple no. 101, Gneuss, 'Preliminary List', no. 244. It is also described in Mynors, *Durham Cathedral Manuscripts*, pp. 28–9 (no. 22), and Gneuss, *HHEM*, pp. 85–90. It is the core and basis of the present edition, which replaces Stevenson's unreliable edition (*The Latin Hymns*) of 1851.

Part A

1r–43r	Latin hymnal with Old English interlinear gloss
43v–45v	proverbs in Latin and Old English
46r–55v	Latin monastic canticles with Old English interlinear gloss
55v	two fragments of hymns (Latin, s. xiv)

Part B

56r	blank
56v	line drawing of Dunstan and Æthelwold, in colour
fols. 57–126	Ælfric's Grammar, without the Glossary; 121v–122v *Incipiunt quinque declinationes*[9]
127r	fragment of a hymn (*Felix per omnes*, s. xi), pen trials
127v	exlibris (s. xvii)

The two parts of the manuscript, A and B, were bound together at an early date. This is proved by the entry on 2r (s. xiii): 'Hoc volumen continet ymnarium. canticularium. et in anglica lingua Donatum et quedam alia.' Even earlier evidence is the hymn fragment dating from the eleventh century[10] on 127r, at the end of the Grammar, which is clearly intended to supplement the hymnal.

The binding itself is of nineteenth-century date and a little too tight, so that it is sometimes difficult to read words extending beyond the ruled inner margin. The size of the pages is 235 × 156 mm, that of the written space in Part A 164 × 100 mm. Part A has nineteen lines per page. The leaves have been ruled on the hair side and for the most part the quires are made up so that the hair side faces outwards.[11] On thick leaves the ruling has been retraced in pencil.

Part A (fols. 1–55) seems to have been made up originally of seven quaternions and at first contained only the hymnal and the monastic canticles. Quires 2–7 are complete. The third leaf and the sixth in the seventh quire are singletons.

---

[9] For this text, see H. Gneuss, 'The Study of Language in Anglo-Saxon England', *Bulletin of the John Rylands University Library of Manchester* 72 (1990), 3–32, esp. 6, n. 11.

[10] This is Hy 151, Gneuss's Hy 87a, a hymn included in V and perhaps originally in C; see p. 46. It is sometimes found in English hymnals of the post-Conquest period; see Gneuss, *HHEM*, p. 78. The fragment includes stanzas I and II up to 'fortia solvunt'. It was considered to be too late to be included in the edition of Hy 151 below, pp. 452–5.

[11] This is rather unexpected for an eleventh-century Christ Church manuscript; cf. T. A. M. Bishop, *English Caroline Minuscule*, pp. xii and xxv–xxvi, and *idem*, 'Notes on Cambridge Manuscripts', *Transactions of the Cambridge Bibliographical Society* 3 (1959–63), 93–5 and 412–23, esp. 420–1.

The first quire now consists of seven leaves. Of these fols. 2 and 5, a bifolium, are supply leaves. The first leaf, now a singleton, contains the original beginning of the hymnal, written by the first scribe (D_1). It was rejected after rubrication, but before illumination of the first initial, *O*, had been carried out,[12] possibly because the initial *P* of Hy 3 on the verso was too clearly visible through the parchment. It was replaced by fol. 2, written by the second scribe (D_2). It seems that fol. 1 was conjugate with the original fol. 5, which is not extant, and therefore the whole bifolium (fols. 1 and the former fol. 5) was replaced, but fol. 1 was retained as a flyleaf.

Fols. 3 and 4 are a bifolium; fols. 6 and 7 are now single leaves. If the first quire was originally a regular quaternion, as seems probable, then the first two leaves must have been cut out, perhaps because they were blank (see pl. I and fig. 1).

On the whole, the original text of fol. 1 is the same as that of fol. 2, which replaced it. However, as D_2 writes a larger hand, the doxology of *O lux beata* (Hy 1/9–12) had to be omitted. The rubrics to Hy 1 and 3 are also missing. On the other hand, D_1 had left Hy 2/8 unglossed by mistake and the gloss was supplied by D_2. There are other minor differences. Compared to D_2, D_1 has a stronger preference for þ to ð in all positions, word-initial, -medial and -final. Since it was used as a flyleaf, fol. 1 is not in good condition and is partly illegible, even under ultraviolet light.

With the exception of fols. 2 and 5 the entire Latin text of the hymnal and the monastic canticles was written by D_1. D_1 is almost certainly identical with the hand which glossed most of the text. The text is in Caroline minuscule, while the Old English gloss is written in Insular minuscule with a narrower pen, as was usual in the eleventh century; it is the case also in J and V. D_1's Caroline minuscule is very regular, upright and comparatively round.[13] In his Insular minuscule the bodies of letters are relatively small and round and the ascenders and descenders fairly long.[14] The descenders often turn to the left. Long *s* is regular. Sometimes Insular letter forms penetrate into the Caroline minuscule of the Latin,

[12] See below, p. 34.

[13] On the origins and general character of eleventh-century English Caroline minuscule (Style IV), see Dumville, *English Caroline Script*, pp. 111–40.

[14] On developments in eleventh-century Insular minuscule, see D. N. Dumville, 'Beowulf Come Lately: Some Notes on the Palaeography of the Nowell Codex', *ASNSL* 225 (1988), 49–63.

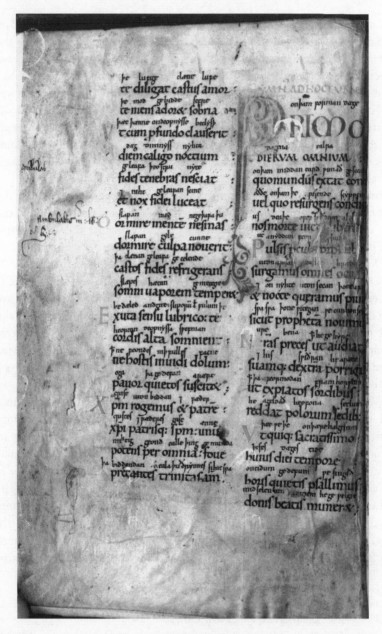

Ia   Durham Cathedral Library, B. III. 32, 1v

Ib   Durham Cathedral Library, B. III. 32, 2r

31

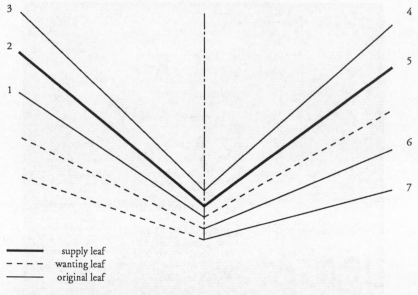

supply leaf
- - - - wanting leaf
———— original leaf

1   Quire 1 (fols. 1–7)

especially on fol. 29. Latin glosses written by D_1 in Caroline minuscule, but with the pen used for the Old English gloss, occur sporadically in interlinear or marginal position throughout the hymnal and canticles. The most frequent gloss is *o* to indicate a Latin vocative. Often the Latin glosses are themselves glossed in Old English.

D_2 wrote not only the text and gloss on fols. 2 and 5, including Hy 1, 2, 3/1–16, 12/10–25, 13, 14 and 15/1–22, but also the gloss to Hy 31 and 91–4 and the gloss to three canticles, 19, 20 and 21.[15] D_2's letter forms are broader and larger in both his Insular and his Caroline minuscule. According to Ker, the character of this hand points to St Augustine's and is related to the script of the missal Cambridge, Corpus Christi College 270.[16] Both D_1 and D_2 belong to the first half of the eleventh century.

A third hand of the eleventh century, D_3, is responsible for glosses to Hy 35, 40, 44/21–8 and 45/17–20 and fragmentary glosses to Hy 37 and

[15] See Korhammer, *MC*, pp. 14–15.
[16] Ker, p. 147. See also N. R. Ker in a letter quoted by Gneuss, *HHEM*, pp. 89–90. The missal is ed. M. Rule, *The Missal of St. Augustine's Abbey* (Cambridge, 1896), which includes a facsimile of a page as a frontispiece.

54. D_3 writes badly with a scratchy pen and two kinds of ink, one very dark and the other light brown.

A fourth hand, also of the eleventh century, D_4, has entered Latin prose paraphrases of Hy 1/1–8, 2, 3/1–20, 4/13–16 and 99/1–2 in the margins of fol. 2 and 35r and added syntactical glosses, sometimes called 'paving letters', to Hy 63/1–4 and 99 on 21v and fol. 35, all in Caroline minuscule.[17] Most of the Latin glosses to Hy 1, 2, 3, 4, 5, 6, 7 and 14 on fols. 2–5 were written either by D_4 or by a very similar hand. Because the lack of space cramps the writing of these glosses, it is difficult in some cases to distinguish the glosses by D_1 and D_4.[18] There are also corrections by the scribes themselves and others by several hands that do not seem to date from much later.

The hymnal and the canticles are arranged in two columns. The end of the verses and of the lines of writing often coincides, but D_1 did not consistently aim at this effect. D_2, however, begins each verse at the head of the line and with a capital letter on 2v and continues to do so on fol. 5. The end of each verse is mostly indicated by a *punctus elevatus* until 6r and with a single dot from that point on.[19] The ends of stanzas are marked almost exclusively with a semicolon.

Most hymns have rubrics. The initials of the hymns are red, green and blue. Most of them are plain, others have a little ornamentation. The first line – or sometimes first couple of lines – is in capital letters. The importance of some major feasts is indicated by a larger initial for the first of the hymns appropriate to them and a larger number of lines at the beginning of these hymns appear in display script.[20]

[17] These are syntactical glosses according to the sequential system; see F. C. Robinson, 'Syntactical Glosses in Latin Manuscripts of Anglo-Saxon Provenance', *Speculum* 48 (1973), 443–75, esp. 453 and 462, and M. Korhammer, 'Mittelalterliche Konstruktionshilfen und altenglische Wortstellung', *Scriptorium* 34 (1980), 18–58, esp. 37–8.

[18] D_1 and D_4 have, however, a distinctive *g*. The lower arc of this letter is attached to the right side of its belly and usually starts high up in D_4's writing, while in D_1's it begins on the left side and from below. D_4 also frequently uses an Insular *d* with an almost vertical upper stroke that ends in an abrupt turn to the right.

[19] A *punctus elevatus* consists of a dot lightly ticked above. For a discussion of punctuation in medieval English manuscripts, see P. Clemoes, *Liturgical Influence on Punctuation in Late Old English and Early Middle English Manuscripts*, Cambridge University, The Department of Anglo-Saxon, Occasional Papers 1 (Cambridge, 1952); see also L. Treitler, 'Reading and Singing', pp. 186–208.

[20] These feasts are Hy 32 (Advent), 36 (Christmas), 43 (Epiphany), 62 (Benedict), 67_1

The first initial in the hymnal on 2r, the *O* of *O lux beata*, contains a drawing of personified Light as a woman wearing a wreath of rays of light and carrying a torch in her hand. According to Temple, this derives from an iconographic tradition depicting the sun and displays some resemblance to the style of the Bury Gospels, London, British Library, Harley 76 (?Canterbury, s. xi[in]).[21] There is no heading for the hymnal as a whole and no explicit either. In the first stanza of *Iesus refulsit* (Hy 43) neumes are interlined.[22]

On 43v–45v, which were originally blank, a collection of forty-six proverbs from various sources, the so-called 'Durham Proverbs', has been entered by another, rather clumsy, hand of the eleventh century.[23] The proverbs are given in Latin and Old English.

On the blank lower half of 55v, following the canticles, a hand of the fourteenth century entered the first line of the hymn *Iesu salvator saeculi* and erased it again, the scribe presumably having realized that the hymn was already included in the hymnal.[24] He then added the first stanza of *Iam Christe sol iustitiae* below.[25]

The manuscript was consulted by Joscelyn for his dictionary in the sixteenth century.[26] A certain Thomas Aynesworth is named as owner on 1r in a hand of the sixteenth or seventeenth century. On 127r a note says: 'This book belongeth to Richard Shuttleworth of Forcet Esq.: and was lent to me by him May 19. 1676 Geo Davenport'. A little below the name is repeated as 'Geo: Davenport' in a different script. Shuttleworth died in

---

(Passiontide), 70 (Easter), 73 (Ascension), 76 (Pentecost), 79 (Pentecost, Tierce), 86₁ (John the Baptist), 87 (Peter and Paul), 95 (Michael), 98 (All Saints). Tierce is the most important Hour at Pentecost; see below, p. 312 (Hy 97, III). Hy 1, 3 and 102 also have special ornamentation; Hy 102 is the first hymn of the *commune sanctorum*; see pp. 24–5.

[21] Temple no. 101. For the 'Bury Gospels', see Temple no. 75, and J. Backhouse in *The Golden Age of Anglo-Saxon Art*, ed. Backhouse *et al.*, no. 58.

[22] See below, p. 98.

[23] The proverbs are ed. O. Arngart, *The Durham Proverbs: an Eleventh Century Collection of Anglo-Saxon Proverbs*, Lunds Universitets Arskrift 1, NF 1, 52, 2 (Lund, 1956) and again in 1981 as 'The Durham Proverbs'. He concludes that the Latin version is translated from the Old English (see p. 6 of his 1956 edition). Doubt was cast on this conclusion by T. A. Shippey in a paper read to the conference of the International Society of Anglo-Saxonists (ISAS) in Durham in 1989.

[24] *Iesu salvator saeculi* is Hy 98 without stanzas I and II. This is the form in which it was current after the Norman Conquest; see Gneuss, *HHEM*, p. 79.

[25] *ICL* no. 7469; cf. Gneuss, *HHEM*, p. 78.

[26] Gneuss, 'Zur Geschichte des Ms. Vespasian A. I', p. 131 and n. 1.

1681. Forcet is in the North Riding of Yorkshire. Davenport was chaplain to Bishop Cosin of Durham.[27] The manuscript probably made its way into the Durham Cathedral Library between 1705 and 1714, for it was not mentioned by Wanley in 1705 and, according to Thomas Rudd's catalogue, it was presented by Thomas Warton, who died in 1714.[28]

The hymns for St Augustine of Canterbury (Hy 83–5), which are not found elsewhere, and a modification of the text of Hy 130 for the Dedication of the Church, invoking St Augustine instead of Mary, would sufficiently indicate that the hymnal is from Canterbury even if this were not supported by all the other evidence.[29] According to Hohler, they are clear evidence that it was written at St Augustine's itself.[30] However, the hymn to St Augustine definitely attested for St Augustine's in Anglo-Saxon times, *O vere virum beatum*, does not appear in D.[31] On the other hand, the hymn for Dunstan (Hy 82) seems to have been in use only at Christ Church, as Gneuss has pointed out.[32] Nevertheless hand D$_2$ points

---

[27] Gneuss, *HHEM*, p. 90. For Shuttleworth, see *The Victoria History of the Counties of England, Yorkshire: North Riding. I* (Folkestone, 1914), pp. 66 and 71. The owner of D before him, Aynesworth, does not seem to have been from North Yorkshire. At any rate, as M. Y. Ashcroft kindly informed me in a letter dated 20 February 1987, the North Yorkshire County Record Office has no record of a man of that name. On 127r several scribes tried out their pens. One hand wrote 'In nomine patris et filii et spiritus sancti amen' in line 7 and another two lines in *textura* in light green ink at the bottom of the page. These probably named another owner of the manuscript; they have been erased.

[28] Thomas Rudd, *Codicum Manuscriptorum Ecclesiae Cathedralis Dunelmensis Catalogus Classicus* (Durham, 1825), p. 174. Into the copy owned by the Durham Cathedral Library a date, *14. 7. 1845*, has been entered by hand. It probably indicates the time when the manuscript was rebound. Rudd was the librarian of the Cathedral library from 1717 to 1726; see Gneuss, *HHEM*, p. 90. The preface of his catalogue names 1725 as the date of its completion.

[29] For evidence of the use of Canterbury sources in the hymnal gloss, see below, pp. 36–7. For links between other texts in D and Canterbury, see below, pp. 39–40. For the affiliation of the Latin text of the hymns, see below, pp. 67–8. On the language of the hymnal gloss as evidence for the origin of D in Canterbury, see below, pp. 73–7 and 89–91.

[30] C. E. Hohler, 'Some Service Books of the Later Saxon Church', in *Tenth-Century Studies: Essays in Commemoration of the Millennium of the Council of Winchester and 'Regularis Concordia'*, ed. D. Parsons (London and Chichester, 1975), pp. 60–83 and 217–27, esp. p. 220, n. 10.

[31] Hy 161. See Gneuss, *HHEM*, pp. 88 and 114–15, and cf. below, p. 64.

[32] See Gneuss, *HHEM*, p. 245.

to St Augustine's[33] and in view of what has been said about the replacement of fol. 1 of D it is hardly possible that D_1 and D_2 were working in different scriptoria. I will return to this question below.

As for the gloss, it clearly did not originate with the Latin text of D. It derives from a hymnal of the Winchester type since a number of hymns that do not occur in the Winchester type are either not glossed at all or were glossed later by D_2 and D_3.[34]

However, some of the hymns or parts of hymns not included in the Winchester type were nevertheless glossed by D_1. These are Hy 41, 60, 82, 88 (incompletely), 90, 115 and 116 and parts of Hy 45 (stanza III), 66 (stanzas II and VI) and 81 (stanza III). Inevitably the question arises of whether D_1, D_2 and D_3 glossed the additional hymns themselves or whether they were able to fall back on other sources. If so, might all three have used the same source?

There seems to be a source involved in the case of Hy 82, glossed by D_1, and of Hy 31, glossed by D_2. In Hy 82 there are no glosses to lines 14 and 16, apparently because the Latin text of the source was different at that point.[35] The gloss to Hy 31 is in some ways close to the gloss in A, the Vespasian Psalter, but markedly different in others.[36] (Both of the sources in question would hardly have been available anywhere but in Canterbury.)[37]

The fragmentary nature of the glosses to Hy 88 by D_1 and to Hy 37 and 54 by D_3, however, rather seems to indicate that they were attempting to gloss them on their own. So a common source seems rather unlikely even though there are no glaring differences in phonology, graphemics and vocabulary.[38]

Gneuss argues that the existence of such a common source has to be considered in view of the situation in V.[39] In the hymnal Vm, Hy 35, 37, 41, 54, 60, 90–2, 44 (stanzas VI and VII), 45 (stanzas III and V) and 66 (stanzas II and VI), all typical of the Canterbury type, and also Hy 55 and

---

[33] See above, p. 32.

[34] Hy 56_1, 56_2, 59, 69, 78 and 101, Hy 62, stanzas VII–XV, Hy 73, stanzas II, IV, VI and VIII, and Hy 74, stanzas II, IV and VII are typical of the Canterbury Hymnal and are not glossed in D. On the hymns glossed by D_2 and D_3, see above, pp. 32–3.

[35] Gneuss, *HHEM*, p. 244.   [36] *Ibid.*, pp. 124–5.

[37] Hy 82 is restricted to Christ Church; see above, p. 35. The Vespasian Psalter was in Canterbury in the eleventh century; see below, p. 57.

[38] See below, pp. 70 and 79.   [39] Gneuss, *HHEM*, pp. 143–5.

the beginning of Hy 54 (by mistake), were glossed in Old English. The gloss is closely enough related to D to be regarded as a direct copy of D if it were not the case that these glosses have more Kentish forms than Vp, the *Expositio* gloss, and that some of them are not taken over from D.[40] However, the glosses concerned derive not only from D_1, but also from D_2 and D_3. Perhaps the most likely explanation is an intermediate copy between D and V with a strong Kentish colouring.

The hymns for Trinity Sunday, Hy 131–3, in J may also have been directly copied from D and are, at any rate, closely related. J has some additional mistakes that may be due to clumsy attempts at correction. A few words are replaced, perhaps in order to bring the usage closer to that of the main gloss, the gloss to the *Expositio*.[41]

The relation between the hymnal gloss in D and the gloss to the *Expositio* in J and Vp is a very complicated one. Both were apparently copied at Canterbury, but written for a hymnal of the Winchester type. This suggests the possibility of a common Winchester source. They share a common vocabulary which is consonant with that hypothesis, of which more below.[42] On the other hand, Gneuss and Korhammer have extensively commented on frequent, sometimes consistent, divergence between the two glosses.[43] The 'Durham Hymnal Gloss' was apparently revised in Canterbury at some stage.[44] A considerable number of differences could be explained as part of that process and in terms of word geography, but others seem merely to reflect individual preferences. If the *Expositio* gloss and D's hymnal gloss derive from the same source, either the revision of D was extremely thorough or the *Expositio* gloss was substantially revised, too.

Considering that in D a hymnal is combined with a gloss not originally written for it and that contamination is rife in the textual tradition of the hymns anyway, it is to be expected that in D lemma and gloss will not

---

[40] Klappenbach, 'Zu altenglischen Interlinearversionen', §152; Gneuss, *HHEM*, pp. 144 and 164. The Old English glosses to Vm are included by Gneuss together with the corresponding part of Vm in his edition of JVp in *HHEM*, pp. 272, 302–3, 306–8, 314–15, 321–3, 332, 334–5, 338–9, 349–50 and 374–7. They have been collated with D in my editions of the individual hymns.

[41] Gneuss, *HHEM*, pp. 141–2, but cf. Korhammer, *MC*, p. 237, n. 17.

[42] See below, pp. 77–88.

[43] Gneuss, *HHEM*, pp. 152–5, and Korhammer, *MC*, pp. 179–218.

[44] See below, p. 79.

always agree with each other and that the gloss will agree with JVp, among others. Nor is it surprising that corrections in D sometimes agree with JVp. However, a number of cases in which the corrector introduces a reading only transmitted in JVp suggests that he may have had one of these manuscripts or a closely related one to hand.[45] Moreover, in spite of many mistakes and interpretations that are entirely their own, D and JVp do share some traits which, taken together, prove direct contact at some stage. Some Latin glosses by D_1 agree with explanations in the *Expositio*. Both tend to render the historic present by the past tense, using, for the most part, the same verb. There are a small number of common mistakes. They share one double gloss in Hy 28/16. They both render *theologe* as *drihtwurða*, a rare loan formation.[46]

These facts must be considered in the light of the close relationship between the manuscripts D, J and V. J and V are from the same scriptorium, and D, or a closely related manuscript, appears to have been available there. If not, it would be difficult to explain Hy 131–3 in J and the Old English glosses in Vm. If all three manuscripts were from the same scriptorium, the points of agreement between the *Expositio* gloss and the hymnal gloss in D could have arisen as the scribes in turn made use of the other manuscripts or their exemplars; for example, D_1 may well have consulted the exemplar of JVp.

It seems reasonable to suggest that the original of the 'Durham Hymnal Gloss' was written at Winchester and revised at Canterbury, although monasteries outside Winchester, but influenced by Winchester usage, are equally possible places of origin. The gloss is not very likely to have been written in Canterbury itself. Winchester influence may have been felt there, but it is a little improbable that the Winchester hymnal was in use there.[47] The compiler of V or its exemplar went to considerable

---

[45] Gneuss, *HHEM*, pp. 146–50. The readings of his groups d, e, f and g must be carefully assessed for their value as evidence according to the number of manuscripts which share the readings of JVp. See also below, p. 68.

[46] Gneuss, *HHEM*, pp. 148–9. The mistakes adduced are Hy 12/2, 23/3, 42/9, 43/4, 72/12 and 125/9. The last of these is not necessarily wrong, but is a very free translation. Other instances of the rendering of the Latin historic present by Old English past tense in D are Hy 64/15, 65_1/4, 8, 10, 12, 16 and 20. The last of these is not shared by JVp. In Hy 65_1/4 and 8 the tense is the same, but the actual word is different. D has *(ge)beran*, JVp *aberan*.

[47] Gneuss, *HHEM*, p. 71. See above, p. 10. On the influence of Winchester on Canterbury during the episcopates of Ælfheah and Lyfing (1006 × 1020), see Korhammer, 'Origin

trouble to align Vp, the *Expositio* gloss of the Winchester hymnal, to Vm, a hymnal of the Canterbury type. This would appear to indicate that the Winchester type was not in use where he worked, which was probably in Canterbury.[48]

As the gloss could not have originated before the introduction of the New Hymnal into England during the Benedictine Reform, it cannot date from earlier than *c*. 970. A *terminus ante quem* of *c*. 1050 is provided by the palaeographical dating of D_1 and D_2, but a certain amount of time has to be allowed for the process of copying, revision and transmission that resulted in D. The vocabulary of the gloss would agree well with a date of *c*. 1000.[49]

The monastic canticles in D with their interlinear gloss go back to the same archetype as the canticles and gloss following the *Expositio* gloss in J.[50] This archetype differed from the norm in that three supernumerary canticles were added to the usual series of eight sets of three.[51] This supplemented version probably did not correspond to liturgical practice. The accompanying interlinear gloss was originally intended for the normal Anglo-Saxon type.

The Latin text of the canticles of the normal Anglo-Saxon series is related to the canticles that follow the hymnal in B and even more closely to those in Cambridge, St John's College 262 (K.21) (s. xiii/xiv) from St Augustine's. This implies a Canterbury tradition.[52] The interlinear gloss has southeastern dialect forms and its vocabulary has much in common with the gloss to the hymnal preceding it, so the two glosses may share the same history.[53] This links D even more closely to J, and it is

---

of the Bosworth Psalter', p. 179, and Dumville, *English Caroline Script*, pp. 115–16. See also below, pp. 42.

[48] See below, pp. 54–5.   [49] See below, pp. 77–80 and 89.

[50] The canticles and the glosses have been edited in Korhammer, *MC*, pp. 247–368.

[51] What happened, in fact, was that the set of canticles for feasts of several apostles or martyrs and the set for a single martyr, both of which are not paralleled elsewhere in Anglo-Saxon England, were supplemented by those of the canticles more commonly in use which these sets did not include. It is not clear how the presence of these two unusual sets in an otherwise normal series of canticles should be interpreted. Influence from northern France is one possibility. See Korhammer, *MC*, pp. 17–20.

[52] See Korhammer, *MC*, pp. 116–18.

[53] Gneuss, *HHEM*, pp. 152–4, Korhammer, *MC*, pp. 176 and 179–222, Hofstetter, *Winchester*, pp. 114–16 (no. 13). Note, however, that the gloss to the canticles does not show quite so clear signs of having been revised at Canterbury.

remarkable how close and intricate the relationship between the three manuscripts D, J and V is.

There is another possible link between D and Canterbury in the Durham Proverbs, nos. 37 and 39. A similar version of them is found in London, British Library, Royal 2. B. V. They were entered in the manuscript at Christ Church, Canterbury, in the eleventh century.[54]

The copy of Ælfric's Grammar, which was bound together with the hymnal as early as the eleventh century, may also come from Canterbury. Not only does it show southeastern dialect forms, but it also has a frontispiece showing Æthelwold and Dunstan under two arches with a monk kneeling below holding a scroll in his hands. This clearly relates to Ælfric's praise of Dunstan and Æthelwold in his preface as those responsible for the renewal of monastic culture in England.[55] The drawing copies, but recasts in a somewhat less elegant manner, the frontispiece to the *Regularis concordia*, a drawing in London, British Library, Tiberius A. iii (2v). There King Edgar, Æthelwold and Dunstan are depicted in their role as pillars of the Benedictine Reform with a similar monk kneeling before them. Tiberius A. iii is almost certainly from Christ Church, Canterbury.[56]

All this corroborates the evidence of the hymnal and supports the conclusion that manuscript D was written in Canterbury. It does not offer anything absolutely decisive in favour of Christ Church rather than St Augustine's, so the latter possibility still must be considered. The link between the script of D_2 and St Augustine's is the main argument in

---

[54] The proverbs are item b in Ker no. 249. They have been printed by Roeder in *Der altenglische Regius-Psalter*, p. xii. See also 'The Durham Proverbs', ed. Arngart, p. 299, notes to nos. 37 and 39, and below, p. 61.

[55] See *Aelfrics Grammatik und Glossar*, ed. J. Zupitza (Berlin, 1880; repr. with a preface by H. Gneuss, Berlin, 1966), p. 3.

[56] Cf. F. Wormald, 'Two Anglo-Saxon Miniatures Compared', *British Museum Quarterly* 9 (1934–5), 113–15 and pl. 35; *idem*, *English Drawings of the Tenth and Eleventh Centuries* (London, 1952), pp. 45–7, 64 and 68 and pls. 23 and 29; C. R. Dodwell, *The Canterbury School of Illumination 1066–1200* (Cambridge, 1954), p. 5 and pl. 3; *Regularis Concordia*, ed. Symons, p. lv, pl. facing p. ix; D. H. Turner in *The Golden Age of Anglo-Saxon Art*, ed. Backhouse *et al.*, no. 28; and Temple nos. 100 and 101. On the provenance of Tiberius A. iii, see below, pp. 59–60. On southeastern forms in the text of Ælfric's Grammar in D, see M. Angström, *Studies in Old English Manuscripts with Special Reference to the Delabialisation of y (u + i) to i* (Uppsala, 1937), pp. 105 and 109–10.

point. St Augustine's and Christ Church did presumably sometimes exchange books. An exchange of scribes is quite another matter; it is difficult to assess how likely it would have been for a scribe trained at St Augustine's to be transferred to Christ Church.[57]

The contents of the manuscript clearly show that it was used as a schoolbook. This is proved not only by the Old English interlinear gloss and the Latin glosses in the hymnal and canticles and the prose paraphrases and the paving letters in the hymnal, but also by the fact that the manuscript was bound together with Ælfric's Grammar early on. Proverbs, too, were popular texts in class, especially the *Disticha Catonis*, from which no. 1 of the Durham Proverbs is taken.[58]

The hymns themselves as well as the canticles and psalms were among the first things young novices had to learn.[59] They had to know them by heart to take part in the services. Thus D would appear to be a fairly basic schoolbook, something like a teacher's handbook for beginners.

B = *London, BL, Additional 37517 (the 'Bosworth Psalter')*

This manuscript[60] contains computistical material and a calendar (1v–3v), a Roman psalter and canticles with incomplete Old English interlinear glosses (4r–104r), a hymnal (105r–128r) and monastic canticles (129r–135r).

Most of the Latin text was written in a late phase of Anglo-Saxon Square minuscule at the end of the tenth century. The decoration of the manuscript, which includes four elaborate psalm initials, has features typical of tenth-century Canterbury.[61] The Old English glosses are in Insular minuscule of the early eleventh century. The calendar was added later, but was intended for manuscript B from the start. It was written in Caroline minuscule in the period between 988 and 1008. It is a Christ

---

[57] Cf. Dumville, *English Caroline Script*, p. 91.

[58] O. Arngart, 'Durham Proverbs 17, 30, 42', *Notes and Queries* 227 (1982), 199–201, esp. 201; 'Durham Proverbs', ed. Arngart (1981), p. 295 (note to no. 1).

[59] Gneuss, *HHEM*, p. 195.

[60] The manuscript is Ker no. 129, Gneuss, 'Preliminary List', no. 291, and Temple no. 22. It has been thoroughly discussed by Gasquet and Bishop, *The Bosworth Psalter*, and Korhammer, 'Origin of the Bosworth Psalter' and most recently Dumville, 'On the Dating', p. 45. See also Gneuss, *HHEM*, pp. 104–5. The hymnal has been edited by Wieland as *The Canterbury Hymnal*.

[61] Temple, pp. 48–9 (no. 22).

Church calendar, as Korhammer has proved.[62] This type of calendar may have been introduced in Canterbury by Dunstan[63] and replaced with a type influenced by Winchester usage under Archbishops Ælfric or Ælfheah (995 × 1012).[64]

The rest of the manuscript is almost certainly from Christ Church as well. Both the hymnal's being of the Canterbury type and the actual text of the monastic canticles, which has been shown to be related to that in D and J,[65] point to Canterbury. In the psalter the division of the psalms for reading at Matins is indicated by a line of red capitals at the beginning of each section with a consistency unusual for Anglo-Saxon manuscripts and which B shares with London, British Library, Arundel 155 (Canterbury, Christ Church, s. xi^1).[66]

Even more importantly, the main hand of the Latin text is identical with the scribe of the Sunbury Charter (London, Westminster Abbey, Muniments Room X), dated 962.[67] This charter, a tenth-century copy of the original made later than 968, was written either in Westminster or more probably in Christ Church.

Christ Church was in close contact with Westminster, so the criteria pointing to Canterbury would probably not exclude B's having been written at Westminster. There is some indication that the manuscript was in Westminster in the thirteenth century.[68] Nevertheless, B is impressive enough to be a product of a great scriptorium such as Christ Church. The only possible reason for preferring Westminster as its place of origin is that B is a monastic manuscript whereas it has not been entirely proved that there were Benedictines at Christ Church during the 970s and 980s.[69]

---

[62] Korhammer, 'Origin of the Bosworth Psalter', pp. 175–80.

[63] The connection with Dunstan rests on the assumption that the calendar is based on that of Glastonbury. Dumville, *Liturgy*, pp. 39–65, thinks that assumption doubtful.

[64] Korhammer, 'Origin of the Bosworth Psalter', pp. 179–80. Dumville, *English Caroline Script*, p. 115, suggests that the change took place during the pontificates of Ælfheah or Lyfing, 1006 × 1020.

[65] Korhammer, *MC*, pp. 115–18.

[66] Ker no. 135, Gneuss, 'Preliminary List', no. 306, Temple no. 66, and J. M. Backhouse in *The Golden Age of Anglo-Saxon Art*, ed. Backhouse *et al.*, pp. 72 and 74 (no. 57).

[67] P. H. Sawyer, *Anglo-Saxon Charters: an Annotated List and Bibliography*, Royal Historical Society Guides and Handbooks 8 (London, 1968), no. 702.

[68] Korhammer, 'Origin of the Bosworth Psalter', p. 187.

[69] Cf. Korhammer, 'Origin of the Bosworth Psalter', pp. 181–2, and Dumville, *English Caroline Script*, p. 100.

The hymnal in B is the oldest example of the complete cycle of the New Hymnal in England. It represents an early stage of the monastic Canterbury type, the later stages of which can be traced in D and Vm. There is no heading or explicit, but the hymns themselves all have rubrics. The first stanzas of Hy 13, 122 and 123 have neumes.

C = *Cambridge, Corpus Christi College 391 (the 'Portiforium of St Wulstan')*

This manuscript[70] contains computistical material and a calendar (pp. 1–23), a Gallican psalter with canticles and a litany (pp. 24–226), a hymnal (pp. 227–78), monastic canticles (pp. 279–93), a collectar (pp. 295–560), prayers, exorcisms and similar texts (pp. 560–620, mainly Latin), a supplementary section to the collectar on various parts of the Office (pp. 620–712) and prognostics and similar texts (pp. 713–21, mainly Old English).

The hymnal is on four quires, 15 to 18, three quaternions and one binion.[71] The original quire 18 was lost or removed; it was replaced in the late twelfth or early thirteenth century by a single bifolium. In the main, the manuscript is the work of two scribes.[72] C_1 wrote the text up to p. 372, including the hymnal, the prayer on pp. 580–1 and probably the Old English on pp. 613–17 and 713–21. C_2 wrote the rest of the Latin texts from p. 373 onwards, with the exception of pp. 591–612, written by C_3, and pp. 581–91, written by C_4. C_3 also wrote the Old English text on pp. 601–3 and 611–12. These hands are of the second half of the eleventh century.

---

[70] The manuscript is Ker no. 67, and Gneuss, 'Preliminary List', no. 104. For descriptions of the manuscript, see further James, *Catalogue of the Manuscripts in the Library of Corpus Christi College* II, 241–8; and Gneuss, *HHEM*, pp. 106–8. The manuscript was extensively discussed by Frere in *The Leofric Collectar*, ed. Dewick and Frere II. An edition of the collectar and the Offices is in *The Portiforium of Saint Wulstan*, ed. Hughes. Except for a few textual notes in Gneuss, *HHEM*, the readings of the hymnal have not been published before; but see below, p. 44, n. 73.

[71] Although the collations by James, *Catalogue of the Manuscripts in the Library of Corpus Christi College* II, 242 and by Frere in the *The Leofric Collectar*, ed. Dewick and Frere II, xiii, disagree at some points, they do not disagree in this section of the manuscript.

[72] There are some unresolved questions regarding the palaeography of the manuscript; see *The Portiforium of Saint Wulstan*, ed. Hughes II, viii, and *The Durham Collectar*, ed. Corrêa, p. 127.

The manuscript was in Worcester in the thirteenth century. Evidence that it was also written in Worcester consists in the invocation of the two Worcester saints Oswald and Ecgwine in the prayer on pp. 589–99 and the three otherwise unattested hymns to St Oswald in the hymnal on pp. 256–7.[73] Moreover, C_3 and C_4 connect the manuscript to a group of manuscripts clearly from the same scriptorium, and most of these manuscripts contain evidence to link them to Worcester one way or another.[74]

For a number of texts contained in C a Winchester source has been suggested. These are the calendar, two of the prayers, the monastic canticles, the collectar and, of course, the hymnal, since it is of the Winchester type.[75]

The computistical table on pp. 22–3 is for the years 1064 × 1093. The *terminus ante quem* for the calendar is 8 October 1089, date of the translation of St Oswald. It is likely, though, that the manuscript was in fact written in 1065; the antiphon 'O radix Iesse', normally sung on 18

---

[73] The hymns, Hy 157–9 (Gneuss's Hy 60a-c) are for St Oswald of Worcester, *pace* Gneuss, *HHEM*, p. 107. They have been previously printed by Frere in *The Leofric Collectar*, ed. Dewick and Frere II, 607. The name of Oswald in these texts is written in capitals to give it particular prominence. Other saints are not so treated.

[74] Hand C_3 is also found in Cambridge, University Library, Kk. 3. 18; hand C_4 closely resembles a script found in Oxford, Bodleian Library, Hatton 113 and 114, in Cambridge, Corpus Christi College 146, London, British Library, Cotton Tiberius A. xiii and Oxford, Bodleian Library, Junius 121. These manuscripts are listed in Gneuss, 'Preliminary List', nos. 22, 637, 638, 366 and 644. On the liturgical script used in Worcester, see T. A. M. Bishop, *English Caroline Minuscule*, p. 20, n. 1. On Cambridge, Corpus Christi College 146 and 391, see Hartzell, 'An Eleventh-century English Missal Fragment', pp. 77–8 and n. 80. On the dating of the additions to Corpus Christi College 146, see N. R. Ker, 'The Provenance of the Oldest Manuscript of the Rule of St. Benedict', *Bodleian Library Record* 2 (1941–9), 28–9, repr. with a note by A. G. Watson in N. R. Ker, *Books, Collectors and Libraries: Studies in the Medieval Heritage*, ed. A. G. Watson (London, 1985), pp. 131–3.

[75] For the calendar, see *The Leofric Collectar*, ed. Dewick and Frere II, 587–602. On the prayers, see T. H. Bestul, 'The Collection of Private Prayers in the "Portiforium" of Wulfstan of Worcester and the "Orationes sive Meditationes" of Anselm of Canterbury', in *Les Mutations socio-culturelles au tournant des XIe–XIIe siècles*, ed. Foreville, pp. 355–64, who strangely assumes that the manuscript itself is from Winchester. On the collectar, see Wulfstan of Winchester, *The Life of St Æthelwold*, ed. Lapidge and Winterbottom, pp. cxix–cxxi. On the hymnal, see above, p. 10. Dumville, *English Caroline Script*, pp. 4–5, n. 15 and p. 57, is rather sceptical about the influence of Winchester on Worcester.

44

December, is prescribed there for the fourth Sunday in Advent and the two dates coincided in that year.[76]

C represents a stage in the development towards the breviary, as it assembles in a single manuscript most of the liturgical books needed for the Office. MacLachlan identifies it with a similarly comprehensive book mentioned as a personal possession of St Wulfstan in his *vita*.[77]

The assembled liturgical texts are not altogether homogeneous. The collectar, which ultimately goes back to a Flemish source[78] and may derive from a Winchester source, is not only expanded, but also modified by the additions on pp. 680–712. So the modifications may represent innovations or genuine Worcester usage as opposed to Winchester usage. The hymnal, too, does not altogether agree with the collectar. There are hymn incipits for normal Sundays in the collectar as well as an incomplete account of the feasts up to and including Passiontide. In the additions to the collectar there are hymn incipits for normal weekdays (pp. 685–700) and for the *commune sanctorum* (pp. 621–56). They are all based on a Winchester-type hymnal.[79] Nevertheless they disagree with the Winchester-type hymnal of C – and with Ælfric and the *Regularis concordia* – with regard to Sundays in Lent. Here they are closer to the Canterbury type and H, but also to later usage in the New Hymnal of post-Anglo-Saxon times, since Hy 54, 55, 57 and 58 are prescribed instead of the common hymns for Sundays in winter.[80] Hy 54, *Sic ter quaternis*, does not appear in the hymnal of C at all. The collectar appears more innovative than the hymnal in this case.

The hymnal is the only complete hymnal of the Winchester type extant. It is unusual in its organization of the hymns in that it separates the *proprium sanctorum* from the *proprium de tempore*. The heading of the hymnal is 'Incipiunt hymni ambrosiani canendi per singulas horas

---

[76] Cf. *The Portiforium of Saint Wulstan*, ed. Hughes II, vi.

[77] L. McLachlan, 'St. Wulstan's Prayer Book', *Journal of Theological Studies* 30 (1929), 174–7.

[78] On the collectar, see *The Leofric Collectar*, ed. Dewick and Frere II, and *The Durham Collectar*, ed. Corrêa, pp. 126–8. Cf. *The Portiforium of Saint Wulstan*, ed. Hughes II, viii–xxv.

[79] See the index of hymn incipits in *The Portiforium of Saint Wulstan*, ed. Hughes II, 92. Cf. Gneuss, *HHEM*, pp. 107–8.

[80] For the treatment of Sundays in Lent in the different types of Anglo-Saxon hymnal, see above, p. 11.

secundum constitutionem patris nostri Benedicti.' Almost all the hymns have rubrics. There are numerous mistakes in the text and few corrections. The latter are by several not much later hands.

Several changes were made to the hymnal by three hands of the twelfth and thirteenth centuries. On p. 264, Hy 66 was erased and replaced by the longer version typical of the Canterbury hymnal. An additional stanza of Hy 65_2 was also added. On p. 265, Hy 109 was erased and replaced by Hy 109 and Hy 104_2, stanza I. C_1 had presumably given only the incipit of Hy 104_2 at that point.[81] Hy 125 from line 3 onwards and Hy 126–9 had been on the lost quire 18 and were replaced on the supplied bifolium. At the same time four hymns current in post-Conquest England were added. Hy 151 with neumes was added in the blank space on p. 252. There is a remote possibility that this hymn had already been added to the hymnal during the Anglo-Saxon period and was lost together with the rest of quire 18, so that the later addition would constitute a replacement.[82]

The manuscript has Anglo-Saxon neumes by three different hands. The neumes to the additional parts on the Office on pp. 661–84 are by the hand which made additions in Worcester to an eleventh-century pontifical, Cambridge, Corpus Christi College 146. The neumes on pp. 315–620 (which includes most of the collectar) and a few on later pages are by the same hand as the neumes in the fragment of an eleventh-century missal from Worcester, now London, British Library, Royal 5. A. XII, fols. iii–vi. The neumes in the hymnal appear to be either by this scribe or the third hand (which does not seem to be found elsewhere).[83]

The neumes are unevenly distributed among twelve hymns. There are neumes to the first stanza of Hy 4, 34, 46, 77 and 87. In the case of Hy 3, 32, 45 and 79 parts of the second stanza have neumes also; in Hy 76 it is

---

[81] For these changes, cf. the edition of the hymns in question and for Hy 66, see above, p. 15.

[82] The only Anglo-Saxon hymnal in which Hy 151 is extant is Vm; cf. the edition of the hymn.

[83] Susan Rankin kindly advised me on the dating of the neumes in C. See her article 'Some Reflections on Music at Late Anglo-Saxon Worcester' in *St Oswald of Worcester: Life and Influence*, ed. N. Brooks and C. Cubitt (London and New York, 1996, pp. 325–48. On Cambridge, Corpus Christi College 146, see S. Rankin in *Cambridge Music Manuscripts*, ed. Fenlon, no. 5, especially p. 19 and Rankin, 'Neumatic Notations in Anglo-Saxon England', p. 136. See also above, p. 44, n. 74.

the first and third stanza that have neumes. These additional neumes appear to be motivated by text-conditioned changes in the application of the melody, to take account of an extra syllable in a line, for example. On the other hand in Hy 158 and 123 not even the whole first verse has neumes. Why these particular hymns received neumes is not clear. The neumes to Hy 47 and 55 are Norman in style and are probably part of the post-Conquest revision of the hymnal.

On p. 656 of the collectar, the incipit of Hy 1, Hy 1/1–2, has been glossed in Old English.[84]

H = London, BL, Harley 2961 (the 'Leofric Collectar')

This manuscript[85] contains a collectar (2r–217v), a hymnal (218r–251r) and sequences (251v–256v).

The manuscript is incomplete and ends in the middle of a sequence. The hymnal and the collection of sequences are on the last five quires, namely 28–32.[86] These were quaternions, but the last leaf of quire 30 is missing and the size of the gap in the text indicates that a whole quire was lost after it. The missing leaves contained the hymns for Easter, Ascension, Pentecost, John the Baptist, Peter and Paul and probably Laurence.

The manuscript was mainly written by one hand, H_1; a second, H_2, wrote fols. 153 and 185, a third, H_3, fols. 194–8, and a fourth, H_4, fols. 234–56. These are all of the eleventh century. There are corrections by several almost contemporary hands.

---

[84] See Ker, p. lxiv. On p. 665 of the collectar there is an interlined Old English note: 'half þes' ('half this') and 'her is wona' ('here is a gap'), separated by something that could be read as *ā* and may stand for *antiphona*. The incipit to an antiphon, 'Haec est dies', is directly above. After I had informed him of the note, Dr D. McDougall of the *Dictionary of Old English* kindly sent me a reproduction of that page so I could check my reading. Dr McDougall, in a letter dated 21 March 1988, was of the opinion that the indistinct letter is *&* and that the note has to do with the abbreviation of the rubric 'IN EUUAN' below.

[85] The manuscript is Ker no. 236, and Gneuss, 'Preliminary List', no. 431. *The Leofric Collectar*, ed. Dewick and Frere is a complete edition of the manuscript and includes a thorough discussion of its contents. See further Gneuss, *HHEM*, pp. 108–9; Drage, 'Bishop Leofric'; A. G. Watson, *Catalogue of Dated and Datable Manuscripts c. 700–1600 in the Departments of the British Library* (London, 1979), no. 718; and Rankin, 'From Memory to Record', pp. 97–112.

[86] On the collation of the manuscript, see Drage, 'Bishop Leofric', p. 369.

In the margin of fol. 1, Samuel Knott, vicar of Combe Raleigh in Devon from 1661 to 1698, has left a note that he obtained the manuscript at St Peter's in Exeter. He also mentions an inscription on the lost torn last leaf of the manuscript which called H a gift of Leofric. Thus this manuscript can probably be identified with the 'collectaneum' that figures in the list of gifts of Bishop Leofric to his cathedral at Exeter.[87] The collectar derives from a Flemish source and is ultimately based on the *Liber capitularis* of Bishop Stephen of Liège.[88] Frere therefore assumed that the manuscript was compiled by Leofric himself, who had been educated in Lotharingia.[89] However, Leofric was not the only one who had connections with Flanders and Lotharingia at that time and the collectar in C independently betrays Flemish influence.[90] Other features that indicate that the manuscript was intended for Exeter from the beginning are the prominent role of Mary Magdalene in the collectar and the fact that the manuscript is for secular canons, such as served the cathedral at Exeter; but what clinches the matter is that the hands H_1, H_3 and H_4 connect H with a group of about two dozen manuscripts, many of which are clearly connected with Leofric and the liturgical and local interests of Exeter.[91] So H, like the others, must have been written at the scriptorium there during Leofric's episcopacy from 1046 to 1072.

H's collectar offers hymn incipits for the whole liturgical year. These are not based on the hymnal that follows it, but on a different one.[92] Still, the

---

[87] M. Förster, 'The Donations of Leofric to Exeter', in *The Exeter Book of English Poetry*, ed. R. W. Chambers, M. Förster and R. Flower (London, 1933), pp. 10–32, esp. 25, n. 78. Cf. Conner, *Anglo-Saxon Exeter*, pp. 13–16. H does not quite fit into the pattern that Conner discerns, namely that the volumes inscribed as gifts of Leofric are typically not the ones written at his scriptorium.

[88] On the collectar, see *The Leofric Collectar*, ed. Dewick and Frere II, and *The Durham Collectar*, ed. Corrêa, pp. 125–6.

[89] *The Leofric Collectar*, ed. Dewick and Frere II, xii. On Leofric's connection with Lotharingia, see F. Barlow, *The English Church 1000–1066: a History of the Later Anglo-Saxon Church*, 2nd ed. (London, 1979), pp. 81–4.

[90] Cf. Ortenberg, *The English Church and the Continent*, pp. 21–94. On the collectar in C, see above, p. 45. On a point of contact between the liturgies of Exeter and Fulda, see Conner, *Anglo-Saxon Exeter*, p. 189.

[91] The scriptorium of Exeter has been comprehensively treated in Drage, 'Bishop Leofric'. Cf. Conner, *Anglo-Saxon Exeter*, pp. 1–20. On the importance of Mary Magdalene in Exeter, see *The Leofric Collectar*, ed. Dewick and Frere II, xxiii.

[92] Cf. the index of hymns in *The Leofric Collectar*, ed. Dewick and Frere II, 650–2. See also above, pp. 13–15. The information contained in the hymn incipits is made use of in

differences are minor when compared with the monastic types of Canterbury and Winchester. In the hymn incipits in the collectar, as in the hymnal, there are hints of continental influence.[93]

The hymnal in H is the only (fairly) complete Anglo-Saxon hymnal for secular clerics. It is symptomatic that in Hy 91/3 *monachorum* 'of the monks' is replaced by *populorum* or, alternatively, *clericorum*. The fact that Hy 62–4 for Benedict do nevertheless appear in H could well indicate that it was itself originally derived from a Benedictine hymnal.

The hymnal has neither heading nor explicit. The rubrics in the part written by H₁ are missing. H₄, on the other hand, seems to have filled in the rubrics as he wrote.

H₄'s Caroline minuscule is rather irregular, but he was experienced with neumes and is responsible for most of those in Exeter manuscripts, including the ones in H. In H's hymnal the neumes come in three blocks of hymns. These are numbers 36–7, 64–99 and 109–22 in H.[94] Usually there are neumes for the whole first stanza.

J = London, BL, Cotton Julius A. vi

This manuscript[95] contains a Latin computus including a metrical calendar and Easter tables (fols. 2–17), an *Expositio hymnorum* with an Old English interlinear gloss (19r–71r), three hymns for Trinity Sunday with

the comments on liturgical usage in the edition. The collectar does not include Hy 61, 90–3 and 107–16. Hy 62–4, the hymns to St Benedict, are also not included except for Hy 62/69–72, which is, however, used for other saints. The collectar also includes *Sidus solare revehit (AH* 52, 253–4) for St Mary Magdalene, *Signum crucis mirabile (ICL* no. 1535) for the Exaltation of the Cross and *Praelata mundi culmina* for SS Peter and Paul *(ICL* no. 12348). The text of these is apparently not extant in Anglo-Saxon manuscripts. Often in the collectar alternative hymns are offered so that it looks as if the hymn incipits had undergone revision.

93 See above, p. 15.
94 On neumatic notation in Exeter manuscripts, including H, see Rankin, 'From Memory to Record'. On the neumes in H, see below, pp. 96–103, and cf. the table of hymns in H (below, pp. 475–8).
95 The manuscript is Ker no. 160, Gneuss, 'Preliminary List', no. 337, and Temple no. 62. It is also described by Mynors, *Durham Cathedral Manuscripts*, no. 21, Gneuss, *HHEM*, pp. 91–7; and Dumville, 'On the Dating', p. 47. Cf. also Dumville, *Liturgy*, p. 20, n. 30. The text of the *Expositio hymnorum* has been edited by Gneuss, *HHEM*.

an Old English interlinear gloss (71r–72v) and monastic canticles with an Old English interlinear gloss (72v–89v).

The original text of the manuscript is by two scribes: fols. 2–17 (the computus) by J_1 and fols. 19–89 (the hymnal and monastic canticles) by J_2. J_2 probably wrote the Old English gloss as well as the Latin text. This scribe can be dated to the middle of the eleventh century or a little earlier. J_1 can be dated to the early years of the eleventh century. He has been connected with the script of Christ Church. J_2 is either identical with or very closely related to the second scribe in V, namely V_2.

There are two twelfth-century additions on fols. 18–19 by two different hands. The first entered the hymn *Assunt o socii festa diei* on 18r, and the second wrote three pieces from the liturgy of Easter Sunday with notation on 18r–19r. To make room for them the beginning of the *Expositio* on fol. 19 was erased. In the late eleventh century, the hymn *O genetrix aeterni* and a fragment of the poem *Ad mensam philosophiae* were added on fol. 90.[96]

This manuscript made its way at some point into the Durham Cathedral library. It does not appear in the twelfth-century catalogue, but is identified in two late fourteenth-century catalogues as a possession of the Cathedral.[97]

The computus seems to have been compiled originally for 969–1006. The Easter tables were apparently later extended to 1044. The metrical calendar, called Hampson's Metrical Calendar, has recently been connected with Canterbury. It is also found in London, British Library, Cotton Galba A. xviii (?Old Minster, Winchester, s. x^{in}) and Cotton Tiberius B. v (Old Minster, Winchester or Canterbury, s. xi^{in}).[98] J shares the five hexameters

[96] See Gneuss, *HHEM*, pp. 92–4. The poem (*ICL* no. 188), may constitute a tenuous link between J and Canterbury; cf. Gneuss, *HHEM*, pp. 96–7.

[97] It is identified by the signature 'A' and the first words on fol. 2, 'principium iani'. See *Catalogi Veteres Librorum Ecclesiae Cathedralis Dunelmensis, Catalogues of the Library of Durham Cathedral*, ed. J. Raine, Surtees Society 7 (London, 1838), 33 and 111.

[98] For the metrical calendar, see P. McGurk, 'The Metrical Calendar of Hampson: a New Edition', *Analecta Bollandiana* 104 (1986), 79–125. The attribution to Canterbury is in Dumville, *Liturgy*, pp. 1–38. Dumville discusses recent work on the calendar and analyses the relation of J to Tiberius B. v. and to Oxford, Bodleian Library, Junius 27 (?Winchester, s. x^{in}), both of which he also would like to attribute to Canterbury. Cotton Galba A. xviii is Gneuss, 'Preliminary List', no. 334, and Temple no. 5. Cotton Tiberius B. v. is Ker no. 193, Gneuss, 'Preliminary List', no. 373, and Temple no. 87. Junius 27 is Ker no. 335, Gneuss, 'Preliminary List', no. 641, and Temple no. 7.

preceding each month in the metrical calendar, the 'Versus de mensibus', with London, BL, Cotton Galba A. xviii.[99] An unexplained feature of the calendar is the prominence given to 30 April, the feast of St Erkenwald, by a golden cross in the margin.[100]

J is famous for the cycle of illustrations in the calendar showing the Labours of the Months, the first of their kind in England. They are closely related to a similar cycle in Tiberius B. v, so that the illumination forms another link between the two manuscripts.[101]

The text and the gloss of the monastic canticles in J go back to the same archetype as those in D, an archetype which probably belongs to Canterbury.[102]

The extremely close relationship between the hymns for Trinity Sunday in J and D has already been mentioned. The text and gloss of the *Expositio hymnorum* is in its turn very closely related to that in V and they may be copies of a common exemplar.[103] The fact that the *Expositio hymnorum* is based on a hymnal of the Winchester type and the language of the gloss, originally pure West Saxon, suggest that *Expositio* and gloss came together to Canterbury from elsewhere, although a significant number of Kentish spellings have been introduced during the copying of J.[104] Because of the strong links between D and J, it seems highly probable that J was written in Canterbury and at Christ Church, if D was written there.

The beginning of the *Expositio* is defective because of the erasure on fol. 19; Hy 1 and the first six stanzas of Hy 3 up to 'crememur' are missing. Bits of Hy 3 are still legible. Because of the loss of one leaf after fol. 55, the latter part of Hy 86_2, the whole of Hy 86_3 and the beginning of Hy 87 are missing as well.[105] The incipits of the hymns (i.e. of the metrical originals) are used as rubrics for their prose counterparts.

---

[99] J. Hennig, 'Versus de Mensibus', *Traditio* 11 (1955), 65–90.

[100] See Gneuss, *HHEM*, p. 96, and Dumville, *Liturgy*, p. 21.

[101] Cf. Temple, nos. 62 and 87.

[102] See above, pp. 39–40, and Korhyammer, *MC*, pp. 17–19.

[103] See Gneuss, *HHEM*, pp. 135–41.

[104] On the language of the *Expositio* gloss, see also below, pp. 77–88, as well as Klappenbach, *Zu altenglischen Interlinearversionen*, Gneuss, *HHEM*, pp. 163–88, and Hofstetter, *Winchester*, pp. 101–3 (no. 10).

[105] Cf. the edition of the hymns in question.

V = *London, BL, Cotton Vespasian D. xii*

This manuscript[106] contains a combined hymnal and *Expositio hymnorum* with an Old English interlinear gloss (fols. 4–120) and monastic canticles accompanied by a version with re-arranged word order and an Old English gloss (fols. 125–55).

Two hands of the mid-eleventh century wrote the Latin text of the hymnal and canticles; the second, V_2, begins on 100v. V_1 is probably identical with the hand that writes the Old English gloss up to 91r and V_2 with the hand that writes the gloss from 92v onwards. (There is no gloss on 91v–92r.) Latin glosses to the metrical text of the first seven hymns are by a nearly contemporaneous hand, V_3.

In V, a hymnal of the Canterbury type, Vm, has been combined with the *Expositio hymnorum* based on the Winchester type in such a way that each hymn is followed by its prose version, glossed in Old English and closely related to J. If the hymn in question was not found in the *Expositio*, its – metrical – text was glossed using another source. The relation of this source to D has already been discussed.[107] Hymns and parts of hymns for which no gloss was available either in the *Expositio* or in the textual tradition of D remain unglossed, with the exception of Hy 37 from line 3 onwards and Hy 90/13–16. These were apparently glossed by the scribe (V_1). The gloss to Hy 37 is full of mistakes.

Fols. 118–24 (the fifteenth quire) may have been added as an afterthought to provide more space for additions to the hymnal by hand V_2 on 117v–119. V_2 adds a hymn for Trinity Sunday, three hymns for St Edmund, a hymn for the Invention of the Cross and a hymn for St Laurence. They are followed by *O pater sancte* on 120v by a hand of the eleventh century.[108] This supplement expands V's hymnal with hymns for feasts not specifically provided for before. Subsequent additions, however, presuppose the introduction of the revised New Hymnal after the Norman

---

[106] The manuscript is Ker no. 208, and Gneuss, 'Preliminary List', no. 391. It is also described in Gneuss, *HHEM*, pp. 98–101. The *Expositio hymnorum* has been edited by Gneuss, *HHEM*.

[107] See above, pp. 36–7.

[108] The hymns by V_2 are Hy 152–6 and Hy 88. See the edition of the respective hymns. *O pater sancte* is Hy 132; it was considered to be too late to be collated.

Conquest and the first block on 120v–123v represents an attempt to update as well as to expand the hymnal by nine hymns, some of which had meanwhile replaced hymns current in Anglo-Saxon times.[109] These are possibly all by the same hand (of the late eleventh or early twelfth century) and include *Ave Dunstane* (Hy 82) with neumes that are still Anglo-Saxon in style. Other additions by hands of the late eleventh to thirteenth century follow. Many of the additions on 120v–124v are accompanied by notation. Among post-Conquest additions to the hymnal on 155v–156v are two hymns for Mary Magdalene, *Lauda mater ecclesia* and *Aeterni patris unice*, by a hand of the twelfth century.[110]

The monastic canticles are each in their turn followed by a version with re-arranged word order. The new order follows the same lines as the prose of the *Expositio hymnorum*. Since this re-arrangement does not seem truly helpful, given that the canticles are already in prose, it can hardly have been done independently of the *Expositio*.[111] The Old English gloss accompanies the re-arranged version just as in the hymnal section.

The connection between the *Expositio* and the re-arranged canticles is confirmed by the close agreement of the two interlinear glosses where spelling, phonology and vocabulary are concerned.[112] The language was originally pure West Saxon, into which a number of Kentish spellings have been introduced in the process of copying. The text of the canticles and that of the re-arranged versions disagree, but both are related to the canticles in C. This textual tradition may have emanated from Winchester;[113] the *Expositio hymnorum* is also based on the Winchester type of hymnal. It is generally agreed that hymnal, canticles and interlinear glosses must derive either from Winchester or from a centre strongly influenced by Winchester.

---

[109] See above, p. 8, and Gneuss, *HHEM*, pp. 75–80.

[110] See Gneuss, *HHEM*, pp. 79–80 and 99. The notation in Vm for Hy 20, 70, 73, 149, 150 and 151 is of Norman type and probably are to be seen in the same context as the additions at the end of the hymnal. The neumes for Hy 69, however, are of the Anglo-Saxon style. I owe thanks to Susan Rankin for this information on the neumes in V.

[111] Gneuss, *HHEM*, pp. 152–4, and Korhammer, *MC*, p. 37. The canticles have been edited by Korhammer, *MC*, pp. 247–368.

[112] See Klappenbach, *Zu altenglischen Interlinearversionen*, Gneuss, *HHEM*, pp. 163–4, and Korhammer, *MC*, pp. 151–245. See also above, p. 51 and n. 104.

[113] Korhammer, *MC*, pp. 118–22.

The history of the manuscript before it entered the Cotton collection is not known except that it was probably used by Joscelyn.[114]

V is obviously from the same scriptorium as J. Together with the connection of the gloss in Vm to manuscript D and the Kentish forms in the interlinear glosses, this points to Canterbury, and especially to Christ Church, if the attribution of J is correct. The addition of the hymns to Dunstan on 120v–121r and to Mary Magdalene on 155v–156r may indicate that V was at Canterbury in the early twelfth century.[115]

The evidence is nevertheless not so strongly in favour of Canterbury that the question of whether it is contradicted by the hymns to St Edmund on 118r–119r does not have to be considered. On the face of it, they certainly suggest a connection with Bury St Edmunds even though St Edmund was one of the more popular Anglo-Saxon saints. As they were written by V₂, they could either have been copied from the exemplar together with the hymnal, or could be an afterthought of V₂ himself. Korhammer assumes that they were in the exemplar and constructs a theory based on them about the route by which the Winchester influence (witnessed in various ways by the contents of V) reached Canterbury.[116] According to his theory, the *Expositio* and the canticles together with their glosses came to Canterbury from Bury and were originally written in Ely or Peterborough.[117] He prefers one of these two reformed monasteries connected with Æthelwold to Winchester itself as the place of origin of the glosses since, according to him, some features of their language deviate from normal usage in both Winchester and Canterbury.

As the Latin text of the canticles in V does not seem to be from Canterbury, but the arrangement of the canticles presupposes the combination of the hymnal with the *Expositio*, Korhammer proposes that a Winchester-type hymnal was originally combined with the Winchester-type *Expositio* and was only later replaced by the Canterbury type. However, considering the nature of the differences between the Canterbury and Winchester types, a compiler in that case would hardly have gone to

---

[114] On the later history of the manuscript, see H. Gneuss, 'Ergänzungen zu den altenglischen Wörterbüchern', *ASNSL* 199 (1962), 17–24, esp. 17–19.

[115] Gneuss, *HHEM*, p. 100.   [116] Korhammer, *MC*, pp. 235–45.

[117] Korhammer's assumption that the gloss is too early to have been written at Bury itself will have to be reconsidered in the light of arguments by Dumville, *English Caroline Script*, pp. 30–48, who, however, connects Bury with the group of reformed monasteries associated with Oswald.

the trouble of such a replacement since all he needed to do was to add the missing hymns at the end. He was, after all, writing a book not for liturgical service, but for teaching or study. It should also be kept in mind that the text of the *Expositio* in J is very closely related to V and that J does not have a 'metrical' hymnal. (It also has no hymns to St Edmund and a different set of canticles.) It does not seem very likely that J was copied from such a complex book as V's exemplar and its predecessors must have been, according to Korhammer's theory.

If the canticle gloss was initially conceived for a normal canticle text, it would not have been too difficult to adjust to the version with re-arranged word order. Nevertheless, it is certainly puzzling that the canticles in V combine two different texts, neither of which was apparently in use in the centre where the manuscript was presumably written, namely Canterbury.

Regardless of the accuracy of Korhammer's scenario, it is perhaps more likely that V's exemplar came from Bury, directly or indirectly, than that V was written in Bury or intended for Bury in spite of its Canterbury sources and Canterbury connections. Moreover, one would tend not to expect a Canterbury-type hymnal at Bury. It is even possible that the Edmund hymns are a misleading clue.[118]

The combined hymnal-cum-*Expositio* is introduced with excerpts from Isidore's *De ecclesiasticis officiis* and *Etymologiae* on the subject of hymns and hymn writers on 4r. It is followed on fol. 4 by two distichs beginning: 'Incipiunt ymni ...'[119] Rubrics precede the hymns; the prose versions have none of their own.

Ri = Leeds, Brotherton Library (formerly Ripon Cathedral s. n.)

Two fragments of an eleventh-century hymnal[120] in English Caroline minuscule were found in the binding of a copy of Virgil's *Bucolica*, printed in Antwerp in 1543 (Ripon Cathedral, xiii d. 39). They have been cut horizontally from two bifolia so that altogether we have fragments of eight

---

[118] There is no obvious connection between the cult of St Edmund and Canterbury, but perhaps Dunstan's involvement with Abbo's *Passio S. Eadmundi* could be considered a link. See Abbo of Fleury, 'Life of St Edmund', ed. Winterbottom, pp. 67–8. See also below, p. 64.

[119] Gneuss, *HHEM*, pp. 199 and 265.

[120] The manuscript is Ker no. 372, and Gneuss, 'Preliminary List', no. 696. See also Gneuss, *HHEM*, p. 103.

pages of the original manuscript. The first strip of parchment measures 93 × 45 mm, which is less than the original written space, so that all lines are defective at the beginning or the end. The first page contains Hy 44/7–11, the second Hy 44/22–8 with a doxology and part of a rubric, the third Hy 64/15–19 and the fourth Hy 62/8–11. The second fragment measures 160 × 50 mm and gives us the head of each page and complete lines of text. The first page contains Hy 72/43–4 with a doxology and Hy 73/1 with a rubric, the second Hy 73/19–20, 25–7 and part of 28, the third Hy 76/18–22 and the fourth Hy 77/7–11. All the text is by one hand except for Hy 44 from line 22 onwards. The text by the main hand is glossed in Latin except for the first two words of Hy 44/8, which are glossed in Old English. The position of Hy 64 before Hy 62 and the abbreviation of the text of Hy 73 would agree with a hymnal of the Winchester type.[121] The doxology of Hy 44 agrees with C, the hymnal from Worcester.[122] The provenance of the hymnal is unknown.

EXCERPTS FROM HYMNALS

The two manuscripts that come under this heading are both early witnesses; in neither case can we be absolutely certain about the specific form of the hymn cycle from which they were excerpted.[123]

A = London, BL, Cotton Vespasian A. i (the 'Vespasian Psalter')

This is the only source, albeit an incomplete one, for the text of the Old Hymnal in England.[124] Three hymns of the Old Hymnal were entered on the last empty pages, 153r–154v, of the manuscript of a Roman psalter with canticles at some time in the first half of the eighth century: *Splendor*

---

[121] See above, p. 13, and cf. below, pp. 259–60 and 265.   [122] Cf. the edition of Hy 44.

[123] See above, pp. 4 and 7.

[124] The manuscript is Ker no. 203, and Gneuss, 'Preliminary List', no. 381. *The Vespasian Psalter*, ed. Kuhn, is a complete edition and includes the hymns. There is a facsimile: *The Vespasian Psalter. British Museum Vespasian A. I*, introduction by D. H. Wright and A. Campbell, EEMF 14 (Copenhagen, 1967). See also E. A. Lowe, *Codices Latini Antiquiores II: Great Britain and Ireland*, 2nd ed. (Oxford, 1972), pp. 21 and 51; Gneuss, 'Zur Geschichte des Ms. Vespasian A. I'; J. J. G. Alexander, *Insular Manuscripts: 6th to the 9th Century*, A Survey of the Manuscripts Illuminated in the British Isles 1 (London, 1978), 55–6 (no. 29), and Gneuss, *HHEM*, pp. 17–19.

paternae gloriae, *Deus creator omnium* and *Rex aeterne domine*, for Lauds, Vespers and Matins respectively (OHy 8, 26 and 3). They were written in uncial script by the main scribe of the manuscript. The hymns as well as the psalter and canticles were glossed in Insular minuscule in a Mercian dialect in the ninth century. It is not clear whether the gloss to the hymns is by the scribe or was copied from an exemplar. A was at St Augustine's, Canterbury, at least from the eleventh century on. It might even have been written in Canterbury in spite of the Mercian gloss, since the relations between Mercia and Kent were very close in the eighth and ninth centuries.

Rex aeterne is found only once in Anglo-Saxon manuscripts of the New Hymnal, namely in D. The version there differs considerably from A so that D cannot have copied directly from A, but a few shared readings suggest a tenuous Canterbury tradition across the centuries.[125]

E = Durham, Cathedral Library, A. IV. 19 (the 'Durham Ritual')

Among the additions made *c.* 970 to a Southumbrian collectar of the first half of the tenth century by six members of the community at Chester-le-Street, there are hymns which belong to the earliest sources for the New Hymnal in England.[126] They are by three of the scribes.

The fifth scribe ('E') wrote *Auctor salutis* (Hy 68) in Caroline minuscule over erasure within the collectar on 53v (p. 106). The third scribe ('C') wrote a group of hymns for occasions from Lent to Easter on the last leaf of the original collectar, fol. 65 (pp. 129–30): *Auctor salutis* (Hy 68), *Audi benigne* (Hy 55), *Vexilla regis* (Hy 67₁, 67₂) and *Ad cenam agni* (Hy 70). These have no connection with the surrounding material. The remaining hymns were written by Aldred, the famous glossator of the Lindisfarne

---

[125] Gneuss, *HHEM*, pp. 124–5. See above, p. 36.

[126] The manuscript is Ker no. 106, and Gneuss, 'Preliminary List', no. 223. The old complete edition *Rituale Ecclesiae Dunelmensis*, ed. Lindelöf, has been superseded only for the collectar proper by *The Durham Collectar*, ed. Corrêa, so the only hymn included there is Hy 68 on pp. 224–5. The facsimile is *The Durham Ritual: a Southern English Collectar of the 10th Century with Northumbrian Additions*, ed. T. J. Brown, EEMF 16 (Copenhagen, 1969). The manuscript is also described by Mynors, *Durham Cathedral Manuscripts*, no. 106, and by A. S. C. Ross, E. G. Stanley and T. J. Brown, 'The Durham Ritual', *Evangeliorum Quattuor Codex Lindisfarnensis*, with introductions by T. D. Kendrick, T. J. Brown, R. L. S. Bruce-Mitford, H. Roosen-Runge, A. S. C. Ross, E. G. Stanley and A. E. A. Werner (Olten, 1960) II.ii, 25–32.

Gospels and the 'Durham Ritual'. They are hymns for ordinary days of the week: *Iam lucis* (Hy 7), *Nunc sancte* (Hy 8), *Rector potens* (Hy 9), *Rerum deus* (Hy 10), *Rex Christe clementissime* (stanza XI of Hy 72 with a doxology) and *O lux beata* (Hy 1) on fol. 77 (pp. 153–4), followed by appropriate collects and chapters, and *Te ante lucis terminum* (Hy 11) on fol. 82 (pp. 163–4). The intrusion of the stanza of a hymn for Easter, Hy 72, is unexplained. Aldred glossed the hymns, in red ink.

This collection of hymns has been interpreted in conflicting ways. They certainly do not represent a complete hymnal. Whatever else is missing, stanzas I–X of Hy 72 are undoubtedly lacking. With Hy 68, E includes one of the hymns that are found in Anglo-Saxon England, but not in France.[127] Like H, the book is a non-monastic document.

SPECIAL OFFICES

Hours of All Saints, Hours of the Dead, Hours of Our Lady, Hours of the Trinity and Hours of the Holy Cross are found in Anglo-Saxon manu-scripts.[128] Originally these devotions were probably practised in private. They supplemented the canonical hours and were modelled on them. They spread and some of them became an official part of the liturgy in individual monasteries. On the Continent this was a development of the ninth and tenth centuries. In England the Hours of All Saints and of the Dead are prescribed in the tenth century in the *Regularis concordia*, but in a version that did not include hymns.[129]

The Hours of the Virgin developed on the Continent later than these other Little Offices, and are correspondingly found in English manuscripts no earlier than the eleventh century. There are three such Anglo-Saxon manuscripts: London, BL, Cotton Tiberius A. iii (T) and London, BL, Royal 2. B. V (R), both of which will be discussed in detail in this chapter, and London, BL, Cotton Titus D. xxvii (New Minster, Winchester, s. xi[1]).

---

[127] See above, pp. 21 and 23.

[128] See the *The Prymer*, ed. Littlehales, esp. vol. II, which also contains E. Bishop, 'On the Origin of the Prymer'; Tolhurst, *Introduction to the English Monastic Breviaries*, pp. 2–3 and 46–137, esp. 120–9; and Gneuss, *HHEM*, pp. 109–10. Cf. Leclercq, 'Fragmenta Mariana', and *idem*, 'Formes anciennes de l'Office Marial' and particularly Clayton, *Cult of the Virgin*, pp. 65–81.

[129] 'Regularis Concordia', ed. Symons and Spath, chs. 19, 56, 91 etc. Cf. E. Bishop, 'Origin of the Prymer', pp. xxii–xxiv.

In Titus D. xxvii only one Hour is provided for. For the single hymn, Hy 66, only an incipit is given.[130]

These three manuscripts are all monastic. Later on, the Hours of the Virgin were taken over by the secular clergy and also became an essential text for the private devotions of the laity, the core of the Prymer or Book of Hours. The Prymers of Sarum and York, the two usages most widespread in medieval England, were, however, not based on any of the Anglo-Saxon Hours of the Virgin, although they appear to have influenced monastic devotions.[131] The tradition may to some extent have been disrupted by the Norman Conquest.

The Hours of Our Lady with a complement of eight hymns were the most elaborate of the Hours in use in Anglo-Saxon England. R and T are also the only manuscripts to give the texts of the hymns, with the exception of Hy 1 in the Office of the Holy Trinity in Oxford, Bodleian Library, Douce 296.[132] Other Hours in Anglo-Saxon manuscripts which give the incipits of hymns are an Office of All Saints in T with Hy 99 for Vespers and Hy 98 for Lauds and two Offices with a single Hour, the Office of the Holy Trinity with Hy 76 and the Office of the Holy Cross with Hy 71, in Titus D. xxvii.[133]

T = London, BL, Cotton Tiberius A. iii

The Hours of Our Lady in this manuscript (107v–115v) originally stood at the end of a miscellany including the Benedictine Rule and the *Regularis concordia*, which was written in the eleventh century.[134] Christ

---

[130] Cotton Titus D. xxvii is Ker no. 202, and Gneuss, 'Preliminary List', no. 380. The single Hour is edited by Leclercq, 'Formes anciennes de l'Office Marial', pp. 101–2, and in *Ælfwine's Prayerbook*, ed. Günzel, pp. 53–5 and 133–6 (no. 51). For a possible connection between this Hour and Æthelwold, which would date the Hour back to the tenth century, see Clayton, *Cult of the Virgin*, pp. 67–70, and Wulfstan of Winchester, *Life of St Æthelwold*, ed. Lapidge and Winterbottom, p. lxix. See also *The Durham Collectar*, ed. Corrêa, pp. 114–16.

[131] See *The Prymer*, ed. Littlehales II, lv–lxxiii.   [132] See below, p. 63.

[133] Cf. Gneuss, *HHEM*, pp. 111–13, and *Ælfwine's Prayerbook*, ed. Günzel, pp. 53–5 and 128–33 (nos. 49–50).

[134] The manuscript is Ker no. 186, and Gneuss, 'Preliminary List', no. 363. *Horae*, ed. Dewick, is a facsimile and diplomatic edition of the Hours. See also *The Prymer*, ed. Littlehales II, lxxv–lxxxiii; Tolhurst, *Introduction to the English Monastic Breviaries*, pp. 114–19 and 121–4; Gneuss, *HHEM*, p. 111; and Clayton, *Cult of the Virgin*, pp. 70–7.

Church, Canterbury, is indicated as the place of origin of the manuscript in various ways. The Hours are clearly a Christ Church service, too.[135] They were written by the scribe identified by Ker as the fourth hand in T, who also wrote 27r–37v, 46v–56v, 96r–107v, and possibly 118v–168v.[136]

The Hours contain a hymn for each canonical hour and quote the complete text. The hymns in question are:

Matins	*Quem terra*	Hy 65
Lauds	*Ave maris stella*	Hy 66
Prime	*Maria mater domini*	Hy 90
Tierce	*Gabrihel dei*	Hy 91
Sext	*Maria celi regina*	Hy 92
None	*Maria virgo virginum*	Hy 93
Vespers	*O quam glorifica*	Hy 89
Compline	*Christe sanctorum decus*	Hy 97

According to Tolhurst, the Hours of Our Lady in Tiberius A. iii must at least partly have been meant to be said in choir.[137] On the other hand, the prayers of Prime and, according to Dewick, the *benedictiones* of Matins, seem to be intended for private devotions.[138] A similar distinction between the Hours was made in the usage of Sarum as described by Bishop.[139] The Hours of the Virgin and the other Offices could be said before or after the proper canonical Hours. In the case of Vespers and Lauds in Tiberius A. iii, they must have followed them.

As far as the hymns for Matins, Lauds and Vespers are concerned, T agrees with the thirteenth-century *consuetudines* of Fleury on the *servitium Marie* on Saturdays except for the period from the Octave of Epiphany to Candlemas. In Fleury, instead of Hy 65 only the second part, Hy 65$_2$, was

---

[135] The litany included in the Hours is definitely from Canterbury; see *Anglo-Saxon Litanies of the Saints*, ed. M. Lapidge, HBS 106 (London, 1991), 71 and 174–7. See *Horae*, ed. Dewick, col. 58 on the invocation of St Margaret in the litany. The wording of the collects suggests Christ Church; see *Horae*, ed. Dewick, cols. 34 and 43–4, and cf. Korhammer, 'Origin of the Bosworth Psalter', p. 178.

[136] Ker no. 186 (p. 248).

[137] Tolhurst, *Introduction to the English Monastic Breviaries*, p. 121.

[138] *Horae*, ed. Dewick, pp. xiii–xiv.

[139] E. Bishop, 'On the Origin of the Prymer', pp. xxxvi–xxxvii.

used.[140] In the later Middle Ages it seems that Hy 65_1 was commonly sung at Matins and Hy 65_2 at Lauds.[141]

Hy 97 for Compline is surprising as it is really a hymn for the Archangel Michael. The choice is probably due to the naming of Gabriel, the angel of the Annunciation, in the third stanza and the invocation of Mary in the fifth. Hy 91–3 may have been composed in England,[142] so perhaps the hymns for Matins, Lauds and Vespers were taken over from a continental source, while the hymns for the Little Hours were compiled in England.

R = London, BL, Royal 2. B V

A quire of three bifolia, fols. 1–6, and a single leaf (fol. 7) are bound in front of the 'Royal Psalter' or 'Regius Psalter', a tenth-century manuscript containing a Roman psalter with an Old English interlinear gloss and Latin scholia, which may be from Winchester or Worcester.[143] The single leaf (fol. 7) contains introductory material to the psalter, but the ternion contains a prayer on 1r and the complete Hours of the Virgin on 1r–6r, both written in a hand of the first half of the eleventh century. The prayer entreating the intercession of Mary, St Machutus and St Eadburg proves that the ternion was written in Winchester, probably in New Minster (later Hyde Abbey). The Hours and the psalter were in Christ Church, Canterbury, in the eleventh century, where additions were made to them.[144]

The text of the Hours differs considerably from that of T. There are differences not only between the hymns selected, but also between the lessons, collects, antiphons etc. However, there are major points in which T and R agree against the most common post-Conquest types of the

---

[140] *Consuetudines Floriacenses*, ed. Davril, chs. 509–12.

[141] *The Prymer*, ed. Littlehales II, lv–lvii.   [142] See above, p. 24.

[143] The manuscript is Ker no. 249, and Gneuss, 'Preliminary List', no. 451. There is a facsimile of the Hours and a diplomatic edition in *Horae*, ed. Dewick. See also G. F. Warner and J. P. Gilson, *Catalogue of Western Manuscripts in the Old Royal and King's Collections*, 4 vols. (London, 1921) I, 40–1; Ker, *Medieval Libraries of Great Britain*, pp. 104 and 202; *The Prymer*, ed. Littlehales II, lxxv–lxxxiii; Roeder, *Der altenglische Regius-Psalter*; Sisam and Sisam, *The Salisbury Psalter*, pp. 52–6; Gneuss, *HHEM*, p. 112; and Clayton, *Cult of the Virgin*, pp. 70–7.

[144] It was at Christ Church that the proverbs were written in R; see above, p. 40.

Hours. According to Tolhurst, R's Hours are more strongly influenced by the Office of the secular clergy and consequently progress further in a development which slowly reduced the typically monastic traits of the Hours of the Virgin.[145] There are no clues in R to indicate whether an Hour was said in choir or privately.

The Hours contain the complete text of the hymns prescribed. These are as follows:

Matins	*Maria mater*	Hy 90
Lauds	*O quam glorifica*	Hy 89
Prime	*A solis ortus*	Hy 44 / stanzas I–III
Tierce	*Domus pudici*	Hy 44 / stanzas IV–VI
Sext	*Quem terra*	Hy 65 / stanzas I–IV
None	*Beata caeli*	Hy 65 / stanzas V–VIII
Vespers	*Ave maris*	Hy 66

O quam glorifica is repeated for Compline. So no Hour has the same hymn as in T. Hy 66 appears in the abbreviated version of the Winchester type, without the second and sixth stanzas.[146] It is a Vespers hymn and it is noteworthy that the Hour of the Virgin in Titus D. xxvii, which also prescribes Hy 66, is intended to be said at Vespers. This is a Winchester manuscript, too.[147] On the other hand, Hy 66 at Vespers seems to have been common in later times.[148]

The division of Hy 44 and Hy 65 is unusual; indeed it is unparalleled in Anglo-Saxon England. That Hy 44 is selected as a hymn for Mary, a not entirely obvious choice, is comparable to its use at Candlemas in the Winchester type and in H.[149] Apart from the standard hymns Hy 65, 66 and 89, R and T also share the rare hymn Hy 90. In R it appears in the longer version otherwise only attested in D.[150] The inclusion of this hymn suggests that the Hours were not borrowed from a French source in their present form. Perhaps they were compiled in England.

---

[145] Tolhurst, *Introduction to the English Monastic Breviaries*, pp. 123–4.
[146] See above, p. 13.
[147] See above, p. 59.
[148] *The Prymer*, ed. Littlehales, II, lv–lvii. Cf. Leclercq, 'Fragmenta Mariana', and *idem*, 'Formes anciennes de l'Office Marial'.
[149] See above, p. 13.
[150] See above, p. 12 and cf. the edition of the hymn in question.

Do = Oxford, Bodleian Library, Douce 296 (S.C. 21870)

A single hymn, *O lux beata trinitas*, appears in an incomplete Office of the Trinity in this manuscript (128r), where it is assigned to first Vespers.[151] The Office (127v–130) was appended in the eleventh century to a manuscript containing a calendar, a psalter, canticles and a litany, which is probably from Crowland Abbey. The date of the calendar is approximately between 1015 and 1036.

SAINTS' HYMNS IN HAGIOGRAPHICAL *LIBELLI*

A hagiographical *libellus* contains the *vita* of a saint, but may also include other material pertaining to him (or her) such as hymns.[152] Even texts on other saints might find their way into it.

Cu = Cambridge, Corpus Christi College, 183

This manuscript is a collection of texts on St Cuthbert.[153] Bede's verse and prose lives are followed by an incomplete liturgical section (92v–95v), which includes the hymn *Magnus miles mirabilis* (Hy 61) on 92v–93r. All these texts are by the same hand.

The manuscript can be dated to the period between 934 and 942. It is presumably the manuscript which is recorded as a gift from King Athelstan to the community of St Cuthbert at Chester-le-Street.

---

[151] The manuscript is Gneuss, 'Preliminary List', no. 617, and Temple no. 79. See also A. G. Watson, *Catalogue of Dated and Datable Manuscripts c. 435–1600 in Oxford Libraries*, 2 vols. (Oxford, 1984), no. 471, and Gneuss, *HHEM*, p. 113.

[152] On this type of book, see Dumville, *Liturgy*, pp. 108–10.

[153] The manuscript is Ker no. 42, Gneuss, 'Preliminary List', no. 56, and Temple no. 6. See also *Two Lives of St. Cuthbert*, ed. Colgrave, pp. 20–1; *Cambridge Music Manuscripts*, ed. Fenlon, no. 1; S. Keynes, 'King Athelstan's Books', in *Learning and Literature in Anglo-Saxon England*, ed. Lapidge and Gneuss, pp. 143–201, esp. 180–5; Robinson, *Catalogue of Dated and Datable Manuscripts*, no. 137; D. Rollason, 'St. Cuthbert and Wessex: the Evidence of Cambridge, Corpus Christi College MS 183', in *St. Cuthbert, his Cult and his Community to AD 1200*, ed. G. Bonner, D. Rollason and C. Stancliffe (Woodbridge, 1989), pp. 413–24; Gneuss, *HHEM*, p. 113; and Dumville, *Liturgy*, pp. 106–7. The hymn is included in the edition 'The Durham Services in Honour of St. Cuthbert', in *The Relics of St. Cuthbert*, ed. C. F. Battiscombe (Durham, 1956), pp. 155–91.

Jo = Cambridge, St John's College, F. 27 (164)

Into a tenth-century manuscript of texts on St Benedict, parts of rhymed offices for St Augustine of Canterbury, an unnamed saint and Abbot Hadrian of St Augustine's were added in the eleventh century, including a hymn for St Augustine (Hy 161) on fol. 15.[154] They are written on leaves originally left blank (15r–16r) within the account of St Benedict's translation to Fleury by Adrevald of Fleury (d. 878). The Office for St Augustine (fol. 15) is by a single hand, while various hands were at work on the following texts, possibly reflecting ongoing composition. The Office for Hadrian clearly indicates that the additions were made at St Augustine's, Canterbury. The hymn is attested again in Cambridge, St John's College 262 (St Augustine's, s. xiv[in]), where it is assigned to Lauds. It does not seem to have been used outside St Augustine's.

La = London, Lambeth Palace 362

This is a quire of twelve leaves which brings together texts relevant St Edmund, the martyred king of East Anglia.[155] It dates from the eleventh century and, except for 9r, is all by one hand. Two hymns and a mass have been inserted into Abbo's *Passio S. Eadmundi* on fol. 11, after his preface. The hymns, *Laurea regni* (Hy 154) and *Laus et corona* (Hy 155), have rubrics in uncial script and are preceded by a description of their metrical form in minuscule.

On the face of it, the manuscript seems to be from Bury St Edmunds, whose patron the saint was, but there are links to Canterbury. The hymns are otherwise only attested in V, probably a Canterbury manuscript, and further texts on St Edmund added in the fourteenth century seem to be connected with the monastery of St Augustine's.

---

[154] The manuscript is Gneuss, 'Preliminary List', no. 153. See also Gneuss, *HHEM*, pp. 114–15; M. R. James, *A Descriptive Catalogue of the Manuscripts in the Library of St. John's College, Cambridge* (Cambridge, 1913), pp. 197–9; and M. R. James, *The Ancient Libraries of Canterbury and Dover* (Cambridge, 1903), p. 534.

[155] The manuscript is Gneuss, 'Preliminary List', no. 514. There is an unreliable edition of the hymns in *Corolla Sancti Eadmundi: the Garland of Saint Edmund, King and Martyr*, ed. F. Hervey (London, 1907), pp. 84–8. On the manuscript, see M. R. James and C. Jenkins, *A Descriptive Catalogue of the Manuscripts in the Library of Lambeth Palace: the Medieval Manuscripts* (Cambridge, 1932), pp. 489–91; Ker, *Medieval Libraries of Great Britain*, pp. 21 and 47; and Gneuss, *HHEM*, p. 114.

OTHER MANUSCRIPTS OF RELIGIOUS INTEREST

This category includes miscellaneous items: a troper, a homiliary and a biblical epic. They were evidently felt to be related enough in subject matter for hymns to be added to them.

W = Cambridge, Corpus Christi College 473 (the 'Winchester Troper')

This member of the pair of 'Winchester Tropers'[156] was written in the Old Minster, Winchester, in the first half of the eleventh century. It may have been compiled by Wulfstan the Cantor. Among the additions made to it on blank leaves of the last quire is a set of the first stanzas of hymns, four in number, Hy 67_2, 73, 79 and 123. The stanzas are written in a hand of the eleventh century which is not responsible for any of the other additions. The rubrics and the initials of the stanzas are missing. Ample space was left for the notation, which is both neumatic and alphabetic; the entry is mainly concerned with the melody and the omitted stanzas were irrelevant.

Bo = Oxford, Bodleian Library, Bodley 342 (S.C. 2405)

The first hymn for St Mary Magdalene to be attested in England, *Laudes Christo* (Hy 162), has been entered at the bottom of 206r of this manuscript, where approximately a third of the page had been left blank.[157] The manuscript is the second volume of a two-volume homiliary containing mainly Ælfric's *Catholic Homilies*, and the entry is in the first of two quires added to it in Rochester in the eleventh century. The hymn

---

[156] The manuscript is Ker no. 72, and Gneuss, 'Preliminary List', no. 116. In the edition *The Winchester Troper*, ed. Frere, the stanzas are on p. 97. See James, *Catalogue of the Manuscripts in the Library of Corpus Christi College* II, 411–12; Robinson, *Catalogue of Dated and Datable Manuscripts*, no. 170; H. Husmann, *Tropen- und Sequenzenhandschriften*, Répertoire international des sources musicales B. 5. 1 (Munich, 1964), pp. 150–1; *Cambridge Music Manuscripts*, ed. Fenlon, no. 4; Holschneider, *Die Organa von Winchester*; and Gneuss, *HHEM*, p. 116.

[157] The manuscript is Ker no. 309, Gneuss, 'Preliminary List', no. 569, and Temple no. 30. See also O. Pächt and J. J. G. Alexander, *Illuminated Manuscripts in the Bodleian Library Oxford 3: British, Irish, and Icelandic Schools* (Oxford, 1973), no. 42; K. Sisam, 'MS. Bodley 340 and 342: Ælfric's *Catholic Homilies*', *RES* 7 (1931), 7–22, *RES* 8 (1932), 51–68 and *RES* 9 (1933), 1–12; and Gneuss, *HHEM*, p. 116.

may have been written by a continental scribe of the eleventh century in Rochester. The hymn itself is not likely to be continental, since later attestations are apparently all English. The hymn was first noticed by Wanley.

Cm = Cambridge, University Library, Ff. 4. 42

The 'Cambridge Iuvencus', a manuscript of Iuvencus's rendering of the gospels, was written by a scribe with an Irish name, Nuadu, at a Welsh centre in the late ninth century and glossed by a number of hands of the late ninth to early eleventh centuries (Welsh and Irish material was also added).[158] The last glosses are by a hand which seems to be from the west of England, perhaps from Worcester. The first leaf contains miscellaneous entries including introductory matter to Iuvencus's poem. On 1v, Hy 1 is found, by an Insular hand, apparently Welsh and of the tenth century. This hand also wrote some of the notes on the evangelists and the gospels which precede the hymn. The rubric to the hymn, however, seems to be by another hand. The New Hymnal would presumably have been introduced into Wales from England.

TEXTUAL RELATIONSHIPS AMONG THE MANUSCRIPTS

As hymns were texts that monks and canons learned by heart in childhood and sang in choir at least once a year, if not daily, it is not to be expected that a stemma in the classical sense could be constructed for the hymnals; contamination is ubiquitous.

However, JVp, the manuscripts of the *Expositio hymnorum*, are a different case since the re-arrangement of the word order has for the most part

---

[158] The manuscript is Gneuss, 'Preliminary List', no. 7. See W. M. Lindsay, *Early Welsh Script*, St Andrews University Publications 10 (Oxford, 1912); T. A. M. Bishop, 'The Corpus Martianus Capella', *Transactions of the Cambridge Bibliographical Society* 4 (1964–8), 257–75, pls. xx–xxii, particularly p. 258 and pl. xx; *idem*, *English Caroline Minuscule*, p. 19; P. Clemoes, *Manuscripts from Anglo-Saxon England: an Exhibition in the University Library Cambridge to Mark the Conference of the International Society of Anglo-Saxonists August 1985* (Cambridge, 1985), p. 21; and M. Lapidge, 'Latin Learning in Dark Age Wales: Some Prolegomena', in *Proceedings of the Seventh International Congress of Celtic Studies*, ed. D. E. Evans, J. G. Griffith and E. M. Jope (Oxford, 1986), pp. 91–107, esp. 98–9.

preserved the text from contamination and it has been copied mechanically. As the manuscripts are also closely related,[159] it is usually easy to reconstruct the common archetype and the hymnal on which it was based. JVp must for the most part be treated as a single witness to the text of a hymn.

On the other hand, the situation in D, where the text is combined with a gloss written for a different type of hymnal,[160] is especially conducive to contamination and so, to a lesser degree, is the combination of a hymnal and a glossed *Expositio* based on a different hymnal in V.[161]

In fact, even the procedure of counting the number of times the different hymnal manuscripts agree and disagree with each other is problematical, not only because the divergent readings are of widely varying importance. The hymnals are collections of texts and, although there is a common core, no Anglo-Saxon hymnal contains exactly the same hymns as any other, whereas quite a few of the hymns common to the hymnals are not fully represented because C and H are defective at different points.[162] Moreover, each hymn text might independently be influenced by another version; after all, in liturgical practice hymns occurred singly, not in a group. For example, in Hy 67_2 CDBVm repeatedly agree with each other as against JVpE, an otherwise unusual grouping.

It is therefore not surprising that the manuscripts diverge from each other in unpredictable and erratic ways.[163] The distinction between secular and monastic hymnals and between Canterbury and Winchester types is not by any means neatly maintained on this level.

With all due caution it may be said, however, that there does seem to be a tendency for D to agree with B. If only the text attested in all hymnals – including the *Expositio* – is taken into account and complications of later corrections or divergent glosses are ignored, there are eight cases in which D and B agree as against VmCJVpH, that is, against the other hymnals. In a further five cases they agree against the other hymnals and against another manuscript (E, R, Ri or T) at the same time.[164]

---

[159] See above, p. 51.   [160] See above, p. 36.   [161] See above, p. 52.

[162] See above, pp. 43 and 47.

[163] Cf. *culpa noverit* DBVmC] *culpam noveris* VpH, *culpam* (corrected to *culpa*) *noverit* A (Hy 2/22); *permanet* DCJVp] *permanent* VmH (Hy 39/10); *quem* DC] *quam* BVmJVpH (Hy 48/5) and so on.

[164] *donet et patris pietate nobis* DB] *donet et nobis patris pietate* Vm, *donet et nobis pietate sola*

Compared to the number of divergent readings in the text as a whole, thirteen is hardly frequent. However, if again only the text attested in all the hymnals is considered, we find that DVm only agree six times, DH five times, DJVp once and DC never, while B under these conditions only agrees three times with Vm.[165]

Furthermore, it may be noted that under these conditions the Canterbury-type hymnals (B, D and Vm) agree as against CJVpH and another manuscript or manuscripts (E, R, Ri or T) at the same time in six, possibly seven, cases; they agree against CJVpH in two cases and against CJVp, but not H, in five cases.[166] This does suggest a particular textual tradition for the Canterbury type of hymnal, however elusive, and a tenuous relationship between hymnal type and textual affiliation, although this would be difficult to prove statistically.

CJVpH (Hy 6/7); *tunc* DB] *quod* Vm, *ut* C, om. JVp, & H (Hy 27/2); *sicut* DB] *uti* VmCJVpH (Hy 32/10); *quod homo natus ex deo* DB] *homo natus ex deo es* VmCJVpH (Hy 38/26); *precamur* DB] *precemur* VmCJVpH (Hy 51/9); *regnat* DB] *regnas* VmCJVpH (Hy 104₂/16); *laetis* DB] *laetus* VmCJVpH (Hy 124/12);

   Christo ... nato DB] *Christum ... natum* VmCJVpHR (Hy 44/3–4); *caro* DB] *carne* VmCJVpHRRi (Hy 44/7); *fulgent mysteria* DB] *fulget mysterium* VmCJVpH, *fulge mysterium* E (Hy 67₁/2); *regnum* DB] *celum* VmCJVpHT (Hy 97/4); *et* DB] *ad* VmCJVpHT (Hy 97/11). Cf. also *nec ... nec* DB] *non ... non* VmJVpH, *nec ... non* C (Hy 119/14).

[165] *nascendo* DVm] *nascentem* BCJVpH (Hy 38/19); *Christi* D, *Christo* Vm] *sponsi* BCJVpH (Hy 58/12); *regulis* DVm] *regulas* BCJVp, *regulare* H (Hy 62/18); *portans* DVm] *portas* B, *plaudis* CJVpHE (Hy 67₂/12); *vota* DVm] *votis* BCJVpH (Hy 98/27); *resolvat* DVm] *revolvat* BCJVpH (Hy 100/14);

   proprio videre DH] *proprio videret* BVmC, *meruit videre* JVp (Hy 7/11); *arduum* DH] *ardua* BVmCJVp (Hy 62/14); *gloriam* DH] *gloria* BVmCJVp (Hy 102/3); *gloriam* DH] *gloria* BVmCJVp (Hy 124/18); *ex* VmCJVp] omitted DH, erased B (Hy 67₂); *magni* DJVp] *magno* BVmC (Hy 74/9); *omnium* BVm] *omnia* DCJVpH (Hy 32/14); *pellantur* BVm] *pellat* DCJVpH (Hy 34/3); *seculis* BVm] *seculi* DCJVpHE (Hy 68/8).

[166] *ut sint acceptabilia* DBVm] *ut fructuosa sint tuis* CJVpHE (Hy 55/19); *nectaris* DBVm] *nectare* CJVpHE (Hy 67₂/10); *portans* DVm, *portas* B] *plaudis* CJVpHE (Hy 67₂/12); *triumphum* DBVm] *triumpho* CJVpHE (Hy 67₂/12); *pro* DBVm] *et* CJVpHE (Hy 67₂/15 = doxology of Hy 67₁ in CJH); *est* CJVpHE] om. DBVm (Hy 67₂/7), but *est* may be an addition in JVp.

   Sic DBVm] *Hic* CJVpH (36/13). DBVm agree as against CJVpH on the doxology of Hy 62. Cf. also Hy 6/7.

   nec DBVmH] *ne* (Hy 26/13); *claustra* DBVmH] *claustrum* CJVp (Hy 39/10); *vos* DBVmH] *nos* CJVp (Hy 49/4); *nostra* DBVmH] *nostro* CJVp (Hy 95/15); *&* DBVmH] *ac* (Hy 98/15). Cf. also *lactas* DBVmHRT] *lacta* CJVp (Hy 65₂/4).

To venture any statement on Ri in its fragmentary state would be foolhardy, but it may be pointed out that its extant readings do not agree with DB[167] – a very slight corroboration of the suggestion that this hymnal may have been of the Winchester type.

As for E, R and T, it is difficult to discern a pattern, however much one might expect R to agree with the Winchester type and T with the Canterbury type, considering the provenance of R and T.[168]

The text of the Cuthbert hymn in Cu agrees completely with DVm, but that may not be of any great significance.[169]

[167] Ri does not agree with DB in Hy 44/7, 73/1 and 73/21–4 and on the doxology of Hy 44 and 72. See above, pp. 55–6.

[168] Cf. the apparatus to the edition of Hy 1, 7–11, 65_1-68, 70, 7, 89–93 and 97. See above, pp. 59–61 and 61–2.

[169] Cf. the edition of Hy 61.

3

The language of the 'Durham Hymnal Gloss'

The assumption that the 'Durham Hymnal Gloss' was originally produced at Winchester or a centre influenced by Winchester *c*. 1000 and subsequently revised at Canterbury is supported by the language of the gloss.

ORTHOGRAPHY, PHONOLOGY AND MORPHOLOGY

The phonology of the 'Durham Hymnal Gloss', although conforming largely to Late West Saxon standards, has some markedly southeastern or Kentish features. These were first noticed by Chapman and Wildhagen.[1] Gneuss analysed them in depth and Korhammer showed that the monastic canticles in D share the same phonological features, as his theory of the common origin of the hymnal and the canticles gloss would lead one to expect.[2] This agrees with the fact that the manuscript was written in Canterbury and with the assumption that the glosses achieved their final form in Canterbury.[3] There is no noticeable phonological difference between glosses by D_1 and D_2, but there are no definite southeastern phonological forms in glosses by D_3, which have some peculiarities of their own.[4]

---

[1] H. W. Chapman, *An Index to the Old English Glosses in the Durham Hymnarium*, Yale Studies in English 24 (New York, 1905), iii, and Wildhagen, 'Psalterium Romanum', p. 457, n. 4. In *Latin Hymns*, ed. Stevenson, p. viii, the gloss is called ordinary Late West Saxon. E. von Schaubert, *Vorkommen, gebietsmäßige Verbreitung und Herkunft altenglischer absoluter Partizipialkonstruktionen im Nominativ und Akkusativ* (Paderborn, 1954), pp. 134–7, tries to prove that the gloss is of Anglian origin, but is refuted by Schabram, *Superbia*, pp. 104–5, and Gneuss, *HHEM*, pp. 161–2.

[2] Gneuss, *HHEM*, pp. 157–61; Korhammer, *MC*, pp. 158–74.

[3] See above, pp. 37–9.   [4] See below, p. 77.

Late West Saxon features

Among the Late West Saxon features of the gloss are a number of occurrences of Late West Saxon smoothing of the Old English long diphthong *ēa* before velar *c*, *h*, *g* to *ē*, for example *gebēcnest, forebēcnum*.[5] The group *weor-* almost always appears as *wur-*, which is also typical of Late West Saxon texts, although the phenomenon was more widely spread in the Middle English period. Examples of this are *swurd* 'sword' and *wurþment* 'honour'.[6] Earlier *weoruld* 'world', however, in most instances appears as *woruld*, the usual form in Late West Saxon texts.[7] The group *sel* sometimes appears as *syl*, but not as often as one would expect in a strictly Late West Saxon text; *sellan* 'give' is more frequent than *syllan*.[8]

---

[5] *Gebecnest* 86₂/12; *forebecnum* 64/11; *ecne* 65₁/18 (*hehstan* (41/14) and *nextan* (33/13) may also belong here, if they derive from unumlauted forms, or belong to the forms cited below in n. 20). This phonological change had already begun in Early West Saxon. See SB §121, Campbell §312, Hogg §§5. 119–23, and for *nextan* in particular SB §86, 4. For *smegan* 33/10, see SB §121, n. 3. Diacritics indicating vowel length will be used in the text, but not in the footnotes of the section on phonology, for technical reasons. References to the 'Durham Hymnal Gloss' in this chapter are given without preceding 'Hy'.

[6] *Swuran* 62/20, *swurplættas* 68/5; *swurd* and inflected forms 4/23, 67₁/10, 82/15, etc. (six times); *towurpende* 68/9; *towurpon* 128/14; also *wurþ* 31/32 (by D₂), 67₂/22, 104₂/8 and *wurþ* (adj.) 42/5, *wurþfull* (four times), *wurþfullice* (twice), *wurþian* (seven times), *wurþment* (sixteen times). See SB §113a, Campbell §321 and Hogg §5.184. For the short diphthong in *sweora* 'neck', see SB §113, n. 4, and Campbell §241.2, n. 5. There are inverted spellings with *wyr* for *wur* reflecting the Late West Saxon change of *wyr* to *wur* in *wyrðmynt* 32/25, 41/17, 87/22; see SB §118, n. 1, Campbell §324 and Hogg §5.185. For *þwyre* (19/12; D actually reads *þryre*), cf. Kitson, 'Geographical Variation', pp. 18–21, who says the root vowel is long. If I understand Kitson aright, the occurrence of *þwyre* together with the form *betwux(-)* for *betweox*, of which there are five instances in the 'Durham Hymnal Gloss' (28/12, 39/27, 63/19, 66/22, 126/5), indicate that a text is from the northwest of the West Saxon dialect area; cf. 'Geographical Variation', pp. 11–21. If that is correct, these spellings in the 'Durham Hymnal Gloss' would presumably have to derive from the original.

[7] *Wurolda* 94/4; *wurolde* 31/71; *wurulda* (corrected to *worolda* by D₁) 65₁/9; also *weorulde* 63/24; *werulde* 87/2; but mostly *woruld* (fifty times). On these forms, see SB §§110, n. 3, 113b and nn. 4 and 7, and 117; Campbell §§210, 1, 323 and n. 3; Korhammer, *MC*, pp. 164–6, Hogg §§5.110 and 5.186.

[8] *Selen* 'gift' is never *sylen*, *self* 'self' is twelve times *self*, five times *sylf* (3/30, 4/15, 35/7 (by D₃), 92/11 (by D₂), 95/5), *sellan* seventeen times *sel-* (one case by D₂), ten times *syl-*, *sellend* is *syllend* (58/6, 60/1). See SB §124, Campbell §325 and Hogg §5.171, n. 2.

An unusual feature is that *niht* 'night' is often spelled *nyht*; rounding is not to be expected before a palatal spirant.[9] On the other hand the form *byþ* for older *biþ* 'is', after a labial and in unaccented position, is frequent in Late West Saxon.[10] The subjunctive *sī* instead of *sie*, *sȳ* is found in both Late West Saxon and Kentish.[11]

Late West Saxon *-nisse*, *-nesse* for the old suffix *-nes* appears only in a minority of cases.[12]

A late form of the dative plural of the personal pronoun, *heom*, occurs beside *him*.[13] Late forms of the demonstrative pronoun are acc. sg. masc. *þæne* and the dat. sg. masc. *þan* with the Late Old English weakening of final *m* to *n*.[14] The vowel *æ* in *þæne* instead of expected *o* may be explained by analogy to other forms of the pronoun, such as *þæt*, or be compared to forms like *þænne* 'then' and *mænige* 'many', which are also found in the hymn gloss in D.[15] These late forms are apparently found in all dialects.

There is a single case of a spelling with *u* for the labiodental spirant *f* in intervocalic position: *giuernysse*. This is a phenomenon found from the tenth century onwards.[16]

These are all features that the 'Durham Hymnal Gloss' shares with the Late West Saxon texts of the period, when it was written.

---

[9] *Nyht* and inflected forms: 2/18 (by D_1, D_2 *nihta*), 3/7 (by D_1, D_2 *nihte*), 4/8, 5/1, 12/6, 14/11 (by D_2), 29/13, also *nyhtlic* 4/7, *nyhtlicre* 31/49 (both by D_2). See SB §31, n. 3, Campbell §301, and Hogg §§5.114 and 167.

[10] *Byþ* 4/23 (by D_2), 4/28 (by D_2), 44/27 (by D_3), 122/25. See SB §427.2 and n. 8 and Hogg §5.173.

[11] *Si* 2/32 (omitted by D_2), 3/36, 31/72 (by D_2), 40/17 (by D_3), 40/19 (by D_3), 55/20. See SB §427, nn. 2 and 3, Campbell §768d, Hogg §§5.146 and 167, n. 1.

[12] For example thirteen spellings of *þrynnes* (1/1 D_1 *-nes*, but D_2 *-nys*) contrast with six times *-nys* (26/1, 31/69 (by D_2), 53/13, etc.), twice *-nis* (1/heading, 131/14). See SB §142n. However, *-nis*, *-nys* occasionally occurs in Kentish; cf. Campbell, §384.

[13] *Heom* 36/18, 98/7. See SB §334 and Campbell §703.

[14] *Þæne* (6/4, 14/11, 30/10, 31/18, 31/23 etc., twenty-five cases in all) occurs besides five cases of *þone*: 3/7, 3/8, 18/9, 66/19, 73/28. See SB, §337, n. 2, Campbell, §380. *Þan* occurs in 39/21, 70/31 and 129/13. See SB §§187 and 337, nn. 2 and 4.

[15] *Þænne* 2/17, 7/13, 30/12, 33/9, 34/13, etc. (twelve cases), *þanne* in 27/20, but only once *þonne* in 13/11; *mænige* 31/35 (by D_2) and by analogy *mænigu* 77/10, 81/2, 100/4, *gemænigfyld* 86₃/7. See SB §79, n. 3, Campbell §380.

[16] *Giuernysse* 57/7. See SB §194.

72

Non-West-Saxon and Non-Standard Features

A distinctive feature of the interlinear gloss that deviates from the Late West Saxon standard spelling of the vowels is that *æ* appears as the result of *i*-umlaut of *a* before a nasal, for example *acænned* 'born', *ængel* 'angel'. Whereas in the Middle English period this phonological development is restricted to Essex and the southeast Midlands, it is found in a wide range of southern Old English manuscripts. Nevertheless it appears to be avoided by many West Saxon scribes. It cannot be used to assign D to any particular territory.[17]

A characteristically southeastern phonological change is that of *y* and *ȳ* (of whatever origin) to *e* and *ē*. The change took place in Kentish in the early tenth century. Many instances of this are found in the interlinear gloss, for example *senna* 'sins', or *brēda* 'brides'.[18]

---

[17] The instances in the 'Durham Hymnal Gloss' are *andfænge* 55/19; *acænde* 47/6, 125/2, 126/3; *acænned* (and inflected forms) 33/3, 36/4, 36/26, 38/13, 38/19, 38/26, 42/4, 42/3, 43/5, 44/4, 86₁/11, 90/5, 125/17, 127/2, 127/10; *acænnende* 36/12; *ændan* 27/15; *ænde* 42/14, 71/4, 102/18, 131/13; *ændeberdnyssa* 22/7; *ængel* (and inflected forms) 38/18, 52/10, 63/9, 65₁/10, 70/10, 72/16, 72/21, 73/17, 75/13, 89/6, 95/5, 96/3, 97/1, 97/13, 97/18, 124/11, 132/7, 133/15; *ængellice* 98/13; *ængliscre* 82/3; *ængliscra* 82/21; *ænglisra* (*sic*) 116/2; *ageansænd* 122/27; *ancænneda* 27/3, 36/2; *ancænned* 46/1, 60/2, 68/1, 82/25, 82/27; *ancænnedre* 87/17; *ancænnedan* 99/26; *asænd* 1/4 (D₂ only), 34/9, 97/14; *asændaþ* 98/8; *awænde* 45/24; *awændende* 66/8; *bænd* 22/15; *besænctan* 20/4; *besæncan* 43/17; *cænde* 65₁/12; *forscræncte* 25/15; *forþæncende* 124/10; *gelængdum* 74/29; *heahængel* 95/2; *mænn* 28/8; *mænnisclice* 75/8; *mænnisces* 97/2; *gemængende* 42/7; *ongeansændst* 25/3; *sænd* 66/7; *onasænd* 76/14; *srængþ* (*sic*) 8/5, *strængþ* 58/15; *strængesta* 72/5; *geþæncþ* 13/11; *unawændendlice* 117/19; *uncænnedan* 99/25; *ungewæmmedum* 36/11; *ungewæmmed* 44/15, 47/8; *wæmme* 55/16; *gewæmmednyssa* 126/16.

See SB §96, n. 8, Campbell §§193d and 291, and Hogg §5.78 (1). This was a matter of some debate. Gneuss, *HHEM*, pp. 160–1, and Korhammer, *MC*, p. 161, n. 7, discuss this feature in D and give bibliographical references. Cf. also Hallander, *Old English Verbs in* -sian, pp. 327 and n. 2, 328 and nn. 2 and 4; *Wulfstan's Canons of Edgar*, ed. R. Fowler, EETS 266 (London, 1972), xxi; *The Salisbury Psalter*, ed. Sisam and Sisam, 13–14.

[18] See SB §31, n. 1, Campbell §288, and Hogg §5.194. The instances in D, grouped according to the origin of the vowels are as follows.

(a) Short *y* by *i*-umlaut of *u*: *ændeberdnyssa* 22/7; *ætstentan* 62/18; *ætstente* 15/14; *asendrigende* 4/8; *begerde* 29/11; *berþene* 106/3; *beterndum* 79/7; *brece* 129/11; *cenehelm* 118/2, 124/2; *dede* 108/3; *dedon* 20/13 (SB §429, nn. 1 and 3, and Campbell §768); *efele* 122/30; *geendeberdiende* 28/8; *endeberdnysse* 86₁/7; *gefelde* 80/4; *gefeldest* 76/26; *gefeldon* 122/8; *feligdon* 119/7; *feligende* 38/35; *gefell* 26/18; *gefelled* 19/15, 117/28; *gefellede* 80/5,

There are also a number of inverted spellings like gedȳfe 'quiet'.[19]

Except in West Saxon, the result of *i*-umlaut of the long and short diphthongs *ea* and *ēa* is *e* and *ē*. There are a number of instances of this in the interlinear gloss in D, for example *gehwerfan* 'return', *gehēr* 'hear!'[20]

87/19; *forþeldegode* 121/10; *ferwyt* 8/8; *geþeld* 119/16; *merige* 126/12; *merigum* 127/19; *oferfelle* 81/3; *ofþreccan* 16/16; *ofþrece* 11/7; *renas* 22/8; *sengodon* 20/16, 55/9; *senna* 45/15, 76/27; *senne* 18/15, 30/6, 87/10, 104₁/2, 112/3, 114/3; *sennum* 98/24, 102/11; *scetefingre* 86₂/12; *scettelsas* 102/10; *sprettinge* 19/5; *sterunga* 19/12; *utrene* 39/19; *wensumlicor* 82/10; *werhta* 125/1; *ymbrenum* 43/13; also in *hyseberþre* 44/17, assuming that this represents *hysebyrþre* (a *hapax legomenon*), cf. Bäck, *The Synonyms for 'Boy'*, p. 180.

(b) Short *y* of other origin (see Campbell §288): *nete* 15/20, 19/16; *netende* 86₃/2 (SB §116, Campbell §265); *werste* 13/16 (SB §114a and n. 2, Campbell §149); *afersiaþ* 99/21; *gefern* 47/1, 62/5, 79/13; *hera* 72/18; *þesne* 16/16; *gef* 4/27; SB §22, n. 2; for *gef*, see Korhammer, *MC*, p. 161. Instances in unstressed syllables may be due to weakening of the vowel: *embhwerft* 36/8; 63/17, 89/9; *emhwerfte* 33/3; *embhwerfte* 58/2; *embhwerftes* 86₂/13, 87/5 (Campbell §372; for the prefix, see SB §102, n. 3); *forwerde* 32/5; the second syllable of *weorþmynt* is -*ment* in thirteen of nineteen occurrences. *Ðwernyssa* (62/7) for *ðweor(h)nyssa* might also belong here, if the vowel is analogous to the verb *þwyrian* and is not in some way due to scribal confusion of *weor*-, *wur*-, *wyr*-; cf. SB §118, n. 1, and Gneuss, *HHEM*, p. 159. Kitson would probably interpret *ðwernyssa* as a Mercianism; cf. Kitson, 'Geographical Variation', pp. 18–21 on *þweores*, *þwyres*, *þweres*.

(c) Long *y* by *i*-imlaut of long *u*: *breda* 126/7; *bredbure* 32/10, 39/13, 86₁/14; *bredgumum* 126/8; *beclesed* 31/13; *clesinga* 71/9; *embscredde* 44/6; *fer* 77/5; *ferenre* 22/3; *feste* 65₁/15; *seferlice* 15/23, 18/10; *sefre* 2/16, 18/7, 27/6, 123/6.

(d) Long *y* of other origin: *ingehedes* 31/28 (with compensatory lengthening; Campbell §243–4).

[19] Inverted spellings of short *e*: *asynd* 1/4 (D₂ only), 41/7; *onasynd* 16/9; *andyttaþ* 32/16; *cynnestra* 98/11; *cynnestran* 47/3; *cynnystre* 97/17; *geedcynnede* 38/33; *fyrmystum* 40/4 (or weakening of unstressed vowel); *hylle* 3/23; *gehylp* 98/10; *hyraþ* 36/20; *lydenwaru* 80/10; *tobrycaþ* 17/3, 29/14; *yfenlyttan* 99/20.

Inverted spellings of long *e*: *gedyfe* 12/8; *bryme* 35/2; *brymde* 123/3; *brymþ* 124/7; *gefyrrædene* 41/8, 103/18; *gefy...de* 86₂/2 (i. e. *geferde*).

[20] Umlauted short *ea*: *geonhwerfende* 50/6; *gehwerfan* 46/18; *gehwerfde* 70/22; *gehwerfþ* 21/7 (corrected to *y*, by D₁), 127/7; *ongeancerryd* 4/24; *serwiendan* 12/18. See SB §105, Campbell §200, 1–2, and Hogg §5.82. It is not clear whether *eormingas* 72/8 represents a form with or without umlaut. It could be a confused spelling of West Saxon *yrmingas*.

Umlauted long *ea*: *æþretnysse* 25/12; *begem* 12/8, 21/12, 26/3, 36/7, 60/3; *begeme* 15/17, 110/3; *begemende* 129/2; *gedreme* 2/14 (D₂ only); *hefigtemnyssa* 129/5; *hefigtemnyssum* 19/3 (D₂) (third syllable); *geher* 55/1; *gehere* 3/9 (D₁ only); *gehersumige* 19/13; *gehersumigeende* (*sic*) 62/23; *gelefaþ* 31/24, 46/18, 82/9; *gelefende* 65₁/12; *gelefendra* 94/10 (D₂), 99/22, 103/10, 117/22; *gelefendum* 17/10; *tobrete* 16/15; *toles* 18/15, 63/4; *tolesan* 4/32. See SB §106, Campbell §200, 5, and Hogg §5.82.

Forms like *gedweld* are typically Kentish, since breaking to *ea* did not take place in front of *l* in Anglian.[21]

Another non-West Saxon trait, more typical of Mercian and Kentish than of Northumbrian, is the lack of palatal diphthongization of *e*, *æ*, *ē*, *ǣ* after palatal *c*, *g*, *sc*. Again there are a number of instances of this in D's gloss, for example *agæf* 'gave' (West Saxon *ageaf*), *ageldaþ* 'pay' (West Saxon *agieldaþ*, *agyldaþ*), *gǣres* 'year's' (West Saxon *gēares*).[22]

Not many cases of the raising of *æ*, *ǣ* to *e*, *ē*, characteristic of Kentish from the tenth century onwards, are found in the gloss in D: *afestnode* 'made fast', *wēpna* 'weapons'.[23]

There are a few forms in *eo*, *ēo*, which appear to lack *i*-umlaut of *io* and *ī̄o*: *heorde* 'shepherd', *geseohpe* 'sight', *hēowe* 'colour', *nēowiende* 'renewing' and *feoht* 'fights' (3 sg. pres. ind.).[24] (The latter may also be compared to *gehelpst* 'help' (2 sg. pres. ind.), which once occurs for regular *gehilpst* and can be explained by analogy to *gehelpe* and *gehelpaþ*.)[25] Such forms occasionally occur in West Saxon texts, but it is marginally possible that here they represent re-West-Saxonized forms in *io*. *Io* would be regular in Kentish in that position. (The spelling *io* is avoided in the 'Durham

---

[21] *Fotwelmas* 53/11; *gedweld* 16/12; *gedwelde* 24/4; *gedweldra* 4/11; *gedweldum* 106/2; *geweldende* 7/5 (but *geweldest* 71/16 is probably a misspelled form of *wel(e)gian*); *well* 15/3; *welle* 87/19; also perhaps *getwifeld* 86₃/6, if the unstressed vowel was not weakened. Cf. Korhammer, *MC*, p. 162. Anglian forms would usually have *æ*; see SB §§85 and 96, 4, Campbell §§143 and 193, Hogg §5.82.

[22] Lack of palatal diphthongization:

(a) of Early Old English æ: *agæf* 67₂/16; *cæstergewara* 48/8, 48/10, 86₂/2, 98/26; *cæstergewaran* 49/2; *cæstergewaru* 86₃/17; *cæstergewarum* 41/12; *gescæft* 46/7, 75/9, 104₂/9; *gescæfta* 11/2, 23/1, 28/5, 50/8; *gescæfte* 132/10; with *i*-umlaut: *sceppend* 2/1, 20/1.

(b) of Early Old English e: *ageldaþ* 3/12; *ageldende* 49/11; *andget* 8/5, *begeten* 27/17; *borhgeldum* 31/47 (D₂); *gelp* 25/14, 108/3; *samodgeddunge* 90/11;

(c) of early Old English long æ: *forgæfe* 31/26 (D₂); *gæres* 36/14; *gærlice* 127/7; *undergæte* 86₁/14; either lack of palatal diphthongization or Late West Saxon smoothing: *scæp* 51/8; *scep* 82/13, 86₂/6; *scepa* 119/13.

See SB §§90–1, Campbell §187, and Hogg §§5.50–5. Since these are presumably Kentish, not Anglian forms, *æ* must be an inverted spelling for *e*; cf. below.

[23] Raising of Germanic *a*, Old English *æ*: *afestnode* 67₁/5; *arfestan* 3/7 (D₁); *infereld* 65₂/10 (or weakening of vowel in unstressed syllable). Raising of West Germanic long *a*, Old English *æ*: *wepna* 122/9. Inverted spellings: *gedræfdon* 16/2; *sælosta* 13/1; *þæs* 129/9; and cf. above n. 22. See SB §52, Campbell §288, and Hogg §5.189.

[24] Early Old English *io*: *heorde* 82/13, 87/9; *geseohpe* 96/3. Early Old English long *io*: *heowe* 76/9; *neowiende* 81/11, *feoht* 122/12. See SB §107 and Hogg §5.83.

[25] *Gehelpst* 33/3. See SB §371 and Campbell §734.

Hymnal Gloss' as in standard Late West Saxon, whereas it occurs in the manuscripts of the *Expositio* gloss, probably written at the same centre.) Such superficial West-Saxonization may also have taken place in *nēoxtan* 'next, last' and in *genēolǣce* 'approach', if these spellings represent Kentish *ē*, broken to *īo* instead of West Saxon *ǣ*, broken to *ēa*.[26]

Back mutation occurs only where it is regular in West Saxon except for a case of *a*-umlaut in front of a liquid, *beoraþ* 'carry', and a case of *u*-umlaut before a dental, *underwreopod* 'supported'.[27] Such forms may occur sporadically even in West Saxon texts.

The unrounding of the second element of original *eo* in *heanon* 'from here' may be Kentish, although unrounding occurs sporadically in West Saxon, too.[28]

As for the consonants, the instances where *t*, mainly in final position, is spelled *d* as in *gead* 'gate' are not a dialectal feature, but a scribal idiosyncrasy, which is either shared by D_1 and D_2 or derived from the exemplar. Comparable cases are found in the Aldhelm Glosses of the Brussels manuscript, which are of heterogeneous character phonologically.[29]

The assimilation of the final consonants in *stefn* 'voice' to *stemn*, common in Late West Saxon texts, is avoided in this gloss with remarkable consistency.[30]

The most characteristic feature of the inflection in D is that the optative plural regularly ends in *-an*, for instance *biddan* 'let us (you, them) pray'.[31] There are also a number of preterite plurals in *-an*, e.g. *bǣran* 'carried'.[32] While these endings are found sporadically in all dialects, a high proportion of them is a characteristic feature of Kentish and a number of West Saxon manuscripts.[33]

---

[26] *Neoxtan* 8/8, *geneolæce* 19/14. See SB §35, n. 1, and Campbell §276.

[27] *Beoraþ* 31/40; *underwreopod* 41/4. See SB §110, Campbell §§210–1, and Hogg §5.105, esp. p. 159, n. 3.

[28] *Heanon* 68/9, 87/24. See SB §35, n. 2, Campbell §281.

[29] *Ædbræd* 65₂/5; *ædbrodene* 43/31; *behad* 93/2 (D_2); *gead* 128/10; *oferswiþdesd* 68/12; *ormæde* 94/8 (by D_2); *tolysdesd* 104₂/8; *wurþmend* 43/34. See SB §224, n. 2, and *The Old English Glosses of MS. Brussels, Royal Library 1650*, ed. L. Goossens, Verhandelingen van de Koninklijke Academie voor Wetenschappen, Letteren en schone Kunsten van Belgie, Klasse der Letteren 76 (Brussels, 1974), 108.

[30] Korhammer, *MC*, p. 166. The word occurs frequently; cf. 2/14, 4/31, 34/1 etc.

[31] *Biddan* 1/6, 26/7, 47/13, 98/16, 98/28, 111/1.

[32] *Bæran* 65₁/8; *fortrædan* 119/10; *gelæstan* 133/16; *þurhforan* 128/14; *wæran* 72/17.

[33] Korhammer, *MC*, pp. 170–1, and Hogg §6. 60.

This phenomenon appears to be distinct from the general weakening of inflectional vowels in Late Old English, such as *þingon* for *þingum*, of which there are comparatively few traces in D.[34]

The unsyncopated 3 sg. *cigeþ* 'calls' would normally be non-West Saxon, but as syncopation is otherwise regular, a single occurrence is hardly significant.[35]

There are two instances of the weak genitive plural being transferred to strong nouns, *dagena* and *tidena*. *Dagena* is found in many texts including West Saxon ones according to Campbell; *tīdena*, from an *ō*-stem with a long root vowel, is much rarer.[36]

To sum up, this predominantly Late West Saxon gloss has a number of non-West Saxon features, presumably introduced by the copyists. That these non-West Saxon features are Kentish is shown most clearly by the high number of instances of *e*, *ē* for *y*, *ȳ*, but also by a sprinkling of forms like *gedweld* and *afestnode*.

A minor puzzle is that D_1 seems to experience difficulties with spelling the word *neorxnawang* 'paradise'.[37]

A note on the spelling of D_3 may be added. The consistency with which D_3 spells the past tense of weak verbs of the second class with *u* is unusual: for example, *apracude* 'horrified'. Forms with *u* occur beside the regular ones in *o* in Late West Saxon, but are usually sporadic.[38]

VOCABULARY

Several studies on the geography and distribution of Old English words include an examination of the 'Durham Hymnal Gloss'[39] and have yielded

---

[34] By D_1: *besceawede* 42/3; *losede* 128/5; *bodeden* 122/7 (ind.); *gelæccon* 25/8 (subj. pres.); *gefrætewion* 100/6 (opt. pres.); *cion* 18/9 (inf.); *þingon* 118/4, 121/8 (dat. pl.).

[35] *Cigeþ* 18/4. See SB, §358, 2 and n. 6.

[36] *Dagena* 3/1 (by D_1 and D_2), 13/2 (by D_2), 15/4 (by D_2), 77/15, *dægena* 26/19; *tidena* 4/ 3, 53/2, 71/4. See Campbell §§572 and 586 and also SB §§237, n. 4, and 269, nn. 1 and 5.

[37] *Nearxnewange* 57/5; *neoxnewange* 70/24; *nerxnewange* 42/4.

[38] *Apracude* 44/22; *gegaderudon* 35/14; *geneasude* 40/15; *polude* 40/12, 44/21, 44/23. See SB §413, n. 3.

[39] For evaluations of the vocabulary of the 'Durham Hymnal Gloss', see Scherer, *Geographie und Chronologie*, p. 45; Rauh, *Wortschatz*, p. 47; Schabram, *Superbia*, p. 104; Wenisch, *Spezifisch anglisches Wortgut*, p. 327, and especially Gneuss, *HHEM*, pp. 186–90, Korhammer, *MC*, pp. 232–5, and Hofstetter, *Winchester*, pp. 106–13 (no. 12).

the result that the vocabulary of the gloss is basically Late West Saxon. Within Late West Saxon it has clear affinities with the Winchester vocabulary.

The Winchester vocabulary, described by Gneuss and Hofstetter,[40] is defined as the attitude that some writers display towards certain groups of synonyms available in Late West Saxon. Some of these synonyms are consistently preferred, others are used sparingly and a third group is actively avoided. The influence of the Winchester vocabulary may be traced widely among Late West Saxon texts, but it is strictly adhered to by Ælfric, at least in his non-alliterating prose, by the Lambeth Psalter gloss and the *Expositio hymnorum* gloss. It is followed not quite as strictly by the translation of the Rule of Chrodegang. These four pieces of writing may be thought of as the core of the Winchester group, to which the interlinear version of the Benedictine Rule should be added as a fifth member.[41] This does not imply that they were all written at Winchester, but rather that the Winchester vocabulary itself is conceived of as having originally been taught in the school of the Old Minster, Winchester, since part of it seems to go back to preferences and innovations of Æthelwold himself.[42] It appears to have its roots in the practice of habitually translating a Latin lemma with a specific Old English word. Teachers would have passed this vocabulary on to their pupils; from there it would have gone on spreading.

Seebold prefers to explain the Winchester vocabulary as due in part to dialectal features shared by Winchester and Kent and going back to settlement by the Jutes. He calls these elements 'Jutish'. Unlike Gneuss and Hofstetter, he believes that they prove that documents in which they occur were actually written either in Winchester or in Kent.[43]

The 'Durham Hymnal Gloss' is clearly influenced by the Winchester

---

[40] Gneuss, 'Origin', and Hofstetter, *Winchester*, esp. pp. 2–20.

[41] Hofstetter, *Winchester*, pp. 38–66 (no. 3), 84–8 (no. 7), 101–3 (no. 10) and 94–100 (no. 9 and 117–23). The number of works which are significantly influenced by the Winchester vocabulary according to Hofstetter is twenty-three (*Winchester*, pp. 28–155).

[42] Hofstetter, *Winchester*, pp. 30–6 (no. 1).

[43] E. Seebold, 'Winchester und Canterbury: zum altenglischen Sprachgebrauch', *Anglia* 107 (1989), 52–64; *idem*, 'Was ist jütisch?' and 'Kentish'. It is unfortunately impossible to discuss this theory here as thoroughly as it deserves. Although some points are clearly valid, there are problems, too. The main one is that we know very little indeed about the Jutes and what language they might have spoken, as Seebold himself admits ('Was ist jütisch?', pp. 338 and 343). Another problem is that it seems to involve assigning too many linguistically disparate texts to Winchester and Canterbury.

vocabulary; however, it also diverges markedly from it in places. Although its vocabulary is basically West Saxon, it does not always agree with the West Saxon norm.

There are a few words in the gloss that may be characteristic of texts of Canterbury origin. These are of two kinds, those that are found only in works presumed to be from Canterbury and those that these works share with poetry and Anglian prose. The latter may have been introduced during the period of Mercian influence in Canterbury in the eighth and ninth century. Wildhagen saw in them possible traces of an ecclesiastical idiom common to Mercian and Kentish.[44] Seebold, however, believes that the Kentish population actually spoke Mercian – with a 'Jutish' strain.[45]

Apart from the 'Durham Hymnal Gloss', works that appear to have such Canterbury vocabulary according to Hofstetter are the Arundel prayer gloss, the interlinear version of the Benedictine Rule and the Aldhelm glosses in the Brussels and Digby manuscripts and, to a lesser degree, the Salisbury Aldhelm glosses and the Prudentius glosses in the Boulogne manuscript.[46] All of these have links to Canterbury, Kent or the southeast.

This Canterbury vocabulary is less distinctive than the Winchester vocabulary. Some fairly rare words are involved. The authors and scribes, who generally tried to adhere to the Late West Saxon standard in their spelling, might have tended to avoid frequent Kenticisms in their vocabulary.

That the 'Durham Hymnal Gloss' should have Late West Saxon and Winchester vocabulary and contain Canterbury words, too, fits the theory that it was written at Winchester or a centre influenced by Winchester and revised at Canterbury. It should be pointed out, however, that the gloss by D_2 and D_3 seems to share all the characteristics of the text by D_1.[47] Not all the Winchester words in the gloss, as it now stands, derive from the original. Some were introduced in Canterbury.

---

[44] Wildhagen, 'Psalterium Romanum', pp. 436–7.

[45] Seebold, 'Was ist jütisch?', p. 343, and 'Kentish'. This should be treated with caution. Kentish need not have been a distinct dialect in AD 500 and could nevertheless have to be considered one 300 years or more later. Moreover, as the seat of the archbishop, who often came from elsewhere, Canterbury was subject to outside influences. Texts written there probably give a distorted picture of the linguistic situation in Kent.

[46] Hofstetter, *Winchester*, pp. 108–10, 117–23 (no. 14), 129–41 (nos. 17 and 18), 438–41 (nos. 214 and 215) and 449–50 (no. 219).

[47] See below, pp. 81–2 and 86–9, but cf. pp. 84 and 90 and p. 86, n. 73.

After these general statements on the vocabulary of the 'Durham Hymnal Gloss' the specific words on whose occurrence they are based must be discussed.[48]

Late West Saxon words and Winchester vocabulary

There are a number of words in the 'Durham Hymnal Gloss' which are only attested in Late West Saxon. Among these are *æthre(g)dan* 'take away', *angsum* 'afraid', *forþyldegian* 'bear', *gehwæde* 'small', *getimbrung* 'fabric', *teart*, *teartlic* 'harsh', *wæfels* 'clothing' and *wiputan* 'outside'.[49] Predominantly Late West Saxon are *gehende* 'near' and *pæslic* 'fitting'.[50] The verb *begi(e)man* 'take care of' is predominantly Late West Saxon and frequent in the Lambeth Psalter, but is used only once (each) by Æthelwold in his translation of the Benedictine Rule and by Ælfric.[51] The verb *besargian* 'grieve, sympathize' is Late West Saxon; the derived noun *besargung* is

---

[48] As this part of the chapter is completely based on previous research, it seemed unnecessary to give references to any Old English text other than the 'Durham Hymnal Gloss' itself. However, since some of the research pre-dates Venezky and Healey's *Microfiche Concordance to Old English*, attempts have been made to check the results of these works against it, where this could be done within a reasonable amount of time (excluding extremely frequent words, statements about semantic distinctions and the like). Statements in Scherer, *Geographie und Chronologie*, and Rauh, *Wortschatz*, especially have not been quoted without confirmation, as they are sometimes extremely unreliable.

[49] *Auferre, ferre, rapere, subtrahere, tollere* – *æthre(g)dan* 43/31, 45/16, 65₂/5, 67₂/8, 71/8, 119/22. See Rauh, *Wortschatz*, p. 33. *anxius* – *angsum* 2/8. See Scherer, *Geographie und Chronologie*, p. 26; *Lambeth-Psalter*, ed. Lindelöf I, 55; and Gretsch, *Die Regula Sancti Benedicti*, p. 320. *sufferre* – *forþyldegian* 121/10. See Korhammer, *MC*, pp. 189–90. *parvus* – *gehwæde* 44/23 (by D₃). See Scherer, *Geographie und Chronologie*, p. 30; Rauh, *Wortschatz*, p. 36; and Gretsch, *Die Regula Sancti Benedicti*, pp. 342–3. *fabrica* – *getimbrung* 75/19 (by D₂). See Scherer, *Geographie und Chronologie*, p. 29; Gretsch, *Die Regula Sancti Benedicti*, p. 356; and Seebold, 'Regional gebundene Wörter', p. 271. *acer, asper* – *teart(lic)* 3/24, 15/15. See Gretsch, *Die Regula Sancti Benedicti*, p. 354. *tegimen* – *wæfels* 86₂/5. See Rauh, *Wortschatz*, p. 39, and Gretsch, *Die Regula Sancti Benedicti* p. 360. *extra* – *wiputan* 55/13. See Korhammer, *MC*, pp. 208–9. Note, however, that according to Venezky and Healey, *Microfiche Concordance to Old English*, *gehwæde* appears in the Kentish Glosses (OccGl 49 (Zupitza), 6.16 and 24.30).

[50] *Gehende* – *prope, proxime* 18/2, 18/8, 35/4. See F. Wenisch, 'Sächsische Dialektwörter in *The Battle of Maldon*', *Indogermanische Forschungen* 81 (1976), 181–203. *Congruus* – *pæslic* 29/10. See Scherer, *Geographie und Chronologie*, pp. 23–4, and Gretsch, *Die Regula Sancti Benedicti*, pp. 357–8.

[51] *Gubernare, intendere, attendere* – *begiman* 12/19, 15/17, 21/12, 26/3, 36/7, 60/3, 110/3,

found once in the 'Durham Hymnal Gloss' and the *Expositio* gloss in corresponding passages and otherwise only in texts by Ælfric.[52] The adverb *eornostlice* 'so, then' is Late West Saxon and very frequent in Ælfric and the West Saxon Gospels.[53]

As for the Winchester vocabulary, the 'Durham Hymnal Gloss' agrees with the usage of the Winchester group as defined by Hofstetter in using *behreowsung* 'penitence', *gearcian* 'prepare, provide', *gelapung* 'church, congregation', *miht* 'miraculous power', *modig, modignes* 'proud, pride', *oga* 'fear' and *gerihtlæcan* 'make straight spiritually, correct'.[54] It also avoids such alternative expressions for these concepts as are not used in texts of the Winchester group. On the other hand it disagrees with the Winchester group in its use of words for 'crown', 'martyr' and 'dare' and partially disagrees in its use of words for 'crush, destroy'.

The prefixed forms *behreowsian* 'repent' and *behreowsung* in Late West Saxon, after the time of Æthelwold, replaced *hreowsian* and *hreowsung*. In using *behreowsung* – the verb 'repent' does not occur – the 'Durham Hymnal Gloss' agrees not only with the Winchester group, but also with the Aldhelm glosses of the Abingdon group and Wulfstan, where the prefixed forms are not, however, used exclusively. On the other hand the *Rule of Chrodegang* uses only the simple forms.[55]

Gearcian 'prepare' was early recognized as typical of the vocabulary of Ælfric. It is consistently preferred to *gearwian* by texts of the Winchester group but not used by Æthelwold. Seebold considers it 'Jutish'.[56]

123/19, 129/2. See Rauh, *Wortschatz*, p. 33, and Gretsch, *Die Regula Sancti Benedicti*, p. 324.

[52] *Dolere, condolere – besargian* 32/5, 104₂/9, *compassio – besargung* 108/2. See Scherer, *Geographie und Chronologie*, p. 27, and Gretsch, *Die Regula Sancti Benedicti*, pp. 326–7. The verb seems to be restricted to texts either influenced by the Winchester vocabulary or written in Canterbury; cf. Venezky and Healey, *Microfiche Concordance to Old English*.

[53] *Ergo – eornostlice* 4/17, 31/65 (by D₂), 43/21, 51/9, 54/5 (by D₃), 60/13, 65₁/9, 74/21, 80/1, 129/1. See Rauh, *Wortschatz*, p. 35, and Gretsch, *Die Regula Sancti Benedicti*, pp. 334–5.

[54] Hofstetter, *Winchester*, pp. 6–20. To the list of Winchester vocabulary in Gneuss, 'Origin', pp. 76–7, he adds *behreowsian* (cf. Gneuss, 'Origin', p. 80), *gearcian*, *oga*, *tobrytan* and *tocwysan*, but rejects *afeormian*, *blissian* and *forswælan*. For these, see below, pp. 84–5, 86 and 88.

[55] The relevant gloss in the 'Durham Hymnal' is *penitentia – behreowsung* 57/10. See Scherer, *Geographie und Chronologie*, pp. 22 and 26; Gretsch, *Die Regula Sancti Benedicti*, p. 325; and Hallander, *Old English Verbs in* -sian, pp. 362–4.

[56] The word is attested in the 'Durham Hymnal Gloss' in the following instances: *prestare,*

Late West Saxon *gelaþung* translates *ecclesia* in texts of the Winchester group whenever the congregation of the church and not its buildings are meant. This use post-dates Æthelwold.[57]

Before the end of the tenth century *miht* translates *virtus* in its meaning 'miraculous power, miracle' only in Northumbrian; West Saxon used *mægen* for the concept. After the time of Æthelwold *miht* appeared beside *mægen* in Late West Saxon. The preponderant use of *miht*, as in the 'Durham Hymnal Gloss', is characteristic of the Winchester group.[58]

Translation of *superbus* 'proud' and *superbia* 'pride' by *modig* and *modignes* rather than by *ofermod* and its derivatives is consistent already in Æthelwold's translation of the Benedictine Rule. It became characteristic of the texts of the Winchester group.[59]

The preferred word for 'fear' in texts of the Winchester group is *oga*, which is considered 'Jutish' by Seebold. *Egesa*, which occurs in poetry, Anglian prose and some Late West Saxon texts, is avoided, but *ege* is not. The latter is a word restricted to West Saxon and, possibly, to West Mercian. It occurs once in the 'Durham Hymnal Gloss'.[60]

The Late West Saxon word *gerihtlæcan* is for the most part found in

---

prebere, parare, adhibere, exhibere – *gearcian* 13/4, 24/6, 46/12, 55/7, 57/15, 62/10, 62/63, 62/65, 66/17, 66/18, 86$_2$/5, 89/7, 119/18. See Dietrich, 'Abt Aelfrik', pp. 544–5, n. 140; Korhammer, *MC*, p. 221; Hofstetter, *Winchester*, pp. 8–9 and *passim*; Seebold, 'Was ist jütisch?', pp. 345–6, and 'Kentish', pp. 417–18.

[57] The attestations in the 'Durham Hymnal Gloss' are *ecclesia* – *gelaþung* 4/15, 57/9, 82/22, 94/8 (by D$_2$), 103/5, 115/1, 117/5, 122/5. See MacGillivray, *Influence of Christianity*, pp. 28–9, *Lambeth Psalter*, ed. Lindelöf II, 55; Gretsch, *Die Regula Sancti Benedicti*, p. 333; and Hofstetter, *Winchester*, pp. 9–11 and *passim*.

[58] The relevant glosses in the 'Durham Hymnal' are *virtus* – *miht* 'miraculous power': 32/25, 38/5, 39/24, 53/12, 62/1, 81/5, 95/21, 96/2, 96/11, 98/29, 102/16, 104$_2$/14, 123/17; 'virtue': 39/11, 62/67, 76/16, 100/6; *virtus* – *mægen* 'miraculous power': 42/14. See Gneuss, *Lehnbildungen*, p. 72; Käsmann, ' "Tugend" ', p. 59 and *passim*; Gretsch, *Die Regula Sancti Benedicti*, pp. 347–9; Hofstetter, *Winchester*, pp. 11–14 and *passim*; and Seebold, 'Kentish', p. 415.

[59] The attestations in the 'Durham Hymnal Gloss' are *superbus* – *modig* 108/3; *modignes* – *superbia* 7/11. See Schabram, *Superbia*, pp. 104–6; Gretsch, *Die Regula Sancti Benedicti*, pp. 351–3; Hofstetter, *Winchester*, pp. 17–18 and *passim*; and Seebold, 'Kentish', pp. 415–16.

[60] The relevant glosses in the 'Durham Hymnal Gloss' are *pavor, horror* – *oga* 2/28, 7/6, 34/14, 117/9; *timor* – *ege* 128/3. See Hallander, *Old English Verbs in -sian*, pp. 143–57; Hofstetter, *Winchester*, p. 14 and *passim*; and Seebold, 'Was ist jütisch?', p. 345, and 'Kentish', p. 419.

texts of the Winchester group. It means 'improve, correct, straighten out' and translates *dirigere*. Formations with prefixed *ge-* and suffixed *-lǣcan* are considered by Seebold to be 'Jutish'.[61]

In all these points the vocabulary of the 'Durham Hymnal Gloss' agrees with that of the Winchester group. It also agrees with it in preferring *tobrytan* as the translation for *(con)terere* 'crush'. Another word favoured by the Winchester group in this context is *tocwysan*, a Late West Saxon word considered by Seebold to be 'Jutish'. This also occurs once in the 'Durham Hymnal Gloss'. However, *forprǣstan*, too, occurs once and use of this verb is avoided in texts of the Winchester group, while it is characteristic of the Vespasian Psalter gloss, the Aldhelm glosses and the interlinear gloss of the Benedictine Rule and so may be seen as a link between Mercian and the usage of Canterbury.[62]

The 'Durham Hymnal Gloss' does not follow the usage of the Winchester group at all in its choice of words for 'crown'. Texts of the Winchester group make a distinction between an actual and a metaphorical, abstract or spiritual crown, *cynehelm* and *wuldorbeag*. Probably both are Late West Saxon words. The 'Durham Hymnal Gloss' uses *cynehelm* six times and *wuldorbeag* only once. Five of the six instances of *cynehelm* are definitely metaphorical and the sixth is a border-line case, while the one instance of *wuldorbeag* is doubtfully metaphorical, as the laurel wreaths concerned are very concretely envisaged. On the other hand the 'Durham Hymnal Gloss' agrees with the Winchester vocabulary in using only *gewuldorbeagian* as the corresponding verb 'to crown'.[63]

---

[61] The attestations in the 'Durham Hymnal Gloss' are *dirigere, corrigere – gerihtlǣcan* 4/26, 53/12, 86₃/12, 95/14, 95/27, 97/16. See Scherer, *Geographie und Chronologie*, p. 22; Gretsch, *Die Regula Sancti Benedicti*, pp. 353–4; Gneuss, *HHEM*, p. 169; Korhammer, *MC*, pp. 197–8; Hofstetter, *Winchester*, pp. 14–15, 51, 107 and *passim*; and Seebold, 'Was ist jütisch?', pp. 346–50, and 'Kentish', pp. 419–20.

[62] The relevant glosses are *terere, atterere, conterere – tobrytan* 7/11, 16/12, 16/15 (wrongly glosses *terreat*), 19/12, 55/13, 96/12; *quatere – tocwysan* 128/13; *conterere – forprǣstan* 31/38. See Gretsch, *Die Regula Sancti Benedicti*, pp. 337–8 and 357; and Hofstetter, *Winchester*, pp. 15–16, 109 and *passim*. On *tocwysan* in particular, see Scherer, *Geographie und Chronologie*, p. 28; Rauh, *Wortschatz*, p. 38; and Seebold, 'Kentish', p. 416.

[63] The relevant glosses are *corona, sertum – cynehelm* 75/28, 118/2, 121/2, 124/2, 126/1 (metaphorical), 86₃/5 (ambiguous); *laurea – wuldorbeag* 119/19, *coronare, laureare, decorare – gewuldorbeagian* 42/6, 86₃/5, 87/8. See J. Kirschner, 'Die Bezeichnungen für Kranz und Krone im Altenglischen' (privately printed PhD dissertation, Ludwig-Maximilians-Universität, Munich, 1975), pp. 226, 230 and 266–8; Rauh, *Wortschatz*, p. 34;

The 'Durham Hymnal Gloss' does not use the loan word *martyr*, which the texts of the Winchester group prefer for 'martyr'. The usual word in D is *prowære*, a word found in poetry and Anglian texts and in the Arundel prayer gloss from Canterbury. *Cypere* occurs four times in the 'Durham Hymnal Gloss', although it appears not to have been used by the original glossator. This word is otherwise restricted to the early works of Ælfric, the *Expositio* gloss and the Arundel prayers, and this seems to imply that its use was limited to Winchester and Canterbury. In the 'Durham Hymnal Gloss' it is used only of St Stephen, and this use roughly corresponds to Ælfric's use of the word.[64]

Finally *audere* 'dare' is translated the single time that it occurs as *pristlæcan*, whereas the texts of the Winchester group avoid that word and use *dyrstlæcan*. *Pristlæcan* appears to be West Saxon, Mercian and Kentish. Both words belong to the type of formation in -*læcan* considered by Seebold to be 'Jutish'.[65]

Apart from the words defined by Hofstetter as characteristic of the Winchester vocabulary, there are others which were used in the same texts, but which are more widely found than the Winchester vocabulary proper. One of these is *afeormian* 'purify, cleanse'. Its use spread in Late West Saxon after the time of Æthelwold, but it remained a southern word. It was used instead of *geclænsian*, but usually did not oust the older word completely, except in the *Expositio* gloss. In the 'Durham Hymnal Gloss' and the gloss to the monastic canticles in D and J *geclænsian* is used to translate *mundare*, while synonymous Latin words are rendered by

---

Gneuss, *HHEM*, p. 185; Gretsch, *Die Regula Sancti Benedicti*, pp. 362–4; and Seebold, 'Kentish', p. 416.

[64] The relevant glosses are *martyr* – *cypere* 40/2, 40/4, 40/20 (by D₃ in all three cases), *protomartyr* – *se forma cypere* 41/2 (shared by Vm), *martyr* – *prowære* 42/9, 86₃/3, 88/1, 98/21, 99/13, 117/2, 117/13, 117/30, 118/1, 118/9, 119/18, 120/1, 121/3, 121/15 (*pro-* by D₁, completed by another hand), *protomartyr* – *se forma prowære* 42/2, *passio* – *prowung* 51/6, 67₂/14. See MacGillivray, *Influence of Christianity*, p. 52; Gneuss, *HHEM*, pp. 182–3; M. R. Godden, 'Ælfric's Changing Vocabulary', *English Studies* 61 (1980), 206–23, esp. 208–9, 220–2 and 222, n. 1; Hofstetter, *Winchester*, pp. 42–3, 106 and 108–9; and Seebold, 'Kentish', pp. 414–15.

[65] The relevant gloss is *audere* – *pristlæcan* 93/5. See Gretsch, *Die Regula Sancti Benedicti*, pp. 332–3; Hofstetter, *Winchester*, p. 44 and *passim*; and Seebold, 'Was ist jütisch?', pp. 348–9, 'Kentish', pp. 422–7, and 'Regional gebundene Wörter', pp. 257–60.

afeormian. The reason may be morphological in that *mundare* is derived from the adjective *mundus* as *geclænsian* is derived from *clæne.*[66]

The preference of *geagnian* 'possess' over *agnian* and the increased use of the word as compared to *agan*, especially to render Latin *possidere*, are features of the texts of the Winchester group, Ælfric in particular.[67]

Angin was the preferred word of Æthelwold for 'beginning' and later spread until in strictly Late West Saxon texts it replaces older *fruma* and *frymþ* everywhere except in prepositional expressions. It is particularly dominant in texts by Ælfric. In the 'Durham Hymnal Gloss' *angin* is always used except once in the phrase *on fruman.*[68]

The exclusive use of *leahtor* to translate *vitium* 'vice' was apparently an innovation of Æthelwold's. His preference influenced Winchester use, although the word did not oust *unþeaw* altogether. The 'Durham Hymnal Gloss' has only *leahtor.*[69]

Translation of *discipulus* by the loan formation *leorningcniht* prevailed after some experimentation in the period after Æthelwold.[70]

The single instance of *prudens* 'clever' in the 'Durham Hymnal' is

[66] The relevant glosses are *abluere, expiare, purgare – afeormian* 3/11, 13/16, 21/14, 23/6, 27/16, 41/11, 45/16, 46/15, 57/17, 75/15, 98/24, 119/22; (*e*)*mundare – geclænsian* 19/10, 25/10, 60/7. See Rauh, *Wortschatz*, p. 32; Gneuss, 'Origin', p. 77, and *HHEM*, p. 190; Gretsch, *Die Regula Sancti Benedicti*, pp. 327–8; and Korhammer, *MC*, pp. 188–9.

[67] The attestations of these words in the 'Durham Hymnal Gloss' are *possidere – geagnian* 72/42, 117/12, 121/12; *possidere – agnian* 87/8. See S. Ono, 'Word Preference in the Old English Verbs of Possessing', *Anglo-Saxonica, Beiträge zur Vor- und Frühgeschichte der englischen Sprache und zur altenglischen Literatur, Festschrift für Hans Schabram zum 65. Geburtstag*, ed. K. R. Grinda and C.-D. Wetzel (Munich, 1993), pp. 279–88.

[68] The relevant glosses are *cardo, exordium, initium, primordium, principium – angin* 14/8, 22/11, 36/3, 44/1, 90/7, 90/8; *in primordio – on fruman* 31/5. See D. Whitelock, 'The Authorship of the Account of King Edgar's Establishment of Monasteries', in *Philological Essays. Studies in Old and Middle English Language and Literature in Honour of Herbert Dean Merritt*, ed. J. L. Rosier (The Hague, 1970), pp. 125–36, particularly 134–5, and Korhammer, *MC*, pp. 211–13.

[69] The attestations of the word in the 'Durham Hymnal Gloss' are *vitium – leahtor* 62/66, 125/14. See Käsmann, '"Tugend"', pp. 43 and 60; Gretsch, *Die Regula Sancti Benedicti*, pp. 343–5; Hofstetter, *Winchester*, pp. 270–1; and Seebold, 'Regional gebundene Wörter', p. 272.

[70] The attestations in the 'Durham Hymnal Gloss' are *discipulus – leorningcniht* 72/29, 77/4. See MacGillivray, *Influence of Christianity*, pp. 43–51; Scherer, *Geographie und Chronologie*, p. 22; Bäck, *The Synonyms for 'Boy'*, pp. 125–31; O. Martz, *Die Wiedergabe biblischer Personenbezeichnungen in der altenglischen Missionssprache*, Beiträge zur englischen

translated by *snoter*. In Late West Saxon this use of *snotor* is found in the texts which Seebold calls the southern English 'Benedictine group', which to a great extent overlaps, but does not altogether coincide with, the Winchester group.[71]

The word for 'to understand, perceive' in the 'Durham Hymnal Gloss' is *undergietan*, which is mainly Late West Saxon. It is frequent in texts of the Winchester group, but also found elsewhere. Although not an early formation, it is considered 'Jutish' by Seebold. Together with *understandan* it tends to replace earlier *ongietan*.[72] The prefix *on-/and-*, perhaps already weakened phonologically and semantically, seems sometimes to have been replaced by *under-* for reinforcement. The 'Durham Hymnal Gloss' always has *underfon* 'take up, receive', not *onfon*, except in two cases which are not by D_1.[73]

The word for 'altar' in the 'Durham Hymnal Gloss' is *weofod*, not the loan word *altare*, and that agrees with the usage of the Winchester group.[74]

In these preferences the 'Durham Hymnal Gloss' agrees with the Winchester group (and other texts). There are others in which it at least partially disagrees. The Winchester group prefers *blissian* 'rejoice, be glad' to older *fægnian*, which, at least in Ælfric, is only used for 'jubilate', that is, the vocal expression of joy. The 'Durham Hymnal Gloss' agrees with this for the most part, but has one instance of *fægnian* glossing *gaudere*.[75]

Although the usual word for 'son' in the 'Durham Hymnal Gloss' is, of course, *sunu*, it has an unusually high proportion of *bearn* in that meaning for

Philologie 33 (Bochum-Langendreer, 1939), 55–6; Gneuss, *HHEM*, pp. 178–9; and Gretsch, *Die Regula Sancti Benedicti*, pp. 345–7.

[71] The relevant gloss is *prudens – snoter* 123/5. See Seebold, 'Die altenglischen Entsprechungen von lat. *SAPIENS* und *PRUDENS*', *Anglia* 92 (1974), 291–333, esp. 321–7, and *idem*, 'Kentish', p. 416.

[72] The relevant glosses are *sentire – undergietan* 44/20, 86_1/14, 133/12. Cf. Ono, '*Undergytan*', and Seebold, 'Kentish', p. 418.

[73] In the 'Durham Hymnal Glosses' *underfon* occurs twenty times; *onfon* occurs in 31/30 (by D_2) and 35/10 (by D_3). See Ono, '*Undergytan*', p. 571; and Seebold, 'Kentish', p. 416.

[74] The relevant glosses are *ara – weofod* 67_2/29, 70/6 and 129/10. See Gretsch, *Die Regula Sancti Benedicti*, pp. 361–2.

[75] The relevant glosses are *gaudere, exultare, conlaetari – blissian* 23/15, 36/20, 48/10, 66/20, 80/5, 93/12 (D_2); *gaudere, iubilare, plaudere – fægnian* 47/10, 65_2/2, 72/3. See K. Ostheeren, *Studien zum Begriff der 'Freude' und seinen Ausdrucksmitteln in altenglischen Texten (Poesie, Alfred, Aelfric)* (Heidelberg, 1964), pp. 250–1; Gneuss, *HHEM*, p. 190; and Gretsch, *Die Regula Sancti Benedicti*, p. 336.

a non-poetic context, particularly a Late West Saxon one. However, Æthel-wold's translation of the Benedictine Rule and the interlinear version of the Rule are even more exceptional in consistently using *bearn*. A plural meaning 'children' occurs once in the 'Durham Hymnal Gloss'. According to Jordan, *cild* is more common in that meaning in Late West Saxon, although this has been doubted.[76] The word *cild* was also extended to boys of a certain age in Late West Saxon, but had a rival in *cnapa*, which was preferred for 'boy' in texts of the Winchester group after the time of Æthelwold, but not exclusively. In the 'Durham Hymnal Gloss' only *cild* is used.[77]

For 'guilt' the 'Durham Hymnal Gloss' uses *gylt* for the most part, but *scyld* in a fair number of instances. Earlier *scyld* was almost completely ousted by *gylt* in texts of the Winchester group and also a number of other Late West Saxon texts so that the 'Durham Hymnal Gloss' may be a little con-servative here. It may be Canterbury texts in particular that retain *scyld*.[78]

For 'sloth, lethargy' the 'Durham Hymnal Gloss' uses *slæwþ*. According to Tetzlaff, from Æthelwold onwards this word was often replaced by *asolcennes*.[79] The corresponding adjectives, *slaw* and *asolcen*, both occur once each in the 'Durham Hymnal Gloss'.[80]

---

[76] The glosses in question are *filius, natus, partus, proles – bearn* 63/22, 74/18, 76/31, 82/22, 82/26, 86$_1$/15, 120/12, 125/1, 125/17, 132/2, 133/3; *tudder ł bearn* 27/4; *filius, genitus, natus, partus – sunu* 1/10, 8/2, 15/31, 32/26, etc. (32 times; twice by D$_2$: 31/4, 31/67; twice by D$_3$: 40/4, 40/18). The plural 'children' is in Hy 82/22. See Jordan, *Eigentümlichkeiten*, pp. 96–7; Bäck, *The Synonyms for 'Boy'*, pp. 11–16, Gretsch, *Die Regula Sancti Benedicti*, pp. 320–2; and Gneuss, *HHEM*, p. 174.

[77] The relevant glosses are *puer, puerulus, parvulus – cild* 43/9, 62/9, 62/22. See Jordan, *Eigentümlichkeiten*, p. 96, Bäck, *The Synonyms for 'Boy'*, pp. 45–8; and Gretsch, *Die Regula Sancti Benedicti*, pp. 327–9.

[78] The relevant glosses are *reatus, scelus – scyld* 30/6, 34/15, 48/15, 86$_1$/3, 86$_2$/11, 100/5, 113/4, 120/6, 131/7; *culpa, debitum, delictum – gylt* 2/22, 4/16, 4/28, 13/12, 14/11, 15/12, 22/15, 23/10, 25/13, 30/8, 34/10, 46/5, 66/23, 75/22, 81/12, 119/22, 125/14, 127/14. See Gretsch, *Die Regula Sancti Benedicti*, p. 338–40, and cf. G. Büchner, *Vier altenglische Bezeichnungen für Vergehen und Verbrechen (Firen, Gylt, Man, Scyld)* (privately printed PhD dissertation, Berlin Free Univ., 1968).

[79] The relevant glosses are *torpor – slæwþ* 3/5, 26/14. See G. Tetzlaff, 'Bezeichnungen für die Sieben Todsünden in der altenglischen Prosa. Ein Beitrag zur Terminologie der altenglischen Kirchensprache' (unpubl. PhD dissertation, Berlin Free Univ., 1953), pp. 117–18. In fact only Ælfric seems to use the word frequently; cf. Venezky and Healey, *Microfiche Concordance to Old English*.

[80] *Torpidus – slaw* 34/5; *deses – asolcen* 18/6.

'Dispel, keep off' is usually rendered by *adræfan*, more rarely by *utadræfan* and *utanydan*. These are all mainly Late West Saxon. The verb preferred in the Winchester vocabulary appears to be *utanydan*, while *adræfan* occurs, for example, in the Aldhelm glosses.[81]

The preferred word for 'sweet' in the Winchester vocabulary appears to be *werod* rather than *swete* or *wynsum*. This preference does not seem to be altogether shared by the 'Durham Hymnal Gloss'.[82]

Some words that occur in D are not used in as wide a range of texts as the Winchester vocabulary. The word *cypere* has already been mentioned; *forswælan* 'burn' is another. It is used consistently in the Lambeth Psalter and the *Expositio* gloss, rather sparsely by Ælfric and very rarely anywhere else. The 'Durham Hymnal Gloss' at any rate has two instances of it, as opposed to two instances of *forbærnan*, the alternative word.[83]

Ælfric himself prefers the words *gefredan* 'feel' and *hreppan* 'touch' to *felan* and *hrinan*. The 'Durham Hymnal Gloss' has one instance each of these.[84]

There may be a tendency in the 'Durham Hymnal Gloss' to follow Ælfric's practice of using *faran* 'go' only in the present tense and *feran* 'go' only in the past so that they become a single verb, as it were. The gloss is not consistent in this, however.[85]

Ælfric is the first to use the noun *utlaga* 'outlaw', whereas *utlah* is found from the early tenth century onwards, but was originally confined to legal

---

[81] The relevant glosses are *pulsus – utanydd* 3/5, 19/3, 33/8; *pellere, repellere, depellere, expellere – adræfan* 6/6, 17/7, 23/13, 27/14, 28/9, 34/3, 57/8, 64/6, 66/11, 75/27, 76/17, 86₃/10, 95/13, 96/13, 97/10, 99/8, 111/3, 128/4; *pulsus – utadræfd* 86₃/14, 111/2 (mistakenly glossing *pulsa* from *pulsare*). See Gneuss, *HHEM*, p. 183.

[82] The relevant glosses are *dulcis – werod(lic)* 5/4, 133/11; *dulcedo – weorodnyss* 82/6; *suavis – wynsum* 48/3; *balsamum – swetnys* 82/7; *mellifluus – hunigswete* 82/8; *suavissonus – swetswege* 50/7. See Gneuss, *HHEM*, pp. 184– 5.

[83] The relevant glosses are *adurere, perurere – forbærnan* 19/9, 29/10; *(con)cremare – forswælan* 3/24, 33/6. See Gneuss, *HHEM*, p. 169, and Korhammer, *MC*, pp. 193–4.

[84] These are *sentire – gefredan* 129/8; *tangere – hreppan* 67₂/4; cf. also *contactus – hrepung* 38/23. See Dietrich, 'Abt Aelfrik', p. 544, n. 140. *Gefredan* may be West Saxon, *hreppan* predominantly West Saxon. *Gefredan* also seems to be a word preferred by Alfred. Cf. Venezky and Healey, *Microfiche Concordance to Old English*.

[85] The relevant glosses are *petere – gefaran* 43/15 (pret.); *intrare – infaran* 21/3, 65₂/7 (pres.); *coire – samodafaran* 80/9 marginal gloss (past participle); *penetrare – þurhfaran* 71/9 (pres.), 94/3 (by D₂), 128/14 (pret.); *intrare – inferan* 44/10 (by D₃) (pret.); *ire, petere – (ge)feran* 40/16, 45/5, 47/16, 86₂/2 (pret.). See *Homilies of Aelfric: a Supplementary Collection*, ed. J. C. Pope, EETS 259–60 (1967–8) I, 101, and Korhammer, *MC*, p. 187.

texts. That the 'Durham Hymnal Gloss' should translate *exul* three times with *utlaga* in contexts completely divorced from the original associations of the Scandinavian loan word is quite unusual for its supposed date, *c.* 1000.[86]

Canterbury words

Among the words in the 'Durham Hymnal Gloss' that may be characteristic for texts from Canterbury *prowære, forpræstan* and *scyld* have already been mentioned. The others listed by Hofstetter are *breman, epian, hrif, nænig, rædgift, stig* and *prinen*.[87] Except for the rare words *rædgift* and *prinen*, these are also found in Anglian texts and can be used as evidence of the link between Canterbury and Mercian.

Breman 'celebrate' does not usually appear in strictly Late West Saxon texts, which have *mærsian*. Other Canterbury texts in which *breman* occurs are the Aldhelm glosses and the interlinear version of the Benedictine Rule.[88]

Traditionally *epian* 'breathe' is Anglian and poetic, *orpian* West Saxon. In the 'Durham Hymnal Gloss' both words occur only once each. Non-poetic, non-Anglian documents that use the noun *epung* are Æthelwold's translation of the Benedictine Rule and the interlinear version from Canterbury.[89]

The preferred word for 'womb, abdomen' in Late West Saxon appears to be *innop*, to which *wamb* loses ground. *Hrif* is on the whole less frequent, but appears in the Aldhelm glosses from Canterbury. The 'Durham Hymnal Gloss' uses all three of these words.[90]

Nænig 'not any, none' is usually an Anglian word.[91]

[86] These instances are *exul – utlaga* 3/29, 13/10, 48/11. See Gneuss, *HHEM*, p. 184.

[87] Hofstetter, *Winchester*, pp. 108–10.

[88] The attestations in the 'Durham Hymnal Gloss' are *celebrare – breman* 43/4, 49/13, 86$_3$/17, 123/2, 124/7, 129/3. See Gneuss, *Lehnbildungen*, pp. 80–1; *HHEM*, pp. 174–5; Gretsch, *Die Regula Sancti Benedicti*, pp. 349–50; and Hofstetter, *Winchester*, pp. 97–8.

[89] The relevant glosses are *spirare – epian* 39/26; *spirare – orpian* 82/7. See Jordan, *Eigentümlichkeiten*, pp. 54–5; Scherer, *Geographie und Chronologie*, pp. 13 and 18; and Gneuss, *HHEM*, p. 176.

[90] The relevant glosses are *alvus – hrif* 39/9, 44/19, 65$_1$/20; *venter – wamb* 44/11, 65$_1$/16, 86$_1$/13; *penetrale, venter, viscus – innop* 39/8, 44/9, 65$_1$/8, 67$_1$/5, 80/5, 89/7, 92/8 (by D$_2$), 117/17, 119/12. See Gneuss, *HHEM*, p. 178.

[91] The word is attested in the 'Durham Hymnal Gloss' only once: *nemo – nænig* 31/54 (by

Rædgift 'senate, council' is a loan formation, which is otherwise only attested in the Aldhelm and the Prudentius glosses from Canterbury.[92]

Stig 'path' does not appear to be a strictly Late West Saxon word. Other Canterbury texts in which it occurs are the interlinear version of the Benedictine Rule, the Arundel prayers and the Aldhelm glosses. It is also poetic and Anglian. It only occurs once in the 'Durham Hymnal Gloss', the more common word being *sipfæt*. The usual meaning of this, of course, is 'journey' and as 'path' it is rare outside poetry, does not occur in Anglian prose and is avoided by texts of the Winchester group.[93]

Prinen 'threefold' elsewhere only occurs in other Canterbury works, the *Regularis concordia* gloss and the Arundel prayers.[94]

Another word that belongs here, not mentioned by Hofstetter, is *hinderscipe* 'badness', which is otherwise only attested in the Aldhelm glosses.[95]

The translation of *caro* 'flesh' by *lichoma* is a trait the 'Durham Hymnal Gloss' shares with one other Canterbury work, the interlinear version of the Benedictine Rule, and also with Anglian texts.[96]

Sefa 'mind, perception' is rare and usually Anglian outside poetry, but it also occurs in the Aldhelm glosses from Canterbury. Beside *sefa* the 'Durham Hymnal Gloss' uses the common West Saxon word *andgi(e)t*.[97]

The use of *stræl* for 'arrow, dart' beside *flan* appears to be a characteristic

---

D_2). See Wenisch, *Spezifisch anglisches Wortgut*, pp. 189–205 and 327; *The Life of St. Chad: an Old English Homily*, ed. R. Vleeskruyer (Amsterdam, 1953), p. 32, n. 1; and K. Jost, *Wulfstanstudien*, Schweizer Anglistische Arbeiten 23 (Bern, 1950), 159–62.

[92] This word also occurs once only in the 'Durham Hymnal Gloss': *rædgyft – senatus* 87/8. See Gneuss, *HHEM*, p. 180.

[93] The relevant glosses are *iter, semita, trames – sipfæt* 66/18, 73/3, 86₃/11, 95/28; *callis – stig* 86₃/12. See Gneuss, *HHEM*, pp. 153 and 179–80; and Korhammer, *MC*, pp. 190–2.

[94] The word is attested three times in the 'Durham Hymnal Gloss': *trinus – prynen* 86₃/18, 96/23, 123/20. See Gneuss, *HHEM*, p. 183.

[95] It occurs only once in the 'Durham Hymnal Gloss': *nequitia – hinderscipe* 122/10. See Gneuss, *HHEM*, p. 178.

[96] The relevant glosses are *caro – lichoma* 39/22, 44/7 (twice), 72/38, 74/12, 87/20; *caro – flæsc* 12/11, 31/20, 39/7, 67₁/3 (twice), 70/16, 75/15 (twice), 75/16. See Gneuss, *HHEM*, p. 176; Gretsch, *Die Regula Sancti Benedicti*, pp. 336–7; and Korhammer, *MC*, pp. 194–5.

[97] The relevant glosses are *sensus – sefa* 21/12, 46/11, 76/13, 95/26; *sensus – andgit* 2/25,

of Kentish texts.[98] *Stræl* is otherwise Anglian; *flan* occurs in West Saxon and in some Mercian texts. Both occur in poetry.

The use of the rare *eorendel* in the 'Durham Hymnal Gloss' to translate *aurora* 'dawn' may possibly belong here, too, since none of its few attestations is in strictly West Saxon prose.[99]

4/29, 8/5, 15/8, 27/13, 27/18. See Gneuss, *HHEM*, p. 180, and Hofstetter, *Winchester*, pp. 233–4, n. 11.

[98] Actually the 'Durham Hymnal Gloss' has *stræle*, presumably a weak feminine, if the form is correct: *spiculum – stræle* 30/3. The other word also occurs once: *telum – flan* 32/24. Cf. Seebold, 'Regional gebundene Wörter', pp. 267–71.

[99] There are two instances in the 'Durham Hymnal Gloss': *aurora – eorendel* 15/30, 30/1. See Gneuss, *HHEM*, p. 175.

4

Musical notation in the Anglo-Saxon hymnals

An integral part of any hymn is the melody to which it is sung. As the earliest medieval notation does not date from before the ninth century, it is true of the melodies even more than of the texts of hymns that their early history has to be reconstructed from much later material.[1]

All conclusions, therefore, about the earliest melodies, those by St Ambrose and those of the Old Hymnal, must remain speculative. Dreves and others have assumed that Ambrose's original melodies are preserved in the notoriously conservative Ambrosian liturgy of Milan, Ambrose's own diocese.[2] Stäblein isolated from among the Milanese stock of melodies a group which, he thought, represented the original Milanese style. He did not necessarily ascribe them to Ambrose, although they are associated with his texts.[3]

There is even less to go on for the early history of the melodies of the New Hymnal up to the late tenth century, but Bullough and Corrêa assume that the degree of uniformity which prevails within the musical tradition *c.* 1000 is due to the standardization attempted by the imperial chapel of Louis the Pious in the early ninth century.[4]

Within the mainstream of medieval church music, the so-called Gregorian chant,[5] hymn melodies are a special case because they are sung to

[1]   Treitler, 'Reading and Singing', pp. 141–72.
[2]   G. M. Dreves, *Aurelius Ambrosius, 'der Vater des Kirchengesanges'*: *eine hymnologische Studie*, Stimmen aus Maria Laach, Ergänzungshefte 58 (Freiburg, 1893), 88–142. Cf. Stäblein, p. 503. On Ambrose, see above, pp. 1–2.
[3]   Stäblein, pp. 503–4.
[4]   Bullough and Corrêa, ' Texts, Chant', pp. 507–8. Cf. above, pp. 6–7.
[5]   On Gregorian chant, see, for example, M. Huglo, 'Le chant gregorien. A: étude historique', in *Précis de musicologie*, ed. J. Chailley, 2nd ed. (Paris, 1984), pp. 121–9;

texts that are stanzaic in form and have a given metrical or rhythmical verse structure.[6] Some of the consequences for the composition are immediate; for example, each stanza is sung to the same melody and the melodic line will normally take account of the end of the verse. Others are less obvious.

Some melodies are closely associated with a single text so that it is possible to conclude that text and melody were originally composed for each other. Frequently, however, texts are sung to a number of different melodies and vice versa. While such a practice is not restricted to hymns, but also found with liturgical prose, the fact that most hymns are composed in metrical or rhythmical Ambrosian verse allowed melodies to be transferred from one hymn to another with unparalleled ease. In the same way a tune composed for a hymn in Sapphics, the second most frequent verse form, could be freely used for all other hymns of the kind. By the twelfth century at the latest it was also usual to sing the same text to different tunes on different liturgical occasions.[7] To know that a hymn was sung to a certain tune in Anglo-Saxon England does not mean that it was the only melody in use for it even in the same church. On the other hand, texts of other hymns not transmitted with Anglo-Saxon notation could have been sung to the same tune.

For approximately a third of the hymns in the present edition we have some information on the tunes to which they were sung. Only in one case, Hy 43, is the information derived from manuscript D itself.[8] There is notation for two hymns in V, three hymns in B and four in W, but most of the relevant notation is in C and H, so there is more information on Worcester and Exeter than on Canterbury or Winchester.[9]

Wagner, *Einführung in die gregorianischen Melodien*; and now above all D. Hiley, *Western Plainchant: a Handbook* (Oxford, 1993), esp. 140–8 (on hymns), 310–11 (on hymnals), 351 (on Anglo-Saxon neumes) and 580–4 (on England). He emphasizes the importance of Corbie for the Anglo-Saxon tradition. On the introduction of Gregorian chant in England, see S. Rankin, 'The Liturgical Background of the Old English Advent Lyrics: a Reappraisal', in *Learning and Literature*, ed. Lapidge and Gneuss, pp. 317–40.

[6] See R. Steiner, 'Hymn §II: Monophonic Latin' in *The New Grove Dictionary of Music and Musicians*, ed. S. Sadie, 20 vols. (London, 1980) VIII, 838–40, and Stäblein, 'Der lateinische Hymnus'. The latter will eventually be superseded by the forthcoming entry by K. Schlager.

[7] Cf. Stäblein, pp. 71–6. Note also the treatment of Hy 128 as opposed to Hy 127 and 129 in H, see below, p. 96. These are *divisiones* of a single hymn.

[8] On notation in D, see above, p. 34.

[9] On notation in B, W, C, H and V, see above, pp. 43, 65, 46–7, 49 and 53.

The notation is in adiastematic or half-diastematic neumes, that is neumes without staves.[10] This means that the notation does not give any information on absolute pitch or on precise intervals. Spaced out above a line of text, it records the number of notes per syllable of text. If there is more than one note to a syllable, the movement of the melodic line within it is indicated; otherwise adiastematic notation can only distinguish the lowest notes of a melody or melodic passage from the higher ones. In addition, there are various ways of indicating a particular kind of phrasing for a note or sequence of notes by special neume forms. Unlike modern notation, the system is designed as a mnemonic or supplementary aid, helping the reader, for example, to apply a tune he already knows by heart to a particular piece of text and especially useful for highly melismatic melodies, since these exhibit the kind of phenomena which the neumes are best able to record. The oldest hymn tunes may have established a tradition of comparative plainness; at any rate, the hymns on the whole tended to be less melismatic than other liturgical music. Hymn tunes are, therefore, not obviously suited to adiastematic notation and the informa-tion the neumes convey to the uninitiated modern reader is often disappointingly sparse. Only in W are the neumes combined with alphabetic notation and thus more informative.[11]

As the hymns are so relatively plain and early notation tells us so little about them, these records have not been a focus of musicological interest. The great hymnologist among musicologists, Bruno Stäblein, has only

[10] On neumes, see M. Huglo, 'Le noms de neumes et leur origine', *Etudes Grégoriennes* 1 (1954), 53–67; S. Corbin, *Die Neumen* (Cologne, 1977), esp. ch. 3 (on English neumes); B. Stäblein, *Schriftbild der einstimmigen Musik*, Musikgeschichte in Bildern 3. 4 (Leipzig, 1975), esp. pp. 32–3 and 114–17 (on English neumes). Pl. 9 is a facsimile of H, 77v–78r, with comments on p. 116. On the interpretation of neumes, see W. Arlt, 'Anschaulichkeit und analytischer Charakter: Kriterien der Beschreibung und Analyse früher Neumenschriften,' in *Musicologie médiévale: notations et séquences. Actes de la table ronde du C.N.R.S. à l'Institut de Recherche et d'Histoire des Textes 6–7 septembre 1982*, ed. M. Huglo (Paris, 1987), pp. 29–55, and K. Schlager, 'Aenigmata in campo aperto. Marginalien zum Umgang mit Neumen', *Kirchenmusikalisches Jahrbuch* 77 (1993), 7–15. On Anglo-Saxon neumes, see further Rankin, 'Neumatic Notations in Anglo-Saxon England'.

[11] On the system of alphabetic notation in the Winchester Troper W, see *The Winchester Troper*, ed. Frere, p. xli, Holschneider, *Die Organa von Winchester*, pp. 89–90; and A. Holschneider, 'Die instrumentalen Tonbuchstaben im Winchester Troper', in *Festschrift Georg von Dadelsen zum 60. Geburtstag*, ed. T. Kohlhase and V. Scherliess (Neuhausen-Stuttgart, 1978), 155–66.

dealt with records that allow precise reconstruction. His English material is all post-Conquest, and unfortunately much of his research remained unpublished.[12]

If the information that the Anglo-Saxon neumes provided was to be made use of, the procedure that suggested itself was to compare the corpus of hymn melodies edited by Stäblein on the basis of diastematic notation with the Anglo-Saxon material. The earliest hymnals edited by Stäblein are those of Moissac in Aquitania and of Kempten in Germany;[13] both are dated to approximately AD 1000 and therefore approximately contemporaneous with the Anglo-Saxon neumes. His earliest English hymnal is that of Worcester in the thirteenth century and his earliest French hymnal, since Aquitanian tradition can hardly be held to represent the French in AD 1000, is that of Nevers in the twelfth century.[14] They are further removed in time, but closer in spatial terms. It seemed best to start with these four and to compare the melodies included closely with the features of tunes recorded by the Anglo-Saxon neumes, beginning with those that accompanied the same text, but proceeding to those that did not. If that yielded only negative results and also if the text of an Anglo-Saxon tune was not included in these four hymnals, the rest of Stäblein's corpus was checked for all tunes associated with that text and these were in their turn compared to the neumatic material.[15]

The results of such a comparison were of varying kinds. In some cases the Anglo-Saxon neumes agreed perfectly with Stäblein's tune and the features recorded in them were so characteristic that there could be no

[12] The projected second volume of his edition, the first volume of which is quoted throughout as 'Stäblein', never appeared. For further research and confirmation of my results in this chapter Stäblein's materials, kept at the Stäblein-Archiv at the University of Erlangen, should be consulted. A first cursory check, with the kind assistance of Dr Andreas Haug, revealed no major discrepancies.

[13] The manuscripts are Vatican City, Biblioteca Apostolica Vaticana, Rossianus 205 and Zürich, Zentralbibliothek, Rh. 83. The Moissac hymnal may be somewhat later than AD 1000.

[14] The manuscripts are Worcester Cathedral Library, F. 160 and Paris, Bibliothèque Nationale, nouv. acq. lat. 1235. There is a facsimile of the Worcester manuscript: *Le Codex F. 160 de la bibliothèque de la Cathédrale de Worcester, antiphonaire monastique (XIIIᵉ siècle)*, ed. A. Mocquereau, Paléographie musicale I, 12 (Tournai, 1922). In the rest of the chapter 'Worcester hymnal' means this thirteenth-century hymnal, not C.

[15] This project could never have been undertaken without the invaluable counsel and assistance of the musicologist Dr Fred Büttner. Any mistakes that may have crept in are my own, however. The *modus operandi* is illustrated below, pp. 98–101.

doubt that this was, in fact, the same melody. In other cases there was obviously no agreement at all. Sometimes the neumes were too unspecific to allow positive identification. Mostly, however, there was some agreement and some deviation.

This is hardly surprising. In a musical tradition which was transmitted orally, in spite of the existence of certain kinds of notation, variation is not unlikely and Stäblein often records a different version for each hymnal. Unfortunately in neumatic notation fairly minor variations can obscure the basic identity of a tune. In each case it had to be considered whether the agreements were characteristic enough to outweigh the deviations or not and all the variants recorded by Stäblein were checked. It cannot be altogether excluded that in one case or another, another melody might be found that agrees with the same set of neumes as well or even better.

These are the results of the comparison for H:

Hy	39	44	48	51	54	55	56	58	60	64
Stäblein no.	406	53	?112	413	?14	411	412	?127	54	?

Hy	66	67	68	95	96	97	98	99	100	102
Stäblein no.	149	32	55	?	?	146	?158	?	?	114

Hy	103	104–6	117	118	119	120	121	122	123	124
Stäblein no.	115	152	115	405	159	405	150	?	423	419

Hy	125	126	127/129	128	138	139	140	141	142	143
Stäblein no.	425	?115	?	146	?705	178	170	?	12	56

Hy	144	145
Stäblein no.	518	70

Question marks preceding Stäblein numbers indicate that the neumes diverge from Stäblein's recorded versions significantly in places, but the identification may nevertheless be undertaken with a fair amount of confidence.

This means that of thirty-eight different tunes recorded in H thirty-two could with more or less certainty be identified with melodies edited by Stäblein. Of these three, Stäblein nos. 406, 419 and 425, were known to Stäblein only from the Worcester hymnal. A further three, Stäblein nos. 146, 405 and 411, are said by him to be attested only in a restricted territory, which in each case includes England, northern France and Germany, but not Italy.[16] If Stäblein records more than one version of a

[16] Stäblein, pp. 561–4.

tune, the version in H does not usually agree with any of them, but appears to share the largest number of features with the Worcester hymnal, although in some cases there are distinct parallels with the Nevers hymnal.[17] The melodies not identified are, with the exception of Hy 96, associated with texts not found in the Worcester hymnal.

So far H looks distinctly English, but there are foreign touches as well. The tunes of *O Nazarene* (Hy 139) and *Rex Christe factor* (Hy 142) are as singular in medieval England as their texts, naturally, as they appear to be the original tunes of those hymns and exclusively associated with them.[18] *Gaude visceribus* (Hy 144) also appears with its original tune, which is remarkable, because according to Stäblein this tune is restricted to Germany.[19] Its presence may perhaps be considered in the light of possible Lotharingian influence on H.[20]

The results of the comparison between the notation in the hymnal of C and the edition of Stäblein are as follows:

Hy	3	4	32	34	45	46	76	77	79–81
Stäblein no.	410	?	?23	402	409	?	?17	64	?71

Hy	87	123	157
Stäblein no.	152	?	?

Of the twelve hymns with neumes in C eight represent tunes that can be tentatively identified. Two of those which could not be identified are associated with texts that are not in the Worcester hymnal printed by Stäblein, Hy 46 and 157. Hy 157 is a rare Oswald hymn, which also has notation for the first line only. Hy 123 has even more defective notation.[21]

Of the eight identified tunes Stäblein no. 409 was known to Stäblein only from Worcester. According to him two of the eight, Stäblein nos. 402 and 410, were in use in restricted territories including England and Germany and excluding Italy; one of these, no. 410, is not attested in France.[22] There are no features in C which Stäblein's evidence might lead one to consider not English. All tunes except two are found in the Worcester hymnal and those two, Stäblein nos. 17 and 64, are attested in

---

[17] The parallels with the Nevers hymnal are strongest in H's versions of Stäblein nos. 56, 146, 149, 150 and 151 (with due caution because of the limits of the evidence).
[18] Stäblein, pp. 552 and 506. [19] *Ibid.*, pp. 575–6. [20] See above, pp. 46–7.
[21] On the patterns of C's notation, see above, pp. 46–7.
[22] Stäblein, pp. 541 and 560–4.

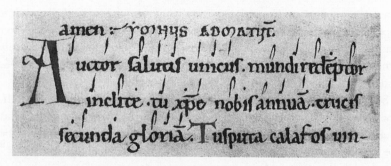

IIa   London, BL, Harley 2961, 239v

Nevers. Again most melodies appear to be closer to the versions of the Worcester hymnal than to any others.

One of the three hymns with neumes in B, Hy 123, had already been identified by Gasquet and Bishop as a melody transmitted in the Worcester hymnal, Stäblein no. 422_1.[23] The other two remain unidentified; one of them belongs to a comparatively rare hymn, Hy 122.[24] The tunes in V for Hy 69 and 82 remain unidentified. The text of Hy 82 is not included in Stäblein. D's tune for Hy 43 has not been found; the text is not included in the Worcester or Nevers hymnals. All four hymns in the Winchester Troper (W) have been identified, one rather tentatively:[25]

Hy	67_2	73	79	123
Stäblein no.	32	4	?71	423

The number of hymns for which we have more than one set of Anglo-Saxon neumes is fairly small. Hy 123 is exceptional, in that there are neumes in four manuscripts, although the neumes in C are only to half a line of verse and the beginning of the melody is syllabic and so impossible to identify. H and W are closely related, but B represents a different melody.

The tunes in H and W for Hy 67 and in C and W for Hy 79 are related. The tunes for Hy 122 in B and H are not the same. For the closely related texts of Hy 87 and 104–6 C and H respectively have versions of Stäblein no. 152. On the face of it, this looks as though the repertories of C, H and W (Worcester, Exeter and Winchester) might go back to a

---

[23] Gasquet and Bishop, *The Bosworth Psalter*, p. 12.   [24] See above, pp. 23 and n. 83.

[25] The tune to Hy 79 agrees closely with that in C, but there are significant variants in lines 1 and 4, which are not recorded by Stäblein for his no. 71.

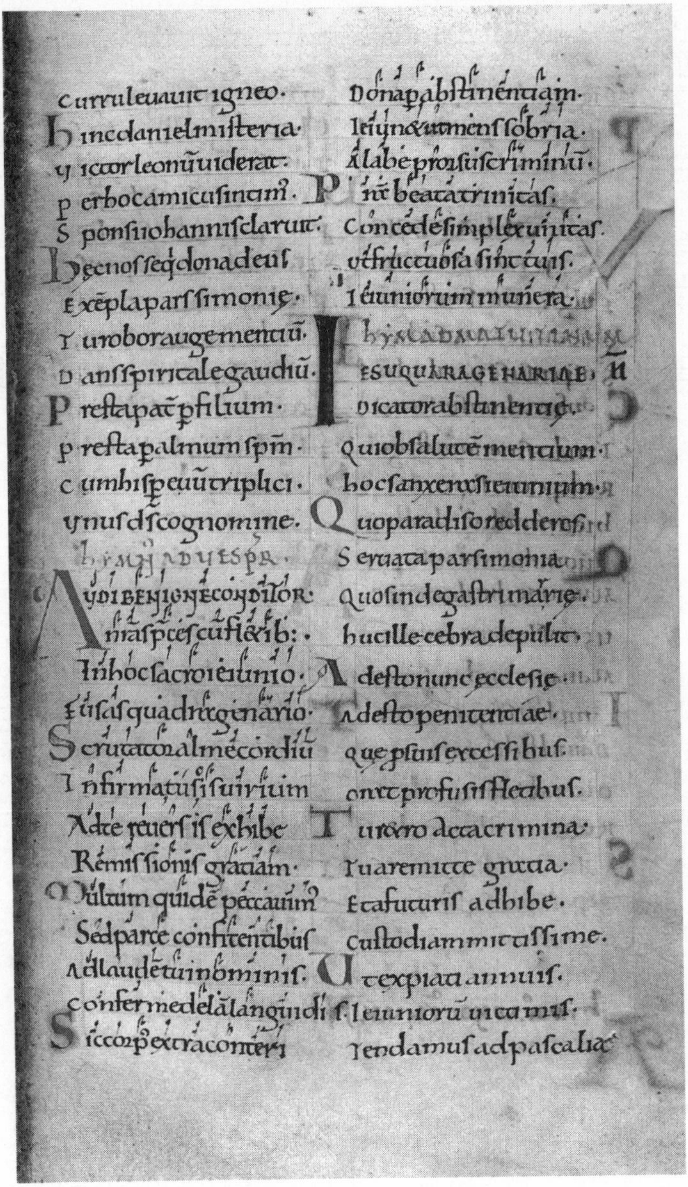

IIb Cambridge, Corpus Christi College 391, p. 245

2a   Stäblein no. 55₃ (Worcester, s. xiii)

2b   Stäblein no. 55₂ (Nevers, s. xii)

common tradition in spite of local variation, while B (from Canterbury) belongs to a different one. This would be based on the assumption, however, that Hy 122 and 123 were not sung to several different tunes, depending on the liturgical occasion. (It should also be noted that Stäblein no. 55 was added in eleventh-century Norman neumes above Hy 55 in C, which is joined to Stäblein no. 411 in H, whatever may be the precise significance of that.)

There were certainly differences in usage in Anglo-Saxon England, although it is impossible to gauge their extent. Whether there was any correlation between the type of hymnal used, monastic or secular, Canterbury type or Winchester, and the tunes remains a matter of speculation.

Although it is otherwise impossible to go into detail within the framework of this introduction, table 1 demonstrates how the version of Stäblein no. 55 in H agrees with the Norman neumes entered above Hy 55 in C, comparing them with the Worcester hymnal and the Nevers hymnal, and illustrates the relation between the Anglo-Saxon and Norman neumes and the hymns edited by Stäblein. Table 1 should be compared with pls. IIa and IIb and figs. 2a and 2b.

The Anglo-Saxon and the Norman versions of Stäblein no. 55 appear to agree more closely than they agree with either the Worcester or the Nevers hymnal. The Worcester hymnal seems a little closer to the neumatic versions than the Nevers hymnal. C seems a little closer to the Worcester hymnal than H. These observations are, of course, limited to the aspects of the melody that are conveyed by the neumes.

The feature which H and C share, that regardless of differences they are on the whole both closer to the thirteenth-century Worcester hymnal than to any other, seems to indicate some kind of continuity beyond the Norman Conquest and not only of local Worcester tradition, as H is from Exeter. The four melodies, three in H, one in C, which were known to Stäblein only from Worcester, are probably an example of Worcester's particular conservativeness. The conditions for their preservation were most propitious in the one diocese which William the Conqueror left in the hands of an Anglo-Saxon bishop, namely Wulfstan II at Worcester. The significance of the other parallels between C and H and the later Worcester hymnal is much less clear. Not only is there not enough other later English material in Stäblein, but there is also very little on northern and western France and Flanders. It is impossible to venture any conclusions on what the Benedictine reformers might have borrowed from

Table 1   *Neumes to Hy 68 in H: points of agreement and divergence with later version of Stäblein No. 55*

			H	C	Worcester	Nevers
Line 1						
Syllable	1	pes		v	v	x
	2	virga		v	v	v
	3	clivis		v	v	v
	4	virga		v	v	v
	5	pes		v	x	v
	6	virga		v	x	v
	7	pes		v	v	x
	8	virga		v	v	v
Line 2						
Syllable	1	punctum liqu.		v	v	v
	2	pes		v	v	v
	3	clivis		v	x	v
	4	punctum		v	x	v
	5	clivis		v	v	v
	6	pes		v	v	v
	7	clivis		v	v	v
	8	punctm		v	v	v
Line 3						
Syllable	1	pes		v	v	x
	2	punctum		v	v	v
	3	virga		v	v	v
	4	clivis		v	v	v
	5	punctum		v	v	v
	6	punctum liqu.		v	v	x
	7	pes		v	v	x
	8	virga		v	v	v
Line 4						
Syllable	1	pes		v	v	v
	2	pes		v	v	v
	3	punctum		v	v	v
	4	clivis		v	v	v
	5	punctum		v	v	v
	6	clivis		?	?	v
	7	pes		v	v	x
	8	virga		v	v	v

v   *agrees*   x   *does not agree*
?   *agreement doubtful*   liqu. *liquescent form*

102

Fleury, Ghent or Corbie and what the Normans might have brought with them.[26] How distinctly English was the Anglo-Saxon tradition? Is Worcester in all cases being particularly conservative in preserving Anglo-Saxon tradition after the Conquest and did the Conquest constitute a major break in tradition elsewhere? It is impossible to say as yet.

It might be promising to look among the Anglo-Saxon material for musical peculiarities which Stäblein has called typical of Worcester or of England.[27] Although as a whole hymn melodies may have developed from plain to more elaborate, the Anglo-Saxon versions of melodies are not by any means plainer than the later Worcester ones.

With regard to hymns for which there are no neumes in Anglo-Saxon sources it may be said that if the same melody is given for the text in the hymnals of Worcester and Nevers it is quite likely to have been in Anglo-Saxon use; if the Worcester hymnal has a melody peculiar to itself, it may well be an Anglo-Saxon survival. As a minor point it may be added that its apparent attestation in H tends to disprove Stäblein's ascription of his no. 70 to the Cistercians.[28]

Finally, here is a list of all the melodies in Stäblein which have been identified in Anglo-Saxon sources:[29] Stäblein no. 4 (W), 14 (H), ?17 (C), 23 (C), 32 (H,W), 53 (H), 54 (H), 55 (H), 64 (C), ?71 (C, W), ?112 (H), 114 (H), 115 (H), 127 (H), 146 (H), 149 (H), 150 (H), 152 (C, H), ?158 (H), 159 (H), 170 (H), 402 (C), 405 (H), 406 (H), 409 (C), 410 (C), 411 (H), 412 (H), 413 (H), 419 (H), 422 (B), 423 (H, W) 425 (H), ?705 (H).

---

[26] Cf. above, pp. 15–22. On Wulfstan, see Stenton, *Anglo-Saxon England*, pp. 660 and 680.

[27] Stäblein, pp. 560–1, and *idem*, 'Der lateinische Hymnus'.

[28] Stäblein, p. 521.

[29] A comparison of the Anglo-Saxon material with that in W. Lipphardt, 'Das Hymnar der Metzer Kathedrale um 1200', in *Festschrift Bruno Stäblein zum 70. Geburtstag*, ed. M. Ruhnke (Kassel, 1967), pp. 160–77, brought no further results.

5

Editorial procedures

The following is a critical edition of the 'Durham Hymnal' together with the text or collation of all that has been preserved in manuscript form of the tradition of liturgical hymns in Anglo-Saxon England. It is arranged as follows.

First, the Latin text of the 'Durham Hymnal' (D) is given with its interlinear gloss. The text is very conservative, but if the original reading of the manuscript is obscured by damage or later corrections, I have attempted to reconstruct it and in rare cases I have supplied Latin text to fill a gap in the manuscript. Reconstructed letters and words are in italics. Supplied text is in square brackets. Asterisks in the Latin text mean that there is a mistake in the following word. Asterisks in the interlinear gloss mean that the gloss fails to translate the lemma accurately. Abbreviations are expanded without comment, except for 7 'and', *l* 'vel', *s.* 'scilicet' and *i.e.* 'id est'.

Next comes a very literal prose translation. Sometimes a deviating reading of other Anglo-Saxon manuscripts is translated in brackets.

The subsequent paragraph gives the relevant information on the liturgical use of the hymn, its author and its metre, the manuscripts in which the hymn is found and its notation, if there is any. For rhythmical verse Dag Norberg's system of notation is used.[1] References for melodies are to numbers in Stäblein's edition. The bibliographical references cited are the bibliography of Schaller and Könsgen (*ICL*), and the editions in the *Analecta Hymnica* (*AH*) and the editions by Bulst and by Walpole. A reference to *AH* preceded by *cf.* refers to the printed text of an individual manuscript (not to a critical edition).

---

[1] D. Norberg, *Introduction à l'étude de la versification médiévale*, Studia latina Stockholmiensia 5 (Stockholm, 1958).

The first section of the textual apparatus deals with manuscript D and treats the Latin text, the Old English gloss and Latin glosses separately. In printing Latin glosses, some of their lemmata are inserted for clarification; these are in brackets.

The second section lists variant readings of all other Anglo-Saxon manuscripts (including those of the *Expositio hymnorum*) containing the text of the hymn. Previous editors are occasionally referred to. The section includes Latin and Old English glosses in the hymnals of Vm and Ri. As JVp contain a prose version their readings are of no value as to word order. The explanatory additions made in JVp are not listed and the Old English gloss in them is only alluded to if it seems to render a reading divergent from the Latin text.

The commentary includes a selection of sources and parallels for the hymn, mainly from the Vulgate[2] and from other hymns. This is in great part derived from Walpole's commentary. There are also selected references to readings of continental manuscripts in *AH* and Bulst. The deviations of the Old English glosses from their lemmata are commented on.

Appended as Hy 134–62 are editions of those hymns which are not found in the 'Durham Hymnal', but are otherwise transmitted in Anglo-Saxon manuscripts, omitting a few saints' hymns that may not have been in liturgical use. They are grouped by manuscript source (H, Vm, C, B, Jo and Bo).

I have consulted the original manuscripts in all cases except for the fragment Ri from Ripon (now Leeds) and the hymns from Cambridge, Corpus Christi College 183 (Cu) and 473 (W). In those cases I have used photographs (Ri) or microfilms (W, Cu).

---

[2] The Vulgate is quoted according to *Biblia sacra iuxta Vulgatam versionem*, ed. R. Weber, 3rd ed. (Stuttgart, 1983). A little punctuation had to be introduced to make the quotations comprehensible, as this edition prints the text *per cola et commata*.

Text, translation, commentary and apparatus

List of Manuscript Sigla

A	London, BL, Cotton Vespasian A. i
B	London, BL, Additional 37517
Bo	Oxford, Bodleian Library, Bodley 342
C	Cambridge, Corpus Christi College 391
Cm	Cambridge, University Library, Ff. 4. 42
Cu	Cambridge, Corpus Christi College 183
D	Durham Cathedral Library, B. III. 32
Do	Oxford, Bodleian Library, Douce 296
E	Durham Cathedral Library, A. IV. 19
H	London, BL, Harley 2961
J	London, BL, Cotton Julius A. vi (*Expositio hymnorum*)
Jo	Cambridge, St John's College F. 27
La	London, Lambeth Palace 362
R	London, BL, Royal 2. B. V
Ri	Leeds, Brotherton Library, formerly Ripon Cathedral s. n.
T	London, BL, Cotton Tiberius A. iii
V	London, BL, Cotton Vespasian D. xii
Vm	hymnal in V
Vp	*Expositio hymnorum* in V
W	Cambridge, Corpus Christi College 473
D_1, D_2	first hand in D, second hand in D
[ ]	supplied text
( )	editor's comment in printed Latin gloss
*	corruption in Latin text; inaccuracy of Old English gloss

1

clypung   to   þære halgan   þrynnisse
[1r] INVOCATIO AD SANCTAM TRINITATEM

eala þu   þu eadige þrynnes
I   *O*   LUX, BEATA TRINITAS

7 ealdorlic   annys
ET PRINCIPALIS UNItas,

eallunga sunne aweggewit *seo* fyrenne
iam   sol recedit igneus;

onageot l asænd leoht   heortum
infunde   lumen cordibus.   4

þe on ærnemergen herigan   leoð
II   *Te m*a*ne*   laudent carmina,

þe we biddan   on æfene
te deprecemur vesperi,

þe ure   eadmod   wuldor
te nostra supplex gloria

geond ealle   *herigað worulde
per cuncta *laudent secula.   8

gode fæder sy wuldor
III Deo patri sit gloria

7 his   anum suna
eiusque soli filio

mid gaste   frofer
cum spiritu paraclyto

nu   7 on ecnysse
et nunc et in perpetuum.   12

sy hit swa
Amen

I O Light, blessed Trinity and sovereign Unity, already the fiery sun is setting; therefore fill our hearts with light.

II May songs praise you in the morning; may we pray to you in the evening. May our humble 'Gloria' praise you throughout all the ages!

III Praise be to God, the Father and his only Son together with the Holy Ghost, now and in eternity. Amen.

109

The hymn is to be sung on the first Vespers of Sunday, i.e. on Saturday evening. This is also implied by B's rubric, as the hymn there follows Hy 2. Hy 2 replaced Hy 1 during the summer; see above, pp. 24–5. The hymn is anonymous. It is in Ambrosian iambic dimeter. No melody has been transmitted for it in Anglo-Saxon manuscripts. It is extant in the hymnals of BCDHVm, and the *Expositio hymnorum* in Vp, but has been erased in J. It is also transmitted in E, Cm and Do. It is glossed in Latin in both D and V. In D this hymn, Hy 2 and part of Hy 3 exist in two versions (both glossed), the first written by D_1 and later used as a flyleaf and, replacing it, a version by D_2 beginning on 2r. The version by D_1 has sustained considerable damage. The edition is based on D_1.

Bibliographical references: *ICL* no. 10920; *AH* 51, 38-40 (no. 40); Walpole no. 79.

Apparatus to D   Latin text: Heading: *om. D_2*; 1 O] *om. in D_1*; 5 Te] T *om. or illegible D_1*; mane] a *damaged D_1*; 8 cuncta] *second* c *added below in D_2*; laudent] n *by another hand on erasure of one letter D_2*; 10-12 *om. D_2*.

Old English gloss: Heading: *om. D_2*; 1 *no traces of a gloss to* LUX. eala ... eadige] *om. D_2*; þrynnes] ðrynnys D_2; 2 annys] *second* n *badly damaged D_1*, annyss D_2; 3 seo *om. or illegible D_1*; 4 asænd] D_1, asynd D_2; 5 þe *damaged and illegible D_1*; 8 herigað] herigan D_2; 10–13 *om. (together with lemma) D_2*; 13 *no traces of gloss to* te et D_1.

Latin gloss: by D_4 on 2r: 1 s. vera (*lux*) s. o (*beata*) s. et o (*trinitas*) 2 maxima o deus scilicet & une, 3 (*recedit*) s. a nobis ardens, 4 (*lumen*) tuum (*cordibus*) s. nostris 5 s. deprecemur 6 te *deprecamu (u erased) possumus carmine laudum vespertinalibus horis.

Prose version by D_4 in the margin on 2r: I O beata lux trinitas & unitas principalis iam recedit igneus s. *i.. (two illegible letters)* sol lumen infunde cordibus II In mane te cum *carmina laudent te s. nos deprecamur vesperi te nostra gloria supplex per cuncta secula laudent.

BVmCVpHECmDo   Heading: Item alius ymnus *B, no rubric VmCVpH*, Ymnus ad vesperum in dominica nocte *E*, O lux beata *by another hand Cm*, Ymnus *Do*; 2 principalis] gloriosa *Cm*; 3-4 *om. Cm*; 3 igneus] ignibus *E*; 4 *At this point the following stanza is inserted in BVm:* Iam noctis tempus advenit / noctem quietam tribuens / diluculo nos respice / salvator unigenite. 5 Te] e *Do*; laudent] laudum *VmVpHDo*, ladunt *C*; carmina] carmine *CDo (also original lemma of the gloss in Vp)*; 7 supplex] pplex *illegible Cm*; 8 laudent] laudet *BVmCVpHDo*, laudat *E (but the gloss, giheriaþ, may translate* laudant). 9–12 *om. E*, 9 Deo] do *Cm*, eo *Do*; sit] t *illegible Cm*; 10-12 *om. B*; 10 -que] *om. Cm*; 11 spiritu] spu *Cm*; 12 in perpetuum] imperpetuum *Do*; perpetuum] perfetua, *last letter almost illegible Cm*; Amen] *om. BVmC, probably by another hand, in E.*

Vm Latin gloss: 1 splendor & o immortalis deitas 2 & o auctoralis *potententia 3 ad presens longe abiit flammeus 4 inmitte radium precordiis 5 *orte dico preconiorum cantico

6 s. ut (*te deprecemur*) inprecamur vesperi orto 7 cernua (*gloria*) modulatio 8 per universa &
ut glorificet.

Commentary   Latin: 1-2 *Cf. Hy 26/1-2. 4 Cf. Hy 15/7f. BVm's additional stanza is
attested by* AH *for south Italy.* 5 *The variant readings are paralleled on the Continent –* AH *reads*
laudum carmine. *Note that this is also the reading of the Latin gloss in D, while the prose version
in D contaminates the variants.* 8 laudent, *although shared by Cm and one continental manuscript
(according to* AH), *seems to be a mistake due to* laudent *in line 5. Note, however, that it is re-
established after correction to* laudet *by another hand in D₂ and that the prose version by D₄ has*
laudent, *too.* Old English: 8 herigað *incorrectly renders* laudent, *itself apparently a mistake; D₂
has the correct optative. Maybe there was a reading* laudant, *though; cf. the gloss in E.*

2

YMNUS AD VESPERAM

ó
eala þu god   sceppend   ealra þinga
I   DEUS, CREATOR OMNIum

7 heofones reccend gefrætuigende
polique   rector vestiens

dæg   mid wlitegum leohte
diem decoro   lumine,

nihte   slæpes   gyfe
noctem soporis *gratiae,   4

liþa   toslopene þæt stilness
II   Artus solutos ut quies

do   geswinces gewunan
reddat laboris   usui

7 mod   gewæhte *he geliþewæce
mentesque fessas   allevet

7 *heofunga   he tolyse ancsume*
luctusque solvat ancxios,   8

þancas   geendedum eallunga dæge
III   Grates peracto   iam   die

7 nihte   of upspringe bena
& noctis exortu   preces,

mid gewilnungum scildige þæt þu gefultumige
votis   reos   ut adiuves,

lofsang   singende   we gelæston
ymnum canentes solvimus.   12

111

þe heortan *niwolnyssum hleoþrion
IV Te cordis yma   concinant,

þe stefn gedryme swege
te vox canora concrepet,

[1v] þe lufige   clæne lufe
    te diligat castus amor,

þe mod   gebidde sefre
te mens adoret sobria,   16

þæt þænne on deopnysse beclysþ
V Ut cum profundo   clauserit

dæg   dimnyss nyhta
diem caligo noctium,

geleafa þeostru   nyte
fides tenebras nesciat

7 niht geleafan scine
et nox fidei   luceat.   20

slapan   mod   ne geþafa þu
VI Dormire mentem ne sinas,

slapan   gylt   cunne
dormire culpa noverit,

þa clænan geleafa gecelende
castos   fides refrigerans

slæpes hætan   gemetegie
somni vaporem temperet.   24

bedæled andgite sliporum ɫ fulum
VII Exuta sensu lubrico

þe heortan deopnyssa swefnian
te cordis alta   somnient,

þæt ne feondes niþfulles facne
ne   hostis invidi *dolum

oga   þa gedefan aræ re
pavor quietos suscitet.   28

crist   uton biddan 7 fæder
VIII Christum rogemus   et patrem

cristes 7 fæderes   gast
Christi patrisque spiritum

ænne   mihtig geond ealle þing
unum potens per   omnia.

ó
gemunda þa bidd*e*ndan eala þu ðrynnes
Fove   precantes,   trinitas.   32

si hit swa
amen

I God, o creator of all things and ruler of the sky, who clothes the day
with beautiful light and invests night with the gracious gift of sleep,

II so that rest returns our limbs to their use in labour only after
relaxation and relieves the weary spirit and banishes anxious grief,

III we give you thanks, now that the day is ended, and our prayers at
nightfall, singing our songs of praise with devotion so that you may
assist the guilty.

IV May our song rise up to you from the depths of our hearts, may our
voice sound your praise melodiously. May our chaste love be devoted
to you, may our hearts adore you soberly

V so that our faith knows no shadows and night shines with light
before our faith, when the darkness of night in its profoundness
brings the close of day.

VI Do not allow the spirit to sleep; let it be guilt that learns to sleep.
May faith keep the chaste cool and control the steam and miasma of
sleep.

VII Free of our endangered perceptions, may we dream of you in the
depths of our hearts so that fear may not startle us from sleep by the
trickery of the envious Enemy.

VIII Let us pray to Christ and the Father and to the Spirit of Christ and of
the Father, a single being powerful in all things. Take under your
protection those who pray to you, o Trinity.

This hymn by St Ambrose of Milan was sung at the first Vespers of
Sunday, i.e. on Saturday. It replaced Hy 1 in summer. In the Old Hymnal
it was sung daily at Vespers; it is OHy 26. The metre is Ambrosian
iambic dimeter. No melody has been transmitted in Anglo-Saxon manuscripts. The text is included in the hymnals of the New Hymnal
BCDHVm, the *Expositio hymnorum* of the New Hymnal JVp and the Old
Hymnal manuscript A. There are two versions of the text in D and the

113

edition is based on D_1. Latin glosses and a Latin prose version accompany the text in D.

Bibliographical references: *ICL* no. 3544; *AH* 50, 13 (no. 7); Bulst, pp. 42 and 183 (II, 4), Walpole no. 5.

Apparatus to D   Latin text: Heading: *on 2r* i F *(i.e.* 1 Feria) *very faint and in Gothic lettering;* YMNUS AD VESPERAM] D_2, *in* D_1 *only a few traces of colour are left of the rubric;* 1 DEUS CREATOR OMNI-] *also in* Capitalis D_2; DEUS] Dds *a small circle in the initial may represent an abbreviation mark, the second* d *is damaged* D_1; 4 gratiae] *first a damaged* D_1, e *erased* D_2; 13 concinant] *second* n *damaged* D_1; 15 *beginning of 2v* D_2; 27 dolum] dolo, *second* o *altered from* u, *suspension mark erased above* D_2; 30 Christi] i *erased from* m D_2.

Old English gloss: 1 eala ... sceppend] *om.* D_2; 2 gefrætuigende] gefrætwigende D_2; 5 stilness] stylness D_2; 11 scildige] scyldige D_2; gefultumige] t *damaged* D_1; 13 niwolnyssum] nywolnyssum D_2; hleoþrion] hleoðrian D_2; 14 gedryme] gedreme D_2; 18 dimnyss] dimnys D_2; nyhta] nihta D_2; 24 gemetegie] he metegie D_2; 25 andgite] andgyte D_2; 31 mihtig] h *on erasure of* g *in lighter ink* D_1; 32 biddendan] e *badly damaged by hole* D_1.

Latin gloss: *Glosses by* D_1: 1 ó] *also by* D_2; 32 ó] *also by* D_2.

Glosses by D_4 *on fol.* 2: 1 s. ó *(Deus)* s. rerum 2 s. o *(rector)* ornans te dico 11 i. desideriis 13 intima 22 i. iubeas 25 *(Exuta)* ipsa dico 26 *(alta)* s. secreta.

Prose version by D_4 *in the margin:* I s. O deus omnium creator & poli rector vestiens cum decoro diem lumine et in noctem cum gratia soporis. II Solutos 's. *st' *(added in the margin with a caret mark)* artus ut reddat quies laboris usui 'et mentes fessas' *(added in the margin with a caret mark)* ille allevet & s. ille solvat ancxios & luctus. III Iam grates peracto die et preces exortu noctis cum votis ut tu adiuves reos & nos solvimus ymnum canentes. IV Te concinant cordis yma te canora vox concrepet te castus amor diligat te sobria mens *adorat *(corrected to* adoret *by suprascript* e). V Ut cum clauserit in profundo diem caligo noctium, et nesciat fides tenebras & nox luceat fidei. VI Ne sinas mentem dormire s. ne sinas dormire culpa noverit s. ne sinas castos fides refrigerans et s. *ille *(or* vie?) temperet somni vaporem. VII s. O homo esse te exuta lubrico sensu ne somnient cordis alta, ne invidi hostis dolo suscitet pavor (r *blotted*) quietos. VIII Rogamus Christum et patrem Christi et patris spiritum unum potens per omnia, fove precantes, s. o trinitas.

BVmCJVpHA   Heading: Hymnus ad vesperam. In sabbato sancto *B*, IN SABBATO YMNUS. AD VESPERAS *Vm*, HYMNUS DOMINICIS AD VESPERUM. SABBATO *C*, DEUS CREATOR *J*, *no rubric VpH*, HYMNUM VESPERTINUM *A*; 1 Deus] s *and contraction mark almost illegible H*; 2 vestiens] vestigens, g *expunged H*; 4 gratiae] gratia *BVmCJVpH*, gratiam, m *erased A*; 5 Artus] a *corrected from* Q *(?) by* V_1 Vm; solutos] solutus, us *abbreviated C; second* o *on erasure A*; 6 laboris] *om. JVp*, labores *with suprascript* i *by the glossator A*; 8 ancxios] anxios, *abbreviated* us *H*; 9 Grates] *corrected from* gratis *by glossator A*; iam] *om. JVp*; 10 exortu] exortum, m *expunged, probably by text hand A*; preces] a *(?) erased after* r *A*; 11 adiuves] adiubes *A*; 13 concinant] concinent *JVp*, concinat *H*, n *erased, but replaced by glossator A*; 14 concrepet] increpet *JVp*; 17 Ut] Et *BA, in B a later hand corrects to*

Ut; profundo] profunda *VmCJVpHA*; 20 fidei] fidelis *corrected from* fideli *by another hand* A; 21 sinas] sinat *C*; 22 culpa noverit] culpam noveris *JVpH*, culpam noverit, m *erased* A; 23 castos] castis *H*, castus *A*; refrigerans] refrigerens *J*; 26 somnient] sompniet, *corrected to* sompnient *by H₁ H*; 27 dolum] dolo *BVmCJVpHA*; 31 unum] unus *VmCJVpH*; 32 amen] *om. BC, A adds* Gloria tibi pater.

Commentary   Latin: 1 *Cf. II Maccabees I.24.* 2–3 *Cf. Ps. CIII.2, 6 and 19–20.* 4 gratiae *in D instead of* gratia *is unattested elsewhere and must be a mistake copied by D₂ from D₁ or their exemplar.* 11 *Cf.* voti reus *Virgil, Aeneis, V.237. Bulst reads* voti, *but* votis *is attested by* AH *for the Continent.* 17 Et *instead of* ut *is attested by* AH. *Bulst reads* profunda. 20 *Bulst reads* fide reluceat, *but* fidei *(and in one case* fideli*)* luceat *is attested by* AH *for the Continent.* 22 culpam *is attested for two continental manuscripts by* AH. 23 *Bulst reads* castis, *noting the variant reading* castos. 27 *Bulst reads* nec, *but* ne *is attested by* AH *for the Continent.* 28 *Cf.* quiesces et suavis erit somnus tuus, ne paveas repentino terrore *Prov. III.24–5.* 29 *Bulst reads* rogamus *as the Latin gloss, but notes* rogemus *as a variant reading.* Old English: 7 he *should be fem. and agree with* stilness. 13 niwolnyssum *should be nom. pl.*

3

YMNUS AD NOCTURNAM

s. die

on þam forman dæge dagena   ealra
I   PRIMO   DIERUM OMNIUM,

on þam middaneard wunað gesceapen
quo   mundus   extat condit*us*

oððe on þam þe arisende   scyppend
vel quo   resurgens conditor

us   deaþe   oferswiðdum alys*de*
nos morte vict*a*   liberet,   4

útanyddum feor   *slæw*þum
II   Pulsis   procul torporibus

uton arisan ealle   hrædlic*or*
surgamus omnes ocius

7   on nyhte uton secan   þone arfestan
& nocte   qu*e*ramus pium,

swa swa þone witegan we cunnon secan
sicut   prophetam novimus,   8

ure   bena   þæt he gehyre

III Nostras preces ut audiat

7 his   swiðran he aræce

suamque dextram porrigat,

þæt þa afeormodan fram horwum

ut expiatos   sordibus

he ageldað heofona   setlum

reddat   polorum sedibus,   12

þæt we þe   on þære halgestan

IV Ut quique sacratissimo

þises   dæges tide

huius diei tempore

on tidum gedefum we singað

horis   quietis psallimus,

mid selenum eadigum he gewelgie

donis   beatis muneret.   16

eallunga nu   þu fæderlice beorhtnyss

V [3r] Iam   nunc, paterna   claritas,

þe we biddaþ   genihtsumlice

te postulamus affatim,

aweggewite galnyss gehorwigende

absit   libido sordidans

7 ælc   dæd   derigendlic

omnisque actus noxius,   20

þæt ful ne sy oþþe slipor

VI Ne feda sit vel lubrica

gefegednyss ures   lichoman

conpago nostri corporis,

þurh þa   hylle   on fyrum

per quam averni ignibus

we selfe beoð forswælede teartlicor

ipsi crememur   acrius.   24

for þy   alysend   we biddaþ

VII Ob hoc, redemptor, quesumus,

þæt man ure   þu adilegie

ut probra nostra deluas,

lifes eces   behefnyssa

vitę perhennis commoda

us   welwillende þu þurhteo
nobis benignus conferas,   28

on þam flæsces fram dæde útlagan
VIII   Quo   carnis actu   exules

gewordene heo sylfe heofanbiggende
effecti   ipsi cęlibes,

swa swa we anbidiaþ   forþalotene
ut   prestolamur cernui,

lofu   we singan wuldres
melos canamus glorię.   32

getiþa   fæder þu arfæstesta
IX   Presta, pater piissime

7 fæder   gemaca   áncenneda
patrique compar unice

mid   gaste   frofer
cum spiritu paraclito

7   nu   7   on ecnysse
& nunc & in perpetuum.   36

si hit swa
amen

I On the first day of all, on which the world was altogether created and on which the creator risen again conquered death and freed us from it,

II let us all rise very quickly, completely shaking off lethargy, and let us seek at night the Mild One, as we know the Prophet to have done,

III so that he may hear our prayers, extend his right hand to us and return those who have been cleansed of filth to their seats in heaven

IV and that he may reward with blessed gifts all of us who sing at this most holy time of day during the quiet hours.

V Even now, Splendour of the Father, we plead with you eagerly that sullying lust and all harmful acts may be far from us

VI lest the confines of our body be disfigured or unsafe, for which we ourselves would be most fiercely burnt in the fires of Hell.

VII Therefore we ask you, Saviour, to wash away our sins, grant us the pleasures of eternal life with your goodwill

VIII so that we who were exiled because of the acts of the flesh shall become dwellers in heaven, as we humbly hope, and sing songs of praise.

IX Grant this, most loving Father, and you, Only-Begotten equal to the Father, together with the Holy Ghost now and in time everlasting.

This hymn was sung at Matins (Nocturn) on Sundays in winter. It is anonymous and written in Ambrosian iambic dimeter. The melody transmitted in C is Stäblein no. 410. The text is included in the hymnals of BCDHVm and the *Expositio hymnorum* JVp. In D there are again two versions of the hymn up to line 16 and the edition is based on D_1. There are Latin glosses in V and D; in D there is also a prose version of the hymn.

Bibliographical references: *ICL* no. 12515; *AH* 51, 24-6 (no. 23), Walpole no. 62.

Apparatus to D   Latin text: Heading: *om. D_2*; 2 conditus] -us *concealed by the tight binding D_1*; 3 conditor] r *concealed by the tight binding D_2*; 4 victa] a *completely faded D_1*; liberet] et *almost illegible D_1*; 5 torporibus] t *and* u *badly damaged D_1*; 7 quęramus] queramus D_2; 8 novimus] s *badly damaged D_1*; 11 expiatos] ex *added later by D_2 in D_2*; 12 sedibus] e *badly damaged D_1*; 23 quam] *the suspension mark apparently added after the glossing stage*; 26 deluas] i *written above* e *probably by D_4.*

Old English gloss: 3 þe] *om. D_2*; arisende] a *damaged or erased D_1*; 4 oferswiðdum] ð *badly damaged D_1*; alysde] de *missing or altogether faded D_1*; 5 útanyddum] útanyddum D_2, m *badly damaged D_1*; slæwþum] slæ *illegible*, m *badly damaged D_1*; 6 hrædlicor] cor *very faint*, or *illegible D_1*; 7 nyhte] nihte D_2; arfestan] arfæstan D_2; 9 gehyre] gehere D_2; 12 ageldað] *a* wynn erased between a *and* g D_2; 27 *the only Old English gloss by D_4*: hyðða *glossing* commoda.

D Latin gloss: *by D_4 on 2v*: 2 (*quo*) s. die 3 (*quo*) s. die 5 i. pigritiis 6 i. velocius 7 s. in *sorando s. deum 8 s. david quesisse s. *principe 10 i. suum s. ut adiutorium (*porrigat*) 11 i. purgatos de peccatis 12 s. nos 13 i. quicumque omnes s. nos dico s. in (*sacratissimo*) 15 s. & in nocturnis 'in tribulationibus' (*added in the margin*) 16 s. nos i. ditet 17 s. o (*claritas*) 18 s. assidue 19 s. a nobis 20 i. nocens 21 ut *turbis luxuriosa 22 *ondino (*above* conpago) s. corpus 23 's. peccata ł que' (*in the margin*) i. inferni *sale (*above* ignibus) 24 s. nos i. incendamur (i. incendamur *repeated and erased*) 25 propter hoc s. o (*redemptor*) i. rogamus 26 s. vitia i. purges 27 s. utilia 28 'i. & ut dones' (*gloss in the margin*) 29 s. de (*actu*) 'i. alieni nos dico' (*in the margin*, i *of* dico *expunged, suprascript* u) 30 i. facti s. nos i. *celeste 31 i. sicut i. humiles ł supplices 32 i. carmina s. tibi 33 s. o (*pater*) 34 s. o (*unice*).

Prose version in the margin by D_4: I Primo omnium dierum in quo *exta mundus conditus vel quo conditor resurgens nos liberet victa morte. II Procul pulsis torporibus surgamus omnes ocius et queramus nocte pium sicut novimus 's. querere' (*added above the line*) prophetam. III Nostras preces ut audiat & porrigat suam dextram ut expiatos s. á sordibus

118

polorum sedibus reddat. IV Ut quique in sacratissimo huius diei tempore in quietis horis psallimus cum beatis donis muneret. V Iam paterna nunc claritas te postulamus affatim absit sordidans libido et omnis actus noxius.

Probably by another hand on the lower margin, connected to line 7 by caret marks: media nocte surgebam ad confitendum tibi.

BVmCJVpH   *Heading and 1–22 erased J*; Heading: *no rubric BVpH*, YMNUS AD NOCTURNOS *Vm*, HYMNUS AD NOCTURNOS *C*; 4 liberet] liberat *Vm*; 7 nocte] *om. Vp*; 10 dextram] dexteram *CVp*; 11 ut] et *VmVpH*; expiatos] piatos *C*; 13 Ut] U *illegible Vm*; sacratissimo] *last letter erased C*; 17 Iam] *om. Vp*; 22 conpago] cumpago *C*; 23 per quam] *erased with the preceding lines J*; quam] -que *(abbreviated) Vm*, quem *H*; averni] averne *Vm*; 24 ipsi crememur] *erased with lines 1–22 J*; 25 quesumus] *om. J, om., space left for the word Vp*; 26 deluas] diluas *Vm*; 27 commoda] comoda *Vm*, commodet *H*; 28 benignus] benigne *C*; 31 prestolamur] r *suprascript V₁ Vm*; 32 canamus] camus *C*; 34–6 *om. C*; 34 patri-] patris- *BVmJVp*; 36 & nunc et in perpetuum] regnans per omne seculum *BVmJVpH; BJVpH add* Amen.

Vm Latin gloss: 1 principali i. die ymerarum singularum [*sic*] 2 constat (*one letter erased after* s) creatus ł cretus 3 aut s. in (*quo*) *omergens operator 4 mortales superata redimat 5 extrusis eminus desidiis 6 elevemus nos cuncti agilius 7 atque sub umbra requiramus clementem 8 ceu vatem scimus s. quesisse 9 oramina quatinus auscultet 11 purificatos i. mundatos s. ā ħ inmunditiis (*another* ħ *suprascript*) 12 recuperet i. restituat s. nos sedilibus 13 quatinus i. nos i. s. in sanctissimo 14 istius lucis hora 15 temporibus tacitis canimus 16 datibus felicibus ditet vel recompenset 17 hac hora i. s. o divina illustratio 18 te ipsum flagitamus abunde 19 desistat i. d... (*gap*) i. fedans commaculans 20 universaque actio nocuus 21 non fetida i. contaminata 22 compositio somatis 23 inferni i. herebi *flammeus 24 nos s. ut *conoremabimur durius ł rigidius 25 quapropter s.o. liberator supplicamus 26 quatinus deliquia i. purges 27 aeterna i. utilitatis ł benefi... (*rest of the word concealed in the binding*) 28 nos i. misericors i. *condonis & ut largiaris 29 quatinus humanitatis reatu alieni 30 facti nos *celestis 31 s. & sicut expectamus humiles 32 laudem modulemus *verationis.

Commentary   Latin: 4 *Cf. Hos. XIII.14*. AH *reads* liberat, *attesting* liberet *for continental manuscripts, too*. 6–8 *Cf. Ps. CXVIII.55–6 and 62. Verse 62 is quoted in the marginal gloss in D. The Psalmist – David – is the 'prophet'*. 11 AH *reads* et hic piatos, *attesting, however,* et expiatos *as the most widely spread reading*. 24 *For* conoremabimur *in the Latin gloss of Vm read* concremabimur. 26 AH *reads* diluas, *attesting also* deluas (*twice*). *The two words may not have been kept entirely distinct*. 30 *Cf. Matt. XXII.30*. 32 *For* verationis *in the Latin gloss of Vm read* venerationis.

4

YMNUS AD MATUTINAM

ó
eala þu ece   gescæfta   scyppend

I   ĘTERNĘ RERUM conditor,

nihte   7 dæg   þu þe gewissast
noctem diemque qui   regis

7 tidena   þu selst tida
& temporum das   tempora,

þæt þu geliðewæce aþrytnysse
ut alleves   fastidium,   4

bydel   dæges nu   swegð

II   Preco diei   iam sonat

nihte   deopre   þurhwacol
noctis profunde pervigil,

nyhtlic   leoht wegferendum
nocturna lux   viantibus

fram nyhte nyht   *asendrigende
a   nocte noctem segregat.   8

þisum astyred   dægsteorre

III   Hoc excitatus lucifer

tolysþ heofan   fram dymnisse
solvit polum caligine,

þysum ælc   gedweldra werod
hoc   omnis errorum   chorus

weg   to derigenne forlæt
viam nocendi   deserit,   12

þisum scypman mægnu gaderað

IV   Hoc nauta   vires   colligit

7 sæs   geliþewæcað brymmas
pontique mitescunt freta,

þisum se sylfa stan   gelaþunga
hoc   ipsa   petra aecclesiae

[3v] crawendum gylt   adyligode
canente   culpam deluit.   16

uton arisan eornostlice hrædlice

V   Surgamus ergo   strenue;

    hana   þa *licgenda awecð
gallus iacentes   excitat

    7 þa slapolan   he þreað
et somnolentos increpat.

    cocc   þa wiþsacendan cit
Gallus negantes   arguit.   20

    hanan crawendan hopa *gehwerþ
VI **Gallo canente spes redit,**

    adligum hæl bið ongeangesend
aegris salus refunditur,

    swurd   scaðan   byþ behydd
mucro latronis conditur,

    aslidenum geleafa ongeangecerryd
lapsis fides revertitur.   24

    ó
    eala þu hælend þa ætslidan beheald
VII   **Iesu,   labentes respice**

    7 us   geseonde gerihtlæc
& nos videndo corrige!

    gef þu behealdst slidas   feallaþ
Si respicis, lapsus cadunt

    7 mid wope gylt   byþ tolysed
fletuque culpa solvitur.   28

    þu leoht scin   andgitum
VIII **Tú lux refulge sensibus**

    7 modes   slæp   tosceac
mentisque somnum discute!

    þe ure   stefn ærest   swege
Te nostra vox primum sonet

    7 behat we tolesan þe
& vota solvamus tibi.   32

    gode fæder sy wuldor
Deo patri sit gloria

I O eternal creator of the material world, you who rule night and day and appoint their time to the seasons to relieve us from monotony,

II now the herald of day is audible, who was watchful throughout the unfathomable night and, as a light at night to the wayfarers, divided night from night.

III Woken by him, the morning star frees the sky of darkness. Because of him, the whole band of errors leaves the path of harmful action.

IV Because of him the sailor gathers strength and the expanses of sea grow mild. When he, the herald, crowed, the Rock himself, the foundation of the Church, washed guilt away by his weeping.

V Therefore let us arise with vigour. The cock is waking up the lie-abeds and chiding the sleepy. The cock is accusing those who practise denial.

VI When the cock crows, there is hope again; health is restored to the sick, the dagger of the robber is sheathed and faith returns to the fallen.

VII Jesus, take heed of those who falter and correct us as you watch over us. If you watch over us, the fall itself falls away and guilt is washed away with tears.

VIII Shine as a light in our perceptions and drive away the somnolence of the spirit. Our voice shall name you first of all and we shall pay our devotions to you.

This hymn was sung at Sunday Lauds in winter. In the Old Hymnal it was a Matins hymn; it is OHy 2. It is by St Ambrose of Milan and is written in Ambrosian iambic dimeter. The melody transmitted in C is so far unidentified. The text is included in the hymnals of BCDHVm and the *Expositio hymnorum* of JVp. There are Latin glosses in D and Vm; in D there is also a Latin prose version of stanza IV. The first three lines in Vm have been glossed with an Old English gloss related to the one in D.

Bibliographical references: *ICL* no. 421; *AH* 50, 11 (no. 4); Bulst, pp. 39 and 182 (II, 1).

Apparatus to D   Latin text: 8 segregat] t *by D₂ on erasure.*

Latin gloss: *By D₄*: 1 deus pater 3 s. qui mutationum vicissitudines 4 leves (*fastidium*) s. hominum 5 i. gallus allegorice Christus 6 i. presentis seculi ignorantie i. tenebrose 7 i. mundana claritas peregrinantibus 9 (*Hoc*) s. precone sonante i. vocatus i. illuminatio fidei 10 purgat 11 s. *precon sonante i. peccatorum multitudo 12 i. iter nobis (*nocendi*) i. relinquit 13 (*Hoc*) s. precone sonante quilibet rector ecclesie 14 i. maris ł mundi mansuescunt i. maria ł unde 15 (*hoc*) s. precone i. infirmitas *sclicet petrus 16 (*culpam*) s. negationis per penitentiam & fletum 17 i. agiliter 18 s. nos s. sua admonitione 20 s. surgere *tebra adoratione 21 i. Christo i. predicante (*spes*) s. salutis 22 tristibus ł tyriosis i.

restauratur 23 (*mucro*) qui morte nudatur i. diaboli 24 (*lapsis*) in peccato i. peccantibus ł
*ress s. resurgenda penitendo redit 25 s. nos in fide 26 i. castiga sic fecisti patrum in
passione 27 i. peccata 28 (*fletuque*) nostro expiatur 29 s. o (*lux*) (*sensibus*) s. nostris 30 anime
pigritiam aufer 31 i. ante omnia s. iam 32 i. preces nos reddamus.

Prose version of stanza IV in the margin of 3r: Canente gallo ille qui navigat resumit vires
*cio appropinquare diem et tunc quiescit mare. Canente *galla flevit Petrus et flendo lavit
culpam negationis.

BVmCJVpH   Heading: Ymnus ad Matutinam *B, no rubric VmpH,* YMNUS AD
MATUTINUM *C,* ETERNE RERUM CONDITOR *J;* 5 sonat] sonet *JVpH;* 6 profunde]
profundo *H;* 8 a] ac *JVp;* 9 excitatus] excitato *B, two letters (*er, ci*?) erased after* ex *at the end
of a line J, space for two letters Vp;* 17 strenue] *added above by* V_1 *VmVp,* strennue *CJH;* 19
somnolentos] *originally* sompnolentes, *second* e *corrected to* o *by* V_1 *Vm,* sompnolentes *H,*
somnolentes *J;* 20 arguit] arguat *H;* 23 latronis conditur] lacronis conditor *H;* 24
revertitur] *by another hand (?) H;* 25 labentes] paventes *B;* 26 corrige] corrigi *C;* 27 lapsus]
laxus *Vm;* 29 refulge] refulget *C;* 30 mentis-] mentes- *C;* somnum] somnium *J;* 33 *B adds:*
eiusque soli filio / cum spiritu paraclyto / et nunc et in perpetuum // Amen. *Vm adds:*
eiusque soli filio.

Vm Old English gloss: 1 eala] *without corresponding Latin lemma* o *by* V_1; gescæfta]
gesceafta; 2 7 dæg] dæig 7; gewissast] gewissat; 3 *gloss ends with* tidena; *from here on the
Latin text is entered at every line, whereas before every second line was left for the gloss.*

Vm Latin gloss: 1 s. o sempiterne naturarum 2 qui gubernas 3 s. qui horarum *confer
horas 4 ut leve facias tedium 5 nuntius modo canit 6 intime ł alte (*noctis*) pernox 7 lumen
iterantibus ł viatoribus 8 separans 9 (*Hoc*) s. precone phosphorus 10 relaxat obscuratione 11
(*hoc*) s. precone *excitate vitiorum grex ł cetus 12 studium *pecandi amittit 13 (*hoc*) s.
precone *excitato virtutes *congeris 14 ponti mansuescunt cerula (*one letter erased after* e) 15
(*hoc*) s. precone s. gallo ipse petrus pastor ęcclesię 16 resonantę maculam abluit (*followed by
erasure of one letter*) 17 erigamus nos *era (*above* ergo) naviter 18 alier *pulsantes excitatos
reddit 19 *desidiosus ammonet 20 nolentes surgere corripit 21 *resonantes fiducia *affuit
22 egrotis medicina s. & restituitur 23 ensis ł gladius furis s. & occulitur ł occultatur 24
peccatis virtus s. & redditur 25 s. o salvator ruentes conspice ł intuere 26 (*nos*) s. *labentus
miserendo emenda 27 si videris s. nos crimina cadunt ł evanescunt 28 planctu crimen
donatur 29 s. o iubar resplende s. nostris ingeniis 30 cordis *pigruum excute 31 laus
*dignis i.e. *optimuum laudet 32 desideria persolvamus.

Commentary   Latin: 8 *The original reading of D was probably* segregans, *as in the gloss and
in BVmCJVpH.* 12 *Bulst reads* vias, *but AH attests* viam *in continental manuscripts.* 15–16 *Cf.
Luke XXII.60-2, Matt. XVI.18–19.* 15 *Bulst reads* ipse, *AH attests* ipsa *for two continental
manuscripts.* 16 *Bulst reads* diluit. 20 *For* tebra *in D's Latin gloss read* crebra. 24 *For* ress *in
D's Latin gloss read* reis. 25 *Cf.* Dominus respexit Petrum *Luke XXII.61. Bulst reads*
labantes, *noting the variant readings* labentes *and* paventes. *Old English:* 18 *For* licgenda *read*
licgendan.

5

[3r] YMNUS AD NOCTURNAM

I on nyhte arisende   uton wacian ealle
   NOCTE SURGENTES   vigilemus omnes,

   symle   on sealmsangum   uton smeagen and
   semper in psalmis   meditemur atque

   mid mægenum eallum   drihtne uton singan
   viribus   totis   domino canamus

   werodlice lofsangas
   dulciter ymnos,   4

II þæt þam arfæstan cyninge   samod singende
   Ut pio   regi   pariter canentes

   mid hys halgum   we geearnian healle
   cum suis sanctis   mereamur aulam

   ingan   heofones   samod 7 eadig
   ingredi caeli,   simul & beatam

   adreogan lif
   ducere vitam.   8

III getiþe þæt us   godcundnes sy eadige
   Prestet hoc nobis   deitas   beata

   fæderes 7 suna   7 samod   þæs halgan
   patris & nati   pariterque sancti

   gastes   ðæs   hlynþ on eallum
   spiritus, cuius   reboat in om*ni*

   wuldor middanearde
   gloria mundo.   12

   sy hit swa
   AMEN

I Let us rise up at night and let us all wake. Let us all meditate
   singing psalms and let us sweetly sing hymns to the Lord with all
   our might,

II so that by singing together for the gracious King we may deserve to
   enter the court of heaven with his saints and to lead happy lives with
   them.

III May the blessed Deity grant us this, the Father, the Son and also the
   Holy Ghost, whose glory resounds throughout the world. Amen.

This hymn replaces Hy 3 as the hymn for Sunday Matins (Nocturn) in summer, as implied by the 'item' of B's rubric; see above, pp. 24–5. It is anonymous, although Alcuin has been suggested as its author. Its metre, Sapphic stanza, is unusual for a ferial hymn. No melody has been transmitted from Anglo-Saxon manuscripts. The text is included in the hymnals of BCDHVm and the *Expositio hymnorum* of JVp and glossed in Latin in D and Vm.

Bibliographical references: *ICL* no. 10238; *AH* 51, 26–7 (no. 24), Walpole no. 63.

Apparatus to D   Latin text: 7 &] ac *written above, possibly by* D_4.
  Latin gloss: *by* D_4 1 s. in (*Nocte*) s. nos (*surgentes*) 2 laudibus 4 laudes 5 (*regi*) s. nostro concorditer s. nos (*canentes*) 7 intrare s. mereamur s. ut *adiutem 8 (*vitam*) omnium bonorum 11 i. resonatur.

  BVmCJVpH   Heading: Item ymnus ad nocturnam *B*, YMNUS AD NOCTURNOS *Vm*, HYMNUS AD NOCTURNUM *C*, NOCTE SURGENTES *J*, *no rubric VpH*; 2 meditemur] meditemut *Vm*; 4 ymnos] ymnus *C*; 7 &] ac *JVp*, ad *H*; 11 reboat] *interlined above by* J_1 (*before the glossing had taken place*) *J*, roboat *C*; amen] *not in BVmCJVp, but in H*.
  Vm Latin gloss: 1 s. hora noctis lectulo amonentes exsurgentes cuncti 2 iugiter psalmodiis (*corrected from* psaalmodiis*)* rimemur ł scrutemur necne 3 fortitudinibus *cantu persolvamus 4 ameniter laudes 5 sereno bono uná modulantes transigere omne tempus 6 ut merita habeamini 7 intrare poli pariter 9 annuat istud divinitas 10 genitoris ac geniti simulque 11 flaminis intonat in universo 12 *lauus honor sic fiat.

Commentary   Latin: 1 amonentes *in the Latin gloss to Vm may render the exhortative mode of* surgamus. 3 viribus totis *cf. Luke X.27.* 7 *The correction to* ac *in D agrees with JVp, cf. also H.* 12 sic fiat *in the Latin gloss to Vm apparently glosses* amen, *but the lemma is not in Vm, which indicates that the gloss is a copy.*

6

YMNUS AD MATUTINAM

efne   nu   nihte   ys aþinnod sceadu
I   ECCE IAM NOCTIS   tenuatur umbra,
leohtes dægrima   glitinigende scinþ
  lucis aurora   rutilans   coruscat;
mid hogungum eallum   uton biddan ealle
  nisibus   totis   rogitemus omnes

þæne ælmihtigan
cunctipotentem. 4

þæt god ure gemiltsod ælce
II [4r] Ut deus nostri miseratus omnem

he adræfe adle he forgyfe hæle
pellat languorem, tribuat salutem,

he selle 7 fæder mid arfæstnysse us
donet & patris pietate nobis

ricu heofona
regna polorum. 8

getiþie þæt us
Prestet hoc nobis

I Behold, how the darkness of night is thinning now and daybreak is glinting, shining red with its light. Let us all with all our heart pray to the Almighty

II that God be merciful on us and that he may drive away all illness and grant us health and that with the love of a father he may give us the kingdom of heaven.

This hymn replaces Hy 4 at Lauds on Sunday during the summer, see above, pp. 24–5. It is linked to the preceding Hy 5 by metre (Sapphic stanza), number of stanzas and liturgical function and is presumably by the same anonymous author. No melody has been transmitted from Anglo-Saxon manuscripts. Hy 6 is included in the hymnals of BCDHVm and the *Expositio hymnorum* of JVp and glossed in Latin in D and Vm.

Bibliographical references: *ICL* no. 4156; *AH* 51, 31–2 (no. 31), Walpole, no. 70.

Apparatus to D Latin gloss: *by D₄* 2 i. prima apparitio dei i. splendet 4 s. secundum 6 s. a nobis infirmitatem ł angorem 7 paterna *clementiam.

BVmCJVpH Heading: hymnus ad matutinam *B*, YMNUM AD LAUDES *Vm*, HYMNUS AD MATUTINUM *C*, ECCE IAM NOCTIS *J*, *no rubric VpH*; 2 aurora] a *on erasure by another hand (not mentioned by Gneuss) J*; 5 nostri miseratus] *om. Vp*; nostri] noster *H*; 6 languorem] languore *C*; tribuat salutem] *om. Vp*; tribuat] tribut *B*; 7 donet et patris pietate nobis] *thus also B*, donet et nobis pietate patris *Vm*, donet et nobis pietate sola *JVpH* (*JVp with the sequence re-arranged according to prose) as well as C, but the latter with the wrong initial:* Nonet *etc.*; 9 *om. JVp*; *Vm adds*: deitas beata.

Vm Latin gloss: 1 hac hora nunc comminuitur ł minuatur (*umbra*) ł scena ł figura ł obscura 2 (*lucis*) ł phosphori (*misplaced above* umbra) (*aurora*) matutina splendens relucet (*one letter erased after* re) 3 conatibus ł.ł conaminibus. flagitemus universi 4 omnes tonantem 5 quatinus misericors factus 6 expellat marcorem concedat s. nobis sanitatem 7 conferat s. pro clementia s. sua 8 gaudia cęlorum.

Commentary   Latin: 2 aurora ... rutilans *cf. Hy 72/1.* 3 nisibus totis *cf. Hy 5/3.* 5 *H's* noster *is paralleled on the Continent.*

7

YMNUS AD PRIMAM

eallunga leohtes   upaganum tungle
I   IAM   LUCIS   ORTO   SIDERE

god   uton biddan eadmodlice
deum precemur supplices,

þæt on dægþerlicum dædum
ut in diurnis   actibus

us   he gehealde fram derigendlicum
nos servet   a   nocentibus;   4

tungan   geweldende he gemetegige
II   Linguam refrenans temperet,

þæt ne sace oga   onswege
ne   litis horror insonet,

gesihþe gehleowende he *þurhteo
visum fovendo   contegat,

þæt heo ne idelnysse   hlade
ne   vanitates hauriat.   8

beon clæne heortan incundnessa
III   Sint pura cordis intima

aweggewite 7 gewitleast
absistat   & vechordia,

flæsces tobryte modignesse
carnis terat   superbiam

drences and metes spearness
potus cibique   parcitas,   12

þæt þænne dæg aweggewít
IV   Ut cum dies abscesserit

127

7 nihte hlot ongeanbringþ
noctemque sors reduxerit,

middaneardes þurh forhæfednysse
mundi per abstinentiam

*hy selfe singan wuldor
ipsi canamus gloriam.   16

gode fæder sy wuldor
Deo patri sit gloria

I As the daystar has now risen, let us pray humbly to God that he may preserve us from harm in our daily activities.

II May he bridle our tongue and teach it moderation to prevent horrible strife from noisily arising. May he protect and shield our sight from perceiving vain things.

III May the heart be pure within and may foolishness be far from us. May the sparing use of meat and drink crush the pride of the flesh

IV in order that, when day is departed and fate has brought night back again, we may be cleansed by our abstinence (*or*: empowered by our withdrawal from the world) and sing his glory.

This hymn is to be sung at Prime daily throughout the year. It is an old hymn, cited by Cassiodor, was possibly part of the Old Hymnal (OHy 16) and was taken over into the New Hymnal from the beginning. It is an anonymous hymn. It is in Ambrosian iambic dimeter. No melody is transmitted from Anglo-Saxon manuscripts. Hy 7 is included in the hymnals BCDHVm, the *Expositio hymnorum* JVp and in E. It is glossed in Latin in D and Vm.

Bibliographical references: *ICL* no. 7500; *AH* 51, 40-1 (no. 41), Walpole, no. 81.

Apparatus to D Latin gloss: *by* D_4 1 diei i. sole 3 i. *dialibus 4 i. custodiat s. ipse deus s. actibus. 5 (*Linguam*) s. nostram s. ipse deus (*temperet*) 7 i. protegendo s. ipse deus i. cooperiat 8 s. ille visus (*vanitates*) i. videat. 9 i. casta (*intima*) interiora i. secretius 10 (*vechordia*) i. dementia mala mortalitas 11 (*terat*) i. domet 14 s. tui vicissitudo (*misplaced above* noctemque) 15 casti i. nitidi 16 (*ipsi*) s. nos s. deo (*canamus*).

BVmCJVpHE Heading: Ymnus ad primam *B*, YMNUS AD PRIMAM *VmC*, IAM LUCIS *J*, AD PRIMAM *Vp*, *no rubric H*, Incipit ymnus ad primam horam *E*; 2 precemur]

precamur *E*; 3 in] *letters illegible to me, but Lindelöf has the word E*; 4 a nocentibus] annocentibus *CJ*; 5 Linguam re-] *illegible according to Lindelöf, but can be seen with the help of ultraviolet light, except for* L *E*; 6 insonet] insonat *E*; 7 visum] *just legible, illegible according to Lindelöf E*; 8 vanitates] vanitatis *CH*; 11 terat] terret *E*; superbiam] superbia *CH*; 13 Ut] Et *Vp*; abscesserit] abscescerit, c *expunged B*; 14 sors] sol, s *altered from* r, *one letter erased after the word (alterations not mentioned by Lindelöf) E*; reduxerit] *in red uncials on erasure E*; 15 abstinentiam] abstinemtiam *Vm*, abstinentia *C*; 16 gloriam] gloria *C*; 17 *om. JVp*; Deo] ō *Vm; E continues*: eiusque soli filio / cum spiritu paraclito / nunc et in perpetuum / regnat per omne seculum.

Vm Latin gloss: 1 ecce luminis exorta iubare 2 postulemus summissi 3 quatinus in diurnalibus factibus 4 custodiat a nocuis ł a nocituris. 5 membrum loquele (*first* e *on erasure*) restringens ut mensuret 6 seditionis pavor resonet 7 (*visum*) luminum favendo ut emendet 8 (*vanitates*) ineptias 'ł fatuitates' (*mistakenly placed above* contegat) admittat ł videat 'hunc oculis ' (*in the margin, mistakenly directed for insertion in the line below*) 9 fiunt munda interna 10 discedat amentia 11 contumaciam 12 poculi & esce frugalitas 13 quando recesserit 15 per parsimoniam 16 (*ipsi*) sibi modulemus laudem.

In the right margin the words Virgilius Haurit *and* locum vicem *are written.*

Commentary   Latin: 5 linguam refrenans *cf. Ps. XXXIII.14, Jas. I.26.* 8 *According to* AH *CH's* vanitatis *is paralleled in one continental manuscript – a partitive genitive or a reflection of the Vulgar Latin sound change of* -is *to* -es? 9 cordis intima *cf.* cordis yma *Hy 2/13.* 17 *E's doxology combines two alternative fourth lines; it can hardly have been sung in this form. The marginal comment in Vm appears to be a reference to Virgil,* Aeneis, *IV.661:* hauriat hunc oculis ignem crudelis ab alto *and to refer to* hauriat *in line 8. Old English:* 7 he þurhteo *means 'may he carry through, perpetrate' instead of 'may he cover, protect'. The inaccuracy may be due to the fact that* fovendo *means roughly the same as* contegat *and the glossator did not wish to use the same gloss twice; another possibility is that the glossator misunderstood the text and assumed that God was asked to confer sight, not blindness (to the world), as blindness usually stands for sin in these texts.* 15 *Note that* mundi *is ambiguous and may also be the nom. pl. of the adjective meaning 'clean'; it is glossed as such in the Expositio gloss.* 16 ipsi *is glossed without regard to the context; it should be* we selfe.

8

YMNUS AD TERTIAM

ó

nu   eala þu halige   us   gast

I   NUNC   SANCTE NOBIS SPIRITUS,

an   fæderes mid suna

unus patris cum filio,

gemedema hræd   beon ongebroht

dignare promptus ingeri

129

urum   geondgoten breoste
nostro refusus   pectori.   4
muð tunge   mod   andget *srængþ

II   Os, lingua, mens, sensus, vigor
andetnysse   swege
confessionem personet,
byrne ł bladesige on fyre   soþlufu
flammascat   igne karitas,
ontende   ferwyt ł bryne neoxtan
accendat ardor   proximos.   8

getiþa   fæder þu arfæstesta
Presta, pater piissime

I   Holy Spirit, you who are One, both of the Father and the Son, deign now readily to enter our breast and to fill it.

II   May our mouth, tongue and mind, our thought and our energy all together resound confessing you. May charity burn within us as with fire; may our ardour kindle the enthusiasm of our neighbours.

Hy 8 was sung daily at Tierce, except for the seasons when other hymns were provided for the Hour, Lent and Pentecost. It is anonymous and is in Ambrosian iambic dimeter. No melody has been transmitted from Anglo-Saxon manuscripts. It is included in hymnals BCDHVm and the *Expositio hymnorum* JVp and is glossed in Latin in Vm.

Bibliographical references: *ICL* no. 10768; *AH* 50, 19-20 (no. 18), Walpole, no. 16.

BVmCJVpHE   Heading: Hymnus ad tertiam *B*, AD TERTIAM YMNUS *Vm*, HYMNUS AD TERTIAM *C*, NUNC SANCTE NOBIS *J*, *no rubric VpH*, Incipit ad tertiam horam ymnus *E*; 1 SPIRITUS] spiritu *C*; 4 pectori] pectore *E*; 5 lingua] *one letter* (m.?) *erased after the word Vm*; mens, sensus] mensensus *CH*; 6 confessionem] confessione *C*; personet] personent *Vm*; 7 flammascat] flammescat *B*, flamescat *VmCJVpE*; 8 accendat] ascendat *C*; proximos] proximus *C*; 9 *om. JVp, E continues:* Patrisque compar unice / cum spiritu paraclito / et nunc et in perpetuum.

Vm Latin gloss: 1 modo s. o agie pneuma eo quod 3 dignum ducas citius illabi ł 4 remissus cordi 5 oscillum lingula ingenium robur 6 fidem orthodoxam concrepet 7 calescat lare ł foco amor 8 inflammet incensio omnes mortales.

Commentary   Latin: 6 *Vm's* personent *agrees with* AH; *however* personet *is also attested there.* 7 flammescere *is the classical form; cf.* L. Dieffenbach, Novum Glossarium Latino-

Germanicum mediae et infimae aetatis *(Frankfurt-on-Main 1867) s. v.* flammascere. Old
English: 5 *For* sræng read stræng.

9

YMNUS AD SEXTAM

ó   ó

eala þu reccend mihtig   eala þu soþfæsta god

I   RECTOR POTENS,   VERAX DEUS,

þu þe gemetegast gescæfta gewrixl

qui temperas rerum vices,

mid beorhtnyssa ærnemergen þu *tihst

splendore   mane   instruis

7 mid fyrum middæg

& ignibus meridiem.   4

adwæsc   lias   saca ł ceasta

II   [4v] Extingue flammas litium,

afyrsa hætan   derigendlice

aufer calorem noxium,

þurhteo hæle   lichomena

confer salutem corporum

7 soþe   sibbe   heortena

veramque pacem cordium.   8

getiþa   fæder þu arfæstesta

Presta, pater piissime

I Mighty ruler, truthful God, you who govern change in the things of
the world, you array morning in its splendour and midday in its fiery
heat.

II Extinguish the flames of discord and banish the hurtful heat, grant
us the health of our bodies and true peace in our hearts.

This hymn was sung daily at Sext except during Lent and at Pentecost and
goes back to the times of the Old Hymnal (OHy 20). It is anonymous and
written in Ambrosian iambic dimeter. No melody has been transmitted in
the Anglo-Saxon manuscripts. The text is included in the hymnals of
BCDHVm, the *Expositio hymnorum* JVp and the entries by Aldred in the
'Durham Ritual' (E).

Bibliographical references: *ICL* no. 14075; *AH* 50, 20 (no. 19); Walpole no. 17.

Apparatus to D   Latin text: 7 corporum] *corrected by D₁ from* corporem *by suprascript* u.

BVmCJVpHE   Heading: Ymnus ad sextam *B*, YMNUS AD SEXTAM *Vm*, HYMNUS AD SEXTAM *C*, RECTOR POTENS *J, no rubric VpH*, Incipit ymnus ad sextam horam *E*; 2 temperas] a *altered from* e *by H₁ H*; vices] vice *C*; 3 splendore] splendorem *E*; 4 meridiem] eri *illegible E*; 5 Extingue] extinge *E*; flammas] flamas *C*; 6 aufer] confer, *struck through and corrected to* aufer *in Gothic cursive Vm*; calorem] calore *C*; 7 salutem] salute *C*; 8 cordium] concordiam *E*; 9 *om. JVp, VmC omit* piissime. *E is very indistinct. Lindelöf reads*: presta pater piissime / patrisque compar unice / cum spiritu. . . *The last line may read*: & s̄ p̄ am *(et spiritus paraclitus amen)*.

Commentary   Latin: 5 *With* flammas litium *cf. Ecclesiasticus XXVIII.11*: homo enim iracundus incendit litem. Old English: 3 tihst *cannot be from defective* *teogan *(SB §415e), 'to arrange', as that is a weak verb ii; it must be from* teon *and mean 'you educate', which is inappropriate for* instruis *here.*

10

YMNUS AD NONAM

     ó
 gescæfta eala þu god fæsthafol strængþ
I RERUM DEUS, TENAX VIGOR

 unastyrod on þe þurhwunað
 inmotus in te permanet

 leohtes dægþerlices tida
 lucis diurnę tempora

 mid æfterfyligendnyssum geendigende
 successibus   determinans;   4

 forgyf beorhtne æfen
II Largire clarum vespere,

 on þam lif *næfre ne fealle
 quo vita nusquam decidat,

 ac mede   deaþes haliges
 sed pręmium mortis sacrę

 ece   onwunige wuldor
 perennis instet gloria.   8

 getiþa fæder þu arfæstesta
 Presta, pater piissime

132

I God of all things in the world, in you an enduring force is lodged forever, immovable, determining the periods of daylight in their sequence.

II Grant us a clear evening so that life may not fail at any point, but let everlasting glory then be imminent, the reward for a holy death.

This hymn was sung daily at None except in Lent and at Pentecost. It is anonymous and written in Ambrosian iambic dimeter. No melody has been transmitted in Anglo-Saxon manuscripts. The text is included in the hymnals of BCDHVm, the *Expositio hymnorum* JVp and the entries by Aldred in the 'Durham Ritual' (E).

Bibliographical references: *ICL* no. 14183; *AH* 50, 20 (no. 20); Walpole no. 18.

BVmCJVpHE   Heading: Hymnus ad nonam *B*, AD NONAM HYMNUS *Vm*, HYMNUS AD NONAM *C*, RERUM DEUS *J*, *no rubric* VpH, Incipit ymnus ad nonam horam *E*; 2 permanet] t *altered to* ns *probably by the corrector of Hy 9/6 Vm*, permanens *JVpE*, permanes *H*; 4 determinans] *so E, Lindelöf wrongly has* diterminans; 5 vespere] vesperi *J*, vesperum *E*; 6 vita] vitam *H*; 8 perennis] perennet, *corrected to* is *possibly by another hand C*; instet] instat *E*; 9 *om. JVp; E adds*: patrisque compar unice / cum spiritu paraclito / et nunc et in perpetuum // amen *with* amen *possibly by another hand.*

Commentary   Latin: 2 *Cf. Wisdom, VII.27. JVpE's reading* permanens *agrees with* AH, *which also reports* permanet *in continental manuscripts.* Old English: 4 æfterfyligendnyssum *is a hapax legomenon, presumably a nonce formation.* 6 næfre *may render* nunquam, *which is a reading attested by AH, but not found in Anglo-Saxon manuscripts.*

11

YMNUS AD COMPLETORIUM

þe   leohtes ær   geendunge
I   TE LUCIS ANTE TERMINUM,

gescæfta scyppend we biddaþ
rerum creator, poscimus,

þæt gewunelicre mildheortnyssa
ut solita   clementia

þu sy wealdend to heordrædene
sis presul ad custodiam.   4

feor   aweggewitan swefna
II Procul recedant   somnia

7 nihta   gedwymeru
& noctium fantasmata

7 feond   urne   ofþrece ł ofsete
hostemque nostrum comprime,

þæt ne beon besmitene lichoman
ne   polluantur   corpora.   8

               ó
getiða   fæder eala þu ælmihtiga
III Presta, pater   omnipotens,

þurh hælend crist   drihten
per Iesum Christum dominum,

þe   mid þe on ecnyssa
qui tecum in perpetuum

rixað   mid halgan gaste
regnat cum sancto spiritu.   12

                                    amen.

I Before the end of daylight, Creator of all things, we ask you to watch
over us, to guard us with your accustomed mercy.

II Let the dreams and illusions of the nights withdraw far away and
crush our enemy so that our bodies shall not be soiled.

III Grant this, almighty Father, by the Lord Jesus Christ, who reigns
with you in eternity together with the Holy Ghost.

This hymn was sung daily at Compline in summer, alternating with Hy
12 in winter. In H, the non-monastic hymnal, however, the arrangements
for Compline are more complex and Hy 11 is often restricted to weekdays.
It is anonymous and written in Ambrosian iambic dimeter with a
rhythmical doxology (4 × 8pp). The hymn goes back to the period of the
Old Hymnal (OHy 31). No melody has been transmitted in the Anglo-
Saxon manuscripts. The text is included in the hymnals of BCDHVm, the
Expositio hymnorum JVp and Aldred's entries in the 'Durham Ritual' (E).

Bibliographical references: *ICL* no. 16086; *AH* 51, 42–3 (no. 44);
Walpole no. 83.

Apparatus to D   Latin text: 6 noctium] c *suprascript by D₁, t on erasure.*

BVmCJVpHE   Heading: Ymnus ad completorium *B*, YMNUS AD COMPLETORIUM *Vm*, ALIA HYMNUS AD COMPLETORIUM *C*, TE LUCIS ANTE TERMINUM *J, no rubric VpH*, Ymnus ad complendum *E*; 3 custodiam] custodia *C*; 6 noctium] noxium *CE*; 8 ne] nec *C*; polluantur] pulluantur *B*; 9 omnipotens] piissime *E*; 11 perpetuum] perpetuo *E*; 12 sancto spiritu] spiritu sancto, *but order reversed by suprascript signs H*; amen] *om. VmCJ.*

Commentary   Latin: *The reasons for C's heading* ALIA *is that Hy 11 follows Hy 12 here. 3* solita *is a metrical irregularity. 5–9 Cf. Hy 140/13–16, Hy 2/27–8, 34/3.*

12

YMNUS AD COMPLETORIUM

ó
eala þu crist   þu þe leoht   eart 7   dæg
I   CHRISTE,   QUI LUX ES ET DIES,

neahte þeostru   þu *oferhelast
noctis tenebras detegis

7 leohtes leoht   þu eart gelyfed
lucisque lumen crederis

leoht   eadig   bodiende
lumen beatum predicans,   4

ó
we biddaþ eala þu halga drihten
II   Precamur,   sanctę domine,

bewere   us   on þissere nyhte
defende nos in hac   nocte.

sy us   on þe rest
Sit nobis in te requies;

gedyfe   nihte   forgyf
quietam noctem tribue,   8

þæt ne hefi   slæp   onhreose
III   Ne   gravis somnus irruat

þæt ne feond   us   undercreope
[5r] nec   hostis nos subripiat

þæt ne flæsc him geðafigende
nec   caro illi consentiens

135

us þe scyldige gesette
nos tibi reos   statuat.   12

eagan slæp   underfon
IV Oculi somnum capiant –

heorte to ðe æfre   wacige
cor   ad te semper vigilet.

swiðra þin gescilde
Dextera tua protegat

þeowan   þa ðe þe lufigað
famulos, qui te diligunt.   16

bewerigend ure   beseoh
V Defensor noster, aspice,

þa serwiendan ofþrice
insidiantes   reprime;

begém   þine þenas
guberna tuos famulos,

þa ða mid blode *þa gebohtest
quos sanguine mercatus es.   20

                              o
gemun þu ure   eala ðu drihten
VI Memento nostri,   domine,

on swarran þisum lichoman
in gravi isto corpore.

*þa ðe eart bewerigend sawle
Qui es defensor animę,

ætbeo þu us   drihten
adesto   nobis, domine.   24

gode fæder sy wuldor
Deo patri sit gloria

I Christ, you who are both light and day, you who draw away the shadows of the night and are believed to be the light of light itself, you who proclaim the light of bliss,

II we pray to you, holy Lord, protect us this night. May we find rest in you; grant us a quiet night,

III that sleep may not fall on us heavily nor the enemy creep up on us nor the flesh consent to him and thus proclaim us guilty before your eyes.

IV Let the eyes take their rest – may our heart always stay wakeful for you. May your right hand protect your servants, who love you.

V You who are our protector, watch us and hold off from us those who are plotting against us; guide your servants, whom you have purchased with your blood.

VI Keep us in mind, Lord, in this body which weighs on us. You who are the protector of the soul, be with us, o Lord.

This hymn was sung daily at Compline in winter, alternating with Hy 11 in summer. In H it is largely restricted to weekdays. It is anonymous and written in rhythmical Ambrosian hymn verse (4 × 8pp). No melody has been transmitted in the Anglo-Saxon manuscripts. It goes back to the period of the Old Hymnal (OHy 30). The text is included in the hymnals BCDHVm and the *Expositio hymnorum* JVp.

Bibliographical references: *ICL* no. 2217; *AH* 51, 21–3 (no. 22), cf. *AH* 27, 111–12 (no. 75); Bulst, pp. 98 and 191 (VI, 9); Walpole no. 61.

Apparatus to D   Latin text: 9 gravis] s *on erasure by another hand*; 10 D_2 *takes over from 5r on*; 11 nec] c *erased*; consentiens] ens *on erasure (of* ET*?), but probably by* D_2, TI *are capitalized and placed somewhat in front of the rest of the line like verse initials and are possibly a later insertion.* Old English gloss: 11 geðafigende] gende *erased*.

BVmCJVpH   Heading: Ymnus ad completorium *B, no rubric VmpH,* HYMNUS AD COMPLETORIUM *C,* CHRISTE QUI LUX J; 2 noctis] *om.* JVp; 7 in te requies] interrequies *H*; 8 quietam] quieam *C*; 10 nec] ne *BJVp*; hostis] s *altered from* t *by* V_1 Vm; 11 nec] ne *B*; consentiens] consentiat *C,* consentiens, ens *expunged, at written above by* H_1 *H*; 13 somnum] somnium *B*; 25 *om.* VmJVp, BH *omit* sit gloria.

Commentary   Latin: 1, 3–4 *Cf. Hy 15/2–4.* 1 *Bulst reads* die, *noting* dies *as variant.* 4 *Bulst reads* beatis, *noting* beatum *as variant.* 6 *The line is metrically irregular. Bulst reads* defende nocte ac die, *but notes the Anglo-Saxon reading as variant.* 10–11 *The reading of BJVp,* ne, *is noted as variant by Bulst.* 11 *Bulst reads* consentiat, *but notes the variant* consentiens. 14 *Cf. S. of S. V.2. Bulst reads* semper ad te, *noting the variant* ad te semper. 17 *Cf.* protector noster aspice *Ps. LXXXIII.10.* 22 *Cf.* corpus enim quod corrumpitur adgravat animum *Wisdom IX.15.* Old English: 2 *The glossator has confused* (con)tegis *and* detegis. 20 þu *is confused with* þa. 22 *For* swarran *read* swaran, *cf. SB §231.4 and n. 3.* 23 þu *is again confused with* þa.

13

YMNUS AD VESPERAM

ó
leohtes eala þu scyppend se sælosta
I LUCIS   CREATOR OPTIME,

leoht   dagena   forðbringende
lucem dierum proferens,

on anginnum leohtes niwes
primordiis lucis novę

mideardes gearcigende ordfruman
mundi   parans   originem,   4

se   ærnemergen *geðeodnes *æfenes
II Qui mane   iunctum vesperi

dæg   beon geciged þu bebeotst
diem vocari   precipis,

sweart   þrosm onaslit
tetrum chaos inlabitur,

geher bena   mid wopum
audi preces cum fletibus,   8

þæt ne mod   gehefegod mid leahtre
III Ne   mens gravata crimine

lifes sy útlaga lace
vitę sit exul   munere,

þonne hit naht ecelices   geðæncð
dum   nil perenne cogitat

7 hit self gyltum hit gewriþ
seseque culpis illigat.   12

hefona   cnysse þæt incunde
IV Cęlorum pulset intimum,

liflic   hit nime mede
vitale tollat   pręmium,

þæt we forbugan ælc þing derigendlices
vitemus   omne   noxium,

þæt we afeormian ealle   þæt werste
purgemus omne pessimum.   16

ó
getiða   fæder þu arfæsteste
Presta, pater piissime

138

I Excellent creator of light, you who bring forth the light of day, who let the world begin with the first emergence of newly created light,

II you who command that morning when it is joined together with evening should be called 'day', now ugly black disorder looms, hear our prayers interspersed with weeping:

III Let not the spirit oppressed with its sin be a stranger to the gift of life, not thinking of anything eternal and entangling itself in sins.

IV But may it knock at the innermost of heavens and carry off the reward of life. Let us avoid all harmful things, let us cleanse ourselves of all that is worst in us.

This hymn was sung at Vespers on Sunday except in Lent. It is anonymous and written in Ambrosian iambic dimeter. No melody is transmitted in the Anglo-Saxon manuscripts. The text is included in the hymnals BCDHVm and the *Expositio hymnorum* JVp.

Bibliographical references: *ICL* no. 9041; *AH* 51, 34–5 (no. 34); Walpole no. 73.

Apparatus to D   Old English gloss: 2 dagena] a *altered from* æ *by erasure*; 7 onaslit] t *on erasure of* d; 10 lace] e *on erasure of* b; 13 *one letter erased in front of* cnysse (þ, p *or wynn?*); 16 werste] r *altered from* s *by erasure*; 17 þu] *corrected, apparently by* D₂, *from* þa *by suprascript* v.
    Latin gloss: 17 ó] *inserted between* pater *and* piissime *with the same pen as used for the gloss.*

    BVmCJVpH   Heading: Hymnus ad vesperam *B*, HYMNUS AD VESPERUM *VmC*, LUCIS CREATOR *J, no rubric VpH*; 1 OPTIME] obtime *C*; 4 originem] oniginem, *but* n *possibly a deformed* r; n *followed by two erased letters, the first of which may be* a *C*, orriginem *J*, origine *H*; 7 tetrum] tetrhum *Vp*; 11 cogitat] cogltat *Vm*; 12 illigat] alligat *JVp*; 14 vitale] t *illegible J*; 15 vitemus] i *suprascript by* J₁ *J*; 17 *om. JVp*; Presta] resta *C*.

Commentary   Latin: *The hymn is based on Gen. I.1–5.* 1 *For* creator optime *cf. Hy* 20/1. 8 *Cf. Hy* 55/2. Old English: 5 geðeodnes *should agree with* mane *(acc. sg. ntr.); the dative* vesperi *is mistaken for a genitive.* 11 *The partitive genitive* ecelices *is independent of the case of the lemma, accusative.* 15–16 *Strictly speaking, the four clauses of this stanza are main clauses, but interpreting the latter two as consecutive (or final?) is semantically justifiable.*

14

FERIA SECUNDA. AD NOCTURNAM

of slæpe   geliðewæhtum liðum
I SOMNO REFECTIS ARTUBUS

forsewenum bedde we arisað
spreto cubili surgimus,

ó
us   eala ðu fæder singendum
[5v] nobis,   pater,   canentibus

ætbeon þe we biddað
adesse te deposcimus.   4

þe tunge   ærest   hleoðrige
II Te lingua primum concinat,

þe modes   fyrwet gewilnige
te mentis ardor ambiat,

þæt dæda   æfterfyligendra
ut actuum sequentium

ó
eala ðu halige   beo ðu anginn
   tu, sancte, sis   exordium.   8

abugan þeostru   leohte
III Cędant tenebrę lumini

7 niht   dægðerlicum tungle
et nox diurno   sideri,

þæt gylt   þæne þe nyht inbrohte
ut culpa, quam   nox intulit,

leohtes aslide   mid lace
lucis labescat munere.   12

we biddað þæt ylce eadmode
IV Precamur idem   supplices,

dara   þæt ealle   þu ofaceorf
noxas ut omnes amputes

7 muðe þe herigendra
et ore te canentium

þu sy geherod on ecnysse
lauderis   in perpetuum.   16

ó
getiða   fæder eala þu arfæstesta
Presta, pater   piissime

I Now our limbs are refreshed with sleep, we forsake the bed chamber and arise. Father, be with us, we pray, as we sing.

II Let the tongue sing of you first of all, let the ardour of the spirit yearn towards you so that you may be the source of all our subsequent actions, holy one.

III Let the shadows give way to light and the night to the daystar so that the guilt with which night has infected us may yield to the gift of light.

IV This is what we humbly pray for, that you may cut us off from all sin and thus be praised forever by the mouths of those who sing of you.

This hymn was sung at Matins (Nocturn) on Mondays. It is anonymous and written in Ambrosian iambic dimeter with some irregularities in the third and fourth stanzas. No melody has been transmitted in the Anglo-Saxon manuscripts. The text is included in the hymnals of BCDHVm and the *Expositio hymnorum* JVp.

Bibliographical references: *ICL* no. 15532; *AH* 51, 27–8 (no. 25); Walpole no. 64.

Apparatus to D   Latin gloss by D₄: 1 de (*somno*) recreatis a labore diei i. membris 2 i. relicto lectulo 3 s. & (*nobis*) i. laudantibus 4 presente i. oramus 5 (*lingua*) nostra ante omnia i. cantet 6 s. & (*te*) desiderium i. cupiat 7 (*actuum*) s. nostrorum i. prevenientium 8 i. initium 9 locum dent peccati *poenitentiam datur 10 i. ignorantia claritati 11 s. cedat (*culpa*) vanitatis nostra tempus *delinquente 12 confessionis *fugiit i. dono 14 i. culpas 'i. repellas a nobis' (*in the margin, identified as belonging above* amputes) 15 (*et*) si de mundo i. laudencium 16 (*lauderis*) condigne.

BVmCJVpH   Heading: hymnus ad nocturnam *B*, FERIA SECUNDA. YMNUM AD NOCTURNOS *Vm*, FERIA SECUNDA. HYMNUS AD NOCTURNUM *C*, SOMNO REFECTIS *J*, no rubric *VpH*; 5 concinat] concinant, *first* c *corrected from* n *J*; 7 actuum] ad tuum *Vm*; 16 in perpetuum] imperpetuum *Vm*; 17 *om. CJVp*, BH *omit* piissime.

Commentary   Latin: 2 *Cf.* cubile spernere Prudentius, Cathemerinon, *I.10*; 5 *Cf. Hy 4/ 31. J's reading* concinant *is paralleled once on the Continent according to* AH. 11 *For* delinquente *in D's Latin gloss read* delinquentie. 12 *For* fugiit *in D's Latin gloss read* fugit *or* fugat? 14 *Cf.* ... noxas nec omnes inputet ... Prudentius, Peristefanon, *V.560.*

15

YMNUS AD MATUTINAM

     ó

eala ðu beorhtnyss fæderlices   wuldres

I   SPLENDOR PATERNĘ GLORIÆ,

of leohte leoht   forðbringende

de luce lucem proferens

leoht leohtes 7 well   leohtes

lux lucis & fons luminis,

dæg dagena   onleohtende

dies dierum inluminans   4

     7 soð   sunne onaslíd

II   verusque sol, illabere

scinende on beorhtnysse ecere

micans nitore   perpeti

7 leoma   þæs halgan gastes

iubarque sancti   spiritus

onasend urum   andgytum

infunde nostris sensibus.   8

     mid gewilnungum we ciað   þe fæder

III   Votis   vocemus te patrem,

fæder eces   wuldres

patrem perennis gloriae,

fæder mihtigre   gyfe

patrem potentis gratiae,

gylt   he gewriðe sliporne ł fulne

culpam religet   lubricam,   12

he gehiwige dæda   stranglice

IV   informet actus strenuos,

teð   he ætstente þæs æfestigan

dentes retundat invidi,

mislimp he gesundfullige tearte

casus secundet   asperos,

he sylle to donne gyfe

donet gerendi gratiam,   16

     mod   he begeme 7   he gewissige

V   Mentem gubernet & regat.

þam clænan geleaffullan lichoman
Casto,   fideli   corpore

geleafa on hætan wealle
fides calore   ferveat,

facnes   attru   *hit nete
Fraudis venena nesciat.   20

7 crist   us   sy mete
VI   Christusque nobis sit cibus

7 drenc   ure   sy geleafa
potusque noster sit fides;

        bliþe uton drincan seferlice
[6r] loeti bibamus   sobria*e*

druncennesse gastes
ebrietatem spiritus.   24

bliþe dæg þes gewite
VII   Letus dies hic transeat;

clænnyss sy swa swa ærnemergen
pudor sit ut   diluculum,

geleafa swa swa middæg
fides velut   meridies,

*æfenglommumge mod nyte
crepusculum   mens nesciat.   28

dægrima rynas   upalymþ
VIII   Aurora cursus provehit –

eorendel eall   forðstæppe
aurora tota prodeat,

on fæder eall   se suna
in patre totus filius

7 eall   on worde fæder
& totus in verbo pater.   32

gode fæder sy wuldor
Deo patri sit gloria

I You, who are the splendour of your Father's glory, who bring forth light from light, who are the light of light and the source of light, who irradiate the day of days

II and are the true sun, descend into us, shining in your ever-lasting brightness and infuse our minds with the rays of the Holy Ghost.

III In our prayers we call on you as the Father, the Father in his perpetual glory, the Father with his potent grace. May he restrain dangerous sin,

IV may he inform energetic action and dull the teeth of the Envious One, may he turn harsh adversity to good and bestow the grace on us to act well.

V May he guide and rule the mind. May faith glow with fervour within a body kept chaste and faithful and be a stranger to the poison of deceit.

VI May Christ be our food and faith be our drink; let us joyfully and soberly drink in the intoxication of the spirit.

VII May this day pass in joy. Let shame be, as it were, our early morning twilight, faith our noon and may our mind not know the dusk of evening.

VIII The dawn is advancing in its course – let the Dawn manifest itself completely, the Son altogether in the Father and the Father altogether in the Word.

This hymn by St Ambrose of Milan was sung at Lauds on Mondays. It is written in Ambrosian iambic dimeter. In the Old Hymnal (OHy 8) it was sung daily at Lauds. No melody has been transmitted in the Anglo-Saxon manuscripts. The text is included in the hymnals of the New Hymnal BCDHVm, the *Expositio hymnorum* JVp and the Old Hymnal manuscript A.

Bibliographical references: *ICL* no. 15627; *AH* 50, 11–12 (no. 5), cf. *AH* 2, 29–31; Bulst, pp. 40 and 182–3 (II, 2); Walpole no. 3.

Apparatus to D   Latin text: 14 retundat] d *partly erased and a damaged, accidentally?* 23 *from here on the text is again by* D_1; loeti] o *erased, but legible under ultraviolet light; a later hand added a* cauda *to* e; sobriae] *one letter, probably* e, *erased after* a, *the same corrector added a suspension mark;* 33 gloria] g *damaged by a tear in the parchment.*
Old English gloss: 26 clænnyss] clænniss, y *suprascript by* D_1.
Latin gloss: 7 o, *possibly with an accent, erased in front of* gastes.

BVmCJVpHA   Heading: hymnus ad matutinam B, AD LAUDES *Vm*, YMNUS AD MATUTINUM C, SPLENDOR PATERNE GLORIE *J*, *no rubric* VpH, HYMNUM AD MATUTINOS A; 2 *after* de *erasure of one or two letters* C; proferens] praeferens A; 4 dies]

diems *with incorrect* m-stroke *(not mentioned by Dewick)* H; dierum] die *followed by the erasure of one letter* C, diem H; 6 perpeti] perpetim *VmC*, perpetim, m *expunged* H; 8 nostris sensibus] nostrisensibus *C*; sensibus] bus *abbreviated, later expanded, probably by another hand* A; 12 religet] redegit A; 13 informet] t *on erasure* J; strenuos] strennuos *CJH*; 14 dentes] dentis C, dentem A; retundat invidi] dat inv *possibly by the corrector of line 33. This is at the end of the line and the rest of* invidi *is cut off. At the beginning of the next line* invi *and* i *appear to have been erased* A; retundat] retundet B; 15 casus] cassus C, c *on erasure* A; 18 casto] castos A; fideli] fidele, e *erased and replaced by* i A; 21 Christus-] spiritus; -que] e *on erasure* A; 23 sobriae] sobriam *VmJVp*; 26 diluculum] deluculo A; 27 meridies] meridiems *with incorrect* m- *stroke (Dewick:* meridies*)* H; 29 provehit] proveat *JVp*; 30 tota] totus *VmJVpA*; 33 *om. CJVp,* A *reads:* Gloria tibi pater gloria unigenito cum sancto spiritu in sempiterna saecula; *another hand inserted* una *in front of* cum.

Commentary   Latin: 1 *Cf.* qui cum sit splendor gloriae eius *(i.e. of God) Heb. I.3.* 4 CH's diem *is attested by* AH *for the Continent.* 7–8 *Cf. Hy 4/29.* 12 *With* lubricam *cf. Hy 3/21, Hy 30/4, 33/8. Bulst reads* releget, AH *attests* religet *for the Continent.* 14 *With* invidi *cf. Hy 2/ 27.* 23–4 *Cf.* et nolite inebriari vino in quo est luxuria sed implemini spiritu *Eph. V.18.* 23 *Bulst reads* sobriam. 29–30 *D's* tota *seems unparalleled, but* provehat *(cf. JVp) is attested besides* prodeat *for the Continent by Bulst and AH.* 31–2 *Cf.* non credis quia ego in Patre et Pater in me est *John XIV.10.* Old English: 20 hit *agrees with* mens (mod), *not with* fides (geleafa).

16

YMNUS AD VESPERAM

ó
eala þu ormæte   heofones scyppend
I   INMENSE CÆLI CONDITOR,

þu þe gemengednyssa þæt hi ne gedræfdon
qui, mixta   ne confunderent,

wæteres flod   todælende
aquę fluenta dividens

heofonan þu forgeafe gemære
cęlum dedisti limitem   4

getrymmende stowe   mid heofonlicum
II   firmans   locum cęlestibus

7 samod   eorþan riþum
simulque terrę rivulis,

þæt yþ   ligas   gemetegie
ut unda flammas temperet,

eorþan moldan þæt he ne tostence
terrę solum ne dissipet,　　　　　　　　　　　8

　　onasynd　nu　　þu arfæstesta
III　infunde nunc, piissime,

　　selene　ecere　　gyfe
　　donum perennis gratiae,

　　*facnyss　niwes þæt ne gelimpum
　　fraudis novę ne　　casibus

　　us　gedweld tobryte eald
　　nos error　atterat vetus.　　　　　　　　12

　　leoht　geleafa gemete
IV　Lucem fides　inveniat;

　　swa leohtes　leoma bringe
　　sic luminis iubar ferat,

　　　s. fides
　　þes geleafa ydelnysse ealle　*tobrete
　　hęc　　vana　　cuncta terreat,

　　　s. fidem
　　þesne geleafan leasinga nane ne ofþreccan
　　hanc　　falsa　nulla comprimant.　　　16

　　getiþa　fæder þu arfæstesta
　　Presta, pater piissime

I Infinite creator of the sky, you who divided the floods of water in two so that they should not mix and cause confusion and who set the sky as a boundary,

II establishing a place both for the streams of heaven and those of the earth so that the water might mitigate the flaming solar heat and might not dissolve the soil of the earth,

III inspire us now, most merciful one, with the gift of your perpetual grace lest the old error crush us so that we fall again through new deceit.

IV Let our faith reach the light; may it bring a ray of brightness. May it put all vain things to flight and may it not be suppressed by any lies.

This hymn was sung on Mondays at Vespers. It is anonymous. Its metre is that of the Ambrosian hymn verse (iambic dimeter). No melody has been transmitted from Anglo-Saxon manuscripts. The text is included in the hymnals of BCDHVm and the *Expositio hymnorum* of JVp.

Bibliographical references: *ICL* no. 7765; *AH* 51, 35–6 (no. 35), Walpole no. 74.

BVmCJVpH   Heading: Feria II. Ymnus ad Vesperam *B*, YMNUS AD VESPEROS *Vm*, FERIA IIIᵃ. HYMNUS AD VESPERUM *C*, INMENSE *J*, *no rubric VpH*; 2 confunderent] confundere *C*; ne] nec *J*; 3 aquę] atque *C*; fluenta] t *on erasure C*; dividens] divins, ns *erased and* dens *added above the line by a correcting hand C*; 4 limitem] limen *with possible erasure of one letter* (i?) *between* l *and* i *Vp*; 7 unda] unde *H*; flammas] flamma, s *inserted above by a corrector C*; 8 *interlined subsequently by another hand B* (*not mentioned by Wieland*); 11 casibus] cassibus *C*; 12 atterat] aterreat *C*; 17 *om. JVp*; piissime] *apparently added later by* B₁ *B, om. C.*

Commentary   Latin: *The hymn is based on Gen. I.6–10.* 5 *Cf.* verbo Domini caeli firmati sunt *Ps. XXXII.6.* 8 *Cf. Gen. IX.11.* Old English: 5–6 *In the lemma* celestibus ... rivulis *is probably dative, but the ablative implied by the gloss* mid *does seem possible.* 11 *For* facnyss *read* facnes, *genitive of* facn. 15 *The gloss* tobrete *is due to a mistaken reading of* terat *for* terreat, *cf. line 12.*

17

ó
eala þu efenhlytta fæderlices   leohtes

I   CONSORS PATERNI LUMINIS,

leoht þu self leohtes 7 dæg
lux ipse lucis & dies,

niht   singende we tobrycaþ
noctem canendo rumpimus,

ætwuna þu biddendum
assiste   postulantibus.   4

afyrsa þeostru   moda

II   Aufer tenebras mentium,

aflyg heapas   deofla
fuga catervas demonum,

adræf   slapolnyssa
expelle sompnolentiam,

þæt ne þa sleacgiendan he ofhreose
ne   pigritantes   obruat.   8

147

ó
[6v] swa eala þu crist us eallum

III   Sic,   Christe, nobis omnibus

þu gemiltsige gelefendum
indulgeas   credentibus,

þæt hit fremige biddendum
ut prosit   exorantibus,

þæt   hleoþrigende we singað
quod precinentes psallimus.   12

Presta, pater piissime

I You who partake equally of the Father's splendour, who are yourself the light of light and yourself the day – we are breaking in upon the night with our song – assist those who pray to you.

II Remove the darkness obscuring our minds, put the hordes of evil spirits to flight, drive out sleepiness, lest it overwhelm the indolent.

III Forgive all of us who believe in you, o Christ, so that what we sing and chant before you may profit us in our earnest prayer.

This hymn was sung on Tuesdays at Matins (Nocturn). It is written in Ambrosian hymn verse (iambic dimeter). No melody has been transmitted in Anglo-Saxon manuscripts. The text is included in the hymnals BCDHVm and the *Expositio hymnorum* JVp.

Bibliographical references: *ICL* no. 2649; *AH* 51, 28 (no. 26); cf. *AH* 2, 30 (no. 3), Walpole no. 65.

Apparatus to D   Latin text: Heading: *The scribe left no space for the missing rubric.* 6 catervas] s *added later, probably by* D_1 *with the pen used for the gloss.*

BVmCJVpH   J *continues from Hy 15 without indicating that a new hymn begins.* Heading: hymnus ad nocturnam *B*; FERIA TERTIA YMNUS *Vm*, HYMNUS AD NOCTURNUM *C, no rubric JVpH*; 2 ipse lucis] lucis ipse *C*; 4 assiste] *one or two letters erased after* adsiste *in C*; 6 fuga] foga *with* o *erased and suprascript* u *by* V_1 *in Vm*; 7 sompnolentiam] a *on erasure by a different hand C*, sompnolentium *H*; 8 pigritantes] pigritantis *C*, ig *added above the line by* H_1 *H*; obruat] obriat *C*; 13 *om. JVp, C omits* piissime.

18

AD MATUTINAM

    fugel   dæges bydel
I ALES DIEI NUNTIUS

    leoht   gehende   bodað
  LUCEM propinquam precinit.

    us   arærend   moda
  Nos excitator mentium

    eallunga crist   to life   gecigeþ
  iam   Christus ad vitam vocat.   4

    afyrsiaþ   he cleopað bedd
II 'Auferte', clamat, 'lectulos

                 s.o
    adlige *mid slæpe eala ge asolcene
  aegros, soporos,   desides

    7 clæne 7 rihte 7 sefre
  castique recti ac sobrii

    waciaþ   nu ic eom gehende
  vigilate! Iam sum   proximus.'   8

    þone hælend uton cion mid stefnum
III Iesum   ciamus vocibus

    wepende biddende   seferlice
  flentes, precantes sobrię.

    geornfull halsung l bén
  Intenta supplicatio

    slapan   heorte clæne   *forbeode
  dormire cor   mundum vetat.   12

        ó
    þu eala crist   slæp   tosceac
IV Tu,   Christe, sompnum dissice,

    þu tobrec   nihte   bendas
  tu, rumpe noctis vincula,

    þu toles   senne   ealde
  tu, solve peccatum vetus

    7 niwe   leoht   ongebring
  novumque lumen ingere.   16

  Deo patri sit gloria

I The winged herald of day cries out to announce that daylight is near. He who wakes the souls, Christ, is even now summoning us to life.

II 'Put away', he cries, 'the beds, which are for the sick, the drowsy and the slothful, and be wakeful, chaste, just and sober! I am already very close.'

III Let us invoke Christ with our voices, in tears and praying soberly. May our intent prayer prevent our pure hearts from sleeping.

IV Christ, dispel sleep, break the chains of night, annihilate the old sin and infuse us with your new light!

This hymn was sung at Lauds on Tuesdays. It is an extract from Prudentius's *Cathemerinon* I, consisting of stanzas 1, 2, 21, and 25. The metre is Ambrosian hymn verse (iambic dimeter). No melody is transmitted in Anglo-Saxon manuscripts. The text is included in the hymnals of BCDHVm and the *Expositio hymnorum* of JVp.

Bibliographical references: *ICL* no. 532; *AH* 50, 23 (no. 22), cf. *AH* 2, 30 (no. 4), Walpole no. 20.

Apparatus to D   Latin text: 8 proximus] x *written on erasure (possibly of* r) *by* D_1.

BVmCJVpH   Heading: ad matutinam *B*, YMNUS AD LAUDES *Vm*, HYMNUS AD MATUTINUM *C*, ALES DIEI NUNTIUS *J*, *no rubric VpH*; 2 propinquam] *last letter erased; another hand retraced* a *and added a suspension mark C*; precinit] percinet *C*; 3 Nos] Nox *C*; 4 vitam] vita *C*; 6 aegros, soporos] aegro sopore *Vm*, egrosopore *C*, egros sopores *H*; 7 casti-] caste- *JVp*; recti ac sobrii] recte ac sobrie *JVp*; 9 ciamus] sciamus *on erasure by another hand C*; 10 precantes] *om. Vp*; 12 vetat] veat *C*; 13 dissice] discute *Vmp*; 16 ingere] in generi *with final letter erased C*; 17 *om. JVp, C reads* Praesta pater.

Commentary   Latin: 1 *Cf. Hy 4/5. 6 The reading of VmC is attested by* AH *for the Continent. The divergence of the manuscripts is caused by the startling attribution of the qualities associated with the occupants of the beds with the beds themselves. 7 JVp's reading is attested by* AH *for the Continent. 8 Cf. I Cor. XVI.13 and I Pet. V.8. 13 Compare Hy 4/30. Vmp have taken over* discute *instead of* dissice. *16 Cf. Hy 39/26.* Old English: *5 The lemma of* bedd *is not a true diminutive, but synonymous with* lectus, *originally with affective overtones. The gloss is therefore accurate. 6* mid slæpe *glosses a reading comparable to VmC. Note that* aegros sopore, *the precise equivalent of the gloss in D, is attested by* AH *for the Continent. 12* forbeode *should be indicative.*

19

YMNUS AD VESPERAM

ó
eorþan   eala þu ormæte sceppend
I TELLURIS   INGENS CONDITOR,

middaneardes moldan þu þe *generigende
mundi   solum qui   eruens

utanyddum wæteres hefigtemnyssum
pulsis   aquę molestiis

eorþan þu sealdest unawendendlice
terram dedisti   inmobilem,   4

þæt sprettinge gelimplice forðbringende
II ut germen aptum   proferens

mid geolowum wlitige blosmum
fulvis   decora floribus

wæstmbære on wæstme heo wære
fecunda fructu   sisteret

7 fodan   gecwemne heo ageafe
pastumque gratum redderet,   8

modes   forbærndes wunda
III mentis perustę vulnera

geclænsa mid grénnysse gife
munda virore   gratiae,

þæt dæda mid wope *he adilegie
ut facta fletu   deluat

7 sterunga *þryre *he tobrete
motusque pravos atterat.   12

hæsum þinum hit gehersumige
IV Iussis tuis obtemperet,

nanum yfelum hit geneolæce
nullis malis approximet,

     mid godum beon gefelled hit geblissige
[7r] bonis   repleri   gaudeat

7 deaþes dæde hit nete
& mortis actum nesciat.   16

Presta, pater piissime

151

I Immense creator of the earth, who raised up the soil of the world, dispelling the troublesome waters, and established the ground as immovable,

II so that it might bring forth its proper growth and be adorned with bright flowers, then become fertile with fruit and yield welcome food,

III purify the wounds of our scorched heart with the fertility of your grace so that it may wash away the committed acts through tears and suppress any corrupt stirrings.

IV May it obey your commands, may it come near no evil, may it rejoice to be filled with good and may it be ignorant of the act that leads to death.

This hymn was sung at Vespers on Tuesdays. It is anonymous and written in Ambrosian hymn verse (iambic dimeter). No melody has been transmitted in the Anglo-Saxon manuscripts. The text is included in the hymnals of BCDHVm and the *Expositio hymnorum* JVp.

Bibliographical references: *ICL* no. 16140; *AH* 51, 36 (no. 36), Walpole no. 75.

Apparatus to D   Latin text: 7 fructu] c *altered from the first minim of* m *or* n *by* D_1.

BVmCJVpH   Heading: hymnus ad Vesperam. feria. iiiᵃ *B*, YMNUS AD VESPEROS *Vm*, FERIA iiiᵃ HYMNUS AD VESPERUM *C*, TELLURIS INGENS *J, no rubric VpH*; 2 mundi] *om. together with its gloss and later added in the margin, probably by* V_1 *Vp*; 3 aquę] atque *C*; 4 inmobilem] mobilem *C*; 5 aptum] actum *Vm*; 7 fructu] fructum *C*; 8 pastumque] partumque *H*; 10 virore] vigore *Vm*; 11 deluat] e *expunged and* i *written above the line; the whole line is on erasure and appears to be by another hand C*; 12 atterat] aterat, *with the second* t *interlined, probably by the corrector of line 11 C*; 13 obtemperet] temperet, *but the Old English gloss translates* obtemperet *JVp*; 14 nullis] s *inserted later by* C_1 *C*; approximet] aproximet *second* p *interlined by the corrector of lines 11–12 C*; 17 *om. JVp, B continues*: patrisque compar unice, *CH omits* piissime.

Commentary   Latin: *The hymn is based on Gen. I.11–13. 4 Cf.* orbem terrae qui non commovebitur *(Ps. XCII.1) and similarly Ps. CIII.5 (iuxta Hebraeos). 9 B seems to have regarded* per-uste *as two words. 11 AH reads* diluat *as the correcting hand in C, but little distinction seems to have been made between* deluere *and* diluere *in Later Latin.* Old English: *2* generigende *glosses* eruens *in its common meaning of 'rescuing'. 11–12 If the subject of the Latin clause is* viror *or* gratia, *both Old English pronouns should be* heo, *referring either to* grennyss *or* gife. *If* mens/mod *were taken as subject, the pronoun should be* hit. *12 For* þryte *read* þwyre *(from* þweorh).

152

20

YMNUS AD NOCTURNAM

ó
gescæfta eala þu sceppend se selosta
I RERUM   CREATOR optime

7 wissigend ure   beseoh
rectorque noster, respice;

us   fram stilnesse derigendlicre
nos a   quiete noxia

þa besænctan mid slæpe alys
mersos   sopore   libera.   4

ó
þe eala þu halige crist   we biddaþ
II Te,   sanctę *Criste, poscimus,

gemiltsa þu leahtrum
ignosce tu criminibus.

to andettene   we arisaþ
Ad confitendum surgimus

7 *yldinge nihte we tobrecað
morasque noctis rumpimus,   8

mod   7 handa   we ahebbaþ
III mentes manusque tollimus,

witega   swa swa on nihtum
propheta sicut   noctibus

us   to donne   bebeot
nobis gerendum precipit

and   mid dædum demde
Paulusque gestis   censuit.   12

þu gesihst yfel þæt þæt   we dedon
IV Vides   malum, quod gessimus.

diglu   ure   we geyppaþ
Occulta nostra pandimus.

bena   geomrigende we asendaþ
Preces gementes fundimus.

forgyf   þæt þæt we sengodon
Dimitte, quod   peccavimus.   16

Presta, pater piissime

I Excellent creator of the world and our guide, regard us; free us, who are sunk in sleep, from our sinful repose.

II We pray to you, holy Christ, forgive our sins. We arise to confess and interrupt our rest,

III we lift up our hearts and hands, as the prophet commands us to do in the night and as Paul sanctioned it by his actions.

IV You see the wrongs committed by us. We lay our secrets open before you. We pour out our prayers amid lamentation. Absolve us from that in which we have sinned.

The hymn was sung at Matins (Nocturn) on Wednesdays. It is anonymous. The metre is Ambrosian hymn verse (iambic dimeter). No melody has been transmitted in the Anglo-Saxon manuscripts. The text is included in the hymnals of BCDHVm and the *Expositio hymnorum* JVp.

Bibliographical references: *ICL* no. 14180; *AH* 51, 28–9, (no. 27), Walpole no. 66.

Apparatus to D   Latin text: 16 peccavimus] *possibly one letter erased after* i *at the end of the line in the manuscript.*

Old English gloss: 9 ahebbaþ] bb *on erasure of* pp *or double-wynn*; 13 gesihst] s *inserted later, possibly by* D_1.

BVmCJVpH   Heading: hymnus ad nocturnam *B*, FERIA QUARTA. YMNUS *Vm*, HYMNUS AD NOCTURNUM *C*, RERUM CREATOR *J, no rubric VpH*; 1 RERUM] *initial* R *altered from* I *B*; 11 nobis] vobis *J*; gerendum] geredum *C*; precipit] pręcepit *H*; 13 Vides] Fides *H*; 14 Occulta] oculta *C*; 17 *om. JVp, B continues*: patrisque compar unice / cum spiritu paraclyto, *VmCH omit* piissime.

Commentary   Latin 1–2 *Cf. Hy 2/1.* 1 *Cf. Hy 13/1.* 9–10 in noctibus extollite manus vestras *Ps. CXXXIII.2.* 11 *H's past tense makes sense and is attested by* AH *twice for continental manuscripts, but ruins the metre.* 12 media autem nocte Paulus et Silas adorantes laudabant Deum *Acts XVI.25.* Old English: 8 yldinge *'delay' renders the most usual meaning of* mora.

21

YMNUS AD MATUTINAM

niht   7   þeostru   7   genipu
I NOX ET TENEBRÆ ET NUBILA,

gemengednyssa middaneardes 7 gedrefeda
confusa   mundi   & turbida,

leoht infærþ hwitað heofon
lux intrat, albescit polus,

crist   cymþ aweggewitaþ
Christus venit, discedite.   4

dymnes eorþan is toslitan
II Caligo terrę scinditur

geslægen þære sunnan mid leoman
percussa solis   spiculo

7 þingum eallunga bleoh gehwyrfþ
rebusque iam   color redit

andwlitan scinendes tungles
vultu   nitentis sideris.   8

       ó
þe eala þu crist   ænne we cunnon
III Te,   Christe, solum novimus;

þe mid mode clænum 7 anfealdum
te mente   pura   & simplici

wepende singende we biddaþ
flendo, canendo quesumus,

begém   nurum sefum
intende nostris sensibus.   12

synt   feala þinga mid degum begleddode
IV Sunt multa   fucis   illita,

þa   leohte *beoþ afeormode þinum
quę luce purgentur   tua;

ó
eala þu leoht easternes tungles
    tu, lux eoi   sideris,

      andwlitan mid liþan onleoht
[7v] vultu   sereno   inlumina.   16

Deo patri sit gloria

155

I Night, Gloom and Clouds, confusion and turmoils of the world, light is entering, the sky is growing bright, Christ is coming, depart!

II The darkness of earth is rent apart, pierced by the arrowing ray of the sun. Things receive back their true colour through the aspect of the shining daystar.

III Christ, we know you alone. We pray to you with a simple and pure mind, weeping and singing: concern yourself with our thoughts.

IV Much is stained with varnish which should be cleansed by your light. Light of the morning sun, shed your light on us with a serene countenance.

The hymn was sung at Lauds on Wednesdays. It is an extract from Prudentius's *Cathemerinon* II, consisting of lines 1–8, 48–9, 52, 57, 59–60 and 67–8. The metre is Ambrosian hymn verse (iambic dimeter). No melody has been transmitted in the Anglo-Saxon manuscripts. The text is included in the hymnals of BCDHVm and the *Expositio hymnorum* JVp.

Bibliographical references: *ICL* no. 10629; *AH* 50, 23–4 (no. 23), Walpole no. 21.

Apparatus to D   Old English gloss: 7 gehwyrfþ] gehwerfþ, e *expunged and* y *written above it by* D_1.

BVmCJVpH   Heading: ymnus ad matutinam *B*, YMNUS AD LAUDES *Vm*, HYMNUS AD MATUTINUM *C*, NOX ET TENEBRE ET NUBILA *J, no rubric* VpH; 3 intrat] r *damaged J*; albescit] abescat *C*; 5 Caligo] celigo *with* e *corrected to* a *by* C_1 *C*; 6 percussa] percusso *H*; spiculo] o *corrected from* a *by* J_1; 11 *one letter* (o, e?) *erased after* flendo *Vm*; 13 fucis] fusis *C*; 14 luce] mente *Vm*; 15 eoi sideris] eoi sideri *Vm*, eo ysideris *with a small erasure after* eo *H*; 17 *om.* CJVp, *H has* Presta pater piissime.

Commentary   Latin: 6 *Cf.* radiorum spicula *Prudentius*, Hamartigeneia, *87.7 Cf.* rebus nox abstulit atra colorem *Virgil,* Aeneis, *VI.272; cf. Hy 23/1–2.* 9 *Cf.* Deus meus cognovimus te *Hos. VIII.2.* 11 AH *reads* flendo et canendo, *so the erasure in Vm may be of* &. Old English: 7 *Note the scribe's attempt to keep to the Late West Saxon standard.* 14 *The glossator has missed the subjunctive.*

22

YMNUS AD VESPERAM

ó
heofones eala þu god haligesta
I CAELI   DEUS SANCTISSIME,

þú ðe scinendne   trendel   heofones
QUI LUCIdum centrum poli

mid beorhtnyssa amytst ferenre
candore   pingis igneo

geecende *mid wlitegum *leohte
augens decora   lumina,   4

on þam feorþan dæge þu ðe ligen
II quarto   die qui flammeam

þære sunnan hweogul gesettende
solis   rotam constituens

þæs monan þenigende   ændeberdnyssa
lunę   ministrans ordinem,

*wiþscriþole renas   tunglena
vagos   recursus siderum,   8

þæt nihtum   oþðe *leohtes
III ut noctibus vel   lumini

todales   geendunga
diremptionis terminum,

of anginnum 7 monþa
primordiis & mensium

tacn   he sealde þæt swuteloste
signum daret   notissimum,   12

onleoht   heorte manna
IV inlumina cor   hominum,

adryg   horu   moda
absterge sordes mentium,

tolys   gyltes bænd
resolve culpę vinculum,

awend hefas   leahtra
everte moles criminum.   16

Presta, pater piissime

157

I Most holy God of the sky, you who adorn the shining centre of the sky with fiery brightness, enhancing the beautiful lights,

II you who established the fiery disc of the sun on the fourth day, who gave the ordered ways of the moon and the erratic paths of the stars (*CJVp:* made the wandering courses of the stars attendant upon the ordered path of the moon),

III in order that the sun should draw a dividing line between night and day and that the moon should give a well-known sign indeed for the beginning of the months,

IV give light to the heart of mankind and cleanse the defilement of their souls, loosen the chain of guilt and lift the burden of our sins from us.

This hymn was sung at Vespers on Wednesdays. It is anonymous and written in Ambrosian hymn verse (iambic dimeter). No melody has been transmitted in the Anglo-Saxon manuscripts. The text is included in the hymnals of BCDHVm and the *Expositio hymnorum* JVp.

Bibliographical references: *ICL* no. 1791; *AH* 51, 36–7 (no. 37), Walpole no. 76.

Apparatus to D   Latin text: 7 ministrans] *second n erased*; ordinem] *corrected to* ordini *by erasure of* e *and two minims of the* m.

BVmCJVpH   Heading: hymnus ad vesperam Feria iiii[ta] B, YMNUS AD VESPERAS Vm, HYMNUS AD VESPERUM C, CELI DEUS SANCTISSIME J, *no rubric* VpH; 3 pingis] pign, is *inserted above, probably by* C_1 *C*; 4 decora lumina] decore lumine Vm, decora lumina, *but a in both cases by a later hand* C, decoro lumine J *(agreeing with the gloss in* JVp*)*. 5 quarto] Quarta Vm; 6 constituens] Cconstituens Vp; 7 ministrans] ministras JVp; ordinem] n *on small erasure* B, ordine, e *erased to* i Vm, ordini *with final letter on erasure (possibly of* n*)* C, ordini JVp; 9 lumini] luminis, s *erased* Vm; 10 diremptionis] diremptiones B, direptionis JVp; 11 mensium] mentium CH; 12 daret] darent BC; 13 Inlumina] Iinlumina *with the second i erased* J; 14 mentium] metium *with* n *inserted above by* V_1 Vp; 17 *om.* JVp, Vm *omits* piissime, C *omits* pater piissime.

Commentary   Latin: *The hymn is based on Gen. I.14–19.* 4 AH *reads* decori lumina, *but also attests* decoro lumine *for continental manuscripts.* 6 *For* solis rotam *see, for example,* Prudentius, Cathemerinon, *XII.5.* 7 AH *reads* ordini, *but also attests* ordinem. 9 luminis *in* Vm, *also presupposed by the gloss in* D, *is attested for the Continent by* AH. 12 *Cf.* et sint in signa *... Gen. I.14.* 15 *Cf.* Hy 18/14–5. *Old English:* 4 mid wlitegum leohte *glosses the reading* *extant in J and underlying the gloss in JVp.* 8 *For* wiþscriþole *read* widscriþole. 9 leohtes *glosses the original reading of Vm; it is used metaphorically for 'day' which is probably the reason for the confusion.* 11 primordiis *was probably mistaken for an ablative, as the glossator usually translates datives literally.*

23

FERIA V. YMNUS AD NOCTURNAM

   niht   sweart gescæfta   oferhelað
I NOX ATRA RERUM CONTEGIT

   eorþan bleoh   ealra
   terrę colores omnium.

   *us andettende we biddaþ
   Nos confitentes poscimus

      ó
   þe eala þu rihtwisa dema   heortena
   te,   iustę   iudex cordium,   4

   þæt þu afyrsige mán
II ut auferas   piacula

   7 horu   modes   þu afeormige
   sordesque mentis abluas

          ó
   7 þu forgife eala þu crist   gife
   donesque,   Christe, gratiam,
   þæt beon afligede leahtras
   ut arceantur   crimina.   8

   mod   efne *aswinc þæt arleasa
III Mens, ecce, torpet impia,

   þæt   gylt slít   derigendlic
   quam culpa mordet noxia;

   forsworcennyssa *mid dædum niman
   obscura   gestis   tollere

   7 þe alysend   secan
   & te, redemptor, querere.   12

   adræf   þu dymnessa
IV Repelle, tu, caliginem

   wiþinnan   ealra   swiþost
   intrinsecus quam maxime,

> þæt on eadigum hit blissige
> ut in beato gaudeat
> hit beon gelogod leohte
> se collocari lumine.
>
> 16
>
> Presta, pater piissime

I Black night has covered with a pall all the colours of the things of the earth. We confess your name and pray to you, just judge of hearts,

II that you may remove our sins and wash away the impurities of our mind and grant us grace, o Christ, so that all transgressions may be warded off from us.

III See how numb our impious heart is, which is torn by its pernicious guilt. You fully intend to take away the darkness and make it seek you, redeemer. (*Or, according to JVp:* It is eager to lift the darkness and to seek you, redeemer.)

IV Dispel the blackness within as far as possible, so that it (i.e. the heart) may rejoice to be installed in the light of bliss.

This hymn was sung at Matins (Nocturn) on Thursdays. It is anonymous and written in Ambrosian iambic dimeter. No melody is transmitted in the Anglo-Saxon manuscripts. The text is found in the hymnals of BCDHVm and the *Expositio hymnorum* of JVp.

Bibliographical references: *ICL* no. 10621; *AH* 51, 29 (no. 28), Walpole no. 67.

Apparatus to D Latin text: 1 ATRA] R *on erasure*; 11 gestis] s *altered to* i *by another hand.*

Old English gloss: 9 aswinc] c *altered to* t, *probably by another hand.* 11 mid] d *damaged by the following erasure;* dedum] *erased; the second letter was probably* e. *There seems to have been a supernumerary letter before* u.

BVmCJVpH Heading: ad nocturnum *B*, FERIA. V. YMNUS AD NOCTURNOS *Vm*, HYMNUS AD NOCTURNUM, *last word on erasure C*, NOX ATRA *J, no rubric VpH;* 2 colores] calores *CH;* 3 confitentes] *Dewick mistakenly has* confitens *H;* 4 iustę] uis te *J;* 5 ut] et *corrected to* ut *by* V₁ *Vp;* 6 mentis] mentes *C;* abluas] ablues *J;* 11 obscura gestis] obscuragesti *Vm;* gestis] gestit *with* t *on erasure by another hand C,* gestit *JVp;* 17 *om. JVp, VmC omit* piissime.

Commentary   Latin: 1–2 *Cf. Hy 21/7–8. 4 Cf.* Deus iudex iustus *Ps. VII.12, note also* scrutans corda *in verse 10.* 11 *The alteration of D agrees with JVpC.* gestis, *whether meaning 'with deeds' or 'you fully intend', may well be a mistake of the scribe, but Vm and the correction in C suggest a more general confusion at this point.* Old English: 3 nos *was not recognized as nominative.* 9 *For* aswinc *read* aswint. 11 dedum *was presumably erased when the lemma was altered.*

24

YMNUS AD MATUTINAM

    leoht   efne   arisþ   ænlic
I [8r] LUX, ECCE, SURGIT AUREA;

   blacigende ateorige blindnyss
   pallens   fatescat cecitas,

   seo us selfe on *scefe   lange
   quę nosmet in preceps diu

   gedwelde teah   mid wegleasum
   errore   traxit devio.   4

   þis   leoht liþe ɫ smilte *he forgife
II Hęc lux serenum   conferat

   7 clæne   us *he gearcige him selfum
   purosque nos prestet   sibi.

   naht ne sprece we   facenfullices
   Nichil loquamur subdolum,

   wealcan we forsworcenlices naht
   volvamus obscurum   nichil.   8

   swa eall ayrne   dæg
III Sic tota decurrat dies,

   þæt ne tunge   leas   ne   hand
   ne   lingua mendax nec manus

   ne eagan syngian slipere
   oculive peccent lubrici,

   þæt ne dara lichoman besmite
   ne   noxa corpus inquinet.   12

   besceawære ætwunaþ wiþufen
IV Speculator adstat desuper,

   se þe us   dagum eallum
   qui nos diebus omnibus

161

7 dæda   ure   besceawaþ
actusque nostros prospicit
fram leohte þam forman oþ æfen
a   luce prima   in vesperum.   16

Deo patri sit gloria

I See, the golden light is springing up! May the blindness devoid of colour give way that has for a long time been drawing us towards the abyss, astray and erring.

II May that light grant fair weather and keep us pure for its own purposes. Let us not say anything deceitful. Let us not revolve dark thoughts within.

III May the whole day pass in such a way that neither our tongue, prone to lies, nor our hand nor our wandering eyes commit a sin so that no guilt may defile our body.

IV A watchman is at hand up above, who regards us and our actions each day from daybreak until evening.

The hymn was sung at Lauds on Thursdays. It is an extract from Prudentius's *Cathemerinon* II, consisting of lines 25, 93–4 and 96–108. The metre is Ambrosian hymn verse (iambic dimeter). No melody has been transmitted in the Anglo-Saxon manuscripts. The text is included in the hymnals of BCDHVm and the *Expositio hymnorum* JVp.

Bibliographical references: *ICL* no. 9114; *AH* 50, 24–5 (no. 25), Walpole no. 22.

BVmCJVpH   Heading: ymnus ad nocturnam *B*, YMNUS AD LAUDES *Vm*, HYMNUS AD MATUTINUM *C*, LUX ECCE *J, no rubric VpH*; 2 fatescat] fatescit *B*; 8 nichil] ichil *J*; 9 decurrat] decurat *J*; 10 ne] nec *Vm*; lingua] línguam *with the accent crossed out; an illegible word by another hand has been erased above C*; 11 -ve] ne *Vm*, nec *C*; 17 *om. JVp*.

Commentary   Latin: 2 AH *reads* facessat, *attesting both* fatescat *and* fatescit *for continental manuscripts.* 10 AH *reads* ne ... ne, *attesting also* nec ... nec *for the Continent.* 11 *The readings of Vm and C are attested by* AH *for the Continent.* Old English: 3 *According to classical usage, while the adverb* praeceps *means 'precipitately', the noun means only 'slope, abyss'.* 5–6 *The subject of the clauses is* leoht *and so the pronouns should be neuter. While the glossator may be thinking of Christ as 'Light', it is not clear whether he understood line 5 and recognized* serenum *as a noun.* 7–8 *The partitive genitives represent idiomatic rather than strictly literal glossing.*

162

25

YMNUS AD VESPERAM

o
micele   eala þu god mihte
I MAGNE   DEUS POTENTIAE,

þu þe of wæterum *upasprunge cynn
qui ex aquis   ortum   genus

dælmælum ongeansændst wæle
partim   remittis   gurgiti,

dælmælum þu upahefst on lyftum
partim   levas   in aera   4

þa besenctan on wæterum ofþriccende
II dimersa   limphis   inprimens,

þa upawegenan to heofonum *onbelædende
subvecta   cęlis   irrogans,

þæt cynrene of anum forþatogen
ut stirpe una   prodita

mistlice hi gelæccon stowa
diversa rapiant   loca,   8

forgyf   eallum   þeowtlingum
III largire cunctis servulis,

þa   geclænsað yþ   blodes
quos mundat unda sanguinis,

nytan   slide   leahtra
nescire lapsum criminum

ne   forberan deaþes   æþretnysse
nec ferre   mortis tedium,   12

þæt gylt   nænne   ofþricce
IV ut culpa nullum deprim*at*,

nænne   up ne ahebbe idel gelp
nullum levet   iactantia,

þæt forscræncte mod   þæt ne fealle
elisa   mens ne   concidat,

þæt upahafene mod   þæt ne hreose
elata   mens ne   corruat.   16

[8v] Presta, pater piissime

I God of great power, you who send the race born from the waters in part back into the deep and in part lift it up into the air,

II immersing some in the waves and plunging them into them, raising some into the skies and assigning them there, so that those derived from one stock take up different places,

III grant all your servants, whom the flow of your blood has purified, not to experience a falling off into sin and not to suffer foul death

IV so that guilt will not weigh anybody down and nobody will be puffed up by vanity, so that the crushed heart will not be cast down nor the overweening heart suffer a fall.

This hymn was sung at Vespers on Thursdays. It is anonymous. Its metre is Ambrosian iambic dimeter. No melody has been transmitted in the Anglo-Saxon manuscripts. The text is included in the hymnals of BCDHVm and the *Expositio hymnorum* of JVp.

Bibliographical references: *ICL* no. 9187; *AH* 51, 37–8 (no. 38), Walpole no. 77.

Apparatus to D   Latin text: 13 deprimat] at *by another hand on erasure.*
   Old English gloss: 3 l *erased in front of* wæle.

BVmCJVpH   Heading: hymnus ad vesperam. feria .v. *B*, AD VESPEROS YMNUS *Vm*, HYMNUS AD VESPEROS *C*; 3 partim] partem *C*; gurgiti] i *on erasure (of* a*?) C*; 4 partim] partem *C*; aera] aerae *with the final* e *erased C*; 5 inprimens] inprimis *H*; 6 irrogans] irrogas *B*; 8 diversa] *small erasure after* di *C*; rapiant] rapians, s *erased and* t *written above by another hand C*; 11 lapsum] lapsus *Vmp*, lapsis *J*; 12 nec] ne *C*; 13 deprimat] deprimet *H*; 15 ne] nec *C*; 16 ne] nec *C*; 17 *om.* JVp, VmC *omit* piissime.

Commentary   Latin: *The hymn is based on Gen. I.20–3. 3 If the original reading of C were* gurgitis, *parallels would be attested by* AH *for the Continent. 6 B's* irrogas *is attested by* AH *for only one continental manuscript. 7 There is a hiatus here. 10 For* unda sanguinis *cf. Hy* 67_2/12 *and 143/17. 11 The gloss in JVp presupposes a reading* lapsus, *which is attested by* AH *for the Continent. 13 Perhaps the original reading of D was* deprimet, *cf. H. 15 Cf.* adlevat Dominus omnes qui corruunt et erigit omnes elisos *Ps. CXLIV.14 and* ne in superbia elatus in iudicium incidat diaboli *I Tim. III.6. Old English: 4 The gloss makes no distinction between the Latin accusative and ablative after* in. *6* onbelædan *for* irrogare *is rather imprecise.*

26

FERIA VI. YMNUS AD NOCTURNAM

ó
eala þu   þrynnysse   annyss
I   TU, TRINITATIS UNITAS,

embhwerft mihtelice þu þe gewissast
orbem   potenter qui regis,

begém   herunga lofsangas
attende laudum cantica,

þe   we hlyniende syngaþ
quę excubantes psallimus.   4

witodlice of bedde we samodarisaþ
II Nam   lectulo consurgimus

nihte   gedefre tide
noctis quieto tempore,

þæt we biddan   wunda
ut flagitemus vulnerum

fram þe læcedom   ealra
a   te medelam omnium,   8

*on   þam facne swa hwæt deofla
III quo fraude   quicquid demonum

on nihtum   we agyltan
in noctibus deliquimus,

adrige   þæt heofonlice
abstergat illud celitus

þines miht   wuldres
tuae potestas gloriae.   12

ne ne lichoma wunige horig ɫ ful
IV Nec corpus adsit   sordidum

ne   slæwþ onwunige heortena
nec torpor instet   cordium

7 leahtres   besmitennysse
& criminis contagio

acolige   bryne gastes
tepescat ardor spiritus.   16

ó
for þy eala þu alysend   we biddaþ
V Ob hoc,   redemptor, quesumus:

gefell mid þinum us   leohte
reple tuo   nos lumine,
þurh þæt   dægena embrynum
per quod dierum circulis
nanum we hreosan on dædum
nullis ruamus   actibus.   20

Presta, pater piissime

I You, oneness of the trinity, who govern the world in your might, lend your ear to the hymns of praise that we sing while keeping watch.

II For we arise from our bed in the quiet hours of the night to implore you to heal all wounds,

III so that whatever sin we committed at night, impelled by the deceit of demons, the might of your glory from heaven will clear it away.

IV And may the body not come here defiled nor numbness of heart descend on us and the ardour of our spirit grow lukewarm through the infection of sin.

V Therefore, redeemer, we ask you: fill us with your light so that by its grace we will not fall in any of our actions, as the days roll by.

The hymn was sung at Matins (Nocturn) on Fridays. It is anonymous. Its metre is Ambrosian iambic dimeter (with hiatus in lines 4 and 8). No melody has been transmitted in the Anglo-Saxon manuscripts. The text is included in the hymnals of BCDHVm and the *Expositio hymnorum* of JVp.

Bibliographical references: *ICL* no. 16594; *AH* 51, 29–30 (no. 29), Walpole no. 68.

Apparatus to D   Latin text: 6 noctis] n *inserted above by* D_1; 16 tepescat] *written as* te pescat, *later connected by a horizontal stroke*; 20 ruamus] *originally* ruamur, r *altered to* s *by* D_1.
Old English gloss: 11 adrige] *one or two letters erased between* a *and* drige.

BVmCJVpH   Heading: ad nocturnam *B*, FERIA VI *Vm*, HYMNUS AD NOCTURNUM *C*; 3 laudum] ladum *C*; 4 quę] qui *CH*; excubantes] excusantes *C*; 8 a] ad *VmCH*; 13 Nec] ne *CJVp*; sordidum] sordium *J*; 14 nec] ne *JVp*; torpor] torpet *C*; 20 ruamus] ruamur *BVmCJVpH*; 21 *om. JVp; VmC omit* piissime. *H has*: Pater pater piissime.

Commentary Latin: 7–8 *Cf.* Hy 31/59–60. 8 *The lemma to the Old English gloss in JVp* (æt þe) *also appears to have been* ad te *and this is also attested by* AH *for continental manuscripts.* 13 AH *reads* ne, *attesting* nec *for the Continent as well.* 19 *Cf.* dierum circulo Hy 56_1/3. 20 ruo *can be both transitive and intransitive; the scribe may have been thinking only of the intransitive use, when he made the correction. On the other hand* AH *(and many continental manuscripts) reads* ruamus. Old English: 9 *The gloss does not recognize* quo *as an equivalent of* ut.

27

YMNUS AD MATUTINAM

ó
eala þu ece   heofones wuldor
I   ETERNA CELI   GLORIA,

eadig hiht deadlicra
beata spes mortalium,

                ó
þæs hean ælmihtigan eala þu ancænneda
celsitonantis   unice

7 clæne tudder Ɩ bearn mædenes
casteque proles   virginis,   4

syle swiþran   arisendum
II   da dexteram surgentibus;

arise   eac swilce mod   sefre
exsurgat &   mens sobria

7 byrnende   on lofe   godes
flagransque in laude dei

þances hit agylde neadwise
grates rependat debitas.   8

upasprungen scinþ   dægsteorra
III   Ortus   refulget lucifer

7 geondstred leoht   he cyþ
sparsamque lucem nuntiat.

fealþ   dimnyss nihta
Cadit caligo noctium.

leoht halig   us   onleohte
Lux sancta nos inluminet   12

7 wunigende urum   andgitum
IV   manensque nostris sensibus

nihte *he adræfe worulde
noctem repellat sęculi

7 ælcan ændan dæges
[9r] omnique fine diei

afeormoda *he gehealde breost
purgata servet pectora.   16

begeten eallunga ærest geleafa
v   Quęsita iam primum fides

awyrtwalige deopum andgitum
radicet altis sensibus,

gesundfullod hiht samodblissige
secunda spes congaudeat,

þanne mare *wunige soþlufu
tunc maior extat caritas.   20

Deo patri sit

I Everlasting glory of heaven, blessed hope of mortal beings, only
begotten Son of the one who thunders on high and child of the
chaste virgin,

II lend your right hand to those who are arisen. May the heart also
soberly arise and, ardent in its praise of God, yield up the thanks it
owes.

III The morning star is risen and shining, it announces the spreading of
light. The darkness of night is cast down. May the blessed light
inspire us

IV and, abiding in our thoughts, drive out the night of this world. And
may it guard our purified breast from any close of day.

V May faith now first be gained and become rooted deep in our minds,
may hope be joined to it next in joy; then love will surpass them.

This hymn was sung at Lauds on Friday. The hymn is anonymous. The
metre is Ambrosian iambic dimeter with some slight irregularities.
The lines are in abecedarian order. No melody has been transmitted in the
Anglo-Saxon manuscripts. The text is included in the hymnals of
BCDHVm and the *Expositio hymnorum* of JVp.

Bibliographical references: *ICL* no. 140; *AH* 51, 32–4 (no. 32), Walpole
no. 71.

Apparatus to D   Latin text: 3 celsitonantis] D_1 *at first wrote* tom, *but corrected himself.* 20 extat] extet *with* e *on erasure by another hand.*

Old English gloss: 20 wunige] *last two letters damaged by erasure of the lemma.*

BVmCJVpH   Heading: ad matutinam *B*, YMNUS AD LAUDES *Vm*, HYMNUS AD MATUTINUM *C*, ETERNA CELI *J, no rubric VpH*; 1 ĘTERNA] AETERNE *C*, Aaeterna *JVp (in J the first* A *is struck through)*, Aterna *Vm*; 2 mortalium] mortaliṁ *C*; 3 celsitonantis] *second* i *on erasure C, written as two words VpH*; 4 caste-] casti- *C*; virginis] virgines *H*; 6 exsurgat] exurgat *BVmJVp*; 7 laude] laudem *H*; 8 rependat] perenni *C*; 11 Cadit] cadat *JVp*; 20 tunc] quod *Vm*, ut *C, om. JVp, &* H; extat] exstet *C*; 21 *om. Vm*, Deo patri sit gloria *BCH*.

Commentary   Latin: 1–2 *Cf.* quod est Christus in vobis spes gloriae *Col. I.27.* 3 AH *reads* celsi tonantis. 7 AH *reads* laudem *(which is metrically preferable) as H does.* 9 ortus *was originally* hortus *with hypercorrect aspiration.* 10 sparsam *originally had prothetic* i. 17–20 *Cf.* nunc autem manet fides, spes, caritas. tria haec. maior autem his est caritas *I Cor. XIII.13, also Hy 117/21–2.* 20 quod *and* et *are also attested by* AH *for continental manuscripts. D must originally have read* extat *as BVmJVpH.* extet *is attested by* AH *for the Continent.* Old English: 20 wunige *glosses* extet, *agreeing with the correction in D.*

28

YMNUS AD VESPERAM

			ó	
	scyppend	mannes	eala þu god	
I	PLASMATOR HOMINIS		DEUS,	

þu þe ealle þing ana   geendeberdiende
qui cuncta solus ordinans

moldan   þu hætst forþateon
humum iubes   producere

slincendes 7 wilddeores cynn
reptantis & fęre   genus,   4

þu þe micele   gescæfta *lichomena
II qui magna rerum   corpora

on cwidu bebeodendes libbende
dictu   iubentis   vivida,

þæt hi þeowian be   endebyrdnysse
ut serviant per ordinem,

underþeodende þu sealdest mænn
subdens   dedisti   homini,   8

169

adræf   fram þeowum þinum
III repelle a   servis tuis,

swa hwæt swa þurh unclænnysse
quicquid   per inmunditiam

oþðe on þeawum hit tiht
aut moribus   se suggerit

oþþe on dædum hit betwuxsette
aut actibus   se interserit.   12

syle gefeana   meda
IV Da gaudiorum premia,

syle gyfa   lac
da gratiarum munera.

tolys   sace bendas
Dissolve litis vincula,

gewriþ   sibbe wære ł wedd
asstringe pacis fędera.   16

Presta, pater piissime

I God, who fashioned man, you who alone appoint all things and order the earth to bring forth the race of the reptile and of the wild beast,

II you who gave to man the huge bodies of forms come to life at your word, when you commanded it, and subjugated them to him so that they shall serve him each in its place,

III drive away from your servants whatever insinuates itself into our behaviour or creeps into our actions with its impurity.

IV Give us the reward of your joys and grant us the gift of your grace. Free us from the bonds of strife and knit us tightly together in compacts of peace.

This hymn was sung at Vespers on Fridays. It is anonymous. The metre is Ambrosian iambic dimeter with slight irregularities. No melody has been transmitted in the Anglo-Saxon manuscripts. The text is included in the hymnals of BCDHVm and the *Expositio hymnorum* of JVp.

Bibliographical references: *ICL* no. 12039; *AH* 51, 38 (no. 39), Walpole no. 78.

Apparatus to D   Old English gloss: 7 endebyrdnysse] endebyrnysse, d *inserted above by*
D₁; 9 a *erased between* adræf *and* fram; þeowum] þoowum, o *corrected to* e *above by D₁*.

BVmCJVpH   Heading: feria vi. hymnus ad vesperam *B*, YMNUS AD VESPERAS
Vm, HYMNUS AD VESPERUM *C*, PLASMATOR HOMINIS *J, no rubric VpH*; 2 solus]
soluus, *i.e.* u *with* us-*abbreviation C*; 4 &] *om.*, e *erased in front of the following word C*; fęre]
ferre *H*; 10 inmunditiam] inmundiam, *first* i *erased from* u *C*; 11 suggerit] sugerit *H*; 16
asstringe] abstringe *Vm*; 17 *om. JVp, CH have*: Deo patri.

Commentary   Latin: *The hymn is based on Gen. I.24–31.* 1 *Cf. Hy 31/6 and 18.* 3–4
producat terra animam viventem in genere suo *Gen. I.24.* 4 *H's* ferre *is attested by* AH *for*
continental manuscripts. 15 *Cf. Hy 22/15.* 16 *Vm's* abstringe *is also attested by* AH *for the*
Continent. Cf. Isa. LIV.10, Ezek. XXXVII.26. Old English: 5 *The genitive plural is wrongly*
carried on from gescæfta.

29

SABBATO. YMNUS AD NOCTURNAM

ó
healicra   eala god   mildheortnysse
I   SUMME   DEUS CLEMENTIAE

7 middaneardes wyrhta seares ł cræftes
mundique   factor machinę,

an   mihtylice
unus potentialiter

7 þrylic   hadelice
trinusque personaliter,   4

ure   arfæstum mid   lofsangum
II   nostros piis   cum canticis

wopas *welwillendlice underfoh
fletus *benignis   suscipe,

*on þam heortan *clænre fram horwum
 quo   cordæ *puro sordibus

þe we brucon   cystiglicor
te perfruamur largius.   8

lendenu 7 lifre   adlige
III   Lumbos iecurque morbidum

forbærn mid fyre þæslicum

171

adure igni   congruo,

begerde þæt hi beon ecelice
accincti ut sint   perpetim

gælsan asindrodum *þære wyrstan
[9v] luxu remoto   pessimo,   12

þæt we þe   tida   nyhta
IV ut, quique horas noctium

nu   hleoþrigende we tobrycaþ
nunc concinendo rumpimus,

mid selenum eadiges eþeles
donis   beatę patriae

we beon gewelgode ealle   genihtsumlice
ditemur   omnes affatim.   16

Presta, pater piissime

I God of utmost mercy, maker of the structure of the world, you who are one in power and threefold in person,

II receive with benevolence our weeping together with our devout hymns so that we may enjoy you more fully, when our heart is cleansed of defilement.

III Sear our loins and our diseased liver with the right fire, as is fitting, so that they may be always girt up and evil lust be far from us,

IV in order that we all, each of us who is now breaking in on the hours of the night with his singing, may be sufficiently enriched with the gifts of our blessed home.

This hymn was sung at Matins (Nocturn) on Saturdays. It is anonymous. The metre is Ambrosian iambic dimeter (with some irregularities). No melody has been transmitted in the Anglo-Saxon manuscripts. The text is included in the hymnals of BCDHVm and the *Expositio hymnorum* in JVp.

Bibliographical references: *ICL* no. 15810; *AH* 51, 30–1 (no. 30), Walpole no. 69.

Apparatus to D   Latin text: 5 piis] ius *written on erasure of* iis *by a later hand*; 6 benignis] i *altered by another hand to* e, s *erased.* 7 cordæ] o *altered from* a *by* D*₁*, æ *erased to* e; puro] o *on erasure, probably by another hand.*

    Old English gloss: 2 *unfinished letter erased between* middaneardes *and* wyrhta; 5 arfæstum] fæstum *erased*, æ *and* t *illegible.* 12 wyrstan] r *altered from* s *by* D*₁*.

BVmCJVpH   Heading: ad nocturnam *B*, YMNUS IN SABBATO *Vm*, HYMNUS AD NOCTURNAM *C*; 5 piis] pius *BVmJVp*; 6 benignis] benigne *BVmCJVpH*; 7 cordæ puro] corda pura *C*; 8 largius] largirus *C*; 12 luxu remoto] luxure meto *with* o *on erasure C*; 13 horas] r *altered from* s *by H₁ H*; noctium] noxium *C*; 15 beatę] beates *H*; 17 affatim] effatim *C*; 17 *om. JVp, VmH omit* piissime.

Commentary   5 *The correction in D agrees with* BVmJVp. AH *reads* pius, *but attests* piis *for one continental manuscript.* 6 *D's* benignis *is a slip due to* piis *and* canticis *in line 5.* 7 *The original ending of* puro *in D may have been* -a *as in C. C's* corda pura *is paralleled in continental manuscripts according to* AH. 9–12 *Cf.* accingite lumbos vestros *Isa. XXXII.11 and* sint lumbi vestri praecincti ... *Luke XII.35.* 11 *The metre is irregular.* 13–14 *Cf. Hy 16/3.* Old English: 1 summe *is taken as agreeing with* deus, *not* clementiae. 5 *The erasure is due to the altered lemma.* 6 welwillendlice *accords with the otherwise attested* benigne. *The lemma has been brought into line with it.* 7 quo *has not been recognized as the equivalent of* ut. Clænre *should be neuter dat. sg., but note that the original ending of the lemma may have been* -a. 12 þære *should agree with* gælsan *(masculine).*

30

YMNUS AD MATUTINAM

   eorendel   eallunga geondstret   heofon
I AURORA IAM   SPARGIT polum;

   eorþum dæg onasihþ
   terris dies illabitur.

   leohtes *swege   stræle ł leoma
   Lucis resultat spiculum;

   aweggewite ælc þing slipores ł fules
   discedat omne lubricum.   4

   gedwimor nihte   fealle
II Fantasma noctis decidat,

   modes   scylde ł senne hreosa
   mentis reatus   subruat.

   swa hwæt swa þeostrum *ladlic
   Quicquid   tenebris horridum

   niht brohte *gylte   fealle
   nox attulit culpe, cadat,   8

   þæt ærmergen se   ytemesta
III ut mane   illud ultimum,

þæne we anbidiað eadmode
quod prestolamur cernui,

on leohte us   flowe ł becume
in luce nobis effluat,

þænne *he þæt mid dreame hleoþraþ
dum   hoc canore   concrepat.   12

Deo patri sit gloria

I Dawn is already spreading across the sky. Daylight is stealing over the earth. The dart of light rebounds. Let everything dangerous and slimy depart.

II May the illusion spawned by night topple and the guilt of the heart be overthrown. Whatever horrible instance of iniquity the night brought in its darkness, may it subside,

III so that that last morning, which we humbly await, may be a flood of light to us as this today resounds with our song.

This hymn was sung at Lauds on Saturdays. It is anonymous. Its metre is Ambrosian iambic dimeter. No melody has been transmitted in Anglo-Saxon manuscripts. The text is included in the hymnals of BCDHVm and the *Expositio hymnorum* of JVp.

Bibliographical references: *ICL* no. 1496; *AH* 51, 34 (no. 33), Walpole no. 72.

BVmCJVpH   Heading: ymnus ad matutinam *B*, AD LAUDES *Vm*, HYMNUS AD MATUTINUM *C*, AURORA *J, no rubric VpH*; 2 terris] ternis *C*; 3 resultat] refulget *C*, resultet *H*; spiculum] i *altered to* e *by another hand Vm*, speculum *C*; 4 discedat] *second* d *partly illegible J*; 6 subruat] sobruat *CH*; 7 horridum] harridum *C*; 8 attulit] *the first* t *altered to* d, *apparently by* C_1 *C*; 10 prestolamur] postulamur *C*; 11 luce] lucem *BVmCJVp*; 12 dum] du *C*; canore] canora *JVp*; 13 *om. VmJVp.*

Commentary   Latin: 1 Et iam prima novo spargebat lumine terras Tithoni croceum linquens Aurora cubile *Virgil, Aeneis, IV.*584–5. 3 *VmC's* speculum *is paralleled on the Continent according to* AH. 4 *Cf. Hy 21/4, 140/21.* 5 *Cf.* noctium fantasmata *Hy 11/6.* 9 *Note the hiatus.* 10 *The metre is irregular.* 11 *BVmCJVp's* lucem *is paralleled on the Continent according to* AH. 12 *JVp's* canora *is paralleled on the Continent according to* AH. Old English: 3 swege *renders H's subjunctive.* 4 *Note the partitive genitive, which is independent of the Latin.* 7 *For* ladlic *read* laðlic. 8 gylte *interprets* culpe *as a dat.* 12 hoc *is taken for acc. sg. ntr, rather than nom.*

31

YMNUS AD MATUTINAM

ó
cyning ece   eala ðu drihten
I REX AETERNE   DOMINE,

gesceafta scyppend ealra
rerum creator omnium,

þu ðe wære ǽr   worulde
qui   eras ante secula

æfre   mid fæder sunu
semper cum patre filius,   4

þu ðe middaneardes on fruman
II qui mundi   in primordio

gesceope   mann
Adam plasmasti hominem,

þam þinre anlicnysse
cui tuae imaginis

andwlitan þu sealdest gelicne
vultum dedisti   similem,   8

þæne   deoful   beswác
III quem diabolus deceperat,

feond   mennisces cynnes
hostis humani generis,

þurh æppel   treowes þæs *ealdan
per pomum ligni   vetiti

deaðes scencende drenc
mortis propinans poculum,   12

se ðe   beclesed on þeostrum
IV quique *clausis in tenebris

geomrode on witum
gemebat in suppliciis,

þæs þu hiw   lichoman
cuius tu formam corporis

geniman   gemedemod þu wære
assumere dignatus és,   16

þæt mann   þu alysdest
V ut hominem redimeres,

þæne   ær   eallunga þu gesceope
[10r] quem ante iam   plasmaveras,

þæt us   gode þu geðeoddest
ut nos deo coniungeres

þurh flæsces gemænnysse
per carnis contubernium,   20

þæne   acennedne of fæmnan
VI   quem editum ex virgine

forhtað   ælc   sawul
pavescit omnis anima,

þurh ðæne 7 we arisan
per quem & nos resurgere

estfullum mode   we gelefað
devota   mente credimus,   24

þu ðe us   þurh fulluhta
VII   qui nobis per baptismata

forgæfe forgyfennysse
donasti indulgentiam,

þe   wæron numene mid bendum
qui tenebamur   vinculis

gebundne ingehedes
ligati   conscientiae,   28

þu ðe rode   for   menn
VIII   qui   crucem propter hominem

onfon   gemedemod wære
suscipere dignatus es,

þu sealdest þin   blod
dedisti   tuum sanguinem

ure   hæle   wurþ
nostrę salutis pretium,   32

witodlice wáhreft þæs temples wæs tosliten
IX   nam   velum templi   scissum est

7 eall   eorðe beofode
& omnis terra tremuit.

þu mænige slæpendra
Tu multos dormientium

awehtest   drihten
resuscitasti, domine.   36

176

þu   feondes þæs ealdan mægenu
X   Tu hostis antiqui   vires

þurh rode   deaðes þu forþræstest
per crucem mortis conteris,

mid þære us getacnode on forheafdum
qua   nos signati frontibus

guðfana   geleafan we beorað
vexillum fidei   ferimus;   40

þu hine   fram us   æfre
XI   tu illum a   nobis semper

adræfan   þu beo gemedemod
repellere *dignaberis,

þæt ne æfre   mæge gederigan
ne   umquam possit ledere

alysedum   þinum blode
redemptos tuo   sanguine.   44

ðu ðe for   us to hellwarum
XII   Qui propter nos ad inferos

niþerastigan gemedemod þu wære
descendere dignatus es,

þæt deaðes borhgeldum
ut mortis debitoribus

lifes þu forgeafe lac
vitę donares   munera,   48

þe   on nyhtlicre tide
XIII   tibi nocturno tempore

lofsang   biwepende we singað
ymnum deflentes canimus.

           ó
gemiltsa us   drihten
Ignosce nobis, domine,

gemiltsa andettendum
ignosce confitentibus,   52

forðan ðu gewita 7 dema eart
XIV   quia tu testis & iudex es,

þæne   nænig mæg   leogan
quem nemo potest fallere.

þa diglan ingehyde
Secreta conscientiae

      ure   þu gesihst fotswaðu
[10v] nostrę vides   vestigia.   56

     þu ura   breosta
XV Tu nostrorum pectorum

     ana   aspyrigend   eart
     solus investigator és;

     þu wunda   lutigendra
     tu vulnerum latentium

     god   ætstandest læce
     bonus assistis   medicus.   60

     þu eart ðe   on cuðe tid
XVI Tu és, qui certo   tempore

     sellende ende   worulde
     daturus finem saeculi;

     þu ealra   geearnungum
     tu cunctorum meritis

     rihtwís geedleanend   eart
     iustus remunerator és.   64

               ó
     þe eornestlice þu halga we biddað
XVII Te ergo,   sanctę, quesumus,

     þæt ure   þu hæle wundan
     ut nostra cures   vulnera,

     [þe] þu eart mid   fæder suna
     qui   es cum patre filius

     æfre   mid   þam halgan gaste
     semper cum sancto   spiritu.   68

         sit
     wuldor sy þe   þrynnys
XVIII Gloria   tibi, trinitas,

              s. & ó
     gelíc   an   godcundnyss
     aequalis   una deitas,

     ær   ealle   wurolde
     ante omnia secula

     7   nu   7 on ecnysse
     & nunc & in perpetuum.   72

                       si hit swa
                       AMEN

I Eternal king and lord, creator of all things, you who always were the Son together with the Father before the ages of the world,

II who fashioned Adam, the human being, at the beginning of the world, to whom you gave an appearance similar to your image,

III whom the devil, the enemy of mankind, had deceived, giving him the cup of death to drink by means of the fruit of the forbidden tree

IV and who, imprisoned in darkness, wailed in torment, whose bodily form you deigned to assume

V to redeem man, whom you had before created, to unite us with God by sharing our flesh,

VI you who were born of a virgin and whom every soul regards with awe, you by whose help we also shall rise again, as we devoutly believe,

VII you who granted pardon by baptism to us who were held captive in the chains of our consciousness of guilt,

VIII you who deigned to take the cross upon yourself for man, gave your blood as the price of our salvation;

IX so the veil of the temple tore apart and all the earth trembled. You woke many of those who slept, Lord.

X You crush the strength of the old enemy by the cross of your death, which we carry as a sign on our foreheads, bearing the banner of faith.

XI You shall always deign to drive him away from us so that he shall never be able to harm those who are redeemed by your blood.

XII You who for our sake deigned to descend into hell to grant the gift of life to those destined to die,

XIII to you we sing the hymn in tears at night-time. Forgive us, Lord, forgive those who confess their sins,

XIV for you are the witness and the judge whom nobody can deceive. You see the secret marks on our conscience.

XV You are the only one to examine our heart. You are with us as a good physician for our hidden wounds.

XVI It is you who will let the world end at the appointed time. You are the one who will accord just reward to the deserts of each.

XVII Therefore we ask you, holy one, to cure our wounds, you who are for ever the Son together with the Father and the Holy Ghost.

XVIII Glory be to you, trinity, who are alike one deity, since before all the ages and now and in eternity.

This hymn was already part of the Old Hymnal (OHy 3). It was commonly sung then at Matins (Nocturn). Manuscript A specifies that it is to be sung on Sundays. Non-Anglo-Saxon hymnals of the New Hymnal tend to prescribe the hymn for Easter. Its apparent use as an alternative hymn for Lauds on Saturdays in D is untypical and may not reflect actual usage. The hymn is anonymous and written in rather irregular rhythmical Ambrosian hymn verse (4 × 8pp). No melody has been transmitted in the Anglo-Saxon manuscripts. The text is contained in the excerpt from the Old Hymnal in A. D is the only Anglo-Saxon manuscript of the New Hymnal to include it.

Bibliographical references: *ICL* no. 14234; *AH* 51, 5–7 (no. 2), cf. *AH* 2, 47 (no. 45), Bulst, pp. 92 and 189–90 (VI, 2), Walpole no. 42.

Apparatus to D Latin text: 6 plasmasti] m *on erasure of* t. 38 mortis] is *on erasure of a letter followed by* m; 41 a nobis] *dittographed and expunged*; 48 donares] e *expunged and* i *written above, probably by another hand.*

Old English gloss: 10 feond] o *inserted above with a caret mark by* D_1; 13 se ðe] *on erasure by another hand, the erased letters began with wynn or* p, *possibly followed by* e, *and ended with* e. *The erasure seems too long for* we ðe. 23 we] us *has been erased underneath.* 25 þu ðe] u *and* ð *on erasure*; 40 we] *wynn corrected from* þ; 50 biwepende] bi *erased.* 53 eart] a *inserted above with a caret mark.* 54 leogan] b *erased in front of the word*; 56 fotswaðu] f *erased from* s.

A Heading: HYMNUM DIEBUS DOMINICIS; 7 tuae] tuę *with* ę *on erasure by another hand*; 9 diabolus] o *on erasure by the corrector of line 7*, l *retraced*; 11–14 *om.* A; 17 redimeres] redemeris; 18 ante] *followed by erasure*; 19 ut] et *with* e *on small erasure, but probably by* A_1; coniungeres] coniungeris *with the* i *altered to* e *by* A_1; 23 &] *om.* A; 25 baptismata] baptismum; 35 multos] o *probably by another hand on erasure*; 38 conteris] conterens; 42 dignaberis] dignaveris; 46 descendere] discendere, i *altered to* a *probably by* A_1; 48 donares] donaris; munera] r *on erasure*; 49 nocturno] matutino; 55 conscientiae] conscientia, e *inserted after* a *by another hand*; 56 nostrę] nostra, e *inserted after* a *by the same hand as in the preceding line*; 59 és] *in the margin*, e *written in minuscule, while the text is in uncial script, but probably by* A_1; 60 medicus] medios, *corrected to* medicus *by* A_1; 64 remunerator és] remuneratores, *words later separated by dots*; 69–72 Gloria tibi pater gloria unigenito cum sancto spiritu in sempiterna saecula, *another hand adds* una *in the margin. This is the lemma to a gloss* somud *and belongs in front of* cum.

Commentary   Latin: 3 *Bulst reads* es, *but notes* eras *as a variant reading.* 6–7 *Cf.* et creavit Deus hominem ad imaginem suam, ad imaginem Dei creavit illum *Gen. I.27.* 7 *Bulst reads* tui, *but notes* tuae *as a variant reading.* 11–14 *These lines are paralleled only in one of the manuscripts surveyed in* AH, *an eighth-century collectar from St Gall (St Gall 2). This appears also to be the only manuscript to share A's doxology. Bulst omits the lines.* 13 *D's* clausis *is obviously a mistake for* clausus, *referring to Adam, cf. the gloss.* 19 *Bulst reads* et *like A.* 23 *Bulst omits* et *like A.* 25 *Bulst reads* baptismum, *noting* baptismata *as a variant.* 33 *Cf.* et ecce velum templi scissum est in duas partes *Matt. XXVII.51.* 35 *A's original reading may have been* multis, *which is attested as a variant reading by Bulst.* 38 *Bulst reads* conterens *as in A, noting the variant* conteris. 40 *Cf.* Hy 67₁/1. 42 *Bulst reads* dignaveris *as in A, which requires the assumption of* dignare *beside* dignari *in this text. The two forms would become homophonic in Vulgar Latin. Cf. also the gloss in D.* 49 *Bulst also notes A's variant reading* matutino. 53 *Cf.* iudex *Ps. VII.12,* testis *Rev. I.5 and III.44.* 55 *Bulst also notes A's variant* conscientia. 56 *Bulst reads* videns. Old English: 42 *The subjunctive renders* dignaveris. 50 *The erasure of* bi- *may be motivated by the lack of an object; the prefix usually makes verbs transitive.* 54 *The scribe was considering writing* bileogan; *perhaps this construction of* leogan *with the deceived person in the accusative did not seem quite idiomatic.*

32

YMNUS IN ADVENTU DOMINI. AD VESPERAM

ó
scyppend   eala   þu halga tunglena
I   CONDITOR   ALMĘ SIDERUM,

ece   leoht gelyfendra
aeterna lux credentium,

ó
eala þu crist   alysend   ealra *þinga
Christe, redemptor omnium,

gehyr   bena   eadmodra
exaudi preces supplicum,   4

þu þe besarigende on forwerde
II qui condolens interitu

deaþes losian worulde
mortis perire seculum

þu gehældest middaneard adligne
salvasti   mundum languidum

forgyfende scyldigum læcedom
donans   reis   remedium   8

onsigendum middaneardes æfene
III   vergente   mundi   vesperæ

swa swa brydguma of bredbure
sicut   sponsus de thalamo

útagán   arwurþosta
egressus honestissima

mædenes moder clysinga
virginis matris clausula,   12

þæs   strangre mihte
IV   cuius forti   potentiae

cneowe synt gebigede ealle þing
genu curvantur   omnia,

     heofonlice eorþlice
[11r] caelestia, terrestria,

andyttaþ   mid mihte underþeodde
fatentur nutu   subdita   16

       s. fatetur
setlgang   sunne andet   healdende
V   occasum sol   custodiens,

      s. fatetur
se mona andet   blacunge   healdende
luna   pallorem retinens,

      fatetur
beortnyss s. andet on tunglum scinende
candor   in astris   relúcens

gewisse healdende   *gemæru
certos observans *limite.   20

       ó
þe   we biddað   eala þu halga *cris
VI   Te deprecamur,   agie,

towearde dema worulde
venturi iudex saeculi:

geheald   us   on tide
conserva nos in tempore

feondes fram flanum *geleaflease
hostis a   telis   perfidi.   24

VII
lof wyrðmynt miht wuldor
Laus, honor, virtus, gloria

gode fæder 7 suna
deo patri & filio

samod mid þam halgan gaste
simul cum sancto spiritu

on ece worulde
in sempiterna secula.   28

amen

I Blessed maker of the heavenly bodies, you eternal light for those who believe in you, Christ, redeemer of everyone, hear the prayers of those who beseech you,

II you who, grieving that this world was perishing in ruinous death, healed the sick world and granted a remedy to the guilty,

III you who like a bridegroom coming forth from the wedding chamber left the most noble enclosure of your virgin mother, when the world's evening was drawing to its close,

IV to whose power and strength all things in heaven and earth bend their knee and confess that they are subject to your command,

V the sun by faithfully observing the sunset, the moon by retaining its pale light, the shining splendour of the stars by restricting itself to certain limits.

VI We pray to you, holy one, judge of the world to come, protect us at this time from the darts of the perfidious enemy.

VII Praise, honour, might and glory to God the Father and the Son together with the Holy Ghost forever for all the ages.

This hymn was sung at Vespers in Advent. It is anonymous. The metre is rhythmical Ambrosian hymn verse (4 × 8pp). Rhyme is monosyllabic and not completely regular. The melody transmitted in C is probably a version of Stäblein no. 23. The text is included in the hymnals BCDHVm and the *Expositio hymnorum* of JVp.

Bibliographical references: *ICL* no. 2554; *AH* 51, 46–7 (no. 47), Walpole no. 84.

Apparatus to D   Latin text: 14 curvantur] curvatur, n *inserted above with a caret mark by* D_1; omnia] *the final* a *altered from* u *and the following letter erased, probably by* D_1; 20 observans] -ns *expunged*, t *written above by another hand*; limite] *another hand adds* s *and corrects to* limites. 22 venturi] -i *altered to* -e *probably by another hand.*

BVmCJVpH   Heading: hymnus ad vesperam de adventu domini B, DOMINICA PRIMA DE ADVENTUM (*sic*) DOMINI YMNUS *Vm*, HYMNUS DE ADVENTU DOMINI AD VESPERUM C, CONDITOR ALME SIDERUM *J, no rubric VpH*; 3 redemptor] redeñptor *B*; 6 perire] *om. JVp*; 8 reis] regis *H*; 9 vesperæ] vespera *B*; 10 sicut] uti *VmCJVpH*; 11 egressus] ingressus *C*; 13 forti] fortis *Vm*; 14 curvantur] curvatur *B*, curvantes *JVp*; omnia] omnium *BVm*; 18 pallorem] pallorum *C*; 20 limite] limites *BVmCJVpH*; 22 venturi] venture *VmJVpH*; 24 telis] telo *Vm*, telos *C*; 28 *CJVp omit* Amen.

Commentary   Latin: 3 *The line is identical with Hy* 36/1. 9 *Cf. Hy* 71/4. AH *attests B's* vespera *for the Continent.* 10 *Cf. Ps.* XVIII.6 *and Hy* 39/17. AH *reads* uti. 13–16 *Cf.* ut in nomine Iesu omne genu flectat caelestium et terrestrium et infernorum *Phil. II.10.* 14 *D's exemplar must have had* curvatur omnium *as in B.* AH *attests JVp's* curvantes *and B's* curvatur *for continental manuscripts.* 17 *Cf.* fecit lunam in tempora. sol cognovit occasum suum *Ps. CIII.19.* 22 *For the alteration in D to* venture, *cf. VmpJH.* AH *reads* venture. 24 AH *reads* telo *like Vm.* Old English: 3 manna *as in the gloss of JVp is a better choice than* þinga. 20 gemæru *glosses the correct reading* limites. 21 *For* cris *read* crist, *an explanatory gloss to* agie. 24 perfidi *was apparently mistaken for a nom. pl. masc. instead of gen. sg.*

33

YMNUS AD NOCTURNAM

word   uplic   forþstæppende
I   VERBUM SUPERNUM PRODIENS

fram fæder gefyrn gewitende
a   patre olim exiens,

þu þe acænned embhwerfte gehelpst
qui natus   orbi   subvenis

on ryne *aurnenre tide
cursu   declivi temporis,   4

onleoht   nu   breost
II   inlumina nunc pectora

7 þinre lufe   forswæl
tuoque amore concrema,

gehyrdre þæt bodunge
audito   ut   preconio

184

beon utanydde æt nextan slipornysse
sint pulsa   tandem lubrica,   8

7 dema   þænne siþþan þu ætbist
III iudexque cum post aderis

smegan dæda breostes
rimari facta pectoris

agyldende gewrixl for dyglum
reddens vicem pro abditis

                       s. meritis
7 rihtwisum rice   for godum geearnungum
iustisque regnum pro bonis,   12

na   æt nextan we beon genyrwode mid yfelum
IV non demum artemur   malis

for gehwilcnysse leahtres
pro qualitate   criminis,

               s.sanctis
ac   mid eadigum halgum wilfægene
sed cum beatis   compotes

we beon ece   *heofonbigende
simus perennes celibes.   16

Presta, pater piissime

I O word that proceeds forth on high and once emanated from the
Father, you who by being born came to the assistance of the world,
when time was running out,

II fill our breast with light and consume it with the ardour of your love
so that at last things dangerous and slimy will be dispelled, as soon
as the proclamation of your coming is heard,

III and so that, when you shall hereafter come as a judge to scrutinize
the heart for its past actions and then requite that which was hidden
and give the kingdom to the just according to their goodness,

IV we will not be oppressed with evil then according to the seriousness
of our faults, but together with the saints attain to being dwellers in
heaven forever.

This hymn is prescribed for Matins (Nocturn) in Advent except in C,
where it is assigned to Lauds. It is anonymous. The metre is Ambrosian
hymn verse, either metrical, but highly irregular (cf. lines 4 and 7), or

rhythmical. The verses are linked by monosyllabic rhyme. No melody has been transmitted in the Anglo-Saxon manuscripts. The text is included in the hymnals of BCDHVm and in the *Expositio hymnorum* of JVp.

Bibliographical references: *ICL* no. 17104; *AH* 51, 48 (no. 48), Walpole no. 85.

Apparatus to D   Old English gloss: 3 þu] þa, u *suprascript (by D₁)*; 13 we] wynn *on erasure*.

BVmCJVpH   Heading: ad nocturnam *B*, AD NOCTURNAM YMNUM *Vm*, HYMNUS AD MATUTINUM *C*, VERBUM SUPERNUM *J, no rubric VpH, faint traces of* verbum *written above by another hand in H*; 1 PRODIENS] g *erased between* i *and* e *H*; 3 subvenis] subveni *H*; 7 audito ... preconio] audita ... preconia *Vm*; preconio] *second* o *partly illegible J*; 8 tandem] tande *C*; 12 bonis] bons *B*; 14 pro] p *C*; 15 compotes] coñpotes *B*; 16 simus] simul *H*; perennes] perenni *C*; 17 Laus honor virtus gloria *B*, Presta pater *Vm*, Laus honor *C, om. JVp*, Laus honor virtus *H*.

Commentary   Latin: *1–2 Cf.* ego ex ore Altissimi prodivi *Ecclesiasticus XXIV.5. 7 Vm's reading is that of* AH. *12 Cf.* beati qui persecutionem patiuntur propter iustitiam quoniam ipsorum est regnum caelorum *Matt. V.10. 16 C's reading may be connected with* perenne *being attested by* AH *for continental manuscripts. 17 According to* AH *BCH's doxology was the one mainly in use on the Continent.* Old English: *4* on ryne *should possibly be read* onryne, *cf. the gloss in JVp. Instead of* aurnenre *the present participle would have been preferable. 16 For* heofonbigende *read* heofonbugende.

34

YMNUS AD MATUTINAM

stefn   beorht   efne   swegþ
I   VOX CLARA, ECCE, INTONAT,

forsworcennyssa gehwilce heo þreaþ
obscura   quęque increpat.

heo adræfe feorran   swefnu
Pellat   eminus sompnia;

fram rodere crist   scinþ
ab *ethere Christus promicat.   4

mod   eallunga arisa   þæt slawe
II   Mens iam   resurgat torpida,

      þæt mid horuwe wunaþ gewæht
[11v] quę sorde   extat saucia;

186

<small>tungel scinþ   nu   niwe</small>
sidus refulget iam novum,
<small>þæt hit nyme ælc   þing derigendlices</small>
ut tollat   omne noxium.   8

<small>ufane   lamb   ys asænd</small>
III   Esursum agnus mittitur
<small>forgyfan togyfes gylt</small>
laxare gratis debitum.
<small>ealle   for   miltsunge</small>
Omnes pro indulgentia
<small>stefne   uton sellan mid   tearum</small>
vocem demus   cum lacrimis,   12

<small>oþer siþan þæt þænne scinþ</small>
IV   secundo ut cum fulserit
<small>7 middaneard   oga   befehþ</small>
mundumque horror cinxerit,
<small>na   for   scylde he gewítnige</small>
non pro reatu puniat,
<small>ac   arfæst us   þænne he gescilde</small>
sed pius nos tunc protegat.   16

Deo patri sit gloria

I   A clear voice resounds loudly and reproaches all that is dark. May it drive the dreams away. Christ is shining down from the sky.

II   Let the benumbed mind, which is wounded by defilement, rouse itself. Now a new heavenly body is kindled to remove all guilt.

III   A lamb is sent from high above to release us from our sinful debts without recompense. Let us all raise our voice in tears to obtain pardon

IV   so that, when it blazes up for the second time and terror overwhelms the world, it will not punish us according to our transgression, but benignly protect us then.

This hymn is prescribed at Lauds in Advent except in C, where it is assigned to Matins. It is anonymous. The metre is rhythmical Ambrosian hymn verse (4 × 8pp). The melody transmitted in C is Stäblein no. 402.

The text is included in the hymnals of BCDHVm and the *Expositio hymnorum* of JVp.

Bibliographical references: *ICL* no. 17528; *AH* 51, 48–9 (no. 49), Walpole no. 86.

Apparatus to D   Latin text: 3 Pellat] *a later hand corrects to* pellantur *adding* n *and abbreviated* ur *above the line.*

Old English gloss: 2 forsworcennyssa] e *dittographed, second* e *erased;* 15 gewítnige] *the position of the accent is ambiguous; it is on either the first or the second syllable.* 16 gescilde] i *by partial erasure from* l.

BVmCJVpH   Heading: hymnus ad matutinam *with* -ti- *inserted above with a caret mark by* B_1 *B,* YMNUS AD LAUDES *Vm,* HYMNUS AD NOCTURNUM *C,* VOX CLARA *J, no rubric VpH;* 3 Pellat] pellantur *BVm;* 4 ethere] ethrę *BVmCH;* 5 torpida] torpoda *Vm,* turpida *with* ur-*abbreviation C;* 8 tollat] tolle, *e altered to* a *and* t *interlined, probably by* H_1 *(Dewick:* tolla *and correction to* tollat) *H;* 11 indulgentia] indulgentiam, m *erased Vm;* 13 fulserit] fuerit, ls *interlined by* V_1 *Vp;* 16 tunc] *om. Vm;* 17 aus *(sic)* honor virtus gloria *B,* Laus honor *C, om. JVp,* Laus honor virtus *H.*

Commentary   Latin: 1 *Cf.* ego vox clamantis in deserto *John I.23.* 3 AH *reads* pellantur *as BVm and the corrector in D.* 4 *The metre requires* ethre *with syncope as in BVmCH.* 7 *For* sidus *cf.* sol iustitiae, *Mal. IV.2, or* stella splendida et matutina, *Rev. XXII.16.* 9–10 *Cf.* ecce agnus Dei qui tollit peccata mundi *John I.29.* 17 *BCH's doxology seems to be the one mainly in use on the Continent.*

35

YMNUS IN FESTIVITATE SANCTI ANDREĘ APOSTOLI

us   efne   dæg   endebyrdnysse mid gedafenlicre
I NOBIS, ECCE, DIES ORDINE   congruo

cymð nu   bryme   beorht   luflic
venit nunc celebris,   clarus, amabilis,

on ðam sigriend ofer   heage
quo   victor super alta

astah   gehende tunglu
scandit prope sidera.   4

drihtnes halig   apostol
II Andreas, domini sanctus apostolus

7 broðor   ealdres   æðelys
germanusque Petri,   principis incliti,

ealdor   sylf   werlic
princeps ipse virilis

efenhlytta on martyrdome he wæs
consors martirio   fuit.   8

fiscere   wæs
III   **Piscator fuerat   Petrus & Andreas,**

þaræfter begen onfengon   *embehwyrft 7 weredu
post   ambo rapiunt   orbis   & agmina,

berypton brymmas middaneardes
vastant aequora mundi

7   ricu   7   hi togetugon heofones
*& regna atque trahunt   poli.   12

þa hi   crist   gesiðan   on gangum 7 gelice
IV   **Dum Christum comites   gressibus & pares**

hi begeaton samod   lara   hi gegaderudon
exéquant pariter,   dogmata colligunt,

hys   deað   hi folgedon
eius mortem sequuntur

7 fotswaðu þurh rode
& vestigia per crucem.   16

amen

I Lo, now the celebrated, the illustrious, the lovely day has arrived for us in its turn, as it should, the day on which a victor mounts high above to the vicinity of the stars.

II Andrew, holy apostle of the Lord and brother of Peter, that famous prince, was himself a manly prince and shared the same martyrdom.

III Peter and Andrew had been fishers. Afterwards both also caught multitudes in the world, plundered the seas of this life and drew their catch up to the realms of heaven.

IV As the allies make equal progress and equally follow after Christ, they accumulate learning, they imitate his death and follow in his footsteps by being crucified.

This hymn was only in use in the Canterbury Hymnal, where it is assigned to the Feast of St Andrew (30 November). It is a short version of a much longer hymn which has been ascribed to to Hrabanus Maurus. The metre employed is the fourth Asclepiadeic stanza (two *asclepiadei minores*, a *pherecrateus* and a *glyconeus*). No melody has been transmitted in the Anglo-Saxon manuscripts. The text is included in the hymnals BDVm. Vm also has an interlinear gloss related to D's.

Bibliographical references: *ICL* no. 10274; *AH* 50, 201–2 (no. 150, long version), *AH* 14a, 130 (no. 129, short version).

Apparatus to D   Old English gloss: *This hymn is glossed by D₃.*

BVm   Heading: in natale sancti andreę apostoli *B*, DE SANCTO ANDREA APOS-TOLO YMNUS *Vm*; 16 amen] *om. Vm.*

Vm Old English gloss: 1 endebyrdnysse] ændebyrnysse; 2 beorht] breoht; 3 ðam] þan; heage] hege; 4 astaah gehænde tunge; 5 apostol] ærendraca; 7 broðor] broþer 7; *V glosses* Petri *as* petres *with erasure of one or two letters after* t; æðelys] æþeles; 8 efenhlytta] efynhlytta; wæs] wes; 9 *second half-line glossed:* peter 7 andreas; 10 þaræfter] þæræfter; onfengon embehwyrft] onfengen ymbhwyrfte; weredu] werudu; 11 berypton brymmas] beryptan brymmes; 14 hi begeaton] hio begeatan; samod] *another hand (probably) adds in the margin:* l ætgædere; hi] *V₁ writes* y *above* i; gegaderudon] gegæderedon; 15 hi folgedon] hy folgodon; 16 fotswaðu] fotswaþa; þurh] þruh.

Commentary   Latin: 4 *Cf. Hy 79/1. The line is metrically defective.* AH *has* propere. 5–6 *Cf. Matt. X.2.* 9–12 *Cf. Matt. IV.18 and Mark I.16–18.* 12 AH *reads* ad *for* et, *but the abbreviated version in* AH *14a, 130, originally also had* et. *As it stands,* trahunt *must be taken as the equivalent of* attrahunt. 15–16 *For the death of St Andrew cf. 'Passio sancti Andreae Apostoli', ed. M. Bonnet, in* Acta Apostolorum Apocrypha, *ed. R. A. Lipsius and M. Bonnet (Leipzig, 1898) II, 1, 1–37.* 15 *Cf. John XXI.19. Old English:* 10 *The gen. sg.* orbis *is mistaken for* nom.

36

INCIPIUNT YMNI DE NATALE DOMINI. YMNUS AD VESPERAM

[12r] ó   s.gentium
      eala þu crist   alysend   ealra þeoda
I   CHRISTE, REDEMPTOR OMNIUM,

      of   fæder   fæderes ancænneda
      EX PATRE patris unice,

      ana   ǽr   anginne
      solus ante principium

acænned unasecgendlice
natus ineffabiliter,   4

  es   es
þu eart leoht   þu eart byrhtnyss fæderes
II tu   lumen, tu   splendor patris,

  es
þu eart hiht ece   ealra
tu   spes perennis omnium,

begém   þa þa asendaþ bena
intende, quas fundunt preces

þine *geon embhwerft
tui per orbem   famuli.   8

            s. nostre   ó
gemun þu ure   hæle eala þu ealdor
III Memento,   salutis   auctor,

þæt   ures   gefyrn   lichoman
quod nostri quondam corporis

of ungewæmmedum mædene
ex inlibata   virgine

*acænnende hiw   þu underfenge
nascendo formam sumpseris.   12

swa andweard *ys geseþed dæg
IV Sic presens testatur dies

yrnende geond gæres ymbrene
currens per anni circulum,

       s.tu
þæt þu ana   fram setle fæderes
quod solus a   sede patris

middaneardes hæl þu come
mundi   salus adveneris.   16

               s. laudat   s. diem   & laudat
þysne heofon 7 eorþe hereð þisne dæg sæ 7 hereð
V Hunc celum, terra,   hunc   mare,

    s. diem
þisne dæg eall   þæt on heom ys
hunc   omne, quod in eis est,

ealdor   tocymes þines
auctorem adventus tui

hyrað blissigende mid lofsange
laudat exultans cantico.   20

we   eac swilce we þe halgum þinum
VI   Nos quoque, qui   sancto tuo

alysede   synt   mid blode
redempti sumus sanguine,

for dæge   gebyrdtide þinre
ob diem natalis   tui

lofsang   niwne   we samodhleoþriaþ
ymnum novum concinimus.   24

wuldor þe   drihten
VII   Gloria tibi, domine,

þu þe acænned eart of mædene
qui natus és de virgine,

mid fæder 7 þam halgan gaste
cum patre & sancto   spiritu

on ece   worulda
in sempiterna secula.   28
         amen

I Christ, redeemer of all men, begotten as only Son of the Father by the Father, you who alone were born before the beginning in an inexpressible manner,

II you who are light, you who are the splendour of the Father, you who are the everlasting hope of all, listen to the prayers which your servants recite throughout the world.

III Remember, champion of salvation, that you once took the form of our body upon yourself and were born of an unsullied virgin.

IV So this day today attests, recurring as it does within the year's cycle, that you and you alone came from the seat of the Father to be the salvation of the world.

V Heaven praises this day, the earth and the sea praise it, everything that is in them praises it joyfully with its song as the occasion of your coming.

VI We also, who have been redeemed by your holy blood, sing a new song together in honour of your birthday.

VII Glory be to you, Lord, who were born of a virgin, together with the Father and the Holy Ghost in eternity.

This hymn was sung at Vespers at Christmas. The collectar and hymnal in H prescribe it only for second Vespers and have Hy 44 for the first Vespers on Christmas Eve. The monastic hymnals and the collectar in C, however, clearly intend it for first Vespers. The hymn is written in rhythmical Ambrosian hymn verse (4 × 8pp). No melody has been transmitted in the Anglo-Saxon manuscripts. The text is contained in the hymnals of BCDH and the *Expositio hymnorum* of JVp.

Bibliographical references: *ICL* no. 2221, *AH* 51, 49–50 (no. 50), cf. *AH* 2, 36 (no. 22), Walpole no. 87.

Apparatus to D   Old English gloss: 5 s *erased in front of first* eart; 15 *small erasure after* ana, *possibly of* a; 24 þ *erased in front of* lofsang.

BVmCJVpH   Heading: hymnus in natale domini ad vesperam *B*, IN NATALE DOMINI. YMNUS AD VESPERAS *Vm*, IN NATALE DOMINI AD VESPERAM *C*, CHRISTE REDEMPTOR *J*; 1 REDEMPTOR] redemtor *C*; 5 *first* tu] Mu *C*; tu splendor patris] *om. JVp*; 8 famuli] famulis *C*; 12 nascendo] noscendo *C*; sumpseris] sumpserit *C*; 13 Sic] Hic *CJVpH, however the gloss in JVp is* þus; 16 adveneris] is *on erasure B* (*not mentioned by Wieland*), advenerit *C*; 17 terra] terre *C*; 19 auctorem adventus tui] adventu sui auctoris *JVp*; 20 exultans] exultat *C*; 21 sancto] *om. J*; 25–9 *Vm's doxology is* Laus, honor, virtus, gloria. 26 és] est *C, in H* es *is by another hand*; 28 amen] *om. VmH*.

Commentary   Latin: 1 *is identical with Hy 32/3.* 8 *C's reading* famulis *is attested for continental manuscripts by AH; AH reads* servuli. 9 *Cf. Heb. II.10.* 13 *AH reads* hic, *but also attests* sic *for the Continent.* 17–20 laetentur caeli et exultet terra, commoveatur mare et plenitudo eius *Ps. XCV.11.* 19 *AH attests* auctoris adventus sui *for continental manuscripts.* 24 *Cf. Ps. XCV.1.* 25–9 *Both doxologies seem to have been current on the Continent.* Old English: 8 *For* geon *read* geond; *the omission of the gloss to* famuli *might be connected with C's reading* famulis. 12 *This really should be an inflected ('passive') infinitive. Compare the gloss in JVp:* to acennanne. 13 *The deponent verb is mistakenly glossed as a passive.*

37

YMNUS AD NOCTURNAM

    arisende   to þe   drihten
I SURGENTES AD TE, DOMINE,
    sweartre nihte   on swigean
    atre   noctis silentio
      [12v] vigiliis obsequimur

patrum sequentes ordinem, 4

II   quem nobis dereliquerunt
iure hereditario
ministrantes excubiis
tibi, sanctę paraclite. 8

III   Pari cum patre clarus es,
cum Christo subtilissimus,
multis modis & spiritus
rex mysticus agnosceris. 12

IV   Fragiles carne conspice;
quos ille antiquissimus
suis decepit artibus,
tuis trahe virtutibus. 16

V   Grex tuus tibi deditus
non teneatur crimine,
quem tuo, Christe, sanguine
voluisti redimere. 20

VI   Oves errantes previde,
pastor bone piissime,
ad aulam celsitudinis
tuis reporta humeris. 24

VII   Tabefactus & saucius
abscedat princeps demonum;
perdat predam de faucibus
fur inportunis rabidus. 28

VIII   Exultet Christus dominus.
Psallat chorus angelicus,
laudes sonans in organo
ter 'sanctus' dicat domino. 32

IX   Gloriam tibi dicimus,
pater, una cum filio,
simul cum sancto spiritu;
in trina laude personet. 36

I Lord, we arise to attend you in the silence of the black night and are obedient in keeping our vigil. In this we follow the custom of our fathers,

II which they bequeathed to us as our inheritance, for they served you by keeping watch in the night, o Holy Ghost.

III You are glorious with the Father, who is equal with you, you are very subtle together with Christ and in many ways you are also known as the Spirit, the mystic King.

IV Direct your attention to those who are in the flesh and vulnerable; draw upwards by your wondrous powers those whom that very old one deceived with his tricks.

V Let the flock that is devoted to you not be bound by iniquity, the flock that you, Christ, were willing to redeem with your blood.

VI Watch out for erring sheep, good and most benevolent shepherd; carry them home on your shoulders to the court above.

VII May the prince of demons retreat paralysed and wounded. May the raving thief be deprived of the prey removed from his brutal jaws.

VIII May Christ, the Lord, rejoice in victory. May the angels' choir chant and salute the Lord three times with their 'Sanctus', letting his praises resound in harmony.

IX We say: 'Glory to you, Father, together with the Son and the Holy Ghost. May it resound in threefold praise.'

This hymn is prescribed in the Canterbury Hymnal for the Matins (Nocturn) of Christmas. It is written in rhythmical Ambrosian hymn verse (4 × 8pp) with a tendency to rhyme. No melody has been transmitted in the Anglo-Saxon manuscripts. The text is included in the hymnals of BDVm. The text in Vm has an interlinear gloss, which is related to D, but continues independently.

Bibliographical references: *ICL* no. 15895; *AH* 27, 113–15 (no. 78), cf. *AH* 14a, 25–6 (no. 10).

Apparatus to D   Latin text: 26 abscedat] *possibly an accent on the first* a, *very faint.* 33 Gloriam] *the abbreviation mark for* m *may be by another hand;* 36 *above* personet *another hand* (D₂?) *has interlined* permanens.

Old English gloss: *The gloss to lines 1–2 is written by hand D₃ and stops at the foot of the page.*

BVm   Heading: hymnus ad nocturnam B, *om.* Vm; 4 ordinem] ordine Vm; 17 tibi] *om.* Vm; 25 Tabefactus] Labefactus Vm; 28 rabidus] rapidus Vm; 33 Gloriam] Gloria BVm; 36 trina] trinea Vm; BVm *add* Amen.

V Old English gloss: 2 swigean] swigen; 3 on wecce wæ gehyrsumiað 4 fædera filigende *y ændebyrde 5 þæne us forletan 6 *unglossed* 7 þenigende *of bædde 8 þe halig frefrigende 9 gelic mid fæder breoht þu eart 10 mid criste *smeaþacal 11 mycel mænifeald 7 gast 12 cyningc renisc *ancnawan 13 tydre flæsc besyoh 14 þa se *þa wyrrestan 15 his beswaac 16 þinum teoh mægnum 17 eowod þin *þu sealdest 18 ne syo ymbhæfd mid leahtre 19 *(three or four letters erased)* þæne þine crist mid blode 20 þu woldest alysen 21 scep dweligende *forecum 22 heorde god *arfæste 23 to healle (h *interlined above*) heanysse 24 þinum ongeanber exlum 25 aswunden geworden 7 forworden 26 gewite ealdor deofle 27 forspille hyþe of gomum 28 þeof ungedafenlic gredicg 29 gefægnie crist drihten 30 singe wered *æglic 31 lof swegende on organo 32 þreowa halig cweþe drihtne 33 wuldor þe we secgað 34 fæder *anum mid suna 35 samod mid halgan gast 36 on þriofealda lofe swege. swa hit gewurðe.

Commentary   Latin: 2 *Cf.* Hy 23/1. 5 *The metre indicates that* dereliquerunt *is stressed on the third syllable in the post-Classical manner.* 14 *Cf.* serpens antiquus *Rev. XII.9, XX.2.* 21–4 *Cf.* John X *(especially* pastor bonus *in verses 10, 11 and 14) and Luke XV.5.* 26 *For* princeps daemonum *cf. Matt. IX.34, Luke XI.15.* 28 *For* fur *cf. John X.8 and 10.* 33 *AH reads* Gloria.

38

YMNUS AD MATUTINAM

       ó
   gehyr eala þu alysend   þeoda
I   AUDI,   REDEMPTOR GENTIUM,
   gebyrdtide þinre wuldor
   natalis   tui gloriam

          útagán   fram gode
   Bethleem egressus a   deo

              *geeacnung mædenes
   [13r] Marię   partus   virginis.   4

      ó
   eala þu crist   mihta   drihten
II   Christe, virtutum domine,
   na of werlicum sæde
   non ex virili   semine,

godcundnysse anre
divinitatis unius

7 efenlytta þæs halgan gastes
consorsque sancti spiritus, 8

þu eart mihtig ealra hæl
III es potens omnium salus.

on þe gelyfende alys
In te credentes libera.

strang æghwær on gewinne
Fortis ubique in prꬿlio

us synfullan genere
nos peccatores eripe. 12

acænnedne god of gode
IV Genitum deum ex deo

we wundriað on þisum lichoman
miramur in hoc corpore,

mannan gode gelicne
hominem deo similem,

geryne wunderlic
mysterium mirabile. 16

nu we swa swa halige gelyfaþ
V Iam nos, ut sancti, credimus,

wundriað eac swilce ænglas
obstupescunt et angeli

on clænan acænnedne lichoman
casto nascentem corpore

hyrde of mægþe iudan
pastorem ex tribu Iuda. 20

leoht *ageotende forspilledum
VI Lumen refundens perditis

ordfruman *heretogan
Iesse originem ducis,

clæne hrepunga flæsclicre
mundus contactu carneo,

beon þæt þæt þu woldest þu eart
esse quod voluisti, es. 24

gebyrdtide þinre gefea
VII Natalis tui gaudium,

þæt þæt mann acænned of gode
quod homo natus ex deo,

ealle we andettað suna
omnes fatemur filium,

rice fæderlic *þurwunigende
regnum paternum permanens. 28

ece lofu we secgaþ
VIII Perennes laudes dicimus

fæder gode mid sunan
patri deo cum filio,

se ys geciged of egypto lande
qui est vocatus ex Aegypto

þurh his þenas god
per suos famulos deus. 32

geedcynnede of þam halgan gaste
IX Renati sancto spiritu

leoht we geseoþ lace
lumen videmus muneris.

swa þe feligende drihten
Sic te sequentes dominum

hale we beoþ ealne weg
salvi erimus iugiter. 36

Gloria tibi, domine

I Redeemer of nations, hear the glory of the day of your birth, you who came out of Bethlehem from God as the son of the virgin Mary.

II Christ, lord of heavenly powers, you who were not born of male seed and who partake of a single divine essence together with the Holy Ghost,

III you are the efficacious salvation of all. Free those who believe in you. You who are strong in battle everywhere, rescue us sinners.

IV In amazement we behold God begotten by God in this body, a man like God, a wonderful mystery.

V We believe now as the saints do; the angels, too, are awe-struck to see the shepherd of the tribe of Juda born from a chaste body.

VI You who restore the light to those who were lost, you trace your lineage back to Jesse. You are clean of all infection of the flesh. You are what you wished to be.

VII We all bear witness to the joy of your birthday, that you were born of God as a man, we bear witness to the son, to the everlasting kingdom of the Father.

VIII We recite constant praise of God the Father with the Son, who was called out of Egypt for his servants.

IX Reborn through the Holy Ghost, we see light granted to us. Thus in following you as our lord we shall be saved forever.

The hymn was sung at Lauds at Christmas according to the monastic hymnals, while in H (collectar and, possibly, hymnal) it is divided between Matins and Lauds on the Octave and not used on Christmas Day itself. Usually the hymns sung on the Octave are the same as those of the feast and this, rather than H's usage, is probably meant by the reference to the Octave in the rubric to the prose version in V. The hymn is written in rhythmical Ambrosian hymn verse (4 × 8pp) and follows the abecedarian scheme (to S), using two-line units. No melody is transmitted in the Anglo-Saxon hymnals. The text is included in the hymnals of BCDHVm and the *Expositio hymnorum* of JVp.

Bibliographical references: *ICL* no. 1331; *AH* 14a, 26–7 (no. 11).

Apparatus to D   Latin text: 11 Fortis] *originally* fortes, i *interlined above* e, *probably by* D_1; 17 nos] *interlined above by* D_1, *a later hand added a caret mark below; three or four letters erased at the end of the line*; 19 nascentem] *originally* nascendo, -tem *interlined above by* D_1, *original ending expunged*; 29 Perennes] s *inserted with the pen used for glossing*; 36 salvi erimus] *written together and separated by a comma.*

BVmCJVpH   Heading: ad matutinam B, ITEM YMNUS Vm, HYMNUS AD MATUTINUM C, IN OCTABAS DOMINI YMNUS. AUDI redemptor gentium Vp, AUDI REDEMPTOR J; 1 GENTIUM] gntium C; 4 partus] partum C; 6 semine] *added in the margin by* J_1 J; 9 es] *small erasure after* E C; 11 Fortis] forces C; 16 mirabile] mirabili JVp; mysterium] mysterio JVp; 17 Iam] Nam B; 18 obstupescunt] obtupescunt C; 19 nascentem] nascendo Vm, uascentem C; 22 originem] orriginem J; 23 contactu] contacto C; 26 homo natus ex deo es VmCJVpH; 31 ex] *om.* B; 32 per suos famulos] pro suis famulis VmC; 34 muneris] munere C; 35 te] *om.* B; dominum] domine JVp; 37 *om.* JVp; C *continues*: qui natus est; H *continues*: qui natus es *with* es *changed to* est *by a later hand*. BVm *reads* Laus, honor, virtus, gloria, B *continues*: deo patri et filio.

Commentary   Latin: *The prose version in V was accidentally omitted. It was subsequently inserted after the feast of St Stephen and the rubric attempts to justify this placement, as the Octave follows the feast of Stephen.* 7 unius *was clearly stressed on the first syllable.* 11 *Cf.* Dominus fortis et potens, Dominus potens in proelio *Ps. XXIII.8.* 19 *Note that Vm agrees with the original reading of D.* 20 *Cf.* leo de tribu Iuda *Rev. V.5.* 31 *Cf.* Ex Aegypto vocavi Filium meum *Hos. XI.1 and Matt. II.15.* Old English: 4 partus, -i, *'son' is confused with* partus, -us, *'conception, birth'.* 21 *The gloss ignores the prefix* re-. 22 ducis *is from* ducere. *Compare the gloss in* J *(but not Vp):* þu læst. 28 *Read* þurhwunigende.

39

ITEM YMNUS

       ó
   cum   eala þu alysend   þeoda
I   VENI,   REDEMPTOR GENTIUM,

   ætyw   geeacnunge mædenes
   ostende partum   virginis,

   *wundrað eall   worulde
   miretur omne seculum.

       swilc gedafenað geeacnung
   [13v] Talis decet   partus   deum.   4

   na   of werlicum sæde
II Non ex virili   semine,

   ac   of gerynelicum blæde ł gaste
   sed mystico   spiramine,

   word   godes geworden flæsc
   verbum dei factum caro

   7 wæstm   innoþes scán
   fructusque ventris floruit.   8

   rif   toþand   mædenes
III Alvus tumescit virginis,

   *clysing clænnysse þurhwunaþ
   claustra pudoris *permane*t*.

   guþfanan mihta   scinaþ
   Vexilla virtutum micant.

   drohtnaþ on temple   god
   Versatur in templo deus.   12

forþstæppende of bredbure his
IV Procedens de thalamo suo,

clænnyssa heall cynelic
pudoris aula regia,

getwinre ormæte edwiste
gemine gigas substantiæ,

glæd   þæt he yrne weg
alacris ut currat viam;   16

utfæreld his   fram fæder
V egressus eius a   patre,

ongeancyme his to fæder
regressus eius ad patrem

7 utrene   to helle
excursusque ad inferos,

ongeancyme to setle   godes
recursus   ad sedem dei.   20

gelic   þan ecan fæder
VI Æqualis aeterno patri,

lichoman mid sige *befon
carnis   tropheo accingere,

untrumnyssa ures   lichoman
infirma   nostri corporis

mihte   getrymende ecere
virtute firmans   perpeti.   24

binn   eallunga scinþ þin
VII Presepe iam   fulget tuum

7 leoht   niht eþað   niwe
lumenque nox spirat novum,

þæt nan   niht *betwuxsende
quod nulla nox interpolat

7 *geleafan *singalum scine
fidesque   iugis   luceat.   28

wuldor þe   drihten
Gloria tibi, domine

I Come, redeemer of nations, and reveal that a virgin has given birth.
Let all the world behold it in wonder. Such a birth befits God.

II Not by the seed of man, but through mystical inspiration the Word
of God was made flesh and the fruit of the womb flourished.

III The womb of the virgin swells, while the barrier of chastity remains. The banners of her virtues shine out – God is dwelling in his temple,

IV who comes out of his wedding chamber, out of the royal court of modesty, as a giant of a twofold nature in order to run his race joyfully.

V His going forth is from the Father and his return to the Father, his departure is to hell and his re-entry is into the seat of God.

VI You who are equal to the eternal Father, gird yourself with the trophy of the flesh and strengthen the weakness of our body with everlasting power.

VII Now your manger shines forth and the night is suffused with a light not known before. May no night invade it and may constant faith shed its light (*or according to JVp:* may it be lighted with constant faith).

This hymn was sung at Matins at Christmas according to the Winchester Hymnal and H (collectar and hymnal). How it was used in the Canterbury Hymnal cannot be determined, but cf. its use at Compline on the third and fourth Sundays of Advent and on the Vigil of Christmas according to the collectar in H. This is Ambrose's Christmas hymn *Intende qui regis* (OHy 34 of the Old Hymnal) without its first stanza. The omission of the first stanza is general in the New Hymnal. The metre is Ambrosian iambic dimeter. A melody is transmitted in H. This seems to be a slightly simpler version of Stäblein no. 406. The text is included in the hymnals of CDHVm and the *Expositio hymnorum* of JVp.

Bibliographical references: *ICL* no. 8189; *AH* 50, 13–14 (no. 8), cf. *AH* 2, 36 (no. 21), Bulst, pp. 43 and 183 (II, 5), Walpole no. 6.

Apparatus to D   Latin text: 10 permanet] permanent *with* nt *on erasure of a letter without ascenders by another hand.* 19 *A later hand has interlined an* us-*abbreviation mark above and corrected to* excursus usque.

Old English gloss: 9 *one letter erased in front of* rif, *probably* r.

Latin gloss: 15 *in the outer margin by another hand*: Gigas i. vir grandis fortis ł terrigena. *The final* a *apparently altered to* -um, *but the alteration was cancelled by erasure.*

VmCJVpH   *Heading:* ITEM YMNUS *Vm*, HYMNUS AD NOCTURNAM *C*, VENI

REDEMPTOR *J*; 1 REDEMPTOR] redemtor *C*; 7 factum] factum̄ *Vp*, factum est *H*; 10 claustra] claustrum *JVp*, clastrum *with* u *interlined above by* *C₁* *C*; permanet] permanent *VmH*; 11 micant] micat *C*; 13 Procedens] procedat *CJVpH*; de] *om. H*; 15 gemine] germine *C*; gigas] gigans *VmCH*; 16 ut currat viam] occurrit vivam *C*; 18 eius] ei *C*; 19 excursusque] excursus usque *VmCJVpH*; inferos] inferros *C*; 21 patri] patris *C*; 24 perpeti] perpetim *CVm*; 27 quod] quę *C*; 28 fidesque iugis] fideque iugi *CJVpH*; 29 Laus honor virtus *VmH*, *JVp omit*.

Commentary   Latin: *4 Bulst reads* deo, *but notes the variant* deum. *7 Cf. John I.44. Bulst reads* factum est *as in H. AH attests omission of* est *only in one continental manuscript. 10 Before its correction the line in D must have been a contamination of CJVp's* claustrum ... permanet *and VmH's* claustra ... permanent. *Bulst reads* claustrum ... permanet; *the plural is attested by AH for continental manuscripts. 13–20 These stanzas are based on Ps. XVIII.6–7. 13 Bulst reads* procedat e, *but* procedens *and* de *are attested by AH for the Continent also. 16 Bulst reads* occurrat *(cf. C), but notes the variant* ut currat. *19 D's* excursusque *may be due to haplography, but the gloss agrees with it. 27 Bulst reads* interpolet. *28 Bulst reads* fideque iugi. *Old English: 3 The optative is required. 4 The omission of the gloss to* deum *is obviously accidental. 10* clysing *glosses the singular of CJVp. 22 The imperative of the deponent has been mistaken for an active infinitive. 27* betwuxsende *apparently glosses the reading attested in the earliest continental manuscripts:* interpolet. *28* geleafan singalum *apparently glosses the reading in CJVpH.*

40

YMNUS DE SANCTO STEPHANO PROTOMARTIRE

      lofsang   uton singan   drihtne
I YMNUM CANTEMUS DOMINO,

      lofsang   cyðere
      ymnum martyri Stephano,

      criste   swa swa cyninge ealra
      Christo, ut   regi   omnium,

           swa swa fyrmystum cyðere
      Stephano, ut   primo   martiri,   4

      criste   swa fædres anlicum suna
II Christo, ut patris unico,

          swa þeowe
      Stephano, ut vernaculo,

      criste   gode 7 menn
      Christo deo & homini,

swa haligum menn
Stephano, ut sancto homini,   8

    criste   þæt   middanearde acenned
III [14r] Christo, quod mundo   genitus,

    þæt   dead
Stephano, quia mortuus,

criste   þæt   lif   he tobrohte
Christo, quod vitam contulit,

    þæt he deað þolude
Stephano, quod mortem pertulit,   12

criste   þæt he nyðer astah
IV Christo, quia descenderat,

    þæt   he up astah
Stephano, quod ascenderat,

criste   þæt he eorðan geneosude
Christo, quod terras adiit,

    þæt   he heofenas geferde
Stephano, quod celos petiit.   16

si lof gode fæder unacennedum
V Laus patri sit ingenito,

*laf suna ancennedum
laus nato unigenito,

lof si þam haligum gaste
laus sit sancto   spiritui

swa mære getiðiendum cyðere
tanta   prestanti   martiri.   20

I Let us sing a hymn to the Lord, a hymn to Stephen, the martyr, to Christ, because he is the king of all, to Stephen, because he was the first martyr,

II to Christ, because he is the only-begotten son of the Father, to Stephen, because he is his servant, to Christ, who is God and man, to Stephen, because he was a holy man,

III to Christ, because he was born to the world, to Stephen, because he died, to Christ, because he conferred life, to Stephen, because he endured death,

IV to Christ, because he descended, to Stephen, because he ascended, to

Christ, because he came to earth, to Stephen, because he went to heaven.

v Praise be to the Father, who was never begotten, praise to the Son, who is the Only-Begotten, praise be to the Holy Ghost, who granted such great gifts to the martyr.

This hymn was sung on the feast of St Stephen (26 December), probably at Matins as C's rubric prescribes. It is not included in the collectar of H. It is anonymous. Its metre is rhythmical; the first four stanzas are 3 × 8pp, 1 × 9pp, the last stanza is 4 × 8pp. No melody has been transmitted in the Anglo-Saxon manuscripts. The text is included in the hymnals of CDHVm and the *Expositio hymnorum* of C.

Bibliographical references: *ICL* no. 7443; *AH* 51, 226–7 (no. 195).

Apparatus to D   Old English gloss: *This hymn is glossed by D₃.* 15 geneosude] o *damaged and might possibly be* a; 16 geferde] D₃'s e *imperfect and very like* o; 20 getiðiendum] *cross stroke of the* eth *missing, but the letter is not* d.

VmCJVpH   Heading: YMNUS DE SANCTO STEPHANO *Vm*, HYMNUS AD NOCTURNUM *C*, HYMNUM CANTEMUS *J, no rubric VpH;* 1 YMNUM] Yymnum *VmH;* CANTEMUS] canamus *Vm*, ca. . .mus *with erasure of two letters* (re.?) *C;* 4 martiri] martyrum *H;* 5–8 *om. JVp, transposed after lines 9–12 in H;* 5 patris] s *altered from* f *Vm;* 8 homini] martiro *C;* 12 pertulit] protulit *C;* 13 quia] que *C;* 17 patri] patro, o *altered to* i *by V₁ Vm;* 18 nato] *om. JVp;* 19 spiritui] spiritu *C;* 20 prestanti] prestante *C;* martiri] martirii *C*, martiru *H (Dewick reads* martirii*); H adds* AMEN.

Commentary   Latin: *For the account of St Stephen's martyrdom, see Acts VI and VII.* 1 Cf. *Hy 73/1. AH attests* canamus *in one continental manuscript.* 4 AH *reads* martyrum *like H, but attests* martyri *for one continental manuscript.* 18 AH *reads* patris *instead of* nato, *but one continental manuscript shares the reading of JVp.*

41

ITEM YMNUS

   ó
eala þu halga   godes deorwurþe
I   SANCTE, DEI PRETIOSAE
se forma cyþere
protomartyr Stephane,

þu þe on mihte soþre lufe
qui virtute caritatis

underwreoþod æghwanone
circumfultus undique

drihten for feondlicum
dominum pro inimico

þu gebæde folce
exorasti populo, 6

asynd bena for estfullum
II funde preces pro devoto

þe nu gefyrrædene
tibi nunc collegio,

þæt þinre gemiltsod
ut tuo propitiatus

mid þingrædene drihten
interventu dominus

us afeormode fram synne
nos purgatos a peccato

geþeode heofones cæstergewarum
iungat cæli civibus. 12

wuldor 7 wurþment gode
III Gloria & honor deo

oþ ðam *hehstan
usque coaltissimo

samod fæder 7 suna
una patri filioque

7 þam æþelan frofergaste
inclito paraclito,

þæs wyrþment 7 miht
cuius honor & potestas

geond ece worulda
per aeterna saecula. 18

AMEN

I You who are holy and of great worth, first of God's martyrs, Stephen, you who were supported at every point by the miraculous strength of charity and thus prayed to the Lord for the people who were your enemies,

II appeal now with your prayers for the community devoted to you so that God may be appeased by your intervention and, purifying us from sin, may allow us to join the citizens of heaven.

III Glory and honour be to God, the Father, the Son and the glorious Holy Ghost, forever equally most high, whose honour and might shall last world without end.

This hymn was sung on the feast of St Stephen (26 December), probably at Lauds in the Canterbury Hymnal, but according to the collectar in H at Vespers. It is not included in the Winchester Hymnal. It has been ascribed to Eusebius Bruno, bishop of Angers (d. 1081). Its metre is rhythmical, but not quite regular; the structure of the stanza is $3 \times (8p+7pp)$. No melody is transmitted in the Anglo-Saxon manuscripts. The text is included in the hymnals of VmDH. Vm also contains an Old English interlinear gloss related to that in D.

Bibliographical reference: *AH* 48, 83–4 (no. 79).

VmH   Heading: ITEM *Vm*; 3 caritatis] *a small erasure after* c *H*; 11 peccato] peccatis *H*; 13–18 *H has the doxology:* Gloriam patri melodis / personemus vocibus / gloriam christo canamus / gloriam paraclito / qui deus trinus & unus / extat ante secula. amen. 14 usque coaltissimo] usquequo altissimo *Vm*; 18 *Vm omits* amen.

    Vm Old English gloss: 1 halga] haliga; deorwurþe] deorwurde; 2 forma] forme; 5 feondlicum] feonlicum; 7 asynd bena] agyot bene; 8 *a letter erased after* þe; 9 gemiltsod] gemildsod; 12 heofones cæstergewarum] heofnes ceastergewaran; 13 wurþment] wurþmynt; 16 frofergaste] froforgast; 17 wyrþment] wurþmynt; miht] mihta; 18 geond] þurh; worulda] wurulda.

Commentary   Latin: 5–6 *Cf. Acts VII.60.* 11 AH *reads* peccatis *like H, attesting* peccato *for continental manuscripts as well.* 12 *Cf.* Hy 48/7–10. 14 AH *attests* usquequo altissimo *as in* Vm *for the Continent.* Old English: 14 hehstan] *The prefix* co- *is ignored in the gloss, which could indicate that it is based on the reading of* Vm.

42

YMNUS AD VESPERAM

eallunga glitenaþ	halig	dæg	7 beorht	þearle
IAM RUTILAT	SACRATA	DIES	& splendida	valde,

on þam is middanearde gewurþod on eallum   se forma þrowære
quo   mundo   colitur   toto   Stephanus protomartyr,

witodlice dæg se georstenlica   god   besceawede on wangum
namque dies hesterna   deum   conspexit in arvis

s. dies
acænnedne þes dæg   healicre acende *nerxnewange
natum, hęc   Stephanum   celso peperit paradyso.

þes   wurþe   geearnungum   7 *æþelborenysse *him
Hic Stephanus dignus meritis   [14v] & stemmatis   illo,   5

þæt   nama   swegð   scinþ   gewuldorbeagod on wurþmente
quod nomen resonat, fulget   decoratus   honore.

blodige   gemængende *trepas ł werodu   mid þeode reþre
Sanguineas miscens   acies   cum gente feroci

þes sigefæste geearnode beorhte   ongeanbringan sigas
hic victor   meruit   claros   retulisse   triumphos.

              ó
us   eadmode   þrowære eala þu stemenda   þe we biddaþ ealle
Nos humiles, martyr   redolens,   té poscimus omnes:

þæs egeslican þæt ðu do feondes   aidlian   awyrgede
horrendi facias   hostis   vacuisse malignas   10

syrwunga 7   þa   forgyfenysse   for slæge þu agyldst
insidias &, quam veniam   pro cedę rependis,

urum   þas   wommum   eadmodum ongeanbring *muðe we biddaþ
nostris hanc maculis,   prono,   refer,   ore precamur,

7 swa   gode acænnedum þu forgyfe   geþeodan *þam heofonlican
sicque deo nato   tribuas   herere   supernis,

þam sy mærlice   mægen   7 wurðment butan ænde
cui sit magnifice virtus   & honor   sine fine.

                    AMEN

Already the sacred and most brilliant day is gleaming red on which Stephen, the first martyr, is revered all over the world, for yesterday saw God born on earth, this day caused Stephen to be born to paradise above. This Stephen is illustrious, worthy in his merits and exalted by that honour which his name proclaims, the crown. Engaging in bloody warfare with a fierce race, he conquered and deserved the famous victory he gained. We all ask you humbly, martyr sweetly fragrant, let the wicked traps of our dreaded foe be made vain and bestow on our faults that forgiveness with which you countered your murder, as we pray with bowed heads. And grant that we may remain faithful to God, the Son, in heaven, to whom be power and honour in glory without end.

This hymn was sung on the feast of St Stephen (26 December). It was used for Second Vespers in the Winchester and Canterbury Hymnals, but for Lauds according to the collectar in H. It is written in hexameters. The manuscript interpunctuation regularly divides them into stanzas of two verses each and this may reflect the structure of the melody, which is not transmitted in Anglo-Saxon manuscripts. The text is included in the hymnals of BCDHVm and the *Expositio hymnorum* of JVp.

Bibliographical references: *ICL* no. 7544; *AH* 19, 255 (no. 461) (uses VH).

Apparatus to D   Latin text: *The division of the hexameters reflects the scribe's punctuation of the caesura.* 2 quo] o *expunged and a written above by another hand*; 11 pro cedę rependis] *originally written as* procedęre pendis, *but* re *separated by a comma from the preceding word and connected to the following with a stroke, by* D_1? 12 refer ore] *written together and later separated by a comma, by* D_1?

Old English gloss: 12 eadmodum ongeanbring] *written together and separated by a comma, by* D_1?

BVmCJVpH   Heading: hymnus in festivitate sancti stephani protomartyris *B*, ITEM DE SANCTO STEPHANO YMNUS *Vm, no rubric, but it may have accidentally been included in the long preceding erasure C*, IAM RUTILAT *J, no rubric* VpH; 2 quo] qua *BCJVp*; 5 Hic] Sic *BVm*; stemmatis] stematis *CJVpH*; 6 resonat] resonet *J*; 9 Nos] Hos *H*; redolens] redoles *C*; 10 malignas] malignos *CVm*; 12 nostris] nrostris *B*; hanc] hac *C*; 14 AMEN] *om. CJVp*.

Commentary   Latin: 5–6 *Cf.* Martyrum primus in Novo Testamento Stephanus fuit. ... Idem autem ex Graeco sermone in Latinum vertitur coronatus, et hoc prophetice ut, quod sequeretur in re, vaticinio quodam futuri prius in vocabulo resonaret. Passus est enim et quod vocabatur accepit. *Isidore of Seville, VII. xi. 3–4.* Old English: 4 *D_1 is uncertain of the spelling of* neorxnawang, *cf. Hy 57/5, Hy 70/24.* 5 stemma *here means 'wreath'. The glossator does not appear to have understood the reference to the etymology ('quod nomen resonat') of the name* Stephanus. *The glossator also has not realized that* illo *is used adjectivally and belongs to* honore. 7 acies *is inappropriately glossed in its common meaning 'troops'.* 12 pronus *means 'inclined', 'bowed' and therefore, by implication, 'humble',* prono ore, *however, is 'with a (humbly) inclined face', rather than 'with a humble mouth'.* 13 *The glossator seems to have taken the ablative* supernis *for a dative.*

43

YMNUS IN EPIPHANIA DOMINI AD VESPERAM

se hælend scán   ealra
I   IESUS   REFULSIT OMNIUM

arfæst alysend   þeoda
PIUS REDEMPTOR gentium.

eall   cynn   geleaffulra
Totum genus fidelium

lofu   breme   herunga
laudes celebret dramatum.   4

þæne   steorra acænnedne scinende
II   Quem stella natum   fulgida

geswutelaþ scinende on rodere
monstrat micans in ethera

7 tungelwitegan he gelædde forestæppende
– magosque   duxit   previa

his   to   cildcradele
ipsius ad cunabula –   8

hi   feallende   cild
III   illi cadentes parvulum

mid cildclaðum gebædon bewundon
pannis   adorant obsitum

soþne   hi andettan 7 god
verum fatentur   & deum

lac   berende   rynelice
munus ferendo mysticum.   12

teonfealdum þriwa geara   ymbrenum
IV   Denis   ter   annorum ciclis

eallunga on dæle *þeonde
iam   parte   vivens corporis

wæter   he gefor fulluhtes
lympham petit   baptis[15r]matis

eallum   þoliende besmitennysse
cunctis carens   contagiis.   16

se sæliga   besæncan
V   Felix   Iohannes mergere

hine   beofode   on flode
illum tremescit flumine,

mihtig his se   mid blode *his
potens suo qui sanguine

synna   middaneardes adrigan
peccata cosmi   tergere.   20

stefn eornostlice tudder   of heofonum
VI Vox ergo   prolem de polis

geseþde healices fæderes
testatur excelsi patris

miht 7 ætwæs haliges gastes
virtus adestque pneumatis,

haligre forgifestre gyfe
sancti datrix   karismatis.   24

        ó
us   eala þu crist mid eadmodre bene
VII Nos,   Christe, supplici   prece

we biddaþ ealle   gescild
precamur omnes, protege,

þu þe bebeodst readian
qui precipis rubescere

mihtylice wæterfatu wæteres
potenter ydrias   aquę.   28

getiþa welwillendne geornfullum
VIII Presta benignum sedulo

frofer   fultume
solamen adiutorio

7 ædbrodene us   of helle
raptosque nos e tartaro

rixian   do mid þe on heofonan
regnare fac tecum polo.   32

lof   þrynnessa neadwis
IX Laus trinitati debita,

wurðmend miht   wuldor
honor,   potestas, gloria,

ecelice   sy ealla
perenniter sit omnia

geond worulda   woruld
per   seculorum secula.   36

AMEN

I Jesus blazed forth as the benevolent redeemer of all nations. May all the community of the faithful celebrate that with praise and psalms.

II The brilliant star glowing in the sky was the sign that he was born and, moving on before the magi, led them to his cradle.

III They threw themselves down and adored the little child, which was wrapped in swaddling clothes; they bore witness that he was the true God by bringing him a mystic gift.

IV Then, when, as far as his body was concerned, he had lived out the course of three times ten years, he sought the water of baptism, he who was free of all contamination.

V The blessed John trembles at the idea of immersing in the river the one who has the power to wipe away the sins of the universe with his blood.

VI So the voice of the Father above, coming from heaven, testifies that he is his son and the miraculous power of the Spirit, the conferrer of the holy gift, is also present.

VII We all pray to you in suppliant prayer, Christ: protect us, you who, in your power, order the jugs of water to turn red.

VIII Grant us benevolent relief together with constant aid and, having snatched us from hell, let us reign with you in heaven.

IX Praise be to the Trinity, as is proper, and honour, might and glory forever throughout the ages.

This hymn was sung at Epiphany. In the Canterbury Hymnal it is assigned to Vespers, in the Winchester Hymnal to Lauds, in the collectar of H to Matins (Nocturn). It is anonymous and written in Ambrosian iambic dimeter. This is the only hymn with neumes in D. The melody is so far unidentified. The text is included in the hymnals of CDHVm and the *Expositio hymnorum* in CJVp.

Bibliographical references: *ICL* no. 7672; *AH* 51, 51–2 (no. 52), cf. *AH* 2, 79 (no. 105), Walpole no. 90.

Apparatus to D   Latin text: 14 vivens] vigens, g *on erasure of one letter by another hand*; 18 tremescit] e *on erasure of* l *by* D_1; 19 potens] ns *imperfectly erased and altered to* st *by another hand*.

Old English gloss: 6 geswutelaþ] wynn *corrected from* þ; 27 bebeodst] bebidst, i *expunged,* eo *interlined by* D₁; 33 neadwis] *followed by erasure of* s.

VmCJVpH   Heading: ITEM UNDE SUPRA YMNUS *Vm*, HYMNUS AD MATUTINUM *C*, IESUS REFULSIT *J*, *no rubric VpH*; 4 celebret] celebrat *C*; dramatum] g *interlined between* a *and* m *probably by another hand Vm*, dragmatum *C*, g *interlined between* a *and* m *by another hand Vp*; 8 cunabula] conabula *C*; 13 ciclis] *second* i *erased from* u *C*; 14 vivens] viens *J*, vigens *Vp*; 15 petit] petiit *C*; 20 tergere] tangere *Vm*; 21 prolem] r *interlined above by* H₁ *H*; polis] poli *C*; 24 sancti] secli *Vm*; 25 Nos] Nox, N *altered by a later hand from* U *C*; prece] *omitted Vm*; 26 omnes, protege] protege omnes *Vm*; 27 rubiscere] s *altered from* f *Vm*; 29 sedulo] sedulus *C*; 30 adiutorio] adiutorium *C*; 31 e tartaro] et tartara *C*; aetartaro *JVp*; 32 polo] pola *C*; 33 debita] debitas *C*; 35 perenniter] perhennis *Vm*; 36 per] in *Vm*; AMEN] *omitted VmCJVp*.

Commentary   Latin: 5–7 *For* stella ... previa *cf. Hy* 45/6. 11–12 *Cf. Hy* 45/8. 14 *The original reading in D was clearly that of VmCH. Note that the alteration brings the Latin into line with the gloss and JVp.* 19 AH *reads* potest. 27–8 *Cf. Hy* 45/22. 31 *JVp's reading may be connected with AH's* a tartaro. AH *also attests* e tartaro *for the Continent.* 32 *Cf.* conregnabimus *II Tim. II.12.* Old English: 19 suo *is glossed twice due to the separation of the possessive pronoun from its noun in the Latin.*

44

YMNUS AD NOCTURNAM

I   fram þære sunnan *upspringes anginne
A   SOLIS   ORTU   CARDINE

oþ   eorðan gemære
ad usque terrę limitem

criste   uton herigan ealdre
Christo canamus   principi

*acænnedne of   mædene
nato   Maria virgine.   4

II   eadig   ealdor worulde
Beatus auctor saeculi

þeowtlicne lichoman embscredde
servile   corpus   induit,

þæt lichoma lichoman alysende
ut caro *canem liberans

þæt he ne forlure   þa ðe he gescop
ne   perderet, quod condidit.   8

213

clæne moder   innoþas
III   Casta parentis viscera

heofonlic inferde gyfe
cęlestis intrat gratia.

wamb   mædenes gebær
Venter puellę baiolat,

digelnysse þæt heone cuþe
secreta, quę non noverat.   12

hus   clænes breostes
IV   Domus pudici pectoris

tempel   færlice   wæs geworden godes
templum repente fit   dei.

         ungewæmmed nytende   wer
[15v] Intacta   nesciens virum

mid worde heo geeacnode suna
verbo   concepit   filium.   16

acende   hyseberþre
V   Enixa est puerpera,

þæne þe   foresæde
quem Gabriel predixerat,

þæne þe meder   on rife hoppetende
quem matris alvo gestiens

beclysed   undergeat
clausus Iohannes senserat.   20

streowe licgean ðolude
VI   Foeno iacere pertulit,

binne   na   aþracude
pręsepe non abhorruit

gehwædre meolce ðolude
parvoque lacte *passus est,

þurh ðæne   na   fugel hingrað
per quem nec ales esurit.   24

geblissað wered   heofonlicra
VII   Gaudet chorus cęlestium

7 englas singað   gode
& angeli canunt deo

7 openlice   byð hyrdum
palamque fit pastoribus

hyrde   scyppend ealra
pastor, creator omnium.   28

wuldor þe   drihten
VIII Gloria tibi, domine,
þu þe aþwogen eart on ea
qui lotus   es in flumine

I From the point of the sunrise unto the other boundary of the earth
let us sing to Christ, the prince born of the virgin Mary.

II The blessed founder of the world clothed himself in the body of a
slave in order that flesh should free the flesh so that he would not
lose what he had created.

III Heavenly grace enters the chaste womb of the mother; the womb of
a girl carries mysteries of which she did not know.

IV The dwelling of a modest breast suddenly becomes the temple of
God. She who was untouched and never knew a man brought forth a
son by means of the word.

V The woman in childbed gave birth to the one of whom Gabriel had
prophesied, to the one whom John had felt when he, still enclosed in
his mother's womb, leapt for joy.

VI He endured lying in the hay, he did not shrink from the manger and
he by whose power not even a bird suffers hunger was fed with a
little milk.

VII The choir of the celestial beings rejoices and the angels sing to God
and, to the shepherds, the shepherd, the creator of all, is revealed.

VIII Glory be to you, Lord, who were purified in the river.

The Canterbury Hymnal assigns this hymn to the Matins (Nocturn) of
Epiphany, the Winchester Hymnal to the Lauds of Candlemas (*Purificatio
Mariae*, 2. 2.), H and its collectar to the First Vespers of Christmas and
Candlemas. H and its collectar also have stanzas V–VII for the Compline
of Christmas. Moreover stanzas I–VI provide for Prime (I–III) and Tierce
(IV–VI) in the Hours of Mary in R. The hymn represents stanzas A to G
from Sedulius's abecedarian hymn *A solis ortus*. It is written in Ambrosian
iambic dimeter. The melody transmitted in H is a version of Stäblein no.

215

53 similar to version 53₃ (Worcester, s. xiii). The text is found in the hymnals of BCDHVm and the fragment Ri, in the Hours of Mary in R and in the *Expositio hymnorum* in JVp. The text of Ri has been glossed.

Bibliographical references: *ICL* no. 34; *AH* 50, 58–60 (no. 53), cf. *AH* 2, 36–7 (no. 23), *AH* 27, 117–19 (no. 82, i); Bulst, pp. 71 and 187 (IV), Walpole no. 31.

Apparatus to D   Latin text: 1 ORTU] *another hand added* S *at the end*; 4 nato] ū *interlined, correcting to* natum, *and apparently erased again*; 7 canem] r *inserted with a caret mark in front of* n *by another hand*; 8 ne] e *erased and abbreviation mark added above* n (*i.e.* non) *by another hand*; 19 quem] *original abbreviation stroke covered by gloss, repeated to the right*; 23 passus] *second* s *altered to* t *by a later hand; apparently before that, another hand wrote* pastus est *in the margin.*
Old English gloss: 21–8 *glossed by* D₂.

BVmCJVpHRRi   *Lines 7–11 and 22–9 are extant in Ri; the lines are defective.* Heading: hymnus ad vesperam in epiphania domini *B*, IN EPIPHANIA DOMINI YMNUS *Vm*, HYMNUS AD MATUTINUM *C*, A SOLIS ORTUS *J*, *no rubric VpH*, YMNUS AD PRIMAM *R*; 1 ORTU] ortus *BJVpH*; 2 ad] et *H*; 3 Christo] christum *VmCJVpHR*; principi] principem *VmJVpHR*; 4 nato] natum *VmCJVpHR*; Maria] marię *C*; 5 Beatus] e *damaged, but legible B*; 7 caro] carne *VmCJVpHRRi*; canem] carnem *BVmCJVpHRRi*; liberans] erans *missing Ri*; 8 perderet] perdidit, *the ending expunged and* eret *written above perhaps by* H₁ *H*; condidit] didit *missing Ri*; 9 viscera] cera *missing Ri*; 10 gratia] tia *missing Ri*; 11 baiolat] aiolat *missing Ri*; 12 *end of section assigned to Prime; incipit of doxology:* Gloria tibi domine *R*; 13 *beginning of section assigned to Tierce, rubric:* YMNUS AD TERTIAM *R*; 14 repente] *on erasure C*; fit dei] fidei *CH*; 16 filium] l *on erasure H*; 19 gestiens] gestiaens *R*; 20 clausus] clusus *with a* written *above by another hand R*; 21–30 *omitted CJ*; 22 abhorruit] horruit *B*, oborruit *Vm*, obhorruit *Vp*, aboruit *HRi*; 23 parvoque lacte p] *missing Ri*; passus] pastus *BVmpHRi*, passtus *with second* s *erased (Dewick:* pastus) *R*; 24 *R ends; incipit of doxology:* Gloria tibi domine. 25 Gaudet chorus cęl] *missing Ri*; 26 deo] *missing Ri*; 27 palamque fit] *missing Ri*; 28 ator omnium] *missing Ri*; 29–30 Laus honor virtus gloria *BVm*, Gloria patri ingenito / eiusque unigenito / una cum sancto spiritu / in sempiterna secula. amen. *C, omitted JVp, omitted, two lines left blank H*, ā patri, *beginning of line missing Ri.*
    Ri gloss: 7–11 *are glossed. The lines are defective.* 7 sancta (*carne*) sua (*carnem*) peccatricem 8 þæt ne losode (*quod*) s. genus hon(. . .) (*or* hom *from* hominum? *Glosses* condidit.) 9 virginea matris me(. . .) (*glossing* viscera) 10 divina ingreditur 11 uterus po(. . .).

Commentary   Latin: 1–2 *Cf. Ps. CXII.3.* 1 *Bulst reads* ortus *as BJVpH and the corrector in D; AH attests* ortu *for continental manuscripts.* 3–4 *Bulst reads* Christo *etc., but AH attests the accusative for continental manuscripts. The alteration in D aligns the lemma with the gloss and BVmCJVpHR.* 6 *Cf. Phil. II.7.* 7 *D's* caro *seems unparalleled.* 8 *Bulst reads* non, *but AH attests* ne *for the Continent.* 9 *Bulst reads* clausae, *but notes the reading* castae. 14 *Cf. Mal. III.1.* 16 *Bulst reads* creavit; *AH attests* concepit *for continental manuscripts.* 23–4 *Cf. Ps. CXLVI.9 and Luke XII.6.* 23 passus *seems a purely scribal error, but is followed by the gloss.* 26 *Bulst reads* deum, *but* AH *attests* deo *for continental manuscripts.* 29 Ri's *doxology was clearly that of* C. *Old English:* 1 upspringes *glosses the reading of BJVpH and* D's *corrector.* 4 acænnedne *translates the reading found in* VmCJVpHR.

45

YMNUS AD MATUTINAM

s. ó

   feond   arlease

I   HOSTIS HERODES IMPIE,

   crist   cuman to hwi ondrædst þu

   Christum venire quid times?

   ne   gegripþ deadlice

   Non arripit mortalia,

   se þe ricu   selþ heofonlice

   qui regna dat cęlestia.   4

   ferdan tungelwitegan *þi   hi gesawon

II Ibant magi,   quam viderant

   steorran folgiende   forestæppendne

   stellam sequentes previam;

   leoht hi sohton   mid leohte

   lumen requirunt lumine,

   god hi andettan mid lace

   deum fatentur munere.   8

   heap   moddra *swegð

III Caterva matrum personet

   forcorfene bewepende tuddra

   conlisa deflens   pignora,

   þæra   wælhreow þusenda

   quorum tyrannus milia

   criste   gehalgode offrunge

   Christo sacravit victimam.   12

   þwealu   clænes wæles

IV Lavacra puri gurgitis

   þæt heofonlice lamb   æthran

   cęlestis   agnus attigit.

   senna   þe   he ne brohte

   Peccata, quę non detulit,

us   afeormigende he ætbræd
nos abluendo   sustulit.   16

wundrum   sealde geleafan
V   Miraculis dedit fidem

habban hyne god   fæder
habere se   deum patrem

untrume gehælende lichaman
infirma sanans   corpora

7 aweccende lica
& suscitans cadavera.   20

niwe   cynn   mihte
VI Novum genus potentię:

       wæteres readodon   wæterfatu
[16r] aquę   rubescunt hydriae

7 win   gehaten ageotan
vinumque iussa   fundere

awænde yþ   ordfruman
mutavit unda originem.   24

wuldor þe   drihten
VII Gloria tibi, domine,

þu þe aþwogen
qui lotus es

I Herod, wicked enemy, why do you fear the coming of Christ? He who grants the heavenly kingdom will not seize transient things.

II The magi went, following the star which they had seen and which went before them on the way. They seek the light, guided by the light. They confess he is God by their gift.

III Let the crowd of mothers cry out (*other manuscripts:* The crowd of mothers cries out), weeping over their slaughtered children. The tyrant consecrated thousands of them victims to Christ.

IV The lamb from heaven touched the cleansing water of the pure river. Washing us clean, he removed the sins which he himself did not bring there.

V With miracles he provided proof that he had God for his father, when he healed sick bodies and revived corpses.

VI That was a hitherto unknown kind of power: jugs of water turn red and the water, being commanded to pour forth as wine, has changed its original nature.

This hymn was sung at Epiphany. The Canterbury Hymnal assigns it to Lauds, the Winchester Hymnal and H to Vespers. H separates out stanza III for the Matins of Holy Innocents. The hymnal, but not the collectar of H, seems to assign stanza IV to the Compline of Epiphany. These are stanzas H–N of Sedulius's abecedarian hymn *A solis ortus*, following on from Hy 44. It is written in Ambrosian iambic dimeter. The melody transmitted in C agrees with Stäblein no. 409 (Worcester, s. xiii, see Stäblein, p. 561). The text is included in the hymnals of BDVm (the Canterbury Hymnal) and, in a shorter version, in the hymnals of CH and the *Expositio hymnorum* of JVp.

Bibliographical references: *ICL* no. 7284; *AH* 50, 58–60 (no. 53), Bulst, pp. 71–2 and 187 (IV), Walpole no. 31.

Apparatus to D   Latin text: 9 personet] personat, at *by another hand on erasure.* Old English gloss: 17–20 *glossed by D₃.*

BVmCJVpH   Heading: ymnus ad matutinam *B*, ITEM UNDE SUPRA *Vm*, HYMNUS EPIPHANIA DOMINI AD VESPERUM *C*, HOSTIS HERODES *J, no rubric VpH*; 1 HERODES] *omitted in JVp*; 3 arripit] eripit *BC*; 4 *one letter erased after* regna *C*; 5 quam] qua *B*; 6 previam] previa *C*; 9–12 *omitted CJ. This stanza is a separate hymn in H; Vp replaces the omitted stanza by copying it from Vm.* 9 personet] personat *Vm and the stanza copied into Vp*; 11 tyrannus] tirannis *H*; 12 victimam] victima *in the stanza inserted in Vp*; 17–20 *omitted CJH, Vp replaces the omitted stanza by copying it from Vm*; 21 Novum] ovum *H*; 22 aque] atque *C*; rubescunt] rabescunt, a *altered to* u *and* u *interlined above by V₁ Vm*; 23 -que] *replaced by* quando *in JVp*; 24 originem] origine *C*; 25–6 Laus honor virtus gloria *B*, āus honor virtus gloria *Vm*, Gloria tibi domine / qui lotus est *C, omitted JVp. H's doxology is:* Gloria tibi domine / qui natus es de virgine (es *altered to* est *by another hand); the doxology for stanza III reads:* Gloria tibi domine / qui natus es de virgine / cum patre & sancto spiritu / in sempiterna secula / Amen. (es *again altered to* est).

Commentary   Latin: 3 *Bulst reads* eripit *as BC do, but notes the variant* arripit. 5 *Bulst reads* qua venerant *(cf. B's* qua), *but notes* quam viderant *as a variant reading.* 9 *D must originally have agreed with BH's* personet. *The alteration in D aligns the lemma with the gloss and* V. *Bulst reads* personat. 17–18 *Cf. John* V.36. 22 *Cf. John* II.7. Old English: 5 þi *may be the instrumental of the demonstrative pronoun rendering* qua *as in B and in Bulst, unless it is relative* þe *with the vowel dittographed from following* hi. 9 swegð *renders* personat, *agreeing with the corrector in D, V and Bulst.*

46

ITEM YMNUS

fram fæder   ancænned
I A   PATRE UNIGENITUS

to us he com þurh mæden
ad nos venit per virginem

fulluht   on rode gehalgiende
baptisma cruce consecrans,

ealle   geleaffulle acænnende
cunctos fideles generans.   4

of heofonan healic he forðstop
II De celo   celsus prodiit,

he underfeng hiw   mannes
excepit   formam hominis

gescæft   mid deaþe alysende
facturam morte   redimens,

gefean lifes syllende
gaudia vite largiens.   8

        ó
þæt þe eala þu alysend   we biddaþ
III Hoc te,   redemptor, quesumus:

onaslid milde
illabere propitius

7 beorht   urum   sefum
clarumque nostris sensibus

leoht   gearce geleaffullum
lumen prebe fidelibus.   12

wuna mid us   drihten
IV Mane nobiscum, domine,

nihte   deorce   asyndra
noctem obscuram remove.

ælcne gylt   afeorma
Omne delictum ablue,

arfæste læcedom   forgyf
piam medelam tribue.   16

þæne   nu   cuman we cunnon
V Quem iam venisse novimus,

gehwerfan eft   we gelefaþ
redire   item credimus,
þu cynegyrd þine æþele
tu, sceptrum tuum inclitum
mid þinum bewere scylde
tuo   defende clypeo.   20

wuldor þe   drihten
VI   **Gloria tibi, domine,**
þu ðe aþwogen eart
qui lotus   es

I The only-begotten Son came to us from the Father through the virgin, consecrating baptism by the cross and giving life to all the faithful.

II He, the lofty one, came forth from heaven and took upon himself the form of a man. He redeemed his creation with his death, bestowing on it the joys of life.

III Redeemer, we ask this of you: descend benevolently and proffer clear light to our faithful thoughts.

IV Abide with us, Lord. Take away the dark night. Wash away every offence. Grant us gracious healing.

V You who, as we know, came at this time and who, as we believe, will return again, defend your glorious sceptre with your shield.

This hymn was sung at Epiphany. The Winchester Hymnal assigns it to Matins (Nocturn), H to the Vespers of the Octave of Epiphany. When the Canterbury Hymnal used it is unclear. It is anonymous and written in rhythmical Ambrosian hymn verse ($4 \times 8pp$) according to an abecedarian scheme using two-line units. The verses are linked by slightly irregular rhyme or assonance. The melody transmitted in C remains unidentified. The text is included in the hymnals of CDHVm and the *Expositio hymnorum* of JVp.

Bibliographical references: *ICL* no. 20; *AH* 27, 66 (no. 6), cf. *AH* 2, 80 (no. 107), Walpole no. 89.

Apparatus to D   Latin text: 20 clypeo] peo *apparently added later, possibly by* D_1.
   Old English gloss: 9 *erasure of two letters* (te.?, re.?) *in front of* þe.

VmCJVpH Heading: ITEM IN EPIPHANIA YMNUS *Vm*, HYMNUS AD NOCTURNUM *C*, A PATRE UNIGENITUS *J*, *no rubric VpH*; 3 cruce] crucem *C*; 7 facturam morte] factura mortis *C*; 11 sensibus] cordibus *Vm*; 20 defende] defunde *with* e *interlined (probably by* V_1*)* *Vp*; 21–2 Laus honor virtus gloria *Vm, omitted JVp*; 22 *omitted H*; es] est *C*.

Commentary Latin: 3 AH *attests* crucem *as in C for one continental manuscript.* 6 *Cf.* formam servi accipiens, in similitudinem hominum factus *Phil. II.7.* 11 AH *reads* cordibus *like Vm.* 13 *For* mane nobiscum *cf. Luke XXIV.29.* 20 *Cf.* omnis sermo Dei ignitus clypeus est sperantibus in se *Prov. XXX.5.*

47

YMNUS IN PURIFICATIONE SANCTÆ
MARIÆ VIRGINIS

	þæt	werod	scopa	arwurþe	gefern
I	QUOD	CHORUS	vatum	venerandus olim	

mid þam halgan gaste   gyddode gefylled
spiritu sancto   cecinit repletus,

on godes geworden   cynnestran *wunað
in dei factum   genetrice constat

beon
esse Maria.   4

þeos god heofones   7 drihten   eorþan
II Haec deum cęli   dominumque terrae

mæden heo geeacnode   7 heo acænde mæden
virgo concepit   peperitque virgo

7   æfter cenninge   heo geearnode wunigen
atque post partum   meruit   manere

ungewæmmed
inviolata.   8

þæne   se ealde rihtwis   on earmum
III [16v] Quem senex iustus   Symeon in ulnis

on huse *underfengc   *drihnes fægnigende
in domo sumpsit   domini gavisus,

                      meruit
for þy   gewiscodne   he geearnode   geseon
ob quod optatum   proprio *videre

mid eagan crist
lumine   Christum.   12

þu   lustbære gewilnungum   we biddan *biddende
IV   Tu libens   votis,   petimus,   precantum,

kynges þæs ecan   cennestre gefultuma þu
regis aeterni   genitrix, faveto,

*7 beorht þæs healican   *healdende roderes
clara que celsi   renitens   Olymphi

ricu   þu ferdest
regna petisti.   16

sy   gode uran   wlite 7 miht
V   Sit deo nostro   decus & potestas,

sy hæl   ece   sy wurðment ece
sit salus perpes,   sit honor   perennis,

se þe heofones healicra   sitt   on heahnysse
qui poli   summa   residet in arce

þrylic   7 an
trinus & unus.   20

AMEN

I It is well known that in Mary, the mother of God, was fulfilled what
the august throng of the prophets once uttered, filled with the Holy
Spirit.

II As a virgin she conceived the God of heaven and the lord of the earth
and gave birth to him as a virgin – and by her merits remained
inviolate after birth.

III Simeon, the just old man, afterwards took him in his arms with joy
in the house of the Lord because he saw Christ, as he had wished,
with his own eyes.

IV Mother of the eternal king, we ask you, support willingly the
requests of those who pray, you who, shining in your brightness,
sought the kingdom of heaven above.

V Glory and might, eternal grace and everlasting honour be to our
God, who resides in the highest fastness of heaven, both three and
one.

This hymn was sung at Vespers on Candlemas (2 February). In the
collectar of H it was specifically assigned to Second Vespers. It has been

ascribed to Hrabanus Maurus (d. 856); it is written in Sapphic stanzas. The text is included in the hymnals of BCDHVm and the *Expositio hymnorum* of JVp.

Bibliographical references: *ICL* no. 13876; *AH* 50, 206–7 (no. 155), cf. *AH* 2, 39 (no. 28).

Apparatus to D   Latin text: 2 cecinit] *second* c *on erasure of* i; 11 videre] *another hand interlines* t, *correcting to* videret.

BVmCJVpH   Heading: in purificatione sancte marię *B*, YMNUS AD VESPEROS IN PURIFICATIONE SANCTĘ MARIĘ *Vm*, HYMNUS DE PURIFICATIO SANCTE MARIE *C*, QUOD CHORUS VATUM *J*, *no rubric* VpH; 5 Hæc] Hunc *Vm*; 10 domini] domino *C*; 11 ob quod optatum] obtatum op quod *Vm*; optatum] obtatum *CVm*; proprio videre] proprio videret *BVmC*, meruit videre *JVp*; 13 petimus] *omitted B*; precantum] *ending erased and altered to* precanti *Vm*, precantes *JVp*; 15 renitens] retinens *VmVpH* (*but JVp gloss is* scinende), retinens, *but* tin *on erasure (by* C₁*)* C; 17 &] *omitted Vp* (*but not in the gloss*); 19 residet in arce] *dittographed in H*; 20 unus] unuus *B*; Amen] *omitted BVmJVp*.

Commentary   Latin: 6 *Cf.* Ecce virgo concipiet et pariet filium *Isa. VII.14.* 9–12 *Cf. Luke II.25–35, especially 30 and 32.* 11 *For the alteration in D cf.* BVmC. *For the insertion of* meruit *cf.* JVp. AH *reads* proprio videret. 13 AH *reads* precantes, *attesting* precantum *for the Continent as well.* 15 *The spacing suggests that D's scribe may not have recognized* que *as the relative pronoun, cf. the gloss. As for* renitens, AH *attests it for continental manuscripts, but reads* retinens. Old English: 3 *This meaning of* constat (*'is, stays'*) *is inappropriate here.* 13 *For the nominative instead of the genitive plural, cf.* JVp (*Latin and gloss*). 15 *Latin* que *the relative pronoun is mistaken for the conjunction.* healdende *renders* retinens, *the variant reading of* VmCVpH. 19 healicra *stands for (standard spelling)* healicre (*dat. sg.*).

48

YMNUS IN SEPTUAGESIMA, ID EST IN CLAUSULA ALLELUIA

s. est
ys   myrige   leoþ
I   ALLELUIA,   DULCE CARMEN,
7 stefn ece   gefean
    vox perennis gaudii,
            lof   wynsum
[16v] alleluia laus suavis

ys   werodum heofonlicum
est choris   celestibus,

s. alleluia
þæne   singaþ   godes wunigende
quem   canunt dei   manentes

on huse   geond worulda
in domo per   secula.   6

s. nostra
ure   bliþe *mater
II   Alleluia, lęta   mater,

s. supernę s. quę est
cæstergewara
concivis   Hierusalem,

stefn þinra
alleluia, vox tuorum

s. angelorum
cæstergewara blissigendra
civium   gaudentium,

s. iam
utlagan us   wepan neadiaþ
exules nos flere   cogunt

flod
Babilonis flumina.   12

we ne gearniaþ
III   Alleluia non   meremur

nu   ecelice   singan
nunc perenne psallere;

s. noster
us   scylde
alleluia nos reatus

neadaþ forlætan
cogit intermittere.

tima   onwunað on   þam gefremedan
Tempus instat,   quo peracta

we heofigan leahtras
lugeamus crimina.   18

for þi   herigende   we biddaþ
IV   Unde laudando precamur

ó
þe eala þu eadige þrynnes
te,   beata   trinitas,

þæt þinne us geseon
ut tuum nobis videre

s. sanctum
eastran   þu selle   on rodore
pascha   des   [17r] in aethere,

on þam þe   bliþe we singaþ
quo   tibi laeti canamus

godes lof ecelice
alleluia perpetim.   24

swa hit gewurðe
ameN

I Hallelujah, pleasant song, sound of eternal joy, the hallelujah is sweet praise to the heavenly choirs, which those who live in the house of God sing throughout the ages.

II Hallelujah, our joyful mother, fellow citizen of Jerusalem, hallelujah, the cry of your rejoicing citizens, the rivers of Babylon force us exiles to weep.

III We do not deserve to sing hallelujah forever yet. Our offence forces us to interrupt our hallelujah. Now is the time when we should mourn the sins we have committed.

IV Therefore we glorify you, blessed Trinity, and pray you that you may grant us to see your Easter in heaven, where we shall joyfully sing hallelujah to you forever.

This hymn was sung at Vespers at Septuagesima. The collectar in H, however, prescribes it for Compline. It is written in rhythmical verse; the stanza can be described as $3 \times (8p+7pp)$ Cf. Hy 143. The melody transmitted in H could be another version of Stäblein no. 112. The text is included in the hymnals of BCDHVm and the *Expositio hymnorum* of JVp.

Bibliographical references: *ICL* no. 559; *AH* 51, 52–3 (no. 53), cf. *AH* 2, 41 (no. 32).

Apparatus to D   Latin text: 10 gaudentium] a *altered from* i, ti *altered from* d.
    Old English gloss: 17 on] *inserted from below with a caret mark by* D*1*; 20 eadige] a *interlined above by* D*1*.
    Latin gloss: 15 s. noster] *inserted in smaller writing by* D*1*.

BVmCJVpH   Heading: in septuagesima ad vesperam *B*, IN SEPTUAGESIMA
YMNUS *Vm*, HYMNUS IN SEPTUAGESSIMO AD VESPERUM *C*, YMNUS IN LXX
AD VESPERAM *H*, ALLELUIA DULCE CARMEN *J*; 1 DULCE] dulee *H (Dewick:*
dulce*)*; 2 perennis] perhenni *B*, perhenis, *a second* n *inserted above probably by* J₁ *while glossing*
J; 4 *mistaken punctuation after* est *C*; 3 laus *and* s *of* suavis *on erasure B*; 5 quem] quam
BVmJVpH; 6 dei] i *altered from* e, *probably by another hand Vm*; 7 mater] er *on erasure by*
another hand, final letter originally m *H*; 8 *three to four letters ending in* s *erased in left margin H*;
10 gaudentium] gaudium *B*; 14 psallere] sallere *C*; 17 Tempus] tepus *C*; peracta] *final letter*
altered from t *either to* a *or to* o *C*, peracto *H*; 19 Unde] inde *H*; 22 aethere] aethera *VmJVp*;
24 perpetim] perpetuum *C*; ameN] *omitted CJVp*.

Commentary   Latin: *On the* Alleluia *cf. Rev. XIX.1–6, also Ps. CXLVII–CXLIX.* 5 AH
reads quod, *quoting several variants from continental manuscripts, among them* quam. 8 *Only one*
witness on the Continent known to AH *has* concivis, *all others read* concinis. 11–12 *Cf.* Super
flumina Babylonis illic sedimus et flevimus *Ps. CXXXVI.1.* 13–18 *Cf.* In Septuagessima
dimittimus cantica caelestia, hoc est, *Alleluia et Gloria in excelsis deo* usque in vigiliam
Pascae et humiliamur sponte pro peccatis nostris, sicut humiliatus est Hebraicus populus
invitus septuaginta annis serviens regi Babilonis sine voce gaudii et letitie, voce sponsi et
sponse. *Ælfric, 'Aelfrici abbatis epistula', ed. Nocent, ch. 26.*

49

YMNUS AD NOCTURNAM

	mid arfæstum	geyppaþ lofum	
I	ALLELUIA PIIS	EDITE laudibus,	
	cæstergewaran rodorlice	singaþ caflice	
	cives aetherei,	psallite naviter.	
	ece	geyppað mid lofum	
	Alleluia perenne	edite laudibus.	3
	heonon eow eces	leohtes inlendan	
II	Hinc vos perpetui	luminis accolas	
	s. aula		
	hit nime swegende	lofbærum werodum	
	assumet resonans	hymniferis choris.	
	ece	geyppað mid lofum	
	Alleluia perenne	edite laudibus.	6
	eow burh healice	*underfó godes	
III	Vos urbs eximia	suscipiet dei,	

227

		s. angelorum	
seo	bliþum swegþ	sangum	astyrod
quę	letis resonat	cantibus excita.	

    ece
Alleluia perenne   9

	gesæligum geancyrre	gefean nimaþ
IV	Felici reditu	gaudia sumite

	ageldende drihtne	*wuldorfulle *lofu
	reddentes domino	glorificum melos.

    ece
Alleluia perenne   12

        ó

	þe eala þu crist breme	wuldor stefnum
V	Te, Christe, celebret	gloria vocibus

        ó

	urum eala þu ælmihtiga	mid þisum þe we secgaþ
	nostris, omnipotens;	hac tibi dicimus:

    ece   geyppaþ mid lofum
Alleluia perenne   edite   laudibus.   15

I Cry hallelujah, amid solemn praise, citizens of heaven, sing forcefully. Cry hallelujah continuously amid songs of praise.

II As it resounds, it shall admit you from here into choirs singing hymns as dwellers in perpetual light. Cry hallelujah continuously amid songs of praise.

III God's glorious city, roused and resounding with joyful songs, shall receive you.

IV Take up the rejoicing at your happy homecoming and offer the Lord a song, glorifying him.

V You shall be celebrated by the gloria in our voices, almighty Christ. Thus for your sake we say: Cry hallelujah continuously amid songs of praise.

This is the first part of a hymn for Septuagesima. Its eight stanzas were divided between Matins (Nocturn) (Hy 49) and Lauds (Hy 50). It is written in *asclepiadei minores*, three to a stanza, the third being the refrain. The melody transmitted in H is the same as that of Hy 48, i.e. possibly Stäblein no. 112. The text is included in the hymnals of BCDHVm and the *Expositio hymnorum* of JVp.

Bibliographical references: *ICL* no. 564; *AH* 27, 74–6 (no. 19), cf. *AH* 2, 41–2 (no. 33), Walpole no. 92.

Apparatus to D   Latin text: 11 reddentes] *second* d *inserted above with a caret mark, probably by* D_1.

BVmCJVpH   Heading: ymnus ad nocturnam *B*, ITEM YMNUS *Vm*, HYMNUS AD NOCTURNUM *C*, ALLELUIA PIIS *J*, *no rubric Vp*, YMNUS AD NOCTURNAM *H*; 1 ALLELUIA] *dittographed by* J_1 *J*; 4 Hinc] c *interlined above, probably by* V_1 *V*; vos] nos *CJVp*; accolas] accolis *JVp (but the gloss probably renders* accolas), áccolans *H*; 5 assumet] asumet *C*; 6 *C omits* laudibus; 7 Vos] nos *Vp*; 8 letis] litis *H (Dewick:* letis); resonat] rosonat *H*; cantibus] cantib *with abbreviation mark probably by another hand B*; excita] excitans *Vm*, exita *H*; 9 *om. JVp; BH continue* edite laudibus, *CVm continue* edite. 10 Felici] infelici *JVp*; reditu] redditu *H*; 11 reddentes] redentes *BC, first* d *altered from* n *by* V_1 *Vp*; 12 *refrain om. JVp; BH continue* edite laudibus; 13 Te] Rex *C*; celebret] celebre *H*; 14 omnipotens] *Vp expands to* o omnipotens, *the first* o *of* omnipotens *erased (the erasure is not mentioned by Gneuss)*; hac] ac *JVp*; 15 *om. JVp;* edite laudibus] *om. Vm*.

Commentary   Latin: *For the concepts underlying this hymn, cf.* iam non estis hospites et advenae sed estis cives sanctorum et domestici Dei *Eph. II.19, the description of the* civitas Dei *in Rev. XXI.10–72, and the threefold* alleluia *of Rev. XIX.1–4.* 4 AH *reads* accola, *attesting* ac(c)olas *for the Continent as well, but not* accolis. 14 *In* Vp *the* o *indicating the voc. was apparently interpreted as the dittographed first vowel of* omnipotens, *therefore the erasure.* AH *reads* ac *like* JVp, *attesting* hac *only for one continental manuscript.* Old English: 7 underfó *is the subjunctive; the lemma is in the future tense.* 11 *Latin* melos *here retains the Greek inflection, as can be seen from the adjective, and is acc. sg. (ntr). The glossator has taken it for a Latin acc. pl.*

50

YMNUS AD MATUTINAM

	haligne	tunglenes	eallunga eþeles		wlite
I	ALMUM	SIDEREAE	iam	patriae	decus

	s. ó				
	sigefæstan	*heafedes	on þam dream ys	singal	
	victores	capitis,	quo	canor est	iugis.

		ece	geyppað mid lofum		
	Alleluia	perenne	edite	laudibus.	3

	s. alleluia			s. alleluia est	
	þæt	gewæhtum rest		þæt mete 7	drenc
II	Hoc	fessis	requies,	hoc cibus &	potus

gelustfulligende *geonhwerfende   hladungum genihtsumum
oblectans   reducens   haustibus affluis.

ece
Alleluia perenne   6

                ó
*us þe mid swetswegum   eala þu scyppend genihtsumlice
III Nos te suavisonis,   conditor, affatim,

gescæfta leoþum   7 lofe   we geyppað
rerum, carminibus   laudeque pangimus.

ece
Alleluia perenne   9

ó
þe eala þu crist breme   wuldor stefnum
Te,   Christe, celebret   gloria vocibus

I Even now as victors you achieve the holy glory of your heavenly home, where there is perpetual song. Cry hallelujah continuously amid songs of praise.

II This is rest to the weary, this is meat and drink to them, delighting them and bringing them home with rich draughts.

III Creator of the material world, we extol you profusely with sweet-sounding songs and praise.

This is the second part or *divisio* of this Septuagesima hymn; it is assigned to Lauds. For details see under Hy 49.

Apparatus to D   Latin text: 5 reducens] n *erased.*

BVmCJVpH   Heading: ymnus ad matutinam B, *no rubric VmJVp,* HYMNUS AD NOCTURNUM C, YMNUS AD MATUTINAM H; *Vmp indicate the beginning of the* divisio *by an enlarged initial.* 1 sidereae] sidere H; patria] patri & C; 2 victores] victoris H; 3 *om.* JVp; edite laudibus] *om.* Vm; 5 reducens] reduces JVpH; 6 *om.* JVp; BHC *continue* edite laudibus; 7 Nos] Hos Vm; suavisonis] suavissonis Vm, suavis sonis CJVp (*but glossed as one word in JVp*); 8 -que] quę C; pangimus] pagimus C; 9 *om.* JVp; BCH *continue* edite laudibus; 10 *om.* VmJVp, B omits vocibus, HC *omit* gloria vocibus.

Commentary   Latin: 5 *For the erasure in D cf. the gloss and JVpH.* AH *reads* reduces, *attesting* reducens *also for the Continent. All Anglo-Saxon hymnals omit the second stanza of the text in* AH. Old English: 2 capitis, 2 pl. pres. ind. *of* capere, *has been mistaken for the gen. sg. of* caput. 5 geonhwerfende *seems at first glance to render the participle* reducens, *but the choice of verb* *is odd. It may, however, gloss JVpH's reading* reduces, *but interpret it not as 2nd pers. sg. fut. of* reducere, *as the gloss in JVp does* (ongenlætst), *but as acc. pl. of the adjective* redux *'returned, returning'. 7 The emphatic nominative of the pronoun is mistaken for the more common accusative.*

51

INCIPIUNT YMNI QUADRAGESIMALES.
YMNUS COTIDIE AD TERTIAM IN QUADRAGESIMA

        godes on geleafan on þam we libbaþ
I   DEI FIDE,   QUA   VIVIMUS,

        on hihte ecan   on þam we gelyfað
        spe   perenni, qua   credimus,

          þurh soþre lufe gyfe
        [17v] per caritatis gratiam

        criste   uton singan wuldor
        Christo canamus gloriam,   4

        s. Christus
        se   gelædd on tida þære þriddan
II qui   ductus hora   tertia

        to þrowunge onsægednysse
        ad passionis hostiam

        rode   berende *hynþe
        crucis ferens   suspendia

        s. adám
        scæp   ongeanbrohte forloran
        ovem reduxit   perditam.   8

          s. Christum
        we biddað   eornostlice underðeodde
III Precamur ergo   subditi

            s. &
        alysednysse   frige
        redemptione liberi,

             s. nos
        þæt he generige   fram worulde
        ut eruat   a   saeculo,

                      s. diaboli
        þa ðe he tolysde fram handgewrite
        quos solvit   a   cyrographo.   12

sit
wuldor sy þe   þrynnes

IV   Gloria   tibi, trinitas,

s. & ó
gelic   an   godcundnyss
aequalis una deitas,

ær   ealle   worulda
ante omnia saecula

7 nu   7 on ecnessa
& nunc & in perpetuum.   16

I   In our faith in God, by which we live, in the enduring hope, with which we believe, through the grace of charity let us sing glory to Christ,

II   who, when he was led at the third hour to the sacrifice of his passion, in suffering himself to be hung on the cross brought home the lost sheep.

III   So we who are set free by redemption submit ourselves to him and pray to him that he will rescue from the world those whom he released from their bondage.

IV   Glory be to you, o Trinity, you who are one equal deity, since before all the ages and now and forever.

This hymn was sung at Tierce on weekdays in Lent in the Winchester Hymnal and on all days of the week in the Canterbury Hymnal and H. Its metre is Ambrosian hymn verse; stanzas I–IV are somewhat irregular iambic dimeter, the doxology is rhythmical (4 × 8pp). It was already part of the Frankish Hymnal (OHy 36). The melody transmitted in H agrees with Stäblein no. 413_1. The text is included in the hymnals of BCDHVm and the *Expositio hymnorum* of JVp.

Bibliographical references: *ICL* no. 3450; *AH* 51, 64 (no. 63); Bulst, pp. 113 and 194 (VIII, 12), Walpole no. 99.

BVmCJVpH   Heading: hymnus ad .III. cotidie in XL *B*, YMNUS AD TERTIAM IN XL *Vm*, HYMNUS IN XL AD TERTIAM *C*, DEI FIDE QUA VIVIMUS *J*, *no rubric Vp*, YMNUS IN QUADRAGESIMA AD TERTIAM *H*; 2 qua] *dittographed J*; credimus] i *erased from* e *H*; 8 perditam] perdita *C*; 9 precamur] precemur *VmCJVpH*; 15 *Vm adds* & *before* ante; 16 *BH add* amen.

Commentary   Latin: 1–3 *Cf. Hy 117/21–3*. 1 *Cf. Hab. II.4*. 2 *Bulst omits* qua, *but notes it as a variant reading*. 4 *Bulst reads* Christi, *but notes the dative as a variant reading*. 5 *Cf.* erat autem hora tertia et crucifixerunt eum *Mark XV.25*. 8 *Cf. Luke XV.4–6*. 9 *Bulst reads* precemur, *noting the variant* precamur. 12 *Cf. Col. II.14*. 15 *Bulst reads* et ante omne saeculum; *the plural is noted as a variant reading. Note that* et *is necessary to the metre.* Old English: 7 suspendium *'hanging' has been confused with* dispendium *'loss, injury'*.

52

YMNUS AD SEXTAM

		on midne dæg	to gebiddenne ys	
I	MERIDIE	ORANDUM EST		
		7 crist	to halsigenne ys	
	Christusque deprecandus est,			
		þæt he hate us	etan	
	ut iubeat nos edere			
		of hys *hangan	lichoman	
	de suo sancto corpore,			4

		s. Christus		
		þæt he	sy herigendlic	
II	ut ille	sit laudabilis		
		on eallum	folcum	
	in universis populis,			
		se sylfa hefona	drihten	
	ipse cęlorum dominus,			
		se ðe sytt	on heanyssum	
	qui sedet in altissimis,			8

		s. Christus		
		7 selle	us fultum	
III	detque	nobis auxilium		
		suos		
		þurh ænglas	wundorlice	
	per angelos mirabiles,			
		þa æfre	us gehealdan	
	qui semper nos custodiant			
		on eallum life	worulde	
	in omni vita sęculi.			12

	wuldor þe	þrynnes
Gloria tibi, trinitas		

233

I We must pray at midday and implore Christ that he may command us to eat of his holy body

II so that he is to be praised among all nations, he, the lord of the heavens, who resides in the highest heights,

III and that he may grant us help by his wondrous angels, who are to watch over us during our whole life in this world.

This hymn was sung at Sext on weekdays in Lent in the Winchester Hymnal and on all days of the week in the Canterbury Hymnal and H. It is anonymous and written in rhythmical Ambrosian verse (4 × 8pp). It goes back to the Frankish Hymnal (OHy 37). No melody has been transmitted in the Anglo-Saxon manuscripts. The text is included in the hymnals of BCDHVm and the *Expositio hymnorum* of JVp.

Bibliographical references: *ICL* no. 9610; *AH* 51, 65 (no. 64), cf. *AH* 2, 43 (no. 38); Bulst, pp. 113 and 194 (VIII, 13), Walpole no. 100.

BVmCJVpH   Heading: hymnus ad VI^m *B*, ymnus ad sextam *Vm*, hymnus ad sextam *C*, meridie orandum *J*, *no rubric Vp*, YMNUS AD VI *H*; 1 orandum] horandum *C*; 4 corpore] sanguine *Vm*; 8 altissimis] altissimus *H*; 9 nobis] nos *J*; 11 custodiant] custodiat *C*; 13 *om. JVp*.

Commentary   Latin: 1 *Cf.* vespere et mane et meridie narrabo et adnuntiabo et exaudiet vocem meam *Ps. LIV.18*. 2 *Bulst omits* -que, *noting it, however, as a variant.* 6 *Bulst reads* universo populo, *noting the plural as a variant.* 9 *Bulst omits* -que, *noting it, however, as a variant.* 10 *Cf.* ille (*i.e. the angel*) respondit: cur quaeris nomen meum quod est mirabile *Judg. XIII.18*. Old English: 4 *For* hangan *read* halgan.

53

YMNUS AD NONAM

      fulfremedum   þreofealdum getæle
I   PERFECTO TRINO   NUMERO
      on þrymfealdum tidena   geendungum
      ternis   horarum terminis
      lofu   singende neadwise
      laudes canentes debitas

> s.   s. deo
> nonsang secgende we singað
> nonam dicentes psallimus   4
>
>   halige   godes gerynu
> II   Sacrum dei   mysterium
>
>   on clænum healdende breoste
>   puro   tenentes pectore
>
>   s. & tenentes
>   lareowes   regol
>   Petri magistri regulam,
>
>   mid tacne hæle   geyppodne
>   signo   salutis proditam,   8
>
>   7 uton we singan   on gaste
> III   et nos psallamus spiritu
>
>   togeþeodende þam apostolum
>   [18r] adherentes apostolis;
>
>   s. illos
>   þa þe fótwelmas habbað   wanhale
>   qui plantas   habent debiles,
>
>   cristes   mid mihte *hi gerihtlæcan
>   Christi virtute   diligant.   12
>
>   wuldor sy þe   þrynnyss
>   Gloria   tibi, trinitas

I Now that the number three is full, made up of periods of three hours each, we sing, chanting the songs of praise we owe and reciting the Office of None.

II Keeping the sacred mystery of God in a pure heart and the rule of Peter, our teacher, as it was made known to us by the sign, the healing,

III let us also sing, cleaving in our spirit to the apostles. May they love (*VmJVpH:* straighten out) those who have weak feet by the healing power of Christ.

This hymn was sung at None on weekdays in Lent in the Winchester Hymnal and on all days of the week in the Canterbury Hymnal and H. It is written in rhythmical Ambrosian verse (4 × 8pp), is anonymous and goes back to the Frankish Hymnal (OHy 25). No melody has been transmitted in the Anglo-Saxon manuscripts. The text is included in the hymnals of BCDHVm and the *Expositio hymnorum* of JVp.

Bibliographical references: *ICL* no. 11878; *AH* 51, 16–17 (no. 15), cf. *AH* 2, 43–4 (no. 39), *AH* 27, 105 (no. 59), Walpole no. 54.

Apparatus to D   Latin text: 9 et] At, A *by another hand on erasure, probably of* E; 12 diligant] l *altered to* r, *possibly by* D*₁*.

BVmCJVpH   Heading: hymnus ad nonam *B*, YMNUS AD NONAM *VmH*, HYMNUS AD NONAM *C*, PERFECTO TRINO *J*, *no rubric Vp*; 6 pectore] pectori *BVmC*; 8 proditam] prodita *C*; 9 et] at *BVmC*; psallamus] psallimus *JVp*; spiritu] spiritum *H*; 11 habent] habens *C*; 12 diligant] dirigant *VmJVpH*; 13 *om. JVp*; trinitas] *om. C.*

Commentary   Latin: 3 *Cf. Hy 117/3. 5 Cf.* habentes mysterium fidei in conscientia pura *I Tim. III.9. 7–12 alludes to Acts III.1–10, the healing of the lame man, beginning* Petrus autem et Iohannes ascendebant in templum ad horam orationis nonam. *8 C's* prodita *may be a scribal error, but could be connected with AH's* regula ... prodita. *AH also attest* regulam ... proditam *for the Continent. 9 The alteration in D brings it into line with BVmC. AH reads* et. *12 The alteration in D aligns it with the gloss and VmJVpH. AH read* dirigant *and attest* diligant *for two continental manuscripts. 11 Cf.* et consolidatae sunt bases eius et plantas *Acts III.7. Old English: 12* hi gerihtlæcan *renders the reading of VmJVpH.*

54

YMNUS AD VESPERAM

þus ðriwa feower   ys getogen
I   SIC TER QUATERNIS TRAHITUR

tidum dæg to æfene
horis dies ad vesperum,

setlgang   sunne gecyðende
occasum sol   pronuntians

nihte   ongengehwyrfan tida
noctis redire   tempora.   4

we   eornostlice mid tacne drihtnys
II   Nos ergo   signo   domini

uton bewerian clusan   breosta
tutemus   claustra pectorum,

236

þæt na næddre   seo wætige
ne   serpens ille callidus

intoganne onginne   ingang
intrandi temptet aditum,   8

ac   mid wæpnum clænnysse
III   sed armis   pudicitię

mod   underf...
mens fulta   vigil libere
sobrietate comite
hostem repellat inprobum.   12

IV   Sed nec ciborum crapula
tandem distentet corpora,
ne vi per sompnum animam
glorificatam *pulluat.   16

Gloria tibi, trinitas

I Thus in three times four hours the day draws towards evening, as the sun announces that it will set and that the time of night is returning.

II Then let us secure the confines of our breast with the sign of the Lord lest that subtle serpent should attempt to enter within,

III but let the watchful mind, relying on the weapons of modesty, freely, together with its ally, sobriety, repel the wicked enemy,

IV but on no account let surfeit of food distend our bodies lest in sleep it should defile our glory-filled soul by its force.

This hymn was sung at Vespers in Lent in the Canterbury Hymnal. In the collectar of H it is assigned to the first and second Vespers of the first and second Sunday in Lent. The rubric in the hymnal of H, however, assigns it to None without giving further details. The hymn is anonymous, is written in rhythmical Ambrosian verse (4 × 8pp) and goes back to the Frankish Hymnal (OHy 38). The melody transmitted in H is probably a version of Stäblein no. 14 closest to 14₅. The text is included in the hymnals of BDHVm. Vm has an Old English interlinear gloss related to D.

Bibliographical references: *ICL* no. 15308; *AH* 51, 67–8 (no. 67), cf. *AH*

2, 84 (no. 114), and *AH* 11, 18 (no. 17), Bulst, pp. 114 and 194–5 (VIII, 14), Walpole no. 103.

Apparatus to D   Latin text: 16 pulluat] *first* u *closed with a horizontal stroke so as to resemble insular* a, *probably by* D_1. Old English gloss: *The incomplete gloss to this hymn was written by* D_3. *It breaks off abruptly in the middle of the last word.*

BVmH   Heading: hymnus ad vesperam *B, no rubric* Vm, YMNUS AD NONAM *H;* 3 occasum] occasu *H;* pronuntians] pronuntiat *H;* 4 noctis] nostris *Vm;* 6 claustra] casta *H;* pectorum] pectora *VmH;* 10 libere] liberet *H;* 11 sobrietate] sobrietatem *H;* 13 crapula] crapul *on erasure H;* 15–17 *om.* Vm, *a later hand adds:* ne vi per somnum animam / ludificatam polluat. 16 glorificatam] ludificata *B,* glorificata *H;* pulluat] polluat *H.*

Vm Old English Gloss: 1 ðriwa] þreowa; ys] is; 2 æfene] efene; 4 ongengehwyrfan] ongeangehwirfan; 5 drihtnys] drihtnes; 6 uton] utan; 7 na] ne; næddre] neddre, æ *interlined above by* V_1; wætige] wrecenda; 8 intoganne] intogune; onginne] ongynne.

Commentary   Latin: 2 *Bulst reads* vesperum. 3 *Bulst reads* occasu *as in H, noting* occasum *as a variant.* 4 *Bulst reads* noctem ... temporum. 5–8 *Cf. Hy 140, especially 5–8.* 6 *Bulst reads* tundimus, *but notes the variant* tutemus. *He reads* casta pectora *as in H, noting* claustra pectorum *as a variant.* 7 *Cf.* serpens erat callidior cunctis animantibus *Gen. III.1.* 8 *Bulst reads* adtemptet aditus, *giving* temptet *as a variant reading.* 10 *Bulst reads* liberis, *noting the variant* libere. 11 *H's* sobrietatem *is attested by* AH *for the Continent.* 13–16 *Cf. Hy 157/9– 10.* 14 *Bulst reads* distendat. 16 *The strange* palluat *produced by the change in D must represent an awkward attempt to correct to* polluat. *Bulst reads* glorificata *as in H, noting the variant* ludificatam, *cf. B; AH also attests* glorificatam *for the Continent.*

55

ITEM YMNUS

ó
gehér eala þu welwillenda scyppend
I   Audi,   benigne   conditor,

ure   bena   mid wopum
nostras preces cum fletibus

on þisum halgan fæstene
in hoc   sacro ieiunio

geondgotene *feowertigum fealdum
fusas   quadragenario.   4

ó   s. nostrorum
smeagend eala þu halige heortena
II   Scrutator   alme   cordium,

238

                     s. nostrarum

untrumnysse þu wast mægena
infirma   tu scis virium;

to þe gecyrredum gearca
ad te reversis   exibe

forgyfenysse gyfe
remissionis gratiam.   8

micclum   witodlice we sengodon
III **Multum quidem peccavimus,**

ac   ara   andettendum
sed parce confitentibus

to lofe   þines naman
ad laudem tui nominis;

forgyf læcedom   adligum ł seocum
confer medelam languidis.   12

swa *lichoma wiþutan beon tobrytt
IV **Sic corpus extra   conteri**

sele   þurh forhæfednyss
dona per abstinentiam,

fæste   þæt mod syfre
ieiunet ut mens sobria

        fram wæmme eallunga leahtra
[18v] a   labe   prorsus criminum.   16

      ó
getiþa eala þu eadige þrynnes
V **Presta,   beata   trinitas,**

      ó
forgyf   eala þu anfealde annys
concede,   simplex unitas,

þæt beon andfænge
ut sint acceptabilia

fæstena   lac
ieiuniorum munera.   20

        si hit swa
        ameN

I Benign creator, hear our prayers accompanied by weeping, poured out during this holy forty-day period of fasting.

II Blessed one who tries our hearts, you know how weak our strength is. Grant the mercy of forgiveness to those who have returned to you.

III We have indeed sinned a lot, but spare those who confess. Grant healing to the sick to the greater glory of your name.

IV By your gift let the body be so worn out on the outside by abstinence that the sober mind withholds itself completely from defilement by sin.

V Grant this, blessed Trinity, you who are a single unity, allow the sacrifice of our fasting to be acceptable to you.

This hymn for Lent was sung at Vespers on weekdays according to the Winchester Hymnal. The collectar in H assigns it to the First and Second Vespers of the third and fourth Sunday in Lent, but the rubric in H mentions None without giving further details. How the hymn was used in the Canterbury Hymnal is not clear. It is anonymous and written in Ambrosian iambic dimeter. The melody transmitted in H agrees with Stäblein no. 411_1 (Worcester, s. xiii). No. 411_1 was previously assumed by Stäblein to be isolated in England, all other sources of no. 411 known to him being of German provenance (Stäblein, p. 562). The text is included in the hymnals of BCDHVm and the *Expositio hymnorum* of JVp.

Bibliographical references: *ICL* no. 1313; *AH* 51, 53–4 (no. 54), cf. *AH* 2, 42 (no. 34), Walpole no. 93.

Apparatus to D   Latin text: 7 exibe] *spiritus asper above* i, *added by* D_1 *to correct to* exhibe *while glossing.*

BVmCJVpHE   Heading: item alius ymnus *B, no rubric VmpE,* HYMNUS AD VESPERUM *C,* AUDI BENIGNE *J,* YMNUS AD IX *H;* 5 Scrutator] Srutator *Vm;* 6 scis] c *interlined and inserted with a caret mark, apparently by* C_1 *C;* 7 virium] cordium, ɫ virium *interlined above by another hand E;* 7 reversis] reversiis, *first* i *erased C;* 8 remissionis] remisionis *E;* 9 *one letter erased after* quidem *E;* peccavimus] pecavimus *E;* 10 parce confitentibus] arce confit *on erasure; the erased word(s) ended in* s *and contained a sequence of three minims H;* 12 languidis] lauguidis *Vp;* 13 Sic] Hic *B;* 15 sobria] sobriam *H,* ia *illegible E;* 19 ut fructuosa sint tuis *CJVpHE, but the ending of the last word in E is almost illegible.* 20 amen] *om. BVmCJVp.*

Vm Old English gloss: 1 gehér] gehyr; eala] *retained here, although the lemma, the Latin gloss* ó, *is om. in Vm;* welwillenda] welwillende; 3 þisum] þysum; 5 smeagend] smeagedd; eala] *again retained, although the lemma is not;* heortena] heortana; 7 gearca] gearce; 9 sengodon] singodon; 10 andettendum] anddettendum; 12 ɫ seocum] *om.;* 13 lichoma] lichaman; tobrytt] tobrytte; 14 sele] syle; forhæfednyss] forhæfeadnys; 16

240

wæmme] *om.*; 17 eala þu] *om. together with the corresponding Latin* ó; þrynnes] þrynnys; 18 eala] *retained, the corresponding Latin gloss om.*; annys] annyss; anfealde] anfealda; annys] annyss; 19 andfænge] andfenge; 20 si hit swa] *om.*

Commentary   Latin: 5 *Cf.* scrutans corda *Ps. VII.10.* 15 *Cf. Hy 2/16.* 17–18 *Cf. Hy 1/ 1–2.* 19 AH *reads* ut fructuosa sint tuis *(the metrically correct variant).* Old English: 4 quadragenario *seems to be taken for a noun, not an adjective but cf. SB §330.* 13 lichoma *should be in the accusative.*

56₁

ITEM YMNUS

 I   Ex more docti mystico
servemus en ieiunium
denum dierum circulo
ducto quater notissimo.   4

 II   Lex & prophetę primitus
hoc protulerunt, postmodum
Christus sacravit, omnium
rex atque factor temporum.   8

 III   Utamur ergo parcius
verbis, cibis & potibus,
somno, iocis & artius
perstemus in custodia,   12

 IV   vitemus autem pessima,
que subruunt mentes vagas
nullumque demus callido
hosti locum tyrannidis.   16

I Do let us keep our fast as we were taught according to the mystical custom, extended over the very well-known cycle of four times ten days.

II The Law and the Prophets originally revealed it to us; afterwards Christ sanctioned it, the king and maker of all ages.

III So let us indulge more charily in words, food and drink, in sleep and amusement and let us persist more strictly in keeping watch,

IV but let us avoid the evil which creeps into wandering minds and let us give no room to the sly enemy to exert his tyranny.

This hymn for Lent was not in use in the Winchester Hymnal. The collectar in H assigns this first half to Matins (Nocturn) and the second half, Hy 56$_2$, to Lauds of the weekdays and the first two Sundays of Lent. The rubric in the hymnal in H, however, appears to assign the whole hymn to Vespers. How the hymn was used in the Canterbury Hymnal is unclear except that it seems to have been divided along the lines laid down by H's collectar. The hymn is anonymous and written in Ambrosian hymn verse (iambic dimeter). The melody transmitted in H is a version of Stäblein no. 412. The last line, which in this melody may vary considerably (Stäblein, p. 562), seems closest to German sources (412$_2$, 412$_3$). The text is included in the hymnals of BDHVm.

Bibliographical references: *ICL* no. 4745; *AH* 51, 55–6 (no. 55), cf. *AH* 2, 83 (no. 112), Walpole no. 94.

Apparatus to D   Latin text: *The end of the* divisio *after line 16 was not originally marked. Later a hand of s. xiv or xv drew a line across the column at this point and added an abbreviated* presta *(the beginning of the doxology).*

BVmH   Heading: item alius ymnus *B*, ITEM YMNUS *Vm*, IN XL YMNUS AD VESPERAM *H*; 2 en] hoc *interlined above H*; 6 *Vm wrongly indicates (by an initial) the beginning of a new line at* postmodum. 6 protulerunt] pretulerunt *with* pre- *abbreviated Vm*; 8 temporum] teporum *H*; 9 Utamur] Otamur, *the top of the O damaged as if with an inefficient attempt to alter it to* U *Vm*; parcius] partius *Vm*, c *altered from* t *H (not mentioned by Dewick)*; 12 custodia] custodiam *VmH*.

Commentary   Latin: 5–8 *The examples from the Old Testament invoked are Moses on Mt Sinai* (*Exod. XXXIV.28*) *and Elijah* (*II Chron. XIX.8*). *On Jesus, see Matt. V.2.* 6 *AH reads* praetulerunt, *attesting* protulerunt *for only one continental manuscript.* 7 *Cf. Hy 60/14.*

56$_2$

1   Dicamus omnes cernui
     clamemus atque singuli;
     ploremus ante iudicem,
     flectemus iram vindicem.   4

II Nostris malis offendimus
tuam, deus, clementiam.
Effunde nobis desuper,
remissor, indulgentiam.   8

III Memento, quod sumus tui,
licet caduci plasmatis;
ne des honorem nominis
tui, precamur, alteri.   12

IV Laxa malum, quod fecimus,
auge bonum, quod poscimus,
placere quo tandem tibi
possimus in perpetuum.   16

[19r] Presta, beata trinitas

I Let us all bow down and speak and let each of us cry out, let us weep before the judge and turn aside his avenging wrath.

II By our iniquities we have offended against your mercy, God. You who remit sins, lavish your forgiveness on us from on high.

III Remember that we are yours, even though part of a fallen creation. Do not give the honour of your name to another, we pray you.

IV Release us from the sin we committed. Add to the goodness that we ask of you for ourselves so that we may indeed be able to find favour with you in eternity.

This part or *divisio* of the hymn is assigned to Lauds by the collectar of H. For further details see above under Hy 56₁.

Apparatus to D   Latin text: 4 flectemus] e *expunged,* a *interlined by another hand;* 7 effunde] ef *expunged,* in *interlined above by another hand.*

  BVmH Heading: *no rubric BH,* YMNUS *Vm; BH do not indicate the beginning of the* divisio. 4 flectemus] flectamus *H;* 8 remissor] emissor *on erasure H,* 10 plasmatis] plasmati *B;* 13 fecimus] gfecimus *Vm;* 14 poscimus] gessimus *Vm;* 15 quo] quod *BVm;* 16 in perpetuum] hinc & perpetim *Vm.*

Commentary   4 *For the alteration in D cf. H.* AH *also reads* flectamus. 10 *B's* plasmati *is paralleled in continental manuscripts according to* AH. 13–14 *In Vm V₁ apparently began to write* gessimus, *anticipating the verb of the following line, and omitted to erase the traces of his slip.*

Vm's reading gessimus *is itself attested for only two continental manuscripts by* AH. 16 AH *reads* possimus hic (*al.* hinc) et perpetim, *cf.* Vm.

57

ITEM

ó
eala þu hælend feowertigfealdre
I   Iesu,   quadragenariae
gehalgigend forhæfednysse
dicator   abstinentiae,
þu þe for hæle   moda
qui ob salutem mentium
þis gehalgodest fæsten
hoc sanxeras ieiunium,   4

*on þam *nearxnewange þu ageafe
II   quo   paradyso   redderes
gehealdenre forhæfednysse
servata   parsimonia,
þa þe þanon giuernysse
quos inde gastrimargię
hider forspenning adræfde
huc inlecebra depulit,   8

ætbeo þu nu   gelaþunge
III   adesto nunc aecclesiae,
ætbeo þu behreowsunge
adesto poenitentiae,
seo þe for *heorum forgægednissum
quę pro suis   excessibus
gebitt mid agotenum tearum
orat profusis   fletibus.   12

þu *on bæc gedonne leahtras
IV   Tu retro acta   crimina
mid þinre forgyf gyfe
tua   remitte gratia
7 fram toweardum gearce
& a   futuris   adhibe

hyrdrædene liþesta
custodiam, mitissime,   16

þæt afeormode gearlicum
V ut expiati annuis

fæstena   onsægednyssum
ieiuniorum victimis

we efstan to easterlice
tendamus ad paschalia

wurþfullice to wurþigenne gefean
digne   colenda   gaudia.   20

ó
getiþa eala þu fæder þurh suna
VI Presta,   pater, per filium,

getiþa þurh þæne halgan gast
presta per almum   spiritum,

mid þysum ecelice   þreofealdum
cum his   per aevum *tripplici

an   god   on naman
unus deus cognomine.   24

sy hit swa
amen

I Jesus, appointer of an abstinence of forty days, who consecrated this fast with a view to the health of the soul

II so that you might return those to paradise by the means of maintained frugality whom the lure of gluttony banished down here from there,

III support your church now, assist in its penitence; it prays, shedding tears for its excesses.

IV Remit the offences committed in the past through your grace and guard us from them in the future, mildest one,

V in order that having atoned by our yearly sacrifice, the fasting, we may address ourselves to the joys of Easter, which should be worthily celebrated.

VI Grant this, Father, by your son, grant it by the Holy Spirit, you who are together with them one god under the name of three in eternity.

This hymn for Lent was sung at Lauds on weekdays in the Winchester

Hymnal; its precise use in the Canterbury Hymnal is unclear. It is not included in the hymnal of H, but the collectar assigns it to Lauds of weekdays and the third and fourth Sunday in Lent. The hymn is anonymous and written in Ambrosian iambic dimeter (with irregularities in stanza III). No melody is transmitted in the Anglo-Saxon manuscripts. The text is included in the hymnals of BCDVm and the *Expositio hymnorum* of JVp.

Bibliographical references: *ICL* no. 7658; *AH* 51, 58–9 (no. 58), Walpole no. 96.

Apparatus to D   Latin text: 6 parsimonia] *followed by erased* e; 8 inlecebra] inlecebrat, t *erased*; 15 a futuris] *written together; a second* f *inserted from above with a caret mark, probably by another hand, corrects to* affuturis.

Old English gloss: 7 A *word of two or three letters, possibly beginning with* þ, *is erased after* þanon. 11 forgægednissum] forgegednyssum, æ *interlined by* D*₁*. 15 þ *erased after* fram; toweardum] t *erased to make room for correction of the lemma.*

BVmCJVp   Heading: item alius ymnus *B*, ITEM YMNUS *Vm*, HYM AD MATUTINUM *C*, IESU QUADRAGENARIE *J, no rubric Vp*; 1 quadragenariae] QUARA-GENARIAE *C*; 5 quo] uo, *stanza initial missing Vm*; 6 parsimonia] parsimonie *VmJVp (but the JVp gloss seems to presuppose a reading* parsimonia); 7 gastrimargię] gastrimarię *with a third* r *interlined above the second, perhaps by* C*₁* *C*; 10 poenitentiae] peniten *on erasure B*; 15 a futuris] affuturis *JVp*; 16 mitissime] mittissime *C*; 21–4 *om. JVp.* 22–4 *om. VmC*; 23 tripplici] triplici *B*; 14 amen] *om. VmCJVp.*

Commentary   Latin: 2 *Cf. Hy 58/4.* 6 *Cf. Hy 58/14. With the original reading in D compare VmJVp.* 15 *D₁ may not have regarded* afuturis *as a single word, as prepositions are often joined to their nouns, but the alteration in D involves reading it as one word. For the alteration cf. JVp. AH reads* affuturis, *but states that the usual spelling in the manuscripts is* afuturis. 17–18 *Cf. Hy 149/17–18, 157/5–6.* Old English: 5 *Latin* quo *has not been recognized as the equivalent of* ut *here. For* nearxnewange *cf. the difficulties D₁ has with the spelling of the word in Hy 42/4, 70/24.* 11 heorum *wrongly anticipates the ending of the noun.* 13 on bæc *renders the more usual meaning of* retro.

58

ITEM YMNUS

beorht   wlite   fæstenes

I CLARUM DECUS IEIUNII

is geswutelod embhwerfte heofonlice

monstratur orbi   cęlitus,

246

þæt   crist   fosterfæder ealra þinga
quod Christus, altor   omnium,

fram mettum gehalgode forhæbbende
cibis   dicavit abstinens.   4

*þæt   leof gode
II Hoc Moyses carus deo

7 æ   syllend wæs geworden
legisque lator factus est.

þæt   geond lyftu
Hoc Eliam per aera

cræte upahóf on fyrenum
curru levavit igneo.   8

heonon   gerynu
III Hinc Danihel mysteria,

*sygefæst leona   geseah
victor   leonum, viderat.

þurh þæt freond inlica
Per hoc amicus intimus

      cristes   scan
[19v] Christi, Iohannes, claruit.   12

þas us fyligan selenu god
IV Haec nos sequi dona, deus,

bisena   forhæfednysse
exempla parsimoniae.

þu strængð geéc moda
Tu robur auge mentium

syllende *gastlice gefean
dans   spiritale gaudium.   16

getiþa   fæder þurh suna
Presta, pater, per filium

I The bright glory of fasting is shown to the world from above; it was consecrated by Christ, the nourisher of all, when he refrained from food.

II By means of this Moses became dear to God and the giver of Law. This lifted Elijah up through the air on a fiery chariot.

III By means of this Daniel, the victor over lions, gazed on mysteries. For this the closest friend of Christ, John, was famous.

IV Grant us to imitate these examples of frugality, God. Increase the strength of our minds by granting spiritual joy.

This hymn for Lent was sung at Matins (Nocturn) on weekdays according to the Winchester Hymnal. The rubric in H also assigns it to Matins, the collectar in H to Matins of weekdays and the third and fourth Sundays in Lent. Its precise use in the Canterbury Hymnal is unclear. The hymn is anonymous and written in Ambrosian iambic dimeter. The melody transmitted in H for the most part agrees with Stäblein no. 127$_2$. The text is included in the hymnals of the BCDHVm and the *Expositio hymnorum* of JVp.

Bibliographical references: *ICL* no. 2365; *AH* 51, 57–8 (no. 57), Walpole no. 95.

Apparatus to D   Latin text: 7 Eliam] *a spiritus asper above* e, *apparently added by* D$_1$ *while glossing.*
   Old English gloss: 7 geond] o *altered from* n.

BVmCJVpH   Heading: item alius ymnus *B*, ITEM YMNUS *Vm*, HYMNUS AD NOCTURNUM *C*, *no rubric JVp*, YMNUS AD NOCTURNAM *H; J continues without a break.* 2 orbi] orb̃, *to be expanded as* orbis? *C; erasure of* s *after* orbi *Vm*; 9 mysteria] mysterium *Vm*; 12 Christi] sponsi *BCJVpH*, christo *Vm*; Iohannes] ihohannes *Vm*, iohannis *C*; 14 parsimoniae] parssimonię *C*; 15 robur] rorbor *H*; mentium] mensium, *but* s *on erasure by another hand H*; 17 *B continues:* presta per almum spiritum, *VmCJVp continue:* presta per almum spiritum / cum his per evum triplici / unus deus cognomine. *Vm adds* amen.

Commentary   Latin: 3–8 *For the fasting of Jesus, Moses and Elijah, cf. Hy* 56$_1$/5–8. 9–10 *For Daniel's fasting and subsequent visions see Dan. I.8–17; for the lions see Dan. VI.7–23.* 9 AH *reads* mysterium; *the plural seems to be found in only two continental manuscripts.* 11–12 *With* amicus … sponsi, *the reading of BCJVpH, cf.* amicus autem sponsi qui stat et audit eum gaudio gaudet propter vocem sponsi *John III.29; on the fasting of John the Baptist cf. Matt. III.4.* 12 AH *reads* sponsi. Old English: 5 hoc *is mistaken for a nom. (as in line 7) instead of abl.* 10 sygefæst *appears to be a normal rendering of* victor, *but does not normally take an objective gen. as* victor *does here, cf.* Venezky and Healey, Microfiche Concordance to Old English. *Comparison with the gloss in JVp suggests that the glossator in D, too, may have taken* leonum *wrongly as referring to* mysteria. 13 *The glossator takes* dona *for the nom. acc. pl. of* donum, *not the homophonous imperative sg. of* donare. 16 gastlice *may be pl.; one would expect* gastlicne.

59

ITEM YMNUS

I   SUMME SALVATOR OMNIUM,
indultor & peccaminum,
Iesu, quadragenarii
consecrator ieiunii,   4

II   da pectoris munditiam,
corporis castimoniam,
ne valeat inrumpere
corruptor pudicitiae,   8

III   qui protoplastum vetito
illiciens edulio
in huius vitę torridum
detruserat ergastulum.   12

IV   Nos, filii aecclesiae
tuo redempti sanguine,
voce precamur humili,
ne pereamus miseri: 16

V   Sana languentum vulnera,
dum restringuntur corpora,
dele virus malitiae
medela parsimoniae,   20

VI   sicut in sterquilinio
benignitatis oculo
dignatus es revisere
Iob in favilla & cinere.   24

Presta, pater, per filium

I Sublime saviour of all and forgiver of sins, Jesus, hallower of the forty-day fast,

II grant us purity of the heart and chastity of the body lest the corrupter of modesty be able to invade us,

249

III who seduced the first created man with the forbidden fruit and caused him to fall into the desert prison of this life.

IV We, the sons of the church redeemed by your blood, pray to you with humble voices, lest we perish miserably:

V Heal the wounds of those who lie ill at the same time as their bodies grow strong and firm again. Destroy the poison of malice by means of the medicine of frugality,

VI just as you deigned to regard again with kind eyes Job on his dunghill amid dust and ashes.

D is the only Anglo-Saxon manuscript to contain this hymn for Lent. Its precise use is unclear. It is anonymous and written in rhythmical Ambrosian hymn verse (4 × 8pp). The stanzas rhyme aabb. Rhyme is monosyllabic.

Bibliographical references: *ICL* no. 15824; *AH* 51, p. 69 (no. 69).

Apparatus to D   Latin text: 20 medela] medelam, m *erased*; 24 *an incomplete* l *is erased in front of* favilla.

Commentary   3–4 *Cf. Hy 57/1–2.* 12 *Cf.* de ergastulo Aegyptiorum *Exod. VI.6–7*; 21 *Cf.* testa saniem deradebat sedens in sterquilinio *Job II.8.* 24 *Cf.* ago paenitentiam in favilla et cinere *Job XLII.6.*

60

YMNUS

ó
eala þu healica syllend   mede
I   SUMME LARGITOR PREMII,

hiht þu þe eart ancænned middaneardes
spes qui es unica   mundi,

bena   begém   þeowena
preces intende servorum

to þe estfullan cleopigendra
ad te devota clamantum.   4

        ure   þe ingehyd

II Nostra te conscientia

        *hefelice ætspurnan geswutelaþ

[20r] grave offendisse monstrat,

  þa   ðu geclænsa   we biddaþ

quam emundes,   supplicamus,

  fram eallum   manum

ab omnibus piaculis.   8

  gyf þu wiþsæcst hwa forgyfð

III Si *rennuis,   quis tribuet?

  gemiltsa for þam þe mihtig þu eart

Indulge, quia   potens és.

  gyf on heortan *we biddan clænre

Si corde   rogamus mundo,

  gewisslice þu scealt of behate

certe   debes   ex promisso.   12

  eornostlice underfoh   ure

IV Ergo   acceptare nostrum,

  þu þe gehalgodes fæsten

qui sacrasti, ieiunium,

  on þam rynelice   easterlice

quo   mystice paschalia

  we underfon gerynu

capiamus sacramenta.   16

  seo healice us   þæt þurhteo ɫ forgyfe

V Summa nobis hoc conferat

  on godcundnysse þrynnyss

in deitate   trinitas,

  on þæra wuldraþ an

in qua gloriatur unus

  geond *ella   worulda god

per cuncta secula deus.   20

                  amen

I Sublime giver of reward, you who are the only hope of the world, lend your ear to the prayers of your servants, who call on you in devout words.

II Our conscience shows us that we have offended badly. Purify it of all sins, we entreat you.

III If you refuse, who will grant it? Pardon us, for you have the power to do it. If we ask you out of a clean heart, surely you owe it to us because of your promise.

IV Therefore accept our fast, you who sanctioned it, in order that we may receive the sacraments of Easter in the spirit.

V May the most high Trinity confer this on us in its divinity, in which the one God is glorified throughout all the ages.

This hymn for Lent was not in use in the Winchester Hymnal. It is assigned to Compline by the rubric and collectar in H. How it was used in the Canterbury Hymnal is not clear. The hymn is anonymous and written in rhythmical Ambrosian hymn verse (4 × 8pp). The verses are linked by monosyllabic rhyme, half-rhyme or assonance in the pattern aabb. The melody transmitted in H agrees with Stäblein no. 54, especially no. 54₃. Stäblein no. 54 is probably the original melody of Hy 60 (Stäblein, p. 516). The text is included in the hymnals of DHVm.

Bibliographical references: *ICL* no. 15827; *AH* 51, 60–1 (no. 60), Walpole no. 98.

Apparatus to D   Latin text: 4 devota] a *altered to* e *by another hand.*
Old English gloss: 13 underfoh] h *altered from* r.

VmH   Heading: *no rubric* Vm, YMNUS AD COMPLETORIUM *H;* 4 devota] devote Vm, devote, *second* e *on erasure* H *(not mentioned by Dewick);* clamantum] *altered from* clamanti H *(not mentioned by Dewick);* 8 piaculis] *on erasure of* s...ppl..a *(supplicia?)* H *(not mentioned by Dewick);* 9 Si rennuis] *first three letters on erasure* H; 11 Si] te VmH; rogamus] rogari Vm, rogare H; 12 fac nos precamur domine VmH; 13 acceptare] acceptato *on erasure, by another hand* H; 14 qui] quod H; 20 cuncta] cunta H; amen] *om.* Vm.

Vm Old English gloss: 1 eala] *renders a Latin gloss* o *in* Vm; healica] halga; 4 cleopigendra] clyopigendra; 6 hefelice] hefilice; geswutelaþ] gesputelaþ; 9 gyf] gif; 10 gemiltsa] gemildsa; for þam] for ðan; 11 gyf] þe 12 do us we biddað *(the second* d *interlined above by* V₁) drihten 13 underfoh] underfon; 17 þæt] *om.;* þurhteo ł forgyfe] forgyfe; 18 þrynnys] þrynnysse; 19 þæra] þære; wuldraþ] wuldriað; 20 geond] þurh; ella] ealla.

Commentary   Latin: 4 AH *reads* devota. 5–7 *Cf.* sanguis Christi ... emundabit conscientiam vestram *Heb. IX.14.* 11–12 AH *reads* Te corde rogamus mundo / Fac nos, precamur, Domine, *but D's version is likewise attested on the Continent.* Old English: 2 *The glossator always translates* unicus *as* ancænned, *which is only appropriate in referring specifically to the only-begotten Son, Christ.* 4 *A demonstrative pronoun may have dropped out before weakly inflected* estfullan.

252

11 *Vm's gloss* þe *renders Vm's reading* té. we biddan *in D and Vm could either be a subjunctive (and then might be due to the facultative use of the subjunctive in Old English conditional clauses) or result from confusion of the reading of D with the reading of VmH, which has an infinitive.* 12 *Vm's gloss renders Vm's reading* fac nos precamur domine.

61

YMNUS DE SANCTO CUTHBERHTO

I   MAGNUS MILES MIRAbilis
multis effulgens meritis
Cuthberhtus nunc cum domino
gaudet perenni premio.   4

II   Carnis terens incendia
corde credidit domino
caduca cuncta contemnens
caritatis officio.   8

III   Legis mandata domini
laetus implevit opere;
largus, libens, lucifluus
laudabatur in meritis.   12

IV   Fecit manare flumina
fontis signi perpetui,
ubi nulla vestigia
videbantur fonticuli.   16

V   Linguam resolvit vinculis
longo tempore retentam.
Petrosa terra segetem
parvo produxit tempore.   20

VI   *Iillius nos auxilium
[20v] deprecæmur perpetuum,
ut mereamur dicere
sine fine cum gaudio: 24

VII   Gloria patri ingenito,

gloria unigenito
una cum sancto spiritu
in sempiterna secula.   28

I The great and admirable soldier who shines forth through his many merits, Cuthbert, now enjoys his eternal reward with the Lord.

II He crushed the fires of the flesh, for in his heart he had faith in the Lord and so despised everything transitory in his duty to charity.

III Joyfully he fulfilled the commands of the law of the Lord in his works. Generous, eager, a giver of light, he was praised for his merits.

IV He caused a stream from a spring, a sign in perpetuity, to flow where no traces of a spring were before to be seen.

V He released a tongue from its ties which had been paralysed for a long time. In a short time he brought forth a crop from a rocky soil.

VI We pray for his continual help so that we may deserve to say joyfully without end:

VII 'Glory be to the unbegotten Father, glory to the Only-Begotten together with the Holy Ghost throughout all the ages.'

This hymn was sung at the feast of St Cuthbert (20 March). It is anonymous and written in rhythmical Ambrosian hymn verse (4 × 8pp) with extensive use of alliteration. No melody has been transmitted in the Anglo-Saxon manuscripts. The text is included in the hymnals of CDHVm, the *Expositio hymnorum* and, among other material relating to Cuthbert, in Cu. There exists a version of this hymn for St Gregory, see *AH* 14a, 61–2 (no. 51).

Bibliographical references: *ICL* no. 9224; *AH* 11, 103 (no. 173).

Apparatus to D   Latin text: 16 fonticuli] *the second* i *altered from* a *by erasure*; 22 deprecæmur] æ *altered from* a, *probably by* D_1, *and altered to* e *by erasue of the left half of the ligature.*

VmCJVpHCu   Heading: HYMNUS DE SANCTO CUÐBERTO *Vm*, HYMNUS DE SANCTO CUTHBERHTO *C*, MAGNUS MILES *J*, *no rubric VpH*, Incipit hymnus sancti cudberhti episcopi *Cu*; 2 meritis] mirabilis *H*; 3 Cuthberhtus] cuðbertus *Vm*, cuðbryhtus *Vp*, cudberhtus *Cu*; 5 terens] terrens, *the first* r *expunged C*; 11 largus, libens] libens largus

JVp; lucifluus] lucifluis *Vm*; 14 signi] signo *CJVpH*; 15 *Vm adds* per *after* nulla; 16 *H adds*
ubi *at the beginning of the line, this is expunged, probably by H₁*; 18 tempore retentam] retentans
tempore *Vm*; retentam] retentans *Vm*, retenta *H*; 19 terra] terrę *JVpH*; segetem] sagetem *C*;
21 Iillius] Illius *BVmCJVpHCu*; nos] nox, x *expunged and* s *interlined above C*; 22
deprecæmur] deprecamur *VmCJVpHCu*; 24 fine] *om. Vm*; cum] *om. H*; 25–8 *om. JVp*; 26–8
om. VmC; 27–8 *om. Cu*; 28 *H adds* amen.

Commentary *For the two earliest prose vitae of the Saint see* Two Lives of St. Cuthbert: a
Life by an Anonymous Monk of Lindisfarne and Bede's Prose Life, *ed. B. Colgrave (Cambridge, 1940). 13 See the anonymous* vita, *ch. III. 3, Bede's prose* vita, *ch. XVIII. 19 Cf. Bede's
prose* vita, *ch. XIX. For* petrosa *cf. Matt. XIII.5 and 20, Mark IV.5 and 16.*

62

YMNUS IN FESTIVITATE
SANCTI BENEDICTI ABBATIS

ó
eala þu crist   halgena   wlite   7   myht

I   CHRISTE, SANCTORUM   DECUS ATQUE VIRTUS,

lif   7 hiw   weg leoht 7 ealdor
vita & forma,   via, lux & auctor,

eadmoddra behát   7 samod   lofsang
supplicum vota   pariterque hymnum

underfoh mildheort
suscipe clemens,   4

þu ðe þinne gefern   to þe
II   qui tuum dudum   Benedictum ad te

teonde   wunderlice   asindrodest middanearde
attrahens mire   segregasti mundo,

þæt ðwernyssa worulde   wiþsacan   leornigende
ut prava   secli   reprobare discens

þe þæt he folgode
te   sequeretur,   8

þæs   estfull   mod   cildes
III   cuius devotum   animum pueri

gyfe   gearcigende   geleafan swiþrian
gratia prestans   fidei   valere,

on þam swiþrigende wundorlice   mid benum he gefremode
qua valens   mire   precibus peregit

on mode *geleaflice
mente   fideli,   12

siþþan astreccende   fot   on asindrodum
IV   Dein extendens   pedem in remotis

heahnyssa he astah   cwilmigan swiþor willende
arduum scandit   cruciare malens

lichoman liðe   *cildlice   byrnende
corporis artus   iuvenilis ardens

on clænre lufe
casto   amore.   16

he tyde syþþan   menn   eadige
V   Imbuit post hinc   homines beatos

*regoles nearonyssum   mod   ætstentan
regulis artis   animum retundi

7 geoce simle   *drihtne heofona
& iugo semper   domini polorum

underþeodan swuran
subdere   colla,   20

of þam   geornfull þen
VI   e quibus Maurus,   sedulus minister,

of wæle getogenne   cild
gurgite ductum   Placidum *puerulum

*gehersumigeende fæder   of burnan upahafenne
obsequens   patri   latice   levatum

of brymme he teah
aequore   traxit,   24

VII   [21r] in quibus ipse via   rite clarens
actibus sanctum docet   ammonendum,
sic dei iussis   libere *parentum
mente subesse.   28

VIII   Pauperum vita   pietate gliscens,
usibus prębens   fidei calore
instruit corda   ambigua sequentum
fidere semper.   32

IX   Quod probans sanctis   fidei vigore
fratribus iunctis   precibus effusis
vas redundare   oleo fluente
ilico pandit.   36

X   Usibus iustis   pietate instans
   Christo fidendo   fidei valere
   deprecans certi   animam reduxit
   corpore functo.   40

XI   Tunc soror sacra   nimium sequendo
   tardius iussum   retinere malens
   imbre obtentum   valide fluente
   artius vinxit,   44

XII   aridum post quę   residens beatus
   cernit eiusdem   animam sororis
   celsa secreta   petere volucri
   pernicitate;   48

XIII   unde gaudendo   fratribus vocatis
   corpus afferri   tumulo humandum
   precipit dudum   sibi preparato
   mox secuturus.   52

XIV   Pręscius post hęc   finis adfuturi
   promtus insistit   tumulum parare.
   Gratia sumpta   animam remisit
   aethre locandam,   56

XV   cuius ad cęlum   via clara fulgens
   angelo teste   Benedicti esse
   auribus fratrum   resonare visa est
   voce sonora.   60

   þises   eala þu crist   geearnungum we biddað
XVI   Huius, o Christe, meritis,   precamur,
      þæt þu aflyge graman   þu forgyfe *herunge
   [21v] arceas   iram,   tribuas   favorem,
   gyfe   þu gearcige   7 forgyfenysse us
   gratiam prestes   veniamque nobis
   liþe   to eallum
   mitis ad omnes.   64

                 ó
   gearca *bebiddað   god eala þu micele reccend
XVII   Prebe, oramus,   deus,   magne rector,
   þæt geleafa ure   leahtrum wiðstande
   ut fides nostra   vitiis resistat

    7   mihta   gecneordnyssum he þenige
    atque virtutum   studiis   ministret

    mid breoste clænum
    pectore   puro.   68

         wuldor   fæder   uton singan ealle
XVIII   Gloriam patri   resonemus omnes

                              *ó
    7 þe   crist   *ancennede *eala *þu heofonlica
    & tibi, Christe,   genite   superni,

    mid þam   se halga   samod 7 scyppend
    cum quibus sanctus   simul & creator

    gast   rixaþ
    spiritus regnat.   72

         amen

I Christ, you who are the honour and the power of the saints, you who are life and ideal, the way, the light and the champion, accept mercifully the prayers of those who implore you and their hymn,

II you who once miraculously drew your Benedict to you and thereby set him apart from the world so that he should learn to reject the iniquity of the world and follow you,

III for you caused this boy's pious heart to be strong in faith by your grace. Strengthened in this with a faithful heart, he performed miracles in his prayers.

IV Then he set foot in a remote region and climbed a steep height, because he, who burned with chaste love, chose to torment his youthful limbs.

V Later he taught blessed human beings to coerce their mind by strict rules and bow their necks always beneath the yoke of the Lord of heaven.

VI One of these, his devoted servant Maurus, pulled the boy Placidus out of deep water, lifted him up out of the waves and drew him from the water's surface by virtue of his obedience to his Father;

VII thus he, who himself duly excelled in the way, teaches that the monk is to be admonished by the example of action and one should so submit oneself to the commands of God and freely obey.

VIII In a life of poverty he, full of piety, gave an example by his habits in the ardour of his faith and taught the doubting hearts of his followers always to remain faithful.

IX He proved this and by the power of his faith, joined with his holy brothers in pouring out prayers, instantly revealed a vessel to be abundantly filled with oil, to overflowing.

X In his pity he insisted on just practice and, trusting in Christ and in faith that he would prevail, he drew back the soul of a certain man by prayer, when his body had died.

XI Then his saintly sister, who followed him closely, because she preferred to keep him with her, when it was rather late, told him to stay and held him and bound him more strongly to herself by a heavy rainfall.

XII After this, as the saint was sitting in a desert place, he saw the soul of this sister seek the secrets on high with winged speed.

XIII Joyful because of this, he called the brothers and ordered them to bring the body in order to bury it in the grave which had long been prepared for him, and he was soon to follow her.

XIV Afterwards, having foreknowledge of his coming end, he eagerly set about preparing the grave. He received grace and gave up his soul, which was to find its place in heaven.

XV His clear and blazing way to heaven, attested by an angel to be Benedict's, seemed to resound in the ears of the brothers with a strong note.

XVI By his merits, Christ, we pray you to hold off your anger and concede us your favour and, merciful to all, grant us your grace and forgiveness.

XVII We ask you, God, great ruler, let our faith resist sins and serve in the pursuit of virtues with a pure heart.

XVIII Let us all sing glory to the Father and to you, Christ, son of him who is in heaven. Together with these rules the Holy Spirit, the creating spirit.

This hymn was sung at the feast of St Benedict (21 March). The Canterbury Hymnal assigns it to Vespers, the Winchester Hymnal, and probably H, to Lauds. It is anonymous and written in Sapphic stanzas. No melody has been transmitted in the Anglo-Saxon manuscripts. The text is included in the hymnals of BCDHVm and the *Expositio hymnorum* of JVp and in the fragment Ri, as far as that is extant. Only D has the full version of this hymn. The others have an abbreviated one. It is likely that the full version was not, in fact, sung during services in Anglo-Saxon England. The text in Ri is glossed.

Bibliographical references: *ICL* no. 2246; *AH* 14a, 63–5 (no. 53), cf. *AH* 2, pp. 40–1 (no. 31).

Apparatus to D   Latin text: 27 parentum] t *expunged and* d *interlined above by another hand*; 48 pernicitate] *first* e *altered from* i *by* D_1.

BVmCJVpHRi   1–8 *not extant in Ri*; Heading: in festivitate sancti benedicti abbatis *B*, ITEM YMNUS *Vm*, HYMNUS AD MATUTINUM (*first* T *partly illegible*) *C*, CHRISTE SANCTORUM *J, no rubric VpH*; 2 & auctor] salusque, *struck through and corrected to* auctor *in the margin by a considerably later hand Vm*; 6 *change of hand in H*; H_2 *begins with* segregasti; 7 prava] probra *B*; secli] mundi *BVmCJVpH*; reprobare] pro *on erasure of* bro *B*; 8 *Ri begins*; 9 cuius devotum a] *missing Ri*; cuius] huius *JVpH*; 10 gratia prestans fi] *missing Ri*; gratia] gratiam *BVmJVpH*; prestans] prestas *B*; 11 qua valens mire] *missing Ri; Ri ends*. mire] e *erased both in Vm and Vp; a considerably later hand has interlined* a *in Vm and written* a *after the erasure in Vp*; 14 arduum] ardua *BVmCJVp*; scandit] scandens *Vm*; malens] mallens *BCJ*, mallens, *first* l *erased Vmp*, mallens, a *on erasure H*; 15 iuvenilis] invenilis *C*; 17 homines] homine *C*; 18 regulis] regulae *BCJVp*, regulare *H*; artis] arctis *Vm*; animum] animos *BVmJVpH*; retundi] retutid *C*; 19 polorum] po *on erasure, probably by a different hand C*; 21 Maurus] mauris *H*; 22 puerulum] puerum *BVmCJVpH*; 23 obsequens] obsequen, s *interlined above, possibly by another hand C*; 24 aequore traxit] ęquo retraxit *H*; 25–60 *om. BVmCJVpH*; 63 gratiam prestes] *om. in B*; prestes] prestens *JVp*; 65 magne] alme *BVmCJVpH*; 69–72 Laudibus cives celebrant superni / te deus simplex pariterque trine / supplices ad nos veniam precamur / parce redemptis *C; JVpH agree with C, but JVp read* at *for* ad, *while H reads* et (*the gloss in JVp seems to render* et). *H adds* amen. *Vm's doxology is erased and illegible except for initial* G; *a later hand has written H's doxology over it, omitting initial* L; 70 superni] superne *B*; 72 *B adds* amen.

Ri gloss: 8 imitaretur 10 valere 13 (remotis) locis (*preceded by one long illegible gloss*).

Commentary   Latin: *For Benedict's Life, see Gregory*, Dialogi, Book II (*Gregoire le Grand*, Dialogues, *ed. de Vogüé II, 120–249.* 1 *Cf. Hy 97/1.* 2 *Cf. John I.4, XIV.6.* 7 *AH reads* probra mundi, *attesting* prava *and* saecli *for two continental manuscripts.* 9–16 *See Gregory* Dialogi II, *Prologue and ch. 1.* 10 *AH reads* praestas, *attesting* praestans *for the Continent in two cases.* 11 *AH reads* mira, *attesting* mire *for the Continent in two cases.* 14 *AH reads* ardua. 18 *Note that the gloss in JVp probably reflects the reading of DVm,* regulae. *AH reads* animos *as* BVmJVpH. 21–4 *See Gregory*, Dialogi II. 7. 22 puerulum *in D is metrically impossible.*

260

25–60 *According to* AH *these stanzas diverge in a considerable number of readings from the text of those (relatively few) hymnals that contain the full version of this hymn.* 41–60 *See Gregory,* Dialogi II. *33–4 and 37.* 65 *According to* AH alme *is found only in one continental manuscript.* 70 *The Latin gloss* ó *in* D *indicates a vocative, reflecting* B's *reading, not* D's. AH *reads* superne. Old English: 12 *One would expect* geleaflicum. 14 *The final vowel of* heahnyssa *could indicate that the original lemma was* ardua *as in* BVmCJVp, *but may be due to the merging of final vowels in Late Old English.* 15 cildlice *seems to be acc.pl. for expected gen.sg.* cildlices. 18 regoles nearonyssum *renders the reading of* BCJVp. 19 *For* drihtne *read* drihtnes; *the ending may be carried over from* geoce. 22 D's *reading* puerulum *instead of* puerum *does not appear to be reflected in the gloss, but the diminutive often has a weakened force in medieval Latin.* 62 herunge *'praise' is puzzling as a gloss for* favorem. 65 bebiddað *is probably a mistake for* we biddað. 70 *Latin* genite *is confused with* unigenite. þu heofonlica *renders the reading of* B, *which has the voc.* Eala, *glossing the Latin* ó, *presupposes this voc.*

63

YMNUS AD NOCTURNAM

I   þæt þines lifes   lofu
    UT TUAE VITÆ,   BENEDICTE, laudes

    nu   þine wurðfullice   þenas   singan we
    nunc tui digne   famuli canamus,

    heortan unclænre   wom   þu gelimplice
    cordis inpuri   maculam tu apte

    toles   mid bene
    solve precatu.   4

        es
    þu eart muneca   fæder 7 lareow
II   Tu   monachorum   pater & magister,

                        ó   s. benedictus
    heofonlic lif   eala þu halga þu forðatuge
    celibem vitam   sacer   edidisti

    7   lare   gebisnunga   mid tacnum
    atque doctrine   documenta signis

    þu self afandodest
    ipse   probasti.   8

    eala þu swiþe gesælig   fæder þu halga æfre
III   O   nimis felix   pater alme,   semper

    *ængel   on life   on gaste *witega
    angelis vita,   spiritu prophetis,

fæderum   on tacnum   drihtnes þenum
patribus signis,   domini ministris

gelic on gebisnungum
par documentis.   12

hit ys   halig   oþre cuman
IV   Est satis sanctum   alios venire

7 heora criste   saula   gestreonan
& suas Christo   animas lucrari;

ó
eala þu fæder halga   eowde mid hundfealdra
tu pater alme,   grege cum centeno

þu geneosast tungla
appetis   astra.   16

fyrdwicu geond embhwerft   mid sange swegaþ
V   Castra per orbem   cantu   resultant

7 þinum gewritum   sawle beoþ gestrinode
& tuis scriptis   animę lucrantur.

betwux þisum 7 us   samod beon amearcode
Inter has & nos   simul annotari,

halga bide
sancte, precare.   20

þæt fæder getiþige   þæt ilce   fæderes
VI   Hoc pater prestet,   hoc idem parentis

ancenned bearn   him selfum efenece
unicus natus   sibi   comperennis,

þæt se halga blæd   an   god   on ælcere
hoc sacer flatus,   unus deus omni

tide   weorulde
tempore saecli.   24

amen

I In order that we, your servants, may sing now worthily the praise of your life, Benedict, free us from the stain of an impure heart by your prayer.

II You are the father and teacher of the monks. You, the holy one, promulgated the unwedded life and yourself gave proof of your teaching by miraculous signs.

III O most blessed and holy father, who was always equal to the angels in his way of life, to the prophets in his spirit, to the Fathers in his miracles and to the servants of the Lord in his teaching!

IV It is holy enough that others should come and win their own souls for Christ – you, blessed father, seek the stars followed by a flock of hundreds.

V Throughout the world fortresses resound with song and souls are won by means of your writings. Pray for us, o saint, that we, too, may be numbered among them.

VI May the Father grant this, may the only-begotten Son of the Father, who is as eternal as he, grant the same, may the Holy Spirit grant this, they who are one God for all time and all ages.

This hymn was sung at the feast of St Benedict (21 March). In the Canterbury Hymnal it is assigned to Matins (Nocturn), in the Winchester Hymnal and H probably to Vespers. It is anonymous and written in Sapphic stanzas. No melody has been transmitted in the Anglo-Saxon manuscripts. The text is included in the hymnals of CDHVm and the *Expositio hymnorum* of JVp. In D there are syntactic glosses.

Bibliographical references: *ICL* no. 19911; *AH* 19, 87 (no. 133)

Apparatus to D   Latin text: 17 cantu] con *interlined at the beginning of the word with a caret mark,* a *altered to* æ. *Both changes are probably by another hand.* 19 annotari] i *on erasure of* e; 22 comperennis] cōperennis (com- *or* con-).

Old English gloss: 21 *erasure (of* i?) *after* fæderes.

Latin gloss: 1–4 *have syntactic glosses by an approximately contemporary hand; the letters* a *to* h *are interlined indicating a rather clumsy re-arrangement of the verbal sequence along the following lines:* Benedicte, tu solve maculam cordis impuri precatu, (ut) canamus famuli laudes (tuae vitae). *The glossator has not dealt with the words of the first half line; they have been added at the appropriate places in brackets. The adverbs* apte, nunc *and* digne *have been excluded from the re-arrangement, unless* apte *was meant to stay behind* tu *and* nunc digne *behind* laudes. tui *(line 2) is glossed verbally by the same hand:* s. nos.

VmCJVpH   Heading: HYMNUS COMPOSITUS AD LAUDEM PATRIS BENEDICTI *Vm*; HYMNUS DE SANCTO BENEDICTO *C*, UT TUE VITE *J, no rubric VpH*; 1 laudes] laudis *C*; 3 maculam] *second* m *on erasure of* s *Vm*; 7 atque] utque *Vp*; doctrine̜] doctrinam *H*; 10 angelis] angelus *CJVp, abbreviated* angel̄s *H (Dewick expands as* angelis); prophetis] prophetes *CJVp*; 12 par] pars *C*; 14 animas] animos *J*; lucrari] lucrare *H*; 15 cum] nunc *VmCJVpH*; 16 appetis] appetisti *J*; 18 tuis] tui *J*; lucrantur] n *interlined above by J₁ J*; 20 precare] precari *H*; 21 Hoc pater] oc pater *on erasure C*; 23 sacer] s *inserted afterwards by C₁ C*; unus deus] deus unus *VmCH*; amen] *om. JVp*.

Commentary 1–4 *Cf.* Hy 86₁/1–4. 9 *Cf.* Hy 86₃/1. 14 *For* lucrari *cf. I Cor.* IX.19–22. 15–18 *The manuscripts consulted by* AH *diverge here considerably.* 17 concentu, *the reading produced by the change in D, is metrically correct, but cf.* VmCJVpH. 23 *JVp has* unus deus *like D, but the* Expositio *is prose.* AH *reads* Deus unus *like* VmCH. *Old English:* 10 ængel ... witega *renders the reading of CJVp.* 13 *The omission of the gloss to* satis *is apparently accidental.*

64

YMNUS AD MATUTINAM

þam mæran singende   gearlice
I   [22r] MAGNO   CANENTES ANNUA

nu   lofsangas
nunc Benedicto cantica

*þæt we brucan þissere æþelan
       fruamur huius inclyti

freolstide   *mid gefean
festivitatis gaudio,   4

se   scan   swa swa tungel niwe
II   qui fulsit ut   sidus novum

middaneardlice adræfende genipu
*mudana   pellens nubila.

ylde   on þam selfon gemære
Aetatis ipso   limite

he forseah *ylde wæstmbære þing
despexit aevi florida.   8

wundra   foremihtig
III   Miraculorum prepotens,

gehrepod mid halgum blæde
atactus sancto   flamine

he scan   on forebecnum
resplenduit prodigiis

toweardre worulde bodigende
venturo seclo   precinens.   12

na   ær   woruldum cuþ
IV   Non ante saeclis   cognitum

nihte   leoma scán
noctu iubar effulserat,

on þam eall   embhwerft wæs gesewen
quo   totus orbis   cernitur.

Hac sancti flatu vehitur.   16

    sy þrynnesse wuldor
v   Sit trinitati gloria,

    sy ece   7 healicnyss
sit perpes & sublimitas,

    ...   *leohtfæt*   scinende
hanc quę lucernam fulgidam

he forgeaf ure   worulde
donavit nostro sęculo.   20

                    amen

I Now let us share in the joy of this glorious festival and sing our yearly songs to the great Benedict,

II who shone like a new star, driving away the clouds of the world. Even at the threshold of youth he despised the bloom of this world.

III Mighty above all in miracles, for he had been touched by the Holy Spirit, he excelled in portents, prophesying of the world to come.

IV A light not known before to the ages blazed out in the night, in which all the world can be seen. Thus it is moved by the spirit of the Holy One.

V Glory be to the Trinity and everlasting majesty be to it, which gave this shining lantern to our world as a gift.

This hymn for the feast of St Benedict (21 March) is assigned to Lauds in the Canterbury Hymnal, to Matins (Nocturn) in H and probably the Winchester Hymnal. It is a cento from a hymn by Paulus Diaconus, *Fratres alacre pectore*. The metre is rhythmical Ambrosian hymn verse (4 × 8pp). The melody transmitted in H has not been identified. The text is included in the hymnals of CDHVm and the *Expositio hymnorum* of JVp and in the fragment of Ri, as far as that is extant. The text in Ri is glossed.

Bibliographical references: *ICL* no. 9206; *AH* 51, no. 146, pp. 168–9, cf. 2, no. 67, p. 59. For the full version of Paulus Diaconus's hymn see *AH*

50, p. 118; *Poetae latini aevi Carolini*, 4 vols., ed. E. Dümmler, L. Traube and K. Strecker, MGH (Berlin, 1881–1914) I, 14; 'Pauli historia Langobardorum', ed. L. Bethmann and G. Waitz, *Scriptores rerum Langobardicarum et Italicarum*, MGH (Berlin, 1878), pp. 12–192, on p. 67.

Apparatus to D   Latin text: 3 inclyti] *second* i *altered to* o, *probably by another hand*; 4 festivitatis] v *on erasure*; gaudio] gaudium, m *erased and* u *altered to* o, *probably by* D_1; 10 atactus] atacto, us *interlined above by* D_1; sancto] alto, *which was expunged and* sancto *interlined above (by* D_1*);* 12 seclo] *abbreviated as* scło, *abbreviation mark erased and* e *interlined above on erased gloss and inserted with a caret mark behind* s *by another hand*; 16 sancti] i *altered to* o, *by* D_1? 19 hanc quę] *two or three letters erased at the beginning of the line,* hanquę *interlined above on erasure of the gloss;* c *interlined after* n *with a caret mark. Both corrections are by the same hand, apparently not* D_1.

Old English gloss: 4 gefean] gefeam, *the last minim of* m *erased*; 12 worulde] *erased to make room for the correction of* scło; u *and* d *illegible*; 19; . . . leohtfæt] *the beginning of the line up to* fæt *erased to make room for the correction of the Latin. The illegible gloss may have terminated in* þe.

VmCJVpHRi   1–14 *missing in Ri*; Heading: ITEM YMNUS *Vm, no rubric, but space was left for one* C, MAGNO CANENTES *J, no rubric* Vp, YMNUS AD NOCTURNAM *H*; 1 CANENTES] T *om. and inserted afterwards* C; 3 inclyti] inclite *VmCJVpH*; 4 gaudio] gaudiis *VmCJVpH*; 6 mudana] mundana *VmCJVpH*; 10 atactus] afflatus *VmJVpH*, aflatus *C*; sancto] alto *VmCJVp*; 12 venturo] o *altered to* a *by another hand* Vm, ventura *CJVpH*; 13 cognitum] cognitu *J*; 15 *Ri begins*; totus] totis *H*; cernitur] ernitur *missing Ri*; 16 et hec terra conspicitur *VmCJVpH, Ri agrees with VmCJVp, but* picitur *is missing.* 18 sublimitas] itas *missing Ri*; 19 hanc quę] hancqu *with* ę *interlined above* Ri; fulgidam] ulgidam *missing Ri*; 20 amen] *om. CJ*.

Ri gloss: 15 (*quo*) iubare 16 tota (*terra*) quo i. . . (*conspicitur*) 18 aeternalis mag*nitudo* 19 (*quę*) trinitas.

Commentary   Latin: 6 *Cf. Hy 21/1–2.* mudana *in D lacks the abbreviation mark.* 7 *The gloss in JVp, on* anginne, *may reflect a reading attested for the original hymn and by* AH *for Italy,* limine *instead of* limite. 10 AH *reads* adflatus alto, *attesting* adtactus *for continental manuscripts.* 12 *The corrector in D has expanded* scło *to make clear that the syncopated form of the word is required by the metre.* JVp's *prose version, which is not constrained by metre, has the unsyncopated form.* 19 *The original reading in D is irrecoverable. There was space for either* hanc *or* que. Old English: 3 *The lack of a definite article before* æþelan *makes it likely that the gloss renders* inclyte, *the reading of* VmCJVpH. 8 ylde *'age' can hardly be stretched to include 'world' as* aevum *can.* 19 leohtfæt *agrees with the gloss in* JVp. *The preceding gloss could have been* seo þe *rendering* quę, *but the fact that the verb of the clause is accompanied by a pronoun suggests that it was not.* 20 *The pronoun is superfluous, if there was a relative pronoun in the preceding line. In any case* he *is wrong, as the pronoun should agree with* þrynnesse *in line 17.*

65₁

YMNUS IN ADNUNTIATIONE SANCTÆ MARIÆ

þæne eorþe brym roderas
I QUEM TERRA, PONTUS, aethera

wurðiaþ gebiddaþ bodiaþ
colunt, adorant, predicant,

þryfealdne gewissigendne seare ł cræft
trinam regentem machinam

clysing gebær
claustrum Mariae baiulat. 4

þam mona sunna 7 ealle þing
II Cui luna, sol & omnia

þeowiaþ geond tida
deserviunt per tempora,

geondgoten hefones gyfa
perfusa cęli gratia

bæran mædenes innoþas
gestant puellę viscera. 8

wundriað eornostlice worulda
III Mirantur ergo sęcula,

þæt ængel brohte sæd
quod angelus fert semina,

þæt mid earan mæden geeacnode
quod aure virgo concepit

7 on heortan gelefende heo cænde
& corde credens parturit. 12

eadig moder mid lace
IV Beata mater munere,

þæs upplica *cræfeca ł wyrhta
cuius supernus artifex

middaneard mid feste healdende
mundum pugillo continens

wambe under earce wæs belocen
[22v] ventris sub arca clausus est, 16

eadig heofones bodunge
V beata caeli nuntio

ecne   mid þam halgan gaste
fecunda sancto   spiritu,

gewilnod   þeodum
desideratus gentibus

þære   þurh rif   wæs geondsænd
cuius per alvum fusus est!   20

I The encompassing body of Mary bears the one whom the earth, the sea and the heavens revere, adore and proclaim, the one who rules the threefold structure of the world;

II the womb of a girl, filled with the grace of heaven, carries the one whom the moon, the sun and all else serve in their seasons.

III Thus the ages are filled with wonder that the angel conveys the seed, that the virgin conceived by the ear and, having faith in her heart, gave birth.

IV Blessed is the mother in her office, in the ark of whose womb the heavenly demiurge was enclosed, he who holds the world in his fist,

V blessed she who by means of the messenger from heaven became pregnant of the Holy Spirit, by whose womb the desire of nations was brought forth.

This Marian hymn may have been divided between Vespers and Lauds of the Annunciation (25 March) in the Canterbury Hymnal. It was sung at Matins (Nocturn) of Candlemas (2 March) according to the Winchester Hymnal. The collectar in H assigns Hy 65₁ to Matins (Nocturn) and Hy 65₂ to Lauds of Candlemas. The same arrangement may apply in the hymnal of H for Candlemas, but at the Assumption of Mary Hy 65 (65₁?) is assigned to Lauds and at the Nativity of Mary (8 September) the place of Hy 65₂ is taken by Hy 138 at Lauds. In the Hours of Our Lady in R Hy 65 provides for Sext and None, in T for Matins. It has been ascribed to Venantius Fortunatus (sixth century). The metre is Ambrosian iambic dimeter. No melody has been transmitted in Anglo-Saxon manuscripts. The text is included in the hymnals of BCDHVm, the *Expositio hymnorum* of JVp and the Hours of RT.

Bibliographical references: *ICL* no. 13173; *AH* 50, 86–8 (no. 72); cf. *AH* 2, pp. 38–9 (no. 27), Walpole no. 39.

Apparatus to D   Latin text: 17 *punctuation om., although end of verse and line do not coincide.*
Old English gloss: 3 gewissigendne] *first* g *on erasure*; 9 worulda] o *altered from* u *by D₁*.

BVmCJVpHRT   Heading: hymnus ad vesperam. In purificatione sanctę mariae *B*, IN ADNUNTIATIONE SANCTĘ MARIAE *Vm*, HYMNUS AD NOCTURNUM *C*, QUEM TERRA PONTUS *J*, *no rubric VpHT*, YMNUS AD SEXTAM *R*; 1 aethera] &thera *T*; Mariae] maria *C*; luna] lua, n *interlined above with a caret mark, by the text hand R (by a different hand according to Dewick, ed., Horae)*; 8 viscera] viscere, e *altered to* a *by V₁ Vm*; 9 Mirantur] irantur *B*; 10 semina] sema, i *interlined above T*; 11 aure] aurē *H*; 16 *In R the divisio ends and the incipit of the doxology follows:* Gloria tibi domine. 17 *R begins the* divisio *with the rubric:* YMNUS AD VIIII. Beata] Benedicta *BCJVpH*, Benedicta *expunged and* eata *interlined by a later hand R*; 18 fecunda] a *altered from* o *R*; 20 alvum] almum *CH*, v *on erasure R; H adds:* Matrem per integerrimam / opem ferens celerrimam / dissolve Christe vincula / quę nostra nectunt crimina / Gloria tibi domine.

Commentary   Latin: 5–6 *Cf.* fecit lunam in tempora. sol cognovit occasum suum *Ps. CIII.19.* 15 *Cf.* quis mensus est pugillo aquas et caelos palmo ponderavit *Isa. XL.12*; in manu eius fines terrae *Ps. XCIV.4.* 17 AH *reads* benedicta, *attesting* beata *for continental manuscripts as well.* 19 *Cf.* et veniet desideratus cunctis gentibus *Hag. II.8.* 20 *H's additional stanza is attested for the Continent by* AH. Old English: 14 *For* cræfeca *read* cræfteca *from* cræftga *with partial assimilation of palatalized* g *to* c *and development of a parasite vowel* i, *here weakened to* e *(Campbell §434, n. 4, SB §196, 2).*

$$65_2$$

eala þu wuldorfulle fæmne
I   O gloriosa   femina,

healic   ofer   tungla
excelsa super sidera,

se þe þe gescop   foregleawlice
qui te creavit provide,

þu sycst halgum   breoste
lactas   sacrato ubere.   4

þæt þe   unrót   ædbræd,
II   Quod ęva tristis abstulit.

þu agyldst haligre spryttinge
tu reddis almo germine.

infaran   þæt tungla woplican
Intrent ut astra flebiles,

heofones eahþerl   þu eart geworden
caeli   fenestra facta es.   8

s. es
þu eart cynges healic geat
III   Tu   regis alta ianua

7   infereld leohtes scinende
& porta lucis fulgida.

lif   forgifen þurh mæden
Vitam datam per virginem,

þeoda   alysede   fægniaþ
gentes redempte, plaudite.   12

wuldor þe   drihten
Gloria tibi, domine

I Oh glorious woman elevated above the stars, you give suck with your sacred breast to the one who created you in his providence.

II You restore by your holy offspring what sad Eve took away. You have become the window of heaven so that the pitiable ones may enter among the stars.

III You are the high door of the king and the shining gate of light. Rejoice, you redeemed nations, that life was given by the virgin.

This is the section of the hymn that was sung at Lauds of Candlemas according to H and its collectar and may have been sung at Lauds in the Canterbury Hymnal.

Apparatus to D   Latin text: *D₁ continues from Hy 65₁ without a break.* 1 *punctuation om. after this verse, although it ends in the middle of the line;* 3 *punctuation om.*
   Old English gloss: 8 eahþerl} r *on erasure of* l.

BVmCJVpHRT   1 *All manuscripts except H continue on from Hy 65₁ without a break, but Vm has an enlarged initial. In J a separate incipit has been entered by the fifteenth-century hand.* gloriosa] gloria sa, o *interlined above the first* a *by C₁ C; four to six letters erased after* gloriosa *Vp;* 3 qui] qu *T;* 4 lactas] lacta *CJVp,* lactas *altered from* lactans *T;* sacrato] sacrata *C;* ubere] ubera, *altered to* uberae *by C₁ C;* 5 tristis] tristit *Vp;* 6 almo] 1 *interlined above, probably by R₁, R;* 7 Intrent] intres *JVp (gloss to JVp renders* intrent*);* 8 es] est *C;* 9 alta] alti *VmJVp,* a *altered to* i *T;* 13 H *adds a stanza before the doxology:* Cui christe natus virginis / es auctor & mirabilis / nos ipsius suffragiis / dona supernis gaudiis. *BH continue:* qui natus és de virgine *(*es *corrected to* est *by another hand H); VmT continue:* Gloria tibi domine / qui natus és de virgine / cum patre et sancto spiritu / in sempiterna secula. *T adds* amen. *R. omits* domine. *C reads:* Deo patri sit gloria.

Commentary Latin: 6 *Cf. Hy 66/8.* 9–10 *Cf. Hy 66/4.* 9 AH *reads* alti, *attesting* alta *for continental manuscripts as well.* 13 *H's additional stanza is attested for the Continent by* AH. *For* Cui *read* qui.

66

ITEM YMNUS

I   hal sy þu sæ   steorra
AVE,   MARIS STELLA,

godes moder halig
dei   mater alma

7   æfre   mæden
atque semper virgo,

gesælig heofones geat
felix caeli   porta,   4

II   nimende þæt   hal sy þu
sumens illud 'ave'

     of muðe
Gabrielis ore

sænd us on sibbe
funda nos in pace

awændende   *nama.
mutans æve nomen.   8

III   tolys bendas scyldigum
Solve vincla reis;

forðbring leoht   blindum
profer lumen cecis.

yfelu ure   adræf
Mala nostra pelle,

godu ealle   bide
bona cuncta posce.   12

IV   geswutela þe beon moder
Monstra te esse matrem

7 nime   *þu self bene
sumatque ipse precem,

se þe for us   acenned
qui pro nobis natus

271

underfeng beon þin
tulit   esse tuus.   16

lif   gearca   clæne
V   Vitam presta puram,

siþfæt gearca orsorh
iter   para   tutum,

þæt geseonde   þone hælend
ut   videntes Iesum

æfre   we samodblissigan
semper conlaetemur.   20

mæden anfealde
VI   Virgo singularis

betwux eallum   liþe
inter   omnes mitis,

us   mid gyltum tolysede
nos culpis   solutos

liþe   do 7 clæne
mites fac & castos.   24

sy   lof   gode fæder
VII   Sit laus deo patri,

*healic   criste   wlite
   summo Christo decus,

gaste   þam halgan
spiritui sancto,

wurþmynt   þrym   an
honor   [23r] tribus unus.   28

sy hit swa
ameN

I   Hail, star of the sea, holy mother of God and perpetual virgin, blessed gate of heaven,

II   make us secure in your peace, receiving that 'ave' from the mouth of Gabriel and so turning around the name of 'Eva'.

III   Undo the bonds of the offenders, extend light to the blind. Drive away the evil besetting us, request everything good for us.

IV   Prove that you are a mother and may he who undertook to be your son for our sake accept the prayer.

v Grant that our life may be pure, arrange a safe journey for us so that
we may rejoice together forever, when we see Jesus.

vi Incomparable virgin, you who are mild above all others, make us free
of sin and mild and chaste.

vii Praise be to God the Father, utmost glory to Christ and the Holy
Spirit, to the three one honour.

This Marian hymn was sung at Matins (Nocturn) of Annunciation
according to the Canterbury Hymnal, at the feast of the Assumption of
Mary (15 August) according to the Winchester Hymnal and at Compline
of the Nativity of Mary according to the hymnal of H. The collectar
assigns it to Vespers of the Annunciation and the Nativity and Compline
of the Assumption. It was also in use in the Hours of Our Lady for Lauds
(T) or Vespers (R). It is anonymous. The rhythmical metre of its stanzas
can be described as $4 \times 6p$ (with synizesis in line 13). The rhyme scheme
is irregular; the verses are linked by monosyllabic rhyme or assonance. The
melody transmitted in H is a version of Stäblein no. 149. The text is
included in the hymnals of BDHVm and the Hours of T. The *Expositio
hymnorum* of JVp and the Hours of R (the texts representing Winchester
usage) contain a shorter version. The original text in C has been erased and
replaced by the full version in a twelfth-century hand. Stanzas II and VI,
which were copied from Vm into Vp, as they were not extant in the prose
version based on the text of the Winchester Hymnal, have an Old English
gloss related to D.

Bibliographical references: *ICL* no. 1545; *AH* 51, 140–2 (no. 123), cf. *AH*
2, 39–40 (no. 29).

Apparatus to D   Latin text: 8 æve] æ *altered from* a *probably by* D_1; 13 Monstra] *above* a
an oblique stroke and a gloss-sized a *have been interlined and then wiped away;* 26 summo] *above* o
v̄ *has been interlined, possibly by* D_1, *and subsequently erased again;* 28 tribus] b *erased and
corrected to* n *by another hand;* b *only visible under ultraviolet light.*

BVmJVpHRT   Heading: hymnus ad nocturnam *B,* ITEM YMNUS *Vm,* AVE
MARIS STELLA *J, no rubric Vp,* YMNUS AD COMPLETORIUM *H,* YMNUS *RT;* 2 alma]
allma *T;* 5–8 *stanza om. JR, om. and replaced by copying Vm in Vp;* 6 h *erased in front of* ore *T
(not mentioned by Dewick, ed.,* Horae*);* 8 æve nomen] nonmen ẹve *H;* æve] ave *B;* 9 reis] regis
Vm, is on erasure? C; g *erased between* re *and* is *Vp,* reis *is on erasure by another hand* H, g *erased
between* re *and* is? *T;* 10 profer] profert *T;* 12 cuncta] cunta, c *interlined by another hand* T;

14 sumatque ipse] sumat per te *BVmJVpHRT*; precem] *second* e *damaged* J; 17–20 *follow lines 21–4 in HT*; 17 presta] resta J; 18 tutum] tuum B; 21–4 *om. JR, om. and replaced by copying Vm in Vp*; 23 solutos] solutis, i *expunged and* o *interlined above by another hand* T; 24 mites] mitis, i *expunged and* e *interlined by the corrector of line 23* T; 26 summo] summum *JVpT*, sumo H; 27 spiritui] spiritu *Vp*; 28 honor tribus] trinus honor *Vm*; tribus] trinus *VmH*, trinus *altered to* tribus T *(not mentioned by Dewick, ed. Horae)*; ameN] *om. JVp*.

Vm Old English gloss: 5 nimende] unbind; hal sy þu] sy þu hal; 21 anfealde] anfealdan; 22 betwux] betweox; 24 liþe] bilewite.

Commentary   Latin: 1 *Cf.* Maria inluminatrix sive stella maris. *Isidore of Seville*, Etymologiarum sive originum liber *VII. x. 1.* 8 AH *attests* Evae nomen *as in* H *for the Continent.* 10 T's profert *is attested for the Continent by* AH. 14 AH *reads* sumat per te. 17–20 AH *has stanza* V *following stanza* VI *like* HT. 26 *The correction in* D *to* summum *agrees with JVpT and brings the lemma into line with the gloss.* AH *reads* summum, *but notes that the variant reading* summo *was very common.* 28 *For the alteration in* D *to* trinus, *cf.* VmH *and the original reading in* T. Old English: 5 unbind *in* V *represents a dittography of the beginning of the gloss of the following stanza due to confusion during the compilation of Vm and Vp.* 8 nama *is uninflected; it should be accusative.* 14 *The glossator is confused by the oblique introduction of Christ as* ipse. 23 *The preposition* mid *indicates that the glossator has understood this to mean 'dissolute in sin'.* 26 healic *renders the reading of JVpT.*

67₁

YMNUS DE PASSIONE DOMINI AD VESPERAM

        guþfanan   cynges   forþsteppaþ
I   VEXILLA REGIS PRODEUNT,

        scinað   rode   geryne
        fulgent crucis mysteria,

        on þam flæsce flæsces scyppend
        qua   carne carnis conditor

        wæs ahangen   on gealgan
        suspensus est patibulo.   4

        afæstnode mid næglum innoþas
II   Confixa clavis   viscera

        aþenigende handa   *fótswaþu
        tendens   manus, vestigia

        alysednysse   for gyfe
        redemptionis gratia

        wæs geoffrod   onsægednyss
        immolatus est hostia,   8

*on þære he wæs gewundod þærtoecan
III   qui   vulneratur   insuper

*swurde   *heardan speres
mucrone diro   lanceae.

þæt us   he aþwoge fram leahtre
Ut nos lavaret   crimine

útfleow ł arn yþ   of blode
manavit   unda sanguine.   12

gefyllede synt   þa þing þe hleoþrode
IV   Impleta sunt, quę   cecinit

mid geleaffullum leoþe
David fideli   carmine

secgende mægþum
dicendo nationibus:

rixode   fram treowe god
'Regnavit a   ligno deus.'   16

I The standards of the King advance, the mystery of the cross blazes forth on which – on the gibbet – the creator of the flesh was hung in the flesh.

II Here the victim was sacrificed for the sake of redemption, his body pierced by nails, stretching out his hands and feet.

III He is moreover wounded by the cruel point of a spear. So that he might wash us clean of sin a stream of blood flowed from him.

IV It has come to pass what David uttered in veracious song, when he proclaimed to the nations: 'God ruled from a piece of wood.'

This Passiontide hymn was divided between Vespers and Matins (Nocturn) according to the Winchester Hymnal and the hymnal of H and probably also in the Canterbury Hymnal. The collectar in H, however, assigns the whole hymn to Vespers. It is by Venantius Fortunatus (sixth century) and written in Ambrosian iambic dimeter. The melody transmitted in H and W is a version of Stäblein no. 32. Stäblein no. 32 is possibly the original melody of Hy 67 (see B. Stäblein, 'Fortunatus', *MGG* 4 (1955), col. 585). The text is included in the hymnals of BCDHVm, the *Expositio hymnorum* of JVp and the 'Durham Ritual' (E). The Winchester Troper only contains stanza I of Hy 67$_2$.

Bibliographical references: *ICL* no. 17180; *AH* 50, 74–5 (no. 67), cf. *AH* 2, 45 (no. 42); Bulst, pp. 129 and 196 (XI, 3), Walpole no. 34.

BVmCJVpHE   Heading: ymnus ad vesperam *B*, DE PASSIONE DOMINI YMNUS *Vm*, HYMNUS DE PASSIONE DOMINI AD VESPERUM *C*, VEXILLA REGIS *J*, *no rubric Vp*, YMNUS IN PASSIONE DOMINI AD VESPERAM H, YMNUS INFRA XL^{ma} *possibly by another hand E*; 2 fulgent] fulget *VmCJVpH*, fulge *E*; mysteria] misterium *VmCJVpHE*; 3 qua] quo *BVmCJVpHE*; 4 patibulo] patibulum *CE*; 5–8 *erased but mostly legible in Vmp*; 5 clavis] carnis *Vp*; 6 tendens] t *illegible Vm*; manus vestigia] manuūestigia *C*; manus] u *illegible Vm*; vestigia] es *illegible Vm*; 8 *BVmCJVpH add* hic *at the beginning of the line*; immolatus] immolata *BVmJVpH*, est] es *Vm*; 9 qui] quo *BVmCJVpH*; vulneratur] vulneratus *BVmCJVpH*, volunneratus *E*; 10 diro] de dirę *Vm*; lanceaę] anceę *on erasure* H; 12 sanguine] *erasure of two letters in front of* sanguine *B (not mentioned by Wieland)*, ex sanguine *VmCJVpE*; 13 cecinit] concinit *VmCH*, concinit, *but* ł cecinit *interlined above, probably by text hand E*; 14 fideli] *second* i *altered by erasure from* u *Vp*; 16 *BVmE do not indicate the end of the* divisio. *Vp adds* ara. *CJH add* Hy 67₂/13–16 (*J in prose*) Salve ara salve victima / de passionis gloria / qua vita morte pertulit / et morte vitam reddidit (*according to C; variant readings of JH:* vita morte] vita mortem *J*, vita mortem, ita morte *on erasure* H; *H adds* amen.)

Commentary   Latin: 2 *Bulst reads* fulget … mysterium. 3 *Bulst reads* quo. 8 *Bulst reads* hic immolata est. 5–8 *The occasional omission of the second stanza in continental manuscripts is noted by* AH; *cf.* Vmp. 9 *Bulst reads* quo vulneratus. 10 *Vm's* dire *is noted as a variant reading by Bulst.* 12 *Bulst reads* unda et sanguine, *noting the occasional omission of* et. 13 *Bulst reads* concinit. 16 Dominus regnavit a ligno *Ps.* XCV.10 *in the* Vetus Latina, *see* Le Psautier Romain et les autres anciens psautiers latins, *ed. R. Weber, Collectanea Biblica Latina 10 (Vatican, 1953).* Hy 67₂/13–16 *functions as doxology for* Hy 67₁. V's ara *is the beginning of the prose paraphrase of the doxology without the* O *added to indicate the voc.; the accompanying gloss, however, is* eala þu weofod. *Old English:* 6 fótswaþu *renders the most common meaning of* vestigium, *which is inappropriate here.* 9 on þære *renders the reading of* BVmCJVpHE, quo, *taken as agreeing with* patibulo. *This is glossed* gealgan *in line 4, but the glossator is thinking of* rode *glossing* crucis *in line 2 and uses the feminine pronoun.* 10 *The original meaning of* mucro *'point, blade' was less familiar than the poetical 'dagger, sword'.* heardan *seems due to a confusion between* dirus *and* durus.

67₂

treow   wlitig   7   scinende
I   Arbor decora & fulgida,
gefrætewod cynges mid godewebbe
ornata   regis purpura,

gecoren wurþfullum boge
electa digno   stipite

swa halige lima   hreppan
tam sancta membra tangere,   4

eadig þæs on earmum
II **beata, cuius brachiis**

wurð   hangode   worulde
prętium pependit saecli.

wæge   geworden lichoman
Statera facta   corporis

7 uþe l reaflac he ætbræd helle
prædamque tulit   tartaro.   8

ageotende wyrtbræð of rinde
III **Fundens aroma   cortice,**

oferswiþende swæcc   hunigteare
vincens   saporem nectaris,

ecne   on wæstme wæstmbærum
foecunda fructu   fertili,

berende sige   æþelne
portans triumphum nobilem,   12

       ó   s. ó
hal sy þu weofud hal sy þu onsægednyss
IV **Salve,   ara,   salve,   victima,**

be þrowunge wuldre
de passionis gloria,

on þam lif   deaþ   þolode
qua   vita mortem pertulit,

for deaþe lif   he agæf
pro morte vitam reddidit.   16

         amen

I Beautiful and shining tree, adorned with the purple of the king, you
who were chosen to come into contact with so holy limbs with your
venerable timber,

II you are blessed, you on whose arms the ransom of the world has
hung. It became a pair of scales for the flesh and wrested its prey
away from hell.

III You who emit sweet scent from your bark, you who surpass the

277

savour of nectar, you who are rich with fertile fruit, you who bear a noble triumph,

IV hail, altar, hail, sacrificial victim, for the glory of the passion, in which life suffered death and returned life for death.

This is the second part of the Passiontide hymn, which appears to have been generally sung at Matins. The collectar of H, however, assigns it to Lauds of the Invention and the Exaltation of the Cross, feasts not mentioned in the rubrics of the hymnals.

BVmCJVpHEW   Heading: *no rubric BVmpEW*, HYMNUS AD NOCTURNUM *C*, ARBOR DECORA *J*, YMNUS AD NOCTURNAM *H; E has an enlarged initial and begins a new paragraph.* 1 Arbor] rbor *W*; 3 electa] electo *E*; digno] digna *VmCVp*; 4 membra] menbra *Vmp*; *W stops here and adds* amen. 6 saecli] seculi *C (VmHE abbreviate, JVp have* seculi*)*; 7 facta] *followed by* est *inserted from above with a caret mark by a later hand* Vm, facta est *CE (and JVp)*, fata est *H*; 8 tartaro] tartari *VmJVpHE*; 9–16 *by a later medieval hand on erasure Vm*; 9 Fundens] fundis *JVpH*, fundis, *possibly a small erasure between* d *and* i *E*; cortice] r *altered from* x *H*; 10 vincens] vincis *JVpHE*; nectaris] nectare *CJVpHE*; 11 foecunda] iocunda *JVpHE*; fertili] fertuli *H*, l *altered from* i *E*; 12 portans] portas *B*, plaudis *CJVpHE*; triumphum] triumpho *CJVpHE*; nobilem] nobili *JVpHE*; 13–16 *om. J*; 13 salve victima] *om. C*; 14–16 *om. CH*; 16 pro] et *VpE*; amen] *om. BVmp; B adds:* Deo patri sit gloria.

Commentary   Latin: 6 *Bulst reads* saeculi. *The syncopation or lack of it depends on the metrical interpretation of the line. JVp's reading, being prose, is irrelevant here.* 7–8 *Bulst reads* statera facta est corporis / praedam tulitque tartari. *AH attests the omission of* est *in continental manuscripts. JVp could be based on either reading.* 9–12 *Bulst reads* fundis aroma cortice, / vincis sapore nectare, / iucunda fructu fertili / plaudis triumpho nobili. *AH attests* fundens, saporem *and* triumphum *for continental manuscripts.* 13–16 *For the full doxology according to CJH see Hy 67₁.* Like VpE CJH have et *in the verse corresponding to line 16; Bulst reads* et morte.

68

YMNUS AD MATUTINAM

      ó
    eala þu ealdor   hæle   ancænned

I   [23ᵛ]   AUCTOR SALUTIS UNICUS,

    middaneardes alysend   æþele
    mundi   redemptor inclytus,

s.ó
þu crist us gearlic
tu Christe, nobis annuam
rode gesundfulla wuldor
crucis secunda gloriam. 4

þu spátlu swurplættas bendas
II Tu sputa, colaphos, vincula
s.es
7 reþe þu þrowodest swingla
& dira passus verbera
rode willende þu astige
crucem volens ascenderas
ure hæle for intingan
nostrę salutis gratia. 8

heanon mid deaþe deaþ towurpende
III Hinc morte mortem diruens
7 lif mid life forgyfende
vitamque vita largiens
deaþes þen facenfulne
mortis ministrum subdolum
þu oferswiðdesd deoful
deviceras, diabolum. 12

nu on fæderes *swiþþran
IV Nunc in parentis dextera
halige scinende onsægednyssa
sacrata fulgens victima,
gehýr we biddað liflicum
audi, precamur, vivido
mid þinum *alysedum blode
tuo redemptos sanguine, 16

*on þam þe fyligende eallum
V quo te sequentes omnibus
þeawa mid forþstæppinga worulde
morum processu saeculi
ongean eall æswicunga
adversus omne scandalum
rode we beran *guðfana
crucis feramus labarum. 20

ó
tiþa eadige þrynnes
Presta, beata trinitas

279

I You who are the only source of salvation, glorious redeemer of the world, Christ, make the annual celebration of the glory of the cross propitious to us.

II You had already endured being spat at, hit with fists and bound and cruelly beaten and then you willingly mounted the cross for the sake of our salvation.

III Then by your death you destroyed death and gave life by your life and thus you completely subdued the sly servant of death, the devil.

IV You who now shine as the holy sacrifice at the right hand of the Father, hear those who were redeemed by your life-giving blood, we pray,

V so that we may follow you in all our ways, as we proceed through the world, and bear the standard of the cross against all scandal.

This hymn was sung at Lauds at Passiontide. The collectar in H, however, assigns it to Vespers. It is anonymous and written in Ambrosian iambic dimeter (with some irregularities). The melody transmitted in H agrees with Stäblein no. 55₃. This is the melody that Norman neumes in C have for Hy 55. The text is included in the hymnals of BCDHVm, the *Expositio hymnorum* in JVp and in the 'Durham Ritual' (E), where it occurs twice, written by two different hands.

Bibliographical references: *ICL* no. 1297; *AH* 51, 70–1 (no. 71).

Apparatus to D   Latin text: 18 saeculi] s *added to the ending either by another hand or, possibly, by D₁ while glossing.*

BVmCJVpHE₁E₂   *E₁ is written by scribe E of the 'Durham Ritual', E₂ is by scribe C.* Heading: hymnus ad matutinam *B*, ITEM YMNUS *Vm*, HYMNUS AD MATUTINUM *C*, AUCTOR SALUTIS UNICUS *J, no rubric VpE₁E₂*, YMNUS AD MATUTINAM *H*; 1–2 Auctor s *and* inl *retraced by a much later, probably modern, hand E₁; the same hand repeats the first word,* Auctor, *above the line in E₂*; 2 inclytus] inclite *VmH*, inlitus *E₁*; 3 Tu] T *damaged E₁*; annuam] annua *C*; 4 gloriam] gloria *C*, iam *illegible J*; 5 colaphos] colaphas *Vm*, colavos *C*, calafos, f *altered (probably) from* p *H*, calaphos *E₂*; 6 dira] r *damaged E₁*; 9 Hinc] hic *H*; morte mortem] mortem morte *E₁E₂; one or two letters erased in front of* diruens *E₁*; 10 vitamque] que *interlined with a caret mark, probably by another hand E₁*; vita] vitam *CH*; 18 saeculi] seculis *BVm*; 21 *om. doxology CJVp,* Presta pater per filium *H, E₁E₂ read:* Presta pater per filium. / presta per. almum spiritum / cum his per evum triplici. / unus deus cognomine. Amen. *(E₁; variant readings of E₂:* pater *inserted from above with a caret mark, by another hand;* Amen *is added by another hand.).*

280

Commentary   Latin: 5 *Cf.* tunc expuerunt in faciem eius et colaphis eum ceciderunt, alii autem palmas in faciem ei dederunt *Matt. XXVI.67 (and similarly Mark XIV.65).* 18 *With the alteration in D compare the reading of BVm.* AH *reads* saeculis, *the gen. being only attested in a single continental manuscript.* Old English: 9 heanon *for* heonon *occurs again in Hy 87/24 (see Introduction, p. 76).* 12 *For spellings like* oferswiðdesd *see Introduction, p. 76.* 13 *For* swiþþran *read* swiþran. 16 alysedum *has dat. sg. instead of nom. pl.; the ending is carried over from* þinum. 17 quo *was not recognized as the equivalent of* ut. 20 guðfana *is uninflected; it should be acc. sg.*

69

YMNUS IN CAENA DOMINI

I	TELLUS AC ÆTHER IUBILANT	
	in magni cæna principis,	
	quę protoplasti pectora	
	vitae purgavit ferculo.	4

II	Hac nocte factor omnium	
	potentis ad misterium	
	carnem suam cum sanguine	
	in escam transfert animę.	8

III	A celsis surgens dapibus	
	prebet formam mortalibus	
	humilitatis gratia	
	Petri petens vestigia.	12

IV	Pallet servus obsequio,	
	cum angelorum dominum	
	ferendo limpham, lintheum	
	cernit caena procumbere.	16

V	[24r] Permitte, Symon, ablui.	
	Acta figurant mistica,	
	dum summus ima baiulat,	
	qui cinis servet cineri.	20

VI	Lavator thoris accubat	
	verbique favos aggerat,	

quos inter hostem denotat,
necis qui dolos ruminat.   24

VII   Trux lupe, Iuda pessime,
       fers agno miti bassia,
       das membra loris rigida,
       quę sorde tergunt sęcula.   28

VIII   Nexi solvuntur hodie
       carnis ac cordis carcere.
       Tingens sacrato crismate
       spes inde crescit miseris.   32

IX   Victori mortis inclitam
       pangamus laude gloriam
       cum patre ac sancto spiritu,
       qui nos redemit obitu.   36

I Heaven and earth rejoice at the supper of the great ruler which purified the breast of the first created man by the food of life.

II That night the creator of all things transformed his flesh and blood into nourishment for the soul, in a mystery of his might.

III Arising from the heavenly banquet, he gave an example to mortal men when he approached the feet of Peter for the sake of humility.

IV The servant pales at that service, when he sees the lord of the angels carry water and a cloth and cower down before him at that supper.

V 'Allow yourself to be washed, Simon. These actions stand for a mystical meaning. When the highest one supports the lowest, one who is ashes should serve those who are ashes.'

VI The one who performed the washing lies down on the couch and utters abundantly honey-combs of words. In the course of these he marks out the enemy who is plotting murderous deceit.

VII You savage wolf, wicked Judas, you offer kisses to the gentle lamb, you surrender the stiff limbs which purify the world from defilement to leather thongs.

VIII Today those who were in chains are set free from the imprisonment

282

of the flesh and the heart. Thus hope, which salves them with sacred chrism, arises for the wretched.

IX Let us sing glory and honour amid praise to the victor over death, who redeemed us from ruin, together with the Father and the Holy Ghost.

This is a processional hymn for Maundy Thursday. Since it is not a part of the Office, it is not regularly included in the hymnals. It has been ascribed to Flavius (sixth century). The metre is rhythmical Ambrosian hymn verse (4 × 8pp). The neumes in Vm represent an unidentified melody. The text is included only in the hymnals of DVm.

Bibliographical references: *ICL* no. 16142; *AH* 51, 77–80 (no. 76), Bulst, pp. 123 and 196 (X), Walpole no. 40.

Apparatus to D   Latin text: 6 potentis ad] s *and* d *erased, altered to* potenti sat *by another hand*; 8 transfert] s *inserted above, probably by* D_1; 15 lintheum] u *altered to* o *and m-abbreviation erased by* D_1? 27 rigida] d *erased and the first* i *altered to* e *by another hand*; 31 sacrato] o *clumsily altered to* t, *an* ur-*abbreviation interlined above – all probably by another hand.*

Vm   Heading: IN CENA DOMINI YMNUS; 1 ÆTHER] ęthra; iubilant] iubilent; 3 quę] quo; 15 lintheum] linteo; 20 qui] quid; servet] servit; 27 das] dans; membra] menbra; rigida] regia; 28 sorde] sordes; 31 unguem sacratur crismatis; 32 inde] unde; crescit] crescat; 35 ac] &; 36 *Vm adds* amen.

Commentary   *The hymn is based on John XIII.* 1 *Cf. Hy* $65_1/1$. *Bulst reads* aethra iubilent *like Vm; AH attests* aether *for continental manuscripts.* 5 *Cf. Hy* $142/1$. 6 *Bulst reads* potenti sat mysterio *like the corrector in* D; *AH attests* potentis ad mysterium *for the Continent, too.* 15 *Bulst reads* linteo *like Vm and the corrector in* D; *AH attests* linteum *for the Continent.* 16 *Bulst reads* caeno; *AH attests* caena *in two continental manuscripts.* 19 *Bulst reads* baiulo; *AH attests* baiulat *for the Continent.* 20 *Bulst reads* quod, *noting the variant reading* quid *as in Vm.* 22 *Cf.* favus mellis verba conposita *Prov. XVI.24.* 26 *Cf. Matt. XXVI.48–9. D hardly ever confuses* s *and* ss *as in* bassia, *so this may be a slip of the pen.* 27 *Bulst reads* regia; *the only continental manuscript printed in* AH *has* rigida. 28 *Bulst reads* sordes . . . saeculi, *noting* sorde . . . saecula *as a variant.* 31 *Bulst reads* unguen sacratur chrismatis, AH *attests* sacrato chrismate *for the Continent, but notes only one case of* tingens. 35 *Bulst reads* et.

70

INCIPIUNT YMNI DE RESURRECTIONE DOMINI

to   æfengereordunga lambes foregleawes
I   AD CENAM   AGNI PROVIDI

mid gyrlum hwitum *scinendum
STOLIS   ALBIS candidi

æfter oferfærelde sǽ   readre
post transitum Maris Rubri

criste   uton singan ealdre
Christo canamus   principi,   4

þæs   haligne lichoman
II   cuius sacrum corpusculum

on weofode rode   gebrædne
in ara   crucis torridum

mid blode his   readum
cruore   eius roseo

*onbyrgendum we libbaþ gode
gustando   vivimus deo,   8

gescilde   eastran on æfen
III [24ᵛ] protecti paschę vespere

fram awestendum ængle
a   devastante angelo,

generode of þam heardestan
erepti de durissimo

deofles   anwealde
pharaonis imperio.   12

eallunga eastran ure   crist   is
IV iam   pascha nostrum Christus est,

se þe geoffrod   lamb is
qui immolatus agnus est.

syfernysse *þearf
Sinceritatis azima

flæsc his   wæs geoffrod
caro eius oblata est.   16

eala þu *soþlice wurðfull onsægednyss
V O   vera digna hostia,

þurh ða   tobrocene synt helle
per quam fracta   sunt tartara,

alysed   folc gehæft
redempta plebs captivata,

agyfan lifes mede
reddita vitę *pręmio!   20

     þænne arisþ   crist   *on byrgene
VI Cum surgit Christus tumulo,

sigefæst he gehwerfde of helle
victor redit   de barathro

wællhreowne bescufende bend
tyrannum trudens vinculum

7 geopenigende *neoxnewange
& reserans   paradysum.   24

             ó
     we biddaþ   eala þu ealdor ealra
VII Quesumus,   auctor omnium,

on *þissere easterlican gefean
in hoc paschali gaudio:

fram ælcum deaþes onræse
ab omni mortis impetu

þin þu bewerige folc
tuum defendas populum.   28

             ó
     wuldor þe   drihten
VIII Gloria tibi, domine,

þu ðe arise   fram deadum
qui surrexisti a   mortuis,

mid fæder 7 þan halgan gaste
cum patre & sancto   spiritu

on ece   worulda
in sempiterna secula.   32

              sy hit swa
              AMEN

I In expectation of the supper of the prophetic lamb, shining in our white robes after crossing the Red Sea, let us sing to Christ the ruler,

II whose holy body was roasted on the altar of the cross. Consuming it together with his rose-red blood we live before God

III and are thus protected on the evening of Passover from the destroying angel and saved from the most cruel power of the Pharaoh.

IV Now Christ, who was sacrificed as a lamb, is our passover. His flesh has been offered up as the unleavened bread of integrity.

V Oh true and worthy sacrificial victim, by which the underworld was breached, the captive people were redeemed and the prize of life was granted!

VI When Christ arises from the grave, he returns a victor from hell, thrusting off the tyrannous bond and unlocking paradise.

VII We ask you on this joyful occasion of Easter, establisher of all things, to defend your people from each assault of death.

VIII Glory be to you, Lord, who arose from the dead, together with the Father and the Holy Spirit world without end.

This hymn for Eastertide was sung at Vespers. It was already in the Frankish Hymnal (OHy 40). It is anonymous and written in rhythmical Ambrosian hymn verse (4 × 8pp). Rhyme is monosyllabic and presupposes Late Latin pronunciation. The stanzas rhyme aaaa (except for the doxology). No melody has been transmitted in the Anglo-Saxon hymnals. The text is included in the hymnals of BCDHVm, the *Expositio hymnorum* of JVp and the 'Durham Ritual' (E).

Bibliographical references: *ICL* no. 157; *AH* 51, 87–9 (no. 83), cf. *AH* 2, 46 (no. 44) and *AH* 27, 88 (no. 36), Bulst, pp. 116 and 195 (VIII, 16), Walpole no. 109.

Apparatus to D   Latin text: 2 *Another hand adds* ET *at the beginning of the line.* 17 vera] a *altered to* e, *by* D_1? 18 quam] *the* m-*abbreviation erased and placed more precisely over* a; 21 cum surgit] *altered to* consurgit, *probably by another hand*; 23 vinculum] um *altered to* o, *probably by another hand*; 29 *Verse punctuation om. in the middle of the line.*

BVmCJVpE   *E was written by Scribe C of the 'Durham Ritual'.* Heading: hymnus ad vesperam in pascha domini *B,* IN RESURRECTIONE DOMINI *Vm,* HYMNUS DE RESURRECTIONE DOMINI. AD VESPERUM *C,* AD CENAM AGNI PROVIDI *J, no rubric VpE;* 1 CENAM] M *erased Vm;* 2 Vm *adds* et *at the beginning of the line;* 6 torridum] *C abbreviates* or *with the* ur-*abbreviation;* 9 Protecti] P *on erasure of* T *B;* 10 a devastante] ad evastante *J (not mentioned by Gneuss);* 11 erepti] erecti *Vmp;* 12 pharaonis] pharonis *B;* imperio] imperia, a *expunged and* o *interlined above by* J_1 *J;* 13 Christus] christe *E;* 17 vera] vere *VmCJVpE*; 18 fracta] facta *E*; 19 redempta] redempta est *E*; plebs] *interlined above, possibly by another hand, in* *C*; 20 reddita] reddite *C*; vitę] vita *CE*; pręmio] premia *BVmCJVpE*; 21 cum surgit] consurgit *E*; 22 redit] reddit *C*; 23 vinculum] vinculo *BVmJVpE*; 27 impetu] impetum *E*.

Commentary   Latin: 1 *Cf.* beati qui ad cenam nuptiarum agni vocati sunt *Rev. XIX.9.* 2 *Cf.* qui vicerit sic vestietur vestimentis albis *Rev. III.5. For the addition of* & *in D cf. Vm. It was made because the line as it stands is metrically defective. The poet's spoken dialect, however, clearly had prothetic e or i in* stolis. *Bulst has no* et, *but notes it as a later variant reading.* 3 *Cf.* quoniam patres nostri omnes sub nube fuerunt et omnes mare transierunt et omnes in Mose baptizati sunt in nube et in mari et omnes eandem escam spiritalem manducaverunt *I Cor. X.1–3.* 5–16 *See Exod. XII, especially* et edent carnes nocte illa assas igni et azymos panes *Exod. XII.8.* 9 *Bulst reads* vesperum, *which is necessary to the rhyme scheme, but notes* vespere *as a variant.* 13 *Cf. I Cor. V.17.* 17 *The alteration to* vere *in D brings the lemma into line with the gloss and VmCJVpE. Bulst reads* vera, *but notes the variant* vere. 20 pręmio *seems merely a slip due to the next two lines' ending in* -o; *however* AH *cites two continental manuscripts with the same variant reading.* 21 *With the correction in D to* consurgit, *cf. E. Bulst reads* consurgit, *noting the variant* cum surgit. 23 *Cf.* et ligavit eum per annos mille *Rev. XX.2. With the correction to* vinculo *cf. BVmJVpE. Bulst reads* vinculum. 26 *Bulst reads* paschale *and gives* paschali *as a variant.* 29–32 *The doxology is not original and not in Bulst.* Old English: 2 *The ending of* scinendum, *which should be nom. sg., was carried over from the two preceding words.* 8 onbyrgendum *represents an unsuccessful attempt to render the Latin gerund; the gloss in JVp is better:* onbyrgende. 12 deofles *is an interpretative gloss, not a translation. The author of the hymn is making poetical use of the traditional interpretation of the Passage of the Red Sea as a type of baptism and in this context 'Pharaoh' stands metaphorically for the devil.* 15 syfernysse *elsewhere renders* sobrietas. *For* þearf *read* þeorf. 17 soþlice *renders the reading of VmCJVpE,* vere. 21 *One would expect the preposition to be of rather than* on. 23 wællhreowne *may be inverted spelling due to the simplification of double consonants in composition. Cf. SB §231, note 3.* 24 neoxnewange *is another strange spelling of the word, cf. Hy 42/4, 57/5. The case ending is wrong, too.* 26 þissere *is the wrong gender,* gefea *being masculine.*

71

YMNUS AD NOCTURNAM

ó
eala þu hælend ure   alysednyss
I   IESU,   NOSTRA REDEMPTIO,

lufu   7 gewilnung
amor & desiderium,

god   scyppend ealra
deus, creator omnium,

287

mann   on ænde tidena
homo in fine temporum,   4

hwilc þe oferswiðde mildheortnyss
II   quę te vicit   clementia,

þæt ðu bære ure   leahtras
ut ferres   nostra crimina

wællhreowne deaþ   þoligende
crudelem   mortem patiens,

þæt us   fram deaþe   þu ætbrude
ut nos a   morte tolleres   8

helle   clesinga   þurhfarende
III   inferni claustra penetrans,

þine   hæftlingas alysende
tuos captivos redimens,

sigefæst mid sige   æþelum
victor triumpho nobili

to swiþran   fæder *þu sitst
ad dextram patris residens.   12

seo selfe þe *neadað arfæstnyss
IV   Ipsa   te   cogat pietas,

        þæt yfele ure   *þu oferswiðdest
[25r] ut mala nostra superes

arigende   7 wilfægene
parcendo & voti compotes

us   mid þinum anwlitan þu *geweldest
nos tuo   vultu   saties.   16

                ó
wuldor þe   drihten
Gloria tibi, domine

I Jesus, our redemption, love and desire, God, creator of all things, man who is to come at the end of time,

II what mercy mastered you so that you took our crimes on yourself and so suffered a cruel death in order to free us from death

III and entered by force into the dungeons of hell, redeeming your captives, and now sit as a victor in noble triumph at the right hand of the Father?

IV May the same love force you to overcome our evil with leniency and, letting us have our wish, to satisfy us with the sight of your face.

This hymn was sung at Matins (Nocturn) at Eastertide. The collectar in H, however, assigns it to Compline and also to Compline and Matins of the Ascension. It is anonymous and written in rhythmical Ambrosian hymn verse (4 × 8pp). The verses are irregularly linked by assonance and half-rhyme. No melody is transmitted in the Anglo-Saxon manuscripts. The text is included in the hymnals of BCDVm and the *Expositio hymnorum* of JVp.

Bibliographical references: *ICL* no. 7657; *AH* 51, 95–6 (no.89), cf. *AH* 2, 49 (no. 49), Walpole no. 114.

Apparatus to D   Latin text: 12 residens] n *expunged.*

BVmCJVp   Heading: hymnus ad nocturnam *B*, ITEM YMNUS *Vm*, HYMNUS AD NOCTURNUM *C*, IESU NOSTRA REDEMPTIO *J*, *no rubric Vp*; 6 nostra] ostra *by later hand (on erasure?) Vm*; 9 penetrans] enetran *on erasure C*; 12 residens] resides *BJVp*; 14 superes] superas *C*; 16 saties] satias *C*; 17 *om. JVp*; *B adds:* qui surrexisti, *C has:* Quesumus auctor.

Commentary   Latin: 3 *Cf. Hy* 2/1. 4 *Cf.* manifestati autem novissimis temporibus *I Pet. I.20.* 11 *Cf. Hy* 67₂/12, 72/11–12, 73/20. 12 *Cf. Hebr.* I.3. *The correction in D brings the lemma in line with the gloss and BJVp.* Old English: 7 *For* wællhreowne *cf. the note to Hy* 70/ 23. 12 þu sitst *renders the reading of BJVp.* 13 neadað *should be optative. The whole stanza is misinterpreted as a description of the redemption through Christ and* superes *and* saties *glossed as past tense.* 16 geweldest *could be a Kentish form of* gewieldan, *but 'rule' makes no sense here. It probably stands for* gewelgodest, *'that you should enrich'.*

72

YMNUS AD MATUTINAM

dægrima   leohtes   glitenaþ
I   AURORA LUCIS RUTILAT,

heofon mid herungum swegþ
cęlum laudibus   intonat,

middaneard *blissigend fægnaþ
mundus   exultans iubilat,

geomriende hell   þoterað
gemens   infernus ululat,   4

þænne cing se   strængesta
II   cum rex ille fortissimus

289

deaþes   tobrocenum mægenum
mortis confractis viribus

mid fét fortredende   helle
pede   conculcans tartara

he tolysde racentegan *eormingas
solvit   catena   miseros.   8

he   se   beclysed mid stane
III   Ille, qui clausus lapide

wæs gehealdan under cæmpan
custoditur   sub   milite,

sigoriende   mid glengan æþelan
triumphans pompa   nobili

sigefæst he aras of *hwreawe
victor surgit de funere.   12

tolysedum eallunga geomrungum
IV   Solutis   iam   gemitibus

7 helle   sarum
& inferni doloribus,

*for þam þe aras   drihten
quia   surrexit dominus,

scinende   cleopaþ ængel
resplendens clamat angelus.   16

*uróte   wæran þa apostolas
V   Tristes erant apostoli

of   cwale hera drihtnes
de nece sui domini,

þæne   wite   deaþes wællhreowes
quem poena mortis crudeli

*reþe fordemdan   arleasan
servi dampnarunt impii.   20

on worde   geswæsum ængel
VI   Sermone blando   angelus

foresæde   wifum
praedixit mulieribus:

on galilea lande drihten
In Galilea   dominus

to geseonne ys   hrædlicor
videndus est quantocius.   24

þa þa ðe heo eodon hrædlice
VII Illę dum pergunt concite

þam apostolum þæt secgan
apostolis hoc dicere,

geseonde hine libban
videntes eum vivere

heo geeadmettan fét drihtnes
adorant pedes domini. 28

þam oncnawenum leorningcnihtas
VIII [25v] Quo agnito discipuli

on galilea lande ofestlice
in Galileam propere

eodon geseon ansine
pergunt videre faciem

gewilnode drihtnes
desideratam domini. 32

on *beorhtre *easterlicre gefean
IX Claro paschali gaudio

sunne middanearde scan on leoman
sol mundo nitet radio,

þa þe crist eallunga þa apostolas
cum Christum iam apostoli

gesihðe gesawon mid lichamlicre
visu cernunt corporeo. 36

ætiwde him selfum wunde
X Ostensa sibi vulnera

on cristes lichoman scinendum
in Christi carne fulgida,

arisan drihten
resurrexisse dominum

on stefne hi andettaþ swutolre
voce fatentur publica. 40

ó
cyng crist þu mildheortesta
XI Rex Christe clementissime,

þu heortan ure geahna
tu corda nostra posside,

þæt þe lofu neadwise
ut tibi laudes debitas

we agyldan on ælcere tide
reddamus omni   tempore.   44

                    6
wuldor þe   drihten
Gloria tibi, domine

I The dawn of light glitters, heaven resounds loudly with praises, the
exulting world rejoices, groaning hell howls,

II as that most mighty king tramples the underworld under foot so
that the forces of death are crushed and releases the wretched from
their chain.

III He who was shut beneath a stone and guarded there by armed force
arises from the grave as a victor triumphant in his noble glory.

IV Now the groaning and pain in hell is relieved. The shining angel
cries out that the Lord has risen.

V The apostles were sad about the death of their Lord, whom godless
slaves had condemned to the cruel punishment of death.

VI The angel prophesied to the women, speaking gently: 'The Lord is at
once to be seen in Galilee.'

VII When they hastily go to tell this to the apostles, they see that he
lives and adore the feet of the Lord.

VIII When the disciples learn this, they speedily proceed to Galilee to see
the face of the Lord, which they long for.

IX With the bright joyousness of Easter the sun shines its rays on the
world (*or:* with its clear rays), as the apostles now see Christ with
corporeal sight.

X Now the blazing wounds in Christ's flesh have been shown to them,
they declare in open speech that the Lord has arisen.

XI Christ, most merciful king, take possession of our hearts so that we
may always sound your praises as we owe them to you.

This Easter hymn was sung at Lauds. It was already in the Frankish
Hymnal (OHy 41). It is anonymous and written in rhythmical Ambrosian
hymn verse (4 × 8pp). Rhyme is monosyllabic and often embraces the
whole stanza. No melody has been transmitted in the Anglo-Saxon

manuscripts. The text is included in the hymnals of BCDVm, the *Expositio hymnorum* of JVp and the fragment Ri, as far as it is extant. The 'Durham Ritual' (E) contains stanza XI with the doxology. The text in Ri is glossed.

Bibliographical references: *ICL* no. 1498; *AH* 51, 89 (no. 84), cf. *AH* 2, 47–8 (no. 46) and *AH* 27, 107 (no. 65), Bulst, pp. 114–15 and 195 (VIII, 15), Walpole no. 111.

Apparatus to D Latin text: 10 milite] m *altered from* b; 16 resplendens] *originally* rependens, s *and* l *interlined above by* D₁ *while glossing*; 18 *one or two letters* (ni.?) *erased in front of* domini. 20 servi] r *erased*; 25 *This line was punctuated as the end of a stanza, but the semicolon was changed to a dot by erasure.*

BVmCJVpERi *Ri is not extant until line 43.* Heading: hymnus ad matutinam *B*; ITEM YMNUS *Vm*, HYMNUS AD MATUTINUM *C*, AURORA LUCIS *J*, *no rubric Vp*; 8 catena] a pena *VmJVp*, ęno *with one or two letters erased in front and* ap *interlined above by another hand C*; 10 milite] limite *C*; 12 surgit] consurgit *JVp*; 17 Tristes] tristis *C*; 18 sui] summi *B*; 19 crudeli] creduli *C*; 20 servi] sevi *VmJVp*; dampnarunt] dampnamur *C*, dapnarunt *Vp*; impii] impię *CJVp*; 24 quantocius] quemtotius *C*, quam totius *JVp*; 26 dicere] *erasure (of* e*?) between* i *and* c *Vm*; 28 adorant] osculantur *JVp*; domini] dei *JVp*; 29 discipuli] li *altered from* a, *probably by the scribe C*; 30 Galileam] galilea *C*; 33 Claro] o *altered from* a *C*; in paschali] impaschali *Vp*; 36 corporeo] rp *interlined, erasure of one letter between first and second* o *J*, corpore *Vp*; 38 Christi] christo *C*; 40 publica] puplica *C*; 41 *E begins. Rubric:* ymnus de resurrectione iesu christi domini nostri. 43 *Ri begins*; 45 *om. JVp; CRi insert an incipit before the line:* Quesumus auctor omnium *C*, Quesumus auctor *Ri. E continues:* qui surrexisti a mortuis / una cum sancto spiritu / in sempiterna secula amen. *Ri omits* domine.

Ri gloss: 43 (. . .)itas (*glossing* debitas) 44 agamus toto.

Commentary Latin: 1 *Cf. Hy 6/2.* 11 *Bulst reads* nobile, *noting* nobili *as a variant. These forms interchange in Later Latin, but Bulst's form improves the rhyme to the eye.* 15 *Cf.* dicite discipulis eius, quia surrexit et ecce praecedit vos in Galilaeam. ibi eum videbitis. ecce praedixi vobis *Matt. XXVIII.7.* 16 *Bulst reads* splendens, *noting the variant* resplendens. 20 *The erasure to* sevi *in D aligns the lemma with the gloss and VmJVp. Bulst reads* saeui, *noting the variant* serui. 22 *Bulst reads* praedicit, *noting the variant* praedixit. 28 *Bulst reads* osculant. 30 *Bulst reads* Galilaea, *noting the variant* Galilaeam. 33 *Cf. Hy 57/19f. Bulst reads* paschale, *noting* paschali *as a variant. Cf. the note to line 11.* Old English: 3 *Read* blissigende. 8 racentegan *represents* racent-teage *with Late West Saxon smoothing (see above p. 71) and simplification of the double consonant, presumably dat. sg. One would have expected a preposition.* eormingas *may represent* earmingas *or* yrmingas, *see above, p. 74.* 12 *For* hwreawe *read* hreawe. 15 quia *introduces an object clause and should be glossed as* þæt. 17 *For* úrote *read* unrote *with a suspension mark instead of an accent.* 20 reþe *glosses the reading of VmJVp.* 33 beorhtre easterlicre *is the wrong gender; possibly it indicates that* gefean *was substituted for* blisse. 38 scinendum *implies that* fulgida *belongs to* carne, *not to* vulnera. *The glossator agrees here with the gloss in JVp.*

73

YMNUS IN ASCENSIONE DOMINI AD VESPERAM

<small>lofsang   uton singan   drihtne</small>
I   YMNUM CANAMUS DOMINO,

<small>lofsanges niwan nu   swegað</small>
  ymni novi nunc personent:

<small>crist   niwum mid   siðfæte</small>
  Christus novo cum tramite

<small>to   fæderes astáh   þrymsetle</small>
  ad patris ascendit thronum.   4

II   Transit triumpho nobili
     poli potenter culmina,
     qui morte mortem assumpserat
     derisus a mortalibus.   8

<small>apostolas þa   *rynelices</small>
III   Apostoli tunc mystico

<small>on dunan   standende crisman</small>
    in monte stantes crismatis

<small>mid   meder byrhtum mædene</small>
    cum matre clara virgine

<small>þæs hælendes gesawon   wuldor</small>
    Iesu   videbant gloriam   12

IV   ac prosecuti lumine
     laeto petentem sidera
     laetis per auras cordibus
     duxere regem sęculi.   16

<small>þa   *sprecende   ænglas</small>
V   Quos alloquentes angeli:

<small>to hwi tungla standende behealde ge</small>
  'Quid astra stantes cernitis?

<small>hælend þes is   hi cwædon</small>
  Salvator hic est', inquiunt,

<small>hælend mid sige   æþelum</small>
  'Iesus triumpho nobili,   20

VI   a vobis ad caelestia
     [26r] qui regna nunc assumptus est,

venturus inde seculi
in fine iudex omnium.'   24

7 swa toweardne hi sædon
VII sicque venturum asserunt,

swa swa   þisne hi gesawon
quemadmodum hunc viderant

healice heofona heahnyssa
summa polorum culmina

astigan þone hælend scinende
scandere Iesum   splendida.   28

VIII Quo nos, precamur, tempore,
Iesu, redemptor unice,
inter tuos in aethera
servos benignus aggrega.   32

sele us   þider mid singalre
IX Da nobis illuc sedula

estfulnysse efstan
devotione tendere,

on þam þe sittan mid fæder
quo te sedere cum patre

on heahnysse rices we gelyfaþ
in arce   regni credimus.   36

þu beo ure   gefea
X Tu esto nostrum gaudium,

þu ðe eart toweard med
qui es futurum pręmium.

sy ure   on þe wuldor
Sit nostra in te gloria

geond ealle æfre worulda
per cuncta semper secula.   40

      ó
wuldor þe drihten
XI Gloria tibi, domine,

þu ðe astihst ofer tungla
qui scandis super sidera,

mid fæder
cum patre

I Let us sing a hymn to the Lord. May new hymns ring out now; Christ ascends towards the throne of the father by an unheard-of way.

II In his noble triumph and in his might he surmounts highest heaven, he who by death conquered death, scorned by mortals.

III Then the apostles, standing together with the glorious virgin, the mother, on the meaningfully named mountain of Oil, saw the glory of Jesus

IV and they followed him with joyful eyes, as he climbed towards the stars, and conducted the king of the world with their joyful hearts through the air.

V The angels spoke to them: 'Why do you stand and gaze up to the stars? This is the saviour Jesus', they said

VI 'who has been received from among you into the kingdom of heaven in noble triumph. From there he is to come as the judge of all at the end of the world.'

VII And they maintain that he will come in the same manner as they saw this Jesus ascend the greatest heights of heaven in their splendour.

VIII At that time, we pray you, Jesus, who are the only redeemer, in your benevolence gather us in among your servants in heaven.

IX Grant us that we may strive with eager devotion to come where, as we believe, you sit with the Father in the fastness of the kingdom.

X You shall be our joy, you who are our future reward. May our glory be in you forever through all the ages.

XI Glory be to you, Lord, who ascend above the stars, together with the Father.

This hymn was sung at the Vespers of Ascension. It is ascribed to Bede (d. 735) and written in Ambrosian iambic dimeter. The melody transmitted in the Winchester Troper (W) is Stäblein no. 4. The text is included in the hymnals of BCDVm, the *Expositio hymnorum* of JVp and the fragment Ri, as far as that is extant. The version in JVpRi is abbreviated. W contains only stanza I. The text of Ri is glossed.

Bibliographical references: *ICL* no. 7438; *AH* 50, 103–5 (no. 82), cf. *AH* 2, 48–9 (no. 48), Walpole no. 117, Beda, 'Opera rhythmica', ed. Fraipont, pp. 419–23.

Apparatus to D   Latin text: 15 laetis] i *on erasure.*
Old English gloss: 13 *The gloss to line 17 was entered here up to* sprecen. *Then the scribe broke off in the middle of the word and the gloss was erased.*

BVmCJVpRiW   Heading: hymnus ad vesperam in ascensione domini *B, no rubric* VmpW, HYMNUS DE ASCENSIONE DOMINI AD VESPERUM *C,* YMNUM CANAMUS *J,* HYM... IN ASCENSIONE DOMINI, *the rubric very pale and partly illegible, it may continue, but if so, it becomes completely illegible Ri;* 1 YMNUM] mnum *W;* DOMINO] glorie *VmCJVpRiW; Ri ends;* 2 ymni] hymnum *JVp (but the gloss renders* hymni*)*; personent] nt *added by another hand C;* 3 novo] *second* o *added by another hand C;* 5–8 *om. CJVp;* 7 assumpserat] absumpserat *B;* 9 tunc] nunc *Vp;* mystico] mystice *Vm,* mistici *JVp;* 11 virgine] *last letter erased C;* 13–16 *om. CJVp;* 13 ac] hoc *Vm;* 19 *Ri begins;* 20 Iesus] iesu *VmC;* nobili] nobilis *C;* 21–4 *om. CJVpRi;* 25 sicque] s *illegible Ri;* asserunt] aserunt, *second* s *interlined above by another hand Ri;* 26 quemadmodum] quemammodum, o *altered from a minim C;* viderant] ra *illegible Ri;* 27 *Ri ends.* 28 Iesum] iesu *C;* splendida] splendide *Vm;* 29–32 *om. CJVp;* 33 sedula] sedulo *C;* 37–40 *om. BVmC, line 37 added in the margin by a late medieval hand in Vm;* 38 futurum] futurus *JVp;* 41 Gloria] loria *C;* 42–3 *om. C;* 42 scandis] ascendisti *B;* sedes *JVp;* super] supra *BVm;* 43 *om. B,* VmJVp *continue (JVp in prose):* & sancto spiritu / in sempiterna secula.
Ri gloss: 1 carmen resonemus laudis 19 christus dicunt 20 cum victoria inclita 21 taliterque rediturum testantur 22 sicut iesum 23 altissima cacumina.

Commentary   Latin: 1 AH *reads* gloriae. 7 AH *reads* absumpserat, *attesting* assumpserat *for two continental manuscripts also.* 10 *Cf.* a monte qui vocatur Oliveti *Acts I.12.* 13 Vm's hoc *is attested in continental manuscripts.* 16–29 *Cf.* quid statis aspicientes in caelum. hic Iesus qui adsumptus est a vobis in caelum sic veniet quemadmodum vidistis eum in caelum *Acts I. 11.* 25–8 *This stanza is not included in* AH. 20 *Cf.* Hy 71/11. 37–40 *The use of this quasi-doxology is not attested in continental manuscripts according to* AH. *Cf. the apparatus to Hy 74/33 and Hy 75/29.* 39 *Cf.* mihi autem absit gloriari nisi in cruce Domini nostri Iesu Christi *Gal. VI.14.* Old English: *The stanzas not glossed are those omitted in CJVp and (at least as far as lines 21–4 are concerned) Ri.* 9 rynelices *renders the reading of JVp.* 17 *The Latin prefix* al- (ad-) *is not rendered in any way by the gloss.*

74

YMNUS AD NOCTURNAM

I   gewiscod   mid gewilnungum ealra *þinga
   OPTATUS VOTIS   OMNIUM

   halig   onleohte dæg
   sacratus inluxit dies,

   on þam middaneardes hiht   crist   god
   quo   mundi   spes, Christus deus,

   astah   heofonan sticole
   conscendit caelos   arduos.   4

II   Ascendens in altum deus
   propriam ad sedem remeat.
   Gavisa sunt cęli regna
   reditu unigeniti.   8

   miceles   mid sige   gewinnes
III Magni triumpho pręlii

   middaneardes ofslegenum ealdre
   mundi   perempto principe

   fæderes andweardiende andwlitum
   patris pręsentans   vultibus

   sigefæstes lichoman wuldor
   victricis carnis   gloriam   12

IV est elevatus in nubibus
   & spem fecit credentibus
   aperiens paradysum,
   [26v] quem protoplasti clauserant.   16

   eala micel   eallum   gefea
V   O grande cunctis gaudium,

   þæt   bearn   ures   mædenes
   quod partus nostrę virginis

   æfter spátle   swingla æfter rode
   post sputa, flagra, post crucem

   fæderlicum setle ys geþeod
   paternę   sedi iungitur.   20

   uton dón   eornostlice þancas
VI Agamus ergo   gratias

ure hæle *wrecendum
nostrae salutis vindici,

urne þæt he *lichoma upawæh
nostrum quod corpus vexerit

         regiam
*healicne to heofones wuldre cynelicre healle
sublimem ad caeli gloriam.   24

 VII Sit nobis cum celestibus
commune manens gaudium,
illis quod se presentavit,
nobis quod se non abstulit.   28

Nu *gelængdum dædum
 VIII Nunc provocatis actibus

crist   anbidian us gedafenað
Christum expectare nos decet

7 *life *swilcum libban
vitamque talem vivere,

*on þam *he mage heofonan astigen
quę possit cęlos scandere.   32

     ó
wuldor þe drihten
Gloria tibi, domine

I The sacred day longed for by the wishes of everyone has dawned on which Christ, God, ascended the high heavens as the hope of the world.

II God ascends on high and returns to his own seat. The kingdom of heaven rejoices at the return of the only-begotten Son.

III In triumph at the victory in a great battle, because the prince of the world was slain, presenting to the gaze of the Father the glory of the victorious flesh,

IV he was lifted up among clouds and he gave hope to those who believed by opening paradise to them, which the first created human beings had caused to be shut.

V O what great joy it is to everyone that the son of our virgin after the spitting and the beating, after the crucifixion, shares the seat of the Father.

VI Let us therefore utter thanks to the champion of our salvation for carrying our body up to the lofty glory of heaven.

VII May there be abiding joy among us, shared with the dwellers in heaven, because he showed himself to them and because he did not remove himself from us.

VIII Now it is fitting that we should await Christ by summoning ourselves to action and live a kind of life that can ascend into heaven.

This hymn was sung at Matins (Nocturn) of Ascension except in B, the oldest Anglo-Saxon hymnal extant, where it is assigned to Lauds. It is anonymous and written in rhythmical Ambrosian hymn verse (4 × 8pp). No melody has been transmitted in the Anglo-Saxon manuscripts. The text is included in the hymnals of BCDVm and the *Expositio hymnorum* of JVp. The version in the Winchester Hymnal manuscripts (CJVp) is abbreviated.

Bibliographical references: *ICL* no. 11388; *AH* 51, 92–3 (no. 87), Walpole no. 112.

Apparatus to D   Latin text: 9 magni] i *altered from* o *by* D_1 *while glossing.*

   Old English gloss: *The stanzas not glossed correspond to those not contained in CJVp.* 24 healle] a *interlined by* D_1.

BVmCJVp   Heading: ad matutinam B, *no rubric* Vmp, HYMNUS AD NOCTURNUM C, OPTATUS VOTIS OMNIUM J; 1 OPTATUS] OBTATIS C; 3 quo mundi christus spes deus B (*the last three words possibly by another hand*), *also* Vm, *but a later hand has changed the sequence to:* quo christus mundi spes deus *by suprascript letters* (a, b); *this is the same order as in* C. (*JVp has prose order.*) 4 conscendit] ascendit Vp; 5–8 *om.* CJVp; 5 deus] dominus Vm; 8 reditu] redita Vm; unigeniti] uinigeniti, *first* i *expunged* B; 9 Magni] magno BVmC; 10 perempto] redemptor Vm; 11 pręsentans] presentas C; 12 victricis] victrices C; gloriam] glorię C; 13–16 *om.* CJVp; 16 protoplasti] protoplastis B, protoplasto Vm; clauserant] clauserat BVm; 17 cunctis] *om.* JVp; 18 partus] parte C; 23 vexerit] vexerat C; 24 Vm *reads* regiam sublimen (*sic*) ad cęli gloriam, ad *is expunged*, gloriam *struck through and it is indicated that* regiam *should take its place*; ad] *om.* C; gloriam] regiam JVp, gratiam C; 25–8 *om.* CJVp; 25–6 cum] *transposed to before* commune B; 29 At *added at the beginning of the line* B, A *and an illegible letter erased at the beginning of the line* Vm; provocatis] probatis B, provocati C; 31 vitamque talem] vitaque tali BJVp, *altered to* vitaque tali, *probably by another hand* Vm; 32 possit cęlos] cælos possit B; scandere] re *on erasure by* C_1 C; 33 *om.* JVp; Sit laus perpes sit gloria / christo regi qui culmina / cęli transcendit ardua / qua sancta exultant agmina. ameN. Vm; Tu esto nostrum gaudium / qui est futurus premium / sit nostra inter (*sic*) gloria / per cuncta semper sęcula // Gloria tibi domine / qui scandit C.

Commentary   Latin: 3 AH *reads* Christus mundi spes *like C, also quoting BVm's word order for continental manuscripts.* 5 *Cf.* ascendens in altum *Eph. IV.8.* AH *reads* dominus *like* Vm. *9–10 cf. Hy 117/24.* 9 AH *reads* magno *like BVmC, attesting* magni *for the Continent as well. The textual tradition of this line appears to diverge widely.* 13 *Cf.* elevatus est et nubes eum suscepit *Acts I.9.* 16 AH *attests* protoplasto clauserat *also for the Continent.* 24 *The Latin gloss* regiam *in D contains the reading of JVp and alternative reading of Vm.* AH *reads* regiam. 31 AH *reads* vitaque tali, *attesting* vitamque talem *for the Continent also.* 33 *For the extra stanza in C cf. Hy 73/37–40.* Old English: 1 *The prop word* þinga *is badly chosen, since* omnium *is clearly to be interpreted as masc. and referring to persons.* 22 wrecendum *'avenging' renders a meaning of* vindici *not applicable here.* 23 lichoma *is uninflected; it should be acc. sg.* 24 healicne *wrongly takes* sublimem *as referring to* corpus, *instead of* gloriam *(or* regiam*).* 29 gelængdum *'prolonged' either completely misunderstands* provocatis *or is corrupted from* gelangodum *'desired, sent for'.* 31 life swilcum *appears to render the reading of BJVp and Vm (after the correction).* 32 *The subject of the relative clause is* que, *agreeing with* vita; *on* þam *could only be explained by a reading* qua *or* quo, *which is not attested by the Anglo-Saxon manuscripts.*

75

YMNUS AD MATUTINAM

    ó
eala þu ece   cyng þu hehsta
I   AETERNE REX ALTISSIME,

alysend   eac swilce geleaffulra
redemptor &   fidelium,

on þam deaþ tolysed losode
quo mors soluta deperit,

is geseald sige   gyfe
datur triumphus gratiae,   4

astigende domsetl swiðran
II scandens tribunal dexterę

fæderes miht   ealra
patris. Potestas omnium

forgyfen ys þam hælende heofonlice
collata est Iesu   caelitus,

seo þe næs   mænnisclice
quę non erat humanitus,   8

þæt þreofeald *gescæft seara ɫ cræft
III ut trina   rerum machina

heofonlicra   eorþlicra
caelestium, terrestrium
7 hellicra   gesceapen
& infernorum condita
gebige   cneow nu   underþeod
flectat genu iam subdita.   12

bifiaþ   geseonde   ængles
IV   Tremunt videntes angeli
awend   *gewrixl deadlicra
versam vicem mortalium.
leahtrað flæsc   afeormaþ flæsc
Culpat caro, purgat caro,
rixaþ   god   godes flæsc
regnat deus, dei   caro.   16

      ó
þu eala crist   ure   gefea
V   Tu   Christe, nostrum gaudium
wunigende on rodore   gewelegod
manens Olimpho preditum,
middaneardes gewissast þu ðe getimbrunge
mundi   regis   qui   fabricam
       middaneardlice oferswiþende blissa
[27r] mundana   vincens   gaudia,   20

heonon þe biddende   we biddað
VI   hinc   te precantes quesumus:
gemiltsa gyltum eallum
Ignosce culpis omnibus
7 heortan upp   ahefe
& corda sursum subleva
to þe mid heofonlicre gyfe
ad te superna   gratia,   24

þæt þænne readiendum þu onginst
VII   ut, cum rubente   ceperis
scinan   genipe deman
clarere nube iudicis,
wite   þu adræfe neadwisa
poenas repellas debitas,
þu *agyfe cynehelmas forlorene
reddas coronas   perditas   28

þu beo   ure   gefea
*u esto nostrum gaudium

ó
wuldor þe   drihten
Gloria tibi, domine

I Most high and eternal God and redeemer of the faithful, by whom death is destroyed and perishes, triumph is allotted to grace,

II you ascend the judgement seat at the right hand of the Father. Power over all things is bestowed on Jesus from heaven, which was not his by his humanity

III so that the threefold structure of creation, of things in heaven, on earth and in hell, now bends its knee in subjection.

IV The angels tremble to see the fate of mortal men changed. The flesh sins, the flesh purifies, God rules as God made flesh.

V Christ, you who are supreme as our joy in heaven, who guide the structure of the world and surpass the joys of this world,

VI we ask you therefore and pray to you: forgive all sins and lift up our hearts towards you by supernal grace

VII so that you may withhold due punishment and return our lost crowns to us, when you come to shine forth from your reddening cloud of judgement.

This hymn was sung at Lauds of Ascension. The collectar of H, however, assigns it to Matins. It is anonymous and written in Ambrosian iambic dimeter. No melody has been transmitted in the Anglo-Saxon manuscripts. The text is included in the hymnals of CDVm and the *Expositio hymnorum* of JVp, but not the earliest of the hymnals, B.

Bibliographical references: *ICL* no. 422; *AH* 51, 94–5 (no. 88), cf. *AH* 2, 48 (no. 47) and 86 (no. 118), *AH* 27, 96–7 (no. 39), Walpole no. 113.

Apparatus to D   Latin text: 15 Culpat] u *altered from* a *by* D_1.

VmCJVp   Heading: IN ASCENSIONE DOMINI YMNUS *Vm*, HMNUS (*sic*) AD MATUTINUM *C*, AETERNE REX ALTISSIME *J*, *no rubric Vp*; 3 soluta] saluta *C*; 4 gratiae] gratia *C*; 7 Iesu] hiesu *Vm*; 8 humanitus] humanitas *C*; 9 ut] Et *JVp*; 12 flectat]

flecta C; 13 Tremunt] NT *on erasure* C; 14 versam vicem] versa vice *Vm*; 20 vincens] vinces C; 23 sursum] *first* s *altered from* r, *probably by another hand* C; 27 debitas] perditas C; 29 *om.* VmJVp; u] Tu C; 30 *om.* JVp. Gloria] loria C; C *adds:* qui scandit, *Vm continues:* qui scandis super sydera / cum patre & sancto spiritu / in sempiterna secula. amen.

Commentary   Latin: 5–6 *Cf.* arduum tribunal alti victor ascendit patris *Prudentius,* Cathemerinon, *IX.104.* 9–12 *Cf. Phil. II.10.* 14 AH *attests Vm's* versa vice *for the Continent as well.* 25–6 *Cf.* et ecce nubem candidam et supra nubem sedentem similem Filio hominis *Rev. XIV.14.* 29 *The rubricator in D om.* T. *This quasi-doxology is also found in one continental manuscript according to* AH. *Cf.* Hy 73/37–40. Old English: 9 gescæft *is uninflected, should be* gen. pl. 14 gewrixl '*exchange*' *glosses a common meaning of* vicem *not appropriate in this context.* 18 gewelegod *has weakened intrusive* i *in front of* g *(SB §165a).*

76

YMNUS IN PENTECOSTEN AD VESPERAM

ó
cum eala þu scyppend gast

I   VENI,   CREATOR SPIRITUS,

mod   þinra   geneosa
mentes tuorum visita,

gefyll   mid heofonlicre gyfe
imple superna   gratia,

þe   ðu gescope breost
quę tu creasti pectora,   4

þu ðe frofergast   eart gesæd
II   qui paraclytus diceris,

*selene   godes þæs hehstan
donum dei   altissimi,

wyll liflic   fyr   soþlufu
fons vivus, ignis, karitas

7 gastlic   smerung
& spiritalis unctio.   8

þu   seofonfealdre heowe lace ł gyfe
III   Tu septiformis   munere,

swiðran godes þu eart finger
dextrę dei tu   digitus,

þu *eart rihtlice *behát   fæderes
tu   rite   promisso patris

304

spræce   þu gewelgas þrotan
sermone ditas   guttura.   12

onæl   leoht   sefum
IV   Accende lumen sensibus,

onasænd lufe   heortum
infunde amorem cordibus

untrumnyssa ures   lichoman
infirma   nostri corporis

mid mihte getrymende ecere
virtute   firmans   perpeti.   16

feond   þu adræfe *feorran
V   Hostem repellas   longius

7 sibbe   þu selle þærrihtes
pacemque dones protinus.

latteowe   swa þe forestæppendum
Ductore sic te praevio

*þæt we forbugan ælc   derigendlices
vitemus   omne noxium.   20

þurh þe we cunnon sele fæder
VI   Per té sciamus, da, patrem,

we oncnawan 7   suna
[27v] noscamus   atque filium,

þe æghwæþeres gast
te utriusque spiritum

we gelyfan on ælcere tida
credamus omni   tempore.   24

gefyrn   halige   breost
VII   Dudum sacrata pectora

mid þinre þu gefeldest gyfe
tua   replesti   gratia;

forgyf   nu   senna
dimitte nunc peccamina

7 sele gedefa   tida
& da quieta tempora.   28

sy   lof   fæder mid suna
VIII   Sit laus patri cum genito

begra   7 frofergaste
amborum & paraclito,

305

bearn   swa swa þisne   he behét
proles, ut   hunc promiserat,

us   7 nu   he forgyfe
nobis modoque tribuat.   32

                sy hit swa
                Amen.

I Come, spirit, creator, seek out the minds of those who are yours, fill their breasts, which you created, with heavenly grace,

II you who are called the Comforter, gift of God the most sublime, a life-giving spring, a fire, charity and spiritual anointing.

III You are sevenfold in your gifts, a finger on the right hand of God, you duly enrich the throat with the faculty of speech promised by the Father.

IV Kindle light in our thoughts and pour love into our hearts, fortifying the weakness of our body with enduring strength.

V Drive the enemy far, far away and grant us peace continuously. Thus, with you leading us as a guide, may we avoid all harm.

VI Make us know the Father through you and also perceive the Son. May we believe in you as the spirit of both at all times.

VII Once you filled consecrated breasts with your grace; now remit our sins and give us peaceful times.

VIII Praise be to the Father and the Son and the Holy Spirit of both, and may the Son bestow it on us now, as he promised it.

This Pentecost hymn was assigned to Vespers in the Canterbury Hymnal, to Matins (Nocturn) in the Winchester Hymnal. In the collectar of H it is assigned to both. It has been ascribed to Hrabanus Maurus (d. 856) and is written in Ambrosian iambic dimeter. The melody transmitted in C is probably a version of Stäblein no. 17, almost the only melody in use for Hy 76 (see Stäblein, p. 507). The text is included in the hymnals of BCDVm, the *Expositio hymnorum* of JVp and the fragment Ri, as far as that is extant. The text in Ri is glossed.

Bibliographical references: *ICL* no. 17048; *AH* 50, 193–4 (no. 144), cf. *AH* 2, 93–4 (no. 132), Walpole no. 118.

Apparatus to D   Old English gloss: 10 eart] *interlined above by D₁*; 18 þærrihtes] æ *altered from* e.

BVmCJVpRi   *Ri is missing up to line 21.* Heading: hymnus ad vesperam *B*, IN SANCTO PENTECOSTEN. YMNUS *Vm*, HYMNUS AD NOCTURNUM *C*, VENI CREATOR *J, no rubric Vp*; 6 altissimi] altissimus *C*; 7 vivus] *originally* vivos, *erased to* u *C*; 10 dextrę] dexterę *B*, dexte, *unless part of the* virga *among the neumes above the lines constitutes an abbreviation mark C*; 16 perpeti] perpetim *CVmp (the JVp gloss agrees with J)*; 17 repellas] repellat *Vm*; 18 dones] donet *Vm*; 20 noxium] noxius *C*; 21 *Ri begins*; 22 *Ri ends*; 25–32 *om. JVp*; 25–8 *om. BVm*; 26–32 *om. C*; 29–32 Deo patri sit gratia / eiusque soli filio *B*, Deo patri sit gratia *Vm*.

Ri gloss: 18 continuo 19 duce l ducte *(te praevio)* antecessore 20 detestemur nocivum 21 *(te)* o sancte spiritus cognoscamus 22 int..ligamus *(el illegible).*

Commentary   Latin: 6 *Cf.* si scires donum Dei *John IV.10*. 7 *Cf.* fons aquae salientis in vitam aeternam *John IV.14, also* flumina de ventre eius fluent aquae vivae *John VII.38. For* ignis *see* Acts II.3; *for* caritas *see Rom. II.5*. 10 *The line is metrically irregular, but the syncope is necessary. The unsyncopated form in JVp's prose is naturally irrelevant. Cf. Isa. XI.2–3*. 13 *Cf. Hy 4/29*. 15–16 *Cf. Hy 39/23–4*. 26 *Cf. Hy 149/3. Old English:* 6 selene *is the wrong case, unless it is inflected weak.* 11 promisso *has been mistaken for a noun. The glossator was misled by the pattern of the two preceding lines, which have predicative nouns without auxiliary; he has again added* eart *as he did there, overlooking the fact that the clause continues in the next line.* 12 gewelgas *is probably not a Kentish form according to SB §356, n. 1, but a mistake possibly due to the influence of the lemma.* 17 *One would have expected* fyrr *(comparative) instead of* feorran. 20 *The main clause is glossed as if it were subordinate; there should be no conjunction.*

77

YMNUS AD NOCTURNAM

eadiga   us   gefean
I   BEATA NOBIS GAUDIA

geares ongeanbrohte *hwewollast
anni reduxit   orbita,

þa ða gast   frofer
cum spiritus paraclytus

scán   on *leorningcnihtum
effulsit in   discipulos.   4

*fér   ræscendum leohte
II   Ignis vibrante lumine

tungan hiw   brohte
linguę figuram detulit,

wordum þæt hi wæron genihtsume
verbis ut essent   proflui

7 on soþre lufe weallende
& caritate   fervidi.   8

mid gereordum hi spræcon ealra
III Linguis   loquuntur omnium.

mænigu forhtiaþ hæþenra
Turbę pavent gentilium.

niwum wine druncnian tellaþ
Musto   madere deputant,

þa ðe gast   gefylde
quos spiritus repleverat.   12

wæron gefremode þas gerynelican þing
IV Patrata sunt   hęc mistica

eastran geendodre tide
paschę peracto tempore

on halgum dagena getæle
sacro   dierum numero,

on *þære æ   wæs geworden forgyfenyss
quo   legis fit   remissio.   16

þe nu eala þu god arfæstesta
V Te nunc,   deus piissime,

mid andwlitan we biddaþ eadmodum
vultu   precamur cernuo:

onaslíd us   heofonlice
Inlapsa nobis caelitus,

forgyf selene gastes
largire dona spiritus.   20

gefyrn *halig breoste
Dudum sacrata pectora

sy lof fæder mid suna
Sit laus patri cum genito

I The year's circle has brought back to us the blessed rejoicing of the time, when the Comforter Spirit illuminated the disciples.

II It took the form there of a tongue within the quivering light of fire so that they might be eloquent in speech and fervent in their charity.

III They speak in the languages of all people. The crowds of heathens are afraid. They believe those to be intoxicated with young wine whom the Spirit has filled.

IV These sacred mysteries took place when Easter was past for the holy number of days, the number after which remission of the law is made.

V We now pray to you, most loving God, with lowered faces: Descend to us from heaven. Grant the gifts of the Spirit.

This Pentecost hymn was assigned by the Canterbury Hymnal to Matins (Nocturn), by the Winchester Hymnal and the collectar of H to Lauds. It is written in Ambrosian iambic dimeter. The melody transmitted in C is a version of Stäblein no. 64. Stäblein's comments (p. 518) suggest that this melody was limited in its use mainly to northern France and England. The text is included in the hymnals of BCDVm, the *Expositio hymnorum* of JVp and the fragment of Ri, as far as that is extant. The text in Ri is glossed.

Bibliographical references: *ICL* no. 1617; *AH* 51, 97–8 (no. 91), cf. *AH* 2, 50 (no. 51), *AH* 27, 99 (no. 42, one stanza only), Walpole no. 115.

BVmCJVpRi   *Ri is missing up to line 7.* Heading: hymnus ad nocturnam *B*, ITEM YMNUS *Vm*, HYMNUS AD MATUTINUM *C*, BEATA NOBIS *J*, *no rubric Vp*; 4 effulsit] effulserit, er *expunged J*; 7 *Ri begins*; 9 loquuntur] locuntur *BVmC*; 11 *Ri stops after this line.* 12 *The whole line in B is possibly by another hand.* quos] quo *BC*; 16 legis] lege *Vm*; 17–22 *om. JVp*; 18 cernuo] cernui *C*; 21 *C omits* pectora. *BVm continue*: tua replesti gratia / dimitte nunc peccamina / & da quieta tempora. 22 *om. C*; Sit] it *Vm*; laus] lus *B*; *BVm continue*: amborum & paraclyto / proles ut hunc promiserat / nobis modoque tribuat amen.

Ri gloss: 7 habundantes 8 ardentes 9 locutionibus (omnium) gentium 10 mirantur incredulorum 11 estuare affirmant.

Commentary   Latin: 4 *The line is metrically irregular.* 5–6 *Cf.* et apparuerunt illis dispertitae linguae tamquam ignis *Acts II.3.* 11 *Cf. Acts II.13.* 13–16 *Cf.* iobeleus, id est quinquagesimus annus remissionis *Num. XXXVI.4;* 16 *AH reads* lege *as in Vm.* 18 *C's* cernui *is attested by AH for the Continent.* 19–20 *Cf. Hy 15/5–8.* 21–2 *Cf. Hy 76/25–32.* Old English: 2 hwewollast *for* hweowol-last *could be Anglian (SB §89), but looks like a scribal error.* 4 *The glossator does not render the distinction between the abl. and acc. after* in *in any way.* 5 ignis *was mistaken for nom. sg.* 16 on þære *agrees with* tide *instead of* getæle. 21 *The incipit was glossed without keeping the rest of the stanza in mind. Either* halig *is uninflected or* sacrata *was mistaken for a nom. sg. fem.*

78

YMNUS AD MATUTINAM

I   ANNI PERACTIS MENsibus
tanta recurrunt gaudia
votisque dudum credulis
[28r] optatus advenit dies,   4

II   in quo spiritus domini
terras replevit gaudiis,
caelestia adventus sui
mundo decurrunt lumina.   8

III   Sic namque filius dei
apostolis spoponderat,
celsos petisset cum polos,
missurum sanctum spiritum.   12

IV   Adest probatum testibus
apostolorum vocibus,
cum sint diversis oribus
variis locuti gentibus.   16

V   Tanto redempti munere
patris & nati spiritus,
iuges agamus gratias
deo perenni in secula.   20

amen

I Now the months of the year have passed, the time of so much rejoicing comes again and the day long wished for in faithful prayers arrives

II on which the Spirit of the Lord filled the earth with joy and the celestial lights of his coming spread through the world.

III For when the son of God ascended into the heavens on high, he had promised thus to the apostles that he would send the Holy Ghost.

IV This is proved by the witness of the voices of the apostles, when they with their several mouths talked to different nations.

v Since we were redeemed by such a great gift, of the Spirit of the Father and the Son, let us thank eternal God constantly throughout the ages.

This hymn was in use only in the Canterbury Hymnal. It was sung at Lauds at Pentecost. It is anonymous and written in Ambrosian hymn verse (highly irregular iambic dimeter or rhythmical). No melody has been transmitted in the Anglo-Saxon manuscripts. The text is included in the hymnals of BVm.

Bibliographical references: *ICL* no. 816; cf. *AH* 14a, 90 (no. 82), *AH* 27, 99 (no. 43). AH's two texts are each based on only one manuscript.

Apparatus to D   Latin text: 2 gaudia] i *inserted from above with caret mark*; 10 spopond-erat] *second* o *altered from a minim.*

BVm   Heading: ad matutinam *B*, ITEM YMNUS *Vm*; 1 MENsibus] b *illegible Vm*; 5 quo] qua *Vm*; in] *om. Vm*; secula] seculo *Vm*.

Commentary   3–4 *Cf. Hy 74/1.* 7 *According to* AH *the continental manuscripts read* caelestis, *which would avoid the synaloephe.* 9–12 *Cf. Acts I.1–12. This stanza is omitted in* AH *27, no. 43.*

79

YMNUS AD TERTIAM

eallunga crist   tungla   astah
I   IAM   CHRISTUS ASTRA ASCENDERAT

ongeangecyrred þanon þe he com
regressus,   unde   venerat,

behatenre fæderes lace
promisso patris munere

haligne   to sellene gast
sanctum daturus spiritum.   4

simbel   onsah   dæg
II   Sollempnis urgebat dies,

on þam geryne   seofonfealdre
quo   mystico septemplici

embhwerfte beterndum seofon siðan
*orbem   voluto   septies

getacnaþ eadige tida
signat beata tempora,   8

                þænne tid   eallum   seo þridda
III   cum hora cunctis tertia

        færlice   middaneard swegð
        repente mundus   intonat

        gebiddendum apostolum
        orantibus   apostolis

        god   cuman   kyþende
        deum venisse nuntians.   12

        gefern   *halig   *breoste
        Dudum sacrata pectora

        sy   lof   fæder mid   suna
        Sit laus patri cum genito

I Christ had already risen up to the stars and returned to where he
  came from, he who was to give us the Holy Ghost as a gift that he
  promised from the Father.

II The solemn day was imminent on which he ordained the time of
   blessing, the sacred cycle of seven days having elapsed seven times,

III when the world suddenly resounded around them all at the third
    hour and announced to the apostles, as they prayed, that God had
    come.

The Pentecost hymn Hy 79–81 was divided into three parts in the
Canterbury Hymnal and Hy 79 assigned to Tierce (for B the division of
the hymn has to be inferred). In the Winchester Hymnal and the collectar
of H the whole hymn was assigned to Vespers. Alternatively the collectar
of H assigns it to Matins (Nocturn). It is anonymous and written in
Ambrosian iambic dimeter (slightly irregular). The melody transmitted in
C and the Winchester Troper (W) may be related to Stäblein no. 71. The
text is included in the hymnals of BCDVm and the *Expositio hymnorum* of
JVp. The first stanza is included in W.

Bibliographical references: *ICL* no. 7471; *AH* 51, 98–100 (no. 92), cf. *AH*
2, 49–50 (no. 50), Walpole no. 116.

Apparatus to D   Latin text: 7 orbem] em *erased (legible under ultraviolet light), altered to* is *by another hand*; voluto] *the case ending erased and illegible, altered to* us *by the same corrector*; 12 nuntians] ns *erased and altered to* t *by another hand.*
Old English gloss: 10 middaneard] *second* a *altered from* r.

BVmCJVpW   Heading: hymnus ad iii^a in pentecosten *B*, UNDE SUPRA YMNUS *Vm*, HYMNUS *followed by one-and-a-half erased lines C*, IAM CHRISTUS ASTRA *J, no rubric VpW*; 1 IAM] am *W*; 3 promisso] promissa *W*; 4 *W ends.* 6 septemplici] septimplici *Vm*; 7 orbem] orbis *B*, orbe *VmCJVp*; voluto] volutus *BC*; 12 nuntians] nuntiat *BC*; 13–14 *om. BCJVp, Vm reads:* Gloria tibi domine / qui scandis.

Commentary   Latin: 1–2 *Cf.* Filium hominem ascendentem ubi erat prius *John VI.63.* 3 *Cf.* et ego mitto promissum Patris mei in vos *Luke XXIV.49.* 6–8 *Cf. Hy 77/13–16.* 7 *D's* orbem *seems unparalleled. It is probably a mistake for* orbe, *which would agree with the gloss and VmCJVp. If so, the following word surely read* voluto *originally; if not, it may have read* volutum. *The alteration in D is to the reading of B, cf. also C. AH reads* orbis volutus, *attesting* orbe voluto *also for continental manuscripts.* 9–10 *Cf. Acts II.2 and 15.* 12 *With the alteration in D cf. BC. BC's* nuntiat *is attested for the Continent by AH.* Old English: 13 halig *repeats the carelessness of the glossator in Hy 77/21.*

80

YMNUS AD SEXTAM

of   fæderes   eornostlice leohte
I   DE PATRIS ERGO   LUMINE

wlitig   fyr   halig   is
[28v] decorus ignis almus est,

*on þam getriwa cristes   breost
qui   fida   Christi pectora

of hætan wordes gefelde
*colore   verbi *coplevit.   4

gefellede   blissodon   innoþas
II   Impleta gaudent viscera

*geondblawenum halgum leohte
afflata   sancto lumine.

stefna   mistlice   swegdan
Voces diverse intonant,

heo spræcon godes mærða
fantur   dei   magnalia.   8

coitur
of ælcere þeode   *wæron gegæderode wæs samodafaren

III   Ex omni gente   cogniti,

*grecisces lydenwaru *hæþen
Grecis, Latinis,   barbaris,

7 eallum   wundriendum
cunctisque ammirantibus

mid gereordum hi spræcon ealra
linguis   *loquntur omnium.   12

gefyrn *halig   breoste
Dudum sacrata pectora

sy lof fæder mid suna
Sit laus patri cum genito

I Thus from the light of the Father it is that the beautiful holy fire proceeds which filled the breasts faithful to Christ with the fervour of the word.

II Hearts that are filled and inspired with the holy light rejoice. Voices are lifted up in different languages and talk about the wonderful works of God.

III Perceived by people from all nations, Greeks, Romans and barbarians, they speak in the languages of all to the astonishment of everyone.

This part of the Pentecost hymn (Hy 79–81) is assigned by the Canterbury Hymnal to Sext. For further details see under Hy 79.

Apparatus to D   Latin text: 4 colore] *first* o *altered to* a, *possibly by another hand*; coplevit] *the* m-*abbreviation mark above perhaps by another hand.*

Old English gloss: 9 wæs samodafaren] *written by* D₁ *while glossing in the left margin together with the Latin gloss which is its lemma; a set of corresponding marks links both to* cogniti. 12 gereordum] *second* e *interlined with a caret mark by* D₁.

BVmCJVp   *No rubric BVmCJVp; BCJ continue from Hy 79 without a break. Vmp treat it as a separate hymn.* 1 PATRIS] s *added by the rubricator* B; 3 qui] quo *CJVp*; 4 colore] calore *BVmCJVp*; coplevit] complevit *B*, complevit, ant *interlined above, possibly by another hand* Vm, compleant *C*, compleat *JVp*; 6 afflata] afflato *VmC*; lumine] spiritu *VmC*, flamine *JVp*; 7 diverse] diversas *VmC*; intonant] intonat *Vm*, consonant *CJVp*; 8 fantur] fantes *B*; 9 cogniti] cogitur *C*, coitur *JVp*; 10 Grecis, Latinis, barbaris] grecus latinus barbarus *CJVp*; 12 loquntur] locuntur *BVmC*, loquuntur *JVp*; omnium] omnibus *Vm*; 13–14 *om. BCJVp, Vm has:* Gloria tibi domine / qui scandis.

Commentary   Latin: 3 AH *attests CJVp's* quo *for the Continent.* 4 D's colore *is due to scribal anticipation of* o. AH *reads* compleat, *attesting* complevit *for continental manuscripts as well.* 6 VmC's spiritu *is attested by* AH *for the Continent.* 7 AH *reads* diverse consonant, *attesting* intonant *and VmC's* diversas *for the Continent also.* 8 *Cf. Acts II.11.* 9 *The Latin gloss in D represents the reading of JVp.* AH *reads* cogitur, *attesting* cogniti *for the Continent as well.* 10 AH *has the nom. in all three cases, but notes the abl. pl. for continental manuscripts also.* 12 *This line is identical with Hy 77/9.* D's loquntur *has haplography of* u. Old English: 3 on þam *renders the reading of CJVp.* 6 geondblawenum *renders the reading of CVm.* 9 wæron gegæderode *appears to render a reading such as C's.* 10 grecisces, *gen. sg. (masc. or ntr.) or possibly nom. pl. is puzzling, as it seems to imply an unattested reading* Greci. *Perhaps a noun, like* folces *is missing, but 'of the Greek people' would be an unusual way of rendering* Grecis. lydenwaru *is either uninflected or renders the nom. case of CJVp. In the latter case the Old English collective noun is rendering the Latin singular* Latinus. hæþen *apparently renders the reading of CJVp. However, considering the confusion in this line, it may have simply been left uninflected.* 13 halig *shows the same carelessness as in Hy 77/21 and Hy 80/13.*

81

YMNUS AD NONAM

I   iudeisc   þa   ungeleaffull
    IUDEA TUNC INCREDULA

    gewitleasum mænigu gaste
    vesano   turba   spiritu

    balcettan niwes wines oferfelle
    ructare musti   crapulam

    fostercild cristes   þread
    alumnos Christi *concrepet,   4

    ac   on tacnum 7 on mihtum
II sed signis   & virtutibus

    ongeancom 7 lærde
    occurrit   & docet Petrus;

    *leasunga *spræcon   geleafleasan
    falsos   probavit perfidos

            gewittnysse
    Iohelis testimonio.   8

            ó
    þes eala þu crist   nu   frofergast
III Hic,   Christe, nunc paraclytus

315

þurh þe arfæsta us *geneoseþ
per te pius nos visitet

eorþan 7 neowiende anseon
terræ novansque faciem

gyltum *alysedum
culpis solutos recreet.   12

gefyrn *halig breoste
Dudum sacrata pectora

sy lof fæder mid suna
Sit laus patri cum genito

I Then the unbelieving Jewish crowd in the insanity of its mind
exclaims against the disciples of Christ saying that they are sputter-
ing under the effect of too much new wine.

II But Peter confronts them and instructs them by signs and miraculous powers. He proves the infidels wrong by the testimony of Joel.

III May that Comforter Spirit visit us now benignly by your agency,
Christ, and fortify those who are released from sin, thus renewing
the face of the earth.

This part of the Pentecost hymn Hy 79–81 was assigned by the Canterbury Hymnal to None. For further details see under Hy 79.

Apparatus to D   Latin text: 4 concrepet] et *expunged and* at *interlined above by another
hand*.
   Old English gloss: 12 *gloss to* recreet *om*.

BVmCJVp   *No rubric* BVmCJVp; *BCJ continue from Hy 80 without a break*. 2 vesano]
vesana *Vm*; 3 crapulam] crapula *Vm*; 4 concrepet] concrepat *VmCJVp*; 7 falsos] falsa *BJVp*,
falso *Vm*; probavit] profari *BC*, prophari *VmJVp*; 8 iohele teste comprobans *CJVp*; 9–12 *om*.
CJVp; 9 Hic] Sic *Vm*; 11 terræ novansque] novansque terrę *Vm*; 13 *om*. *BVm*; *C continues
(and so do JVp, but in prose):* tua replesti gratia / dimitte nunc peccamina / et da quieta
tempora. 14 Gloria tibi domine *erased B*, Gloria tibi domine / qui scandis *Vm*. *C continues
(and so do JVp, but in prose):* amborum & paraclito / proles ut hunc promiserat / nobis
modoque tribuat.

Commentary   Latin: 3 *Vm's* crapula *is attested by* AH *for the Continent*. 4 *The correction in
D brings the lemma into line with the gloss and VmCJVp*. 7 AH *reads* falso, *attesting* falsa *and*
falsos *for the Continent also. It reads* profari, *but notes* probavit *in continental manuscripts*. 8 *This
refers to Acts* II.17–21, *quoting Joel*, II.28–32. AH *reads* Ioele teste comprobans, *but* Ioelis
testimonio *occurs in continental manuscripts as well*. Old English: 4 þreað *renders the reading of*

VmCJVp. 7 leasunga *renders the reading of BJVp.* spræcon *clearly presupposes the reading of BVmCJVp. It may stand for the infinitive* sprecan *(with two inverted spellings, see above, pp. 75 and 76). However, the past tense may have been substituted for the infinitive, because in Old English the a. c. i. (probably) was not quite idiomatic after* sprecan, *cf. Mitchell,* Old English Syntax, *§3743. If so, the substitution was probably not a conscious decision of the glossator's.* 10 geneoseþ *should be optative.* 12 alysedum *takes over the case ending of the preceding word. Perhaps the glossator expected an abl. abs. The omission of the gloss to* recreet *is probably accidental, but the mistake in glossing* solutos *points to some confusion on the part of the glossator. The gloss to this stanza is not by the original glossator, for the stanza is not included in the Winchester Hymnal.* 13 *The same carelessness is repeated as in Hy 77/21, 79/13 and 80/13.*

82

YMNUS DE SANCTO DUNSTANO EPISCOPO

     hal sy ðu   biscopa
I AVE   DUNSTANE, PRESULUM

     tungel 7 wlite   scinende
     sidus decusque splendidum,

     leoht þæt soþe þeode   ængliscre
     lux vera   gentis Anglice

     7 to gode   latteow forestæppende
     & ad deum dux   praevie.   4

     þu eart hopa þinra   se mæsta
II Tu   spes tuorum maxima,

     weorodnyss eac swilce incunde
     dulcedo necnon intima

     orþiende wyrtbræþa swetnyssa
     spirans odorum balsama

     liflicra   hunigswete
     vitalium melliflua.   8

           ó
     þe   fæder we gelefað
III [29r] Tibi, pater, nos credimus,

     þam   þe naht wensumlicor
     quibus te nil iocundius,

     to þe handa we astreccaþ
     ad te manus expandimus,

     þe   bena we ageotaþ
     tibi preces effundimus.   12

scép þine heorde þu arfæsta
IV Oves tuas, pastor pie,

passim premunt angustię.

swurde þeode hæþenre
Mucrone gentis barbare

necamur, en, cristicole. 16

ó
offra sacerd onsægednysse
V Offer, sacerdos, hostias

criste bena þa gecwemestan
Christo precum gratissimas,

mid þam *glæd leahtra
quibus placatus criminum

he tolyse racentega isene
solvat catenas ferreas, 20

þurh þa ængliscra gemærum
VI per quas Anglorum terminis

7 gelaþunge bearnum
ecclesiæque filiis

7 mægþe geleaflease
& nationes perfide

7 cwyld abugan derigendlice
pestesque cedant noxiæ. 24

ó
þurh þe fæder hiht *ancænned
VII Per te, pater, spes unica,

þurh þe bearn sib ancenned
per te, proles, pax unica

7 gast leoht *ancænned
&, spiritus, lux unica

ætsy us on worulda
adsit nobis in secula. 28
amen

I Hail Dunstan, you star and glorious ornament among bishops, true light of the English nation and leader preceding it on its way to God,

II you are the greatest hope of your people and also an innermost sweetness breathing the honeyed balm of life-giving perfumes.

III We have faith in you, Father, we to whom nothing is more pleasing than you are. We extend our hands to you, we pour out prayers to you.

IV Troubles oppress your sheep on all sides, kind shepherd. See how we, the believers in Christ, are decimated by the swords of the pagan nation.

V O priest, offer up to Christ the sacrifice of most satisfactory prayers, so that by them he may be appeased and release us from the iron chains of our transgressions

VI and so that by them both infidel nations and harmful diseases may recede from the territory of the English and the sons of the church.

VII By your intercession may the Father, our only hope, by your intercession may the Son, our only peace, and the Spirit, our only light, be with us throughout the ages.

This is a hymn for the feast of St Dunstan (19 May). It is anonymous and written in Ambrosian iambic dimeter (with irregularities). Rhyme is monosyllabic; the stanzas rhyme aabb or aaaa except for stanza V. The only other Anglo-Saxon manuscript to contain the hymn is V, where it is, however, a later addition. The neumes in V, though late, are of the Anglo-Saxon type and represent an unidentified melody.

Bibliographical references: *ICL* no. 1540; *AH* 11, 111–12 (no. 188), Gneuss, *HHEM*, pp. 241–5 (critical edition).

Apparatus to D   Old English gloss: 19 l *erased in front of* glæd.

Commentary   Latin: *For the earliest* vitae *of St Dunstan see* Memorials of St Dunstan, *ed. Stubbs. 13–16 The stanza obviously refers to raids of the Danes at the time of its composition (presumably in the reign of Æthelred) and was dropped in all manuscripts from V onwards; cf. Gneuss's edition. 20 For* catenas ferreas *cf. Jer. XXVIII.13–14.* Old English: *13–16 The omission of the gloss to lines 14 and 16 is obviously connected in some way with the omission of the stanza in V and later manuscripts. Perhaps there was an unattested version, in which the stanza was rephrased, before it was dropped completely. 19* glæd *is the standard translation of* placatus *in this gloss. It is especially infelicitous here, as the emphasis is on the process of placating rather than on the result. 20 For* racentega *see the note to Hy 72/8. 25–7* unicus *'sole, only' is the equivalent of* unigenitus *only when referring to the Son. It is a surprising carelessness of the glossator to call the Father and the Holy Spirit 'Only-Begotten'.*

83

YMNUS DE SANCTO AUGUSTINO

I   CAELESTIS AULE NOBILES
mundique recti principis
concorditer ferant deo
laudum trophea precluo,   4

II   qui maxima clementia
genus humanum tartara
terendo vitę reddidit
&, ut hanc sciret, indidit.   8

III   Apostolos nam colligit,
Gregorius de quis venit,
qui filium dat Anglicis
Augustinum fanaticis,   12

IV   non de carnali semine,
sed spiritali vimine,
emisit, ut Cristi decus
conferret acris plebibus.   16

V   Quod ut peręgit omnibus
[29v] deo iuvante nisibus,
vocatur ex tholis poli,
ut colletetur angelis.   20

VI   Hinc té precamur, artifex
opime rerum, supplices,
ut huius ore militis
tuis tuum des servulis.   24

VII   Sit glorię nitor patri,
sit filio lux & iugis,
sit procedenti flamini
ab his venustas luminis.   28

1 Let the nobles of the celestial court and of the true prince of the world offer unanimously praises in honour of his victory to the most glorious God,

II who in his surpassing mercy brought the human race back to life and taught it to know that life, when he crushed Hell.

III For he gathers apostles to himself. From these Gregory is descended, who gives his son Augustine to the idolatrous English;

IV he sent out his son, not by the seed of the flesh, but by spiritual growth, to bring the glory of Christ to fierce nations.

V As soon as he has carried that out with all effort and with the help of God, he is summoned from the vaults of heaven to share there the joy of the angels.

VI Therefore we suppliants pray to you, excellent maker of created things, to give your humble servants what is yours according to the speech of this your soldier.

VII Glory and splendour be to the Father and perpetual light be to the Son. Glowing beauty be to the Spirit that proceeds from them.

This hymn is intended for the Vespers of the feast of St Augustine of Canterbury (26 May). It has been ascribed to Wulfstan, precentor of Old Minster, Winchester, and is written in rhythmical Ambrosian hymn verse (4 × 8pp). Rhyme or assonance are monosyllabic; the stanzas rhyme aabb. D is the only manuscript known to contain the hymn; there are no neumes.

Bibliographical references: *ICL* no. 1787; *AH* 51, 164–5 (no. 141), Wulfstan of Winchester, *Life of St Æthelwold*, ed. Lapidge and Winterbottom, p. xxxvii.

Apparatus to D   Latin text: 21 Hinc] c *interlined above with a caret mark, perhaps by* D₁.

Commentary   *On St Augustine of Canterbury see Beda*, Historia ecclesiastica (Bede's Ecclesiastical History of the English People, *ed. Colgrave and Mynors*), I. 23–33 and II. 1–3.

84

YMNUS AD NOCTURNAM

SUMMA DEI BONITAS,   cęli que septa gubernas
quęque solum firmas,   summa dei bonitas,
laudibus eximiis,   da, Augustinum resonemus,
quem pie sanxisti   laudibus eximiis.
Iure salutifero,   Romae qui nascitur arci,   5
nascimur & quo nos,   iure salutifero
clarus in orbe viget.   Quod contulit ille, dicasti,
quodque polis renitet.   Clarus in orbe viget.
Huius ob alloquium   nobis miserere precamur.
Commoda quaeque para   huius ob alloquium.   10
Impetret ista dies,   mundemur ut actibus imis.
Deinde salutis opes   impetret ista dies.
Gloria magna patri,   semper tibi gloria, nate,
[30r] cum sancto spiritu;   gloria magna patri.

Excellent goodness of God, you who rule the confines of the sky and support the earth, excellent goodness of God, let us sing with the greatest of praise of Augustine, whom you established lovingly in the greatest of praise. He who by beneficial edict was born in the city of Rome and by whose agency we are also born, by beneficial edict he flourishes, renowned in the world. What he brought you have sanctioned and that he shines in heaven. He flourishes, renowned in the world. Because of his intercession have pity on us, we pray. Confer everything good on us because of his intercession. May this day see us purified of our meanest actions and may this day then see us enriched with the treasure of salvation. Great glory be to the Father, glory be to you forever, o Son, as well as to the Holy Spirit; let there be great glory to the Father.

This hymn for the feast of St Augustine of Canterbury (26 May) was intended for Matins (Nocturn) in D. It has been ascribed to Wulfstan, precentor of Old Minster, Winchester (tenth century) and is written in epanaleptic distichs. Unlike the hymns by Bede and Wulfstan in this form (see above, p. 26), the hymn is not abecedarian. D is the only manuscript known to contain the hymn; there are no neumes.

Bibliographical references: *ICL* no. 15796; *AH* 51, 165–6 (no. 142),
Wulfstan of Winchester, *Life of St. Æthelwold,* ed. Lapidge and Winterbottom, p. xxxvii.

Commentary   1–2 *Cf. Ps. CXXXV.5–6, Isa. XLII.5.*

85

YMNUS AD MATUTINAM

I	AVETO, PLACIDIS	PRESUL amabilis,	
	aveto, cęlebri	laude notabilis,	
	aveto, salubri	luce capabilis	
	Augustine placabilis.		4

II	Nobis ista dies	sumptibus innuit,	
	quid tu quis opibus	florueris, situs	
	cum terris redolens	infima presseris,	
	Augustine		8

III	Tu factis renitens	voceque preminens,	
	tu donis rutilans	atque deo placens,	
	tu mundum retinens	astrave possidens,	
	Augustine		12

IV	Non horror nivei	tramitis obstitit,	
	non gressu tepuit	æquoreum iecur	
	te, quem forma boni	ediderat sibi,	
	Augustine		16

V	Iam, pastor superis	indite gazulis,	
	flexis poplitibus	cum prece poscimus,	
	assis quo clipeus	noster in omnibus,	
	Augustine		20

VI	Exhinc subveniat	digna precatio	
	in sublime tuis	prepete servulis	
	quos nutrire studes	fastibus aetheris,	
	Augustine placabilis.		24

VII Assis his, genitor   atque potens deus,
     aptet Christus & haec,   patre deo deus,
     cum flatu patrio,   quo regimur deo,
     Augustine placabilis.   28

           amen

I Hail, bishop to be loved by the peaceable, hail, you who are noteworthy by your great fame, hail, you who are empowered with beneficial light, gentle Augustine.

II This day with its splendour hints to us in what way you flourished and with what resources, when in your fragrance you dwelt down below on earth.

III You shine in the splendour of your deeds and excel in your speech, you are brilliant in your gifts and pleasing to God, you retain the world in your possession and have obtained the stars.

IV The terrors of the snow-covered way were no obstacle, your passion did not grow faint in your progress on the sea in you, whom the pattern of all good had fashioned for itself.

V Now, shepherd possessed of heavenly treasure, in prayer on bent knees we request you to be with us as our shield in all things.

VI May your worthy entreaty from now on help your humble servants quickly upwards, whom you strive to rear for the feasts of heaven.

VII Assist them, Father and mighty God. May Christ, who is God with a Father who is God, also make that possible together with the Spirit of his Father, by whom we are governed as by God.

This hymn for the feast of St Augustine of Canterbury (26 May) is assigned to Lauds in D. It has been ascribed to Wulfstan, precentor of Old Minster, Winchester (tenth century). Its metre is the second asclepiadeic stanza (cf. Hy 119) with the fourth verse used as a refrain. D is the only manuscript known to contain this hymn; there are no neumes.

Bibliographical references: *ICL* no. 1558; *AH* 51, 165 (no. 143), Wulfstan of Winchester, *Life of St Æthelwold,* ed. Lapidge and Winterbottom, pp. xxxvii–xxxviii.

Apparatus to D   19 *punctuation om., although end of verse and line do not coincide.*

Commentary   5 *Cf. Hy 35/1.*

86_1

YMNUS IN NATIVITATE SANCTI IOHANNIS BABTISTÆ

		þæt hi magon	tolætenum	swegan	æddrum
I	[30v]	UT QUEANT LAXIS		RESONARE FIBRIS	

wundra dæda þenas þinra
mira gestorum famuli tuorum,

tolys besmitenys weleres scylde
solve polluti labii reatum,

ó
eala þu halga
   sancte   IOHANNES. 4

s. gabrihel
bydel   of hean   cumende rodore
II Nuntius celso   veniens Olympho

þe fæder mæran   wesan to acennenne
te patri magno   fore nasciturum,

*nama   7 lifes   endeberdnysse *adreogenlices
   nomen & vitę   seriem   gerende

be endebyrdnysse geypte sanges
ordine   promit. 8

he behates   twiniende heofonlices
III Ille promissi   dubius superni

forspilde hrædlice   dreamas spræce
perdidit prompte   modulos loquelę,

ac þu geedstaþelodest   acænned ofslægenre
sed reformasti   genitus perempte

dreamas stefne
organa vocis. 12

wambe *on diglum   geléd *bedde
IV Ventris obstruso   positus cubili

325

þu undergæte cyngc   on bredbure wunigende
senseras   regem   thalamo manentem,

heonon fæder ɫ moder bearnes   geeárnungum æghwæþer
hinc parens   nati   meritis   uterque

digolnyssa geypte
abdita   pandit.   16

I In order that your servants may be able to voice the miracles you did and loosen the cords, remove the sin from the lip that it pollutes, Saint John.

II The messenger coming from high heaven imparts to your great father that you are to be born and announces your name and the ordering of life you are to lead in the proper sequence.

III Because he doubted the heavenly promise, he was at once deprived of the cadences of speech, but when you were born, you restored the instrument of that muted voice.

IV While you rested in the enclosed chamber of the womb, you perceived the king dwelling in his bower. Thus both parents revealed what was concealed by the merits of their son.

This hymn for the feast of St John the Baptist (24 June) was divided up and the first *divisio* sung at Vespers. The hymn has been ascribed to Paulus Diaconus (eighth century). It is written in Sapphic stanzas. No melody has been transmitted in the Anglo-Saxon manuscripts. The text is included in the hymnals of BCDVm and the *Expositio hymnorum* of JVp.

Bibliographical references: *ICL* no. 16894; *AH* 50, 120–3 (no. 96), cf. *AH* 2, 50–1 (no. 52).

Apparatus to D   Latin text: 6 magno] *another hand has interlined v̄ above.*

Old English gloss: 8 geypte sanges] *due to lack of space* geypte *was added in the left margin. A set of corresponding signs indicates that it belongs above* promit. sanges *was squeezed into the margin between* geypte *and the rest of the text in smaller script, perhaps at a later time, and is separated from it by a dot.*

BVmCJVp Heading: ymnus ad vesperam in natale sancti iohannis baptistę *B,* DE SANCTO IOHANNE BAPTISTA YMNUS *Vm,* HYMNUS DE SANCTO ... AD VESPERUM *(name of saint erased) C,* UT QUEANT LAXIS *J, no rubric Vp;* 1 RESONARE] ARE *on erasure C;* FIBRIS] *erasure of 1–2 letters between* fi *and* bris *C;* 2 mira] mirra *C;*

gestorum] iestorum *C*; 3 polluti] pulluti *B*, i *altered from* u *and followed by two erased letters C*; reatum] reatu *C*; 6 magno] magnum *Vm*; 7 gerende] gerendo *C*; 9 promissi] promisi *followed by an erased letter C*; 16 *C and J continue:* Gloria patri genitoque proli / et tibi compar utriusque semper / spiritus alme deus unus omni / tempore secli. *C,* Resonemus omnes gloriam deo patri & tibi o Christe superne genite cum quibus regnat spiritus sanctus & creator simul. *J.*

Commentary   Latin: *For the whole* divisio *cf. Luke I, especially 13–17, 41–5 and 67–9. Heading:* BABTISTÆ *is a spelling common in the Middle Ages, as Professor Stotz has kindly informed me. 6 AH reads* magnum *like Vm and the corrector in D. 16 For the doxology of which J has the prose version see the doxology to Hy 86 by a later hand in Vm (see below, textual note on Hy 86₃/17–24, p. 331) and Hy 88/33–6. The doxologies in C and J are attested by AH for the Continent, but not the one in D (Hy 86₃/17–24). Old English: 1 For the doubling of dentals in* æddrum *see SB §229. 6 As there is no definite article,* mæran *may render* magnum, *the reading of the corrector and Vm, not* magno. *7* nama *is uninflected and should be acc.* adreogenlices *is an unsuccessful attempt to render the Latin gerundive; 'bearable, performable' does not fit. 8* sanges, *clearly an explanatory gloss, may refer either to* seriem, *the word beside it, or to* ordine, *if it is to be inserted above* promit *together with* geypte. *13* diglum *renders* abstruso *rather than* obstruso. bedde *'bed' translates a common, but inappropriate meaning of* cubile. *Cf. the gloss in JVp,* cleofan. *14 For the spelling* cyncg *see SB §215.*

86₂

scræfu westenes	gungum under gearum
I Antra deserti	teneris sub annis
cæstergewara heapas	forfleonde þu gefyrdest
civium turmas	fugiens petisti,
þæt ðu ne mid *leahtre huruþinga	*gewemman lif
ne levi saltem	maculari vita
spræce *þu mihtest	
famine posset.	4

gearcode ruhne	wæfels olfend
II Prebuit yrtum	tegimen camelus
liþum halgum	gyrdel scép
artubus sacris,	stropheum bidentes,
þam burne drenc	fodan
cui latex haustum,	*s*atiata pastum
*hunigum gærstapum	
mella locustis.	8

oþre þæt án giddodan witegena
III Ceteri tantum cecinere vatum

heortan forewitegendra leoman *toweardre
corde presago iubar adfuturum,

þu witodlice middaneardes scylde afyrsigende
tu quidem mundi scelus auferentem

mid scetefingre þu gebecnest
indice   prodis.   12

næs widgilles fæc geond embhwerftes
IV Non fuit vasti spatium per orbis

haligre ænig acenned
sanctior quisquam genitus Iohanne,

se mán worulde geearnode þweandne
qui nefas saecli meruit lavantem

bedyppan on wæterum
tingere limphis.   16

I While yet of tender years you fled from the crowds of the townspeople and went to caves in the desert so that your life at all events might not be polluted by frivolous speech.

II The camel provided a rough garment for the holy limbs, sheep provided a girdle to whom the spring provided drink and dripping honeycombs together with locusts provided food (*Vm*: and honey combined with locusts provided food).

III The other prophets with their prescient hearts only sang of the star that was to be – you point out the one who takes away the sin of the word with your forefinger.

IV In all the vast circumference of the world there was never born anyone holier than John, who was found worthy to lave with water the one who washes away the iniquity of this world.

This section of the hymn for the feast of St John the Baptist, Hy 86, was sung at Matins (Nocturn).

Apparatus to D Latin text: 7 satiata] sociata *with* oc *by another hand on erasure.*

Old English gloss: 3 huruþinga] *is some way removed from its lemma because of spacing problems, but connected with it by a set of corresponding marks.*

BVmCJVp *B has an enlarged initial, Vmp continue without a break.* Heading: *no rubric*

BVmp, HYMNUS AD NOCTURNUM *C*, ANTRA DESERTI *J*; 3 maculari vita] maculare vitam *VmCJVp*; 4 famine] flamine *J*; posset] posses *VmCJVp*; 6–16 *From the second half-line of 6 onwards there is a gap in J.* 6 stropheum] tropheum *Vmp*; 7 satiata] sociata *Vm*; pastum] gustum *Vm*; 8 locustis] locustes *C*; 11 scelus] scelum *C*; auferentem] auferenten *B*, afferentem *C*; 14 quisquam] quisque *C*; 16 *C adds:* Gloria patris.

Commentary   Latin: 3–4 AH *reads* maculare vitam … posses. 6 *Vmp's* tropheum *is attested only once for the Continent by* AH. 7 D *clearly read* satiata *like BCVp.* AH *attests* satiata *for a single continental manuscript.* 11–12 *Cf. John I.29.* 13–14 *Cf. Matt. XI.11.* Old English: 1 *The spelling* gungum *is typically Mercian (SB §92.1a), but certainly possible in West Saxon and Kentish.* 3 leohtre *was probably misread as* leahtre *by the scribe, who expected a noun after the preposition.* gewemman *renders the reading of* VmCJVp; *the following gloss,* lif, *may render either* vita *or the* vitam *of VmCJVp.* 4 þu mihtest *renders the reading of VmCJVp.* 7 *The gloss to* satiata *was probably omitted, because it rendered* sociata, *agreeing with* Vm *and the altered reading in D.* 8 *The case ending of* hunigum *mistakenly anticipates the dative of the following* gærstapum. 10 forewitegendra *may be dat. sg. fem. with* a *explained by the weakening and confusion of final vowels, but probably the scribe assumed that the word agreed with* witegena. *For* toweardre *read* toweardne.

86₃

eala þearle gesælig	7 geearnungum		healic
I O nimis felix	meritisque	[31r]	celse
netende wom	snawitre clænnysse		
nesciens labem	nivei pudoris,		
foremihtig þrowære	7 westenes *bigenc		
prepotens martyr	heremique cultor,		
þu mæsta witegana			
maxime vatum.			4

cynehelmas þreowa on teonfealdum	oþre gewuldorbeagiað		
II Serta ter denis	alios coronant		
geiht geeacnungum	getwifeld sume		
aucta crementis,	duplicata quosdam,		
þryfealdum mid hundfealdum	gemænigfyld wæstme		
trino centeno	cumulata fructu		
þe halig gefrætewiaþ			
te, sacer, ornant.			8

	ó sancte Iohannes		
nu mihtiga	ures geearnungum genihtsumum		
III Nunc potens	nostri meritis opimis		

329

breostes   hearde   stanas   adræf
pectoris duros   lapides repelle,

clincig   *gesmeþiende   siþfæt 7 gebigede
asperum planes   iter & reflexos

gerihtlæc stige
dirige   calles,   12

þæt arfæst middaneardes   *hælend 7   alysend
IV **ut pius mundi   sator & redemptor**

modum   útadræfedum   horuwe   clænum
mentibus pulsa   luvione puris

rihtlice gemedemige   cumende halige
rite   dignetur   veniens sacratos

settan   færeldu
ponere gressus.   16

mid lofum cæstergewaru   bremaþ   heofonlice
V **Laudibus cives   cẹlebrant superni**

ó
þe god   anfeald   7 samod   þrynen
te, deus simplex   pariterque trine,

eadmod   7 *us   forgyfennysse we biddaþ
supplices ac nos   veniam   precamur.

ara   alysedum
Parce redemptis!   20

sy   gode uran   wlite 7 miht
VI **Sit deo nostro   decus & potestas,**

sy hæl   ece   sy wurðment *eces
sit salus perpes,   sit honor   perennis,

se þe heofonas healicra   sitt   on heahnysse
qui poli   summa   residet in arce

þrylic 7 án
trinus & unus.   24

si hit swa
AMEN

I O most happy and excelling in your merits, you who do not know of
any stain on your snow-white modesty, mightiest of martyrs and
inhabitant of the desert, greatest of prophets!

II Wreaths of thirtyfold growth crown others, wreaths of double that size crown some, wreaths heaped with three-hundredfold fruit adorn you, o holy one.

III By your bountiful merits, mighty one, thrust away now the hard stones from our breast, smooth the rugged way and straighten the bent paths

IV so that the benign creator and redeemer of the world, as soon as the pollution is removed from purified minds, may rightly condescend to come and tread there with his holy feet.

V The citizens of heaven exalt you with songs of praise, God who is one and also three, and we suppliants pray for forgiveness. Spare those whom you redeemed!

VI Glory and might be to our God, perpetual happiness and everlasting honour to him, who resides in the uppermost fastness of heaven, both one and three.

This, the third section of the hymn for St John the Baptist, was sung at Lauds. The collectar in H also assigns it to Compline.

Apparatus to D   Old English gloss: 5 þreowa] o *interlined above by* D_1.

BVmCVp   *In J* Hy 86_3, *as part of the preceding* divisio, *was entered on a leaf now missing. B has an enlarged initial; Vmp continue from* Hy 86_2 *without a break.* Heading: *no rubric BVmp,* HYMNUS AD MATUTINUM *C;* 6 aucta] auta *Vm;* 7 trino] trina *VmCVp;* 9 opimis] opmmis, *first* m *altered to* i *C;* 11 planes] plana *followed by erasure of* s *Vm,* planas *C,* planans *Vp;* 12 calles] gressus *B,* callos, o *damaged, perhaps partially erased C;* 14 puris] ris *by another hand on erasure; in the inner margin someone, possibly* C_1, *has written* ris *C;* 17–24 *om. JVp.* C *reads:* Gloria patri. *In Vm the original doxology (only one stanza) is erased and a later hand has written on the erasure:* loriam (*sic*) patri resonemus omnes. / & tibi xpiste genite superne. / cum quibus sanctus simul & creator / spiritus regnat. AMEN.

Commentary   Latin: 5–7 *Cf.* et dabant fructum, aliud centesimum, aliud sexagesimum, aliud tricesimum *Matt. XIII.8.* 7 AH *reads* trina, *attesting* trino *for the Continent as well.* 11 AH *reads* planans, *but also attests* planas, plana *for the Continent.* 17–24 *For the altered doxology in Vm cf. J (see note to* Hy $86_1/16$*) and* Hy 88/33–6. *This and the doxology in C (see note to* Hy $86_1/16$*) are also attested for the Continent by AH, whereas the one in D is not.* Old English: 3 bigenc *is the appropriate translation for* cultus. *The required* nomen agentis *is* bigenga*. The spelling with unvoiced stop in final position (SB §215) suggests that the corruption was already in the exemplar.* 6–7 *The lack of inflection in appositive participles is quite common, see Mitchell,* Old English Syntax *I, §§1434–41.* 11 gesmeþiende *renders the reading of Vp.* clincig *is a* hapax legomenon; *cf. Venezky and Healey,* Microfiche Concordance to Old English. 13 hælend *for* sator *is not literal or accurate; the gloss in JVp has* scyppend. 19 nos *was not recognized as emphatic* nom. 22 perennis *was apparently interpreted as gen. sg., but there may be dittography of* s. 23 healicra *stands for (standard spelling)* healicre.

87

YMNUS IN PASSIONE APOSTOLORUM PETRI ET PAULI

mid ænlicum leohte   7   wlite   rosenum
I   AUREA   LUCE ET DECORE ROSEO,

leoht leohtes ealle   þu geondgute werulde
lux lucis, omne   perfudisti   seculum

gewlitigende heofonan   mid æþelum martyrdome
decorans   cẹlos   inclyto   martyrio

on þisum halgan dæge   þe he selð scyldigum forgifenysse
hac   sacra   die,   quẹ dat reis   veniam.   4

     geatweard heofones   lareow embhwerftes samod
II   [31v] Ianitor cẹli,   doctor orbis   pariter,

deman   worulde   soþe middaneardes leohta
iudices sẹcli,   vera mundi   lumina,

      s. petrus s. paulus
þurh rode   oþer   oðer   mid swurde sigerode
– per crucem alter, alter   ense   triumphat –

lifes rædgyft   gewuldorbeagode hi ahniaþ
vitẹ senatum   laureati   possident.   8

     ó
nu   eala þu gode heorde   mildheort underfoh
III   Iam,   bone   pastor   Petre, clemens accipe

behát biddendra   7 senne   bendas
vota precantum   & peccati vincula

tolys   þe   anwealde betæhtum
resolve tibi   potestate tradita,

mid þam eallum heofonan   mid worde þu beclyst þu geopenast
qua   cunctis cẹlum   verbo   claudis, aperis.   12

     ó
lareow   eala þu æþele   þeawas ty
IV   Doctor   egregie   Paule, mores instrue

7 on mode heofonan   us *gebringe   hoga
& mente polum   nos transferre satage,

oþþæt   fulfremed   sy forgyfen fullicor
donec *perfectus   largiatur plenius

*geidlod   þæt   we be dæle doþ
evacuato,   quod ex parte gerimus.   16

    eala ge elebeames getwinne   arfæstnysse *ancænnedre
V   Olive   bine   pietatis   unice,

on geleafan estfulle   on hihte strange   swiþost
fide   devotos   spe   robustos, maxime

mid welle gefellede   soþre lufe twifealdre
fonte   repletos   caritatis gemine

æfter deaþe   lichoman   biddaþ   libban
post mortem carnis   impetrate vivere.   20

sy þrynnysse   ece   wuldor
VI   Sit trinitati   sempiterna gloria,

wyrðment miht   7   fægnung
honor,   potestas   atque iubilatio,

on annysse   *þam wunaþ   cynedom
in unitate   cui manet imperium

heanon forð 7   nu   geond ece   worulda
extunc   & modo   per aeterna secula.   24

I   Light of light, you have suffused all this world with golden light and rose-red beauty, adorning heaven with renowned martyrdom on this holy day, which grants pardon to the guilty.

II   The gatewarden of heaven as well as the teacher of the world, judges of this world and true lights of the universe, have both gained their laurel wreaths and the senate of life – the one triumphed by the cross, the other by the sword.

III   Now, good shepherd Peter, receive indulgently the requests of those who pray to you and loosen the bonds of sin by the power that was given to you and by which you either close or open heaven to all with a word.

IV   Excellent teacher Paul, teach us moral behaviour and strive to carry us in spirit to heaven against that time when that which is perfect shall be granted more fully and that which we do imperfectly shall be superseded.

v You who are two olive trees of a single piety, devoted in faith, strong in hope, filled most of all with the wellspring of your twinned charity, obtain for us that we shall live after the death of the flesh.

vi Everlasting glory, honour, might and joy be to the Trinity, which in its unity retains its rule, since past times and does so now and will do so in eternity.

This hymn is for the feast of SS Peter and Paul (29 June). It was sung at Vespers, at least according to the collectar in H. It is anonymous, although it has been ascribed to a certain Elpis. It is written in rhythmical iambic trimeter with a regular caesura after the fifth syllable; the stanza can be described as $4 \times (5p+7pp)$. The melody transmitted in C agrees with Stäblein no. 152_2 with only slight deviations. Hy 87 is the usual text of this melody. The text is included in the hymnals of BCDVm and the *Expositio hymnorum* of JVp. Stanzas II and IV were also singled out and recombined with Hy 104_2: Hy 104_1 and 105.

Bibliographical references: *ICL* no. 1439; *AH* 51, 216–19 (no. 188), cf. *AH* 2, 54 (no. 58), Walpole no. 126.

Apparatus to D   Latin text: 4 reis] *one letter erased between* re *and* is, e *and* i *connected by a stroke across the erasure;* veniam] *the* m-*abbreviation appears to be missing but may have merged with the lower loop of the* g *of* forgifenysse; 16 evacuato] o *on erasure (probably of* e).

Old English gloss: 24 geond] d *interlined above by* D_1.

BVmCJVp   *The rubric and 1–2 except for* et roseo decore *were on the same missing leaf in* J *as a large part of Hy 86.* Heading: hymnus in passione petri et pauli B, ITEM HYMNUS Vm, HYMNUS DE SC... (*the last letter,* E *or* I, *and the abbreviation mark erased*) PETRO ET PAULE C, *no rubric* Vp; 2 omne] *followed by an erased* m Vm; 4 reis] *erasure of a letter between* re *and* is C; 5 *one or two letters erased in front of* doctor B; 7 triumphat] triumphans VmJ, triumpha *followed by the erasure of two or three letters* Vp; 10 peccati] peccatis, s *erased* C; 14 nos transferre] nostras ferre C; 15 perfectus] perfectum BVmCJVp; 16 evacuato] o *altered from* a (*not mentioned by* Wieland) B, *last letter* (a?) *erased* C; 18 devotos] devot *followed by an erased* t C; maxime] maximo B, maxima, a *erased* C; 21 trinitati] *final letter* (o?) *altered to* i C; 23 imperium] imperio C.

Commentary   Latin: *For the lives of Peter and Paul as far as they are not treated in the New Testament itself see* Acta Apostolorum Apocrypha, 2 vols., *ed.* R. A. Lipsius (Leipzig, 1891) I, 1–272. 1 *Cf. Hy* 24/1. 2 *Cf. Hy* 15/3. 6 *Cf. Hy* 117/8. 7 *The final cadence seems irregular.* AH *reads* triumphans; *only one continental manuscript has* triumphat. 10–12 *Cf.* quodcumque

334

ligaveris super terram, erit ligatum in caelis, et, quodcumque solveris super terram, erit solutum in caelis *Matth. XVI.19.* 15–16 *Cf.* cum autem venerit quod perfectum est, evacuabitur quod ex parte est *I Cor. XIII.10.* 15 *For* perfectus *in D read* perfectum, *cf. BVmCJVp.* 17 *Cf. Zech. IV.3 and 11–14 and Rev. XI.3–4.* 18–19 *Cf. Hy 117/21–4.* 18 *C's* maxima *is attested for the Continent by* AH. *Old English:* 14 gebringe *seems to be (2 sg.) optative; the glossator may have unconsciously substituted the form the verb would take in a* þæt-clause *for the infinitive.* 16 geidlod *is uninflected, so it probably does not render* evacuato; *cf. the notes on the Latin text of this line in D and BC.* 17 *Once again* unicus *is rendered by* ancænned *regardless of the context, cf. Hy 82/25–7.* 23 þam *should be fem., as* cui *agrees with* trinitati.

88

YMNUS DE PASSIONE SANCTI LAURENTII MARTYRIS

I
þrowæres   cristes   we wurþiað sige
MARTYRIS CHRISTI   colimus   triumphum,

gearlicne timan
annuum tempus   venerando cuius
cernua vocis   prece iam rotundus
orbis adorat.   4

II Pontifex Syxtus   monuit [32r] ministrum
fixus in ligno   crucis: 'Exequéris
me cito poenam   patiendo magnam;
ibis ad astra.'   8

III Tortor iratus   petit, ut talenti
pondus ignoti   manifestet omne,
mente vesana   cupiens vorare
aurea lucra.   12

IV Sprevit hic mundi   peritura dona:
fert opem nudis,   alimenta claudis,
dividit nummos   miseris catervis
corde flagranti.   16

V Igne torquetur   stabili tenore
cordis accensus;   superat minaces
ignium flammas   in amore vitę
semper opime.   20

VI   Uritur post hęc   latus omne testis.
       'Verte', prefecto   loquitur iocunde,
       'corporis partem   laniando coctam
       dentibus atris.'   24

VII   Spiritum sumpsit   chorus angelorum,
       intulit cęlo   pie laureandum,
       ut scelus laxet   hominum precando
       omnipotentem.   28

VIII   Supplici voto   rogitemus omnes:
       Sancte Laurenti,   veniam preceris,
       qui tuum festum   celebrant ubique
       voce vel actu.   32

IX   Gloriam patri   resonemus omnes,
       eius & nato   iubilemus apte,
       cum quibus regnat   simul & creator
       spiritus almus.   36
               amen

I   We celebrate the triumph of Christ's martyr, the date of which each year the world throughout its circumference reveres and adores with humbly voiced prayer.

II   Pope Sixtus, when he was nailed to the wood of the cross, admonished his servant: 'You will follow me quickly and in doing so suffer great pain, you will ascend to the stars.'

III   The furious torturer demanded that he should surrender the whole sum of concealed money, for he in his insane mind wished to consume the golden lucre.

IV   But this man rejected the gifts of the world, which must perish, and brought help to the naked and food to the lame. He, who had an ardent heart, shared out the coins among the crowds of the wretched.

V   In his steady frame of mind he is burnt and tortured by fire and he overcomes the threatening flames of fire in his love for the life that will be fruitful forever.

VI   After this all one side of the martyr is scorched. Pleasantly he says to the prefect: 'Turn the cooked part of my body and tear it with black teeth.'

VII The choir of the angels received the spirit and lovingly carried it to heaven to be crowned with a laurel wreath so that he might effect the remittance of the sins of men by prayers to the Almighty.

VIII Let us all ask in humble prayer: 'Saint Laurence, pray for the forgiveness of those who celebrate your feast anywhere in word or deed.'

IX Let us all sing glory to the Father and let us hymn his son, as is fitting, jointly with whom the Holy Spirit, the creator, reigns, too.

This is a hymn for the feast of St Laurence (10 August). The collectar in H assigns it to Vespers. It is not found in the Winchester Hymnal. It is anonymous and written in Sapphic stanzas. No melody has been transmitted in the Anglo-Saxon hymnals. The text is included in the hymnals of BDVm.

Bibliographical references: *ICL* no. 9384; *AH* 51, 193–5 (no. 172).

Apparatus to D   Latin text: *30* preceris] *the accent on the second syllable was probably added by a later hand.*

BVm   Heading: hymnus de sancto laurentio *B,* YMNUS DE PASSIONE SANCTI LAURENTII ARCHIDIACONI *Vm;* 9 petit] p *altered from* n *B;* 36 *B omits* amen.

Commentary   Latin: *The passion of St Laurence is treated by St Ambrose in the hymn* Apostolorum supparem *(Bulst, p. 51 (II, 13)) and by Prudentius,* Peristefanon II. 21–4 *Cf.* uersate me, martyr uocat, uorate, si coctum est, iubet. *Ambrose,* Apostolorum, *stanza VIII, 3–4;* Converte partem corporis satis crematum ... coctum est *Prudentius,* Peristefanon *II.401–6.*

89

YMNUS IN ASSUMPTIONE SANCTÆ MARIÆ VIRGINIS

	eala hwu	wuldorfullum	leohte þu scinst
I	[32v] O	QUAM GLORIFICA	LUCE coruscas,

	cynrenes davidlices	cynelic tudder
	stirpis Davitice	regia proles,

healic   sittende   mæden
sublimis residens   virgo Maria

ofer   heofoncennede   roderes   ealle
supra celigenas   aetheris omnes.   4

     þu   mid mædenlicum   moder wurðmente
II Tu, cum virgineo   mater honore,

     ængla   *hlæfdige   breostes lofsang
     angelorum domino   pectoris ymnum

     halgum innoþum   clæne þu gearcodest
     sacris visceribus   casta parasti.

                        s. de tuo sancto
     acænned heonon god is   lichoman crist
     Natus hinc deus est   corpore Christus,   8

     þæne   eall   arwurþiende   embhwerft gebitt
III Quem cunctus venerans   orbis   adorat,

     þam nu   rihtlice   cneow is gebiged ælc
     cui nunc rite   genu flectitur omne,

     fram þam we biddaþ   þe cumendre
     a   quo nos petimus   te veniente

           s. nostrorum vitiorum   s. eterne
     aworpenum þeostrum   gefean eces leohtes
     abiectis   tenebris   gaudia lucis.   12

     þæt forgyf fæder   leohtes ælces
IV Hoc largire, pater   luminis omnis,

     suna   þurh agenne   mid gaste halgum
     natum per proprium   flamine sancto,

     se þe mid þe scinende   leofaþ on *rodere
     qui tecum nitida   vivit in aethera

     rixiende 7 *gemeagende   worulda ealle
     regnans ac moderans   secula cuncta.   16

                            amen

I Oh, in what glorious light you shine, royal child of the house of David, Virgin Mary, enthroned on high above all celestial offspring in heaven.

II You, who are a mother and also preserve your maidenly honour, chastely held ready a song of praise from the heart for the lord of the angels, when your womb was made holy. Thus God was born as Christ from a human body,

III he whom all the world reveres and adores, before whom now each knee is bent, as is fitting, whom we ask for the joys of light at your coming, when the shadows are dispelled.

IV Grant this, Father of all light, by means of the Holy Spirit for the sake of your Son, who lives with you in the shining heavens, ruling and guiding all ages of the world.

This hymn was sung at the feast of the Assumption of Mary and assigned to Vespers, at least in the Winchester Hymnal and the collectar of H. The collectar of H also has it for Vespers of the Nativity of Mary. The hymn was also in use in both versions of the Hours of Our Lady for Vespers (T) or Lauds and Compline (R). It is anonymous. Each of the stanza's four verses consists of a hemiepes and an adonius, cf. the second *metrum* in Boethius's *De consolatione philosophiae*, Book I (*ICL* no. 6247). No melody has been transmitted in the Anglo-Saxon manuscripts. The text is included in the hymnals of CDHVm, the *Expositio hymnorum* of JVp and the Hours of RT.

Bibliographical references: *ICL* no. 10997; *AH* 51, 146 (no. 126), cf. *AH* 2, 40 (no. 30).

Apparatus to D   Latin text: 4 aetheris] *spelled with a capital in the manuscript*; 6 domino] *a small erasure after the second* o, *it may have been altered from* a; 14 natum] n *om.*; *a small capital* N *was added in the left margin in front of the word, but at a small distance, probably by* D₁.
   Old English gloss: 6 hlæfdige] *originally* hlæfdigæ, *the left loop of the* æ *erased*.

VmCJVpHRT   Heading and 1–8 *up to* natus *missing in* H *due to loss of leaves.* Heading: IN ASSUMPTIONE SANCTE MARIE YMNUS *Vm*, HYMNUS A SUPREMO SANCTAE MARIAE AD VESPERUM *C*, O QUAM GLORIFICA *J*, *no rubric Vp*, YMNUS *RT*; 2 stirpis] s *damaged T*; davitice] *so also* T *pace Dewick, ed.,* Horae; 4 aetheris] & etheris *Vm*; 5 honore] honorem *C*; 6 domino] domina *Vm*; ymnum] aulam *CRT*; 8 *H begins with* hinc; corpore Christus] co.p... x.., *the rest illegible Vm*; 9 cunctus] cunctis *VmJH*, cuntus *T*; venerans] venerandus *J*, venerandus, *possibly on erasure Vp (not according to Gneuss; the JVp gloss renders* venerans); orbis] i *interlined above by* V₁ *Vp*; adorat] adorant *C*, *one letter erased in front of* t *R (not mentioned by Dewick, ed.,* Horae), adorant, n *erased T*; 13 luminis] liminis? *The word is partly illegible C.* omnis] T *abbreviates as* om̄s *(usually expanded to* omnes); *another hand has added another* s. *Dewick, ed.,* Horae, *expands this as* omnis. 14 flamine] flumine *H*; 15 nitida] n *altered from* m *R*; aethera] ethra *HR*; 16 regnans] *mistakenly repeated, the first* regnans *erased Vm*; moderans] moderam, m *erased C*; 16 amen] *om. JVp*.

Commentary   Latin: 4 *The capitalization of* aetheris *in D is unusual, as* D₁ *does not usually have verse initials.* 6 AH *reads* aulam *like CRT. The metre requires syncope in* angelorum. Old

English: 6 hlæfdige *renders the reading of Vm.* 15 rodere *is sg. instead of pl.; dat. sg. instead of acc. after* on *would be possible, if the participle* scinende *were not acc. pl.* 16 *For* gemeagende *read* gemetgiende.

90

ITEM YMNUS

      moder   drihtnes
I MARIA, MATER DOMINI,

   þæs ecan fæderes suna
   æterni patris filii,

   bring spede us   eallum
   fer opem nobis omnibus

   to þe samod becumendum
   ad te confugientibus.   4

   god   of gode acænnedne
II Deum de deo genitum

   þu acendest suna
   tu genuisti filium;

   se þe næfð   anginn
   qui non habet initium,

   of ðe he underfeng anginn
   ex te sumpsit   exordium.   8

   þisne suna   towundorlicne
III Hunc partum admirabilem

   7 æfre   samodherigendlicne
   semperque conlaudabilem

   gefyrn witegan *samodgeddunge
   olim prophete consono

   heo spræcon mid *bene
   affati sunt oraculo.   12

IV Per Gabrihel archangelum

   de caelo venit nuntium

   electum dei filium.

   Affatus est per ordinem: 16

V 'Ave, Maria inclita,

   tu plena Dei gratia,

concipies per spiritum
& generabis filium.'   20

VI   O virgo beatissima
[33r] per cuncta semper secula,
& tu miranda nimium
& nunc & in perpetuum.   24

VII Qui totum mundum condidit,
in te formatus extitit,
quem mundus totus non capit
in tuo ventre iacuit.   28

VIII Hunc nobis nasci profuit;
a morte nos eripuit,
pro nobis ipse mortuus
& nos per ipsum vivimus.   32

Deo patri sit gloria

I   Mary, mother of the Lord, the son of the eternal Father, bring aid to all of us who seek refuge with you.

II You bore as your son God, begotten by God. He who has no beginning, took his starting point from you.

III In the past the prophets spoke of this wonderful birth, which is forever to be praised, in unanimous predictions.

IV The message regarding the chosen Son of God came from heaven by means of the archangel Gabriel. He spoke in an ordered manner:

V   'Hail, glorious Mary, you are filled with the grace of God, you shall conceive by the spirit and bear a son.'

VI O virgin most blessed throughout all the ages and o you who are to be admired above all both now and forever!

VII He who created the whole world was formed within you. He whom the whole world cannot contain lay in your womb.

VIII It was good for us that he was born; he saved us from death by dying for us and we live through him.

This hymn and Hy 91–3 seem to be intended for the Assumption of Mary in D and V, but the details are unclear. In H they are apparently assigned for Candlemas or possibly Annunciation, but they are not included in the collectar. They provide for the Day Hours of the Office of Our Lady in T, Hy 90 for Prime. In R, which does not include the other three hymns, Hy 90 is assigned to the Matins of Our Lady. It is anonymous and written in rhythmical Ambrosian hymn verse (4 × 8pp). Rhyme is monosyllabic with a tendency to be disyllabic; the stanza rhymes aabb. No melody is transmitted in the Anglo-Saxon manuscripts. The text is included in the hymnals of DHVm and the Hours of RT. In Vm the text is glossed in Old English; the gloss is in part related to the one in D.

Bibliographical references: *ICL* no. 9298; cf. *AH* 14, 110–11 (no. 107), *AH* 23, 77 (no. 119).

Apparatus to D   Latin text: 3 *Punctuation om. after the third verse, although the end of the verse and the line do not coincide.*

VmHRT   Heading: *no rubric VmH,* YMNUS *R,* YMNUS AD PRIMAM *T*; 2 æterni] æterne *T*; filii] filium *Vm*; 3 nobis] n *altered from* v *T*; 4 confugientibus] configientibus *T*; 6 tu] *expunged and* qui *interlined above, probably by another hand H*; 7 habet] habent, n *expunged R*; 8 ex] a *Vm*; 9 Hunc] Tunc *T*; partum] partem *H*, parte *T*; admirabilem] ammirabilem *H*, tam mirabilem *R*, admirabile *T*; 11 consono] *interlined above by another hand R, final* o *altered from* a *T*; 13–32 *om. HT*; 17–32 *om. Vm*; 27 mundus totus] totus mundus *R*; 33 *VmHRT have a different doxology; text according to R:* Gloria tibi domine / qui natus es de virgine / cum patre & sancto spiritu / in sempiterna secula. amen *Vm stops after* virgine. *H stops after* es; es *was corrected to* est *by a later hand. T stops after* domine.

Vm gloss: 2 suna] sunu; 5 acænnedne] acennedne; 10 samodherigendlicne] samodherigedlicne; 12 spræcon] sprecan; 13–16 *are also glossed:* 13 þurh gabriel heahængel 14 of heofenan com bode 15 gecoran godes suna 16 spræcende wæs þurh ændebyrde; *the doxology of Vm is glossed:* wuldor þe drihten / se acenned is of mædene.

Commentary   Latin: *The versions recorded by* AH *from continental manuscripts diverge widely from D after the third stanza.* 7 *Cf. Heb. VII.3.* 17–21 *This stanza recurs as Hy 91/5–9. Cf.* have gratia plena. Dominus tecum . . . ecce concipies in utero et paries filium *Luke I.28 and 31.* 25–32 *This stanza recurs as Hy 92/5–12.* Old English: *Lines 13–33, which remain unglossed in D, are not contained in HT's version of the hymn. Note also that 17–32 are om. in Vm. Originally, of course, there will have been no gloss to this hymn at all, since it is not part of the Winchester Hymnal, but here an intermediate stage, at which the shorter version of the hymn was added and glossed, seems indicated.* 11 consono, *the adjective belonging to* oraculo *has been mistaken for a noun.* 12 oraculo *has been misinterpreted because of associations with* orare *and* oratio *and possibly because the prophets 'address' Christ* (affari).

91

ITEM YMNUS

      godes heahengel
I GABRIHEL, DEI ARCHANGELus,

    ure   hæle bydel
  nostræ salutis nuntius,

  he swegde swa
  intonuit sic Mariam

  gegretende þa halgastan
  salutans sacratissimam: 4

    hal sy ðu   æðele
II 'Ave,   Maria inclita,

    s.és
  þu eart full   godes gyfe
  tu   plena dei gratia,

  þu geeacnast þurh gast
  concipies per spiritum

  7 þu acenst
  & generabis filium.'   8

    eala þu mæden eadigosta
III O virgo   beatissima

    ofer   heofonan gebletsod
  supra cęlos   benedicta,

    gebide for muneca
  exora pro monachorum

    estfullum werode eadmodra
  devoto choro supplicum.   12

I Gabriel, God's archangel, the messenger who announced our salvation, exclaimed thus, when he greeted the most blessed Mary:

II 'Hail, noble Mary, you are filled with the grace of God. You shall conceive by the Spirit and bear a son.'

III O most happy virgin blessed above the heavens, pray for the choir of suppliant monks devoted to you.

This hymn, which is not found outside Anglo-Saxon England, is apparently intended for Assumption in DVm and for Candlemas in H; see above under Hy 90. In T it is assigned to Tierce of the Hours of Our Lady. It is anonymous and written in rhythmical Ambrosian hymn verse (4 × 8pp). Rhyme is monosyllabic; the stanza rhymes aabb. No melody is transmitted in the Anglo-Saxon manuscripts. The text is included in the hymnals of DHVm and the Hours of T. V has an Old English interlinear gloss related to D.

Bibliographical references: *ICL* no. 5461; *AH* 12, 49–50 (no. 75) (uses HV).

Apparatus to D   Latin text: 12 *Another hand, still of the eleventh century, adds* Gloria *in the right margin.*

   VmHT   *VmHT have no rubric. H indents and has a full-sized hymn initial.* 4 sacratissimam] sacratissimum *T*; 5 inclita] t *altered from a T*; 7 concipies] concipes *T*; 10 benedicta] exaltata *H*; 11 monachorum] populorum *and the scribe has interlined* pro clericorum *above H*; 12 *VmH add* Gloria tibi domine, *T adds* Gloria tibi domine / qui natus est.

   Vm Old English gloss: 1 heahængel] heahengel; 2 swegde] swegie; 4 halgastan] *om.*; 5 hal sy þu] syo þu gesund, *mistakenly repeated*; 6 eart] *om.*; 7 þu] þe; 8 acenst] acænst; *Vm glosses* filium *with* suna; 10 heofonan] heofonam; 11 muneca] munecha; 12 estfullum] estfulla.

Commentary   Latin: 5–9 *The stanza repeats Hy 90/17–21.* 10 *Cf.* exaltare super caelos *Ps. CVII.6.* Old English: 4–5 *The omission of the gloss to* sacratissimam *in Vm and the dittography of the following gloss suggest that the gloss to* Ave *was originally* hal sy þu *as in D and that confusion arose, because the two glosses begin with the same three letters.* 6 eart *has no Latin lemma in Vm and could have been omitted for that reason.* 8 *There is no apparent reason for the omission of the gloss to* filium *in D.*

92

          heofones cwén
1 Maria, cęli   regina
    on halignysse wuldorfull
    sanctitate   gloriosa,
    geher bena   þena
    audi preces famulorum
    7 gebida   drihten
    & deprecare dominum.   4

se ðe ealne   middaneard gescóp

II Qui totum mundum condidit,

on ðe gehiwod ł sceapen wunoð
in te formatus   extitit,

þæne eall middaneard ne befehð
quem totus mundus   non capit

on þinum innoðe læg
in tuo   ventre iacuit.   8

þysne us   beon acenned he *foregewissode

III Hunc nobis nasci   profuit;

fram deaðe us he generode
a   morte nos eripuit,

for us   he sylf wæs dead
pro nobis ipse   mortuus

7 we þurh hine   libbað
& nos per ipsum vivimus.   12

I Mary, queen of heaven glorious in your sanctity, hear the prayers of your servants and intercede for them with the Lord.

II He who created the whole world was formed in you. He whom the whole world cannot contain lay in your womb.

III It was good for us that he was born. He rescued us from death by dying for us and we live through him.

This hymn is apparently intended for the Assumption of Mary in DVm and for Candlemas in H. For details see above under Hy 90. In T it is assigned to Sext of the Hours of Our Lady. It is anonymous and written in rhythmical Ambrosian hymn verse (4 × 8pp). Rhyme is monosyllabic; the stanza rhymes aabb. No melody has been transmitted in the Anglo-Saxon manuscripts. The text is included in the hymnals of DHVm and the Hours of T. V contains an Old English interlinear gloss related to D.

Although the hymn is not found outside Anglo-Saxon England, a related one is printed in *AH* 23, no. 121, p. 78 from Munich, Staatsbibliothek, clm 14926 (s. xv), from Sankt Emmeram, Regensburg.

Bibliographical references: *ICL* no. 9296; *AH* 12, 50 (no. 77) (uses HV).

Apparatus to D   Latin text: 12 *An eleventh-century hand adds* Gloria *in the margin as at the end of Hy 91.*

VmHT   *Vm continues onward from Hy 91 without a break; H indents and has a full-sized hymn initial.* Heading: *no rubric in VmH, ymnus T;* 4 dominum] dm̄ *T;* 7 totus mundus] mundus totus *H, Vm has* adorat *in front of* non. *The word is lightly struck through.* 9 Hunc] Nunc *H,* Tunc *T;* nasci] s *altered from* c *by the scribe T;* 11 ipse] esse *T;* 12 &] E *T; H adds* Gloria tibi domine / qui natus est, *T adds* Gloria tibi domine.

Vm gloss: 1 heofones] heofenes; 2 halignysse] halinysse; wuldorfull] wuldorful; 3 geher] gehyr; 4 gebida] gebide; 6 gehiwod ł] *om.;* wunoð] wunat; 8 innoðe] o innoþe; 9 þysne] þisne; acenned] acænned; foregewissode] *Vm breaks off after* fore. 11 dead] deað; 12 we] us.

Commentary   Old English: 9 foregewissode *in D is a* hapax legomenon *and an odd gloss for* profuit. *Perhaps there was an unattested variant* providit.? *In Vm the scribe apparently copied* fore *as equivalent of* pro *and omitted the unsatisfactory half of the gloss.*

93

mæden mædena
I   Maria, virgo virginum,

gehýr   behád þeowena
exaudi vota servorum,

*geornfulre bene   us   geheald
iugi   prece nos conserva

7   ðe *wurðigende help
[33v] ac te   colentes   adiuva.   4

we þristlæcað eadmode biddan
II   Audemus   proni   rogare:

gehýran ure   gemedema
Audire nostros dignare

on þinum lofu   wurðmynte
in tuo   melos honore

7 for ús   þinga
ac pro nobis intercede.   8

geþeod   werodum engelicum
III   Iuncta choris   angelicis,

us   gehæl mid mundbyrdum
nos salva patrociniis,

þæt ecelice   mid   burhleodum
ut perpetim cum civibus

346

we blissian   heofonlicum
gaudeamus celestibus.   12

ó
wuldor ðe   eala ðu drihten
IV Gloria tibi,   domine,
qui natus es

I Mary, virgin of virgins, hear the request of your servants, preserve us by your constant prayer and help those who worship you.

II Bowing down before you we dare to ask: 'Deign to hear our songs in your honour and intercede for us.'

III You who are joined to the choirs of the angels, save us by your advocacy so that we may rejoice continually with the citizens of heaven.

This hymn, which is not found outside Anglo-Saxon England, seems to be intended for the Assumption of Mary in DV and for Candlemas in H. For details see above, under Hy 90. In T it is assigned to None of the Hours of Our Lady. It is anonymous and written in non-metrical Ambrosian hymn verse; the verses are octosyllabic with irregular final cadence. Rhyme is monosyllabic; the stanzas rhyme aabb. No melody has been transmitted in the Anglo-Saxon manuscripts. The text is included in the hymnals of DHVm and the Hours of T.

Bibliographical references: *ICL* no. 9301; *AH* 12, 50 (no. 76, uses HV).

Apparatus to **D**   Latin text: 2 exaudi] a *altered from* o *to insular* a *and later corrected to Caroline* a *by another hand*; 6 Audire] a *possibly altered from* u; 14 qui] q *is a small capital letter.* Old English gloss: 11 *one or two letters erased in front of* ecelice.

VmHT   Heading: *no rubric in VmH*, ymnus *T*; 5 Audemus] Laudemus *Vm*; 8 ac] hac *H*; pro] p *T (not mentioned by Dewick, ed., Horae);* 9 Iuncta] Cuncta *Vm*; 11 perpetim] perpetuum *H*; 12 *Vm adds* in *after* gaudeamus; 14 *om. HT*; natus es] *om. Vm.*

Commentary   Old English: 2 *For* behád *with* d *for* t *see p.* 76. 3 geornfulre *for* iugis *is imprecise, although 'diligent' is implied here.* 4 wurðigende *renders the Latin acc., although* helpan *requires dat. or gen.*

94

ITEM YMNUS

      wæs geworden geat   cristes   þurhfere
I   FIT   PORTA CHRISTI PERVIA,

      gefylled full   mid gyfe
      referta, plena gratia,

      7 þurhfor   cyng 7 þurhwunode
      transitque rex & permanet

      *clysing swa swa heo wæs geond wurolda
      clausa, ut   fuit,   per   sęcula.   4

      cynn   upplices godes ł mihte
II   Genus superni numinis

      forðstop   healle mædenes
      processit aula virginis,

      brydguma alysend   scyppend
      sponsus, redemptor, conditor,

      his ormæde gelaðunge
      suę gigas æcclesiae.   8

      wurðmynt moder 7 gefea
III Honor matris & gaudium,

      *mycel   hiht gelefendra
      inmensa spes credentium

      þurh swearte deaðes drencfatu
      per atra   mortis pocula

      he tolysde ure   leahtras
      resolvit nostra crimina.   12

      gode fæder sy wuldor
      Deo patri sit gloria

I A gate through which Christ may pass has come into being, filled completely with grace, and the king passes through and it remains closed, as it was before, throughout the ages.

II The offspring of the deity in heaven came forth from the royal hall of the virgin, he, the bridegroom, the redeemer, the creator and the giant of his church.

III He, the honour and joy of his mother and the immeasurable hope of those who believe in him, made void our transgressions by draining the dark cup of death.

This hymn seems to be intended for the Assumption of Mary in DVm, although the details are unclear. In H and its collectar it is assigned to Compline of the third and fourth Sunday in Advent and of Annunciation. It is anonymous and written in Ambrosian hymn verse (iambic dimeter) with an irregular third stanza. No melody has been transmitted in the Anglo-Saxon manuscripts. The text is included in the hymnals of DHVm.

Bibliographical references: *ICL* no. 5163; *AH* 27, 118–19 (no. 82, ii), Walpole no. 88.

Apparatus to D   Old English gloss: 12 tolysde] s *on erasure of* l.

VmH   Heading: *no rubric VmH; 9 one or two letters erased in front of* matris*? H*; 13 Laus honor virtus *H*.

Commentary   Latin: 1–4 *Cf.* porta haec clausa erit. non aperietur et vir non transiet per eam, quoniam Dominus Deus Israhel ingressus est per eam eritque clausa *Ezek. XLIV.2–3.* 3–4 *Cf. Hy 39/10.* 6–8 *Cf. Hy 39/13–16, Ps. XVIII.6.* 10 *Cf. Hy 117/22.* 11 *Cf.* calix *Matt. XXVI.39 and 42.* Old English: 1 *The glossator has deviated here from his practice of rendering historic present by the simple past tense. If a distinction is made, it may be one of aspect.* 4 *The attributive participle* clausa *(agreeing with* porta) *is translated as a noun; perhaps it was mistaken for nom. pl. ntr.* 8 *For* ormæde *with* d *for* t, *see p.* 76. 10 mycel *is too weak semantically for* inmensa.

95

YMNUS IN DEDICATIONE BASILICÆ SANCTI MICHAELIS

geryne   tacenbora
I   MISTERIORUM SIGNIFER

          ó   s. michael
heofonlicra   eala þu heahængel
caelestium,   archangele,

þe halsigende   we biddaþ
te supplicantes quęsumus,

þæt us   glæd   þu geneosige
ut nos placatus visites.   4

349

þu sylf mid   halgum   ænglum
II   Ipse cum sanctis angelis,

mid   rihtwisum mid   apostolum
cum iustis,   cum apostolis,

onleoht   stowe   ealne weg
inlustra locum iugiter,

on þære nu   biddende we drohtniað
quo   nunc orantes degimus.   8

clænnestra   ealra
III   Castissimorum omnium

larewa   7   biscopa
doctorum ac pontificum

for us   bena   genihtsuma
[34r] pro nobis preces profluas

estfull   offra drihtne
devotus offer domino,   12

feond   he adræfe þæt þæne reþan
IV   hostem repellat ut sęvum

7 spede   sibbe *gerihtlæce
opemque pacis dirigat

7 ure   samod breosta
& nostra simul pectora

geleafa fulfremed geondscine
fides perfecta perlustret.   16

astigan   ure   þærrihtes
V   Ascendant nostrę protinus

to þrymsetle   stefna wuldres
ad thronum *vocis glorię

7 mod   ure   he uparære
mentesque nostras erigat,

se þe on setle scinð   scinendum
qui sede   splendet fulgida.   20

her   miht   his   wunige
VI   Hic virtus eius maneat,

her fæst ł trum byrne   soþlufu
hic firma   flagret caritas,

her to hæle   behefnyssa
hic ad salutis commoda

350

his   *he becume þenum
suis occurrit   famulis.   24

      gedwyld ealle   he afyrsige
VII   Errores omnes auferat

      7 worigende sefan   he *þreage
      vagosque   sensus corrigat

      7 he gerihtlæce fotswaþu
      & dirigat   vestigia

      ure   sibbe þurh siþfæt
      nostra pacis per semitam.   28

      leohtes on heahnysse scinendre
VIII   Lucis in arce   fulgida

      þas   halgan he awrite leoþ
      hęc sacra scribat   carmina

      7 ure   samod naman
      nostraque simul nomina

      on béc   lifes he gesette
      in libro vitae conserat.   32

                   amen

I Ensign bearer of the heavenly mysteries and archangel, we entreat and request you to visit us in a propitious mood.

II Together with the holy angels, with the just and the apostles, do you yourself illuminate this place continually, where we now dwell in prayer.

III Offer up faithfully the abundant prayers of all the most chaste teachers and bishops to the Lord for us

IV that he may drive away the savage enemy and send us peace for our support and that at the same time perfect faith may shine deep in our breasts.

V May our voices rise up straight to the throne of glory and may he who shines on that blazing seat lift up our minds towards him.

VI May his miraculous power dwell here. May steadfast charity burn here. Here he meets his servants for their ease and salvation.

VII May he dispel all errors and correct wavering judgement and guide our feet on the path of peace.

351

VIII In the glowing fastness of light may he write down these holy songs and also set down our names in the book of life.

This hymn was sung at the feast of the Archangel Michael (29 September). In the Canterbury Hymnal the hymn is assigned to Vespers, in the Winchester Hymnal and H to Matins (Nocturn). It is anonymous and written in rhythmical Ambrosian hymn verse (4 × 8pp). The melody transmitted in H remains unidentified. The text is included in the hymnals of BCDHVm and the *Expositio hymnorum* of JVp.

Bibliographical references: *ICL* no. 9945; *AH* 14a, 83–4 (no. 74).

Apparatus to D   Latin text: 24 famulis] a *may be altered from* u.

BVmCJVpH   Heading: ymnus in sollempnitate sancti michaelis archangeli *B, no rubric Vmp,* HYMNUS AD NOCTURNUM *C,* MISTERIORUM SIGNIFER *J,* YMNUS AD NOCTURNAM *H;* 4 visites] visitet *C;* 6 *second* cum] tum *C;* 7 inlustra] inlustrat *C;* 8 degimus] degemus *Vp,* deimus *H;* 9 Castissimorum] castissimórum, *erasure of 1–2 letters in front of* o *B;* 15 nostra] *last letter erased and altered to* o *Vm,* nostro *CJVp;* pectora] *last letter erased and altered to* e *Vm,* pectore *JVp;* 16 perlustret] maneat *VmCJVp;* 18 vocis] voces *BVmCJVpH;* 20 splendet] p *altered from* l *(Wieland reads* splendet) *B;* fulgida] *on erasure by another hand H;* 21 Hic] hinc *C;* 23 salutis] s *on erasure by another hand H;* commoda] comoda *C,* od *on erasure by another hand H;* 24 occurrit] occurrat *BCJVp;* famulis] famuli *J;* 26 vagosque] vagasque *JVp;* corrigat] *by another hand on erasure H;* 28 nostra] nostras *C;* 30 carmina] crimina *C;* 32 conserat] consecrat *C;* amen] *om. CJVp.*

Commentary   Latin: Heading: *D's rubric means that the date of the feast is that of the dedication of St Michael's basilica in Rome.* 16 AH *reads* muniat, *but attests* VmCJVp's *maneat for one continental manuscript at least.* 18 vocis *in D should be nom. pl.; spellings of the nom. pl. with* i *occur in Later Latin, but are not otherwise found in this gloss.* 24 AH *reads* occurrat. Old English: 14 gerihtlæce *translates* dirigire *in its common meaning 'to correct, make straight', which is not appropriate here.* 24 he becume *renders the reading of BCJVp.* 26 þreage *is used here in its sense 'to chastise'; the glossator clearly wanted to avoid* gerihtlæcan, *because it translates* dirigat *in the next line.*

96

YMNUS AD NOCTURNAM

o

þe eala þu crist   beorhtnyss   fæderes
I TIBI,   CHRISTE, SPLENDOR PATRIS,
lif 7 miht heortena
vita ac virtus cordium,

on geseohþe   ængla
in conspectu angelorum

mid gewilnungum stefne we singaþ
votis,   voce psallimus,

wrixliende   hleoþriende
alternantes concrepando

lofu   we sellaþ mid stefnum
melos damus   vocibus.   6

we samod herigað arwurþigende
II ### Conlaudamus   venerantes

ealle   heofones cempan
omnes caeli   milites,

ac   healicost   ealdor
sed pręcipue primatem

heofonlices werodes
cęlestis   exercitus,

                on mihte
Michaelem in virtute

tobrytende   deoful ł scuccan
conterentem zabulum.   12

mid þam hyrde   feor   adræf
III ### Quo   custode procul pell*e*,

        ó
cyng eala crist   þu arfæstesta
rex   Christe piissime,

ælc   mán   feondes
omne nefas inimici.

clæna   heortan 7 lichoman
Mundos corde & corpore

neorxnewange   agyf *þinre
paradyso   [34v] redde tuo

mid anre mildheortnyssa
nos sola clementia.   18

wuldor   fæder gedrymum
IV ### Gloriam patri melodis

uton swegan   mid stefnum
personemus vocibus,

353

wuldor criste   uton singan
gloriam Christo canamus,

wuldor   þam frofergaste
gloriam paraclyto,

se þe god   þrynen 7 an
qui deus trinus & unus

wunað ær   worulda
extat ante secula.   24

sy hit swa
AMEN

I To you, Christ, glory of the Father, life and strength of hearts, we lift
up our voice in song and in prayer in the sight of the angels, we offer
hymns, declaiming them in turns with our voices.

II We revere all the soldiers of heaven and praise them all together, but
especially the prince of the celestial army, Michael, who by his
miraculous power crushes the devil.

III With him as a guardian, Christ, most loving king, drive away all the
wickedness of the enemy. Purely through your mercy return us to
your paradise, purified in heart and body.

IV Let us raise our voices chanting glory to the Father, let us sing glory
to Christ, glory to the Comforter Spirit, who has existed as God, one
and threefold, since before the ages of the world.

This hymn was sung at the feast of the Archangel Michael (29 September).
In the Canterbury Hymnal it is assigned to Matins (Nocturn), in the
Winchester Hymnal and H to Vespers. It is anonymous and written in a
rhythmical metre; the stanza can be described as $3 \times (8p+7pp)$. The
melody transmitted in H remains unidentified. The text is included in the
hymnals of BCDHVm and the *Expositio hymnorum* of JVp.

Bibliographical references: *ICL* no. 16365; *AH* 50, 207–8 (no. 156).

Apparatus to D   Latin text: 13 pelle] pellas *with* as *by another hand on erasure*; 17 tuo] o
altered to a *by another hand.*

Old English gloss: 15 feondes] o *altered from* n.

BVmCJVpH   Heading: ad nocturnam *B, no rubric* Vmp, HYMNUS DE SANCTE
MICHAHELE ARCHANCELO (*sic*) *C,* TIBI CHRISTE SPLENDOR *J,* YMNUS DE

SANCTO MICHAELE ARCHANGELO *H*; 2 ac] *om. Vm*; 8 caeli] seculi *C*; 9 primatem] primatum *C*; 11 Michaelem] michahele *C*; 13 pelle] pellens *BCH*; 16 Mundos] mundo *VmCH*; 17 redde tuo] redd&uo *C*; 18 nos] n *on erasure of* m *probably by another hand B*; 19 Gloriam] Gloria *C*; 21 gloriam Christo] *om. J (J also omits the repetition of* canamus *in the* Expositio); 23 deus trinus & unus] trinus & unus deus *Vm*; 24 AMEN] *om. VmCJVp.*

Commentary   Latin: 1 *Cf. Hy 15/1.* 2 *AH omits* ac *like Vm.* 13 *The size of the erasure in D suggests that it agreed with VmJVp before the correction rather than with BCH's reading* pellens. pellens *is attested in only one continental manuscript used by AH.* 16 *VmCH's* mundo *is attested by AH for continental manuscripts.* 17 *The alteration to* tua *in D aligns the lemma with the gloss.* Old English: 17 þinre *appears to translate* tua *as the corrector has it. This reading is not otherwise attested in Anglo-Saxon England.*

97

YMNUS AD MATUTINAM

ó
eala ðu crist   halgena   wlite   ængla
I   CHRISTE, SANCTORUM   DECUS ANGELORUM,

ealdor mænnisces   7 cynnes   reccend
autor humani   generisque rector,

us   ece   forgyf welwillende
nobis ęternum   tribue benignum

astigan   rice
scandere regnum.   4

ængel   sibbe   to   þissere
II   Angelum pacis,   Michael, [ad] istam

heofonlice beon asend   uton biddan healle
cęlitus   mitti   rogitæmus aulam,

us   þæt gelomlice   cuman 7 weaxan
nobis ut crebro   veniant & crescant

gesundfulnyssa ealle
prospera   cuncta.   8

ængel   se stranga   þæt feond
III   Angelus fortis,   Gabrihel, ut hostem

he adræfe þæne ealdan   he fleo fram heahnysse
pellat   antiquum,   volitet ab alto,

*oftrædlice tempel   he cume 7 *þisum
sepius   templum   veniat & istud

355

geneosigan ure
visere   nostrum.   12

        ængel   us   læce   hæle
 IV   Angelum nobis   medicum salutis

        asænd of heofonum   þæt ealle
        mitte de caelis,   Raphael, ut omnes

        hæle adlige   7 samod   ure
        sanet egrotos   pariterque nostros

        he gerihtlæce dæda
        dirigat   actus.   16

        heonon godes ures   cynnystre
  V   Hinc dei   nostri   genitrix Maria,

        eall   7 us   werod   ængla
        totus & nobis   chorus angelorum

        æfre   ætwunige   samod 7 seo eadige
        semper adsistat,   simul & beata

        gegaderung eall
        contio   tota.   20

        getiþige þæt us
        Prestet hoc nobis

I Christ, glory of the holy angels, founder and ruler of the human race, grant us to ascend to the bounteous eternal kingdom (*other manuscripts:* by your favour to ascend to the eternal realm).

II Let us pray that the angel of peace, Michael, may be sent from heaven to this hall so that all kinds of prosperity may often come to be ours and may increase.

III May the resolute angel Gabriel fly down from on high to drive away the ancient enemy and may he also come very often to see this sanctuary of ours.

IV Send us the angel Raphael from heaven as physician for our health that he may heal all the sick and also guide our actions.

V Moreover, may the mother of our God, Mary, and all the choir of the angels and also the whole congregation of the blessed be with us always.

This hymn was sung at Lauds of the feast of the Archangel Michael

(29 September). The collectar in H also assigns it to Compline. It also provides for Compline of the Hours of Our Lady in T. It is anonymous and written in Sapphic stanzas. The melody transmitted in H is probably a version of Stäblein no. 146 closest to 146_1 and 146_2. The text is included in the hymnals of BCDHVm, the *Expositio hymnorum* of JVp and the Hours of T.

Bibliographical references: *ICL* no. 2244; *AH* 50, 197–8 (no. 146), cf. *AH* 2, 64 (no. 76).

Apparatus to D   Latin text: 5 Michael, istam] ad *inserted in between from above by another hand with a caret mark*; 6 rogitæmus] æ *altered to* a *by another hand,* m *apparently altered from* l *by D₁*; 7 crebro] b *damaged by the erasure of* æ *in the preceding line and retraced by the corrector*; 17 Hinc] n *inserted from above with a caret mark by D₁ while glossing.*

Old English gloss: 7 gelomlice] lic *damaged at the time of the alteration in line 6.*

BVmCJVpHT   Heading: ad matutinam B, *no rubric* Vmp, HYMNUS AD MATU-TINUM (YMN *and* AD MAT *on erasure*) C, CHRISTE SANCTORUM J, YMNUS AD MATUTINAM H, YMNUS T; 2 rector humani generis & auctor Vm; generisque] generis & CT *(the prose version of JVp has* atque); 3 benignum] benignus BVmCJVpHT; 4 regnum] celum VmCJVpHT; 6 rogitæmus] rogitamus VmJVpH, rog. . ., *rest of word illegible except for a capital* S T; 7 veniant & crescant] veniente crescant Vm; 8 prospera] prospa J *(not mentioned by Gneuss)*; cuncta] cunct *on erasure* C, cunta T; 9 Angelus] Angelum CT; fortis] forti JVp *(but the JVp gloss renders* fortis), pacis T; 10 pellat] pellað T; 11 templum] teplum H; veniat] veniens H; &] ad VmCJVpHT; istud] istum B; 12 visere] viscere T; 15 sanet] sanat H; nostros] nostras C; 16 dirigat] diriget, e *altered to* a *by C₁* C; actus] actos C, *one letter erased after* a? *(not mentioned by Gneuss)* J; 17 Hinc] hic BH; Maria] marię C; 18 nobis] *om.* JVp; 20 contio] conscio C; tota] toto C; HT *add* amen. 21 BVm *continue:* deitas beata. CJVpHT *have no doxology.*

Commentary   Latin: 2 AH *reads* rector humani generis et auctor *like* Vm, *but quotes the reading of* DBH *from two continental manuscripts.* 3 AH *reads* benignus. benignum *in D is probably purely scribal.* 4 AH *attests* caelum *for continental manuscripts.* 5 *The omission of* ad *in D is accidental.* 6 *The alteration in D is to the reading of* VmJVpH. AH *reads* rogitamus. 7 AH *reads* veniente crescant. 9 *Cf.* Gabriel Hebraice in linguam nostram vertitur fortitudo dei *Isidore of Seville,* Etymologiarum sive originum libri VII. *v.* 10. 11 *Cf. Luke I.9–19.* AH *reads* veniens ad *as* H; veniat *and* et *seem to be attested in only one continental manuscript each.* 13 *Cf.* Raphael interpretatur curatio vel medicina dei *Isidor of Seville,* Etymologiarum sive originum libri VII. *v.* 13. 17 *The original reading* Hic *in D agrees with* BH; *the altered reading fits the gloss.* Old English: 3 welwillende *could translate either* benignum *or* benignus *as in* BVmCJVpHT. 11 *No attempt is made to render the comparative;* sepius *need not, however, have strictly comparative force.* þisum *should be acc. sg. ntr., since* istud *agrees with* templum . . . nostrum.

98

YMNUS IN FESTIVITATE OMNIUM SANCTORUM
AD VESPERAM

      freols   woruldum is gewurðod
I   FESTIVA SAECLIS COLITUR

    dæg halgena   ealra
    dies sanctorum omnium,

        þa ðe rixiað   on heofonlicum
    [35r] qui regnant in cęlestibus,

    ó
    eala ðu hælend míd þe gesæliglice
      IESU,   tecum feliciter.   4

    þas we ciaþ   eadmode
II Hos invocamus cernui

         ó
    7 þe   eala þu alysend ealra
    teque,   redemptor omnium.

    heom 7 þe   eadmode
    Illis tibique supplices

    bena   geomriende we asændað
    preces gementes fundimus.   8

       ó
    eala ðu hælend alysend   worulde
III   Iesu,   salvator saeculi,

    alysedum   mid spede gehylp
    redemptis ope   subveni

       ó
    7 *eaþa ðu arfæsta godes cynnestra
    &,   pia   dei genitrix,

    hæle bide earmingum
    salutem posce miseris.   12

    werodu ealle   ængellice
IV Caetus omnes angelici,

    heahfædera   heapas
    patriarchum cunei

    7 witegena   geearnunga
    & prophetarum merita

    us biddan   forgifenyssa
    nobis precentur veniam.   16

fulluhtæra cristes   se forestæppende
V Baptista Christi prẹvius

7 cægbora se roderlica
& claviger æthereus

mid oþrum apostolum
cum ceteris apostolis

us   hi tolysan fram bende leahtres
nos solvant nexu   criminis.   20

werod   halig   þrowæra
VI Chorus sacratus martyrum,

andetnyss sacerda
confessio sacerdotum

7 seo mædenlice clænnys
& virginalis   castitas

us   fram sennum hi afeormian
nos a   peccatis abluant.   24

muneca   helpas
VII Monachorum suffragia

7 ealle   cæstergewara heofonlice
omnesque cives   celici

hi tiþian *benum eadmodra
annuant vota   supplicum

7 lifes hi biddan mede
& vitẹ poscant premium.   28

lof   wurþment miht   wuldor
VIII Laus, honor,   virtus, gloria

gode fæder 7 sunan
deo patri & filio

samod mid þam halgan gaste
simul cum sancto   spiritu

on ece   worulda
in sempiterna sẹcula.   32

si hit swa
ameN

I The feast day of All Saints is celebrated in all the world, the day of
those who reign happily in the heavenly regions together with you, o
Jesus.

II It is these we invoke with bowed heads and it is also you, redeemer of all. As suppliants we address prayers to them and to you, sighing the while.

III Jesus, saviour of the world, assist and aid those whom you redeemed and you, loving mother of God, demand salvation for the wretched.

IV May all the hosts of the angels and the troops of the patriarchs and the prophets by virtue of their merits pray for forgiveness unto us.

V May the Baptist who preceded Christ and the bearer of the keys to heaven release us from the bond of sin in concert with the other apostles.

VI May the holy choir of the martyrs and the priests by virtue of their being confessors and the maidens by virtue of their chastity purify us of our transgressions.

VII May the intercession of the monks and may all citizens of heaven grant the requests of the suppliants and ask the reward of life for them.

VIII Praise, honour, might and glory be to God, the Father and the Son together with the Holy Ghost in eternity.

This hymn was sung at Vespers of the Feast of All Saints (1 November). The hymnal of H, however, appears to assign it to Matins (Nocturn). It is anonymous. Its metre is rhythmical Ambrosian hymn verse (4 × 8pp). Stanzas III–VII show a tendency to rhyme aabb. For indications that they may constitute the original text of the hymn, see the commentary on lines 1–8. The melody transmitted in H may possibly be a version of Stäblein no. 158 with a deviating first line. The text is included in the hymnals of BCDHVm and the *Expositio hymnorum* of JVp.

Bibliographical references: *ICL* no. 5087; *AH* 51, 152–3 (no. 130), cf. *AH* 2, 66 (no. 80).

Apparatus to D   Latin text: 9 saeculi] *on erasure, possibly by another hand*; 13 *one letter erased after* angelici; 24 abluant] n *erased*; 27 vota] a *erased and* is *written over it, probably by another hand*.

BVmCJVpH   Heading: ymnus in festivitate omnium sanctorum *B, no rubric Vmp,* HYMNUS IN NATALE OMNIUM SANCTORUM *C,* FESTIVA SECLIS COLITUR *J,* YMNUS IN FESTUM OMNIUM SANCTORUM *H;* 1 COLITUR] collitur, *second* l *erased*

H; 3 regnant] regnat C; 7 -que supplices] que supplic *on erasure by another hand* H; 9 saeculi] i *on erasure of* o H; 10 redemptis] redemtor B; subveni] subvenis B; 15 &] ac CJVp; 16 precentur] precemur JVp *(but the gloss may well render* precentur); 18 claviger] clavier H; æthereus] aethereis H; 23 virginalis] virginalts Vm; 24 peccatis] i *on erasure* H; abluant absolvant J; 27 vota] votis BCJVpH; 29 gloria] *om.* C; 30–2 *om.* CH; 31– 2 *om.* B; 31 simul] *om.* Vp; 32 amen] *om.* JVp.

Commentary   Latin: 1–8 *These stanzas are only attested by* AH *in English sources (mostly the Anglo-Saxon ones) and a couple of French ones.* 14 *Cf.* cuneus prophetarum *I Sam.* X.10. 15 AH *reads* ac *like* CJVp, *but* et *is also attested on the Continent.* 26 *For* cives *cf.* Hy 48/10–11. 27 votis, *the altered reading in* D, *agrees with* BCJVpH *and the gloss.* vota *is shared with* Vm. Old English: 11 *For* eaþa *read* eala; *it may be due to following* ðu. 27 benum *glosses the reading of* BCJVpH.

99

YMNUS AD NOCTURNAM

ó
eala þu crist   alysend   ealra *þinga
I   CHRISTE, REDEMPTOR OMNIUM,

geheald   þine   þenas
conserva tuos famulos

eadiges   æfre   mædenes
beatae semper virginis

*glæd   halgum benum
placatus sanctis precibus.   4

eadige eac swilce werode
II   Beata quoque agmina

heofonlicra   gasta
caelestium spirituum,

forðgewitene andwyrde
preterita, presentia,

towearde yfelu adræfað
[35v] futura mala pellite.   8

*scopas þæs ecan deman
III   Vates aeterni iudicis

7 apostolas   drihtnes
apostolique domini,

eadmodlice   we biddað
suppliciter exposcimus

361

beon gehælede eowrum benum
salvari   vestris precibus.   12

þrowæres   godes æþelan
IV   Martyres dei   incliti

7 andetteras scinende
confessores lucidi,

eowrum benum
vestris orationibus

us   underfoþ on heofonlicum þingum
nos ferte   in cęlestibus.   16

werod   haligra   mædena
V   Chorus sanctarum virginum

7 muneca   ealra
monachorumque omnium,

samod mid halgum eallum
simul cum sanctis omnibus

yfenlyttan cristes   doþ
consortes Christi facite.   20

þeode   afersiaþ geleaflease
VI   Gentem auferte perfidam

gelefendra   of gemærum
credentium de finibus,

þæt cristes   lofu   neadwise
ut Christi laudes debitas

we gelæstan   glædlice
persolvamus alacriter.   24

wuldor fæder þam uncænnedan
VII   Gloria patri ingenito

7 his   ancænnedan suna
eiusque unigenito

samod mid þam halgan gaste
una cum sancto   spiritu

on ece   worulda
in sempiterna secula.   28

I Christ, redeemer of all men, preserve your servants, placated by the
holy prayers of the perpetual virgin, blessed Mary.

II You also, blessed troops of celestial spirits, dispel evils past, present
and to come.

III You prophets of the eternal judge and you apostles of the Lord, humbly we beg to be saved by means of your prayers.

IV You renowned martyrs of God and resplendent confessors, convey us into the heavenly regions by your appeals.

V You choir of holy virgins and of all monks, let us be partakers in Christ together with all the saints.

VI Move the heathen infidels away from the borders of the faithful so that we may gladly offer up the praise we owe to Christ.

VII Glory be to the Father, who was not begotten, and to his only-begotten Son together with the Holy Ghost in eternity.

This hymn was sung on All Saints' Day (1 November). In the Canterbury Hymnal it is assigned to Matins (Nocturn), in the Winchester Hymnal to Lauds, in H to Vespers. It is anonymous and written in rhythmical Ambrosian hymn verse (4 × 8pp). The melody transmitted in H remains unidentified, although the beginning may have resembled Stäblein no. 53. The text is included in the hymnals of BCDHVm and the *Expositio hymnorum* of JVp. D is glossed in Latin.

Bibliographical references: *ICL* no. 2220; *AH* 51, 150–1 (no. 129), cf. *AH* 2, 66 (no. 81).

Apparatus to D   Latin text: 12 salvari] salvare, e *expunged*, i *interlined above*; 13 incliti] c *altered from a minim*; 14 que *interlined above after* confessores *by another hand*.
    Old English gloss: 21 afersiaþ] *a small erasure between* a *and* f.
    Latin glosses: *There are syntactical glosses (the 'paving letters' type) to the whole hymn except for the doxology, stanza VII. There are also a prose version of the first two lines in the margin and a series of verbal glosses, both interlinear and marginal, all by* D_4.
    The hymn re-arranged according to the suggestions given in the syntactical glosses is as following – the re-arrangement proceeds by stanza, starting afresh with the letter a *at the beginning of each:* I Christe, redemptor omnium, conserva tuos famulos beatae semper placatus sanctis precibus virginis. II Beata agmina caelestium spirituum, quoque pellite preterita presentia futura mala. III Vates aeterni iudicis apostolique domini, suppliciter exposcimus salvari vestris precibus. IV Incliti martyres dei confessoresque lucidi, ferte nos in celestibus vestris orationibus. V Chorus sanctarum virginum monachorumque omnium, facite consortes Christi simul cum sanctis omnibus. VI Gentem auferte perfidam de finibus credentium, ut persolvamus alacriter debitas Christi laudes.
    The marginal prose version of lines 1–2 is as follows: O Christe redémptor omnium s. fidelium / conserva i. omnes Christianos.

The verbal glosses are: 1 s. fidelium 2 s. omnes Christianos 3 s. marię 4 propiciatus 5 .s. o. vos (*agmina*) i. multitudines 6 i. angelorum 7 (*preterita*) s. & (*futura*) 8 s. & (*futura . . .* *pellite*) s. a nobis 9 s. o (*Vates*) i. Christi 11 i. precamur 13 i. testes i. nobiles 14 clari sanctitate 15 per vestras orationes 16 (*in celestibus*) s. habitaculis 17 s. o. (*Chorus*) 20 nos (*consortes*) 21 (*Gentem*) s. hereticorum. ł paganorum 22 i. christianorum 24 i. solvamus (*alacriter*) i. sine metu hostilitatis.

BVmCJVpH   Heading: ymnus ad mat, mat *corrected to* n *by erasure of a minim of* m *and* at (*Wieland does not note the erased letters*) B, *no rubric* Vmp, HYMNUS AD MATUTINUM C, CHRISTE REDEMPTOR J, AD VESPERAM. YMNUS H; 2 tuos] tuus C; 4 sanctis] sanctus (*abbreviated*) C; 7 preterita] preterrita C; 9 iudicis] iudices C; 13 incliti] *second* i *altered by erasure from* o C; 14 confessores] confessoresque BVmCJVpH; 15 *om.* B; 23 Christi] christo Vm, christo *with* i *interlined above by* H₄ H; 25–8 *om.* JVp; 26–8 *om.* C; 27 una] *om.* H; 28 BH *add* amen.

Commentary   Latin: *It is not clear why this comparatively straightforward hymn should merit the extraordinary amount of glossing in D, unless this is a beginners' exercise. The syntactical glosses especially seem quite futile.* 14 que, *omitted in D, but added by the corrector, is presupposed by the gloss.* 20 Cf. *divinae consortes naturae II Pet. I.4.* 21 *Among the paving letters in D a and b, which would presumably have moved* auferte *in front of* Gentem *have been omitted.* Old English: 1 þinga *is a badly chosen prop word,* manna *would have been better. Cf. the Latin gloss* fidelium. 4 glæd, *habitually used to render* placatus, *seems especially inappropriate when the instrument which 'placates' is specified* (precibus). 9 *One of the two possible meanings of* vates, *'poets'* (scopas) *is inappropriate here.* 14 7 *glosses the accidentally om.* que.

100

YMNUS AD MATUTINAM

       ó
  ealra *þinga eala þu crist   samod þinra
I OMNIUM,   CHRISTE,   pariter tuorum

  freols halgena   we wurþiað biddende
  festa sanctorum   colimus precantes

  þas þe þa ðe nu   geearnedon beon geþeodde
  hos, tibi qui iam   meruere iungi,

  ure   gescyldan
  nostra tueri.   4

  bendas ure   scylda   *hi tolysan
II Vincla nostrorum   scelerum resolve.

	leohte mihta	folce gefrætewion	
	Luce virtutum	populos adornent.	
	heo becepan us	arfæstnyssa anre	
	Vindicent nobis	pietate sola	
	ricu heofonlice		
	regna superna,		8

	þæt þam lifes	fúrlang lareowes	
III	ut quibus vitę	stadium magistri	
	bið aúrnen þissera	benum eadigum	
	curritur, horum	precibus beatis	
	scinendum heofones	bosme gelogode [beon]	
	fulgido cęli	gremio locemur	
	on ecum life		
	perpete vita.		12

	wuldor þære halgan	arfæstlice þrynnysse	
IV	Gloriam sanctę	pie trinitati	
	mænigu swege	singe 7 *wealce	
	turba persultet,	canat & resolvat,	
	seo wunigende rixaþ	god án on ælcere	
	quę manens regnat	deus unus omni	
	tide worulde		
	[36r] tempore saecli.		16

amen

I Christ, we celebrate the feast of all your saints together and pray that they who have already earned that they should join you may watch over our affairs.

II Loosen the chains of our crimes. May they, the saints, adorn the nations by the light of their miraculous power. May they claim the celestial realms for us by their kindness alone

III so that by the prayers of those with the help of whom the course of the race of life is run, the race ordained by the teacher (*other manuscripts*: of those with the help of whose teaching the race of life is run), we may be placed in the shining bosom of heaven in eternal life.

IV May the assembly piously chant and sing glory to the Holy Trinity and duly yield it (*other manuscripts*: repeat it), to the Trinity which rules as one God unchangingly for all time in this world.

This hymn was sung at the feast of All Saints (1 November). In the Canterbury Hymnal and H it is assigned to Lauds, in the Winchester Hymnal to Matins (Nocturn). It is anonymous and written in Sapphic stanzas. The melody transmitted in H remains unidentified. The text is included in the hymnals of BCDHVm and the *Expositio hymnorum* of JVp.

Bibliographical references: *ICL* no. 11370; *AH* 11, 61 (no. 93), cf. *AH* 2, 88 (no. 123).

Apparatus to D   Latin text: 9 magistri] *another hand adds* s, *correcting to* magistris.

BVmCJVpH   Heading: hymnus ad matutinum B, *no rubric* Vmp, HYMNUS AD NOCTURNUM C, OMNIUM CHRISTE J, YMNUS AD MATUTINAM H; 3 hos] nos CH; qui iam] quia H; 5 resolve] resolvant BJVpH; 6 populos] populus C, populs *(usually expanded to* populis*)* Vm; adornent] adornant BCJ, adornænt, æ *corrected to* e H; 8 superna] polorum H; 9 Ut] Et BJ; magistri] magistris BVmJVp; 10 curritur] currit Vm; 11 fulgido] fulgendo Vm; gremio] o *on erasure, by another hand* C; locemur] lucemur C; 12 vita] vitam C; 13 trinitati] trinitatis C; 14 persultet] resultet B, persultat C; resolvat] revolvat BCJVpH; 15 regnat] regna C; 16 amen] *om.* VmCJVp.

Commentary   Latin: 5 AH *reads* resolvant. 8 AH *reads* regna polorum *like* H, *attesting* regna superna *for one continental manuscript.* 9–10 *Cf. I Cor. IX.24–6.* 14 AH *reads* resultet, *noting* persultet *twice and* resultat *once among continental variant readings.* AH *also reads* revolvat. Old English: 1 þinga *is superfluous, as* omnium *is not used as a noun.* 5 hi tolysan *glosses* BJVpH*'s variant.* 14 wealce *renders the reading of* BCJVpH.

101

YMNUS IN NATALE SANCTI MARTINI EPISCOPI

I   MARTINE, CONFESSOR dei
valens vigore spiritus,
carnis fatescens artubus,
mortis futurę prescius,   4

II   qui pace Christi affluens,
in unitate spiritus
divisa membra æcclesię
paci reformans unice,   8

III   quem vita fert probabilem,
      quem mors cruenta non ledet,
      qui callidi versutias
      in mortis hora derogat,   12

IV   haec plebs fide promptissima
      tui diei gaudia
      votis colit fidelibus.
      Adesto mitis omnibus.   16

V   Per te quies sit temporum,
      vitae detur solacium,
      pacis redundet commodum,
      sedetur omne scandalum,   20

VI   ut caritatis gratia
      sic affluamus spiritu,
      quo corde cum suspiriis
      Christum sequamur intimis.   24

      Deo patri sit gloria

I Martin, confessor of God strong with the force of the spirit, you who were aware of coming death, when you grew weary in your fleshly limbs,

II you who are rich in the peace of Christ, you who reunited the members of the church, who were divided against each other, together in one peace, in oneness of the spirit,

III you whom life showed to be praiseworthy, whom cruel death could not harm, who scorned the tricks of the sly one in the hour of death,

IV this crowd most readily in its faith celebrates the joyful occasion of your birthday with faithful prayers. Be with them all in your gentleness.

V May tranquillity prevail in these times by your agency, may alleviation of life be conferred by you, may the advantages of peace abound, may all scandal be silenced

VI in order that by the grace of charity we may overflow with the spirit so that we follow Christ with sighs felt from the bottom of our heart.

This hymn is for the feast of St Martin (11 November). The collectar in H assigns it to Matins. The hymn is anonymous and written in Ambrosian iambic dimeter with some irregularities. No melody has been transmitted in the Anglo-Saxon manuscripts. The text is found only in B and D; the hymnal in H has a different hymn for St Martin, Hy 145.

Bibliographical references: *ICL* no. 9329; *AH* 27, 218–19 (no. 154).

B   Heading: in festivitate sancti martini; 1 CONFESSOR] consessor; 3 fatescens] fatiscens; 5 pace Christi affluens] in pace æcclesiæ; 21 ut] Et; 25 Deo] eo.

Commentary   *The earliest Life of St Martin is by Sulpicius Severus (Sulpice Sévère, Vie de St. Martin, ed. J. Fontaine, SChr 133–5 (Paris, 1967–9)).*

102

    blissige   heofon   mid lofum
I EXULTET CĘLUM LAUDIBUS,

    swege   eorðe mid gefeanum
  resultet terra gaudiis:

    þara apostola   wuldor
  apostolorum gloriam

    halige *singan   symbelnyssa
  sacra canunt sollempnia.   4

    ge   worulde rihtwise deman
II Vos saecli iusti   iudices

       7 soþa middaneardes leohta
  [36v] & vera mundi   lumina,

    mid gewilnungum we biddaþ heortena
  votis   precamur cordium,

    gehyrað bena   eadmoddra
  audite preces supplicum.   8

    s.ó sancti apostoli
    ge þe   heofon mid worde beclysaþ
III Qui   cęlum verbo   clauditis

    7 scettelsas his   ge tolysaþ
  serasque eius solvitis,

    us   fram sennum   eallum
  nos a   peccatis omnibus

unbindaþ mid hæse we biddaþ
solvite iussu, quesumus.   12

þæra   *mid bebode ys underþeod
IV Quorum precepto subditur

hæl 7 adl   ealra
salus & languor omnium,

ó sancti apostoli
hælað   seoce   þeawum
sanate ægros moribus

us *agyfende mihtum
nos redentes virtutibus,   16

þæt þænne se dema tobecymð
V   ut, cum iudex advenerit

crist   on ænde worulde
Christus in fine saeculi,

us ecum   gefeanum
nos sempiternis gaudiis

dó   beon wilfægene
faciat esse compotes.   20

gode fæder sy wuldor
Deo patri sit gloria

I   May heaven rejoice with songs of praise, may the earth echo it in its
    rejoicings. This sacred festival celebrates the glory of the apostles in
    song.

II O just judges over this world and true sources of light to the
    universe, we entreat you with prayers from our heart, hear the
    requests of the suppliants.

III You who can lock heaven and unlock its bolts with a word, unlock
    us from all sins by your command, we beseech you.

IV You to whose command the health and the sickness of all is subject,
    heal us, who are diseased in our moral nature, and lead us back to
    the virtues

V   so that Christ, when he arrives as judge at the end of this world, may
    let us participate in everlasting joy.

This hymn was sung at all feasts of apostles. In the Winchester Hymnal it
is assigned to Lauds, in the collectar of H to Lauds and Vespers. It is

intended for Vespers in the hymnal of H. Details of usage in the Canterbury Hymnal are uncertain. The hymn is anonymous and written in rhythmical Ambrosian hymn verse (4 × 8pp). The melody transmitted in H agrees with Stäblein no. 114_3 with two deviations paralleled in versions 114_1 and 114_2. The text is included in the hymnals of BCDHVm and the *Expositio hymnorum* of JVp.

Bibliographical references: *ICL* no. 4866; *AH* 51, 125–6 (no. 108), cf. *AH* 2, 74 (no. 94).

Apparatus to D   Latin text: Heading: *no rubric, but there is two lines' space for one*; 13 subditur] b *on erasure.*

BVmCJVpH   Heading: hymnus in sollempnitate omnium apostolorum B, *no rubric* Vmp, HYMNUS AD MATUTINUM C, EXULTET CELUM J, YMNUS IN NATALE OMNIUM APOSTOLORUM AD VESPERAM H; 2 gaudiis] *om.* J; 3 apostolorum] apostolum B; gloriam] gloria BVmCJVp; 4 canunt] canant JVp; 5 s *erased after* iusti C; 11 a peccatis] appecatis C; 12 solvite] audite Vp; 13 Quorum precepto] *om.* Vp; 14 omnium] hominum BCJ; 16 redentes] reddentes VmCVp; 17 cum] cu H; 18 fine] finem Vp; 19 sempiternis gaudiis] sempiterni gaudii BH; 21 *om.* JVp, C *omits* sit gloria.

Commentary   Latin: 3 AH *attests* gloria *also for continental manuscripts.* 4 AH *reads* canant, *attesting* canunt *for the Continent as well.* 6 Cf. *Hy 103/8.* 9 Cf. *Hy 87/12.* 13–14 Cf. Et convocatis duodecim discipulis suis dedit illis potestatem spirituum inmundorum ut ... curarent omnem languorem *Matt. X.1, cf. also Luke IX.1.* 19 AH *reads* sempiterni gaudii *like BCH, attesting* sempiternis gaudiis *also for the Continent.* Old English: 4 singan *glosses the reading of* JVp. 13 *The gloss* mid bebode *mistakes the dat. for an abl.*

103

ITEM YMNUS

ó
ece   cristes   lac
I   Æterna Christi munera

apostola   wuldor
apostolorum gloria

lofu   singende   neadwise
laudes canentes debitas

mid bliþum uton singan modum
lætis   canamus mentibus.   4

gelaþunga   ealdres
II   Ǽcclesiarum principis

gewinnes sigorlice   heretogan
belli   triumphales duces,

þære heofonlican healle cempan
caelestis   aulę milites

7 soþe middaneardes leohta
& vera mundi   lumina.   8

estfull   halgena   geleafa
III   Devota sanctorum fides,

unoferswiþed hiht gelefendra
invicta   spes credentium,

fullfremed cristes   soþlufu
perfecta Christi caritas

middaneardes sigorað   ealdor
mundi   triumphat principem.   12

on þisum fæderlic   wuldor
IV   In his   paterna gloria,

on þisum willa   gastes
in his   voluntas spiritus,

blissað   on þisum suna
exultat in his   filius,

heofon [is] gefelled mid *gefeanum
celum repletur   gaudio.   16

          ó
þe nu   eala ðu alysend   we biddað
V   Te nunc,   redemptor, quesumus,

þæt on heora gefyrrædene
ut ipsorum consortio

þu geþeode biddende þeowtlingas
iungas   precantes servulos

on ece   worulde
in sempiterna secula.   20

            amen

I Let us sing with joyous hearts of the eternal gifts of Christ, as in (*H:* as of) the glory of the apostles and thus sing the songs of praise we owe them.

II They are the princes of the branches of the church, the triumphant leaders in battle, soldiers of the celestial court and true sources of light in the world.

III The devoted faith of the saints, the unconquered hope of the believers and the perfect love of Christ triumph over the prince of this world.

IV In these the glory of the Father exults, in these the will of the Spirit exults, in these the Son exults and heaven is filled with joy.

V We beseech you now, redeemer, to join the humble servants praying to you to their fellowship forever in eternity.

This adaptation of Hy 117 for apostles was sung on all feasts of apostles. In the hymnal of H it is assigned to Lauds, which may apply equally to the two Canterbury Hymnal manuscripts DV, but is by no means certain. Neither the Winchester Hymnal nor the collectar in H have Hy 103, but the collectar in H has a shorter adaptation of Hy 117 for evangelists and confessors, *Devota sanctorum* (Hy 117, stanzas VI–VIII = Hy 103, stanzas III–V). Hy 117 is probably by St Ambrose and is written in Ambrosian iambic dimeter. The melody transmitted for Hy 103 in H seems to be a version of Stäblein no. 115 closest to 115₄. The text is included in the hymnals of DHVm. Vp's *Expositio hymnorum* conflates Hy 117 with its adaptation Hy 103; see below under Hy 117.

Bibliographical references (for Hy 117): *ICL* no. 411, *AH* 50, 19–20 (no. 17), cf. *AH* 2, 74–5 (no. 95); Bulst 52 and 185 (II, 14), Walpole no. 15. (The editions note readings of Hy 103 in their critical apparatus or commentary.)

VmH   Heading: *no rubric Vm*, YMNUS AD MATUTINAM *H*; 1 ÆTERNA] Aterna *Vm*; 2 gloria] gloriam *H*; 5 principis] principes *VmH*; 7 caelestis] celestes *H*; 14 spiritus] filiu *Vm*; 15 filius] filium *H*; 16 gaudio] gaudiis *H*; 18 ipsorum] illorum *H*; 20 sempiterna] sempterna *H*; amen] *om. Vm.*

Commentary   Latin: *For the whole hymn cf. Hy 117, the original version for martyrs.* 2 gloria, *the reading of DVm, does not appear to be attested on the Continent, according to AH and*

Bulst. 5 principis *in D may be purely scribal and is certainly not original, cf. Hy 117/5.* 18 *Bulst notes both* ipsorum *and* illorum. Old English: 16 *The auxiliary is missing.* gefeanum *glosses the reading of H (cf. also Hy 117/28).*

104₁

DE SANCTO PETRO APOSTOLO

		ó			
	nu	eala þu gode hyrde		mildheort underfoh	
I	IAM	BONE PASTOR,	[37r] Petre,	clemens accipe	

behát biddendra	7 senne	bendas	
vota precantum	& peccati	vincula	

tolys þe	anwealde	betæhtum
resolve tibi	potestate	tradita,

mid þam eallum	heofonan	mid worde þu beclyst þu geopenas		
qua	cunctis celum	verbo	claudis, aperis.	4

I Now, good shepherd Peter, receive indulgently the requests of those who pray to you and loosen the bonds of sin by the power that was given to you and by which you either close or open heaven to all with a word.

This is the first of a series of alternative first stanzas for 104₂ adapting a hymn for apostles to the feasts of individual apostles. In combination with 104₂ this stanza was sung on the feasts of St Peter, presumably at Vespers except on the Nativity of Peter and Paul (29 June), when its place was taken by Hy 87, as in H's collectar. While the rubrics in the hymnals are quite unspecific, the instructions in the collectar are quite complex. Hy 104 is to be sung at Vespers of the Octave of feasts of apostles, Matins of the Octave of the Nativity of Peter and Paul, and at Matins and Vespers of Vincula Petri (1 August). It is also offered as an alternative possibility for Compline and Matins of the Nativity of Peter and Paul. Another feast of St Peter in the Anglo-Saxon liturgical calendar is Cathedra Petri (1 January), but the first version of the hymn in the hymnal in H seems intended for a feast in March. The only date in the Exeter calendar (Wormald, *English Calendars*, no. 7) that approximately fits is the Eastern one for Cathedra Petri on 22 February. Hy 104₁ is taken from Hy 87 and the melody to which Hy 104$_1$ and 104$_2$ were sung agrees with that of Hy 87, i.e. a version of Stäblein no. 152 close to 152$_2$. It is transmitted in H. The text of Hy 104$_1$ is included only in the hymnals of BDH; the other manuscripts avoid repetition of the stanza, since it was given in the context of Hy 87. H, however, includes Hy 104$_1$ twice, a version by scribe H$_1$ and one by scribe H$_4$.

Bibliographical references: *ICL* no. 1439; *AH* 51, 216–19 (no. 188), Walpole no. 126.

BH$_1$H$_4$ Heading: hymnus de sancto Petro apostolo *B, no rubric H$_1$,* YMNUS DE SANCTE PETRE APOSTOLORUM PRINCIPE *H$_4$;* PASTOR] o *on erasure B;* 3 resolve] *so H$_1$ (Dewick wrongly reads* resolvi); 4 *H$_1$ adds* Sit trinitati sempiterna gloria.

Commentary   Latin: *See under the source, Hy 87. The ultimate sources for the lives of the twelve apostles addressed in the Hy 104$_1$ and Hy 105–15 (followed in each case by Hy 104$_2$) are, apart from the Bible, the Acta Apostolorum Apocrypha, ed. Lipsius and Bonnet. Old English: 4 geopenas could be a Kentish archaicism (SB §356, n. 1), but is probably a slip.*

104$_2$

	ó			
	getiþa	eala þu crist	worulda	drihten
I	*Anne,	Christe,	seculorum domine,	
	us	*geond þissera	þe leofa geearnunga	
	nobis per	horum	tibi cara merita,	
	þæt þe we þe ætforan		hefylice agyltan	
	ut, quę te coram		graviter deliquimus,	
	þissera	beon tolysede	mid wuldorfullum benum	
	horum	solvantur	gloriosis	precibus.	4

	ó			
	gehæl	eala þu alysend	gescæft þin æþele	
II	Salva,	redemptor,	plasma tuum nobile	
	geinsegelod mid halgum		andwlitan þines leohte	
	signatum sancto		vultus tui lumine	
	ne þu totoran beon		ne geþafige mid facne deofla	
	nec lacerari		sinas fraude demonum,	

for　þi　deaþes　　*þu tolysdesd wurð
propter quod mortis　　exsolvisti　pretium.　　　　8

　　besariga hæftlingas　　beon þine þeowtlingas
III　Dole　captivos　　esse tuos servulos,

　　tolys　scyldige　　fótcopsede　uparær
　　absolve reos,　　compeditos erige

　　7　þa þe ðu mid blode　　þu alysdest mid agenum
　　et, quos　cruore　　redemisti proprio,

　　　　ó
　　cyng eala þu gode mid þe　　do blissigan ecelice
　　rex　　bone,　tecum　　fac gaudere perpetim.　　　12

　　　　ó
　　sy þe　eala þu hælend　　þu gebletsoda drihten
IV　Sit tibi,　　Iesu,　　benedicte　domine,

　　wuldor miht　　wurðment 7　cynedom
　　gloria, virtus,　　honor　& imperium

　　samod mid　fæder　　7 þam halgan frofergaste
　　una　cum patre　　sanctoque　paraclito,

　　mid þam　*þu rixast　　god ær　worulde
　　cum quibus　regna*t*　　deus ante secula.　　　16

　　　　　　　　　amen

I Grant us, Christ, lord of ages, by the merits of these men, which are dear to you, that that in which we sinned deeply in your eyes may be redeemed by their glorious prayers.

II Creator, save your noble work, which bears the imprint of the light of your holy face, and do not let that be torn apart by the deceit of demons for the sake of which you paid the price of death.

III Regret that your humble servants are captive, acquit the guilty, lift up those who are fettered and let those rejoice with you forever whom you redeemed with your own blood, good king.

IV Glory, might, honour and authority be to you, Jesus, blessed lord, together with the Father and the Holy Spirit. With these he has reigned as God since before the beginning of the world.

This hymn was in use for the feasts of each of the apostles, preceded respectively by an appropriate first stanza selected from among Hy 104$_1$ and 105–16. In the Winchester Hymnal this series of hymns was presumably in use for Vespers except on the Nativity of Peter and Paul. In H it may be for Vespers or Matins – hymnal and collectar diverge at these feasts. The impression the collectar gives that Hy 104_2 was also used separately is probably incorrect. Details of usage in the Canterbury Hymnal are uncertain. The metre agrees with that of Hy 87, from which Hy 104_1 and Hy 105 are taken, i.e. rhythmical iambic trimeter $(4 \times (5p+7pp))$. The melody also agrees with Hy 87, see above under 104_1. The text is included in the hymnals of BCDHVm and the *Expositio hymnorum* of JVp.

Bibliographical references: *ICL* no. 843; *AH* 51, 121–5 (no. 107, includes Hy 104_2 and 106–16).

Apparatus to D   Latin text: 16 regnat] regnas, s *on erasure, probably by another hand.*
Old English gloss: 4 tolysede] o *on erasure.*

BVmCJVpH   Heading: *no rubric BVmJVp,* HYMNUS IN NATALE OMNIUM APOSTOLORUM C, DE APOSTOLORUM H; 1–15 *up to* cum *apparently on erasure in Vm;* 1 Anne] Annue *BVmCJVpH;* 2 horum] huius *H;* cara] caro, o *on erasure by another hand and in its turn altered to* a *C;* 4 horum] huius *H;* solvantur] salvantur *BH,* o *by another hand, probably over an erased* a *C;* 5 nobile] noboles, s *expunged C;* 9 Dole] Doli, i *on erasure B;* 13 Iesu] IESU *C;* 15 *end of apparent erasure in Vm after* una cum; 16 regnat] regnas *VmCJVpH; BCJVp omit* amen.

Commentary   Latin: 1 *The omission of* u *in D is due to haplography with the minims of nn.* 2–4 *H's* huius *is also attested for the Continent by AH.* 10 *Cf.* Dominus solvit conpeditos, Dominus inluminat caecos, Dominus erigit adlisos *Ps. CXLV.7–8.* 16 *D presumably agreed with B originally. The corrector brings the lemma into line with the gloss and the reading of VmCJVpH. AH also reads* regnas. *Old English:* 2 geond *renders the wrong meaning of* per *and should read* þurh. 8 tolysdesd *may represent one of the spellings with* d *for* t *(see above, p. 76) or dittography of* sd. *It glosses a common meaning of* exsolvere, *'loosen, free', which is inappropriate in this context.* 11 *The pronoun appears twice; once with the verb and once in what was apparently felt to be the proper (idiomatic) Old English position in the sentence.* 16 þu rixast *glosses the reading of VmCJVpH.*

105

DE SANCTO PAULO APOSTOLO

        ó
    lareow   eala þu æþele   þeawas ty
I DOCTOR   EGREGIE,   PAULE, mores instrue

7 mode	heofonan	us	gebringan	hoga
& mente	polum	nos	transferre	satage,
oþþæt	fullfremed	sy	forgyfen fullicor	
donec *perfectus		largiatur plenius		
aidlod		þæt we be dæle doþ		
evacuat*a*,		quod ex parte gerimus.		4

Annue, Christe

1 Excellent teacher Paul, teach us morals and strive to carry us in spirit to heaven until the perfect one shall give more fully that which is made vain, because we do it imperfectly (*other manuscripts:* against that time when that which is perfect shall be granted more fully and that which we do imperfectly shall be superseded).

This stanza from Hy 87 was used together with Hy 104$_2$ on feasts of St Paul; see above under Hy 104$_2$ for details. H's collectar has it for Nocturn and Vespers of the *Nativitas Pauli*. Another version in H, H$_1$, which does not appear to continue with Hy 104$_2$, is clearly for the Conversio Pauli (25 January). The melody transmitted in H is the same as for Hy 104 with only very minor differences, as is to be expected. The text is included in the hymnals of BDH. The other manuscripts avoid the repetition of the stanza from Hy 87. H, as has already been mentioned, contains two versions.

Bibliographical references (for Hy 87): *ICL* no. 1439; *AH* 51, 216–19 (no. 188), Walpole no. 126.

Apparatus to D   Latin text: 4 evacuata] evacuato, o *by another hand on erasure.*

BH$_1$H$_2$ Heading: hymnus de sancto Paulo apostolo *B, no rubric H$_1$,* DE SANCTE PAULO *H;* 2 polum] polo *B;* 3 perfectus] perfectum *BH$_1$H$_2$;* 4 evacuata] evacuato *H$_1$H$_2$;* 5 *H$_1$* reads: Sit trinitati sempiterna gloria / honor potestas atque iubilatio.

Commentary   Latin: *This is Hy 87/13–16. It shares the problematical readings of that stanza in the third and fourth line. 4 D probably agreed with B, but cf. Hy 87/15. evacuato agrees with H$_1$H$_2$ and* AH.

106

DE SANCTO ANDREA APOSTOLO

```
        ó
        eala              þu arfæsta      halgena         liþesta
I       ANDREAS PIE,                      SANCTORUM mitissime,

        begyt    urum    gedweldum forgyfenysse
        optine nostris   erratibus veniam

7       þa ðe beoð       gehefegode      mid berþene synne
        &, qui  gra[37v]vamur            sarcina     peccaminum,

        upahefe  mid þinum    þingrædenum
        subleva tuis          intercessionibus.                      4
```

Annue, Christe

I Pious Andrew, most gentle of saints, obtain forgiveness for our errors
and lift us up by your repeated intercession, who are weighed down
by the burden of our sins.

This stanza was combined with Hy 104$_2$ to be sung on the feast of St
Andrew (30 November), see above under Hy 104$_2$. The collectar in H
prescribes it for First Vespers and Matins (Nocturn). The usage of the
Canterbury Hymnal at this feast must have been affected by the
availability of Hy 35, but the details are not clear. Naturally the stanza's
metre agrees with that of 104$_2$ and the melody transmitted in H is the
same as Hy 104 with only very minor differences. The text is included in
the hymnals of BCDHVm and the *Expositio Hymnorum* of JVp.

Bibliographical references: *ICL* no. 755; *AH* 51, 121–5 (no. 107), cf. *AH*
2, 71 (no. 90).

BVmCJVpH   Heading: hymnus de sancto andrea B, *no rubric* Vmp, HYMNUS DE
SANCTE ANDREE APOSTOLE C, ANDREA PIE J, DE S. ANDREE APOSTOLI H; 1
ANDREAS *last letter erased* Vm, ANDREA C; 2 erratibus] errantibus CJ, *one letter erased in
front of* t H; 5 *om.* VmJVp; B *omits* Christe. Annue] nnue C.

Commentary   Latin: 1 AH *reads* Andrea.

107

DE SANCTO IOHANNE APOSTOLO

twifealdre þære heofonlican   healle   leohtfatu
1   BINA   CẸLESTIS   AULE LUMInaria,

eac swilce   se drihtwurðe
Iacobe necnon   Iohannes theologe,

biddað us   forgyfennysse biddendum
poscite nobis   veniam   rogantibus,

þa   com   crist   togyfes sellan earmingum
quam venit Christus   gratis dare miseris.   4

Annue, Christe

1 You two lamps in the celestial palace, Jacob and John the theologian, request that forgiveness for us who entreat for it which Christ came to give freely to the wretched.

This was combined with Hy 104_2 and sung on the feasts of St James the Elder (25 July) and St John (27 December). The stanza is included in the hymnals of BCDHVm and the *Expositio hymnorum* of JVp. For further details see under Hy 104_2 (pp. 375–6).

BVmCJVpH   Heading: de sancto iacobo et iohanne *B, no rubric Vmp*, HYMNUS DE SANCT... (*last letter erased, probably* E) IACOBE ATQUE IOHANNI *C*, BINA CELESTIS *J*, DE S. IACOBI APOSTOLI *H*; 2 theologe] theolege *H*; 4 quam] qua, a *on erasure by another hand C*; 5 *om. VmJVp. B omits* Christe. *C adds:* require unius apostoli.

Commentary   Latin: 5 *The addition in C directs the user to Hy* 104_2.

108

DE SANCTO *IACOBE

ó
eala   þu rihtwise   hælendes broðer drihtnes
1   IACOBE IUSTE,   Iesu   frater domini,

sy þe   arfæst   ofer   us   besargung
sit tibi pia   super nos compassio,

	þa þe scyldige dede	modig	idel gelp	
	quos reos facit	superba iactantia		

	7 befylde	middaneardes wrænnys		
	atque foedavit	mundi	petulantia.	4

Annue, Christe

1 Just Jacob, brother of Christ the Lord, have pity on us in your charity, on us whom arrogant boastfulness has made guilty and whom the shamelessness of the world has besmirched.

This stanza was combined with Hy 104_2 and sung at the feast of St James the Younger (1 June). It is included in the hymnals of BCDHVm and the *Expositio hymnorum* of JVp. For further details see under Hy 104_2 (pp. 375–6).

Apparatus to D Latin text: 3 facit] a *altered to æ and expunged, apparently as an involved way of correcting to e; by* D_1 *or another hand?*

   BVmCJVpH Heading: de sancto iacobo fratre domini *B, no rubric Vmp,* HYMNUS DE SANCT... IACOB... AP., *the final letter of* SANCT *and* IACOB *erased C,* IACOBE IUSTE *J,* DE SANCTE IACOBE APOSTOLI *H;* 2 pia] p *on erasure of 1–2 letters C;* 3 facit] fecit *BVmCJVpH;* 4 foedavit] fedamur *H;* 5 *om.* VmJVp.

Commentary Latin: 1 *Cf.* Iacobum fratrem Domini *Gal. I.19.* 3 *The correction in D agrees with* BVmCJVpH. AH *reads* fecit, *but notes* facit *as a variant reading in continental manuscripts.* Old English: 3 dede *presumably glosses* fecit *as in* BVmCJVpH *and by the corrector in D; however, this glossator might have glossed* facit *the same way, taking it as a historic present.*

109

DE SANCTO BARTHOLOME*O*

	6		
		heofones tungel	ænlic
1	BARTHOLOMEÆ,	CÆLI SIDUS	aureum
	þusend siþan ofer	þære sunnan leoman scinende	
	milies supra	solis	iubar radians,
	uparèr mod	ure	heofonan *drefende
	erige mentes	nostras polo	turbidas

<table>
<tr><td>7 adlige   ure</td><td>gehæl ingehyd</td><td></td></tr>
<tr><td>ægrasque nostras</td><td>sana conscientias.</td><td>4</td></tr>
</table>

Annue, Christe

1 Bartholomew, golden star in the sky that shines a thousand times brighter than the rays of the sun, raise our troubled minds up to heaven and heal our sick conscience.

This stanza was combined with Hy 104_2 and sung at the feast of St Bartholomew (24 August). The stanza is included in the hymnals of BDHVm and the *Expositio hymnorum* in JVp. It has been erased in C and replaced by a more closely written version followed by part of Hy 104_2. For further details see under Hy 104_2 (pp. 375–6).

BVmJVpH   Heading: de sancto Bartholomeae *B, no rubric Vmp,* BARTHOLOMEAE *J,* DE SANCTE BART *followed by abbreviation mark H;* 1 BARTHOLOMEÆ Bartholomeus *B;* 2 milies] miles *B;* radians] iradians *J (not mentioned by Gneuss),* radiens *H;* 4 -que] *om. in JVp (but the gloss to it extant);* 5 *om. VmJVp; B adds:* seculorum domine.

Commentary   Latin: Heading: *In D the name is abbreviated as* BARTHOLOM *and abbreviation mark. Considering the rubric in B and the rubrics of DBCH to Hy 110, it is entirely possible that this stands for* BARTHOLOMEE *or even* BARTHOLOMEI. *The situation in H is similar.* 2 B's miles *is attested twice in continental manuscripts according to* AH. Old English: 3 *Instead of* drefende *the passive participle,* gedrefed, *is required.*

110

DE SANCTO *MATHEAE

<table>
<tr><td>ó</td><td></td><td></td><td></td></tr>
<tr><td>eala   þu halige</td><td>mid twifealdre þeonde gyfe</td><td></td></tr>
<tr><td>1   MATHEE SANCTE,</td><td>BINO   pollens munere,</td><td></td></tr>
<tr><td>mid singalum hælend þinge benum</td><td></td><td></td></tr>
<tr><td>sedulis   Iesum interpella questibus,</td><td></td><td></td></tr>
<tr><td>þæt us on *middanearde</td><td>he begeme gedrefednyssum</td><td></td></tr>
<tr><td>ut nos in mundi</td><td>gubernet turbinibus,</td><td></td></tr>
<tr><td>þæt ne siþðan þæt ece</td><td>forswelge forwyrd</td><td></td></tr>
<tr><td>ne   post æternus</td><td>sorbeat interitus.</td><td>4</td></tr>
</table>

Annue, Christe

1 Saint Matthew, enriched with a double gift, press Jesus closely with requests that he may so guide us in the storms of the world that eternal perdition does not swallow us up later on.

This stanza was combined with Hy 104_2 and sung at the feast of St Matthew (21 September). It is included in the hymnals of BCDHVm and the *Expositio hymnorum* of JVp. For further details see under Hy 104_2 (pp. 375–6).

BVmCJVpH   Heading: de sancto Matheae *B, no rubric Vmp,* HYMNUS DE SANCTE MATHEI APOSTOLI *C,* MATHEE SANCTE *J,* DE SANCTE MATHEĘ *H;* 2 sedulis] sedulus *Vm;* 3 in] *om. B;* gubernet turbinibus] gurbernaturbinibus *C;* 4 post] *one letter erased in front of* st *H;* æternus] ęternos *C,* erternus *H;* sorbeat] be *damaged and illegible Vp;* 5 *om. VmJVp.* Annue] nnue *C.*

Commentary   Latin: Heading: *With the eccentric case ending of* MATHEAE *cf. BH.* Old English: 3 middanearde *should be gen.; the mistaken dat. must be due to the preceding* on.

111

DE SANCTO PHILIPPO

eadmode *we biddan   muð leohtfætes
1 PRONI ROGAMUS,   PHILIPPE, os lampadis,
arfæste *heofonlice   earan *útadræfde deman
  pias cęlestis   aures pulsa iudicis,
þæt ða *þing þe we geearnodon   he adræfe wite
  ut, quę   meremur,   repellat supplicia
7 þa þing þe we biddað   he sylle heofonlice gefean
  &, quę   precamur,   det superna gaudia.   4

Annue, Christe

1 Bowed down before you, Philip, mouth of the lamp, we ask you to assail the favourably inclined ears of the heavenly judge asking that he may withhold the punishment that we deserve and grant the celestial joys we pray for.

This stanza was combined with Hy 104_2 and sung at the feast of St Philip

(1 June). It is included in the hymnals of BCDHVm and the *Expositio hymnorum* of JVp. For further details see under Hy 104₂ (pp. 375–6).

BVmCJVpH   Heading: de sancto Philippo *B, no rubric Vmp,* HYMNUS DE SANCTI philippe *C,* PRONI ROGAMUS *J,* DE S (*with abbreviation mark*) PHILIPPI *H;* 1 PHILIPPE] philimppe *H;* 2 pias cẹlestis] *om. Vm;* pias] pia *H;* cẹlestis] caelestis, ca *and first* s *damaged and partly illegible J;* pulsa] pusa *J;* 3 ut, quẹ] atque *B;* supplicia] supplica *C;* 5 *om.* VmJVp. *B continues:* seculorum domine. *C adds:* require unius apostoli.

Commentary   Latin: 1 *Cf.* Philippus os lampadarum . . . *Isidor of Seville,* Etymologiarum sive originum libri VII. ix. 16. 5 *The addition in C directs the user towards Hy 104₂.* Old English: 1 we biddan *should be indicative.* 2 *The glossator has taken* cẹlestis *as belonging to the following* aures *instead of* iudicis. pulsa, *2 sg. of the imperative of* pulsare, *'knock', has been confused with the homophonous abl. sg. fem. of the past participle of* pellere. *3* þing *is superfluous, as this is not a nominal relative clause, but attributive to* supplicia.

112

[38r] DE SANCTO *TADDEAE

	ó		ó	
	eala þu eadige		7 eala	þu æðele
1	BEATE SIMON	ET	TADDEE	inclite,

geseoþ ure   geomrunga mid tearum
cernite nostros   gemitus cum lacrimis,

7 we þe þurh slide ł senne   geearnodon helle ł cwicsusle
quique per lapsum   *mereamur barathrum,

þurh eow heofona   we geearnian infæreld
per vos cẹlorum   mereamur aditum.   4

Annue, Christe

1 Blessed Simon and renowned Thaddaeus, take heed of our moans together with our tears and may we, who have earned hell by our fall, earn the right to enter the heavens by your agency.

This stanza was combined with Hy 104₂ and sung at the feast of St Simon and St Judas Thaddaeus (28 October). It is included in the hymnals of BCDHVm and the *Expositio hymnorum* of JVp. For further details see under Hy 104₂ (pp. 375–6).

BVmCJVpH   Heading: de sancto simone et iude *B, no rubric Vmp,* HYMNUS IN NATALE APOSTOLORUM SIMONIS ET IUDE *C,* BEATE SYMON *J,* DE SANCTE SYMON ET TADDEĘ *H;* 1 SIMON] syon *H;* TADDEE] tathee *C;* 2 gemitus] i *interlined above by the scribe on a small erasure C;* lacrimis] fletibus *BVmCJVpH;* 3 mereamur] meruimus *BVmCJVpH;* 5 *om. VmJVp; B adds:* seculorum domine.

Commentary   Latin: Heading: *With the case ending of* TADDEAE *in D cf. H.* 3 mereamur *in D is probably a mistake for* meruimus, *a dittography of* mereamur *in the following line, but note that AH reads* promeremur, *attesting* meruimus *twice for continental manuscripts.* Old English: 3 geearnodon *renders* meruimus.

113

DE SANCTO THOMA

	eala þu	*crist	*geonleohtend	sidan
I	O THOMA,	CHRISTI	PERLUSTRAtor	lateris,

þurh þa halgan   þe we biddaþ wundan
per illa sancta   te rogamus vulnera,

þa þe middaneardes ealla   adilogodon leahtras
queͤ mundi   cuncta   deluerunt crimina:

ure   scylde   adrig þinum benum
Nostros reatus   terge tuis   precibus.   4

Annue, Christe

I Thomas, you who surveyed the side of Christ, by those holy wounds, which washed away all the iniquities of the world, we entreat you: wipe away our guilt with your prayers.

This stanza was combined with Hy 104$_2$ and sung at the feast of St Thomas (21 December). It is included in the hymnals of BCDHVm and the *Expositio hymnorum* of JVp. For further details see under Hy 104$_2$ (pp. 375–6).

Apparatus to D   Latin text: 3 deluerunt] *originally abbreviated* deluer̄; *either D$_1$ or another hand afterwards added* t.

BVmCJVpH   Heading: de sancto thomae *B, no rubric Vmp,* HYMNUS DE SANCTE THOME APOSTOLE *C,* O THOMA CHRISTI *J,* DE SANCTE THOMA *H;* 3 deluerunt] diluerunt *C;* 4 reatus] reatos *H;* 5 *om. VmCJVp.*

Commentary   Latin: 1–2 *Cf. John XX.24–9.* Old English: 1 crist *should be gen.; inflection may be lacking because the over-literal rendering of* perlustrator *did not allow the glossator to make sense of its attribute.* geonleohtend *renders the components of the Latin, but* lustrare *means 'look at' as well as 'cast light on'. The gloss to Vp has the appropriate* sceawiend (*J has* sceawian*).*

114

DE SANCTO MATHIA

ó
eala   þu rihtwise   on twelftum   cynesetle
I   MATHIA IUSTE,   DUODENO solio

sittende   mid hlote   us   fram eallum bendum
residens sorte,   nos a   cuntis nexibus

tolys senne   *soþlice leohtes gefeanum
solve peccati,   vere lucis gaudiis

*on þam we brucan   þinum halgum benum
quo   perfruamur   tuis   sanctis precibus.   4

Annue, Christe

I Just Matthias, you who took your seat on the twelfth throne by lot, release us from all the bonds of sin so that by your holy prayers we may enjoy the happiness of the true light.

This stanza was combined with Hy 104_2 and sung at the feast of St Matthias (24 February). It is included in the hymnals of CDHVm and the *Expositio hymnorum* of JVp. For further details see under Hy 104_2 (pp. 375–6).

Apparatus to D   Latin text: 2 *The punctuation of the half-verse after* sorte *is missing, although it does not coincide with the end of the line.*

VmCJVpH   Heading: *no rubric Vmp;* HYMNUS DE SANCTE MATHIAE APOSTOLI C, MATHIA IUSTE J, DE SANCTO MATHIA H; 1 DUODENO] duodene C; 2 cuntis] cunctis *VmCJVpH;* 5 *om. VmJVp; C continues:* seculorum domine.

Commentary   Latin: 1–2 *Cf.* et dederunt sortes et cecidit sors super Matthiam et adnumeratus est cum undecim apostolis *Acts I.26.* 2 *The spelling* cunt- *for* cunct- *is habitual in T, but this is the only case in D.* Old English: 3 vere *was mistaken for the adverb instead of an adjective belonging to* lucis. 4 quo *introduces a final clause and should have been glossed* þæt.

115

DE SANCTO BARNABA APOSTOLO

	ó bydel	eala þu welwillende	7 wlite	gelaþunge
I	PRECO	BENIGNE	ET DECUS	aecclesiæ,

haligre	he geseo þæt yrmða
Barnaba sancte,	cernat ut miserias,

halsa crist	we þoliaþ þa ðe be geearnunge
supplica Christum,	patimur quas merito,

geliþewæc halgum	7 us þinum benum
releva sanctis	nosque tuis precibus.	4

Annue, Christe

1 Kind herald and flower of the church, Saint Barnabas, beseech Christ that he may regard the adversities which we deservedly suffer and comfort us with your holy prayers.

This stanza was combined with Hy 104$_2$ and sung at the feast of St Barnabas (11 June). It is included only in the hymnals of D and H. For further details see Hy 104$_2$ (pp. 375–6).

H   Heading: DE SANCTO BARNABA; 3 Christum] christo.

Commentary   Old English: 2 *The glossator takes* sancte *as belonging to* aecclesiæ, *whereas it probably belongs to* Barnaba *and the Latin text is punctuated accordingly.*

116

DE SANCTO GREGORIO

	ó eala þu halga	geearnungum healicost
I	ALME GREGORI,	MERITIS precipue

fæder *ænglisra	lareow 7 apostol
pater Anglorum,	doctor & apostole,

us æfre þinum	gefultuma helpum
nos semper tuis	adiuva suffragiis,

þæt mid þe *life   we brucan   sigeleane
ut tecum vite   perfruamur bravio.   4

Annue, Christe

I Blessed Gregory, excellent in your merits, father of the English, teacher and apostle, help us always by your support so that we may enjoy the prize of life together with you.

This stanza was combined with Hy 104_2 and sung at the feast of St Gregory (12 March). It is included only in the hymnals of D and H and is clearly of Anglo-Saxon provenance. For further details see under Hy 104_2 (pp. 375–6).

H   Heading: *no rubric*; 1 G R E G O R I] gregorii; 5 Sit trinitati sempiterna.

Commentary   Latin: *See* The Earliest Life of Gregory the Great: by an Anonymous Monk of Whitby, *ed. B. Colgrave (Laurence, 1968) and Bede,* Historia ecclesiastica (Bede's Ecclesiastical History of the English People, *ed. Colgrave and Mynors) I.23–32 and II.1; note especially:* Quem recte nostrum appellare possumus et debemus apostolum, *p. 123 and compare Hy 116/2. The doxology in H is that of Hy 87. Old English: 2 For* ænglisra *read* ængliscra. 4 vite *was mistaken for a dat., but it must be a gen. attribute to* bravio.

117

YMNUS DE MARTYRIBUS

*ó
*eala þu ece   cristes   lac
I   ÆTERNA CHRISTI MUNERA

7 þrowæra   sigas
& martyrum victorias

     lofu   singende   neadwise
[38v] laudes canentes debitas

mid bliþum uton singan modum
lętis   canamus mentibus.   4

gelaþunga   ealdres
II   Æcclesiarum principes,

gewinnes sigorlice   heretogan
belli   triumphales duces,

þære *heofonlice healle cempan
cęlestis   aule milites

7 soþe middaneardes leoht
& vera mundi   lumina   8

      ogan   oferswiðdan worulde
III   terrore victo   saeculi

7 witum   forsewenum lichoman
pęnisque spretis   corporis

deaþes   haliges *wiþerleane
mortis sacrę *compendia

lif   eadig   geahniað
vitam beatam possident.   12

      wæron bescofene on fyre þrowæras
IV Traduntur   igni   martyres

7 *wilddeorum tuxum
& bestiarum dentibus.

gewæpnod wedde mid clawum
Armata sævit   ungulis

cwellæres gewitleases hand
tortoris insani   manus   16

      nacode   gehangodon innoðas
V   Nudata pendent   viscera,

blod   halig   wæs agotan
sanguis sacratus funditur,

ac   þurhwunedon unawændendlice
sed permanent *immobili

lifes eces   gife
vitę perennis gratiæ.   20

      estful   halgena   geleafa
VI Devota sanctorum fides,

unoferswiðod hiht gelefendra
invicta   spes credentium,

fulfremed cristes   soþlufu
perfecta Christi caritas

middaneardes sigorað   ealdor
mundi   triumphat principem.   24

      on þisum fæderlic wuldor
VII In his   paterna gloria,

on *þisun willa   gastes
in   his   voluntas spiritus,

blissaþ   on þisum suna
exultat in his   filius,

heofon bið gefelled mid gefean
cęlum repletur   gaudio.   28

       þe   nu   alysend   we biddaþ
VIII   Te nunc, *redeptor, quesumus,

þæt þrowæra   geferrædene
ut martyrum consortio

þu geþeode biddende   þeowtlingas
iungas   precantes servulos

on ece   worulda
in sempiterna secula.   32

                amen

I Let us sing with joyous hearts of the eternal gifts of Christ and of the victories of the martyrs and so sing the songs of praise we owe them.

II The princes of the branches of the church, the triumphant leaders in battle, soldiers of the celestial court and true sources of light in the world,

III for they overcame the terror of the world and treated the suffering of the flesh with scorn, they have gained blessed life by the short-cut of a holy death.

IV The martyrs are consigned to fire and to the teeth of wild animals. The hand of the insane torturer, armed with hooks, savages them.

V Their intestines are laid bare and hang out, their holy blood is spilled, but they remain immovably committed to the grace of everlasting life (*other manuscripts*: they remain unmoved for the sake of everlasting life).

VI The devoted faith of the saints, the unconquered hope of the believers and the perfect love of Christ triumph over the prince of this world.

VII In these the glory of the Father exults, in these the will of the Spirit exults, in these the Son exults and heaven is filled with joy.

389

VIII We beseech you now, redeemer, to join the humble servants praying
to you to the fellowship of the martyrs in eternity.

This is the oldest hymn for martyrs and was already in use in the Old
Hymnal (OHy 44). In the New Hymnal it was in use for feasts of more
than one martyr. B includes it among the hymns for apostles, which
clearly does not exclude its use for feasts of non-apostolic martyrs as well.
As a hymn for apostles it was later replaced by an adapted version, Hy
103. In B Hy 117 is assigned to Matins and this may hold true for the
Canterbury Hymnal in general. In the hymnal of H it is assigned to
Lauds, but in the collectar to Matins (Nocturn). In the Winchester
Hymnal it was either for Matins or, less probably, for Vespers. The hymn
is probably by St Ambrose of Milan himself. It is written in Ambrosian
iambic dimeter. The melody transmitted in H seems to be the same as
that for Hy 103, but still closer to Stäblein no. 115₄. The text is included
in the hymnals of BCDH and the *Expositio hymnorum* of J. In V Hy 117
and its related version, Hy 103, are conflated. The metrical version of Hy
103, which had no corresponding prose version, since Hy 103 is not part
of the Winchester Hymnal, was joined to a partially re-adjusted prose
version of Hy 117, which is collated below. Hy 117 itself, which must
have existed in the exemplar of Vm, was omitted.

Bibliographical references: *ICL* no. 411; *AH* 50, 19 (no. 17), cf. *AH* 2,
74–5 (no. 95); Bulst, pp. 52 and 185 (II, 14), Walpole no. 15.

BCJVpH   *There is a change of hands in V at the beginning of the clause that corresponds to line
28 in Vp.* Heading: hymnus ad nocturnam B, *no rubric* CVp, AETERNA CHRISTI J,
YMNUS AD MATUTINAM H; 3 canentes] ferentes BJ, *om.* Vp; 4 lętis] leti B; 5–8 *om.* H;
6 BJVp *add* et *at the beginning of the line*; 9 terrore] terrę J; victo] vita B; 10 *om.* Vp; spretis]
spreto C; 11 compendia] compendio BCJVpH; 12 possident] possidet H; 13–20 *om.* Vp; 15
ungulis] ungulas C; 16 tortoris] tartaris C; 17 pendent] pendunt J; 19 immobili]
immobiles BCHJ; 20 gratiæ] gratia BCJ; 21–8 *om.* H; 28 gaudio] gaudiis BJVp; 29
redeptor] redemptor BCJVpH; 30 ut] et B; 32 amen] *om.* BCJVp.

Commentary   Latin: 3 *Bulst reads* ferentes, *with* AH *noting the variant* canentes *for
continental manuscripts.* 6 AH *attests* BJVp's *et for continental manuscripts. In* JVp *et just might be
an independent explanatory addition in the prose version.* 8 *For* vera mundi lumina *cf. Matt. V.14,
Phil. II.15.* 11 *For* compendia *read* compendio *like Bulst,* BCJVpH *and the glosses in D and
JVp.* 12 *Bulst reads* lucem *for* vitam, *noting* vitam *as a variant reading.* 19 immobili *in D is
not attested by Bulst and* BCJH *have* immobiles. 20 *Bulst reads* gratia. 21–3 *For the three
theological virtues cf. I. Cor. XIII.13.* 24 *For* mundi ... principem *cf. John XIV.30 and*

XVI.11. 25 Cf. *Hy 15/1.* 28 AH *attests BJVp's* gaudiis *for only one continental manuscript.* 29 *In* redeptor *in* D *the abbreviation mark for* m *is om.* Old English: 7 *For* heofonlice *read* heofonlican. 11 wiþerleane *renders the correct* compendio. compendium *may mean 'profit' and thence, perhaps, 'remuneration', but here it is much more likely that it means 'shortening' (of life through death) and it is glossed in this way in* J (sceortnysse). 14 wilddeorum *should be gen. pl.; the case ending was transferred from the following* tuxum. 19 unawændendlice *could translate both* immobili *and* immobiles.

118

YMNUS

ó
cyng eala þu æþele   þrowæra
I REX   GLORIOSE MARTYRUM,

cenehelm andettendra
corona confitentium,

*þa ðe forseonde   eorðlice þing
qui   respuentes terræna

þu gebringst to heofonlicon þingon
perducis   ad cęlestia,   4

eare   welwillende þærrihte
II aurem benignam protinus

*geic   urum   stefnum
appone nostris vocibus;

sigas   halige we geyppað
trophea sacra pangimus.

gemiltsa þæt ðe we agyltan
[39r] Ignosce, quod deliquimus.   8

þu oferswiþst on þrowærum
III Tu vincis   in martyribus

arigende   andettærum
parcendo confessoribus,

þu oferswið ure   leahtras
tu vince   nostra crimina

syllende   forgyfennysse
donando indulgentiam.   12

gode fæder sy wuldor
Deo patri sit gloria

I Glorious king of martyrs and crown of those who confess you, who guide towards heavenly things those who despise what is earthly,

II lend a kind ear to our voices straight away; we are celebrating the fruits of holy victory. Forgive that in which we have transgressed.

III You have the victory in the persons of your martyrs while sparing the confessors. Overcome our iniquities by granting remission.

This hymn was sung at feasts of more than one martyr. In the Winchester Hymnal it is assigned to Lauds, in the hymnal of H to Vespers. In the collectar of H it is generally assigned to Lauds, but to Vespers on Holy Innocents (28 December). The details of its use in the Canterbury Hymnal are not clear. It is anonymous and written in rhythmical Ambrosian hymn verse (4 × 8pp). The stanza rhymes aabb. Rhyme is monosyllabic. The melody transmitted in H agrees with Stäblein no. 405$_1$. The melody is restricted to England, Normandy and Germany and this version shows traits typical of Worcester (Stäblein, p. 561). The text is included in the hymnals of BCDHVm and the *Expositio hymnorum* of JVp.

Bibliographical references: *ICL* no. 14273; *AH* 51, 128–9 (no. 112), cf. *AH* 2, 75 (no. 96), Walpole no. 121.

BVmCJVpH   Heading: hymnus in natale plurimorum martyrum *B, no rubric Vmp*, HYMNUS AD MATUTINUM *C*, REX GLORIOSE *J*, AD VESPERAM *H*; 8 Ignosce] iginosce *H*; 12 indulgentiam] indulgentia *C*; 13 *om. VmJVp; Vm adds* AMEN. *C omits* sit gloria.

Commentary   Latin: 2 *Cf. Hy 121/2, 124/2 and 126/1.* Old English: 3 *For* þa *read* þu. 6 *Both* apponere *and* geiecan *can mean 'add', but in this context the gloss is altogether inappropriate.*

<h1 style="text-align:center">119</h1>

<h2 style="text-align:center">ITEM DE MARTYRIBUS</h2>

	halgena	for geearnungum	æþela	gefean
I	SANCTORUM MERITIS		INCLITA	gaudia
	*we geyppað geferan	7 dæda	stranglice	
	pangamus, socii,	gestaque fortia,		

witodlice *weaxð mod   geyppan   mid sangum
nam   gliscit animus   promere cantibus

sigefæstra cynn   þæt selosta
victorum genus optimum.   4

     þas synt   þa ðe healdende   middaneard anþracode
II   Hi sunt, quos retinens   mundus   inhorruit,

     him   witodlice unwæstmbærum   blosme forscruncen
     ipsum nam   sterili   flore   peraridum

     heo forsawon eallunga   7 ðe heo   feligdon
     sprevere   penitus   teque secuti sunt,

       ó
     cyng crist   gode   heofonlice
     rex   Christe bone, cęlitus.   8

     þas for   ðe wodnyssa 7   *reðnyssa
III   Hi pro te furias   atque ferocia

     fortrædan   manna   7 reþe   swingla
     calcarunt hominum   saevaque verbera,

     geswac þisum slitenda   stranglice *hoc
     cessit his   lacerans   fortiter   ungula

     *þæt he ne totǽr innoþas
     nec carpsit   penetralia.   12

     hi wæron geslægene mid swurdum   on þeawa scepa
IV   Cęduntur   gladiis   more   bidentium

     ne   murcnung swegde   ne   ceorung
     nec murmur resonat   nec quęrimonia,

     ac   mid heortan stilre   mod   wel   gewittig
     sed corde   tacito   mens bene conscia

     *geheold   geþeld
     *conserva patientiam.   16

         s. est
     la hwilc stefn   seo   mæg   mid tungan gereccan
V   Quę   vox, quę poterit   lingua   retexere,

     þe   ðu þrowærum   lac   gearcast
     quę tu martyribus   munera preparas,

     *readum witodlice flowendum   blode   wuldorbeagum
     rubri nam   fluido   sanguine laureis

     beoð gewelgode wel   scinendum
     ditantur   bene fulgidis.   20

ó

þe eala þu ðrilic godcundnyss	7 *samod we biddaþ
VI Te, trina deitas	unaque, poscimus,
þæt gyltas þu afeormige	derigendlice þu ætbræde
ut culpas abluas,	noxia subtrahas,
þu selle sibbe þenum	*us eac swilce wuldor
des pacem famulis,	nos quoque gloriam
geond ealla þe worulda	
per cuncta tibi saecula.	24

amen

I Let us sing of the joyous occasion made famous by the merits of the saints and their resolute deeds, comrades, for the heart is inspired to celebrate the best kind of victors in song.

II These are they before whom this world trembled while it still held them, for they despised it altogether as an arid desert of barren flowers and followed you heavenwards, good king Christ.

III These people scorned the rage and the fierce and savage blows of men for your sake. Before them the strongly tearing claw weakened and did not tear their entrails apart.

IV They are cut down with swords in the same way as sheep and neither a murmur nor a complaint is uttered, but the mind conscious of no evil maintains patience with a quiet heart.

V What voice is there that could recount with tongue what gifts you prepare for the martyrs, for, still red with flowing blood, they are endowed with brightly shining laurel wreaths!

VI We ask you, deity both three and one, to wash away our guilt and remove what is harmful, to give peace to your servants and let us also give you glory throughout the ages.

This hymn was sung at feasts of more than one martyr. In the Canterbury Hymnal the hymn must have been assigned either to Vespers or to Lauds, in the Winchester Hymnal to Vespers or Matins. In the hymnal of H it is assigned to Matins, but in the collectar to Vespers. The hymn has been ascribed to Hrabanus Maurus (d. 856). It is written in the second Asclepiadeic stanza (consisting of three lesser asclepiads and one glyconic). The melody transmitted in H agrees with Stäblein no. 159_2 except for a deviation at the beginning of the third line. Hy 119 is apparently the original text of this melody (Stäblein, p. 547). The text is included in the hymnals of BCDHVm and the *Expositio hymnorum* of JVp.

Bibliographical references: *ICL* no. 14680; *AH* 50, 204–5 (no. 153), cf. *AH* 2, 75 (no. 97).

Apparatus to D Latin text: 19 *Punctuation om. after* fluido, *although the caesura and the end of the line do not coincide.*

Old English gloss: 6 unwæstmbærum] d *erased between* n *and* w.

BVmCJVpH Heading: item alius ymnus *B, no rubric* Vmp, HYMNUS IN NATALE PLURIMORUM MARTYRUM *C*, SANCTORUM MERITIS *J*, YMNUS IN NATALE PLURIMORUM MARTIRUM (Y *with abbreviation mark for* YMNUS *has been squeezed in front and is ignored by Dewick*) *H*; 2 fortia] fortii *C*; 4 victorum] um *interlined above with a caret mark by another hand C*; optimum] obtimum *C*; 5 Hi] hu *C*; retinens] retines *H*; 6 peraridum] perarridum *C*; 8 *line on erasure* Vm; 10 calcarunt] calcarum *C*; hominum] *case ending erased, final letter* m *or* n Vm; 11 ungula] ungulas *C*; 12 nec carpsit] necarpsit *H*; nec] ne VmJVp; 13 Cęduntur] Cceduntur *C*; 14 nec ... nec] non ... non VmJVpH, nec ... non *C*; murmur] murmor *C*; resonat] resonant *C*; 16 conserva] conservat VmCH, conservet BJVp; patientiam] patientia *C*; 18 preparas] preparans, n *underlined* Vm; 19 fluido] fluvidos *C*, fluvido *H*; 21 trina] summa VmCJ, sumna Vp *(not mentioned by Gneuss)*; 22 noxia] noxias VmCH; 23 nos] sit BH; gloriam] gloria BVmCH; amen] *om.* CJVp.

Commentary Latin: *The hymn is conceived on the lines of Hy 117.* 11 *Cf. Hy 117/15.* 13 *Cf.* sicut oves occisionis *Ps. XLIII.22 and Rom. VIII.36.* 14 AH *reads* non ... non. 16 *The correct reading is clearly* conservat *as in* VmCH. AH *reads* conservat. 21 summa *is attested by* AH *for two continental manuscripts.* 23 AH *attests* gloria *as a variant reading for continental manuscripts.* Old English: 2 geyppað *should be optative.* 3 weaxð *glosses a common meaning of* gliscere, 'grow'. *(The* JVp *gloss has* gewilnað.) 9 *The glossator assumes that* ferocia *is being used as a noun, whereas it is in fact an attributive adjective.* 12 þæt ... ne *glosses* ne, *the reading of* VmJVp *(and* H?*).* 16 geheold *glosses the correct* conservat *as in* VmCH. 19 *The glossator has wrongly taken* rubri *as a dat. sg. belonging to* fluido *instead of nom. pl.* 21 una *has been mistaken for the adverb instead of an adjective parallel to* trina. 23 nos *(nom.) has been mistaken for an acc.*

120

YMNUS DE UNO MARTYRE

ó
eala þu þrowære godes þu ðe ancennedne
1 [39v] MARTYR DEI, QUI UNICUM

fæderes fyligende   suna
patris sequendo filium

*þu oferswiðst sigorigende   feondum
victis   triumphans hostibus,

sigefæst brucende heofonlicum
victor fruens cęlestibus,   4

þinre bene   mid lace
II tui precatus munere

ure   scylde adilega
nostrum reatum delue

afligende yfeles besmitennysse
arcens mali contagium,

lifes asyndrigende æþrytnesse
vitę removens tedium.   8

tolysede synt nu bendas
III Soluta sunt iam vincula

þines haliges lichoman
tui sacrati corporis,

us tolys fram bendum worulde
nos solve vinclis   saeculi

mid lufe *bearne godes
amore filii dei.   12

gode fæder sy wuldor
Deo patri sit gloria

I Martyr of God, you who triumph, your enemies overcome, by
following the only son of the Father and as a victor partake of the
heavenly,

II wash away our iniquity by the gift of your prayer, warding off the
infection of evil and taking away the weariness of life.

III Now the bonds of your holy body are loosened, loosen us from the
bonds of this world through the love of the Son of God.

This hymn was sung at the feast of one martyr. In the Winchester Hymnal
it is assigned to Matins (Nocturn), in the hymnal of H to Vespers, in the
collectar of H to Matins and Vespers. In the Canterbury Hymnal it may
have been either for Vespers or Matins. It is anonymous and written in
Ambrosian iambic dimeter. The stanza rhymes aabb. Rhyme is mono-

syllabic. The melody transmitted in H agrees with Stäblein no. 405_1 and is the same as for Hy 118. The text is included in the hymnals of BCDHVm and the *Expositio hymnorum* of JVp.

Bibliographical references: *ICL* no. 9360; *AH* 51, 129–30 (no. 113), cf. *AH* 2, 76 (no. 98).

BVmCJVpH   Heading: hymnus in natale unius martyris B, *no rubric Vmp*, HYMNUS AD NOCTURNUM C, MARTYR DEI QUI UNICUM J, YMNUS I. MARTYRIS *(abbreviated)* AD VESPERAM H; 3 triumphans] triumphas B; hostibus] bus *on erasure* B; 6 delue] dilue VmJVp; 12 filii] fili BH; 13 *om.* JVp. B *omits* gloria.

Commentary   Latin: 3 B's triumphas *is attested by* AH *in continental manuscripts.* 8 *Cf.* cum taedio est tempus vitae nostrae *Wisdom II.1.* Old English: 3 victis, *the past participle (abl. pl.), has been confused by the glossator with* vincis. 12 *For* bearne *read* bearnes.

121

ITEM YMNUS

ó
eala þu god   þinra   cempena
I   DEUS, TUORUM MILITUM

hlot 7 cynehelm *mede
sors & corona,   premium,

lofu   singende   þrowæres
laudes canentes martyris

tolys   fram bende leahtres
absolve nexu   criminis.   4

*her   witodlice   middaneardes gefean
II   Hic nemphe *mudi   gaudia

7 geswæsnyssa   derigendlice
& blandimenta noxia

gewitendlice rihtlice *bescufende
caduca   rite   deputans

becom   to heofonlicon þingon
pervenit ad caelestia.   8

wite   he þurharn stranglice
III   Poenas cucurrit   fortiter

7 he forðeldegode werlice
& sustulit   viriliter.

for   ðe ageotende   blod
Pro te refundens sanguinem

þa ecan   gyfa   geahnað
aeterna dona possidet.   12

for þy   mid bene eadmodre
IV Ob hoc pręcatu supplici

           o
þe we biddaþ   eala þu arfæstesta
te poscimus,   piissime:

on þisum sige   þro[wæres]
in hoc   triumpho martiris

forgyf   dara   þeowtlingum
dimitte noxam servulis.   16

lof   7   ece   wuldor
V Laus & perennis gloria

gode fæder 7 suna
deo patri & filio,

þam halgan samod frofergaste
sancto   simul paraclito,

on worulda   woruld
in seculorum secula.   20

             sy hit swa
             amen

I God, the portion and crown and reward of your soldiers, free from the bondage of sin those who sing the praise of the martyr.

II He certainly made his way to heaven by rightly considering the joys and dangerous allurements of the world as vain and fleeting.

III He resolutely passed through trouble and toil and sustained them manfully. Having shed his blood for you, he possesses the eternal gifts.

IV Therefore we entreat you in humble prayer, o most kind one: forgive your humble servants their guilt on this day of the martyr's triumph.

V Praise and everlasting glory be to God the Father and the Son with the Holy Spirit world without end.

This hymn was sung at feasts of one martyr. In the Canterbury Hymnal and the hymnal and collectar of H it was assigned to Lauds, in the Winchester Hymnal to Vespers. In the collectar of H it is also assigned to the Second Vespers of martyrs who were not bishops. It is anonymous and written in Ambrosian iambic dimeter. Rhyme is monosyllabic and slightly irregular, but the stanza generally rhymes aabb. The melody transmitted in H is a version of Stäblein no. 150 closest to 150$_1$. It is restricted to Italy, France and England (Stäblein, p. 565). The text is found in the hymnals of BCDHVm and the *Expositio hymnorum* of JVp.

Bibliographical references: *ICL* no. 3576; *AH* 51, 130 (no. 114a), cf. *AH* 2, 76 (no. 99), Walpole no. 122.

Apparatus to D   Old English gloss: 15 þrowæres] wæres *om. and later added by another hand*; 20 woruld] o *altered from* u.

BVmCJVpH   Heading: hymnus ad matutinam *B, no rubric Vmp*, HYMNUS UNIUS MARTYRIS AD VESPERUM *C,* DEUS TUORUM *J,* YMNUS AD MATUTINAM *H*; 2 sors] sor *H*; corona] corora *B*; 3 martyris] martires *H*; 5 nemphe] nimphe *C*; mudi] mundi *BVmCJVpH*; 7 deputans] duputans *H*; 11 pro] per *J*; refundens] effundens *VmCJVp*, reffundens *H*; sanguinem] sanguine *C*; 12 possidet] possident *Vm*; 17–20 *om. JVp*; 19 simul cum sancto spiritu *H*; 20 seculorum] sempiterna *H*; secula] seculis *Vm; C omits* amen.

Commentary   Latin: 2 *Cf. Hy 118/2.* 8 *Cf. Hy 118/8.* 5 *In* mudi *the scribe of D has omitted the abbreviation mark.* 11 AH *reads* effundens, *attesting* refundens *for continental manuscripts as well.* 19 AH *attests* una cum sancto spiritu *for continental manuscripts, cf. H.* Old English: 2 *The glossator interpreted* premium *as an accusative instead of a nominative.* 5 hic, *the demonstrative pronoun, has been mistaken for homophonous* hic *'here'.* 7 deputare *has a homonym meaning 'cut off' and this may be what the glossator is thinking of. Even so,* bescufende *'casting down' is not very close.*

122

YMNUS DE CONFESSORIBUS

   ó
   eala ðu crist   beorhtnyss   wuldres
I   CHRISTE, SPLENDOR GLORIÆ,
   lofu   we gereccaþ þe
   laudes referimus tibi,

þu ðe mid genihtsumum *wuldre
qui profluo   miraculo

halgena   gefrætewigende cafertun
[40r] sanctorum ornans   atrium,   4

*þu ðe on sibbe gelaðunge
II   qui in pace aecclesiae

blowende on þeawe lilian
florentes more   lilii

bodeden   folce
predicaverunt populo,

þæt hi gefeldon *neorxnewange
ut replerent   paradysum.   8

nimende   wepna wiglice
III Sumentes arma bellica

ongean feondes hinderscipe
contra hostis nequitiam,

scyld   geleafan swurd
scutum fidei, gladium

*gast   *feoht   stranglice
spiritus, pugnant fortiter,   12

on þæra   muþe god   is
IV   in quorum ore   deus est,

on þæra   heortan crist   is
in quorum corde Christus est,

on þæra   mode   arfæstnyss
in quorum mente pietas,

rihtwisnyss 7 soþfæstnyss
iustitia & veritas.   16

upasprungene of myxe dustes
V   Orti   de fece pulveris,

for   godum heora geearnungum
pro bonis suis meritis

gelice   gewordene ænglum
similes facti   angelis

heo brucað beorhtum gefeanum
fruuntur claris   gaudiis.   20

æt þæra   *bana deadra
VI   Ad quorum ossa mortua

400

to micclum cristes wuldre
ad magnam Christi gloriam

niwa weaxað wundra
nova crescunt miracula,

syllende folce helpas
dantes plebi suffragia,   24

þænne byð geseald hæl seocum
VII dum datur   salus languidis,

biþ agolden lif deadum
redditur vita mortuis,

leoht bið ageangesænd blindum
lumen refunditur   cȩcis,

underfoð færeld þa wanhalan
capiunt gressum debiles.   28

o
þe nu we biddað eala þu drihten
VIII Te nunc oramus,   domine,

heora us mid emtrymminge
eorum nos munimine

fram ælcum efele gescyld
ab omni malo protege

7 lif us forgyf
et vitam nobis tribue.   32

amen

I Christ, splendour of glory, we offer up praise to you, who beautify
   your hall with the abundant miracles of the saints

II who flowered in the peace of the Church in the manner of the lily
   and preached to the people that they might fill paradise.

III Having taken up the arms of war against the malice of the enemy,
   the shield of faith, the sword of the spirit, they fight valiantly,

IV they in whose mouth God is, in whose heart Christ is and in whose
   mind there is piety, justice and truth.

V Although they originated from dirt and dust, they became similar to
   angels in return for their good merits and partake of resplendent
   happiness.

401

VI Around their dead bones new miracles spring up to the great glory of Christ, for they give aid to the people,

VII in that health is granted to the sick, life is restored to the dead, sight is returned to the blind and the weak gain the faculty of walking.

VIII We pray to you now, Lord, defend us from all evil by means of their protection and grant us life.

This hymn was presumably in use for feasts of more than one confessor in the Canterbury Hymnal in general; it cannot be determined to which Hour(s) it was assigned. In the Winchester Hymnal and the hymnal of H it was sung at feasts of an apostle, but in the former it was assigned to Matins (Nocturn), in the latter to Vespers. The collectar of H assigns it to Vespers of more than one confessor and of evangelists. The hymn is anonymous and written in rhythmical Ambrosian hymn verse (4 × 8pp). A melody is transmitted in H. The text is included in the hymnals of BCDHVm and the *Expositio hymnorum* of JVp.

Bibliographical references: *ICL* no. 2232; *AH* 14a, 138 (no. 139).

Apparatus to D   Latin text: 12 pugnant] n *expunged, possibly by another hand.*
Old English gloss: 25 seocum] c *interlined above with a caret mark, probably by D₁.*

BVmCJVpH   Heading: item alius ymnus *B, no rubric Vmp,* HYMNUS AD NOCTURNOS *C,* CHRISTE SPLENDOR *J,* YMNUS AD VESPERAM *H*; 4 ornans] ornas *BCJVpH,* n *erased Vm*; 5 qui] ui *C*; 10 nequitiam] nequitia *H*; 12 spiritus] sps *C*; 13 ore] hore *J*; 17 fece] feci *C*; pulveris] pulvere ł ris *B*; 22 ad] et *H*; 24 dantes] *ending erased,* s *just visible, replaced, possibly by V₂, with* ur-*abbreviation Vm,* dentes *H*; plebi] plebis *C*; 28 gressum] gressus *VmC*; 30 munimine] munine *B,* munime *H*; 30–1 nos ... protege] *mistakenly repeated* (protege *immediately follows* nos *in the prose version) J*; 31 ab omni] *dittographed Vm*; 32 *VmCH add:* Deo patri sit gloria, *but H omits* D. *BVmCJVpH omit* amen.

Commentary   Latin: 1 *The line is a syllable short, unless* splendor *had a prothetic vowel; other (continental) versions begin* Christe rex *or* O Christe. 4 *AH reads* ornas *like BCJVpH, attesting* ornans *for one continental manuscript. The critical apparatus of AH, however, is suspect at this point, because its statements are self-contradictory.* 9–12 *Cf. Eph. VI.13–17.* 24 *AH reads* dantur, *attesting* dantes *for one continental manuscript; again the apparatus is suspect.* Old English: 3 *For* wuldre *read, presumably,* wundre. 5 qui *has been mistaken for a singular referring to* CHRISTE. 7 bodeden *shows weakening of final* -on. 8 neorxnewange *has the wrong case ending; the scribe may not know the gender of this word (see p. 77).* 12 spiritus, *the gen., was mistaken for the nom.* feoht *might be uninflected because of resulting confusion. It may, however, render the altered reading* pugnat *and be a non-West-Saxon spelling for 3 sg. pres. ind.* fiht (*SB §122, 1; see above, p. 75*). 21 *The gen. pl. of* bana deadra *is due to the preceding* þæra; *the words should be acc. pl.*

123

YMNUS DE UNO CONFESSORE

I
þes andettære   drihtnes   halig
ISTE CONFESSOR   DOMINI SACRATUS,

freols folc   þæs   *brymde   geond emhwerft
festa plebs cuius   celebrat per   orbem,

todæg bliþe   he geearnode diglo
hodie laetus   meruit   secreta

astigan   hefones
scandere cęli,   4

II
se   arfæst snoter   eadmod   sidefull
qui pius, prudens,   humilis, pudicus,

sefre   clæne   wæs 7 gedefe
sobrius, castus   fuit & quietus,

líf   þa hwile andwerd þe   *gestrangode his
vita dum   pręsens   vegetavit eius

lichaman *liþ
[40v] corporis artus,   8

III
æt haligre þæs   byrgene   oftrædlice
ad sacrum cuius   tumulum frequenter

lima   adligra   nu   hæle
membra languentum   modo sanitati,

on swa hwilcre adle   swa hi *beoð gehefegode
quolibet   morbo   fuerint gravata,

heo beoð geedstaþolode
restituuntur.   12

IV
for ði   nu   ure   werod   on wurðmente
Unde nunc noster   chorus in honore

his   lofsang   singð þisne lustlice
ipsius ymnum   canit hunc libenter,

þæt his arfæstum   geearnungum we beon gefultumode
ut piis eius   meritis   iuvemur

*ælc   geond ylde
omne per   aevum.   16

V
sy hæl   him   wlite 7   miht
Sit salus illi,   decus atque virtus,

se   wiþufan heofones   sittende   heahnysse
qui supra   caeli   residens cacumen

ealles   middaneardes   seare ꝥ cræft begymð
totius mundi   machinam gubernat

þrinen 7 an
trinus & unus.   20

I That sacred confessor of the Lord whose feast the people celebrate throughout the world deserved to ascend joyfully to the secret regions of heaven today,

II he who was pious, prudent, humble, modest, sober, chaste and calm, while present life animated the limbs of his body,

III at whose holy tomb now the parts of the body of the sick are often restored to health, by whatever disease they may have been oppressed.

IV Therefore our choir now sings this hymn in his honour gladly in order that we may be aided by his pious merits throughout the ages.

V Prosperity, honour and power be to him who, residing above the highest heaven, guides the workings of the whole universe as both three and one.

This hymn was sung at the feast of a confessor. In the Winchester Hymnal it was assigned to Vespers and Matins (Nocturn), as the collectar in C shows. The collectar in H agrees, although the rubric in the hymnal of H only mentions Vespers. The usage of the Canterbury Hymnal cannot be precisely ascertained. The hymn is anonymous and written in Sapphic stanzas. There are four sets of neumes for it. The melody transmitted in B is Stäblein no. 422. The neumes entered above the first half-line in C apparently belong to another melody, which remains unidentified. The melody transmitted in H and the Winchester Troper (W) agrees with Stäblein no. 423_1. The text is included in the hymnals of BCDHVm and the *Expositio hymnorum* of JVp. The first stanza is also in W.

Bibliographical references: *ICL* no. 8410; *AH* 51, 134 (no. 118), cf. *AH* 2, 77 (no. 101).

Apparatus to D   Latin text: 17 su *erased in front of* illi; 18 cacumen] *second* c *altered from a minim.*

BVmCJVpHW   Heading: *no rubric BVmpW*, HYMNUS IN NATALE UNIUS CONFESSORIS *C*, ISTE CONFESSOR *J*, YMNUS I. CONFESSORIS AD VESPERAM *H*; 1 ISTE] ste *BW*; 2 celebrat] *om. J*; 4 cęli] caelum *C*; 15 piis] pius *CJ*; 16 omne] onne *B*; 18 residens] residet *C*; 19 totius] totiuus, *i.e. a superfluous* u *in front of the abbreviation mark Vm*; machinam] machinan *B*; gubernat] gubernans *C*; 20 *VmCH add* amen.

Commentary   Latin: 5–6 *Cf.* oportet ergo episcopum inreprehensibilem esse, unius uxoris virum, sobrium, prudentem, ornatum, hospitalem, doctorem, non vinolentum, non percussorem, sed modestum, non litigiosum, non cupidum *I Tim. III.2–3, cf. also Tit. I.7–8 and II.2.* 19 *C's* gubernans *is attested twice in continental manuscripts collated by* AH. Old English: 2 celebrat *is not a historic present, so the use of the past tense is not justified.* 7 gestrangian *'strengthen' for* vegetare *is not quite accurate.* 8 artus *has not been recognized as acc. pl.* 11 beoð gehefegode *should be past tense, rendering the perfect tense of the Latin subjunctive.* 16 ælc *was left uninflected; the glossator overlooked that it ought to agree with* ylde.

124

ITEM YMNUS

ó
eala þu hælend alysend   ealra þeoda
I   IESU,   REDEMPTOR OMNIUM,
ece   cenehelm biscopa
perpes corona presulum,
on þisum dæge mildheortlicor
in hac die clementius
urum   gefultuma þu stefnum
nostris faveto   vocibus.   4

þines haliges naman
II   Tui sacrati nominis
andettære halig   scán
confessor almus claruit,
þæs   brymð gearlice
cuius celebrat annua
estful   folc   simbelnyssa
devota plebs sollempnia,   8

se   rihtlice middaneardes gefean
III qui rite   mundi   gaudia
þises   gewitendlice *forþæncende
huius caduca   *deputans

mid ænglum heofonlicum
cum angelis caelestibus

*bliðe brucð medum
laetis potitur praemiis. 12

þises welwillendlice getiða
IV Huius benigne annue

us fyligan fotswaðu
nobis sequi vestigia,

þises for bene ðeowtlingum
huius precatu servulis

forgyf ðara leahtres
dimitte noxam criminis. 16

ó
sy crist cyng þu arfæstesta
V Sit, Christe, rex piissime,

þe 7 fæder wuldor
tibi patrique *gloriam

mid gaste frofer
cum spiritu paraclito

7 nu 7 on ecnyssa
& nunc & in perpetuum. 20

I Jesus, redeemer of all, everlasting crown of the prelates, be especially favourable to our invocations on this day.

II The blessed confessor of your sacred name achieved renown whose yearly feast day the dedicated people are celebrating.

III He correctly thought the joys of this world fleeting (*other manuscripts*: correctly despised the fleeting joys of this world) and so is gaining his happy reward among the heavenly angels.

IV Grant us with your good will to follow in his footsteps. For the sake of his prayers forgive your humble servants their guilt and offence.

V Glory be to you, Christ, most merciful king, and to the Father and also to the Holy Spirit now as in eternity.

This hymn was sung at feasts of a confessor. In the Winchester Hymnal and H it was assigned to Lauds. Its precise usage in the Canterbury Hymnal is not certain. It is anonymous and written in Ambrosian iambic dimeter. The melody transmitted in H agrees with Stäblein no. 419. Stäblein knew this melody only from the thirteenth-century hymnal of Worcester. However, he indicates the existence of a related, probably derived, Dominican melody (Stäblein no. 185), apparently originating in the north of France (Stäblein, p. 563). The text is included in the hymnals of BCDHVm and the *Expositio hymnorum* of JVp.

Bibliographical references: *ICL* no. 7659; *AH* 51, 133–4 (no. 117), cf. *AH* 2, 76 (no. 100), Walpole no. 123.

BVmCJVpH   Heading: item alius ymnus *B, no rubric Vmp*, HYMNUS AD MATU-
TINUM *C*, IESU REDEMPTOR *J*, YMNUS AD MATUTINAM *H*; 1 OMNIUM]
hominum *JVp*; 3 clementius] clementia *C*; 5 Tui] ui *B*; 9 qui] ui *B*; gaudia] gloriam
VmJVp; 10 caduca] caducam *VmJVp*; deputans] respuens *BVmCJVpH*; 12 laetis] lętus
CJVpH, laetus, a *altered from* o *Vm*; 13 Huius] uius *B*; benigne] benignus *BVmJVpH*; 17
Sit] it *B*, Sic *C; B adds* tibi *in front of* Christe; piissime] *so also* H *(Dewick reads* piisime*)*; 18
tibi] tib *B*; gloriam] gloria *BVmCJVp*; 20 *BVmH add* amen.

Commentary   Latin: 1 *Cf. Hy 36/1 and 99/1.* 2 *Cf. Hy 126/1.* 5–6 *Cf.* confitentium
nomini eius *Heb. XIII.15.* 9–10 *Cf. Hy 121/5 and 7.* gloriam . . . caducam *is attested by* AH
for continental manuscripts. 10 deputans *in D was probably transferred from the similar line Hy
121/7.* AH *reads* respuens, *attesting* deputans *as a variant reading for continental manuscripts.*
12 AH *reads* laetus. 13 AH *reads* benignus. 15–16 *Cf. Hy 121/13 and 15.* 18 *For* gloriam
in D read gloria; *that H and D share this mistake must be coincidence.* Old English: 10
forþæncende *presumably glosses* respuens, *the reading of BVmCJVpH;* deputare *means 'consider',
although contempt is implied by the context, of course.* 12 bliðe *glosses VmCJVpH's reading* laetus.

125

YMNUS DE VIRGI[41r]NIBUS AD VESPERAM

mædenes   eala ðu bearn   7 werhta   moder
I VIRGINIS   PROLES   OPIfexque matris,

mæden þæne gebær   7 heo acænde mæden
virgo quem gessit   peperitque virgo,

mædenes freols   we singað sige
virginis festum   canimus tropheum;

underfoh behát
accipe votum.   4

þeos þin mæden   on tweofealdum eadig
II Haec tua virgo   dupplici   beata

*mid hlote þa ðe heo gewilnode   tydderlicne gewyldan
sorte,   dum gessit   fragilem domare

lichoman had   gewelde *wælhreowne
corporis sexum,   domuit cruentum

on lichaman worulde
corpore   saeclum.   8

þanon ne deað   ne *freond deaðes
III Inde nec mortem   nec amica mortis,

reþe witena   cynn aforhtigende
sæva pẹnarum   genera, pavescens

blode   agotenum   heo geearnode diglu
sanguine fuso   meruit   secreta

astigan heofones
scandere caeli.   12

              ó
þissere for þingrædene   god halga urum
IV Huius obtentu,   deus alme, nostris

ara nu gyltum   leahtres forgifende
parce iam culpis   vitia remittens,

*on þam þe clænes   we swegan haligne
quo tibi puri   resonemus almum

breostes lofsang
pectoris ymnum.   16

wuldor fæder   7 acænnedum bearne
V Gloria patri   geniteque proli

       ó
7 þe   eala þu gemaca   æghwæðeres æfre
& tibi,   compar   utriusque semper

gast þu halga   god an   on ælcere
spiritus alme,   deus unus, omni

tide worulde
tempore saecli.   20

I Child of the virgin and creator of your mother, whom a virgin carried and gave birth to, still a virgin, we sing of the victory feast of a virgin; accept our prayer.

II While this virgin of yours, twice happy in her fate, endeavoured to overcome the frail sex of her body, she bodily overcame the cruel world.

III Therefore she shied away neither from death nor savage kinds of suffering akin to death and so by shedding her blood she earned it to ascend to the secret regions of heaven.

IV Let her obtain from you that you shall spare our guilt now and remit our sins, holy God, so that out of a pure heart we may chant for you the holy hymn.

V Glory be to the Father and his begotten Son and to you, Holy Spirit, forever equal to both – one God – for all ages of the world.

This hymn was sung on feasts of a holy virgin. In the Canterbury Hymnal it is assigned to Vespers and there was apparently no distinction between feasts of one virgin and feasts of several virgins. The collectar of H makes such a distinction and assigns Hy 125 to Vespers and Matins of a single virgin. The usage in the Winchester Hymnal is not certain. The hymn is anonymous and written in Sapphic stanzas. Note that the third and fourth lines of stanzas I–IV originally ended in *-um*. The melody transmitted in H is apparently a version of Stäblein no. 425. Stäblein (p. 564) knew the melody only from the thirteenth-century Worcester hymnal. The text is included in the hymnals of BCDHVm and the *Expositio hymnorum* of JVp.

Bibliographical references: *ICL* no. 17362; *AH* 51, 137–8 (no. 121), *AH* 2, 78 (no. 103).

Apparatus to D   Latin text: 3 *punctuation missing at the end of the verse, although it does not coincide with the end of the line*; 5 *punctuation om. at the end of the verse*; 7 domuit] t *inserted from above with a caret mark by* D*₁ with the pen used for the gloss; punctuation of caesura and at the end of the verse missing, although neither coincides with the end of the line*; 10 pavescens] s *altered from a partially erased* t, *probably by* D*₁ with the pen used for glossing*; 19 *punctuation missing at the end of the verse, although it does not coincide with the end of the line.*

Old English gloss: 7 gewelde] *second* e *interlined above an original* i; 15 *after* haligne *one or two letters are erased.*

BVmCJVpH   Heading: hymnus de virginibus B, *no rubric* Vmp, HYMNUS IN NATALE UNIUS VIRGINIS C, VIRGINIS PROLES J, YMNUS I. VIRGINIS H; 3–20 *missing in C on account of loss of pages and replaced by a scribe of the eleventh or twelfth century*; 6 sorte] sorde H; 9 Inde] Unde BVm; 11 secreta] sacratum JVp; 12 caeli] cẹlum JVp; 13

Huius] Cuius *H*; obtentu] u *on erasure? H*; 14 parce] perarce *(superfluous abbreviation mark)* *C*; vitia remittens] vitiare mittens *Vm*; remittens] rmittens *B*; 15 puri] patri *J*; 20 tempore] temporere *Vm*; *BVmH add* amen.

Commentary Latin: 9 *BVm's* Unde *is attested by* AH *for continental manuscripts.* 11–12 *The rhyme suggests that JVp's reading was the original one.* AH *reads* sacratum ... caelum, *attesting* secreta ... caeli *for continental manuscripts as well.* 12 *Cf. Hy 123/4.* Old English: 6 *The glossator has not realized that* dupplici *and* sorte *belong together so that one of the two prepositions* on *and* mid *is superfluous.* 7 wælhreowne (cruentum) *should agree with* worulde (saeclum), *not* had (sexum). 9 *Presumably the glossator did not recognize* amica *as adjective and took it for the noun* amica, *'female friend', as happened in the JVp gloss.* 15 quo *was not recognized as the equivalent of* ut *here.*

126

ITEM YMNUS

ó
eala ðu hælend cynehelm   mædena

I   IESU,   CORONA VIRGINUM,

þæne   moder seo geeacnode
quem mater illa concepit,

seo   ana   mæden acænde
quę sola virgo parturit,

þas   behát mildheort underfoh
haec vota clemens accipe,   4

þu ðe *fetst   betwux lilian
II   qui   pascis inter   lilia

emhegod *mid werodum mædena
septus   choreis   virginum,

*breda   wlitigende mid wuldre
sponsa decorans gloria

7 *bredgumum agyfende meda
sponsisque   reddens premia.   8

swa hwider swa ðu gæst mædena
III   Quocumque pergis, virgines

folgiaþ   7   lofum
sequuntur atque laudibus

æfter þe singende   he yrnað
post te canentes cursitant

7 lofsangas merige heo swegað
ymnosque dulces personant.   12

þe we biddað   cystiglicor
IV Te deprecamur: largius

urum   togeyc   modum
nostris adauge mentibus

nytan   eallunga ealla
nescire prorsus omnia

gewæmmednyssa wunda
corruptionis   vulnera.   16

Deo patri sit gloria

I Jesus, crown of virgins, whom that mother conceived who was the only one to give birth as a virgin, accept these prayers kindly,

II you who feed among the lilies, surrounded with the dancing of virgins, honouring them with the promised glory (*J*: the bridegroom beautiful in his glory) and giving their reward to the brides.

III Wherever you proceed, virgins follow and praising you they always run after you singing and intone sweet songs of praise.

IV We pray to you: grant our souls in larger measure to be completely free of all knowledge of wounds of corruption.

This hymn was sung at feasts of a virgin. In the Canterbury Hymnal it was assigned to Matins (Nocturn). The collectar in H assigns it to Lauds of feasts of one virgin and Lauds and Vespers of feasts of several virgins and the rubric in the hymnal does not contradict that. The usage in the Winchester Hymnal is not certain. The hymn has been ascribed to Ambrose; it is written in Ambrosian iambic dimeter. The melody transmitted in H is identical with that of Hy 103, i.e. it agrees most closely with Stäblein no. 115$_4$. The text is included in the hymnals of BCDHVm and the *Expositio hymnorum* of JVp.

Bibliographical references: *ICL* no. 7654; *AH* 50, 20–1 (no. 21), cf. *AH* 2, 78 (no. 104), Walpole no. 19.

Apparatus to D   Latin text: 7 sponsa] a *altered from* u *and one letter erased after the word.*
Old English gloss: 6 mædena] a *altered from* u *by* D$_1$ *and followed by an erasure.*

BVmJVpH Heading: hymnus ad nocturnam *B, no rubric Vmp,* IESU CORONA VIRGINUM *J,* YMNUS AD MATUTINAM *H*; 2 quem] que *J*; 5 qui] ui *B*; 7 sponsa] sponsas *B*, sponses *Vmp*, sponsus *J*, sponsans *H*; 8 reddens] redens *H*; 13 deprecamur] te precamur *J*, precamur *Vp*; largius] larius *H*; 14 nostris] *inserted above with caret mark H*; adauge] & auge *H*; 16 corruptionis] curruptionis *B*; 17 *om. JVp*.

Commentary   Latin: 1 *Cf.* in die illa erit Dominus corona gloriae *Isa. XXVIII.5.* 2 AH *reads* concipit *and the metre proves that this was in the original.* 5 *Cf. S. of S. II.16 and VI.2.* 7 *Cf. Isa. LXI.10.* AH *reads* sponsus decorus, *attesting* sponsas decoras *for one continental manuscript.* 9 *Cf. Rev. XIV.4.* 11 *Cf. S. of S. I.3.* Old English: 5 pascis *can be both transitive and intransitive, but is intransitive here.* 6 *The glossator has confused* choreis *with* choris. 7 breda *renders* sponsas, *the reading of B.* 8 *The glossator has taken* sponsis *for the dat. pl. of* sponsus *instead of the dat. pl. of* sponsa.

127

YMNUS IN DEDICATIONE ÆCCLESIÆ

ó
eala þu crist   ealra þinga   wealdend   þu halga
I   CHRISTE,   CUNCTORUM   DOMINAtor alme,

fæderes þæs ecan   acænned fram muðe
patris aeterni   genitus ab   ore,

eadmodra   behát   7 samod   lofsang
supplicum vota   pariterque ymnum

geseoh welwillende
cerne benignus.   4

geseoh þæt þe clænum   god   on wurðmente
II Cerne, quod puro,   deus, in honore

folc   þin eadmod   swegð   on healle
plebs tua supplex   resonat in aula,

gærlice *þæs   gehwerfað to wurþigenne
annua cuius   redeunt colenda

tida   freols
tempora festa.   8

þis hus   rihtlice   þe gehalgod
III Hęc domus rite   tibi dedicata,

ys acænned on þam   folc   gehalgodne
nascitur in qua   populus, sacratum

    *lichoma underfehþ   drincð 7 eadiges
    corpus assumit,   **bibit & beati**

    blodes   drenc
    sanguinis haustum.   12

    her þurhhalige   burnan þa ealdan
IV **Hic sacrosancti**   **latices *veteras**

    adilegiað gyltas   7 losiað   dara
    deluunt culpas,   **perimuntque noxas**

    crisman *soþlice   cynn þæt sy *geedcenned
    crismate vero,   **genus ut creetur**

    cristenra manna
    christicolarum.   16

    wuldor þam healican   swege   fæder
V **Gloria summum**   **resonet parentem,**

    wuldor suna   7 samod   þæne halgan
    gloria natum   **pariterque sanctum**

    gast   mid merigum   *hit dreme   lofsange
    spiritum dulci   **modulemur ymno**

    geond ælce ylde
    omne per aevum.   20

            amen

I Christ, holy ruler of everyone, born from the mouth of the eternal father, look kindly on the prayers of the suppliants and also on their hymn.

II See, God, what your people utter as suppliants in pure honour in the hall whose festive season of the year has returned.

III This house is truly dedicated to you, in which the people are born, receive the sacred body and drink the draught of blessed blood.

IV Here the most holy waters wash off old guilt and annihilate iniquity by the true chrism so that the race of the worshippers of Christ may come to be.

V May the song of glory celebrate the most high Father, may the song of glory celebrate the Son and may we sing equally of the Holy Spirit in sweet songs of praise throughout the ages.

This, the first section of a hymn for the anniversary of the dedication of the church (Hy 127–9), was sung at Vespers. The hymn is anonymous and written in Sapphic stanzas with some metrical irregularities. The melody transmitted in H remains unidentified. The text is included in the hymnals of DHVm and the *Expositio hymnorum* of JVp; it was presumably also included in C, but is now lost.

Bibliographical references: *ICL* no. 2167; *AH* 51, 112–15 (no. 103), cf. *AH* 2, 72 (no. 92) and *AH* 27, 265 (no. 189).

Apparatus to D   Latin text: 1 DOMINAtor] *The scribe began to write* DOMINATor, *erased* T *at the end of the first line and continued with* t *at the beginning of the next one.* 16 christicolarum] a *on erasure, possibly by another hand.*

  Old English gloss: 8 freols] r *on erasure (of* l); 9 þ *erased in front of* gehalgod.

VmJVpH   Heading: *no rubric* VmJVp, YMNUS DEDICATIONIS ECCLESIĘ IN ANNIVERSARIO *H*; 1 CUNCTORUM] cunctarum, a *altered from* o (*not mentioned by Dewick*) *H*; 2 ab ore] ambore, m *expunged H*; 4 *in the right margin by a later hand:* hic deficit, *which was then crossed out J*; 5 honore] *on erasure? H*; 6 resonat] rosonat *H*; 7 annua] annuo *H*; redeunt] revehunt *JVp*; colenda] colendum *VmJVp*; 8 tempora] tepore *H*; festa] festum *VmJVp*, festo *H*; 10 nascitur] noscitur *Vm*; 13 veteras] veternas *VmJVpH*; 14 deluunt] diluunt *VmJVp*; 15 creetur] cretur *J*; 17 resonet] so *interlined above with a caret mark probably by* V₂ *Vm*; 19 modulemur] moduletur *VmJVpH*; ymno] ymnum *Vm*; 20 *JVp omit* amen.

Commentary   Latin: 7 revehunt *in JVp is paralleled on the Continent according to* AH. 7–8 AH *attests* annuo … tempore *for continental manuscripts; cf.* H. 8 AH *attests* festum *for continental manuscripts.* 10 AH *reads* noscitur *like* Vm, *attesting, however,* nascitur *as well.* 13 *For* veteras *in D read* veternas, *as in* VmJVpH. 17–18 Gloria *may also be abl., in which case the subject is* genus *in line 15. It is so understood in the JVp gloss.* 19 AH *reads* moduletur, *attesting* modulemur *for continental manuscripts as well.* Vm's ymnum *is paralleled on the Continent according to* AH. Old English: 6 *The glossator takes* tua *for nom. sg., but for metrical and contextual reasons it is probably abl. and is so translated in the JVp gloss.* 7 þæs *should be* þære, *as the antecedent is* healle. 11 lichoma *should be acc.* 15 soþlice *is apparently the adverb; the lemma, however, is not the adverb* vero, *which usually means 'but', but the adjective* verus *in the abl. case. The prefix* ed- *'again' is an addition by the glossator and changes the meaning. The catechumens are reborn through baptism, but the Christian Church,* genus christicolarum, *is newly established by it.* 17 *The acc. of the lemma is rendered by a dat., a slip rather than a conscious decision, as* þæne halgan gast *below remains in the acc. The difference is between praise to the Father and praise of the Father.* 19 hit dreme *renders* moduletur, *the reading of* VmJVpH, *although the latter must be taken as a passive, not a deponent, except in* Vm's *reading of the line.*

128

AD NOCTURNAM YMNUS

her hæl   seocum   *læcedon   gewæhtum
I   HIC SALUS AEGRIS,   MEDIcina fessis,

leoht   blindum   7 forgifenysse urum
lumen orbatis   veniaque   nostris

[is] *gesæd ætspyrningum   ege   7   gnornung
fertur   offensis,   timor atque meror

ys adræfed ælc
pellitur   omnis.   4

deofles   reþe   losede her reaflac
II   Demonis seva   perit hic rapina;

gemah   scinhiw   forhtað 7   gehæfta
pervicax monstrum   pavet et retenta

lichaman forlætende   flihð   on asindrode
corpora linquens   fugit in remotas

      hrædlicor sceaduwa
[42r] ocius   umbras.   8

þeos stow   witodlice   is geciged heal
III   Hic locus nemphe   vocitatur aula

      eterni
cynges ðæs ecan   7 gead   heofonan
regis   inmensi ianuaque caeli

7 geat   lifes   eþel   geneosigende
portaque vitę   patriam petentes

underfehð ealle
accipit   omnes,   12

þoden þa   nan ne   *tocwise oþþe worigende
IV   turbo quam nullus   quatit aut vagantes

*towurpon windas   7 *þurhforan   scuras
diruunt venti   penetrantque nimbi,

ne   sweartum derað   picen   þystrum
non tetris   ledit   piceus tenebris

hell   aþracigende
tartarus horrens.   16

wuldor *þam healican
Gloria summum

I Here health is given to the sick, remedies to the weary, sight to those bereft of it and forgiveness to our transgressions and all fear and sadness is dispelled.

II The demon's savage raids are put an end to here; the obstinate fiend grows afraid, leaves the bodies he possessed and flies most quickly to distant shadows.

III Truly this place is often called the hall of the immeasurably great king and the gate to heaven and as the door to life it receives all who seek their home.

IV No whirlstorm shakes it nor do straying winds tear it apart or rain showers penetrate here and pitch-black hell filled with the horror of its dark shadows cannot harm it.

This section of the hymn for the anniversary of the dedication of the church Hy 127–9 was sung at Matins (Nocturn). The neumes given in H differ from those for Hy 127 and 129, but agree with those for Hy 97, apparently a version of Stäblein no. 146. For further details see under Hy 127.

Apparatus to D   Latin text: 1 SALUS] U *on erasure.*
Old English gloss: 15 picen] c *altered from minim.*

VmJVpH   Heading: *no rubric Vmp,* HIC SALUS *J,* ALIA *H;* 2 veniaque] veniamque *VmJVp,* q *altered from* t? *H;* 3 atque] *interlined above perhaps by another hand J (Gneuss: by the scribe);* 4 omnis] omnes *(abbreviated) H;* 5 Demonis] s *added later? (not mentioned by Dewick) H;* perit] t *altered from* c? *H;* 7 fugit] fuit *Vm,* g *interlined above J;* 9 nemphe] nempe *H;* 10 inmensi] aeterni *VmH;* ianuaque] niveaque *H;* 12 omnes] omnis *Vm;* 13 aut] haut *Vp both times (aut is repeated in the prose version);* 14 diruunt] dirunt *H;* 17 *om. HJVp.*

Commentary   Latin: 1 *Cf. Hy 4/22.* 2 veniamque *is attested by* AH *for the Continent.* 10 *The Latin gloss* eterni *in D is not explanatory, but an alternative reading, the reading of VmH.* AH *attests* eterni *for only one continental manuscript.* AH *reads* niveaque *like H.* 13 *Cf. Hy 110/3.* Old English: 1 *For* læcedon *read* læcedom. 3 *The auxiliary is missing, moreover* fertur *does not mean 'is said' in this context.* 10 ðæs ecan *renders the variant given in the Latin gloss.* gead *is another of the instances of sporadic spelling with* d *for* t *(see p. 76).* 13 tocwise *is the wrong mode.* 14 *The rendering of the present by the past tense is inappropriate here.* 17 *The acc. is again rendered by dat.; cf. Hy 127/17.*

129

YMNUS AD MATUTINAM

we biddað   eornostlice   o god   þæt liþe
I QUESUMUS ERGO,   DEUS, UT sereno

getiþige anwlitan   þenas   begemende
annuas vultu,   famulos gubernes,

þa ðe þines mid healicre   bremað   wurðmente
qui tui summo   celebrant honore

gefean temples
gaudia templi.   4

nane us lifes   *cwylmige hefigtemnyssa
II Nulla nos vitę   crucient molesta.

beon dagas bliþe   7 glæde   nihta
Sint dies laeti   placideque noctes.

nan   of us   losigendum middanearde
Nullus ex nobis   pereunte mundo

gefrede fyr
sentiat ignes.   8

þes dæg on þam   þe gehalgod
III Hic dies, in quo   tibi consecratam

þu besceawast weofud   *þu forgife ece
conspicis   aram,   tribuat perenne

gefean   us   7 he þeo on langsumum
gaudium nobis   vigeatque longo

tide   brece
temporis usu.   12

wuldor *þan healican
Gloria summum

I Therefore we ask you, God, to favour us, regarding us kindly, and to guide your servants who celebrate the joys that your temple offers with signal honour.

II May no troubles of life pain us. May the days be serene and the nights be peaceful. May none of us be made to feel the fires when the world perishes.

III May this day, on which you regard the altar dedicated to you, bring us everlasting joy and remain effective in use for a long time.

This, the third section of the hymn for the anniversary of the dedication of the church Hy 127–9, was sung at Lauds. The neumes accompanying the text in H are almost identical with the unidentified melody of Hy 127. For other details see under Hy 127.

Apparatus to D Latin text: 3 *Punctuation at the end of the verse om., although it does not coincide with the end of the line.* 6 noctes] *added in the margin together with its gloss; a set of signs indicates the place where it is to be inserted.*

Old English gloss: 6 nihta] *added in margin together with its lemma;* 9 þes] e *altered from* æ.

VmJVpH Heading: *no rubric* VmpH, QUESUMUS ERGO *J; in H the stanza is only marked as a first stanza by a new set of neumes;* 1 sereno] serenum *JVpH;* 2 vultu] vultum *JVpH;* gubernes] gubernans *VmJVpH;* 3 summo] summi *H;* honore] amore *VmJVp,* amando *H;* 5 nos] *om. JVp;* molesta] molestia *JVp;* 6 noctes] noctis *Vm;* 7 pereunte] pereuntque *Vm;* 8 sentiat] sentiant *H;* 9 Hic] Sic *H;* consecratam] consecrato *H;* 11 longo] *first* o *damaged J;* 13 *om. JVp.*

Commentary Latin: 1–2 serenum ... vultum *(JVpH) is attested by* AH *for the Continent as well.* 2 AH *reads* gubernans, *attesting* guberges *for continental manuscripts as well.* 3 AH *reads* amore, *cf.* VmJVp. 5 AH *reads* cruciet molestas, *also attesting* crucient molesta *for the Continent.* Old English: 2 begemende *glosses the reading of* VmJVpH. 5 cwylmige *should be plural; the mistake is probably connected with* AH's *reading* cruciet. 10 *The glossator translates as if the lemma were* tribuas. *This could be due to* conspicis / þu besceawast *in the same verse, but* AH *attests* tribuas, tribue *in continental manuscripts.* 13 þan healican *again is dat. instead of acc., cf.* Hy 127/17 *and* Hy 128/17.

130

ITEM YMNUS

I CHRISTE, CÆLORUM   HABITATOR alme,
   hęc domus fulget   sub honore cuius,
   hostiam clemens,   tibi quam *littamus,
   suscipe laudis.   4

II Omnium semper   chorus angelorum
   in polo *tenet   benedicit alto

| | atque sancti | simul universi | |
| | [42v] sedule laudant. | | 8 |

III Presulis almi   meritis Augustini
     atque istorum   pariter sanctorum
     contine poenam   pie, quam meremur,
     daque medelam.   12

IV   Sic tuam presta   celebrare laudem
     flebilem vitam   miseratus istam,
     fiat ut nobis   licitum videre
     te sine fine.   16

V   Doxa sublimi   maneat parenti,
     eius & nato   pariterque sancto
     pneumati, trino   domino & uno
     semper in aevum.   20
                amen

I   Christ, holy dweller in heaven, in whose honour this house is resplen-
    dent, receive kindly the sacrifice of praise which we offer up to you.

II The choir of all the angels always exalts you in high heaven and all
    saints eagerly praise you, too.

III Through the merits of holy Augustine and those other saints all
    equally, hold back mercifully the punishment we deserve and confer
    healing.

IV Out of compassion for this pitiable life, grant that we may celebrate
    your praise in such a way that it will be allowed to us to see you
    without end.

V   Honour be to the most high Father and to his Son and also to the
    Holy Spirit, to the threefold and single Lord, in eternity.

This is a Canterbury version of a hymn for the anniversary of the
dedication of the church, which is not otherwise found in Anglo-Saxon
England. The adaptation for Canterbury (see Commentary to lines 9–10)
proves that the hymn was really used, but the details are unclear. It is
anonymous and written in Sapphic stanzas. The text in D has no neumes.

Bibliographical references: *ICL* no. 2162; *AH* 51, 115–16 (no. 104).

419

Commentary 3 *For* littamus *read* litamus. 5–6 *Cf.* benedicite Domino *(some manuscripts add* omnes*)* angeli eius *Ps. CII.20.* 6 *For* tenet *read* temet. 7 AH *reads* atque te sancti *which is metrically correct.* 8 AH's *third stanza is omitted.* 9–10 *In* AH *these lines read:* Virginis sanctae meritis Mariae / atque cunctorum pariter piorum; *St Augustine of Canterbury was introduced without attention to the metre.*

131

YMNUS DE SANCTA TRINITATE

eala þu arwurðe   þrynnyss herigendlice
I   O   VENERANDA   TRINItas laudanda,

þearle welwillende   7 *wuldor wurðful
valde benigna   gloriaque digna,

ure   gehyr   bena þam þe
nostras exaudi   preces, quibus tibi

we singað lofsang
canimus ymnum.   4

þe we ciað   7   we biddað
II   Te invocamus   atque adoramus

7 þe   we heryað   þrynnes eadig
teque laudamus,   trinitas beata.

þu us   syle   scylde   ealra
Tu nobis dona   scelerum cunctorum

forgyfenessa
remissionem,   8

þæt we magon   modum   estfullum
III   ut valeamus   mentibus devotis

don *wurðfullum   þe   eac swilce lofu
agere dignas   tibi quoque laudes

dæges 7 nihtes   tidum 7 handwilum
die   ac nocte,   horis & momentis

æfre   secgende
semper dicentes.   12

wuldor ormæte   butan ænde wunigende
IV   Gloria ingens,   sine fine manens

sy þrynnisse   healicre godcundnysse
sit trinitati,   summe deitati

ealle   geond worulda   stefne samod mid anre
cuncta per   secula.   Voce simul una

ealle   secgan
cuncti dicamus   16

     sy hit swa
     amen.

I O Trinity to be venerated and praised, most kind and worthy of glory, hear our prayers, interspersed with which we sing our hymn to you.

II We call upon you and adore you and praise you, blessed Trinity. Grant us the remission of all iniquities

III so that we may also be able to offer adequate praise to you with devoted hearts, uttering it always, by day and night, at each hour and moment.

IV Immeasurable and endless glory be to the Trinity, the most high deity, throughout the ages. Let us all say with one voice together: Amen.

This hymn for Trinity Sunday was sung at Vespers. It is anonymous and written in Sapphic stanzas with a strong tendency to interior rhyme. No melody is transmitted in the Anglo-Saxon manuscripts. The text is appended to the hymnal in D and the *Expositio hymnorum* of J. J has an Old English interlinear gloss closely related to that of D.

Bibliographical references: *ICL* no. 11070; cf. *AH* 14a, 126 (no. 123).

Apparatus to D   Latin text: 10 laudes] *added later, possibly by another hand*.

J   Latin text: Heading: YMNUS DE SANCTA TRINITATE; 6 trinitas] trinas; 13 Gloria] loria.

J   Old English gloss: 1 arwurðe] arwurða; þrynnyss] þrynnes; 2 þearle] swiðe; wurðful] wurðfull; 3 bena] bene; 5 ciað] cygað; 6 heryað] heriað; þrynnes] þrynnys; 7 ealra] eallra; 8 forgyfenessa] forgifennysse; 9 magon] magan; estfullum] gewilnungum; 10 eac swilce] witodlice; 11 nihtes] nihte; handwilum] handhwilum; 12 secgende] sægende; 13 ænde] ende; 14 sy] sye; þrynnisse] þrynnysse; 15 worulda] wurulda; 16 secgan] we cweðað; sy] syo.

Commentary   Latin: 15 *The metre requires* saecla *as in* AH. Old English: 2 *The glossator takes* gloria *for nom. sg., whereas it is clearly the abl.* 10 dignas *belongs to* laudes / lofu, *so that* wurðfullum *should be acc. pl. ntr. The dat. is apparently due to the following* þe. 11 dæges 7 nihtes *in D represents an idiomatic rendering of the Latin temporal ablative.* nihte *in J could be the regular gen. (SB §284, note 3) or be a dat., the conventional equivalent of abl. in the gloss.*

132

[43r] ITEM YMNUS

eala þu *fæter halige   liþe   7   arfæst
I   O   PATEr   SANCTE,   MITIS ATQUE pie,

eala þu hælend crist   bearn arwurðe
o   Iesu   Christe,   fili   venerande

7 frofergast   gast   7 halig
paraclitusque,   spiritus & alme,

god   ece
deus aeternæ,   4

þrynnes halig   7 annys   trum
II   trinitas sancta   unitasque firma,

godcundnys soþ   godnyss ormæte
deitas   vera,   bonitas inmensa,

leoht ængla   hæl   steopcilda
lux angelorum,   salus orphanorum

7 hiht   ealra
spesque cunctorum,   8

*þeowian þe   ealle þing þe ðu gescope
III   serviunt tibi,   cuncta   quę creasti,

þe samod ealle   *herigan gescæfte
te simul cunctę   laudant creaturę.

*us   eac swilce þe   we singað estfullice
Nos quoque tibi   psallimus devoti.

þu us gehýr
Tu nos exaudi.   12

wuldor þe   god   ælmihtig
IV   Gloria tibi,   deus omnipotens,

              micel   7 ece
[trinus et unus]   magnus & eternus,

þe gedafenað lofsang   wurðment lof 7 wlite
te decet   ymnus,   honor,   laus & decus

nu   7 on ecnysse
nunc & in evum.   16

I O holy, mild and loving Father, o Jesus Christ, son to be venerated, o Comforter and Holy Spirit, eternal God,

II holy Trinity and strong oneness, true godhead, immeasurable goodness, light of the angels, salvation of the orphans and hope of everyone,

III everything you created serves you, all creatures praise you together. We, too, sing songs to you devotedly. Hear us.

IV Glory be to you, almighty God, (*V:* threefold and single), great and eternal; hymns, honour, praise and glory are fitting for you now and forever.

This hymn was sung at Matins (Nocturn) on Trinity Sunday. It is anonymous and written in Sapphic stanzas. Monosyllabic rhyme links half-verses and verses in a slightly irregular pattern. No melody has been transmitted in the Anglo-Saxon manuscripts. The text is appended to the hymnals of D and V and the *Expositio hymnorum* of J. The text in V is an addition of the eleventh century. J contains an Old English interlinear gloss closely related to D.

Bibliographical references: *ICL* no. 10975; *AH* 51, 101–2 (no. 95), cf. *AH* 2, 58 (no. 65).

Apparatus to D   Latin text: 1 PATEr] r *interlined above by* D_1; 4 aeternæ] æ *altered from* a.

JV   Heading: YMNUS DE SANCTE TRINITATE AD NOCTURNAM *J, no rubric V;* 2 Iesu] hiesu *V;* 3 &] o *V;* 9 serviunt] S *om. J;* 10 simul] tuę *V;* 13 deus omnipotens] omnipotens deus *V;* 14 trinus et unus] *om. J; V reads:* trinus & unus magnus & excelsus; 16 *JV add* amen.

J Old English gloss: 1 fæter] fæder; 2 bearn] sunu; 3 gast] *om.;* 5 þrynnes] þrynnys; annys] annyss; 6 godnyss] godnys; 8 ealra] eallra; 9 *J adds* 7 *in front of* ealle, *omits the second* þe; 10 samod] ætgædere; 14 micel] mycel; 15 wurðment] wurðmynt.

Commentary   Latin: 3 AH *reads* o *like V, but* et *is also attested.* 7 *Cf.* patris orfanorum *Ps. LXVII.6.* 10 AH *reads* tuae *like V.* 13 *The sequence of words in V is attested by* AH *for continental manuscripts.* 14 *The first half of the verse is missing in D and J. V's* magnus & excelsus *is attested by* AH *for continental manuscripts.* Old English: 1 fæter *is the only instance of* t *for* d *in D; the reverse occurs sporadically in this gloss (see p. 76). Cf. SB §224 and n. 2.* 9 þeowian *should be indicative.* 7 ealle *in J interprets the lemma as* cunctaque. 10 herigan *should be indicative.* 11 *The glossator has mistaken the nominative* nos *for the more common accusative.*

133

ITEM YMNUS

6

hal sy þu to wurþigenne þrynes
I AVE,   COLENDA TRINITAS,

hal sy þu ece   annyss
ave,   perennis unitas,

fæder god   bearn god
pater deus, nate deus

7 god   halig gast
& deus alme spiritus.   4

þas þing þe   nu   gecweme
II Hęc   tibi nunc gratuita

we geyppað   bena
depromimus preconia,

þa   þe   beon gecwemestan
quę tibi sint gratissima

7 us   þa halwendestan
& nobis saluberrima.   8

þe þrylicne æfre   we heriað
III Te trinum semper laudamus

7   ænne   we biddað
atque unum adoramus.

þinre werodre mildheortnysse
Tuę dulcis clementiae

we undergytan emtrymminga
sentiamus   munimina.   12

eala þu þrynnes eala þu annys
IV O trinitas, o   unitas,

ætbeo þu halsigendum
adesto supplicantibus

7 ængla   mid lofum
& angelorum laudibus

underfoh   þæt þæt we gelæstan
admitte, quod   persolvimus.   16

sy hit swa
AMEN

I Hail, Trinity to be revered, hail, everlasting oneness, God Father, God Son and God Holy Spirit.

II We freely offer you these commendations. May they be most pleasing to you and most beneficial to us.

III Always we praise you as the threefold one and adore you as the single one. May we enjoy the protection of your sweet mercy.

IV O Trinity, o oneness, aid those who entreat you and count among the praise of the angels that which we are finishing.

This hymn was sung at Lauds on Trinity Sunday. It is anonymous and written in rhythmical Ambrosian hymn verse (4 × 8pp) linked by slightly irregular monosyllabic rhyme. No melody has been transmitted in the Anglo-Saxon manuscripts. The text is appended to the hymnal of D and the *Expositio hymnorum* of J. J contains an Old English gloss closely related to that in D.

Bibliographical references: *ICL* no. 1539; *AH* 19, 9 (no. 2, based on J and D).

J   Heading: YMNUS IN LAUDIBUS; 5 Hęc] ęc; 7 gratissima] gravissima; 12 munimina] munimia; 16 quod] *interlined above with the pen used for glossing.*

   J Old English gloss: 1 hal sy þu] syo þu gesund; þrynes] þrynnys; 2 sy] wes; annyss] annys; 5 þas] þa; 6 geyppað] geyppuð; bena] bene; 7 gecwemestan] gecwemesta; 9 þrylicne] þrinlicne; heriað] herigað; 11 werodre] weorodre; 12 we] *om.*; emtrymminga] ymtrymminga; 13 þrynnes] ðrinnys; 15 ængla] ængle; 16 sy hit swa] *om.*

134

I   Iesu, redemptor seculi,
    verbum patris altissimi,
    lux lucis invisibilis,
    custos tuorum pervigil,   4

II   tu fabricator omnium,
    discretor atque temporum,
    fessa labore corpora
    noctis quiete recrea.   8

425

III   Te deprecamur supplices,
      ut nos ab hoste liberes,
      ne valeat seducere
      tuo redemptos sanguine,   12

IV   ut, dum gravi in corpore
      brevi manemus tempore,
      sic caro nostra dormiat,
      ut mens sopore nesciat.   16

V   Sit, Christe, rex piissime,
      tibi patrique gloria
      cum spiritu paraclito
      & nunc & in perpetuum.   20
                           Amen

I Jesus, redeemer of the world, word of the most high Father, invisible light of light, wakeful guardian of your own,

II you maker of all and distinguisher of times and seasons, refresh the bodies weary with labour with rest in the night.

III We humbly pray you, deliver us from the enemy that he may not be able to seduce those who are redeemed by your blood

IV so that, while we for a short time remain in our cumbersome body, our flesh may sleep in such a way that the heart knows no sleep.

V Glory be to you, Christ, most merciful king, and to the Father as well as to the Holy Spirit now and forever.

This is a hymn for Compline. From H's collectar it appears that it was sung on some Sundays and at a number of feasts. It is anonymous and written in Ambrosian iambic dimeter. The stanza rhymes aabb. No melody has been transmitted in Anglo-Saxon hymnals. The text is included in the hymnals of B and H. H is followed here.

Bibliographical references: *ICL* no. 7662; *AH* 51, 43–4 (no. 45). The hymn is no. 11a in Gneuss, *HHEM*.

H   *No rubric.*

   B Heading: Item alius ymnus; 13 ut] Et; 16 nesciat] vigilet; 17 Deo patri sit gloria; 20 *B omits* amen.

Commentary   Heading: *The rubric in B implies use for Compline, as the preceding hymn is used for that Hour.* 16 sopore nesciat *in H looks like an obvious mistake for* soporem nesciat, *but the reading is extant as a variant in the Uses of Sarum and York; cf.* Breviarium ad usum insignis ecclesiae Sarum, *ed. Proctor and Wordsworth II, 234. B has* sopore *with another verb.*

135

I   Agnoscat omne seculum
venisse vitę premium.
Post hostis asperi iugum
apparuit redemptio.   4

II   Esaias quę precinit,
completa sunt in virgine,
annuntiavit angelus,
sanctus replevit spiritus.   8

III   Maria ventre concepit
verbi fidele semine.
Quem totus mundus non capit,
portant puelle viscera.   12

IV   Radix Iesse iam floruit
& virga fructus edidit,
foecunda *partim protulit
& *virga mater permanet.   16

V   Presepe poni pertulit,
qui lucis auctor extitit.
Cum patre cęlos condidit,
sub matre pannos induit.   20

VI   Legem dedit qui seculo,
cuius decem precepta sunt,
dignando factus est homo
sub legis esse vinculo.   24

VII   Adam vetus quod polluit,
Adam novus hoc abluit;

VIII

tumens quod ille deiecit,
humillimus hic erigit.   28

Iam nata lux est & salus,
fugata nox & victa mors.
Venite, gentes, credite:
deum Maria protulit.   32

IX

Gloria tibi, domine,
qui natus es de virgine,
cum patre & sancto spiritu
in sempiterna secula.   36

amen

I May the whole world understand that the reward, life, has come.
After the time of the yoke of the brutal enemy redemption has been
revealed.

II What Isaiah sang in prophecy was fulfilled in the virgin. The angel
heralded it; the Holy Spirit filled it wholly.

III Mary conceived in her womb by the faithful seed of the word. A girl
carries inside her the one whom the whole world cannot contain.

IV Now the root of Jesse brought forth a flower and a branch brought
forth fruit. Fertile, it produced offspring and yet the mother remains
a virgin.

V The one who was the originator of light suffers himself to be laid in
a manger. He created the heavens together with his father; under the
care of his mother he is dressed in swaddling clothes.

VI The one who gave law to the world, who issued the Ten Command-
ments, became human and deigned to be constrained by the law.

VII What the old Adam defiled the new Adam cleanses, what the
former, swollen with pride, threw down the latter in his utmost
humility raises up.

VIII Now the light and the salvation is born, the night is dispelled and
death is conquered. Come, o nations, and believe it: Mary gave birth
to God.

IX Glory be to you, Lord, who were born of a virgin, with the Father
and the Holy Ghost in eternity.

This is a Christmas hymn, but its precise use is unclear. It has been ascribed to Venantius Fortunatus (sixth century). It is written in Ambrosian iambic dimeter. The text itself is included only in the hymnal of H, while the hymn is not even mentioned in the collectar of the same manuscript. The text is not accompanied by neumes.

Bibliographical references: *ICL* no. 492; *AH* 50, 85–6 (no. 71); Walpole no. 38.

H 34 es] est, t *added by later hand.*

Commentary 1 *Cf. Hy 39/3.* 5 *Cf. Isa. VII.14.* 13 *Cf. Isa. XI.1 and 10, Rom. XV.12.* 15 *For* partim *read* partum. 16 *For* virga *read* virgo. 25–6 *Cf.* primus homo Adam ... novissimus Adam *I Cor. XV.45.*

136

I   Corde natus ex parentis   ante mundi exordium,
    alpha & o cognominatus,   ipse fons & clausula
    omnium, quę sunt, fuerunt   queque post futura sunt
    seculorum seculis,   4

II   O beatus ortus ille,   virgo cum puerpera
    edidit nostram salutem   feta sancto spiritu
    & puer redemptor orbis   os sacratum protulit
    seculorum seculis.   8

III   Psallat altitudo cęli,   psallant omnes angeli,
    quidquid est virtutis usquam,   psallat in laudem dei.
    Nulla linguarum silescat,   vox & omnis consonet
    seculorum seculis.   12

IV   Ecce, quem vates vetustis   concinebant seculis,
    quem prophetarum fideles   pagine spoponderant.
    Emicat promissus olim.   Cuncta conlaudent eum
    seculorum seculis.   16

V   Te senes & te iuventus,   parvulorum te chorus,
    turba matrum virginumque,   simplices puellule

voces concordes *pudici   perstrepant concentibus
seculorum seculis.   20

VI   Tibi, Christe, sit cum patre   agioque spiritu
     *ymnos, melos, laus perennes,   gratiarum actio,
     honor, virtus, victoria,   regnum ęternaliter
     seculorum seculis.   24
                  amen

I He who was born from the heart of the Father before the beginning
of the world, who is also named the alpha and omega, is himself the
source and end of all that is, has been and will be in the future for
ages of ages.

II Oh, blessed was that birth, when the virgin mother impregnated by
the Holy Spirit bore our salvation and the redeemer of the world
showed his holy face as a boy to the ages of ages.

III May the high heavens sing psalms, may all angels sing them, may
whatever is of any power anywhere sing psalms to praise God. May
no tongue be silent and may each voice join in harmony for ages of
ages.

IV Behold the one of whom the seers sang in past ages, the one whose
coming the reliable writings of the prophets affirmed. The one who
was once promised stands revealed. Let all things praise him together
during the ages of ages.

V Let the old and the young, let the choir of little children, the crowd
of mothers and virgins, the simple girls, let their voices in unison
proclaim you in chaste harmony for ages of ages.

VI May you, Christ, together with the Father and the Holy Spirit have
forever hymn and song and praise accompanied by prayer, the giving
of thanks, honour, power, victory and rule in eternity for ages of
ages.

This hymn was in use at Christmas and Candlemas (the Purification of
Mary, 2 February). The collectar in H prescribes it for the First Vespers of
St Stephen (26 December) and Compline of the Octave of Christmas, the
Vigil of Epiphany, the Vigil of Purification and Purification itself. It is an
extract from Prudentius's *Cathemerinon* IX comprising lines 10–12, 19–27

and 109–11. The verses are written in catalectic trochaic tetrameter. The text is only included in the hymnal of H (apart from manuscripts of the *Cathemerinon*) and is not accompanied by neumes.

Bibliographical references: *ICL* no. 2773; *AH* 50, 25–6 (no. 26), Walpole no. 23.

H   2 o] *written as Greek omega between dots*; 22 perennes] *corrected to* perennis, e *expunged*, i *suprascript*.

Commentary   2 *Cf. Rev. I.8 and* 17. 6 *Cf. Ps. CXLV.*6. 18 *Cf.* laudate eum omnes virtutes eius *Ps. CXLVIII.*2. 19 *For* pudici *read* pudicis. 22 *For* ymnos *read* ymnus.

137

I	Infantum meritis	inclita gaudia	
	pangamus, socii,	gestaque fortia,	
	nam gliscit animus	promere cantibus	
	victorum genus optimum.		4
II	Caeduntur gladiis	more bidentium.	
	Non murmur resonat	non querimonia,	
	sed corde tacito	mens bene conscia	
	conservat *patientia.		8
III	Te, trina deitas	unaque, poscimus,	
	ut culpas abluas,	noxia subtrahas,	
	des pacem famulis –	nos quoque gloria	
	per cuncta tibi secula.		12

amen

I Let us sing of the joys made renowned by the merits of infants and their resolute acts, comrades, for the heart is inspired to celebrate the best kind of victors in song.

II They are struck with swords like sheep. Neither a murmur nor a complaint is uttered, but the mind conscious of no evil maintains its patience with a quiet heart.

III We ask you, deity threefold and single, to wash away our guilt and remove what is harmful, to give peace to your servants – we shall also give you glory throughout the ages.

This is an adaptation of Hy 119 for the feast of the Holy Innocents (28 December). According to the collectar in H it was sung at Lauds. The text is included only in the hymnal of H and is not accompanied by neumes, but was probably sung to the same melody as Hy 119. For further details see under Hy 119 (pp. 394–5).

138

I   Nunc tibi, virgo virginum,
laudes ferimus carminum
teque cęli dominam
resultet hec *plebiculo.   4

II   Tu porta domus fulgida
egressionis inscia
& virga fructu florida
virgoque nato gravida.   8

III   Te nostra sonant carmina,
te angelorum agmina;
infernus tibi ululat
fretumque maris intonat.   12

IV   Lacta, regina, parvulum
ęterni regis filium,
lacta sacrata ubere,
qui te concessit vivere.   16

V   Tu clara stirpe regia
*iure mundi domina,
*desideratus omnibus
tu protulisti gentibus.   20

VI   Tu *tella maris fulgida,
absolve plebis crimina.

Fletus quoque supplicum
inmuta dando gaudio.   24

VII   Laus patri invisibili,
laus eius almo flamini
laus sit unigenito
orbis terrarum domino.   28
            Amen

I Now we offer praise in song to you, virgin of virgins, and these humble folk shall celebrate you as queen of heaven.

II You are the glittering door of the house that has not known anyone to pass through, the branch burgeoning with fruit and the virgin pregnant with a son.

III It is you our songs sing of, you the hosts of angels sing of; hell groans before you and the straits of the sea thunder your name.

IV Give suck to the little son of the eternal king, o queen, give suck from your sacred breast to the one who granted that you should live.

V You, who are glorious because of your royal descent and rightfully the ruler of the world, bore the one whom all nations longed for.

VI You who are the glowing star of the sea, free the people of their guilt. Change the weeping of the supplicants, too, by granting them joy instead.

VII Praise to the unseen Father, praise to his Holy Spirit, praise be to the only-begotten Son, the lord of the world.

This Marian hymn is included in the hymnals of C, H and Vm. H contains the text twice, a version by scribe H_1 for Candlemas and a version by scribe H_4 for Lauds of the Nativity of Mary (8 September). The collectar in H disagrees and assigns it to Matins of the Nativity of Mary (as an alternative to Hy 65_1). In V the hymn is for Candlemas, in C for the Nativity of Mary. The hymn is anonymous and written in rhythmical Ambrosian hymn verse ($4 \times 8pp$). The stanza rhymes aabb. The neumes accompanying H_4 probably represent a version of Stäblein no. 705. The text is based on H_1.

Bibliographical references: *ICL* no. 10775; *AH* 14a, 109 (no. 105). The hymn is no. 47a in Gneuss, *HHEM*.

H₄VC   Heading: YMNUS AD MATUTINAM *H₄*; ITEM YMNUS. DE SANCTA MARIA *V*, HYMNUS DE NATIVITATE SANCTE MARIAE *C*; 1 virgo] *mistakenly repeated V*; 2 ferimus] referimus *V*; carminum] carmina *C*; 3 dominam] domina *H₄C*; 4 plebiculo] plebecula *H₄*, plebicula *VC*; 8 virgo-] virga- *V*; 12 maris] matris *VC*; 15 lacta] lacto *H₄*; sacrata] sacrato *H₄VC*; 17 clara] claustra *C*; 18 iure] iureque *H₄VC*; 19 desideratus] desideratum *H₄VC*; 20 protulisti] pertulisti *C*; 21 Tu] O *VC*; tella] stella, ell *on erasure possibly by another hand H₄*, stella *VC*; 23 supplicum] supplicantum *V*; 24 inmuta dando] inmutando *VC*; gaudio] gaudium *H₄VC*; 26 flamini] flamine *C*; 27 sit] *on erasure possibly by another hand H₄*; 28 *C omits* amen.

Commentary   Heading: *Whereas* natale *in the rubrics to feasts of other saints means the day of their death (the day of their birth to heaven),* nativitas *here really means 'day of birth'.* 4 *For* plebiculo *read* plebicula *like H₄VC.* 5 *Cf. Hy 65₂/10.* 7 *Cf. Isa. XI.1.* 15 *Cf. Hy 65₂/4. AH reads* sacrato. 17 *Cf. Hy 89/2.* 18 *For* iure *read* iureque *like H₄VC.* 19 *For* desideratus *read* desideratum *like H₄. Cf. Hag. II.8 and Hy 65₁/19.* 21 *For* tella *read* stella *like H₄VC.* 24 AH *reads* gaudium.

139

HYMNUS AD COMPLETORIUM

I   O Nazarene, lux Bethleem, verbum patris,
quem partus alvi virginalis protulit,
adesto castis, Christe, parsimoniis
festumque nostrum rex serenus aspice,
[ieiuniorum dum litamus victimam].   5

II   Nil hoc profecto purius misterio,
quo fibra cordis expiatur lividi,
*imtemperata quo *domatur viscera,
arvina putrem ne resudans crapulam
obstrangulate mentis inienium premat.   10

III   Sit trinitati in unitate gloria,
in trinitate *unitate gratia,
potestas, honor atque iubilatio
nostra benigne cum benivolentia

ieiuniorum acceptanti munia.   15
amen

I O man of Nazareth, light from Bethlehem, word of the Father, brought forth by birth from the virginal womb, assist in the period of chaste abstinence and regard our time of celebration in royal satisfaction, while we offer up the sacrifice of fasting.

II Indeed nothing is more purifying than this mysterious rite, by which the heart strings are redeemed from their malice and the unbridled flesh is restrained so that no fat reeking of foul excess can oppress the thought of the stifled mind.

III Glory be to the trinity in unity, thanks be to the unity in trinity, power, honour and jubilation be to it, because it receives our labour in fasting kindly and with goodwill.

This is a hymn for Lent, assigned to Compline. The collectar in H specifies that it is to be sung on the third and fourth Saturday and on the third Sunday in Lent. It is an extract from Prudentius's *Cathemerinon* VII comprising verses 1–10 with an added doxology. The melody transmitted in H is a version of Stäblein no. 178. This is the only known melody for this text (Stäblein, p. 552). The text is included only in H.

Bibliographical references: *ICL* no. 10956; *AH* 50, 28–9 (no. 29); Bulst, p. 59 (III, 5), Walpole no. 25.

Commentary   1 *For* verbum patris *see John I.1.* 3–5 *Cf.* 149/17–19. 5–7 *Cf. Hy* 57/16f. 5 *The omission of this line is clearly accidental.* 8 *For* imtemperata *read* intemperata. *For* domatur *read* domantur. 12 *For* unitate *read* unitati.

140

ITEM ALIUS AD COMPLETORIUM

I   Cultor dei, memento
te fontis et lavacri
rorem subisse sanctum,
te crismate innotatum.   4

435

II   Fac, cum vocante somno
castum petis cubile,
frontem locumque cordis
crucis figura signet.   8

III   Crux pellit omne crimen.
Fugiunt crucem tenebre.
Tali dicata *signet
mens *fructuare nescit.   12

IV   Procul, procul, vagantum
portenta somniorum,
procul esto pervicaci,
prestigiator, astu.   16

V   O tortuose serpens,
qui mille per meandros
fraudesque flexuosas
agitas quieta corda,   20

VI   discede, Christus hic est.
Hic Christus est, liquesce.
Signum, quod ipse nosti,
dampnat tuam catervam.   24

VII   Corpus licet fatiscens
iaceat recline paululum,
Christum tamen sub ipso
*meditabitur sopore.   28

VIII   Gloria ęterno *patei
& Christo, vero regi,
paraclitoque sancto
& nunc & in perpetuum.   32

amen

I You who revere God, remember that you underwent the holy sprinkling with cleansing water and that a mark was made on you with chrismal oil.

II Take care that when sleep calls and you turn to your chaste bed-chamber the forehead and the place where your heart is shall be signed with the figure of the cross.

III The cross keeps off all iniquity. Darkness flees before the cross. If the heart is consecrated by such a sign it cannot waver.

IV Stay far off, far off, phantasms of straying dreams, stay far off, deceiver, with your persistent cunning!

V O writhing serpent, you who disturb quiet hearts by your thousand-fold twisting and your flexible deceptions,

VI depart; Christ is here! Christ is here, dissolve! The sign you know yourself spells damnation for your band.

VII Although the body growing weary may lean back a little and lie down, we shall contemplate Christ even in our sleep.

VIII Glory be to the eternal Father and to Christ, the true king, and the Holy Comforter both now and forever.

In H this hymn for Compline occurs in the section for Lent, in B among the ferial hymns, but may nevertheless be intended for Lent. It is an extract from Prudentius's *Cathemerinon* VI comprising verses 125–53. The melody transmitted in H is a fairly plain version of Stäblein no. 170, the only known tune for the hymn (see Stäblein, 'Hymnus', col. 998). The text follows H.

Bibliographical references: *ICL* no. 2976; *AH* 50, 29–30 (no. 30); Walpole no. 26. The manuscripts consulted in *AH* are all late medieval. The hymn is no. 12a in Gneuss, *HHEM*.

B   Heading: item alius; 4 innotatum] innovatum; 8 figura] a *on erasure*; 11 signet] somno; 12 fructuare] fluctuare; 16 prestigiator] o *appears altered from* u; 26 iaceat] iacet; paululum] paulo; 28 meditabitur] meditamur; 29–32 Deo patri sit gloria; *B omits* amen.

Commentary   2 *Cf.* per lavacrum regenerationis et renovationis *Tit. III.5.* 11 *For H's* signet *read* signo *(and so* AH*);* signet *has slipped in from line 8.* B's *reading is altogether different.* 12 *For H's* fructuare *read* fluctuare. 26 H's *paululum does not conform to the metre, but is a widespread reading on the Continent according to* AH. 28 AH *reads* meditabimur. 29 *For H's* patei *read* patri *(Dewick overlooks the mistake).*

141

HYMNUS AD MATUTINAM

I   Rex angelorum prepotens,
     qui sponte pauper factus es,
     ut nos per evum divites,
     in ethre tecum poneres,   4

II   largire nobis prospera
     crucis sacra sollempnia
     gratesque da *psolvere
     magne tuę clementię,   8

III   qui sustinens obprobria,
     fel, vincla, sputa, verbera
     mortemque, nobis perpetis
     vitę parasti gloriam.   12

IV   Nunc clarus in regno tuo
     nostri memento, quesumus,
     *ut cum latrone perfrui
     da paradisi gaudiis.   16

V   Tecum patrem piissimum
     simulque sancto spiritu
     inferna, terre, sidera
     tremunt, adorant, concrepant.   20

                       amen

I Most mighty king of angels, who became poor by your own will to make us rich in perpetuity and bring us with you to heaven,

II make the holy feast of the cross beneficent for us and let us render thanks to your great mercy,

III for you bore insults, gall, fetters, spittle, blows and death and so made available to us the glory of eternal life.

IV Now you are dwelling in splendour in your kingdom, remember us, we pray, and grant that we may taste the joys of paradise together with the robber.

v Hell, earth and stars tremble before the most kind Father in one
with you and the Holy Spirit, they revere you and resound with your
name.

This hymn is included only in H and is not mentioned in the collectar in
that manuscript. In the hymnal it is assigned to Lauds of Passiontide. It is
anonymous and written in Ambrosian iambic dimeter. The neumes in H
represent an unidentified melody.

Bibliographical references: *ICL* no. 14242; *AH* 51, 69–70 (no. 70).

Commentary   7 *For* psolvere *read* persolvere. *The abbreviation mark is missing.* 9 *Cf. Hy*
68/5–6. 15–16 Cf. Luke XXIII.39–43. 15 For ut *read* et. *17–18 Cf. Hy 65₁/1–2.*

142

ITEM

I   Rex Christe, factor omnium,
    redemptor & credentium,
    placare votis supplicum
    te laudibus colentium.   4

II Qui es creator siderum,
    tegmen subisti carneum
    dignatus hanc vilissimam
    pati doloris formulam.   8

III Ligatus es, ut solveres
    mundi ruentis complices
    per probra tergens crimina,
    que mundus ausit plurima,   12

IV cuius benigna gratia
    cuius per alma munera
    virtute solvit ardua
    primi parentis vincula.   16

V   Cruci redemptor figeris,
    terram sed omnem concutis.

Tradis potentem spiritum;
*nigressit omne seculum. 20

VI *Vox in paterne glorię
victor resplendens culmine,
cum spiritus munimine
defende nos, rex optime. 24

amen

I Christ, king, you who made all and are the redeemer of the believers,
be appeased by the prayers of the supplicants who adore you by
praising you.

II You, who are the creator of the stars, undertook to be clothed in
flesh, deigning to endure this most worthless form with its pain.

III You were bound so as to set free those who were entangled in the
decaying world by iniquities, purifying them of the sins of which
the world had dared to commit many indeed,

IV you, whose benevolent kindness by your holy gifts undid the
burdensome chains of the first father by miraculous power.

V As the redeemer you are nailed to the cross, but make all the earth
shake. You yield up your powerful spirit and all the world grows
dark.

VI Now resplendent as victor on high in the glory of the Father, defend
us by the protection of the Spirit, best of kings.

This hymn is included only in H. It is not found in the collectar of that
manuscript. The rubric assigns it by implication to Passiontide, possibly
to Lauds. It is anonymous and written in Ambrosian iambic dimeter. The
stanza rhymes aabb. The neumes in H represent a version of Stäblein no.
12 combining features of 12_2 and 12_3. This is apparently the original
melody, known hitherto only from Germany and northern Italy and,
according to Stäblein, typically German (Stäblein, p. 506).

Bibliographical references: *ICL* no. 14254; *AH* 51, 71–2 (no. 72).

Commentary   AH *has the first four stanzas in the following sequence: I, IV, II, III.* 12 AH
reads auxit. 14 AH *reads* vulnera. 17–20 *Cf. Matt.* XVII.45 *and* 51. 20 *For* nigressit *read*
nigrescit. 21 *For* Vox *read* Mox.

143

ITEM YMNUS AD MATUTINAM

I Pange, lingua, gloriosi   prelium certaminis
  & super crucis tropheo   dic triumphum nobile,
  qualiter redemptor orbis   immolatus vicerit.   3

II De parentis protoplasti   fraude facta condolens,
  quando pomi noxialis   morte morsu corruit,
  ipse lignum tunc notavit,   ligni iure ut solveret.   6

III Hoc opus nostre salutis   ordo depoposcerat,
  multiformis proditoris   arte ut artem falleret
  & medelam ferret inde,   hostis unde leserat.   9

IV Quando venit ergo sacri   plenitudo temporis,
  missus est ab arce patris   natus, orbis conditor,
  atque ventre virginali   carne factus prodiit.   12

V Lustra sex qui iam peracta   tempus implens corporis
  se volente, natus ad hoc,   passioni deditus
  agnus in crucem levatur   immolandus stipite.   15

VI Hic *accetum, fel, arundo,   sputa, clavi, lancea.
  Mite corpus perforatur;   sanguis, unda profluit,
  terra, pontus, astra, mundus   quo lavantur flumine.   18

VII Crux fidelis, inter omnes   arbor una nobilis,
  nulla silva talem profert   fronde florem, germine.
  Dulce lignum dulces clavos,   dulce pondus sustinet.   21

VIII Gloria & honor deo   atque coaltissimo
  una patri filioque   inclito paraclito,
  cui honor & potestas   in eterna secula.   24
                  amen

1 Sing, tongue, of the battle, the glorious struggle, and speak of that famous triumph on the sign of the victory, the cross, how the redeemer of the world conquered by being sacrificed.

II Filled with pity at the deception imposed on the first created man, our forefather, when he perished in death because he had tasted the harmful fruit, he honoured a tree then with his choice to lift the just punishment connected with a tree.

III This act was required in the plan of our salvation so that he might deflect the tricks of the many-shaped betrayer with a trick of his own and derive healing from the same source from which the enemy had inflicted hurt.

IV When it therefore came to the point that the holy time was fulfilled, the Son, the creator of the world, was sent down from the fastness of his Father and he came forth, made flesh in the womb of a virgin.

V When he had lived out the time of his embodiment, six times five years having passed, he of his own will yielded himself up to suffering, as he had been born for that, and he is lifted up on the cross, on a wooden beam, as a lamb to be sacrificed.

VI Here there are the vinegar, the gall, the reed, the spittle, the nails and the lance. His gentle body is pierced; blood and water flow forth, a stream, by which earth, sea and sky – the world – are washed clean.

VII Faithful cross, tree singular in honour among all others, no wood bears another such flower among foliage and branches. The sweet timber supports sweet nails and a sweet weight.

VIII Glory and honour be to God and to the glorious Spirit that is above all together with the Father and the Son; honour and might be to him in eternity.

The hymn was originally composed to be sung at a procession by Venantius Fortunatus in the sixth century. It remained in use as a processional hymn; only later was it used in the Office for Passiontide. The only hymnal to contain the text is H. The rubric in the hymnal assigns it to Lauds, the collectar to Matins (Nocturn). The neumes in H represent a version of Stäblein no. 56 combining features of 56_2 and 56_3. This is the usual tune of this hymn when it is sung as part of the Office, not used as a processional hymn. The stanzas consist of three trochaic *septenarii*.

Stanzas VII and VIII are also found in Cambridge, Corpus Christi College, 422, p. 316 (personal communication by H. Gneuss). This is a mid-eleventh-century manuscript from Winchester (Gneuss, 'Preliminary List', no. 111); Sherborne is an early provenance for it. I have not been able to collate the two stanzas.

Bibliographical references: *ICL* no. 11583; *AH* 50, 71–3 (no. 66); Walpole no. 33; Venantius Fortunatus, *Venantii Honorii Clementiani Fortunati opera poetica*, ed. F. Leo, MGH Auct. Ant. 4, 1 (Berlin, 1881) II, 3.

H   1 *no punctuation at the caesura;* 7 *no punctuation at the caesura;* ordo] r *altered from* i, o *altered from* n.? 18 lavantur] a *altered to* æ.

Commentary   1–2 *Cf. Prudentius,* Cathemerinon *IX.84–5.* 2 *Cf. Hy 67₂/12.* 6–9 *These are probably allusions to the apocryphal legend of the wood of the cross; cf. the comments of Walpole. Cf. Hy 156/8.* 6 *Cf. Hy 156/8.* 10 *Cf. Gal. IV.4 and Eph.I. 10.* 16 *Read* acetum.

144

IN NATALE SANCTE MARIE

I   Gaude visceribus,   mater, in intimis,
     felix ecclesia,   quę replicas sacra
     sanctę festa Marię –
     plaudant astra, solum, marę,   4

II   cuius magnifica   est generatio,
     cuius vita sacris   claruit actibus,
     cuius vita honorem
     summum fine tenet sine,   8

III quę virgo peperit   virgoque permanet,
     lactavit propriis   uberibus deum
     portantemque gerebat
     ulnis prona trementibus,   12

IV   felix multiplici   laude puerpera,
     regis porta sui   clausa perenniter,
     mundi stella fluentis,
     floris virgula regii.   16

V   Te nunc suppliciter,   sancta theotocos
     regis perpetui   sponsaque, poscimus,

ut nos semper ubique
miti munere protegas. 20

VI Sanctis optineas, virgo, precatibus
pacis presidium dulce diutine
nobis atque beati
regni dona perennia. 24

VII Presta, summe pater, patris & unice
amborumque simul spiritus, annue,
qui regnas deus unus
omni tempore seculi. 28

ameN

I Rejoice in your innermost heart, o mother, happy church, you who celebrate again and again the holy feasts of blessed Mary – may the stars, the earth and the sea hail her,

II whose begetting was glorious, whose life was renowned for holy deeds, whose life has the greatest honour without end,

III for she gave birth as a virgin and is still a virgin, she gave suck with her own breasts to God and carried humbly in trembling arms the one who upholds,

IV a mother blessed in manifold praise, a door for her king that is forever closed, a star for the fluctuating world, a branch with a kingly flower.

V We humbly entreat you now, holy mother of God and bride of the eternal king, to protect us always and everywhere acting for us in your mercy.

VI May you obtain for us the sweet safety of lasting peace and the eternal gifts of the blessed realm with your holy prayer, virgin.

VII Grant this, sublime Father and only-begotten Son of the Father and Spirit of both together, and approve it, you who reign as one god for all time in the world.

This Marian hymn is included only in H; the collectar assigns it to the first Vespers of the Nativity of Mary. The hymn is anonymous and written in the fourth Asclepiadeic stanza. The neumes in H represent Stäblein no.

518, hitherto only known from Germany and Verona (Stäblein, p. 575–6), apparently the original melody of this hymn.

Bibliographical references: *ICL* no. 5500; *AH* 51, 144 (no. 125).

H   2 *Wrong punctuation after* replicas *instead of after* sacra; 4 marę] *corrected by erasure of* i *from* marię; 9–28 *Punctuation becomes very irregular;* 18 perpetui] i *altered to* o, *then back to* i.

Commentary   9 *Cf. Hy 47/6.* 14 *Cf. Hy 94/1–4.* 16 *Cf. Hy 138/7.*

145

DE *SANCTE *MARTINI EPISCOPI

I   Fratres unanimes   federe nexili,
     mecum participes   luminis annui,
     quo solis hodie   fulminat orbita
     Martini revehens   fest*a* celebria,   4

II   cantemus pariter   carmen amabile
      Martini meritis   oppido *nobili.
      Clerus cum populis   consonet organo.
      Grandi nam volupe est   psallere gaudio,   8

III   Martinus quoniam   vota fidelia
       accendit tribuens   cuncta salubria.
       Confert hic famulis   rite canentibus
       stellis aureola   serta micantibus.   12

IV   Cunctis candelabrum   luminis extitit,
      a multis tenebris   mortis & expulit.
      Virtutum statuit   crescere germina,
      in quorum fuerant   pectore crimina.   16

V   His nos subsidiis   undique prediti
     pangamus proprio   cantica presuli.
     Laudemus parili   voce, quod approbat,
     dampnemus vigili   mente, quod improbat.   20

VI   Martinum precibus   gens modo Gallica
      dignis sollicitet   nostraque Anglia.

Martinus faciat   tempora prospera.
Mundi, Christe, salus,   o, tibi gratia.   24
                     ameN

I   Brothers united in spirit with a tightly knit bond, who share with me each year that light with which the sun in its course sparkles today as it brings to us again the renowned feast of Martin,

II   let us sing together a delightful and very glorious song on the merits of Martin. Let the clergy sing in harmony together with the people, for it pleases us to sing with great joy,

III   since Martin inspires faithful prayer by granting everything good for us. On his servants who sing fittingly he bestows lovely golden wreaths with gleaming stars.

IV   He was a candle-stick shining with light to everyone and he drew them often from the shadows of death. He caused seedlings of virtue to sprout in those in whose breast there had been iniquity.

V   Because we are given this assistance at every point, let us sing our songs to our bishop. Let us praise with one voice what he approves of, let us condemn with vigilant attention what he disapproves of.

VI   Let the French people and our England now urge Martin with fitting prayers. May Martin make our times prosperous. Thanks be to you, o salvation of the world, Christ.

This hymn for the feast of St Martin (11 November) is included only in H. It has been ascribed to Hrabanus Maurus (d. 856). It is written in the first Asclepiadeic stanza, consisting of four *asclepiadei minores*. The stanza rhymes aabb. The neumes in H apparently represent an adapted version of Stäblein no. 70. According to Stäblein (p. 521) this melody is Cistercian, which is disproved by its occurrence here half a century earlier.

Bibliographical references: *ICL* no. 5361; *AH* 50, 205–6 (no. 154).

H   4 festa] a *on erasure by another hand?* 5 amabile] *corrected from* ambile *by suprascript* a, *possibly by another hand.*

Commentary   6 *For* nobili *read* nobile. 10 AH *reads* attendit. 14 AH *reads* tenebras. 18 *Blume points out in the notes to AH that Martin was patron of Mainz, which was Hrabanus's diocese as archbishop.* 22 Anglia *replaces* Francia *and other words for the Frankish empire, Germany*

or districts in Germany of the manuscripts consulted by AH. The original reading would agree with
the ascription to Hrabanus.

146

YMNUS IN NATALE DOMINI CANENDUS AD TERTIAM

   I   CHRISTE, hac hora tertia
           tua nos reple gratia,
           caritate & fervidos
           nos nostrosque fac proximos.   4

   II Ille deus paraclýtus
           nostris nunc adsit cordibus
           in hac hora, qui rutilos
           inflammavit apostolos.   8

   III Presta hoc, deus, trinitas,
           una & compar deitas,
           cui laus, virtus, gloria
           nunc & cuncta per secula. amen.   12

I Christ, fill us with your grace at this third hour and make us and our
neighbours fervent in our charity.

II May God in the form of that Comforter be present in our hearts at
this hour who touched the shining apostles with flame.

III Grant this, God, trinity, one and equal deity, to whom be praise,
power and glory now and for all ages. Amen.

V (Vm) is the only manuscript to include this hymn for the Tierce of
Christmas Day (without a prose version). It is anonymous and written in
rhythmical Ambrosian hymn verse (4 × 8pp). The stanza rhymes aabb. V
has no neumes.

Bibliographical references: *ICL* no. 2188; *AH* 12, 14–15 (no. 3). The
hymn is no. 39a in Gneuss, *HHEM*.

Commentary   *Cf. Hy 8. 7–8 Cf. Acts II.2 and 15.*

147

AD SEXTAM. YMNUS.

I   SEXTA etate virgine
qui natus es pro homine,
fac nos octava sumere
ẹtate sortem glorie   4

II   et, qui hac hora mysticum
sedisti super puteum,
fonte tuo nos irriga
atque sole inlumina!   8

Presta hoc, deus, trinitas

I You who were born by a virgin in the sixth age for the advantage of man, make us obtain a share of the glory in the eighth age

II and, you who sat at this hour on the mystical well, water us with your springwater and shine on us with your sun.

V (Vm) is the only Anglo-Saxon manuscript to include this hymn for the Sext of Christmas Day. It is anonymous and written in rhythmical Ambrosian hymn verse (4 × 8pp). The stanza rhymes aabb. Vm does not include neumes.

Bibliographical references: *ICL* no. 14977; *AH* 12, 15 (no. 4). The hymn is no. 39b in Gneuss, *HHEM*.

Commentary   1 *Cf. Dan. II.31–45.* 5–6 *Cf. John IV.3–15, especially verse* 6: sedebat sic super fontem. hora erat quasi sexta.

148

YMNUS. AD NONAM.

I   HORA nona que canimus,
exaudi, Iesu, petimus,

> quam tuus reddit obitus
> sacrosanctum mortalibus. 4

II   Hac hora tuo vulnere
> fons manavit ęcclesię.
> Tua nos iungat inclita
> sancto latroni gratia. 8

> Presta hoc, deus, trinitas

I   Hear what we sing, Jesus, we ask you, at the ninth hour, which your death renders most sacred to mortals.

II   At that hour the wellspring of the church flowed from your wound. May your glorious kindness make us join the holy robber.

V (Vm) is the only Anglo-Saxon manuscript to include this hymn for the None of Christmas Day. It is anonymous and written in rhythmical Ambrosian hymn verse (4 × 8pp). The stanza rhymes aabb. There are no neumes in V.

Bibliographical references: *ICL* no. 7189; *AH* 12, 15 (no. 5). The hymn is no. 39c in Gneuss, *HHEM*.

V   4 sacrosanctum] *originally* sacra sanctum, o *interlined above* a *by* V₂.

Commentary   *1–4 Cf. Matt. XXVII.46, Mark XV.33 and Luke XXIII.44. 5–6 Cf. Hy 67₁/11–12. 8 Cf. Luke XXIII.39–43 and Hy 141/15.*

149

YMNUS IN PASCHA AD PRIMAM

I   TE, LUCIS AUCTOR, personent
> huius caterve carmina,
> quam tu replesti gratia
> anastasi potentia. 4

II   Nobis dies hec innuit
> diem supremum sistere,

quo mortuos resurgere
vitéque fas sit reddere.

8

III Octava prima redditur,
dum mors abunda tollitur,
dum mente circumcidimur
novique demum nascimur,

12

IV cum mane nostrum cernimus
redisse victis hostibus
mundique luxum tempnimus,
panem salutis sumimus.

16

V Hęc alma sit sollempnitas,
sit clara hęc festivitas,
sit feriata gaudiis;
dies reducta ab inferis.

20

Gloria tibi domine

I The songs of this assembly shall proclaim you, origin of light, for you filled it with grace by the potency of your resurrection.

II This day suggests to us that there will be a last day, on which divine law commands that the dead shall rise again and be returned to life.

III The eighth day becomes the first, as death, which abounded, is abolished, as we are circumcised in spirit and born anew indeed,

IV when we see our morning has come again and our enemies are slain, when we despise the debauchery of the world and partake of the bread of salvation.

V Let this ceremony be sacred, let this feast be glorious, let it be celebrated with joy; day is retrieved from the underworld.

This hymn is included only in V (Vm, without a prose version) and assigned there to the Prime of Easter Sunday. It is anonymous and written in Ambrosian iambic dimeter with irregular rhyme. The text in V is without neumes.

Bibliographical references: *ICL* no. 16087; *AH* 27, 87 (no. 35); Walpole no. 110. The hymn is no. 72a in Gneuss, *HHEM*.

V   10 abunda] *second minim of* u *altered to* e; 14 hostibus] h *interlined above with a caret* mark.

Commentary   9 *Walpole illustrates this idea with quotations from St Ambrose and St Augustine.* 11 *Cf. Rom. II.28–9.*

150

I   CHORUS NOVE Hierusalem
*nova meli dulcedinem
promat colens cum sobriis
paschale festum gaudiis,   4

II   quo Christus, invictus leo
dracone surgens obruto,
dum voce viva personat,
a morte functos excitat.   8

III   Quam devorarat, improbus
predam refundit tartarus.
Captivitate libera
Iesum secuntur agmina.   12

IV   Triumphat ille splendide
et dignus amplitudine;
soli polique patriam
unam facit rem publicam.   16

V   Ipsum canendo supplices
regem precemur milites,
ut in suo clarissimo
nos ordinet palatio.   20

VI   Per secla mete nescia
patri supremo gloria
honorque sit cum filio
et spiritu paraclito.   24
                              ameN.

I Let the choir of the new Jerusalem chant a new sweet kind of song and celebrate the feast of Easter with sober rejoicing,

II at which Christ rises up as the unconquered lion, for the dragon was destroyed, and wakes the departed from death, as he calls out with his living voice.

III Cruel hell gives up again the prey that it has devoured. The troops freed from captivity follow Christ.

IV He triumphs gloriously and he is worthy of pomp; out of the land of earth and of heaven he makes one commonwealth.

V Let us pray to this king as his humble soldiers, that he may deploy us in his most splendid palace.

VI Glory and honour be to the supreme Father with the Son and the Holy Spirit for ages without end.

This Easter hymn, perhaps intended for Tierce in Vm, is assigned to the first Vespers of Sundays after Easter in the collectar of H. It has been ascribed to Fulbert of Chartres (d. 1028). If that is correct, it appears to have become popular very quickly. It is written in Ambrosian iambic dimeter. The stanza rhymes aabb. The text is included only in Vm and not accompanied by neumes.

Bibliographical references: *ICL* no. 2153; *AH* 50, 285 (no. 215), cf. *AH* 2, 93 (no. 131). The hymn is no. 72b in Gneuss, *HHEM*.

Commentary   1 *Cf. Rev. XXI.2.* 2 *For* nova *read* novam. *Note, however, that* nova ... dulcedine *is attested among the variants given in* AH. 5 *Cf. Rev. V.5.* 6 *Cf. Rev. XX.*

151

HYMNUS DE SANCTO PETRO PAULOQUE

I FELIX PER OMNES   festum mundi cardines
   apostolorum   prepollet alacriter,
   PETRI beati,   PAULi sacratissimi,

    quos Christus almo   consecravit sanguine,

    aecclesiarum   deputavit principes.   5

II   Hii sunt olive   due coram domino

    et candelabra   luce radiantia,

    preclara celi   duo luminaria.

    Fortia solvunt   peccatorum vincula.

    Portas Olimphi   reserant fidelibus.   10

III Habent supernas   potestatem claudere

    sermone sedes,   pandere splendentia

    limina poli   super alta sidera.

    Linguae eorum   claves celi facte sunt.

    Larvas repellunt   ultra mundi limitem.   15

IV   PETRUS beatus   catenarum laqueos

    Christo iubente   rupit mirabiliter.

    Custos ovilis   & doctor ęcclesię

    pastorque gregis,   conservator ovium,

    arce luporum   truculentam rabiem.   20

V   Quodcumque vinclis   super terram strinxerit,

    erit in astris   religatum fortiter

    et, quod resolvit   in terris arbitrio,

    erit solutum   super celi radium.

    In fine mundi   iudex erit seculi.   25

VI   Non impar PAULUS   huic, doctor gentium,

    electionis   templum sacratissimum,

    *immorte compar,   in corona particeps.

    Ambo lucernę   & decus ęcclesie

    in orbe claro   choruscant vibramine.   30

VII O Roma felix,   que tantorum principum

    es purpurata   pretioso sanguine,

    excellis omnem   mundi pulchritudinem

    non laude tua,   sed sanctorum meritis,

    quos cruentatis   iugulasti gladiis.   35

VIII Vos ergo modo,   gloriosi martyres,

    PETRE beate,   PAULE mundi lilium,

celestis aule   triumphales milites,
precibus almis   vestris nos ab omnibus
munite malis,   ferte super aethera.   40

Gloria deo [...]

I The joyous feast of the apostles prevails with its cheerfulness in all quarters of the world, the feast of the blessed Peter and the most holy Paul, whom Christ consecrated with holy blood and appointed the princes of the Church.

II They are two olives before the Lord and two candlesticks shining with light, two glorious stars in the sky. They undo the strong fetters of sin. They unlock the gates of Olympus to the faithful.

III They have the power to shut the celestial dwellings by their word and to open the shining doorway to heaven above the stars on high. Their tongues have become the key of heaven. They drive back the demons beyond the borders of the world.

IV Blessed Peter miraculously broke the bond of his chains at the command of Christ. Guard of the sheep-fold, teacher of the church, shepherd of your flock and preserver of your sheep, keep away the wild fury of the wolves.

V Whatever he lays in chains on earth shall be strongly bound among the stars and what he acquits by his judgement shall be free above the gleam of the sky. When the universe ends, he will be the judge of this world.

VI Paul is not unlike him; he, the teacher of the pagans, the most holy temple that was chosen, is like him in death and shares the crown with him. Both shine in the world as lanterns and ornaments of the church, sparkling brightly.

VII O happy Rome, you who are clothed in the purple of the precious blood of such great princes, you surpass all the beauty of the world not by your fame, but by the merits of your saints, whom you murdered with your bloodied swords.

VIII So, glorious martyrs, blessed Peter, Paul, lily of the world, victorious soldiers of the celestial court, protect us by your holy prayers from all evil and carry us up above the skies.

This is a hymn for the feast of SS Peter and Paul. The details of its liturgical use, especially in relation to Hy 87, are unclear. It has been ascribed to Paulinus of Aquileia (d. 802). The meter is rhythmical iambic trimeter with a regular caesura ($4 \times (5+7\text{pp})$). The text is extant only in V (Vm, without a prose version). It could have been included in C, but as it stands, the text is a post-Conquest addition. (The neumes in C, which were also added later, represent a version of Stäblein no. 105 combining features of 105_1 and 105_2.)

Bibliographical references: *ICL* no. 5017; *AH* 50, 141 (no. 103), cf. *AH* 2, 53 (no. 56). The hymn is no. 87a in Gneuss, *HHEM*.

V   7 radiantia] *one letter erased between* a *and* d; 41 *Another, later, hand continues, possibly on erasure:* ... per immensa secula / sit tibi nate decus & imperium / honor potestas sancto spiritui. / sit trinitati salus individua / per infinita seculorum secula AMEN. AMEN *is written in Greek letters.*

Commentary   *This hymn and Hy 87 closely resemble each other.* 16–17 *Cf. Acts XII.6–7.* 27 *Cf. Acts IX.15.* 28 *For* immorte *read* in morte. 31–5 *Cf. the poem* O Roma nobilis *(The Oxford Book of Medieval Latin Verse, ed. F. J. E. Raby (Oxford, 1959), p. 190).*

152

I   Adesto, sancta trinitas,
par splendor, una deitas,
qui extas rerum omnium
sine fine principium.   4

II   Te cęlorum militia,
laudat, adorat, predicat,
triplexque mundi machina
benedicit per saecula.   8

III   Assumus & nos cernui
te adorantes famuli.
Vota precesque supplicum
ymnis iunge caelestium.   12

IV   Unum te lumen credimus,
quod & ter idem colimus.

'Alpha & o' quem dicimus,
te laudet omnis spiritus.   16

v Laus patri sit ingenito,
   laus eius unigenito,
   laus sit sancto spiritui,
   trino deo & simplici.   20

AMEN

I Be with us, holy trinity, you who are equal in glory and one deity, who are the beginning of all things and without end.

II The troops of heaven praise, adore and proclaim you and the threefold mechanism of the world blesses you throughout the ages.

III We, too, your humble servants, are here and adore you. Let the prayers and entreaties of the suppliants be joined to the songs of praise of the inhabitants of heaven.

IV We believe that you are a single light, which we also revere as threefold but the same. You whom we call 'alpha and omega', let every spirit praise you.

V Praise be to the Father, who was never begotten, praise to his only-begotten Son, praise be to the Holy Spirit, to the God who is threefold and one.

This hymn for Trinity Sunday is included only in V (Vm) and is not accompanied by neumes there. It is anonymous and written in rhythmical Ambrosian hymn verse (4 × 8pp). The stanza rhymes aabb; sometimes there is assonance only instead of rhyme.

Bibliographical references: *ICL* no. 296; *AH* 51, 102 (no. 96).

V   7 triplex-] e *altered to high* e *(as in ligatures) possibly by* V_2.

153

YMNUS DE SANCTO EADMUNDO REGE ET MARTYRE

I   EADMUNDUS, MARTYR INCLYTUS,
Anglorum rex sanctissimus,
hac luce palmam nobilem
triumphans cęlos intulit.   4

II   Tulit iubar hoc splendidum
opima tellus Anglica,
quo splendet omne sęculum
et cęlis crescit gaudium.   8

III   *Quorum murmur pauperum
exaudiat, sacrarium
et ad cęlestis perferat
regis pius causidicus.   12

IV   Favorem Christi cęlitus
nostris piaclis impetret,
orbs ut gravata sentiat
donativum indulgentie.   16

V   Precantum votis annuat
pater deus cum filio
simul cum sancto spiritu
per seculorum secula.   20

AMEN

I Eadmund, the renowned martyr, the most saintly king of the English, on this day triumphantly bore his splendid token of victory up to heaven.

II It was the fruitful land of England that brought forth that shining star by which the whole world is illuminated and the joy in heaven is increased.

III May he hear the complaints of the poor among his people and report them at the temple of the king of heaven as their kind advocate.

IV May he obtain Christ's sympathy with our sins from heaven so that the oppressed world can experience the gift of indulgence.

V May God, the Father with the Son and the Holy Spirit, grant the prayers of those who invoke him, for ages and ages.

This hymn for the Vespers of the feast of St Eadmund (20 November) is included only in V (Vm, without a prose version). It is anonymous, if clearly Anglo-Saxon, and written in rhythmical Ambrosian hymn verse (4 × 8pp). The text is not accompanied by neumes.

Bibliographical references: *ICL* no. 4268; *AH* 19, 122 (no. 196).

Commentary *For the* vita *of Eadmund, see Abbo of Fleury, 'Life of St. Edmund', ed. Winterbottom.* 9 AH *emends to* Tuorum, *but it should be* Suorum.

154

AD NOCTURNAM

I LAUREA REGNI   REDEMITUS OLIM
   REX EADMUNDUS,   decus orbis huius,
   nunc suis adsit   famulis, precamur
   supplici voto.   4

II Hac die cęli   fruitur secretis,
    qua triumphalem   meruit coronam
    nactus ex Dani   *gladius tyranni
    sanguine palmam,   8

III cuius exsectum   caput ore prono
     trux lupus fovit   famulatus illi,
     donec ad notum   rediit cadaver
     vulneris expers.   12

IV *nde, rex martyr,   tibi, magnus heres,
    integer membris   maculeque *puris,
    fungeris digno   meritis honore
    talibus hymnis.   16

v Sit honor patri   iugis & perhennis,
   qui tuos signis   decorat triumphos,
   cuius obtentu   *piis ipse parcat
   trinus & unus.   20

AMEN

I May King Eadmund, who once was crowned with the laurels of
   kingship and was an ornament of this world, assist his servants now,
   we entreat in humble prayer.

II He enjoys the benefits of the mysteries of heaven on this day, on
    which he earned the crown of the victory, for he gained the prize by
    his blood shed by the swords of the tyrant, the Dane.

III When his head was cut off and his face lay on the earth, a grim wolf
     cared for it and served him, until it was returned to his renowned
     body, unharmed by wounds.

IV Therefore, king and martyr, great heir, whole in your limbs and free
    of defilement, you enjoy the honour appropriate to your merits in
    such hymns.

V Ready and perpetual honour be to the Father, who honours your
   victory with signs. May he, who is threefold and one, kindly spare us
   because you have obtained it for us.

The hymn for St Eadmund (20 November) is included in the manuscripts
V (Vm) and La. V (Vm) assigns it to Matins. It is anonymous, but
certainly Anglo-Saxon, and written in Sapphic stanzas. The texts are not
accompanied by neumes.

Bibliographical references: *ICL* no. 8785; *AH* 19, 123 (no. 197).

La   Heading: YMNUS IN HONORE SANCTI EADMUNDI Dicolos tetrastrophos
saphici endecasyllabi cum quarto versu adonio; 1 REDEMITUS] redimitus; 4 supplici]
supplice; 6 qua] quam; 7 gladius] gladiis; 13 nde] Unde; 14 puris] purus; 17 iugis] gis *on
erasure by text hand, last erased letter was* s; 19 piis] pius; 20 La *omits* amen.

Commentary   Heading: *The subtitle in La is a definition of the Sapphic stanza.* 2
EADMUNDUS *scans as four syllables.* 7 *Read* gladiis *as in La.* 13 *Read* Unde *as in La. The
stanza initial is omitted.* 14 *La's reading* purus *preserves the Horatian tag (Horace, Carmina, I.
xxii. 1).* 19 *La's* pius *is metrically correct.*

459

155

AD MATUTINAM

I   LAUS ET CORONA MILITUM,
Iesu, tibi certantium,
huius triumpho subditis
intende regis martyris.   4

II   Hac rex EADMUNDUS die
*raptos cruento scammate
sese *flagorum stigmati
cęlo *reptus exuit.   8

III   *Devictus acri stipite
loris cruentis undique
*Danis tribunal execrat
ac numen eius inprobat,   12

IV   qui *terebratis spiculis
regis cruorem conbibit,
quem pro suis fidelibus
velle mori conicimus.   16

V   Nos hac EADMUNDUS die,
rex martyr, aptet gratie,
qua perfruamur celitum
bonis per omne seculum.   20

AMEN

I Jesus, you who are the renown and the crown of the soldiers who fight for you, look on the subjects of this king and martyr on the occasion of his triumph.

II On this day King Eadmund was taken away from the blood-stained arena, divested himself of himself in the face of his laceration with goads and was received into heaven.

III Tied to the cruel stake with strips of leather stained everywhere with blood, he curses the council of the Dane and reviles his god.

IV The Dane drinks the blood of the king after he has been pierced with javelins. We suppose he wanted to die for his faithful followers.

V May Eadmund, the king and martyr, make us ready for grace so that we shall thereby enjoy the benefits of the inhabitants of heaven throughout the ages.

The hymn for St Eadmund is included in V (Vm) and La. V assigns it to Lauds. It is anonymous and written in Ambrosian iambic dimeter. The stanza rhymes aabb; sometimes there is assonance instead of rhyme. The texts are not accompanied by neumes.

Bibliographical references: *ICL* no. 8793; *AH* 19, 123 (no. 198).

La Heading: ITEM ALTER monocolos tetrastrophos iambici dimetri acatalectici quod est dictum archilochicum; 6 raptos] raptus; 8 reptus] reptus, ce *interlined with caret mark probably by another hand*; 9 Devictus] Devmctus; 11 Danis] Dani; 14 conbibit] combibit.

Commentary Heading: *The subtitle in La is a definition of Ambrosian iambic dimeter.* 5 EADMUNDUS *scans as four syllables.* 6 *For* raptos *read* raptus. 7 *For* flagorum *read* flagrorum. 8 *For* reptus *read probably* receptus, *as the corrector in La does; note that V and La agree in this obvious mistake.* 9 AH *emends to* Devinctus. 11 *For* Danis *read* Dani. 13 AH *emends to* terebrati.

156

I Salve, crux sancta,   salvæ, mundi gloria,
vera spes nostra   vere ferens gaudia,
signum salutis,   salus in periculis,
vitale lignum   vitam portans omnium.   4

II Te adorandam,   te crucem vivificam
in te redempti,   dulce decus seculi,
semper laudamus.   Semper tibi canimus
per lignum servi,   per te, lignum, liberi.   8

III Originale   crimen *netans in cruce,
nos & a pravis,   Christe, munda maculis.

461

Humanitatem miseratus fragilem
per crucem sanctam lapsis dona veniam. 12

IV Protege, salva, benedic, sanctifica
populum cunctum crucis per signaculum.
Morbos averte corporis & animę.
Hoc contra signum nullum stet periculum. 16

V Sit deo patri laus in cruce filii,
sit coęqualis laus sancto spiritui.
Civibus summis gaudium sit angelis,
honor sit mundo crucis exaltatio. 20

AMEN

I Hail, holy cross, hail, glory of the world, our true hope, which truly brings joy, sign of salvation, salvation in danger, life-giving wood that bears the life of all.

II It is you, cross, who should be adored, it is you, who give life, that we always praise, for we were redeemed in you, sweet glory of the world. We are always singing to you, we who became slaves because of a piece of wood and became free through you, who are a piece of wood.

III Christ, you who destroyed original sin on the cross, cleanse us also of evil defilement. Have pity on frail mankind and grant forgiveness to those who have fallen by the holy cross.

IV Protect, heal, bless and sanctify all the people by the sign of the cross. Prevent ailments of the body and the soul. In the face of this sign no danger shall persist.

V Praise be to God the Father in the cross of the Son; equal praise be to the Holy Spirit. May the exaltation of the cross be a joy to the citizens high above, the angels, may it be honour to the world.

The text of this hymn is included only in V (Vm). The collectar in H says that it is to be sung at Vespers and Matins of the Invention and the Exaltation of the Cross (3 May and 14 September). The hymn is by Heribert of Eichstätt. The metre is rhythmical and the stanza can be described as $4 \times (5p+7pp)$. The text is not accompanied by neumes.

Bibliographical references: *ICL* no. 14547; *AH* 50, 291–2 (no. 223).

V   *No rubric.* 18–19 *All punctuation om.*

Commentary   9 *For* netans *read* necans.

157

HYMNUS DE *SANCTI OSWOLD EPISCOPI

I   REX ANGELORUM,   dominator orbis,
     palma sanctorum,   decus & corona,
     laus tibi, quia   rutilat OSWALDUS
     presul in astris.   4

II   Hunc ut descendens   iubar arce poli,
     Criste, splendere   populo iussisti
     inthronizatum   solio decenter
     pontificali.   8

III Hic mítis, castus   humílísque, largus,
     gemma & vite   speculumque legis
     multis ad fructus,   sibi ad coronam
     iure refulsit.   12

IV   Qui postquam felix   meruit coruscos
     scandere cęlos,   medicine dona
     contulit *egros,   sua *quo non pollent
     membra, sacello.   16

V   Hic te pro nobis   rogitet tonantem,
     cui laus, virtus,   honor atque perpes,
     qui trinus regnat   deus *adque unus
     omne per evum.   20

                         *ammen

I King of the angels, ruler of the world, prize, glory and crown of the
saints, praise be to you because Bishop Oswald blazes among the
stars.

II Like a star descending from the fastness of the sky, Christ, you ordered this man to give the people light, fittingly enthroned on the seat of a bishop.

III This man, mild, chaste, humble and generous, a jewel of life and a mirror of the law, sparkled with light so as to benefit many and justly gain a crown for himself.

IV After he happily ascended into radiant heaven by his merits, he conferred gifts of healing on the sick, who have no power over their limbs, in the chapel.

V May he entreat you in our favour, the thunderer, to whom be praise, might and everlasting honour, who reigns as God, threefold and one, throughout the ages.

This hymn for Vespers of St Oswald of Worcester (28 February) is included only in C. It is anonymous, apparently of Worcester origin, and written in rhythmical Sapphic stanzas (3 × (5p+6p), 5p). Only the first line has neumes. The tune could not be identified.

Bibliographical references: *The Leofric Collectar*, ed. Dewick and Frere II, 607. The hymn is no. 60a in Gneuss, *HHEM*.

C   Heading: SANCTI] *the last letter erased, might also be* E; 7 inthronizatum] *second* i *interlined above, correcting the original* o, z *on erasure, both corrections probably by text hand;* decenter] r *erased from* m; 9 humílísque] *one letter erased after first* i, ue *erased and replaced by abbreviation mark by the text hand;* 10 speculumque] ue *erased and replaced by abbreviation mark by text hand;* 17 Hic te] rite *added above by another hand;* 19 adque] atque *interlined above by the correcting hand of line 17.*

158

HYMNUS AD NOCTURNUM

I   CELI VERNANTEM PATRIAM,
     lucis inmensam gloriam,
     Oswaldum sanctum dulcibus
     letis canamus cantibus;   4

II   gemma vite qui fulserat,
       hac in vita dum manserat,
       archipresul angelicis
       semper intentus studiis.   8

III   Scala fuit & aurea
       *plurens tollens ad sidera,
       ubi triumphat domini
       ante thronum altissimi.   12

IV   Hoc polo perstillantia
       iam promisere miracula
       eius ad glebam dantia
       *egis *cara* malagmata.   16

V   Cuius prece propitius
       sit nobis Christus dominus,
       trinum & unum omnia
       quem laudant deum secula.   20

I Let us sing in sweet and joyous songs of our home in heaven, where it is spring, about the immeasurable glory of light and about Saint Oswald,

II who shone like a jewelled bud on the vine, while he was still in this life, an archbishop who was always intent on his angelic purposes.

III He was also a golden ladder leading a multitude up to the stars, where he enjoys his victory before the throne of the highest Lord of all.

IV This the miracles that filter down from heaven have now made us believe, which grant invaluable cures to the sick in his territory.

V May Christ the Lord be inclined towards us by his prayer, whom all the ages praise as God threefold and one.

This hymn for the Matins of St Oswald (28 February) is included only in C. It is anonymous, apparently of Worcester origin, and written in rhythmical Ambrosian hymn verse (4 × 8pp). The stanza rhymes aabb. The text is not accompanied by neumes.

Bibliographical references: *The Leofric Collectar*, ed. Dewick and Frere II, 607. The hymn is no. 60b in Gneuss, *HHEM*.

C   4 letis] *another hand interlined* letí *above*; 10 plurens] *another hand, probably the correcting hand of Hy 157, interlined* plures *above*; 16 egis cara malagmata] *run together and later separated by a dot and a comma.* e *and* ca *are on erasure by another hand and the correcting hand of Hy 157 and line 10 has interlined* egris *and* cara *above.*

Commentary   10 *Read* plures *like the corrector.* 16 *Read* egris *like the corrector.*

159

AD MATUTINUM

I   INCLITE PATER   super astra *pollent,
     SANCTE OSWALDE,   domini dilecte,
     presul & alme,   venerandus orbe
     salve per evum.   4

II   Tu nos a cunctis   precibus *dilectis
     múnda per Christum,   petimus, tonantem
     nosque alumnos   proprios guberna
     ut pater almus.   8

III Tu nos peccatis   releva iacentes,
     nobis & opem   tribue paternam,
     clemens & procul   mala cuncta pelle,
     pastor honeste.   12

IV   Sint nobis cuncta   bona per te dona,
     *nostre & vita   domini pax crescat
     et post hanc vitam   capiat nos clara
     aula polorum.   16

V   Prestet hoc pater   deus *adque natus,
     spiritus sanctus,   cui laudem dicat
     omne, quod spirat,   pię trinitati
     cuncta regenti.   20

AMEN

I Renowned father, you who are powerful in the realm above the stars, Saint Oswald, beloved of the Lord and holy bishop, hail as one who is forever to be revered by the world.

II Purify us of all committed sins by your prayers, we pray, in the name of Christ the Thunderer and guide us, your pupils, as our holy father.

III Lift us up, for we lie prostrate because of our guilt, grant us your fatherly help and mercifully keep all harm far from us, noble shepherd.

IV May we receive all good gifts through you, may the peace of the Lord increase in our life and the bright palace of heaven receive us after this life.

V May God, the Father and the Son and the Holy Spirit, grant this; may every being that breathes speak its praise, for the kind trinity rules all.

This hymn for Lauds of St Oswald (28 February) is included only in C. It is anonymous, clearly of Worcester origin and written in rhythmical Sapphic stanzas (3 × (5p+6p), 5p). The text is not accompanied by neumes.

Bibliographical references: *The Leofric Collectar*, ed. Dewick and Frere II, 607. The hymn is no. 60c in Gneuss, *HHEM*.

C   1 pollent] *corrected by another hand to* pollens *by an interlined* s; 9 iacentes] s *on erasure, probably by another hand*; 17 adque] *another hand interlines* q *above, followed by an unusual abbreviation mark* (que *or* quia?).

Commentary   1 *For* pollent *read* pollens *like the corrector*. 5 *For* dilectis *read* delictis. 7 alumnos proprios *means the community at Worcester*. 14 *Either* nostra *must be read for* nostre *or* vite *for* vita. 17 *For* adque *read* atque.

160

I   Summe confessor   sacer et sacerdos,
    temporum metas   rota torquet anni.
    Tempus est nobis   tibi consecratum
    pangere festum.   4

II   Presul insignis   meritisque clare,
te sacra cleri   populique turba
corde prostrato   pietate poscit
vernula patrem: 8

III   Vota cunctorum   relevans in aula
regis aeterni   foveas utrumque
ordinem, cuius   pius exstitisti
pastor in urbe.   12

IV   Questibus cuncti   referunt gementes
gesta culparum   lacrimisque pandunt
pessime mentis   animęque nigrę
crimina dira,   16

V   digna que poena   revocat in hora,
nostra cum dira   miseros perurget
pandere mundo   variante facta
celitus ira.   20

VI   Tu procul casus   prohibe tonantes,
pelle peccata,   tenua furorem.
Pestis et morbus,   petimus, recedat
sospite cive.   24

VII   Moribus cunctis   moderare vitam,
confer et sudam   placidamque mentem.
Corda virtutum   meditentur arma
munere Christi.   28

VIII   Sancte, tu prebe,   quoties rogaris,
profluos fructus   pluviasque largas.
Credimus cuncta   domino favente
te dare posse.   32

IX   Credimus Christum   pretium laborum,
premium iustum   studiis dedisse,
a quibus artus   etiam solutos
morte bearis.   36

X   Gloriam Christo   patulo canamus
ore prestanti   sive dominanti,

tanta qui pollet   deitate simplex,

trinus et unus.   40

AMEN

I Supreme holy confessor and priest, the turning wheel of the year makes the time of each season come round again. It is time for us to celebrate the feast that is dedicated to you.

II Bishop excellent and renowned for your merits, the holy assembly of the clergy and the people entreats you as a father with humbled heart and with devotion as your slave:

III May you carry the prayers of all up into the court of the eternal king and may you support both orders, as you used to be their kind shepherd in the town.

IV Lamenting and sighing, everyone reports his guilty actions and amid tears reveals the terrible sins of his wicked mind and black soul,

V which a fitting punishment is going to recall to us in the hour when the dreadful anger of heaven forces us in our misery to disclose our actions, after the world has changed.

VI Keep thundering misfortune far away from us, drive off sins and quiet frenzy. Let plague and illness recede from us, we pray, and the citizens be preserved from them.

VII Guide our life in all our habits and confer on us a serene and quiet mind. Let our hearts meditate on the weapons of the virtues by the gift of Christ.

VIII Grant abundant harvest and ample rainfall, saint, every time you are asked for them. We believe that you can give us everything, if God is in favour of it.

IX We believe that Christ gave you a reward for your efforts, a just recompense for your endeavours, in which you are happy, even if your limbs are resolved in death.

X Let us open our mouths wide and sing glory to Christ, giver and ruler, who can do such great things, who is one in his divinity, threefold and single.

469

This hymn for the feast of a single confessor is included only in B. Its precise use is unclear. It is anonymous and written in Sapphic stanzas. The text is not accompanied by neumes.

Bibliographical references: *ICL* no. 15813; *AH* 27, 260–2 (no. 184), cf. *AH* 2, 77 (no. 102). The hymn is no. 124a in Gneuss, *HHEM*.

B   *Space is left for a rubric at the beginning.*

161

I   O vere virum beatum,
    o vere magnificum,
    qui missus ad predicandum
    Christi evangelium
    quondam armis bellicosum
    subgecit oceanum.   6

II Cuius regna Augustinum
    predicant theologum,
    quo doctore laudant Christum
    regnantem in saeculum,
    quibus et nos concinamus
    AMEN in perpetuum.   12

I   Oh what a truly blessed, what a truly glorious man, who was once sent to preach the gospel of Christ and conquered the violent ocean in battle!

II His realms celebrate Augustine, the scholar of theology, because of whose instruction they praise Christ the ruler forever. Let us, too, sing 'amen' together with them everlastingly.

The text of this hymn for the feast of St Augustine of Canterbury (26 May) is included only in Jo and not accompanied by neumes. It is anonymous and attested only for St Augustine's. The metre is rhythmical; the stanza can be described as $3 \times (8p+7pp)$. All lines rhyme in *-um* except for the assonance in line 11.

Bibliographical reference: Gneuss, *HHEM*, pp. 114–15.

Jo   *No rubric;* 7 regna Augustinum] a augus *on erasure of* augus.

Commentary   6 *The spelling of* subiecit *with* g *reflects Later Latin pronunciation, not necessarily influenced by Old English.*

162

Laudes Christo

I   Laudes Christo cum canticis
cordis canamus *moduilis,
qui peccatricem Mariam
sponsam fecit sanctissimam.   4

II   Pulsis septem demonibus
hanc septiformis spiritus
implet, pater & filius –
hęc trinitas unus deus.   8

III   Hinc Iesu Christi domini
pedes perfundens lacrimis
rigat, ungit exterius,
qui se mundat interius.   12

IV   Pergit ad crucem dominus.
Lugens Maria sequitur.
Videt pati, videt mori,
sepulcro condi conspicit.   16

V   Sepulto fert aromata
dumque condire properat,
redivivum a mortuis
cernere prima meruit.   20

VI   Ergo, Maria, domini
dei dilecta filii,
impetra nobis miseris,
quod impetrasti lacrimis.   24

471

VII   Sit genitori domino
et eius unigenito
cum spiritu paraclito
gloria, laus atque honor.   28

AMEN

I Let us sing songs of praise accompanied by chanting and by melodies from the heart to Christ, who made the sinner Mary his most holy bride.

II Seven demons were driven out from her, she was filled with the Spirit in its seven forms, the Father and the Son, the trinity, one God.

III Therefore she moistens and bathes the feet of the Lord Jesus Christ with tears, she anoints on the outside the one who purifies her within.

IV The Lord is on his way to the cross. Mary follows, mourning. She sees him suffer, she sees him die and watches as he is entombed in the grave.

V She brings spices to him, after he is buried, and as she hastened to embalm him, she earned the privilege of being the first to see him risen alive again from among the dead.

VI So, Mary, beloved of the Son of God, the Lord, obtain for us in our misery what you obtained by your tears.

VII Glory, praise and honour be to the Lord, the Father and his only-begotten Son with the Holy Spirit.

This hymn for the feast of St Mary Magdalene (22 July) is included only in Bo. It is anonymous and written in rhythmical Ambrosian hymn verse (4 × 8pp) with monosyllabic rhyme or assonance. The stanza rhymes aabb. The text is not accompanied by neumes.

Bibliographical reference: *AH* 12, 174 (no. 315).

Bo   Heading: *possibly by another hand*; 18 properat] pro *altered from* per.

Commentary   2 *For* moduilis *read* modulis. 5 *Cf. Luke VIII.2.* 9–12 *Cf. Luke VII.37–9.* 15 *Cf. Mark XV.40 and John XIX.25.* 16 *Cf. Matt. XXVII.61 and Mark XV.47.* 17–18 *Cf. Mark XVI.1.* 19–20 *Cf. Mark XVI.9 and John XX.11–18.*

Hymns of the Old Hymnal and the Frankish Hymnal

This table has been adapted from Gneuss, *HHEM*, pp. 23–5. The Mozarabic Hymnal, which is excluded here, apparently resembled the Frankish Hymnal, but shared some hymns with the Old Hymnal.

The following symbols and abbreviations are used:

OHy	number of the Old Hymnal				
NHy	number of the New Hymnal				
D	Distribution				
A	Author				
No	Matins (Nocturn)	I	Prime	Su	Sunday
No (1.)	First Nocturn	III	Tierce	Mo	Monday
No (2.)	Second Nocturn	VI	Sext	Tu	Tuesday
La	Lauds	IX	None	We	Wednesday
Ve	Vespers			Th	Thursday
Co	Compline			Fr	Friday
O	included in witness(es) to the Old Hymnal				
Oe	included in the Old Hymnal as attested for England				
F	included in manuscript(s) of the Frankish Hymnal				
Am	by St Ambrose				
Am?	probably by St Ambrose				

(The distinction between *No (1.)* and *No (2.)* is applicable only to hymnals of the Old Hymnal from Gaul and England. The assignment of Lauds hymns to days of the week is applicable only to the Frankish Hymnal.)

OHy	Hymn incipit	Use	D	A	NHy
1	Mediae noctis tempus	No (1.)	OeF		
2	Aeterne rerum conditor	No (2.)	OeF	Am	NHy 4
3	Rex aeterne domine	No (1.)	OeF		NHy 31
4	Magna et mirabilia	No (2.)	OF		
5	Tempus noctis	No	F		

OHy	Hymn incipit	Use	D	A	NHy
6	Te deum laudamus	La	OeF		
7	Deus qui caeli lumen es	La, Su	F		
8	Splendor paternae gloriae	La, Mo	OeF	Am?	NHy 15
9	Aeterne lucis conditor	La, Tu	OF		
10	Fulgentis auctor aetheris	La, We	F		
11	Deus aeterni luminis	La, Th	F		
12	Christe caeli domine	La, Fr	F		
13	Diei luce reddita	La, Sa	F		
(14)	Fulgentis auctor aetheris	I	O		
15	Venite fratres ocius	I	Oe		
16	Iam lucis orto sidere	I	O		NHy 7
17	Iam surgit hora tertia	III	OeF	Am	
18	Iam sexta sensim volvitur	VI	OF		
19	Bis ternas horas explicans	VI	Oe		
20	Rector potens verax deus	VI	O		NHy 9
21	Ter hora trina volvitur	IX	OeF		
22	Postmatutinis laudibus	I	F		
23	Certum tenentes ordinem	III	F		
24	Dicamus laudes domino	VI	F		
25	Perfectum trinum numerum	IX	F		NHy 53
26	Deus creator omnium	Ve	OF	Am	NHy 2
27	Deus qui certis legibus	Ve	OF		
28	Deus qui claro lumine	Ve	F		
29	Sator princepsque temporum	Ve	F		
30	Christe qui lux es et dies	Co	OeF		NHy 12
31	Te lucis ante terminum	Co	O		NHy 11
32	Christe precamur annue	Co	O		
33	Te deprecamur domine	Co	Oe		
34	Intende qui regis Israel	Christmas	OeF	Am	NHy 39
35	Illuminans altissimus	Epiphany	OF	Am?	
36	Dei fide qua vivimus	III Lent	F		NHy 51
37	Meridie orandum est	VI Lent	F		NHy 52
38	Sic ter quaternis trahitur	IX, Ve Lent	F		NHy 54
39	Hic est dies verus dei	Easter	OeF	Am?	
40	Ad cenam agni providi	Easter	F		NHy 70
41	Aurora lucis rutilat	Easter	F		NHy 72
42	Apostolorum passio	Peter and Paul	Oe	Am?	
43	Amore Christi nobilis	John Evangelist	Oe	Am?	
44	Aeterna Christi munera	Martyrs	OeF	Am?	NHy 117

The Hymnal in H

Although C separates the *proprium de tempore* from the *proprium sanctorum*, the hymnal whose *propria* section differs most widely from the others is H. As a non-monastic hymnal it provides hymns for Compline. It also gives cross-references if a hymn is used on more than one occasion as the other hymnals do not. For these reasons it was thought advisable to list the incipits of the hymns in the sequence in which they occur in H. The statements about liturgical use are based on the rubrics in H. Where rubrics are defective or lacking, they are hypothetical and mainly based on comparison with the collectar in H. They are therefore placed in brackets. Cross-references are indicated as follows: 36', 37', 47' etc.

No.	Hymn Incipit	NHy	Liturgical Use
1	O lux beata trinitas	1	(Vespers, Saturday, winter)
2	Primo dierum	3	(Matins, Sunday, winter)
3	Aeterne rerum	4	(Lauds, Sunday, winter)
4	Deus creator	2	(Vespers, Saturday, summer)
5	Nocte surgentes	5	(Matins, Sunday, summer)
6	Ecce iam noctis	6	(Lauds, Sunday, summer)
7	Iam lucis orto	7	(Prime, daily)
8	Nunc sancte nobis	8	(Tierce, daily)
9	Rector potens	9	(Sext, daily)
10	Rerum deus	10	(None, daily)
11	Lucis creator	13	(Vespers, Sunday)
12	Te lucis ante	11	(Compline, summer)
13	Iesu redemptor seculi	134	(Compline, Sundays, feasts)
14	Christe qui lux es	12	(Compline, winter)
15	Somno refectis artubus	14	(Matins, Monday)
16	Splendor paternae	15	(Lauds, Monday)
17	Immense caeli	16	(Vespers, Monday)
18	Consors paterni	17	(Matins, Tuesday)
19	Ales diei	18	(Lauds, Tuesday)
20	Telluris ingens	19	(Vespers, Tuesday)

No.	Hymn Incipit	NHy	Liturgical Use
21	Rerum creator	20	(Matins, Wednesday)
22	Nox et tenebrae	21	(Lauds, Wednesday)
23	Caeli deus	22	(Vespers, Wednesday)
24	Nox atra	23	(Matins, Thursday)
25	Lux ecce	24	(Lauds, Thursday)
26	Magnae deus	25	(Vespers, Thursday)
27	Tu trinitatis	26	(Matins, Friday)
28	Aeterna caeli	27	(Lauds, Friday)
29	Plasmator hominis	28	(Vespers, Friday)
30	Summae deus	29	(Matins, Saturday)
31	Aurora iam spargit	30	(Lauds, Saturday)
32	Conditor alme	32	(Vespers, Advent)
33	Fit porta	94	(Compline, Advent)
34	Verbum supernum	33	(Matins, Advent)
35	Vox clara	34	(Lauds, Advent)
36	Veni redemptor	39	(Compline, Christmas Eve)
37	A solis ortus	44	(First Vespers, Christmas)
37'	Enixa est	44 (V–VII)	(Compline, Christmas)
36'	Veni redemptor	39	(Matins, Christmas)
38	Agnoscat omne saeculum	135	(?, Christmas)
39	Audi redemptor	38	(Matins and Lauds, Octave of Christmas?)
40	Christe redemptor omnium ex patre	36	(Second Vespers, Christmas?)
41	Corde natus	136	(Second Vespers, Christmas?)
42	Iam rutilat	42	(Matins, St Stephen?)
43	Sancte dei pretiose	41	(Vespers, St Stephen?)
44	Hymnum cantemus domino	40	(Lauds, St Stephen?)
45	Infantum meritis	137	(Lauds, Holy Innocents)
46	Caterva matrum	45, III	(Matins, Holy Innocents)
47	Hostis Herodes	45	(Vespers, Epiphany)
47'	Lavacra puri	45, IV	(Compline, Epiphany)
48	A patre unigenitus	46	(Vespers, Octave of Epiphany?)
49	Iesus refulsit	43	(Matins, Epiphany)
50	Doctor egregie	105	(Conversion of Paul)
37'	A solis ortus	44	(First Vespers, Candlemas)
51	Quod chorus vatum	47	(Second Vespers, Candlemas)
41'	Corde natus	136	(Compline, Candlemas)
52	Quem terra pontus	65_1	(Matins, Candlemas)
53	O gloriosa femina	65_2	(Lauds, Candlemas)
54	Maria mater domini	90	(Candlemas?)
55	Gabriel dei	91	(Candlemas?)
56	Maria caeli	92	(Candlemas?)

No.	Hymn Incipit	NHy	Liturgical Use
57	Maria virgo	93	(Candlemas?)
58	Nunc tibi virgo	138	(Candlemas)
59	Iam bone pastor	104_1	(Cathedra Petri?)
60	Alme Gregori	116	(St Gregory)
61	Magnus miles	61	(St Cuthbert)
62	Ut tuae vitae	63	(Vespers, St Benedict?)
63	Christe sanctorum decus atque virtus	62	(Lauds, St Benedict?)
64	Magno canentes	64	Matins (St Benedict)
65	Cantemus cuncti melodum		Septuagesima (sequence)
66	Alleluia dulce	48	Vespers, Septuagesima
67	Alleluia piis	49	Matins, Septuagesima
68	Almum sidereae	50	Lauds, Septuagesima
69	Dei fide	51	Tierce, Lent
70	Meridie orandum	52	Sext, Lent
71	Perfecto trino	53	None, Lent
72	Sic ter quaternis	54	None, Lent
73	Audi benigne	55	None, Lent
74	Ex more docti	56	Vespers, Lent
75	Summe largitor	60	Compline, Lent
76	O Nazarene lux Bethleem	139	Compline, Lent
77	Cultor dei	140	Compline, Lent
78	Clarum decus	58	Matins, Lent
79	Vexilla regis	67_1	Vespers, Passiontide
80	Arbor decora	67_2	Matins, Passiontide
81	Rex angelorum praepotens	141	Lauds, Passiontide
82	Auctor salutis	68	Lauds, Passiontide
83	Rex Christe factor	142	Lauds, Passiontide
84	Pange lingua	143	Lauds, Passiontide

****

(gap in manuscript)

No.	Hymn Incipit	NHy	Liturgical Use
85	O quam glorifica	89	(Vespers, Assumption of Mary)
86	Ave maris stella	66	Compline (Assumption of Mary)
52'	Quem terra pontus	65_1	Lauds (Assumption of Mary)
87	Gaude visceribus	144	(Vespers) Nativity of Mary
88	Nunc tibi virgo (cf. 58)	138	Lauds, Nativity of Mary
89	Tibi Christe splendor	96	Vespers, Archangel Michael
90	Mysteriorum signifer	95	Matins, Archangel Michael
91	Christe sanctorum	97	Lauds, Archangel Michael
92	Festiva saeclis	98	(Matins) All Saints
93	Omnium Christe	100	Lauds, All Saints

No.	Hymn Incipit	NHy	Liturgical Use
94	Christe redemptor omnium conserva	99	Vespers, All Saints
95	Fratres unanimes	145	St Martin
96	Iam bone pastor (cf. 59)	104_1	St Peter
97	Annue Christe	104_2	(Matins?) Apostles
98	Doctor egregie (cf. 50)	105	St Paul
99	Andrea pie	106	St Andrew
100	Bina caelestis	107	St James (the Elder and St John)
101	Proni rogamus	111	St Philip
102	Iacobe iuste	108	St James (the Younger)
103	Bartholomaee	109	St Bartholomew
104	O Thoma Christi	113	St Thomas
105	Mathaee sancte	110	St Matthew
106	Beate Simon	112	St Simon and St Jude
107	Mathia iuste	114	St Mathias
108	Praeco benigne	115	St Barnabas
109	Exultet caelum	102	Vespers, Apostles
110	Aeterna Christi munera	103	Lauds, Apostles
111	Christe splendor	122	Vespers, Apostles
112	Sanctorum meritis	119	(Matins) Several Martyrs
113	Aeterna Christi munera	117	Lauds, Several Martyrs
114	Rex gloriose	118	Vespers, Several Martyrs
115	Martyr dei	120	Vespers, Single Martyr
116	Deus tuorum	121	Lauds, Single Martyr
117	Iste confessor	123	Vespers, Confessor
118	Iesu redemptor omnium	124	Lauds, Confessor
119	Virginis proles	125	(Vespers) Holy Virgin
120	Iesu corona	126	Lauds, Holy Virgin
121	Christe cunctorum	127	(Vespers) Dedication of the Church
122	Hic salus aegris	128	(Matins) Dedication of the Church
123	Quaesumus ergo	129	(Lauds, Dedication of the Church)

Bibliography

Arngart, O., 'The Durham Proverbs', *Speculum* 56 (1981), 288–300

Bäck, H., *The Synonyms for 'Child', 'Boy', 'Girl' in Old English*, Lund Studies in English 2 (Lund, 1934)

Backhouse, J., D. H. Turner and L. Webster, ed., *The Golden Age of Anglo-Saxon Art 966–1066* (London, 1984)

Bateson, M., ed., 'Indicium regule quomodo', in *Compotus Rolls of the Obedientiaries of St. Swithun's Priory, Winchester*, ed. G. W. Kitchin, Hampshire Record Society 7 (London, 1892), 196–8.

Bishop, E., 'On the Origin of the Prymer', in *The Prymer or Lay Folk's Prayer Book II*, ed. H. Littlehales, EETS 109 (1897), xi–xxxviii

Bishop, T. A. M., *English Caroline Minuscule* (Oxford, 1971)

Brunner, K., *Altenglische Grammatik. Nach der Angelsächsischen Grammatik von Eduard Sievers*, 3rd ed. (Tübingen, 1965)

Bullough, D. A. and A. L. H. Corrêa, 'Texts, Chant and the Chapel of Louis the Pious', in *Charlemagne's Heir: New Perspectives on the Reign of Louis the Pious (814–840)*, ed. P. Godman and R. Collins (Oxford, 1990), pp. 489–508

Bulst, W., ed., *Hymni Latini Antiquissimi LXX. Psalmi III* (Heidelberg, 1956)

Campbell, A., *Old English Grammar* (Oxford, 1959)

Clayton, M., *The Cult of the Virgin Mary in Anglo-Saxon England*, Cambridge Studies in Anglo-Saxon England 2 (Cambridge, 1990)

Colgrave, B., ed., *Two Lives of St. Cuthbert: a Life by an Anonymous Monk of Lindisfarne and Bede's Prose Life* (Cambridge, 1940)

Colgrave, B., and R. A. B. Mynors, ed., *Bede's Ecclesiastical History of the English People* (Oxford, 1969)

Conner, P. W., *Anglo-Saxon Exeter: a Tenth-Century Cultural History*, Studies in Anglo-Saxon History 4 (Woodbridge, 1993)

Corrêa, A., ed., *The Durham Collectar*, HBS 107 (1992)

Cunningham, M. P., ed., *Aurelii Prudentii Clementis Carmina*, CCSL 126 (1966)

479

Davril, A., ed., *Consuetudines Floriacenses Saeculi Tertii Decimi*, CCM 9 (1976)

de Vogüé, A., ed., *Grégoire le Grand, Dialogues*, trans. P. Antin, 3 vols., SChr 251, 260 and 265 (1979–80)

Dewick, E. S., ed., *Facsimiles of Horae de Beata Maria Virgine*, HBS 21 (1902)

Dewick, E. S., and W. H. Frere, ed., *The Leofric Collectar*, 2 vols., HBS 45 and 56 (1914–21)

Dietrich, E., 'Abt Aelfrik. Zur Literatur-Geschichte der angelsächsischen Kirche. I', *Zeitschrift für historische Theologie* 25 (1855), 487–594

Dinter, P., ed., Odilo of Cluny, *Liber tramitis aevi Odilonis Abbatis*, CCM 10 (1980)

Drage, E. M., 'Bishop Leofric and the Exeter Cathedral Chapter 1050–1072: a Reassessment of the Manuscript Evidence' (unpubl. PhD dissertation, Oxford Univ., 1978)

Dreves, G. M., C. Blume and H. M. Bannister, ed., *Analecta Hymnica Medii Aevi*, 55 vols. (Leipzig, 1886–1922) with an index (2 vols.) by M. Lütolf (Bern, 1978)

Dumville, D. N., *English Caroline Script and Monastic History: Studies in Benedictinism, A.D. 950–1030*, Studies in Anglo-Saxon History 6 (Woodbridge, 1993)

   Liturgy and the Ecclesiastical History of Late Anglo-Saxon England, Studies in Anglo-Saxon History 5 (Woodbridge, 1992)

   'On the Dating of Some Late Anglo-Saxon Liturgical Manuscripts', *Transactions of the Cambridge Bibliographical Society* 10 (1991–), 40–57

Fenlon, I., ed., *Cambridge Music Manuscripts, 900–1700* (Cambridge, 1982)

Foreville, R., *Les Mutations socio-culturelles au tournant des XIe–XIIe siècles*, Spicilegium Beccense 2 (Paris, 1984)

Fraipont, J., ed., 'Bedae Opera Rhythmica', in *Bedae Opera III*, CCSL 122 (1955), 405–70

Frere, W. H., ed., *The Winchester Troper from Mss. of the Xth and XIth Centuries*, HBS 8 (1894)

Gasquet, F. A., and E. Bishop, *The Bosworth Psalter* (London, 1908)

Gneuss, H., 'A Preliminary List of Manuscripts Written or Owned in England up to 1100', *ASE* 9 (1980), 1–60

   Hymnar und Hymnen im englischen Mittelalter, Buchreihe der Anglia 12 (Tübingen, 1968)

   'Latin Hymns in Medieval England: Future Research', in *Chaucer and Middle English Studies in Honour of Rossell Hope Robbins*, ed. B. Rowland (London, 1974), pp. 407–24

   Lehnbildungen und Lehnbedeutungen im Altenglischen (Berlin, 1955)

   'Liturgical Books in Anglo-Saxon England and their Old English Terminology', in *Learning and Literature*, ed. Lapidge and Gneuss, pp. 91–141

'The Origin of Standard Old English and Æthelwold's School at Winchester', *ASE* 1 (1972), 63–83

'Zur Geschichte des Ms. Vespasian A. I', *Anglia* 75 (1957), 125–33

Gretsch, M., *Die Regula Sancti Benedicti in England und ihre altenglische Übersetzung*, Texte und Untersuchungen zur Englischen Philologie 2 (Munich, 1973)

Günzel, B., ed., *Ælfwine's Prayerbook (London British Library, Cotton Titus D. XXVI + XXVII)*, HBS 108 (1993)

Hallander, L.-G., *Old English Verbs in -sian: a Semantic and Derivational Study*, Acta Universitatis Stockholmiensis, Stockholm Studies in English 15 (Stockholm, 1966)

Hallinger, K., *Gorze-Kluny: Studien zu den monastischen Lebensformen und Gegensätzen im Hochmittelalter*, 2 vols., Studia Anselmiana 22–5 (Rome, 1950–1)

Hallinger, K., ed., *Consuetudines Cluniacensium antiquiores cum redactionibus derivatis. Corpus consuetudinum saeculi X/XI/XII*, CCM 7. 2 (1983)

Consuetudinum saeculorum X/XI/XII monumenta. Introductiones, CCM 7. 1 (1984)

Hartzell, K. D., 'An Eleventh-century English Missal Fragment in the British Library', *ASE* 18 (1989), 45–97

Hofstetter, W., *Winchester und der spätaltenglische Sprachgebrauch*, Texte und Untersuchungen zur Englischen Philologie 14 (Munich, 1987)

Hogg, R. M., *A Grammar of Old English* (Oxford, 1992–), vol. I

Hohler, C., and A. Hughes, ed., 'The Durham Services in Honour of St. Cuthbert', in *The Relics of St. Cuthbert*, ed. C. F. Battiscombe (Durham, 1956), pp. 155–91

Holschneider, A., *Die Organa von Winchester* (Hildesheim, 1968)

Hughes, A., ed., *The Portiforium of Saint Wulstan*, 2 vols., HBS 89 and 90 (1958–60)

James, M. R., *A Descriptive Catalogue of the Manuscripts in the Library of Corpus Christi College, Cambridge*, 2 vols. (Cambridge, 1912)

Jordan, R., *Eigentümlichkeiten des anglischen Wortschatzes. Eine wortgeographische Untersuchung mit etymologischen Anmerkungen*, Anglistische Forschungen 17 (Heidelberg, 1906)

Jumièges. Congrès scientifique du XIIIe centenaire. Rouen, 10–12 juin 1954 (Rouen, 1955)

Käsmann, H., ' "Tugend" und "Laster" im Alt- und Mittelenglischen. Eine bezeichnungsgeschichtliche Untersuchung' (unpubl. PhD dissertation, Berlin Univ., 1951)

Ker, N. R., *Catalogue of Manuscripts Containing Anglo-Saxon* (Oxford, 1957)

Medieval Libraries of Great Britain: a List of Surviving Books, 2nd ed., Royal Historical Society Guides and Handbooks 3 (London, 1964), with a *Supplement* by A. G. Watson, Royal Historical Society Guides and Handbooks 15 (London, 1987)

Kitson, P., 'Geographical Variation in Old English Prepositions and the Location of Ælfric's and Other Literary Dialects', *English Studies* 74 (1993), 1–50

Klappenbach, H., *Zu altenglischen Interlinearversionen von Prosaparaphrasen lateinischer Hymnen: der Lautcharakter von Cotton Vespasian D XII mit einem Vergleich zu Cotton Julius A VI und Durham-Hs.* (Leipzig, 1930)

Korhammer, M., *Die monastischen Cantica im Mittelalter und ihre altenglischen Interlinearversionen. Studien und Textausgabe*, Texte und Untersuchungen zur Englischen Philologie 6 (Munich, 1976)

'The Origin of the Bosworth Psalter', *ASE* 2 (1973), 173–87

Kuhn, S. M., ed., *The Vespasian Psalter* (Ann Arbor, MI, 1965)

Lapidge, M., and H. Gneuss, ed., *Learning and Literature in Anglo-Saxon England: Studies Presented to Peter Clemoes on the Occasion of his Sixty-Fifth Birthday* (Cambridge, 1985)

Lapidge, M., and M. Winterbottom, ed., Wulfstan of Winchester, *The Life of St Æthelwold* (Oxford, 1991)

Leclercq, J., 'Formes anciennes de l'Office Marial', *Ephemerides Liturgicae* 74 (1960), 89–102

'Fragmenta Mariana', *Ephemerides Liturgicae* 72 (1958), 292–305

Leroquais, V., *Les Psautiers manuscrits Latins des bibliothèques publiques de France*, 3 vols. (Mâcon, 1940–1)

Lindelöf, U., ed., *Der Lambeth-Psalter*, Acta Societatis Scientiarum Fennicae 35. 1 and 43. 3 (Helsingfors, 1909–14)

Rituale Ecclesiae Dunelmensis. The Durham Collectar, Surtees Society 140 (Durham, 1927)

Lindsay, W. M., ed., *Isidori Hispalensis episcopi etymologiarum sive originum libri XX*, 2 vols. (Oxford, 1911)

Lipsius, R. A., and M. Bonnet, ed., *Acta Apostolorum Apocrypha*, 3 vols. (Leipzig, 1891–1903)

Littlehales, H., ed., *The Prymer or Lay Folk's Prayer Book*, 2 vols., EETS 105 and 109 (1895–7)

Louis, R., ed., *Etudes ligériennes d'histoire et d'archéologie médiévales* (Auxerre, 1975)

MacGillivray, H. S., *The Influence of Christianity on the Vocabulary of Old English*, Studien zur Englischen Philologie 8 (Halle a. S., 1902)

Mearns, J., *Early Latin Hymnaries: an Index of Hymns in Hymnaries before 1100* (Cambridge, 1913)

Mitchell, B., *Old English Syntax*, 2 vols. (Oxford, 1985)

Mynors, R. A. B., *Durham Cathedral Manuscripts to the End of the 12th Century* (Oxford, 1939)

Mynors, R. A. B., ed., *P. Vergilii Maronis opera* (Oxford, 1969)

Nocent, H., ed., 'Aelfrici abbatis epistula ad monachos Egneshamnenses directa', in *Consuetudinum saeculi X/XI/XII Monumenta non-Cluniacensia*, CCM 7. 3 (1984), 149–85

Ono, S., '*Undergytan* as a "Winchester" Word', in *Linguistics across Historical and Geographical Boundaries: in Honour of Jacek Fisiak on the Occasion of his Fiftieth Birthday*, ed. D. Kastovsky and A. Szwedek, 2 vols., Trends in Linguistics, Studies and Monographs 32 (Berlin, 1986) I, 569–77

Ortenberg, V., *The English Church and the Continent in the Tenth and Eleventh Centuries: Cultural, Spiritual, and Artistic Exchanges* (Oxford, 1992)

Proctor, F., and C. Wordsworth, ed., *Breviarium ad Usum Insignis Ecclesiae Sarum*, 3 vols. (Cambridge, 1879–86)

Rankin, S., 'From Memory to Record: Musical Notations in Manuscripts from Exeter', *ASE* 13 (1984), 97–112

'Neumatic Notations in Anglo-Saxon England', in *Musicologie médiévale: notations et séquences. Actes de la table ronde du C.N.R.S. à l'Institut de Recherche et d'Histoire des Textes 6–7 septembre 1982*, ed. M. Huglo (Paris, 1987), pp. 129–44

Rauh, H., *Der Wortschatz der altenglischen Übersetzungen des Matthäusevangeliums untersucht auf seine dialektische und zeitliche Gebundenheit* (Berlin, 1936)

Robinson, P. R., *Catalogue of Dated and Datable Manuscripts c. 737–1600 in Cambridge Libraries*, 2 vols. (Cambridge, 1988)

Roeder, F., ed., *Der altenglische Regius-Psalter*, Studien zur Englischen Philologie 18 (Halle a. S., 1904)

Schabram, H., *Superbia. Studien zum altenglischen Wortschatz. I: Die dialektale und zeitliche Verbreitung des Wortguts* (Munich, 1965)

Schaller, D., and E. Könsgen, *Initia carminum Latinorum saeculo undecimo antiquiorum* (Göttingen, 1977)

Scherer, G., *Zur Geographie und Chronologie des angelsächsischen Wortschatzes im Anschluss an Bischofs Waerferths Übertragung der 'Dialoge' Gregors* (Leipzig, 1928)

Seebold, E., 'Kentish – and Old English Texts from Kent', in *Words, Texts and Manuscripts: Studies in Anglo-Saxon Culture Presented to Helmut Gneuss on the Occasion of his Sixty-Fifth Birthday*, ed. M. Korhammer (Cambridge, 1992), pp. 409–34

'Regional gebundene Wörter in Wærferths Übersetzung der *Dialoge* Gregors des Großen', in *Anglo-Saxonica, Beiträge zur Vor- und Frühgeschichte der englischen Sprache und zur altenglischen Literatur, Festschrift für Hans Schabram zum 65. Geburtstag*, ed. K. R. Grinda and C.-D. Wetzel (Munich, 1993), pp. 251–77

'Was ist jütisch? Was ist kentisch?', in *Britain 400–600: Language and History*, ed. A. Bammesberger and A. Wollmann, Anglistische Forschungen 205 (Heidelberg, 1990), 235–52

Sisam, C., and K. Sisam, ed., *The Salisbury Psalter*, EETS 242 (1959)

Stäblein, B., 'Der lateinische Hymnus', *MGG* VI, cols. 993–1018

Stäblein, B., ed., *Hymnen (I): die mittelalterlichen Hymnenmelodien des Abendlandes*, Monumenta Monodica Medii Aevi 1 (Kassel, 1956)

Stenton, F. M., *Anglo-Saxon England*, 3rd ed. (Oxford, 1971)

Stevenson, J., ed., *The Latin Hymns of the Anglo-Saxon Church. With an Interlinear Anglo-Saxon Gloss*, Surtees Society 23 (Durham, 1851)

Stubbs, W., ed., *Memorials of Saint Dunstan, Archbishop of Canterbury*, RS (1874)

Symons, T., ed. and trans., *Regularis Concordia Anglicae Nationis Monachorum Sanctimonialiumque* (London, 1953)

Symons, T., and S. Spath, ed., 'Regularis Concordia', *Consuetudinum saeculi X/XI/XII monumenta non-Cluniacensia*, CCM 7. 3 (1984), 61–147

Temple, E., *Anglo-Saxon Manuscripts 900–1066*, Survey of Manuscripts Illuminated in the British Isles 2 (London, 1976)

Tolhurst, J. B. L., *Introduction to the English Monastic Breviaries: the Monastic Breviary of Hyde Abbey, Winchester VI*, HBS 80 (1942)

Treitler, L., 'Reading and Singing: on the Genesis of Occidental Music-Writing', *Early Music History* 4 (1984), 135–208

Venezky, R., and A. diPaolo Healey, *A Microfiche Concordance to Old English* (Toronto, 1980)

Wagner, P., *Einführung in die gregorianischen Melodien: ein Handbuch der Choralwissenschaft*, 3 vols. (Leipzig, 1911–21)

Walpole, A. S., ed., *Early Latin Hymns* (Cambridge, 1922)

Weber, R., ed. *Biblia sacra iuxta Vulgatam versionem*, 3rd ed., 2 vols (Stuttgart, 1983)

Wenisch, F., *Spezifisch anglisches Wortgut in den nordhumbrischen Interlinearglossierungen des Lukasevangeliums*, Anglistische Forschungen 132 (Heidelberg, 1979)

Wieland, G. R., ed., *The Canterbury Hymnal*, Toronto Medieval Latin Texts 12 (Toronto, 1982)

Wildhagen, K., 'Studien zum Psalterium Romanum in England und zu seinen Glossierungen (in geschichtlicher Entwicklung)', in *Festschrift für Lorenz Morsbach: dargebracht von Freunden und Schülern*, ed. F. Holthausen and H. Spies, Studien zur englischen Philologie 50 (Halle a. S., 1913), 417–72

Winterbottom, M., ed., Abbo of Fleury, 'Life of St. Edmund', in *Three Lives of English Saints*, ed. M. Winterbottom (Toronto, 1972), pp. 65–87 and 91–2

Wormald, P., 'Æthelwold and his Continental Counterparts: Contact, Comparison, Contrast', in *Bishop Æthelwold: his Career and Influence*, ed. B. Yorke (Woodbridge, 1988), pp. 13–42

Yorke, B., ed., *Bishop Æthelwold: his Career and Influence* (Woodbridge, 1988)

General index to the introduction

Index of hymn incipits

After each incipit the following information is given, as far as applicable. *OHy* represents the number of the hymn in the Old Hymnal (see Appendix I). **(N)Hy** represents the number of the hymn in the New Hymnal at the same time as the number of the hymn in this edition. *Sa* or *Yo* mean that the hymn in question was in use in England after the Norman Conquest among the secular clergy following the Use of Sarum or the Use of York. It is then stated whether the melody is represented in Anglo-Saxon neumes and in which manuscript and, for the identified melodies, the number in the Stäblein edition is given. Finally, the page numbers refer to each instance in which the hymn is mentioned in ch. 1 and 2 of the introduction, including references to hymn glosses, but excluding the footnotes on pp. 67–9. It should be noted that only hymns that have a *(N)Hy* number are fully treated in this book. For the others, see Gneuss, *HHEM*. The spelling follows classical norms; *u/v* are distinguished, but not *i/j*.

A patre unigenitus **(N)Hy 46**, Sa, Yo; unidentified melody (C): 17, 21, 22, 46, 97

A solis ortus cardine **(N)Hy 44**, Sa, Yo; Stäblein No. 53 (H): 13, 14, 15, 17, 18, 33, 36, 56, 62, 96, 103

Ad cenam agni providi OHy 40, **(N)Hy 70**, Sa, Yo: 33–4, 53, 57

Adam vetus quod polluit (*divisio of* Agnoscat omne saeculum) Yo

Adesto sancta trinitas **(N)Hy 152**, Sa, Yo: 52

Aestimavit hortulanum Sa

Aeterna caeli gloria **(N)Hy 27**, Sa, Yo

Aeterna Christi munera / apostolorum **(N)Hy 103**, Yo; Stäblein No. 115 (H): 12–13, 14, 22, 96, 103

Aeterna Christi munera / et martyrum OHy 44, **(N)Hy 117**, Yo; Stäblein No. 115 (H): 6, 12, 96, 103

Aeterne lucis conditor OHy 9

Aeterne rerum conditor OHy 2, (N)Hy 4, Sa; unidentified melody (C): 3–4, 6, 24–5, 33, 46, 97

Aeterne rex altissime **(N)Hy 75**, Sa, Yo: 21–2

Aeterni patris unice Yo: 53

Agnoscat omne saeculum **(N)Hy 135**, Yo: 15

Ales diei nuntius **(N)Hy 18**, Sa, Yo

Alleluia dulce carmen **(N)Hy 48**; Stäblein No. ?212 (H): 96

Alleluia piis **(N)Hy 49**

Alme Gregori **(N)Hy 116**: 15, 24, 36, 49

Almum sidereae (*divisio of* Alleluia piis) **(N)Hy 50**

Amore Christi nobilis OHy 43: 4

Andrea pie **(N)Hy 106**, Sa, Yo; Stäblein No. 152 (H): 96, 98, 103

Angulare fundamentum (*divisio of* Urbs beata) Sa, Yo

Anni peractis mensibus **(N)Hy 78**: 12, 14, 22, 36

Annue Christe **(N)Hy 104₂**, Sa, Yo; Stäblein No. 152 (H): 22, 96, 98, 103

Antra deserti (*divisio of* Ut queant laxis) **(N)Hy 86₂**, Sa, Yo: 51

Apostolorum passio OHy 42: 4

Table of hymn numbers

494

Index of abbreviated doxologies

The index includes only those doxologies that are abbreviated in the text of the edition. Bold numbers indicate the page on which the full text appears.

Index of manuscripts cited in the introduction

Index of manuscripts cited in the introduction

Index of Old English words treated in ch.3

This index includes only words discussed as lexical items. The alphabetization ignores the prefix *ge-*. *æ* is alphabetized as *ae*, *þ* after *t*.

GENERAL THEOLOGICAL SEMINARY,
NEW YORK